The Great War a
Humanitarianism

MW00781422

The aftermath of the Great War brought the most troubled peacetime
the world had ever seen. Survivors of the war were not only the soldiers
who fought, the wounded in mind and body. They were also the stateless, the children who suffered war's consequences, and later the victims
of the great Russian famine of 1921–23. Before the phrases "universal
human rights" and "non-governmental organization" even existed, five
remarkable men and women – René Cassin and Albert Thomas from
France, Fridtjof Nansen from Norway, Herbert Hoover from the United
States, and Eglantyne Jebb from Britain – understood that a new type of
transnational organization was needed to face problems that respected
no national boundaries or rivalries. Bruno Cabanes, a pioneer in the
study of the aftermath of war, shows, through his vivid and revelatory
history of individuals, organizations, and nations in crisis, how and when
the right to human dignity first became inalienable.

BRUNO CABANES, a pioneer in the study of the aftermath of war, is
an Associate Professor in the Department of History at Yale University.
His previous publications include *La victoire endeuillée: La sortie de guerre
des soldats français (1918–1920)* (2004).

Studies in the Social and Cultural History of Modern Warfare

In recent years the field of modern history has been enriched by the exploration of two parallel histories. These are the social and cultural history of armed conflict, and the impact of military events on social and cultural history.

Studies in the Social and Cultural History of Modern Warfare presents the fruits of this growing area of research, reflecting both the colonization of military history by cultural historians and the reciprocal interest of military historians in social and cultural history, to the benefit of both. The series offers the latest scholarship in European and non-European events from the 1850s to the present day.

This is book 41 in the series, and a full list of titles in the series can be found at: www.cambridge.org/modernwarfare

The Great War and the Origins of Humanitarianism, 1918–1924

Bruno Cabanes

CAMBRIDGE
UNIVERSITY PRESS

CAMBRIDGE
UNIVERSITY PRESS

University Printing House, Cambridge CB2 8BS, United Kingdom

Published in the United States of America by Cambridge University Press, New York

Cambridge University Press is part of the University of Cambridge.

It furthers the University's mission by disseminating knowledge in the pursuit of education, learning and research at the highest international levels of excellence.

www.cambridge.org
Information on this title: www.cambridge.org/9781107604834

© Bruno Cabanes 2014

First published 2014

Printed in the United Kingdom by Clays, St Ives plc

A catalogue record for this publication is available from the British Library

Library of Congress Cataloguing in Publication data
Cabanes, Bruno.
The Great War and the origins of Humanitarianism, 1918–1924 / Bruno Cabanes.
   pages   cm. – (Studies in the social and cultural history of modern warfare)
Includes bibliographical references and index.
ISBN 978-1-107-02062-7 (hardback)
1. Humanitarianism – History – 20th century.   2. Philanthropists – History – 20th century.   3. World War, 1914–1918.   4. Basic needs – History – 20th century.
5. Human rights – History – 20th century.   I. Title.
BJ1475.3.C33   2014
361.2′6 – dc23   2013032778

ISBN 978-1-107-02062-7 Hardback
ISBN 978-1-107-60483-4 Paperback

Contents

Acknowledgments

My thanks go first to the colleagues and friends who read my manuscript in its entirety or who read individual chapters in progress and provided helpful suggestions and incisive critiques: Stéphane Audoin-Rouzeau, Annette Becker, David Blight, John Horne, Heather Jones, John Merriman, Antoine Prost, Henry Rousso, Leonard V. Smith, Jay Winter – and the two anonymous readers from Cambridge University Press. Others have been generous in sharing documents and references: Peter Holquist, Dzovinar Kévonian, Sandrine Kott, Manon Pignot, Paul-André Rosental, Annemarie Sammartino, Carl Emil Vogt, and Patrick Weil. I thank my friend Professor Piotr Wandycz of Yale University for kindly translating the letters of Polish children to Herbert Hoover. Thanks are also due to Jay Winter who gave me the chance to publish this book in his series at Cambridge University Press.

I am grateful to our many wonderful graduate students at Yale University, a true source of inspiration, and among them: Ahmed Alsoudani, Catherine Dunlop, Julia Elsky, Mattie Fitch, Brian Jordan, Charles Keith, Alice Kelly, Nathan Kurz, Diana Lemberg, Ken Loiselle, Kimberly Lowe, Nicole Mombell, Jacqueline Mosher, Philipp Nielsen, Jason Resnikoff, Miranda Sachs, Vreni Schoenenberger, Sara Silverstein, Gene Tempest (with whom I had the privilege to teach a class on "War and the Environment"), Helen Veit, Charles (Max) Walden, Jennifer Wellington, Rachel White, Lauren Young, and Suyeon Yun.

I am much indebted to Stephanie O'Hara, Associate Professor at the University of Massachusetts at Dartmouth, who turned my manuscript into fluent and elegant English. I owe her so much. My dear friend and colleague Alice Kaplan also read the manuscript chapter by chapter, and her suggestions on style and language were invaluable.

Len Smith offered me the opportunity to present my chapter on Nansen at the conference on The Unfinished Business of War and Revolution, Europe 1918–1919 at Oberlin College in March 2009. Many thanks to Carol Fink, John Horne, Kristin Kopp, Erez Manela,

Annemarie Sammartino, and Tara Zahra for their comments and sugges-
tions. I thank also Stéphane Audoin-Rouzeau for inviting me to present
my research in his seminar at the École des Hautes Études en Sciences
Sociales. I am grateful for his feedback and for the thoughtful questions
I received from Damien Baldin, Franziska Heimburger, Hervé Mazurel,
Emmanuel Saint-Fuscien, and Clémentine Vidal-Naquet.

For my research in Geneva, Oslo, Paris, Cambridge, London, Palo
Alto, Calif., and West Branch, Iowa, I received generous funding from
the Whitney Griswold research fund and from the Macmillan Center at
Yale.

I benefited from the hospitality of the Norwegian Nobel Institute in
Oslo (special thanks to my colleagues Olav Njølstad, Helge Pharo, and
Anne Cecilie Kjelling) and the University of Paris-Sorbonne (thanks to
Édouard Husson). These two wonderful institutions provided a haven
where I wrote the first draft of this book. Thanks to my colleagues
Philippe Burrin and Gopalan Balachandran, with whom I had the privi-
lege of spending the summer of 2008 as Visiting Fellow at the Graduate
Institute of International Studies in Geneva.

The staff of the following libraries and archives deserve special mention: at Yale, the Sterling Memorial Library and the Beinecke Library; in
Geneva, the archives of the League of Nations, the archives of the International Labor Organization, the archives of the International Committee
of the Red Cross, and the State Archives of Geneva; in Paris, the Bibliothèque Nationale de France, the Archives Nationales, the Bibliothèque
de Documentation Internationale Contemporaine (Nanterre); in Oslo,
the library of the Norwegian Nobel Institute and the National Archives;
in Palo Alto, Calif., the Hoover Institution Archives; in West Branch,
Iowa, the Hoover presidential archives; in London, the archives of the
Save the Children Fund.

Finally, many thanks to family in France and friends in Connecticut
for their love and their support.

I would like to dedicate this book to my wife Flora, who remains
my most trusted reader and inspiration, and to our beautiful daughters
Gabrielle and Constance. This book is for you, with all my love.

Introduction: Human disasters: humanitarianism and the transnational turn in the wake of World War I

The Great War in Europe was an unprecedented catastrophe. By mid August 1914, the devastated cities of Dinant and Louvain had already come to symbolize the horror of industrialized warfare. The first reports of the German Army's atrocities in Belgium and France, of massacres, rapes, deportations, and the destruction of hospitals and historic monuments, soon followed.[1] These reports were only confirmed by the brutal military occupations on the western front, in the Balkans, in Central and later in Eastern Europe.[2] From the standpoint of humanitarian law, then, in its infancy, the Great War was nothing but a series of bloody affronts to human dignity. The year 1915 marked a turning point, with its increased violence against civilian populations and the beginning of the Armenian genocide.[3] Even the Armistice brought no relief. In Europe and in the Near East, refugees fled revolutions, civil wars, and persecution. Hundreds of thousands of families suffered famine and epidemics. Meanwhile, millions of wounded and disabled soldiers struggled to return to their civilian lives. And yet in the end, the Great War did more than create disaster. It fostered deep and long-term pacifist feeling among a substantial population, and it made the protection of all the war's victims, civilians and soldiers alike, an absolute necessity—a project that drew to it a surprisingly large and talented group of activists and their supporters.

The timid steps taken in this direction during the peace negotiations were short-lived. In June 1919, Germany acknowledged the Allies' right to prosecute, before military tribunals, those accused of committing "acts in violation of the laws and customs of war."[4] But the *Reichsgericht* or Supreme Court established in Leipzig in 1921 was a mockery of justice: of the initial list of more than 800 accused "war criminals," including

[1] John Horne and Alan Kramer, *German Atrocities, 1914: A History of Denial* (New Haven: Yale University Press, 2001).
[2] Annette Becker, *Les cicatrices rouges, 14–18: France et Belgique occupées* (Paris: Fayard, 2010).
[3] John Horne (ed.), *Vers la guerre totale: le tournant de 1914–1915* (Paris: Tallandier, 2010).
[4] Articles 228 and 229 of the Treaty of Versailles.

the German generals Hindenburg and Ludendorff, the tribunal in fact prosecuted only 45—all of whom were mid-level German Army officers.[5] The other major power that the Allies might have held accountable was Turkey, for crimes committed in the Ottoman Empire against its Armenian minority. However, according to the Hague Convention of 1907, the concept of "war crime" applied only to acts of violence perpetrated by a belligerent state against the soldiers or civilians of another state. This definition of war crimes excluded any state that persecuted its own civilians. The 1919 Commission on the Responsibilities of the Authors of War and on Enforcement of Penalties asked the salient question: if the atrocities committed against Armenians could not be described as "war crimes," were they "crimes against the laws of humanity," as defined in the preamble of the Hague Convention of 1907?[6] The participants at the Paris Peace Conference responded in the negative. In their eyes, "laws of humanity" was too imprecise a concept to have any implications for penal procedure. The United States and Japan bore a historic responsibility for this decision, which was made, no doubt, because the American government considered Turkey a potential bulwark against the Bolshevik threat, and, thus, a potential ally that needed to be appeased. The "crimes against humanity" committed by the Ottoman Empire were explicitly mentioned in Articles 226 and 230 of the Treaty of Sèvres (1920) between the Allies and Turkey. But this treaty was never ratified. Instead it was replaced on July 24, 1923, by the Treaty of Lausanne, which granted amnesty to those responsible for the crimes previously mentioned in the Treaty of Sèvres.[7] As far as attacks on civilian populations were concerned, a sovereign state still could not be prosecuted for crimes committed against its own citizens. The Turks themselves held a number of trials in which soldiers were convicted of violating the Turkish military code, but that was an entirely domestic matter. This protection of national sovereignty lasted until the immediate aftermath of World

---

[5] James F. Willis, *Prologue to Nuremberg: The Politics and Diplomacy of Punishing War Criminals of the First World War* (Westport, Conn.: Greenwood Press, 1982); Jean-Jacques Becker, "Les procès de Leipzig," in Annette Wieviorka (ed.), *Les procès de Nuremberg et de Tokyo* (Brussels: Complexe, 1996), pp. 51–60.

[6] Report presented to the Preliminary Peace Conference by the Commission on the Responsibilities of the Authors of War and on the Enforcement of Penalties (Carnegie Endowment for International Peace, Division of International Law, 1919), quoted in M. Cherif Bassiouni, *Crimes against Humanity: Historical Evolution and Contemporary Application* (Cambridge University Press, 2011), Introduction, xxix–xxx.

[7] Gary Bass, *Stay the Hand of Vengeance: The Politics of War Crimes Tribunals* (Princeton University Press, 2001); M. Cherif Bassiouni, "World War I, 'the war to end all wars' and the birth of a handicapped international criminal justice system," *Denver Journal of International Law and Policy*, 30: 3, 2002, pp. 244–291.

War II, when Article 6 of the London Charter of the International Military Tribunal (dated August 8, 1945) established the procedures for the Nuremberg Trials.

However, this failure to recognize "crimes against the laws of humanity" was counterbalanced by other significant new developments. World War I and its aftermath represent a decisive turning point in the redefinition of humanitarianism: a profound transformation of pre-war humanitarian practices and humanitarian law into an assertion of "humanitarian rights." In a 1922 newspaper article, the Russian Jewish legal scholar Boris Mirkine-Guetzévitch noted with hope for the future: "A contemporary popular legal conscience has been born, which acknowledges aid to refugees, victims of starvation, and victims of epidemics as a task of an international, public nature."[8] This transformative moment in the long development of humanitarianism—meaning both humanitarian action on the ground and humanitarian discourse—is the topic of this book.

Humanitarians in the second half of the eighteenth century sought to ease the suffering of others, whether victims of war, famine, natural disasters, or slavery and other forms of exploitation. They were driven by an ethics of empathy, rooted in their Christian faith, and by changing sensibilities, as illustrated by the success of the sentimental novel, a phenomenon Lynn Hunt has analyzed in her groundbreaking book *Inventing Human Rights: A History*.[9] By the end of the nineteenth century, with the creation of the International Committee of the Red Cross in 1863, the Brussels Conference Act of 1890 prohibiting slavery, and the rise of the practice of humanitarian intervention,[10] humanitarian work had three main characteristics: the role of nation-states, which provided a framework for organizing humanitarian aid;[11] a religious aspect, which saw aid to victims as a charitable act;[12] and lastly, the sociological and ideological origins of humanitarian aid workers, who for the most part

---

[8] "L'émigration," *La Tribune Juive*, 113, February 24, 1922, quoted in Dzovinar Kévonian, "Les juristes juifs russes en France et l'action internationale dans les années vingt," *Archives Juives*, 34: 2, 2001, p. 85.
[9] Lynn Hunt, *Inventing Human Rights: A History* (New York: W.W. Norton, 2007).
[10] Gary J. Bass, *Freedom's Battle: The Origins of Humanitarian Intervention* (New York: Alfred A. Knopf, 2008) and, for a critical reading, Samuel Moyn, "Spectacular wrongs: Gary Bass' *Freedom's Battle*,'" *The Nation*, October 13, 2008; Davide Rodogno, *Against Massacre: Humanitarian Interventions in the Ottoman Empire, 1815–1914* (Princeton University Press, 2012).
[11] David Forsythe, *Humanitarian Politics: The International Committee of the Red Cross* (Baltimore: Johns Hopkins University Press, 1977).
[12] Craig Calhoun, "The imperative to reduce suffering: charity, progress, and emergencies in the field of humanitarian action," in Michael Barnett and Thomas G. Weiss (eds.), *Humanitarianism in Question: Politics, Power, Ethics* (Ithaca: Cornell University Press, 2008), pp. 73–97.

came from civil society or were inspired by religious activism. An initial shift towards "scientific philanthropy" took place in the United States between 1890 and 1910, but it was with the outbreak of the Great War that humanitarianism truly changed.

Indeed, during the period 1914–18, humanitarianism became increasingly organized around transnational networks. It also became more secular, giving rise to a discourse that spoke less of charity and more about human rights. Lastly, humanitarianism relied mainly on a new social group: experts—physicians, engineers, social workers—who took a more and more active role in devising and carrying out humanitarian work, in conjunction with the volunteer groups and missionaries more typically associated with such work.[13] The accomplishments of Herbert Hoover and the Commission for Relief in Belgium is one of the best examples of this professionalization of humanitarian action on the ground.[14] In her work on humanitarianism during the Great War, Annette Becker has amply demonstrated the impact World War I had, as total war, on definitions of victimhood and on the establishment of modern humanitarian aid.[15] I would argue instead that the true turning point can in fact be located in the aftermath of the Great War, when changes already evident grew larger and more radical in nature.

In my previous book on France after World War I, I emphasized a unique period, which I called the *sortie de guerre*—the transition from war to peace. This is a time when individual and collective identities are reorganized in order to adapt to the new requirements of peacetime—especially the soldiers undergoing demobilization, who were the main focus of my research.[16] At the collective level of societies, as well as at the individual level of survivors of the Great War, the transition from war to peace consisted of successive waves of demobilization and remobilization, making the boundaries between war and peace difficult to define.

---

[13] Charles Pelham Groves, "Missionary and humanitarian aspects of imperialism," in L.H. Gann and Peter Duignan (eds.), *Colonialism in Africa* (Cambridge University Press, 1969), Vol. I, pp. 462–496; Alice L. Conklin, "Colonialism and human rights: a contradiction in terms? The case of France and West Africa, 1895–1914," *American Historical Review*, 103: 2, April 1998, pp. 419–442; J.P. Daughton, *Humanity So Far Away: European Empires, International Organizations, and the Discovery of Global Suffering* (Oxford University Press, forthcoming).

[14] George I. Gay and Harold H. Fisher (eds.), *Public Relations of the Commission for Relief in Belgium: Documents*, 2 vols. (Stanford University Press, 1929) and Frank M. Surface and Raymond L. Bland (eds.), *American Food in the World War and Reconstruction Period* (Stanford University Press, 1931).

[15] Annette Becker, *Oubliés de la Grande Guerre: humanitaire et culture de guerre, 1914–1918* (Paris: Noésis, 1998; repub. Pluriel, 2003).

[16] Bruno Cabanes, *La victoire endeuillée: la sortie de guerre des soldats français (1918–1920)* (Paris: Seuil, 2004).

The *sortie de guerre* also constitutes a key period in the history of humanitarianism, especially with respect to ethnic minorities and the survivors of the Armenian genocide.[17] In the space of several years—that is, between 1918 and the mid 1920s—the Western world had to confront global problems on a scale and of a violence unprecedented in the history of the modern world. Millions of veterans and war victims returned home. Suffering from severe physical and psychological wounds, they had important needs, which they made known; yet these needs were generally difficult for society to satisfy. Refugees numbered in the hundreds of thousands; many of them had no material resources or identity papers that would allow them to settle abroad easily. The Allied blockade against Germany and the former countries of the Austro-Hungarian Empire, the revolutions and the breakup of empires in Central Europe, and the agricultural crisis in Russia and the Ukraine all contributed to the rise of widespread famines and epidemics. The social tensions of the post-war era, the economic crisis, and the growth of unemployment stoked the fears of millions of workers, who sought to have new social rights recognized.

In other words, humanitarianism, already deeply shaken by the war, was henceforth faced with a significant new challenge: the transnational aspect of the transition from war to peace. No one could claim to be able to handle the issues of the post-war period with the conceptual tools, the same material resources, or the same organizational structures as the early twentieth century. Although humanitarianism had long been an international activity, it now changed its scale, and also its nature.[18] The movement of displaced populations, the interdependency of different parts of the world, and the globalization of the post-war world all suggested that the questions facing that world could no longer be addressed at a national or international level; instead, such questions needed to be taken up at a transnational level. The potential risks associated with humanitarian disasters were also too great to be considered at the level of nation-states or their representatives. This transnationalization of humanitarianism is undoubtedly one of the major trends of the post-war era.

---

[17] Dzovinar Kévonian, *Réfugiés et diplomatie humanitaire: les acteurs européens et la scène proche-orientale pendant l'entre-deux-guerres* (Paris: Publications de la Sorbonne, 2004); Eric D. Weitz, "From the Vienna to the Paris system: international politics and the entangled histories of human rights, forced deportations, and civilizing missions," *American Historical Review*, 113: 5, December 2008, 1313–1343; Keith David Watenpaugh, "The League of Nations' rescue of Armenian genocide survivors and the making of modern humanitarianism, 1920–1927," *American Historical Review*, 115: 5, December 2010, pp. 1315–1339.

[18] Kevin Grant, Philippa Levine and Frank Trentmann (eds.), *Beyond Sovereignty: Britain, Empire, and Transnationalism, c.1880–1950* (Basingstoke: Palgrave Macmillan, 2007).

In parallel with the development of transnational humanitarian practices, the post-war transition period also saw a new kind of humanitarian narrative emerge. The expression of empathy for war victims led progressively to a new discourse on the rights of these victims. Legal scholars shaped this discourse of rights, as expressed by the victims themselves and by their representatives, into various forms of legal theory: the violence of the war and the post-war period as a violation of the law; the right to aid and protection for victims; the right to compensation for the violence that had been suffered. The first question I explore concerns the relationship between humanitarian practices and humanitarian narrative, and the assertion of humanitarian rights. In other words, how did humanitarian aid on the ground grow into a reformulation of victims' rights? Another question concerns the specific nature of these rights: were they humanitarian rights, defined within a specific context—war, political persecution, natural disaster—and applied to a collective group of victims, identified as such (and if so, according to what criteria)? Or, were these rights what we might call human rights, defined as universal and inalienable for each individual as a human being?[19]

In fact, the evolution in humanitarian practices in the wake of World War I went hand in hand with a shift in ways of thinking about victims' rights. Not only that, the practitioners and the thinkers influenced one another: legal scholars who worked for the League of Nations, who published in journals of international law, and who worked for organizations such as the Hague Academy of International Law were inspired by what humanitarian aid workers on the ground were doing; aid workers in their turn affirmed the need to recognize the humanitarian rights of victims. In this book, each of the chapters on the evolution of humanitarian aid practices—to veterans, refugees, victims of the Russian famine, etc.— is thus framed within an analysis of how humanitarian discourse, and especially the emerging discourse on human rights, was evolving.

The rights of man, humanitarian rights, the rights of workers, children's rights, the defense of a people's well-being and moral welfare— in the early 1920s, such concepts were far from self-evident. Several social groups collaborated on this work of redefinition and codification, which explains the diversity of the terminology they used. These groups included experts from new international organizations such as the League of Nations and the International Labor Office, created by the peace

---

[19] On "humanitarian rights" and "human rights," see Marco Sassoli, "Le droit international humanitaire, une *lex specialis* par rapport aux droits humains?" in Andreas Auer, Alexandre Flueckiger and Michel Hottelier, *Les droits de l'homme et la constitution: études en l'honneur du Professeur Giorgio Malinverni* (Geneva: Schulthess, 2007), pp. 375–395.

treaties of 1919: scholars of international law, scattered throughout the war but active during the 1920s;[20] networks of physicians and specialists of social issues, who worked for the leading international humanitarian organizations, old and new—the International Committee of the Red Cross (1863), the Near East Relief (1919), and the Save the Children International Union (1920).[21] A group of international activists and legal scholars, including Alejandro Álvarez, André Mandelstam, Nicolas Politis, René Cassin, Georges Scelle, and many others, gave rise to a legal discourse that would revolutionize humanitarian work. If we briefly examine this group of thinkers from a sociological standpoint, we can see an overrepresentation of Russian, Russian-Jewish, Greek, and Central European jurists, all exiled from their country of origin or having immigrated to France, as well as French jurists specializing in international law—in other words, legal scholars with a personal experience of exile or persecution as a member of an ethnic minority, and marked by the universal principles of 1789 and the tradition of the Rights of Man.[22]

All these activists and experts started from the premise that rights had suffered major setbacks during World War I. They sketched out a plan of action: to develop transnational protections for populations that had been threatened or attacked or who were otherwise vulnerable, in wartime or peacetime. They expressed the hope that the newly formed League of Nations would work towards the codification and protection of these rights. In their view, the international organizations founded in the peace treaties represented a third way, between the narrow-minded nationalism that was still very powerful after the war, and the revolutionary internationalism on the rise since the Russian Revolution. It was critically important to respond to the Bolshevik threat and to stabilize Europe, which had been shaken by the chaos of war and the post-war period. Rights activists thus contributed to "recasting Bourgeois Europe," to use the title of Charles Maier's groundbreaking study of the 1920s.[23] Their humanist utopia is one of the least well-known and most unexpected legacies of World War I, a brutal conflict carried out in the name of

---

[20] Jean-Michel Guieu, "Les juristes français, la Société des Nations et l'Europe," in Jacques Bariéty (ed.), *Aristide Briand, la Société des Nations et l'Europe, 1919–1932* (Presses universitaires de Strasbourg, 2007), pp. 185–199.

[21] Davide Rodogno, Bernard Struck and Jakob Vogel (eds.), *Shaping the Transnational Sphere: Networks of Experts and Organisations, 1840–1930* (New York: Berghahn Books, forthcoming).

[22] Dzovinar Kévonian, "Les juristes, la protection des minorités et l'internationalisation des droits de l'homme: le cas de la France (1919–1939)," *Relations Internationales*, 149: 1, 2012, pp. 57–72.

[23] Charles Maier, *Recasting Bourgeois Europe: Stabilization in France, Germany and Italy in the Decade after World War I* (Princeton University Press, 1975).

the defense of nations. Although the innovations of these activists, legal scholars, and experts were of lasting importance for legal scholarship and humanitarian practice alike, they have remained nearly invisible. Why has this historic shift been so thoroughly misunderstood? There are several reasons. First of all, most legal scholars and experts in the 1920s worked within the framework of international organizations such as the League of Nations and the International Labor Office. Historians have tended to neglect the social history of international work during the post-war period, concentrating instead on questions of collective security or the rights of minorities.[24] Only very recently has the scholarly study of major international organizations been revived. Thematic studies of refugees, health policy, the international struggle against forced labor and prostitution, on the one hand, and the study of networks of experts who gravitated around these organizations, the circulation of reformist ideas, and the creation of international standards have begun to renew our sense of the post-war era.[25] The history of the 1920s remains significantly underdeveloped, in contrast to the large amount of scholarly work devoted to World War I and the 1930s. Because the questions of disarmament and peace have dominated historical debate, other major issues at stake in the post-war period have been forgotten. These include: reparations for suffering inflicted during the war, the struggle for social justice, the fight for human dignity—all subjects at the heart of scholarship on international law and the work of humanitarian organizations in the 1920s.

There is another reason for the lack of awareness of a new international politics of rights after World War I, and it is even more illuminating than the reasons I have just given. Here we come to the debate on the nature

[24] For a synthesis of this new history of international relations, see Zara Steiner, *The Lights that Failed: European International History, 1919–1933* (Oxford University Press, 2005). On the central question of the rights of minority groups, see Carole Fink, *Defending the Rights of Others: The Great Powers, The Jews, and International Minority Protection, 1878–1938* (Cambridge University Press, 2004).

[25] Susan Pedersen, "Back to the League of Nations," *American Historical Review*, 112: 4, October 2007, pp. 1091–1117. The new history of the League of Nations and other post-war international organizations is so rich that I can only cite a few studies here. Among them is the work of Barbara Metzger (her doctoral thesis, "The League of Nations and human rights: from practice to theory," University of Cambridge, 2001, unfortunately not yet published), Sandrine Kott, Jasmien Van Daele, Isabelle Lespinet-Moret, Pierre-Yves Saunier, Thomas Cayet and Vincent Viet on the International Labor Office; Dzovinar Kévonian, Claudena Skran and Keith David Watenpaugh on refugees; Paul Weindling, Paul-André Rosental, Marta Aleksandra Balinska and Martin David Dubin on health policy; Dominique Marshall, Joëlle Droux and Emily Baughan on children's rights; Kevin Grant and James P. Daughton on forced labor—and many others.

of the rights that were defended in the early 1920s: were they human-itarian rights, or human rights? For some 15 years, numerous studies have focused on the history of human rights, which now constitutes an academic field, at the intersection of the history of ideas, legal history, and the history of international relations.[26] This field is not without its controversies, especially when the question of humanitarian rights ver-sus human rights is at issue. Some scholars, such as Mark Mazower and Keith David Watenpaugh, claim that there is neither progression nor continuity between the era of humanitarian rights and the modern era of human rights;[27] others, such as Barbara Metzger, take the view that the humanitarian work of the League of Nations was in practice struc-tured by human rights.[28] The works published in this field all share a genealogical perspective that can be summed up by a single question: when did human rights as we know them today first come into being? In other words, when did human rights become the universal utopia that now serves as a reference point in international relations and drives the work of activists all over the world?

Such a driving question clearly has its limitations. For those who see the Universal Declaration of Human Rights of 1948 as a decisive turn-ing point, there is a risk of falling into a kind of moralizing and tri-umphant discourse, celebrating the prophets of human rights and over-looking the hesitations and inconsistencies of their struggle during and after World War II.[29] Conversely, demystifying the study of human rights, an approach best illustrated by Samuel Moyn's *The Last Utopia: Human*

[26] For a preliminary approach, see Louis Henkin, *The Age of Rights* (New York: Columbia University Press, 1990); Jan Herman Burgers, "The Road to San Francisco: The Revival of the Human Rights Idea in the Twentieth Century," *Human Rights Quarterly*, 14: 4, November 1992, pp. 447–477; Paul Gordon Lauren, *The Evolution of International Human Rights: Visions Seen* (Philadelphia: University of Pennsylvania Press, 1998); Kenneth Cmiel, "The recent history of human rights," *American Historical Review* 109: 1, February 2004, pp. 117–135; Lynn Hunt, *Inventing Human Rights*; Stefan-Ludwig Hoffmann (ed.), *Human Rights in the Twentieth Century* (Cambridge University Press, 2011); Akira Iriye, Petra Goedde and William I. Hitchcock (eds.), *The Human Rights Revolution: An International History* (Oxford University Press, 2012).
[27] Mark Mazower, "The strange triumph of human rights," *New Statesman*, February 4, 2002; *No Enchanted Palace: The End of Empire and the Ideological Origins of the United Nations* (Princeton University Press, 2009); Watenpaugh, "The League of Nations' res-cue" and *Bread from Stones: The Middle East and the Making of Modern Humanitarianism* (University of California Press, forthcoming).
[28] Barbara Metzger, "Towards an international human rights regime during the inter-war years: the League of Nations' combat of traffic in women and children," in Grant *et al.* (eds.), *Beyond Sovereignty*, pp. 54–79.
[29] For a critical reading of this historiography, see especially Mazower, "The strange tri-umph," *New Statesman*; *No Enchanted Palace*. See also Kirsten Sellars, *The Rise and Rise of Human Rights* (Stroud, UK: Sutton Publishing, 2002).

Rights in History,[30] also carries some risks. Since, according to Moyn, human rights did not become established as the "last utopia" until the 1970s, when other utopias such as anti-colonialism and Marxism were threatened or in decline, pre-existing ways of codifying human rights take on lesser importance by comparison. Consider, for example, the Universal Declaration of Human Rights of 1948, which Moyn eloquently describes as a "funeral wreath laid on the grave of wartime hopes."[31] If we adopt his point of view, the gains made in human rights in the 1920s will seem relatively modest.

I would like to propose a different perspective, and take up this question not from the perspective of a historian of human rights, but from the perspective of a historian of World War I and of the transition from war to peace. Instead of viewing the politics of rights in the 1920s as an incomplete version—less universal, less mobilizing, less efficient—of the utopia of human rights as we know it today, I argue that it should be understood in light of the traumatic experience of the Great War. The redefinition of rights in the 1920s must be re-situated in the dramatic context of the post-war period; as such, it is not a *step* in the history of rights but a *key moment* in shaping attitudes and values—what the historian John Horne has called "cultural demobilization," that is, the pacification of minds and the progressive restoration of peaceful relationships with former enemies.[32] Although it may seem at first glance a minor utopia within the broader framework of the twentieth century, humanitarian rights in the 1920s indeed represent a decisive turning point when seen from the perspective of those who survived the collective disaster that was the Great War. In the transitional period of the early 1920s, taking up the question of humanitarian rights became a way of turning away from war. These rights were an active part of the culture of the post-war transition period, with its unique aspirations for a lasting peace and for justice; they should be studied and analyzed as such, using the tools and methods developed in the past several decades by cultural historians of World War I.[33]

The history of human rights (almost exclusively the work of American historians) and the cultural history of the Great War seem mutually

---

[30] Samuel Moyn, *The Last Utopia: Human Rights in History* (Cambridge, Mass.: Belknap Press of Harvard University Press, 2010).

[31] *Ibid.*, p. 2.

[32] John Horne, "Démobilisations culturelles après la Grande Guerre," *14–18 Aujourd'hui* (Paris: Noésis, 2002), pp. 49–53.

[33] Jean-Jacques Becker (ed.), *Histoire culturelle de la Grande Guerre* (Paris: Armand Colin, 2005); Jay Winter and Antoine Prost, *Penser la Grande Guerre. Un essai d'historiographie* (Paris: Seuil, 2004); *The Great War in History, Debates and Controversies, 1914 to the Present* (Cambridge University Press, 2005).

unaware of each other, even when they focus on the same time period. The former is part of a transnational approach;[34] it studies the evolution of legal categories such as the transition from the idea of "humanitarian rights" to "human rights," and the way in which the circulation of ideas and the growth of transnational organizations produced shared knowledge and ideals. The latter is based on national or comparative history; its goal is to analyze the emergence of "cultures of war" in 1914–18 and their reformulation after the war; it seeks to explain how the violence of the Great War marked collective discursive productions and sensibilities.[35] By bringing these two historiographical traditions together, or, more precisely, by using the tools of the cultural history of the Great War to reflect on the history of human rights, we can better understand the true meaning and consequences of the debates over the politics of rights during the 1920s.

Those who codified and diffused the politics of rights in the aftermath of the Great War did not intend to provide a legal foundation for the new international organizations. More fundamentally, at stake for them was an imperative to turn away from war, to break with the "nationalization of rights" that had endured during the conflict, and to recreate a shared humanist culture. In 1914–18, each of the belligerent nations used the law to disqualify enemies, to exclude them from the community of civilized nations.[36] In his book *Qui a voulu la guerre?* [*Who Wanted the War?*] the sociologists Émile Durkheim and Ernest Denis used the vocabulary of penal law to put the German people as a whole on trial: "It is thus she [Germany] who is the great guilty party . . . The guilt of Germany appears in the fullest light [. . .] Everything proves it and nothing excuses or attenuates it."[37] During the war itself, many legal scholars, specialists of international law in particular, worried about the consequences the

[34] There is a rich bibliography on this idea, and on the distinction between "transnational history" and "global history." For a preliminary approach, see Bayly *et al.*, "*AHR* conversation: on transnational history," *American Historical Review*, 111: 5, December 2006, pp. 1441–1464, and Akira Iriye and Pierre-Yves Saunier (eds.), *The Palgrave Dictionary of Transnational History* (Basingstoke: Palgrave Macmillan, 2009).

[35] Stéphane Audoin-Rouzeau and Annette Becker, "Violence et consentement: la 'culture de guerre' du premier conflit mondial," in Jean-Pierre Rioux and Jean-François Sirinelli (eds.), *Pour une histoire culturelle* (Paris: Seuil, 1997), pp. 251–271. For more recent work, see Stéphane Audoin-Rouzeau, "Les cultures de guerre," in Benoît Pellistrandi and Jean-François Sirinelli (eds.), *L'histoire culturelle en France et en Espagne* (Madrid: Casa Velásquez, 2008), 289–299.

[36] On the functioning of this "nationalization of law" during the Great War, see Annie Stora-Lamarre, "La guerre au nom du droit," *Revue d'histoire du XIXème siècle*, 30, 2005, pp. 150–160.

[37] Emile Durkheim and Ernest Denis, *Qui a voulu la guerre? Les origines de la guerre d'après les documents diplomatiques* (Paris: Armand Colin, 1915), pp. 61–63.

conflict would have on their discipline. In 1916, one of the great theorists of pre-war international law, the Frenchman Antoine Pillet, offered the following disillusioned observation: "Nothing thus remains of what had seemed to be most solidly established, and we servants of international law have come to this, to wondering if something can be rebuilt after this great destruction."[38] Redefining rights meant opening a space for transnational dialogue, a space that had disappeared during the war. It meant reaffirming the meaning and function of law after having used it for nationalist purposes and, in a way, denaturalizing it.

This work of redefinition was begun by experts at the League of Nations and the International Labor Office in Geneva, together with experts at new institutions such as the Union Juridique Internationale (Paris, 1919), the Hague Academy of International Law (1923), and the Institut des Hautes Études Internationales (Geneva, 1927; known today as the Graduate Institute of International and Development Studies). Many of the legal scholars who took part in defining the "war of law" in 1914–18 were also responsible for creating new international standards after the war. Historians of the law and of international relations have tended to forget that these legal scholars also *experienced the war firsthand*. Some, like Georges Scelle and René Cassin, were drafted in the summer of 1914. For Scelle, "[World War I] was the most significant event the world had seen since the fall of the Roman Empire."[39] Others lived under German occupation. Many had to go into exile, fleeing war and persecution. Those who did not fight nonetheless had to break off professional and intellectual relationships, sometimes even friendships, with colleagues abroad. For all of them, the prospect of peace could not and did not mean a simple return to the status quo of the pre-war era.

World War I resulted in an unprecedented crisis of national sovereignty, which affected nearly all the former belligerent countries. Most affected were of course the Russian, Austro-Hungarian, German, and Ottoman Empires, which had now disappeared, producing territorial dislocation, a singular identity crisis, and the obligation to grant new rights to minority groups and to redefine the state's protective role, now transferred to other organizations, such as the Church or private charities.[40] The outbreak of the Russian Revolution rendered existing legal structures

---

[38] Antoine Pillet, "La guerre actuelle et le droit des gens," *Revue Generale de Droit International Public*, 1916, p. 12.

[39] Georges Scelle, *Le pacte des nations et sa liaison avec le Traité de paix* (Paris: Librairie du Recueil Sirey, 1919).

[40] On this crisis of sovereignty in Europe following the Great War, see Annemarie H. Sammartino, *The Impossible Border: Germany and the East, 1914–1922* (Ithaca: Cornell University Press, 2010), Introduction, pp. 1–17.

ineffective in a world where violence prevailed. The creation of new states gave rise to new national rights, breaking with those of the former empires. How could an individual's rights be guaranteed in countries that did not hesitate to persecute their own citizens or strip them of their nationality, as was the case with the Bolshevik regime and its supposed opponents, and in Turkey's treatment of the survivors of the Armenian genocide?

In the case of a victorious country such as France, where actual sovereignty was not an issue, it is more accurate to speak of a crisis in the legitimacy of the nation-state. The veterans of the Great War brought this crisis into sharp focus. "They have rights over us," declared Georges Clemenceau, the French *président du Conseil*, in reference to French veterans of World War I; he did not specify what those rights might be. To ensure their rights, French veterans had to rely on their veterans' associations more than they did on the state.[41] A crisis of sovereignty was at work in the milieu of internationalist legal scholars, who sought to found their discipline anew after the war. The great French jurist Georges Scelle appealed to his colleagues "to reject the idea of sovereignty deliberately and definitively, for it is false and it is harmful";[42] others, who were less radical, attacked only the idea of *absolute* sovereignty. In any event, for all these jurists, the individual and his rights deserved absolute priority in international law.

In 1918–19, the American President Woodrow Wilson himself saw a universalized liberal individual as the true locus of sovereignty in the post-war world. "International law has—may I say it without offense?—been handled too exclusively by lawyers. Lawyers like definite lines. [. . .] They like charted seas, and if they have no chart, hardly venture to undertake the voyage," he declared in May 1919. "Now we must venture upon uncharted seas to some extent in the future. In the new League of Nations, we are starting out upon uncharted seas . . . " For Wilson, the new world order had to go hand in hand with a rebuilding of international law, based on new standards. Conversely, his Secretary of State Robert Lansing favored international law of the pre-war era, based on the results of agreements made between nation-states. In an article in the *American Journal of International Law*, Lansing warned against the dangers of "Wilsonianism"—without actually calling it that: "We cannot ignore the dangerous possibility that moderate forms [of internationalism] may

[41] Antoine Prost, *Les anciens combattants et la société française, 1914–1939* (Paris: Presses de la Fondation nationale des Sciences Politiques, 1977).
[42] Georges Scelle, "Une ère juridique nouvelle," *La paix par le droit*, July–August 1919, pp. 297–298.

under certain influences develop into extreme [forms] and threaten our political institutions."[43]

The redefinition of rights in the 1920s was also a consequence of the chaos in Europe after the war. Because the problems of the post-war period were in essence transnational, any potential solutions would have to be transnational as well—hence the attempt to bring several countries together in dealing with crises. The League of Nations and its satellite organizations such as the International Labor Office, as well as humanitarian organizations such as the International Committee of the Red Cross, made it their task to coordinate responses to crises in the unstable climate that prevailed after the war. The case of Russian refugees is a good example. In the early 1920s, between 750,000 and 2 million refugees were amassed on the Polish–German border, and around Constantinople and Athens. Their high concentration in these areas, combined with their lack of legal status as stateless persons and their disruptive effect on the labor force were a cause of shared concern for all nations in the West. Thus, the League of Nations decided to create a High Commission for Refugees in 1921, then the Nansen Certificate, first issued to Russian refugees in July 1922 and extended to include Armenian refugees (1924) and Assyrian and Assyro-Chaldean refugees (1928).

The work of international legal scholars and the policies drafted by international organizations in Geneva should not, in the end, overshadow the role of another participant in the development of rights: the humanitarian sector. Following the Great War, this sector underwent a profound restructuring, which resulted from the breadth of technical and financial means now available, an increasingly scientific approach to international relief aid, and the growing impact of humanitarian issues on public opinion.[44] World War I strengthened the solidarity among countries and their allies, as well as the feeling of belonging to a global world. Activists from humanitarian organizations played a key role in these debates over rights, which is something that most historical studies of the 1920s tend to overlook. These activists' experience in the field enriched their conception of international humanitarian law. Thus, the Save the Children International Union called on the League of Nations to acknowledge children's rights. In other cases, the victims of war mobilized in order to

---

[43] Arthur S. Link, *The Papers of Woodrow Wilson* (Princeton University Press, 1966–1994), Vol. 58, pp. 598–600; Robert Lansing, "Some legal questions of the peace conference," *American Journal of International Law*, 13, 1919, p. 632, cited by Leonard V. Smith, "The Wilsonian Challenge to International Law," *Journal of the History of International Law*, 13: 1, 2011, pp. 206, 208.

[44] Kévonian, *Réfugiés et diplomatie humanitaire*.

ensure their own rights. Beginning in 1924, French and German veterans met in Geneva for meetings of the Conférence Internationale des Associations de Mutilés et Anciens Combattants [International Conference of Associations of Disabled War Veterans] (CIAMAC). Precursors of what we today would refer to as non-governmental organizations (NGOs), these groups of citizens were formed in order to put pressure on states and defend common goals on an international scale.

The development of transnational rights in the 1920s was not a faceless movement. It was embodied by men and women—jurists, aid workers, diplomats, activists—all deeply marked by their experience of the war. The French legal scholar and disabled combat veteran René Cassin defended the rights of his fellow victims of the war—his comrades in arms—first within the scope of veterans' associations and then at the League of Nations in Geneva. Albert Thomas, former Minister of Munitions in the French government's *union sacrée* of 1914–17, went on to run the International Labor Office in 1920, where he undertook a profound reform of international social law. The Norwegian explorer and diplomat Fridtjof Nansen, named High Commissioner for Refugees by the League of Nations in 1921, created a passport for Russian refugees in 1922, an act that revolutionized the status of stateless persons. The American philanthropist and businessman Herbert Hoover organized the two largest humanitarian operations of the early twentieth century, the first dedicated to providing relief in Belgium and Central Europe during the war, the second to providing aid to famine-stricken Russia in 1921–23. The English activist Eglantyne Jebb mobilized British public opinion in support of Austrian and German children suffering from the devastating effects of the Allied blockade—at a time when public opinion was otherwise quite hostile to Germany. Jebb founded the Save the Children Fund in May 1919. Thanks to her efforts, the League of Nations ratified a fundamental document in September 1924: the Declaration of the Rights of the Child.

The respective struggles of Cassin, Thomas, Hoover, Nansen, and Jebb shed light on the refinement and redefinition of rights in the post-war period. As a group, these men and women and the organizations they led fostered the rights of victims of war; the rights of workers, insofar as social justice is the best guarantee of international peace, as the founding charter of the International Labor Organization (ILO) put it (1919); the rights of stateless persons, who found themselves in legal limbo in the chaos of the post-war period, and who had to be reintegrated as quickly as possible into international regulations; the rights of victims of famine and epidemic, in the name of ideas still in embryonic form, such as the "right to mutual aid for all peoples in cases of calamity," as René Cassin phrased it in 1925;[45] and finally, the rights of children, who represented both innocent victims of the violence of war and the ultimate beneficiaries of post-war reconciliation.

These transnational rights had their own limitations. For example, they could only be put into practice through the goodwill of nation-states. Although they were acknowledged on an international level, this did not mean they were universal: in the area of labor law, for example, Western workers were treated better than workers in the colonies or in less industrialized countries, as the policies drafted by the ILO reveal. It would be wrong to see these transnational rights as more modern than they actually were, to conflate the legal redefinition of rights of the 1920s with the 1948 Universal Declaration of Human Rights, or to confuse the ILO of 1919 with its 1944 renewal via the Philadelphia Declaration, or to meld the humanitarian aid work of the interwar period (as efficient and scientific as it was) with the major humanitarian programs of 1950–60. Transnational rights as defined in the 1920s were based on ideas that were themselves still somewhat vague. These rights were the result of negotiations, influences, confrontations, and compromises. But there is no doubt that, as policy became practice, they changed the lives of hundreds of thousands of people after the war. Countless Russian and Armenian refugee families were saved from certain death because they could emigrate with a Nansen passport—and this is but one example.

In their own time, René Cassin, Albert Thomas, Fridtjof Nansen, Herbert Hoover, and Eglantyne Jebb all enjoyed a worldwide reputation. Just as there had been a "Wilsonian moment" after the Great War, there was also a "humanitarian moment"—that is, a period of several years in which important collective expectations were consolidated.[46] In the same way that President Wilson's Fourteen Points speech and his projects for rebuilding international relations inspired an almost unparalleled wave of enthusiasm, figures such as Hoover and Nansen, among others, gave rise to great hopes during the post-war period. The Hoover Archives at Stanford University contain sacks that had been used to send wheat to Belgium, Poland, and Russia as part of humanitarian assistance pro-grams; children in those countries decorated the empty sacks in Hoover's honor and sent them back to the United States to convey messages of thanks. The Nansen archives in Oslo have preserved letters from Russian refugees imploring the High Commissioner to lend them money or to

---

[45] Commission d'étude du projet Ciraolo, June 27–29 1925, p. 19, quoted in Antoine Prost and Jay Winter, *René Cassin* (Paris: Fayard, 2011), p. 100.

[46] Erez Manela, *The Wilsonian Moment: Self-Determination and the International Origins of Anticolonial Nationalism* (Oxford and New York: Oxford University Press, 2007).

help them settle abroad. Without the charisma and determination of their founders, it is likely that the Nansen Passport and the aid programs to famine victims in Russia would never have seen the light of day. These men and women did not act independently, of course. They knew each other, worked together, and shared ideas—Nansen and Hoover during the humanitarian crisis in Russia, for example, or Cassin and Thomas, defending veterans' rights under the auspices of the International Labor Office. More than that, though, they set up networks in which international civil servants, diplomats, and jurists could make use of the work being done on the ground by doctors and social workers. The personal history of these leading figures in post-war humanitarianism, the history of transnational rights, and the history of major international institutions and the networks of experts they put in place are all closely connected. Without the context of Hoover's Quaker roots or the philanthropic circles that Jebb's family was involved in, how can we understand the moral roots of the Commission for Relief in Belgium (CRB) or the Save the Children Fund (SCF), both major humanitarian enterprises, the former during the war and the latter after it? In the area of labor law, Albert Thomas cannot be separated from the reformist socialism of the pre-war period, from the experts at the Ministry of Munitions, which he ran from 1916 to 1917, or from the circle of experts at the International Labor Office. The rights of war victims would not have been acknowledged without the strong pressure brought to bear by veterans' associations all across Europe. Finally, the rights of refugees, promoted by Nansen, have to be understood in light of his Scandinavian origins, since a small country like Norway saw the defense of humanitarian rights as a better alternative to traditional diplomacy, because it was one that allowed smaller countries to have an important influence on international relations.

The experience of the Great War lay at the heart of this movement for rights. For Cassin, Thomas, Nansen, Hoover, and Jebb, as for all their contemporaries, it was a foundational moment. The war stirred up deep feelings against injustice and it gave rise to transnational standards for the protection of vulnerable populations. That is why we must begin with World War I, in order to understand how a brutal conflict carried out in the name of defending nation-states led to new kinds of humanitarian concerns and to assertions of humanitarian rights as the property of all those caught up in the cauldron of war.

1 "Rights, not charity": René Cassin and war victims

"The war left deep and permanent scars on me, and on many of my comrades . . . I could not accept the idea that national solidarity towards disabled veterans would be restricted to a kind of charitable handout."
René Cassin, Nobel Peace Prize Lecture, Oslo, December 10, 1968

At the end of World War I, an entire generation of veterans struggled to return to civilian life. Their ranks had been decimated by the considerable losses sustained during the conflict. In Europe, 10 million men lost their lives in combat; 20 million were wounded; 8 million suffered from various kinds of disabilities. The families who welcomed them home were often at a loss to cope with the severity of the soldiers' injuries and trauma, with their own inability to care for them, and with the impossibility of returning to pre-war life. These psychological problems were compounded by economic difficulties when a demobilized soldier was disabled, or when a family's principal provider had been killed in action. Widows, often young, numbered in the millions. There were nearly 6 million orphans when the Armistice was signed, and likely 3 million more in the years that followed, as veterans died from the consequences of their injuries.

For all of these "war victims,"[1] the recognition of their rights would be decisive: the right to a pension, to medical care, to a job. Indeed, these rights could take on paramount importance, since economic circumstances and living conditions were so difficult in the early 1920s. In the eyes of survivors of the Great War, the questions of justice and dignity were also at stake: in all countries, veterans called for "rights, not charity." But how could these rights be defined in the wake of a conflict with so many victims? The social legislation inherited from the nineteenth century was no longer suitable for the situation, especially with new and equally important issues at stake in the post-war period:

---

[1] *Victime de guerre* or "war victim" is a generic term, used in the French pensions law of 1919, and which, at the time, referred to both soldiers and civilians. See Annette Becker, "Conclusion," in David El-Kenz and François-Xavier Nérard (eds.), *Commémorer les victimes en Europe, XVIème–XXIème siècles* (Paris: Champ Vallon, 2011), pp. 328–329.

18

the reconstruction of regions that had been destroyed, the political management of victory or defeat, the peace conference, the suppression of revolutionary and counter-revolutionary movements. In fact, the recognition of victims' suffering was not the central issue, although the need for this recognition was certainly crucial. It was also necessary to provide legal grounds for their demands for compensation, which required political will—significant legislative work and the intervention of numerous legal scholars, including experts on labor law or occupational health.[2] In the immediate post-war period, the concept of "victim" had not yet been solidified and the idea of a "right to compensation" remained rather vague.[3]

A definition of the rights of war victims in fact consisted of two parts. Legal scholars had first to evaluate *a posteriori* the damage inflicted on people by the conflict, the severity of the damage, and the eventual chances of recovery. They thus defined society's responsibility for this damage, by virtue of which victims could obtain compensation. In France, the concept of compensation can be understood in light of the work of Léon Bourgeois, the theorist of *solidarisme*, a very influential philosophy at the end of the nineteenth century. In reaction to the rise of chronic poverty, Bourgeois wanted to encourage better social cohesion and redefine the social contract.[4] Assistance to war victims fitted in with this line of thought.[5] The Republic, both a warlike and maternal figure, as Maurice Agulhon's work has amply demonstrated,[6] was there to protect the weakest and to repair the damage wrought by the war. "The idea

---

[2] In the case of France, for example: legal scholars such as Charles Valentino (who wrote an important dissertation on *Accidents du travail et blessures de guerre* [*Workplace Accidents and War Wounds*], Bordeaux: impr. Y. Cadoret, 1917), Marcel Lehmann (*Le droit des mutilés* [*Disabled Veterans' Rights*], Paris: Librairie Bernard Grasset, 1918) and René Cassin.

[3] Annette Becker, "Les victimes, entre 'innocence,' oubli et mémoire," *Revue suisse d'histoire*, 57: 1, 2007.

[4] Several recent studies have focused on Léon Bourgeois, shedding new light on how important his influence was on politicians of the Third Republic. See especially Marie-Claude Blais, *La solidarité. Histoire d'une idée* (Paris: Gallimard, 2007) and Serge Paugal (ed.), *Repenser la solidarité. L'apport des sciences sociales* (Paris: Presses Universitaires de France, 2007). On Bourgeois' role in post-war international milieus, see Marie-Adelaide Zeyer, *Léon Bourgeois, père spirituel de la Société des Nations. Solidarité internationale et service de la France (1899–1909)*, Dissertation, École des Chartes, 2006.

[5] The first mention of the idea of "compensation" for victims of the war appeared in a law passed on December 26, 1914. It concerned "those who were victims of property damage" when the Germans invaded, and it presented the state as the final means of recourse, when private insurance failed to compensate the individual who had suffered the damage.

[6] Maurice Agulhon, *Marianne au combat. L'imagerie et la symbolique républicaines de 1789 à 1880* (Paris: Flammarion, 1979). Translated by Janet Lloyd as *Marianne into Battle: Republican Imagery and Symbolism in France, 1789–1880* (Cambridge University Press, 1981).

of solidarity between Frenchmen was only a philosophy before the war, a
philosophy that the war turned into a collection of harsh and clear experimental truths," is how the representative Léon Bérard summed it up in a
speech to the Chamber of Deputies in July 1917. Moreover, the concept
of compensation also had a diplomatic dimension that should not be
overlooked. In the case of France, if the state could be held responsible
for the damage done to victims, the ultimate debtor was Germany, who
would have to undertake "all pensions or compensations for the military
victims of the war . . . and for those whom these victims provided for."[7]

A posteriori compensation of damages, then, but also an anticipation
of future risks. In effect, between the two wars, a new legal category
was born, whose outlines were still rather vague: the vulnerability of
war victims. By vulnerability, a legislator meant the losses or limitations
resulting from war, the different kinds of handicaps that rendered victims
fragile and exposed them, *a priori* this time, to additional risks, whether of
a physical nature (for example, deteriorating health) or of a social nature
(such as job loss). The risks encountered by victims after the war imposed
on society a duty to assist, to take care of, and to protect them.[8] For the
historian, the progressive introduction of this idea of vulnerability shows
that legal scholars of the 1920s had already understood what current
historiography continues to underline: one can never completely escape
from the effects of a total war like World War I.

The definition of a right to compensation was thus inseparable not
only from the establishment of medical categories, which were constantly
evolving during the conflict, but also from the establishment of moral
norms, which could valorize some kinds of injuries and neglect others,
and, more globally, from the establishment of the social status of victims.[9] To take one well-known example, the status of those with physical
injuries was completely different from the status of those with psychological wounds, both during and after the war. For as much as the visibility
of bodily injuries facilitated the realization of the damage inflicted on
disabled soldiers, psychological wounds were tainted with the suspicion
that they were faked, or they were considered dishonorable.[10] In the same

---

[7] Annex 1 of Article 232 of the Treaty of Versailles: disabled veterans, war widows and
orphans are mentioned in Category 5 (see Pierre Renouvin, *Le traité de Versailles*, Paris:
Flammarion, 1969).

[8] Brian Turner, *Vulnerability and Human Rights* (Pennsylvania State University Press,
2006).

[9] Didier Fassin and Richard Rechtman, *L'Empire du traumatisme* (Paris: Flammarion,
2007). Translated by Rachel Gomme as *The Empire of Trauma: An Inquiry into the
Condition of Victimhood* (Princeton University Press, 2009).

[10] George L. Mosse, "Shell-shock as a social disease," *Journal of Contemporary History*, 35:
1, January 2000, pp. 101–108.

way, in defeated countries, the disfigurement of severely wounded veterans was perceived as emblematic of defeat: they bore its signs on their bodies. In other words, the rights of war victims were at the intersection of several discourses, often competing ones: those of the legislator, the physician, and the victim himself, when he could express himself. However, in the wake of World War I, the initiative for a consideration of victims' rights came from veterans and veterans' associations rather than from the state. It is thus they who constitute the focal point of this chapter.[11]

In the 1920s, many veterans felt they had been abandoned; the defense of their rights sounded like a cry of anger against this abandonment, anger that resulted from any number of causes: powerlessness to cope with the devastation of physical suffering, social isolation, blows to self-esteem, loss of virility, and feelings of shame. As it happens, this cry of anger that is so important for understanding the general tone of the war's immediate aftermath has, over time, become difficult for us to hear. In "victorious" countries, national memory has altered the reality of the post-war transition period, wrongly presented as a moment of national unity. The difficulty of reintegrating into post-war society has been progressively eclipsed by the official rhetoric of the 1920s, which glorified conquering soldiers as heroes. It is only recently, in fact, that we have rediscovered how chaotic the veterans' return actually was, and understood that the recognition of their rights was only achieved after long and difficult battles.[12] In the defeated nations, images of veterans begging in the streets of German and Austrian cities, and then the Nazi mythology stigmatizing civilian ingratitude towards demobilized soldiers had as its consequence the complete distortion of the reality of the return home in 1918.[13] In fact, not only were former soldiers well and truly

---

[11] The historiography is especially rich here. For a preliminary approach, see Stephen R. Ward (ed.), *The War Generation: Veterans of the First World War* (Port Washington, NY: Kennikat Press, 1975).

[12] For a general overview, see Hans Mommsen (ed.), *Der Erste Weltkrieg und die europäische Nachkriegsordnung: Sozialer Wandel und Formveränderung der Politik* (Cologne: Böhlau, 2000), and Stéphane Audoin-Rouzeau and Christophe Prochasson (eds.), *Sortir de la Grande Guerre. Le monde et l'après-1918* (Paris: Tallandier, 2008).

[13] Richard Bessel, "Die Heimkehr der Soldaten. Das Bild der Frontsoldaten in der Öffentlichkeit der Weimarer Republik," in Gerhard Hirschfeld, Gerd Krumeich and Irina Renz (eds), *"Keiner fühlt sich hier mehr als Mensch..." Erlebnis und Wirkung des Ersten Weltkriegs* (Essen, 1993), pp. 221–240; Sabine Kienitz, "Beschädigte Helden. Zur Politisierung des kriegsinvaliden Soldatenkörpers in der Weimarer Republik," in Jost Dülffer and Gerd Krumeich (eds.), *Der verlorene Frieden. Politik und Kriegskultur nach 1918* (Essen, 2002), pp. 199–214. Nils Löffelbein is currently writing a dissertation entitled "Der Nationalsozialismus und die Invaliden des Ersten Weltkrieges," Heinrich-Heine-Universität, Düsseldorf.

celebrated upon their return to Germany, but the Weimar Republic rather quickly set up a significant aid system for disabled veterans, widows, and war orphans, which made it one of the most protective sets of legislation in post-war Europe.[14] Finally, historiography has often privileged an administrative approach to the question of veterans' rights, without always fully taking into account its social and human implications. The familial, private dimension of the return home of disabled veterans has long been neglected in favor of a more global approach, that of the policies concerning veterans' aid.[15]

In comparison with the great social and political crises of the early 1920s, the question of veterans' rights has often been considered a secondary problem. However, in more than one respect, it was a central element in the slow and chaotic transition period following the Great War. The question of veterans' rights was first of all a factor in the stability of post-war societies: former soldiers were in essence men transformed by their experience of violence, men who were marginalized because they had been kept separate from the civilian world, and men who were demanding because they expected explicit signs of recognition from the societies welcoming them home.[16] Ensuring them rights, especially the weakest among them such as the severely wounded and the disabled or their families, meant lessening potential arenas of conflict and social trouble, although the state's direct intervention may not have sufficed to guarantee their loyalty.[17] In a general way, compensation has always been perceived as insufficient with respect to the damage suffered—something well understood by the German psychiatrist Karl Abraham, as early as 1918.[18] The extent and the nature of the aid given, as well as the means used to provide it, all differed significantly from one country to another, but the rights granted to veterans always bore witness to a desire to maintain control over former soldiers and assign them a collective identity.

Veterans' rights were also closely connected to the economy of war and post-war reconstruction: during the conflict, the wounded had to be allowed to return to a working life as soon as possible, and their

[14] Deborah Cohen, *The War Come Home: Disabled Veterans in Britain and Germany, 1914–1939* (Berkeley: University of California Press, 2001), Chapter 4.
[15] A notable exception is Marina Larsson's pioneering work, *Shattered Anzacs: Living with the Scars of War* (Sydney: University of New South Wales Press, 2009).
[16] On the psychological implications of recognition, see the work of the psychiatrist Claude Barrois, especially *Psychanalyse du guerrier* (Paris: Hachette, 1999).
[17] Cohen, *The War Come Home*, Chapter 2.
[18] *Zur Psychoanalyse der Kriegsneurosen* (Leipzig: Internationaler Psychoanalytischer Verlag, 1919).

families had to be able to pursue their participation in the war effort. After the war, victims of the conflict had to be able to contribute, as best they could, to the work of rebuilding. This was the aim of setting aside jobs in industry for disabled veterans; this was also the goal of the technicians who invented new prostheses, which were not designed with either aesthetic goals in mind or with perfectly restoring bodily function. Instead, they were designed to be adapted to the disabled man's professional needs. Rather than a mechanical hand, a disabled veteran could be fitted with an extremity in the form of a claw, pincers, or a hammer. Thus the concern was less with seeking to restore the disabled man to his pre-war identity than with allowing him, symbolically at least, to return to working life.[19]

Lastly, the question of veterans' rights had a specifically political dimension. In a country like France, where soldiers had also been citizens since the establishment of universal male suffrage in 1848, such rights were connected to the status of citizen. It was as citizen-soldiers that numerous French soldiers proposed appealing to the Chamber of Deputies in order to put an end to the useless, deadly offensives of 1917, as Leonard V. Smith has shown in his study on the French mutinies in 1917.[20] "We serve the army as a representation of the state, and we serve the state as a representation of the sovereign people," the mutineers explained. "We are citizens, we are therefore free to express our feelings, the values that we defend," as the cooper Louis Barthas summarized it in his war diaries, which provide good examples of this assumption of direct democracy.[21] In this way, French soldiers differed from British or German soldiers, not all of whom enjoyed the right to vote. Once back at home, French veterans continued to invoke their status as citizens while asserting their rights. In their eyes, the aid given to them had no connection to welfare nor to a form of public generosity nor to a logic of recompense, but, instead, was intimately tied to their rights. This is the true significance of Georges Clemenceau's famous statement in November 1917: "These Frenchmen whom we were constrained to throw into battle, 'ils ont des droits sur nous' [we owe them rights]," a

---

[19] Joanna Bourke, *Dismembering the Male: Men's Bodies, Britain and the Great War* (University of Chicago Press, 1996).

[20] Leonard V. Smith, *Between Mutiny and Obedience: The Case of the French Fifth Infantry Division during World War I* (Princeton University Press, 1994).

[21] Leonard V. Smith, "Remobilizing the citizen-soldier through the French army mutinies of 1917," in John Horne (ed.), *State, Society and Mobilization during the First World War*, (Cambridge University Press, 1997), pp. 144–159. See also *Les carnets de guerre de Louis Barthas, tonnelier, 1914–1918* (1st edition, 1978; repub. Paris: La Découverte, 2003).

relatively vague formulation nonetheless, which does not define the precise nature of these rights or the way in which the nation will honor its debt.[22]

The case of France is therefore a particular one. In what follows, I want not only to describe how French veterans' rights were structured after the Great War, but also to demonstrate that what was at stake for veterans transcended the context of the 1920s and the national context of France. Two radical claims lay at the heart of veterans' associations' fight for the decent treatment of disabled soldiers and families in mourning: the redefinition of war victims' rights and peace between nations, both of which required that the absolute sovereignty of states be called into question. In other words, a state that sent millions of men to the battlefields could not be the only guarantor of the rights of these men upon their return. The state needed a goad and a watchdog—namely, veterans' associations. By virtue of the sacrifices they agreed to make on the battlefields, the veterans of the Great War earned the moral authority to assert their rights. In the aftermath of the war, the profound significance of the effects of combat was at work, surpassing the somewhat technical character of the debates over veterans' rights.

One man played an essential role in the definition and promotion of the rights of victims of the Great War: the French legal scholar René Cassin. Along with Eleanor Roosevelt, Charles Malik, P.C. Chang, and John Humphrey, he was one of the founders of the Universal Declaration of Human Rights in 1948.[23] Severely wounded in 1914, Cassin experienced the disorganization of the health services at the beginning of the war and the carelessness of public authorities in providing material assistance to soldiers who emerged from the war as disabled. He himself suffered little since he had the means to regain his place in society, but many around him found themselves victimized. His fight for the improvement of veterans' rights was also the fight of all the veterans' associations that were founded, even before the war was over.

When Cassin was a participant in the French delegation to the League of Nations in 1924, he initiated a dialogue with veterans from other countries, including former enemy powers such as Germany and Austria,

---

[22] Antoine Prost, "Ils ont des droits sur nous," in Jean-François Muracciole and Frédéric Rousseau (eds.), *Combats. Hommage à Jules Maurin historien* (Paris: Michel Houdiard éditeur, 2010), pp. 369–380.

[23] Mary Ann Glendon, *A World Made New: Eleanor Roosevelt and the Universal Declaration of Human Rights* (New York: Random House, 2001); Habib C. Malik (ed.), *The Challenge of Human Rights: Charles Malik and the Universal Declaration* (Oxford: Charles Malik Foundation, 2000); Clinton Timothy Curle, *Humanité: John Humphrey's Alternative Accounts of Human Rights* (University of Toronto Press, 2007).

in order to defend these rights on an international scale and promote peace. René Cassin's personal journey and his political role thus led him to raise questions about several forces specific to the post-war period: the link between veterans' rights and the promotion of human dignity; the transition from the defense of veterans' rights at a national level to a transnational level, and the relationship between the rights of the war's victims and the defense of peace.

French veterans' associations and the victims of the Great War

In the month of August 1914, Cassin was a young legal scholar, 26 years old, pursuing his studies in order to take the highly competitive national examination known as the *agrégation*.[24] From a Jewish family near Bayonne in Southwestern France, close to the Spanish border, he attended law school in Aix-en-Provence, and then settled in Paris in 1908. He then divided his time between writing a thesis on civil law, which he defended in the spring of 1914, and a position as editor at the law journal *Recueil des Lois et Décrets*, better known as the *Recueil Sirey*. His friends were mostly students like him, who met in a group called the "Ihering Circle," an intellectual club where members would present their work in progress. Among them was Paul Ramadier, who would become the first *Président du Conseil* of the Fourth Republic, and Marcel Plaisant, whom Cassin would meet up with again during the 1920s when the former was France's representative at the League of Nations. On August 1, 1914, France entered into war. Several hours after notices announcing the general mobilization were posted on the walls of Paris, Cassin took the train to Antibes to join his assigned regiment, the 311th Infantry.

One month later, he was fighting in the Argonne and the Hauts-de-Meuse, at the time of the extremely violent clashes typical of the end of the "war of movement." Many friends died around him, as he recalled in public in September 1940, in a moving speech delivered on the BBC, after he had joined the Free French:

I can still see you even now, Captain Woignier, a Catholic from Lorraine with a fiery soul; when you closed your eyes in death, you gazed on your native land, and I can still see you, Vandendalle and Pellegrino, fearless and blameless, peaceful gardeners with bright red blood, like your beautiful flowers. I can see you, Garrus,

---

[24] The *agrégation* is a highly competitive national examination administered in a variety of subjects. Those who succeed on the *agrégation de droit* are guaranteed a position as a law professor in the French higher education system.

a humble day laborer from the hills of the Var, you, the freethinking poacher, who volunteered for dangerous patrols, and you, Samama, prosecuting judge who thought it important, because you were Jewish, not to seek a safer position.[25]

On October 12, the regiment received the order to lead a night raid on the Chauvoncourt barracks, near Saint Mihiel. When they arrived about a hundred meters from their goal, the front-line companies suddenly found themselves bathed in enemy searchlights. Under heavy fire from the barracks' defenders, battle continued until two o'clock in the morning.[26] Cassin fell, hit by several bullets. He was wounded in the abdomen and thought he was going to die. He asked a soldier in his company to let his father know, and he asked a priest to pray with him. The night turned to morning, and he survived. He was quickly evacuated, not to a neighboring hospital, but to the area where he had first reported for duty after being called up, in accordance with military regulations. What followed was an absurdly long journey of 600 kilometers back to Antibes. On October 17, he underwent an operation and remained a convalescent for 6 months. He was formally discharged in March 1916.[27]

Despite the severity of his injuries, Cassin was fortunate. He benefited from the support of his family and friends. He rapidly returned to civilian life, and with military honors: a commendation, the *Croix de Guerre*, and the *Médaille militaire*. By January 1916, he found a job as a lecturer in civil law at the law school in Aix-en-Provence. He therefore did not suffer from the solitude, the lack of recognition, and the financial hardship that afflicted many other disabled soldiers. The fate of many French soldiers wounded in the fall of 1914 was often much darker than Cassin's. Until the reforms initiated in 1915 by Justin Godart, the Under-Secretary of State, the army's medical system seemed to be completely overwhelmed by the influx of wounded men during the first months of the war.[28] From a medical standpoint, most military doctors neglected to take into consideration the risk of infection caused by pieces of shell or shrapnel.[29] An

---

[25] *Cahiers de l'Union Fédérale*, 377, November 1987, "René Cassin au Panthéon," quoted by Prost and Winter, *René Cassin*, p. 32.
[26] *Journal des Marches et Opérations* (JMO), 311ème Régiment d'Infanterie, Service Historique de la Défense, 26N747/1.
[27] René Cassin, *La pensée et l'action* (Paris: Éditions F. Lalou, 1972), pp. 192–195.
[28] The work of Justin Godart, named Under-Secretary of the State Health Service on July 1, 1915, was important: in particular, he undertook the setup of organizations specializing in examining the discharge dossiers of each military region and systematizing the way soldiers were discharged, as well as the creation of prosthetic fitting centers and physical therapy centers for disabled veterans. See Prost, *Les anciens combattants et la société français*, Vol. I, pp. 8 ff.
[29] Sophie Delaporte, *Les médecins de la Grande Guerre, 1914–1918* (Paris: Bayard, 2003).

official report by the Hygiene Commission of the Chamber of Deputies in May 1915 describes the problem: "Without taking into account whether they were seriously wounded or not, men were assigned randomly to uncomfortable train cars with bad suspension, bad brakes, bad lighting, and that had not been disinfected; they often reached their destination only after a journey of several days."[30] The wounded were crowded into rearguard hospitals, where they waited over many months before they could be discharged. The legislation on discharges and pensions was completely inadequate for a conscript army. At most, it made it possible to handle some hundred cases a month, not the tens of thousands of cases that had accumulated by the end of 1914. Yet this legislation remained in place until 1919.[31] Even more serious was the fact that the spirit of the 1831 law had become obsolete. Indeed, soldiers had to provide positive proof that their wounds were due to the war and not other causes. Suspicion often won out over compassion. In the absence of eyewitnesses or a correctly filled-out evacuation document, the military commissions of the Great War showed themselves to be overly picky. At most, they granted to wounded men a pension so small that it did not allow them to cope with the rising cost of living.[32] It was in this climate of growing discontent that the first veterans' associations were born. In Paris, they were organized by 1915, whether on the basis of categories (the type of injury, or the injured man's profession) or according to the hospital where they had been treated.[33] In the provinces, disabled men were not as numerous, and tended to organize themselves in general associations: Saint-Etienne, February 1916; Nancy, April 1916; Orléans, February 1917. René Cassin joined the

[30] Archives du Service de Santé, Val de Grâce, ASS 574, pp. 20–21, quoted by Antoine Prost, "Le service de santé militaire pendant la Première Guerre mondiale," in Annette Wieviorka (ed.), *Justin Godart, un homme dans son siècle* (Paris: CNRS éditions, 2004), p. 147.
[31] French deputies had in mind a reform of the 1831 law as early as December 1914; a draft was proposed in November 1915, but the work of the bill's sponsor, Pierre Massé, deputy from the Hérault, and then Georges Lugol, deputy from the Seine-et-Marne, was completed only at the war's end: the pensions law was passed on March 31, 1919.
[32] According to the *Journal des mutilés* (February 10, 1918), the price of basic necessities had multiplied by a factor of 2.5 during the length of the war in French cities with more than 100,000 residents. Between July 1914 and July 1917, the index of the price of goods grew by 183 percent (see Statistique générale de la France, *Annuaire statistique*, 55ème volume, 1939, partie rétrospective, 151).
[33] One of the first major associations, l'Association Générale des Mutilés de la Guerre (General Association of Disabled War Veterans) was founded at the Maison-Blanche hospital in Paris. Places for medical care, but also places of boredom and of waiting, where discontent grew, hospitals and physical therapy centers provided especially favorable conditions in which discharged soldiers could give voice to their demands.

disabled veterans' association of Aix-en-Provence in March 1916, more out of concern for his former comrades in arms than from personal need, since his teaching job provided him a comfortable salary:

In this city in mourning, Aix, I saw war widows; I saw our injured comrades who were starting to be invalided out, those from the battle of the Marne, and then the battle of Verdun; and my barber, who had lost his left hand, told me that the disabled in that area had begun to demonstrate, because with a provisional allowance of 1.50 francs per day, they were living in poverty, no longer able to exercise their professions. He, for his part, had been lucky enough to be rehired by his boss . . . I was the assistant secretary of the association, since I didn't want to put myself forward. I wanted to help without drawing attention to myself. At the time I was a newlywed and had a crushing workload. We created the Aix association, and then others in the small surrounding villages . . . The widows, even those who had jobs, were not used to going out, and a woman dressed in mourning who went into a café was frowned upon. They really had to be courageous![34]

By joining together, the victims of the war sought to put pressure on public authorities to obtain a reevaluation of their pensions. Until the 1919 law, pensions were below the bare minimum wage. A soldier who was on 100 percent disability received 3.25 francs per day in 1915 and 4.80 francs per day in 1918. This was less than the minimum wage of the lowest paid factory workers during the war those—"specially assigned" whom soldiers saw as *planqués* or "shirkers."[35] These war pensions were far less than the salary of more highly skilled workers, who could earn 15–25 francs per day.[36]

Some former soldiers were condemned to poverty. Many employers hesitated to hire a disabled veteran, who would produce less than an able-bodied man and who risked causing accidents. The *Journal des mutilés* [Disabled Veterans' Newspaper], founded in 1916 by the *Association des mutilés de guerre* [Association of Disabled War Veterans], reported the following conversation between the boss of a car factory now making weapons, and a severely wounded former soldier who had come to ask him for work: "You are disabled, obviously, but that's not our fault. You have to understand that we are obligated above all to consider the inter-ests of our company and that we are trying to avoid being hampered by cripples."[37] Humiliated, disabled veterans tended to keep to them-selves and to become discouraged. Men originally from the countryside,

---

[34] Cassin, "Fragments autobiographiques," *La pensée et l'action*, p. 197.
[35] Charles Ridel, *Les Embusqués* (Paris: Armand Colin, 2007).
[36] Gabriel Perreux, *La vie quotidienne des civils en France pendant la guerre* (Paris: Hachette, 1966), p. 161, quoted by Prost, *Les anciens combattants et la société français*, Vol. I, p. 19.
[37] *Journal des Mutilés*, March 1, 1917, p. 3.

on the other hand, had more chances of finding farm work. They also reintegrated more quickly into their families, who protected them when they came home. Veterans' associations did not lose any time, moreover, in promoting a return to the land, which was preferable to city life, that symbol of all ills. Agricultural camps created for disabled soldiers and war orphans thus had a therapeutic, pedagogical, and moralizing vocation. For the *Association Nationale des orphelins de guerre* [National Association of War Orphans], for example, "the salvation of the [French] race" would occur through "the resurrection of the soil and of agriculture, of the healthy and fertile life of the countryside."[38]

In addition to greater material support, former soldiers also wanted better moral recognition for the sacrifices they had made. On top of feeling useless after the severity of their injuries forced them to leave fellow soldiers at the front, they also felt the shame of being taken for cowards by civilians who knew nothing of war. Some called for symbolic rights, such as reserved seats on public transport—which still exist— or the creation of special insignia that would allow for them not to be confused with the *embusqués* or shirkers, who had stayed safely on the home front.[39] The rights sought by severely wounded soldiers thus were not limited to confronting the material difficulties of wartime; such rights also had to allow for shaping the collective identity and maintaining the honor of those who would benefit from them.

From the outset, the founders of veterans' associations firmly believed that they were leading a noble fight, legitimized by the blood spilled on the battlefields.[40] Their actions as citizens and as veterans were meant to fight society's indifference and the miserly mindset that prevailed, as they saw it, in the Chamber of Deputies and in government offices.[41] From the war's outset, the ingratitude of the home front thus became a preferred theme in trench journalism, then in the newspapers of veterans' associations.[42] In October 1917, in the *Journal des mutilés*, an editorial

---

[38] Olivier Faron, *Les enfants du deuil. Orphelins et pupilles de la nation de la première guerre mondiale (1914–1941)* (Paris: La Découverte, 2001), pp. 64–65. This exaltation of the purificatory aspect of the campaign was a commonplace of war literature. On this topic, see in particular Bourke, *Dismembering the Male*.

[39] *Journal des Mutilés*, February 15, 1917, p. 2.

[40] On the origins of this discourse, see John Horne, "L'impôt du sang: republican rhetoric and industrial warfare in France, 1914–18," *Social History*, 14: 2, May 1989, pp. 201–223.

[41] On this rhetoric, quite typical of veterans, see Antoine Prost, "Combattants et politiciens. Le discours mythologique sur la politique entre les deux guerres," *Le Mouvement social*, 85, October–December 1973, pp. 117–154.

[42] Stéphane Audoin-Rouzeau, *Les combattants des tranchées* (Paris: Armand Colin, 1986); for a study of the internal function of this discourse in the veterans' milieu, see Prost, *Les anciens combattants et la société français*, Vol. III, pp. 174–178.

writer opined: "What we need now are offices where disabled veterans, widows, and orphans will be treated with respect, offices where employees, instead of rejecting a request due to a minor error on the form, will hasten to correct the error and right a wrong. And if Alexandre Ribot [former *Président du Conseil* from March to September 1917] does not find civil servants capable of simply doing their duty in wartime, let him send them to the front. There, they can defend their leather seats themselves."[43]

The newspapers of veterans' associations played an essential role, beginning with the first years of the movement. In response to the diversity of individual situations, they reinforced the idea of a "community of experience" and utilized strategies that sensitized people to victims' suffering.[44] They published page-long stories of the mishaps affecting this or that injured veteran; here, an amputee forced to beg in the streets; there, a soldier who had been invalided out but who was now mistaken for a shirker. All while applauding the decision to reserve seats in the subway for blind and disabled veterans in December 1915, the *Journal des mutilés* denounced civilians' attitude:

Thanks to you, Monsieur le Préfet, we will no longer see disabled veterans bullied, we will no longer see them struck by the vigorous fists of patriots by proxy in monstrous attacks; people will no longer have the right to read and re-read the same lines for half an hour without noticing the man suffering in front of them, leaning on his crutches or holding on to his cane, keeping his balance on a wooden leg with difficulty and pain.[45]

Over time, this newspaper became an important one. It sought to put the expertise of specialists in administrative law at the public's disposal so that veterans could navigate the maze of laws and regulations.[46] In its first issue, published in May 1916, the paper addressed its readers in the following terms: "Do you have a claim to make? Write to us. Do you

---

[43] Paul Birault, "Une loi de gratitude," *Journal des Mutilés*, October 6, 1917.

[44] On this idea, see especially the work of the political scientist Christophe Traini, "Les victimes entre émotions et stratégies," in Sandrine Lefranc and Lilian Mathieu (eds.), *Mobilisations de victimes* (Presses universitaires de Rennes, 2009).

[45] *Journal des Mutilés*, December 1, 1917.

[46] During this period, many booklets were published such as *Pour obtenir une pension militaire. Ce qu'il faut savoir, ce qu'il faut faire. Guide indispensable aux veuves, orphelins et réformés* [*How to Get a Military Pension: What to Know, What to Do. An Indispensable Guide for Widows, Orphans, and Discharged Soldiers*] (Paris, 1915) here and below; *Guide de la victime de guerre (pensions, gratifications, allocations)* [*The War Victim's Guide (Pensions, Bonuses, Allowances)*] (Paris, 1916); *Guide pratique des droits des militaires et de leurs familles victimes de la guerre aux recours, pensions, gratifications et autres avantages accordés par l'État* [*Practical Guide to the Rights of Soldiers and their Families Who Have Been Victims of the War, to Pensions, Bonuses, and Other Advantages Granted by the State*] (Paris, 1917).

need advice? Write to us. To obtain satisfaction . . . write to us. Do you need information? Write to us. For anything . . . write to us."[47]

In November 1917, a meeting of all the veterans' associations was held at the Grand Palais in Paris, with the goal of forming a national union. But the small provincial associations, afraid of being overshadowed by the Parisian movements, organized a second meeting in Lyon in February 1918: the *Union Fédérale* (UF) was then born, and René Cassin would play an increasingly important role in it beginning in March 1919. During the meeting at the Grand Palais, the military physician Charles Valentino, who also held a doctorate in law,[48] was instrumental in arguing that the principle of compensations should prevail over that of welfare.

What is at issue is whether the veteran wounded in combat, who saved his country, will constantly be at the mercy of the government's generosity, or whether he will on the contrary be able to present himself before the nation as a true creditor! When a man comes home disabled and when he has shed his blood, [. . .] this constitutes his right not to charity but to compensations for the damage he has suffered.[49]

He drew lengthy applause. The principle of compensation, which the attendees passed by a unanimous vote, was defended by the associations during all the debates in the Chamber of Deputies; it ended up being written into the beginning of Article 1 of the Law of March 31, 1919.

This law represented considerable progress with respect to the legislation inherited from the July Monarchy (1830–48). First of all, it put an end to the disabled veteran's obligation to prove the origin of his wounds, and instituted the principle of presumption of origin, which worked to his advantage.[50] No more need to look for witnesses to attest that a wound had been received during the heat of battle. This new provision also applied to war widows, as long as their husband's decease was officially registered—an often long and painful process given the large number of soldiers missing in action. The new law also made pension calculations more equitable, by replacing the old pension classes of 1831 with a new system of rating disability, in increments of 5 percent, going up to 100 percent disability. It was modeled on the French law of 1898 concerning workplace accidents. It is doubtless easy to stress the somewhat absurd character of these judgments: is the loss of a leg more serious than the loss

---

[47] *Journal des Mutilés*, May 6, 1916.
[48] Charles Valentino, secretary-general of the UF from 1918, became director of the pensions bureau in 1920.
[49] *Journal des Mutilés*, December 8, 1917.
[50] Presumption of origin was already affirmed in the law of December 9, 1916 concerning special temporary allowances for discharged soldiers (réformés no. 2).

of an arm? How can the relative damage linked to the loss of a thumb, a hand, or the right instead of the left hand be evaluated? However, at the time, the scientific appearance of the disability evaluation system by and large convinced veterans. Increases were included based on the number of children and dependents. Finally, the rights of war widows and orphans were officially recognized.

At the very moment when the law on compensations was being discussed in the Chamber of Deputies, another problem arose: the progressive demobilization, by age groups, of 5 million French soldiers, following the Armistice. This brought other rights to light, which differed from disabled soldiers' rights. This large-scale operation required faultless logistics on the part of the state: demobilization had to take place at a steady rhythm but without giving Germany the feeling that the French were disarming; it required sending men home, liquidating stocks of material, and organizing the occupation of the Rhineland. Since the demobilization of each echelon depended on the preceding one, it was impossible to give soldiers a precise timetable for their freedom. The men became impatient, worrying about the difficulties awaiting them upon their return: would their wife still be there? In what condition would they find their farm? Would their old boss take them back? Moreover, they came up against the cavils and quirks of a bureaucracy that they did not understand well.

Here is one example among many. In theory, the Law of November 22, 1918 affirmed the right of returning soldiers to take up their old jobs. The passage of this legislation, only 11 days after the signing of the Armistice, is one indication of its perceived importance by French legislators. However, this law, which appeared at first glance quite favorable to the rights of veterans, came with a condition: in order to be hired by a former employer, the veteran had to send him a registered letter in the 2 weeks following his discharge. After that, he lost all claim to this right. Now, how many returning soldiers forgot this formality during the joy of reuniting with their families? Two weeks was not long to readapt to civilian life. Moreover, quite often, the company where the demobilized soldier used to work had disappeared. It might have gone bankrupt during the war, or the boss might have been killed in battle. A cartoon published as early as 1917 in the *Journal des mutilés* expressed the soldiers' fears: two men were shown talking in their trench, with one saying, "War, ok, well and good. But what about after the war?"[51]

In early 1919, the discourse on rights occupied a major place in veterans' rhetoric and in Parliament. The veterans' associations, which were

---

[51] *Journal des Mutilés*, October 6, 1917, p. 1.

quite influential in France during the interwar period,[52] were split into two large groups, with some defending the specific interests of disabled veterans (the UF was the most powerful), while the others welcomed the demobilized soldiers upon their return home, such as the *Union Nationale des Combattants* (UNC), founded on November 11, 1918 with the support of the army, the Catholic Church, and the business world. The UNC already numbered nearly 100,000 members in February 1919. During this entire period, discontent reverberated among both recently demobilized soldiers and those still waiting to be demobilized. In the explosive context of the major strikes of spring 1919, the Clemenceau government wanted at all cost to avoid a situation where the social crisis and veterans' resentment might combine and stimulate revolutionary conditions. In March 1919, the government instituted a demobilization bonus of 250 francs, supplemented by 20 francs for each month spent at the front. It also waived taxes due during the war for veterans and war widows, if their income was less than 5,000 francs; once home, many demobilized soldiers had found a letter from the tax bureau waiting for them, demanding back taxes.[53] Finally, efforts were made to honor soldiers on their return and to help them avoid the bureaucratic headaches that the first waves of demobilized soldiers had fought with. The weight of symbolism in this definition of veterans' rights has over time become for us largely unfamiliar.[54] However, it remains essential. Otherwise, how can we understand that men worn out by the war years could take umbrage at the "Abrami suit," the badly cut suit of clothes given to them upon discharge? Or that they could complain in their letters about being welcomed in demobilization centers by young soldiers who had not seen combat?

For disabled veterans' associations, however, the question of pensions remained the top priority, since the amount set by the Law of March 31, 1919 was rapidly revealed to be insufficient in light of the rising cost of living.[55] But how could the government be persuaded to agree to a

---

[52] Antoine Prost justly reminds us that veterans' associations had four to five times as many members as trade unions did in France at the beginning of the 1930s.

[53] Prost, *Les anciens combattants et la société français*, Vol. 1, p. 52.

[54] Should this growing inability to understand be set against the demilitarization of European society, as seen in James Sheehan's masterful study, *Where Have all the Soldiers Gone? The Transformation of Modern Europe* (Boston: Houghton Mifflin, 2008)? Generally speaking, the moral categories that prevailed at the outset of the Great War, particularly the idea of sacrifice, have been modified by the professionalization of the army over several decades and by a kind of banalization of the military as a profession. On this theme, see Eric Deroo (ed.), *Le sacrifice du soldat* (Paris: CNRS éditions, 2009).

[55] The Chamber had initially adopted a standard of 2,400 francs per year for a soldier declared 100 per cent disabled, which was more or less equal to the cost of living for

reevaluation of the amount of the pension? If pensions worthy of the name were to be put in place, perhaps it would be best to begin with a distinction between those who had seen combat and those who had not, between those who had fought in the trenches and those who had worked desk jobs, because they were disabled before the war? Justice or equality: this was another element of the post-war debates. At the annual meeting of the UF in Nancy in May 1921, René Cassin forcefully challenged this proposition. Professor at the School of Law in Lille, he had become, in May 1920, the secretary-general of the UF, then its vice-president, under the president, Henri Pichot, a schoolteacher from the Loiret department in north-central France. They directed the largest veterans' association in France. "We had to be vigilant because some wanted to use disabled veterans for political reasons, even violent ones," he remembered. "We never accepted this and at that moment we took a uniquely republican position: we would obtain everything through the law, through democratic means!"[56] For Cassin, to establish a hierarchy among veterans of the Great War was inconceivable. All had served their country, whether by their work or with their blood: no one could contest the spirit of equality among veterans.[57] It was up to the state to find the necessary resources to provide them what it owed.

What was at stake in these debates of the immediate post-war period was important. By ardently defending the principle of compensation, veterans' associations asserted that the state was not, in their eyes, a supreme tribunal that could distribute rights to its soldiers according to its good pleasure.[58] In reality, the rights enjoyed by veterans were already imposed on the state by reason of its contract linking it to its citizens, in a series of reciprocal obligations. Moreover, rights resulted from damages incurred during the conflict, whatever their nature: ruined health, job loss, delay in career advancement. Enshrining the principle of compensations in law thus implied a redefinition of what it meant to be a victim of war. As the *Journal des mutilés et réformés* [Disabled and Discharged Veterans' Newspaper] put it: "Officer, junior officer, or

a year, estimated at 2,500 francs. But inflation naturally tended to reduce veterans' buying power sharply at the beginning of the 1920s. See Prost, *Les anciens combattants et la société français*, Vol. I, p. 55.
[56] Cassin, "Fragments autobiographiques," p. 201.
[57] Rapport au Congrès de Nancy, May 15–17, 1921, pp. 126–134, quoted by Prost and Winter, *René Cassin*, p. 55.
[58] This theme appears again in discussions over measures for retired veterans, begun in 1930. In 1933, Cassin reaffirmed the legitimacy of these measures: "This is not generosity on the part of the State towards victims of the war and veterans, but the compensation for personal damages." (Rapport au Congrès de l'UF à Limoges, June 3–7, 1933)

ordinary soldier; worker, farmhand, employee, or boss, the equal nature of their sacrifices was indisputable. And the equal sacrifice calls for equal compensations, according to the principles of true democratic justice."[59] In June 1793, the Convention had led the way by promoting severely wounded regular soldiers to the rank of second lieutenant so that they could benefit from decent pensions and be admitted as residents to the national military hospital and retirement home, L'Hôtel national des Invalides.[60] At the time, a "sacred debt" incurred by the nation with respect to its defenders was spoken of; the term was largely taken up again in political discussions after the Great War.[61] The 1919 law went much farther than the 1793 law, since it guaranteed the same treatment to all veterans.

The rights of victims and the origins of the French welfare state

The debate over veterans' rights following the Great War thus led to a renegotiation of the bond between the state and its citizens, but it was not restricted to this one point. Studies of other post-war periods, in particular the post-war transition period following the American Civil War, have sought to theorize the link between the development of veterans' pensions and the development of the welfare state, stressing the role of veterans' lobbying, the rivalry between political parties to capture the veterans' vote, and the creation of a large bureaucracy in charge of pensions.[62] In the case of France after the Great War, the establishment of rights for veterans also tended to increase the state's role in such

---

[59] *Journal des Mutilés*, June 1, 1917.

[60] Isser Woloch, "A sacred debt: veterans and the state in Revolutionary and Napoleonic France," in David Gerber (ed.), *Disabled Veterans in History* (Ann Arbor: University of Michigan Press, 2000), pp. 145–162, and his book *The French Veterans from the Revolution to the Restoration* (Chapel Hill, University of North Carolina Press, 1979).

[61] In addition to Clemenceau's 1917 speech, where he affirmed that veterans "have rights over us," Aristide Briand, in his inaugural speech of 1921, reminded his audience that disabled veterans and the families of soldiers killed in combat were "the nation's first creditors." Cassin took up this expression in an article published in *La France mutilée*, January 30, 1921.

[62] Theda Skocpol, *Protecting Soldiers and Mothers: The Political Origins of Social Policy in the United States* (Cambridge, Mass.: Harvard University Press, 1992). Calling into question the idea that the welfare state developed in the United States in the 1930s, Skocpol points out that the federal government devoted a quarter of its spending to pensions between 1880 and 1910. In 1910, more than 560,000 disabled veterans, and more than 300,000 widows, orphans, and dependents received federal aid, while thousands of veterans received care in specialized facilities. See also Megan J. McClintock, "Civil War pensions and the reconstruction of union families," *Journal of American History*, 83 (September 1996), pp. 456–80. The classic work on post-Civil War pensions remains

different domains as veterans' access to medical care, the right of disabled
soldiers to work, and the training of veterans for reentry into the work
force . . . This change, begun during the war, did not take place without
some tension: historically, the source of social policy in France has been
traced to the rise of mutual aid societies in the nineteenth century, at the
local level, and not, as is generally believed, to the tradition of a centralized state.[63] Thus, the expansion of the state's social role in 1914–18 was
viewed with suspicion. Many felt it risked creating a large bureaucratic
and technocratic machine that would distance itself from veterans and
be deaf to their expectations.[64]

Veterans' associations in particular were quite aware of this danger.
René Cassin, who had directed the UF since 1922, took a close interest
in the *Office national des mutilés et réformés* or ONM [National Bureau of
Disabled and Discharged Veterans], founded in 1916 in order to coordinate the efforts of various aid organizations working with victims of the
war.[65] Initially part of the Ministry of Labor, then the Ministry of Pensions in 1920, the ONM financed rehabilitation programs for disabled
veterans, convalescent homes for the severely wounded, and welcome
centers for war orphans, both in Paris and provinces, thanks to depart-
mental committees created by prefects.

In order to understand the social weight of this organization, we must
recall the extraordinary philanthropic movement born during the war, the
thousands of private foundations or buildings bequeathed for the use of
disabled veterans, war orphans, and war widows. In 1916, for example,
there existed more than 3,000 charitable organizations in Paris, each
with their own boards, benefactors, and volunteers: *Œuvre nationale de
protection en faveur des femmes et enfants victimes de la guerre* [National
Charity for the Protection of Women and Children War Victims]; *Œuvre
de secours aux enfants* [Help the Children Charity]; *Œuvre de l'hospitalité*

John William Oliver, *History of the Civil War Military Pensions, 1861–1865* (Madison:
University of Wisconsin Press, 1917). On the question of African-American soldiers,
see Donald Shaffer, *After the Glory: The Struggles of Black Civil War Veterans* (Lawrence:
University Press of Kansas, 2004).

[63] Paul V. Dutton, *Origins of the French Welfare State: The Struggle for Social Reform in
France (1914–1947)* (Cambridge University Press, 2002). The history of the retreat of
private aid in face of the power of the state in matters of social protection has notably
been studied by Henri Hatzfeld, *Du paupérisme à la sécurité sociale* (1971, repub. Presses
universitaires de Nancy, 1989).

[64] For a general overview, see Fabienne Bock, "L'exubérance de l'État en France de 1914
à 1918," *Vingtième siècle. Revue d'histoire*, 3, July 1984, 41–51.

[65] Jean-François Montès, "L'office national des anciens combattants et victimes de guerre:
création et actions durant l'entre-deux-guerres," *Guerres mondiales et conflits contemporains*, 205, January–March 2002, pp. 71–83.

familiale [Familial Hospitality Charity]... [66] Some had been founded at the end of the nineteenth century and continued their work after the summer of 1914; many others were born out of the momentum of national unity of the Great War. This burst of generosity needed to be controlled and managed; this was the role of the ONM, which was recognized as a public institution by legislation on January 2, 1918.

The veterans' priority was thus rapidly to take control of the ONM. In February 1918, only six representatives from charities in charge of disabled veterans and six from disabled veterans' associations were part of an executive board comprising sixty members. A year later, ten additional representatives from disabled veterans' organizations joined the executive board of the ONM. Among them were several important figures in the veterans' movement: André Maginot, Henri Pichot, and of course René Cassin. Disabled veterans occupied an increasingly large place in government offices of France's *départements*, but they were irritated by having to depend on the government to nominate them to their post. According to the veterans, the future of the ONM lay in the election of representatives, and in a management system shared between the state and veterans' associations.

Here we see one of the arguments already advanced in the debate over pensions: veterans held a moral authority that came from their experience as citizen-soldiers. It should thus fall to them and to them alone to outline a policy on aid to war victims, and not to bureaucrats to decide on such a policy in their place. In October 1920, a new reform increased the number of representatives at the head of the ONM to eighty, half of whom would henceforth be disabled veterans or war widows. In addition to the equal number of members of veterans' associations and representatives of the state, the process of the selecting of the former was especially interesting. Disabled veterans' associations and war widows chose a slate of candidates for representatives to the ONM, who were then voted on by the associations' membership. In other words, the very principle of social democracy, specific to France, saw the light of day in this organization and it would be taken up by works councils in 1945.[67]

But aid policies were not restricted to disabled veterans; they also applied to their families and to the families of soldiers killed in action. Several days after mobilization, the Law of August 5, 1914 had anticipated the conflict's impact on families. It awarded a sum of 1.25 francs

---

[66] Faron, *Les enfants du deuil*; Frank Gilson has a dissertation in progress, "Les œuvres de guerre à Paris et dans le département de la Seine pendant la Grande Guerre," under the direction of Stéphane Audoin-Rouzeau, Paris, École des Hautes Études en Sciences Sociales.

[67] Antoine Prost, "Ils ont des droits sur nous," p. 376.

per day to the wives of soldiers who had been deployed, supplemented by half a franc per day per child under the age of 16.[68] In so doing, legislators were only following a model inherited from the end of the nineteenth century, which based social assistance on the family unit, with respect to the number of dependent children.[69] In a country such as France, suffering from a low birth rate, the risk of a war that would turn into a "demographic blood-letting" was taken quite seriously. In founding the *Secours National* [National Aid Society] by the end of 1914, the mathematician Paul Appell wanted to come to the aid of the victims of war and "ensure the lives of those indispensable to the future of the French Race."

The Law of August 5, 1914 nonetheless rapidly proved to be inadequate. It was not enough to support the families of soldiers financially while they were deployed. After the very heavy losses of the summer and fall of 1914, countless war orphans needed help: along with the children of severely wounded soldiers, they initially only benefited from a pension called *secours annuel* or "annual assistance," going back to a law passed in April 1831.[70] What was required was not only to dust off the nineteenth-century legislation but also to adapt it to the context of total war: such was the meaning of the law that Léon Bourgeois proposed to the Senate on April 1915, leading 2 years later to the Law of July 27, 1917, which established the *Office national des pupilles de la nation* [ONP, or National Bureau of Pupils of the Nation].

A distinction should be made between the terms *orphelin de guerre* or "war orphan," and *pupille de la nation* or "pupil of the nation." The former refers to all children whose fathers were killed in combat but also to those whose fathers died later from their injuries. A child could thus be born well after the war, in the 1920s or even the 1930s, and be considered a war orphan; this unusual situation shows the extent to which identities could fluctuate during this period, and how the distinction between wartime and peacetime is impossible to delineate. War orphans benefited indirectly from the pensions law of March 31, 1919. The pension of a war widow was simply augmented by virtue of how many children she had, up to the age of 21. The status of *pupille de la nation* was more

---

[68] The law of August 5, 1914 remained in effect until October 1919. It affected nearly 4 million French families during World War I.

[69] On the opposition between France and Great Britain, and their structures, that of the parental unit and the male breadwinner, see the classic study by Susan Pedersen, *Family, Dependence, and the Origins of the Welfare State: Britain and France (1914–1945)* (Cambridge University Press, 1993).

[70] Several decrees in the fall of 1914 gave special consideration to the widows and orphans of civil servants killed in combat; they received half of the fallen soldier's salary, but this arrangement was set to end at the cessation of hostilities.

complex. These were children whose main provider, whether their father, mother, or other adult, was no longer capable of seeing to their needs, due to death, or to an injury or illness resulting from war or aggravated by it. *Pupilles de la nation* were thus not necessarily orphans. The law of July 1917 renewed a legal category that had appeared for the first time in France under the Revolution and then under the Empire—that of adoption by the nation—even if it did not have the same sense as it did in the eighteenth and nineteenth centuries.[71] In order to obtain the status of *pupille de la nation*, the child's legal representative had to initiate the request, which then had to be accepted by the civil court of the district where the applicant resided. This adoption by the state was symbolic in nature: with the citation "Died for France" on the father's death certificate, the corresponding citation "adopted by the nation" was added to the child's birth certificate. It could be accompanied by material assistance from the state, but this was not automatic.

What is especially interesting for our purposes here with respect to victims' rights was the way in which those who drafted the Law of July 27, 1917 wrote it in such a way that *pupilles de la nation* could not be confused with *pupilles de l'Assistance publique*, or wards of the state. Under the Third Republic, the *Assistance publique* (Social Services) was developed with the goal of receiving mistreated and neglected children, and reintegrating them into society.[72] Helping neglected children was part of a larger context of the increasing intervention of the republican state into family life, which occurred in particular via the establishment of compulsory education, the regulation of child labor, and the growing intolerance of domestic violence. Under the guise of regulating familial disorder, the boundary between public and private space thus tended to fade. Bureaucracy removed children from paternal authority. It placed them in foster families, often in the countryside, in hopes that they would be able to escape the bad instincts inherited at birth and become good citizens thanks to working and living in a healthy environment. The ultimate goal of the *Assistance publique* was to transform children "into honest people and to make them love their social milieu and their profession." There was no concept of social compensations for orphan wards of the

---

[71] The first case of public adoption was that of Suzanne Lepeletier de Saint-Fargeau, 11 years old, whose father was assassinated in 1793 by a bodyguard who criticized him for having voted in favor of the execution of Louis XVI. In December 1805, Napoléon had adopted as *pupilles de la nation* the children of officers and ordinary soldiers who had died at Austerlitz. A long tradition was thus set in place, applied successively to victims of the July Days of 1830, June 1848, and the war of 1870–71.

[72] Ivan Jablonka, *Ni père, ni mère. Histoire des enfants de l'Assistance publique (1874–1939)* (Paris: Seuil, 2006).

state; the state protected them, certainly, but it also kept them in a sort of rural proletariat and stigmatized them throughout their life. Wards of the state remained second-class citizens.

Nothing of the sort applied to *pupilles de la nation*. First, legislators took care that the status of these *pupilles* did not authorize state intervention in the private sphere. The recognition of the rights of children, as victims of the war, would not harm the rights of the family. As early as the law of July 5, 1915, paternal authority was transmitted to the mother, whose role tended to expand during and after the war, as recent studies of war widows have shown.[73] Moreover, the consideration accorded by society to *pupilles de la nation* differed completely from that accorded to wards of the state. The legislator Léon Bérard was quite clear on this point: "For reasons of moral appropriateness that are obvious to everyone, it was simply not possible that sons of soldiers who fought in the war be in the same legal category as 'foundlings' or 'neglected children.'" The legal scholar René Querenet specified, "One of the preoccupations of the law's authors was that [*pupilles de la nation*] not be subsumed into the same group as wards of the state [*pupilles de l'Assistance publique*]. It was not charitable assistance that the law provided along with the title of pupil of the nation, it was a right . . . "[74]

And since it was a right, all *pupilles de la nation* had to be on equal footing. "It is a law of Brotherhood and not charity," the legislator said. "It applies to rich and poor. The state has incurred a sacred debt towards the *pupilles de la nation*. The law ensures the same title of honor to all these children, however unequal their fortunes. It brings them closer together with a patent of nobility conferred on them that calls to mind the sacrifices of their fathers, who died to ensure our safety." It was thus quite appropriate that on July 14, 1918 a great ceremony took place all over France to mark the inauguration of the law concerning *pupilles de la nation*. The parallel between France at war and Revolutionary France was carefully stressed through the use of a common vocabulary: the defense of Liberty, the indivisibility of the Nation, the veneration of heroes who died in combat, and the emergence of a new elite destined to renew the country: "The law brings them closer together by conferring on them patent of nobility that calls to mind the sacrifices of their fathers, who

---

[73] Peggy Bette, "Des maîtresses en leur demeure? Le pouvoir de tutelle des veuves de guerre au sein de la sphère familiale au lendemain de l'Armistice (1918–1921)," in Bruno Cabanes and Guillaume Piketty (eds.), *Retour à l'intime au sortir de la guerre* (Paris: Tallandier, 2009), pp. 245–257.

[74] René Querenet, Conférence faite au Comité d'entente des œuvres venant en aide aux veuves et aux orphelins de la guerre (Paris, 1918).

died to ensure our safety."[75] In other words, the right to compensation stems from a "fictive kinship"[76] that elevates them above their status as simply victims, in order to make them children of the entire nation— hence the debates about whether or not their status as *pupilles de la nation* should end upon reaching the age of majority: since the state adopted these children as its pupils, should it not act as a father who would continue to care for them their entire life? For war orphans, on the other hand, obtaining a pension was explained more simply, in terms of a blood relationship to a soldier killed in action or who died as a result of his wounds.

As in the case of veterans, the state's intervention on behalf of war orphans grew out of an intense private-sector mobilization that dated back to the start of the war. Certain charities were secular and republican in nature, such as the *Œuvre des Pupilles de l'École publique*, which was initially founded to aid children in the public school system whose fathers had been killed in action or severely wounded. Others, of a Christian nature, such as the *Œuvre des Bons Enfants* [Charity for Good Children], sought to link war orphans to the image of Christ as a child. In a country like France, where the question of secularism still inspired heated debate, secular and religious charities were often at odds with each other, especially when it came to sharing public funds. In the Catholic newspaper *La Croix*, for example, the journalist Jean Guiraud stigmatized the *Œuvre des Pupilles de l'École publique* as being "run by a Jew, M. Xavier Léon," and the army orphanage as "run by a Jewess, Mlle Weil," who would pressure war widows to enroll their children in secular schools in exchange for the promise of financial help.[77] Inversely, the secular camp denounced the hidden influence of Catholic associations on families in mourning.

At the same time, solidarity in favor of young victims of the war extended well beyond national boundaries. The Great War gave emigrants of French origin the opportunity to restore their ties to France, ties that had been neglected for several decades. In July of 1917, the orphans of the Alpes-de-Haute-Provence *département* received 5,000 francs from the French expatriate colony in Puebla, Mexico, which had been established there during Napoleon III's failed 1861–67 military expedition. The conflict also gave rise to a significant demonstration of solidarity from American philanthropists, who acted in a variety of ways in order to

---

[75] Quoted by Faron, *Les enfants du deuil*, pp. 118–119.
[76] This "fictive kinship" plays an important role in dealing with collective grief in the 1920s and 1930s, as Jay Winter has shown in "Forms of kinship and remembrance in the aftermath of the Great War" in Jay Winter and Emmanuel Sivan (eds.), *War and Remembrance in the 20th Century* (Cambridge University Press, 1998), pp. 25–40.
[77] *La Croix*, May 7, 1918, quoted by Faron, *Les enfants du deuil*, p. 81.

supply food to people under German occupation (under the leadership of Herbert Hoover, as I will discuss in Chapter 4), to help refugees and then to participate in the rebuilding of destroyed French villages (Anne Morgan and her association, the American Friends of France), and to come to the aid of war orphans (the Fatherless Children of France association). In 1917, a group of American patrons acquired the château of the marquis de Lafayette, situated in the little village of Chavaniac in the Haute-Loire *département*. Several years later, Edith Carow Roosevelt, the widow of President Theodore Roosevelt, gave funds earmarked for "all the *Pupilles de la Nation* from Saint-Quentin and its region."[78] Her son Quentin, a pursuit pilot, had been killed in aerial combat on July 14, 1918 in the skies above the *département* of Aisne.

In the end, the return to peace nonetheless raised the risk that this burst of philanthropic goodwill would dry up, dependent as it was on the generosity of various benefactors. In addition, the *Office national des pupilles de la nation* [National Bureau of Wards of the Nation], created in 1917, suffered from significant regional differences in the way children were helped, with those in some areas getting better assistance than those in other areas. By increasing pensions, the Law of March 31, 1919 provided an initial answer to all these questions.[79] In all the debates concerning the definition of the rights of victims of the Great War, René Cassin played a leading role. He was sometimes nicknamed the "father of *pupilles de la nation* [wards of the Nation]." As a legal scholar, he took part in the negotiations over legislative and statutory documents, as did his colleagues Lehmann, Pichot, and Valentino. His efforts sometimes ran up against the inertia of certain legislators, as he recalled in an autobiographical text: "[For them], war was like a vast parenthesis that the last cannon's blow in 1918 had closed, and when I met with an elderly senator—an intelligent man—to discuss the matter of the *pupilles de la nation*, telling him that severely wounded soldiers needed their children to be cared for (for there were the dead and also the very severely wounded), he replied, 'I thought the situation of these brave men would improve with time.' I pointed out to him, '*Monsieur le Sénateur*, legs do not grow again!'"[80]

---

[78] Olivier Faron, "Aux côtés, avec, pour les pupilles de la Nation. Les formes de mobilisation en faveur des orphelins de la Première Guerre mondiale," *Guerres mondiales et conflits contemporains*, 205, January–March 2002, p. 20.
[79] Pensions varied according to the rank of the deceased. For ordinary soldiers, it was a mere 300 francs per year and per orphan, which is very little. The base rate went up to 500 francs per year in 1922 (see A. Scherrer, *La condition juridique de l'orphelin de la guerre de 1914–1919* [Nancy: Berger-Levrault, 1933]).
[80] Cassin, *La pensée et l'action*, p. 203.

Cassin did not forget that he wielded a kind of moral authority conferred on him by veterans of the war, especially the members of the UF, of which he was president from 1922. One of his priorities was to obtain equal control of governmental offices between representatives of veterans' associations and public officials. This was done in October 1920 for the ONM, which gave veterans' associations a historic responsibility: the ONM's mission was now to distribute funds among hundreds of veterans' associations and physical therapy centers, and to give loans to disabled soldiers to buy a piece of land or housing. Cassin followed all this work closely, in his capacity as vice-president of the ONM. On the other hand, veterans' associations remained a minority on the executive board of the *Office national des pupilles de la nation* (ONP) Over time, the defense of the rights of victims of the war ended up being concentrated within a single organization: the *Office national des anciens combattants* [National Veterans' Bureau] was incorporated into the ONM in 1933, in order to found the *Office national des mutilés, anciens combattants et victimes de la guerre* [National Bureau of Disabled Veterans, Veterans, and War Victims], which in turn absorbed the ONP in January 1935.

Reintegrating disabled veterans into society: a common goal for all veterans

Beginning in the early 1920s, the question of the rights of war victims expanded beyond the strictly national framework and acquired an international dimension. This was the time of the first major veterans' meetings devoted to war victims' rights. These rights took on new meaning: by creating dialogue among veterans from different countries, on subjects as fundamental as physical therapy, financial compensations, and access to a job, veterans no longer situated themselves on the grounds of categorical claims—that is to say, rights specific to a social group. Rather, they focused more attention on the relationship between veterans' rights and human dignity. In becoming more international, veterans' discourse on their rights became more universalizing, and, in a way, more radical. According to them, it was no longer a particular country, in the name of a pact linking citizens and public power in time of war, that was indebted to its own veterans for their sacrifices on the battlefields—as indicated, for example, by the May 1920 demonstrations of disabled veterans in all the major German cities.[81] All the former warring countries owed

---

[81] These demonstrations brought thousands of people together in the streets of major cities, and they were especially impressive. Soldiers with several facial disfigurements were at the head of a parade in Berlin in May 1920, followed by amputees leaning on

inalienable rights to their veterans, in the name of universal principles such as justice and dignity.

One point deserves special emphasis because it is fundamental. The dialogue among veterans did not originate from any initiative coming out of Geneva. It arose out of the veterans' associations themselves, which were increasingly convinced that the well-being of their members depended on a common defense of their rights, across national borders. By sharing information on social policy in each country, these associations could better put pressure on their governments. Moreover, a growing number of Allied veterans had understood that, if a lasting peace was to be obtained, the democratic institutions of the Weimar Republic had to be supported and everything had to be done to avoid German veterans' movements being mired in a desire for revenge and in nationalist hatred.[82] In the countries formed out of the breakup of the Austro-Hungarian Empire, the deterioration of the food situation and financial instability threatened demobilized soldiers and their families.[83] With time, all of Central Europe would descend into chaos.

In January 1921, the leaders of Britain's National Federation of Discharged and Demobilised Sailors and Soldiers petitioned the ILO, founded in 1919 with Article XIII of the Treaty of Versailles, in order to promote social justice throughout the world. They requested that the ILO organize a conference on the rights of disabled veterans. Several months later, the UF, then under the leadership of Henri Pichot, took up the British project during its meeting in Nancy (May 15–17, 1921). In the summer of 1921, the ILO conferred with different veterans' associations across Europe in order to organize a conference in Geneva.[84]

A man by the name of Adrien Tixier would play a crucial role in this enterprise. Like Cassin, he was a disabled veteran. On August 28, 1914, while the Battle of the Marne raged, Tixier was gravely wounded. He was only 21. His left arm was amputated up to the shoulder. His body remained riddled with shards of shrapnel. For more than 30 years, his life was "a proud dialogue with pain," as Léon Blum would later say in a speech delivered at Tixier's funeral in February of 1946. After his discharge in 1914, Tixier chose to become a schoolteacher, working in the

their crutches and about fifty disabled soldiers in wheelchairs, pushed by their wives or mothers. Widows and orphans also took part in this "march against forgetting." See Robert Weldon Whalen, *Bitter Wounds: German Victims of the Great War, 1914–1939* (Ithaca: Cornell University Press, 1984).

[82] Prost, *Les anciens combattants et la société français*, Vol. 1, p. 75.

[83] Manfried Rauchensteiner, "L'Autriche entre confiance et résignation, 1918–1920" and "La Hongrie, 1918–1920: dix gouvernements en vingt mois," in Audoin-Rouzeau and Prochasson (eds.), *Sortir de la Grande Guerre*, pp. 165–206.

[84] ABIT, MU/7/2/2; Commission internationale des mutilés, 1921.

Albi region. He then devoted all his energy to the defense of disabled war veterans and became one of the leaders of the veterans' movement. Tixier was a republican and a socialist, like many inhabitants of the Limousin where he grew up, in Haute-Vienne, and the *département* he later lived in, the Tarn, where Jean Jaurès had been elected as a representative to the Chamber of Deputies in 1885. In 1919, Albert Thomas, the Socialist Party candidate for Jaurès' seat, met Tixier. Several months later, when Thomas was named director of the International Labor Office, he called on Tixier to come to Geneva and put him in charge of issues concerning disabled war veterans.[85]

In June 1921, Tixier received a letter from Paul Vaillant, secretary-general of the *Fédération socialiste des Côtes du Nord*, who sent him the resolutions adopted at the UF meeting in Nancy. The idea of an international effort on behalf of disabled veterans was not new: as early as the end of the war, the Permanent Inter-Allied Committee had created a prosthetics research laboratory in Brussels. But, generally speaking, French veterans were disappointed by the inertia of this organization.[86] Moreover, and this was doubtless the most extraordinary part, the UF wanted to meet with representatives from the Central Powers: "For the first time, officially, so to speak [. . .] enemy combatants of yesterday will meet face to face, somewhere other than on the battlefield, to collaborate on a task of mutual recovery and justice."[87]

For the members of the ILO's executive board, partnership with disabled veterans had many advantages. The veterans were obviously the ones most affected by developments in prosthetics and by new laws formulating social policy—laws aimed at them, covering insurance, pensions, and jobs. The veterans provided the ILO with additional legitimacy. Albert Thomas, its director, called them "experts from the practical point of view."[88] Nor could the sheer number of disabled war veterans be overlooked (there were more than 8 million of them, out of the 20 million men in Europe wounded by the war), along with the weight of their role in veterans' associations and their impact on public opinion. Their organizations were powerful: the veterans' movement was structured around the disabled veterans' groups, beginning with the severely

---

[85] Henry Hauck, "En souvenir d'Adrien Tixier," *La Revue socialiste*, February 1956.
[86] The leaders of the ILO also criticized the work of the Inter-Allied Committee. In a report dated September 1922, Tixier gave the following account of a conference that the Committee held in Ljubljana and in Belgrade: "More or less meaningless results. Some vague wishes were expressed, after ineffectual discussions, held in trains and hallways . . . On the other hand, the three Yugoslav capitals were all visited, there were dozens of receptions, lunches, dinners, speeches, and toasts" (ABIT/MU/2/2/0).
[87] ABIT, MU/7/2/2, Letter from Vaillant to Tixier, June 30, 1921.
[88] ABIT, MU/7/1, Thomas' speech in March 1922 to the first meeting of the experts.

wounded who had been demobilized during the war. In the end, in all of post-war Europe, injured and disabled veterans had become particularly visible in the public sphere. "Living monuments to the war dead," in the words of the novelist Joseph Roth, they movingly embodied the presence of war in post-war societies. Support for disabled veterans could have a favorable effect at a time when international organizations were still in a fragile state due to the refusal of the United States to participate, the strength of nationalism, and the criticisms of militant Communists.[89]

In reality, veterans' groups as a whole did not turn to the ILO to ask for international cooperation. Close to the French Communist Party was the *Association républicaine des anciens combattants*, or ARAC [Republican Association of Veterans]. The ARAC refused, and would continue to refuse, to work with the bourgeois institutions that had grown out of the Treaty of Versailles. The writer Henri Barbusse, who financially supported the association with the royalties from his best-seller *Le Feu* (*Under Fire*, 1916), was its secretary-general. In a letter to Tixier, he wrote: "We do not believe as you do that the poverty and injustice endured by soldiers of the proletariat can actually be fought via annual conferences held under the auspices of and with the official participation of the representatives of governments responsible for the people's poverty and for war."[90] At the other end of the political spectrum, some French veterans' associations rejected the very idea of working with German veterans. This was the case of the *Union nationale des combattants*, or UNC [National Veterans' Union], which, after the UF, comprised the second largest veterans' association. This association developed a nationalist discourse that left no room for cooperation with former enemies.

The same attitude could be found among the *Association générale des mutilés de la guerre* [General Association of Disabled War Veterans], the oldest of the veterans' associations, founded in the summer of 1915. In a letter to Tixier, its director, General Malleterre, former director of the Invalides military hospital and retirement home in Paris, expressed his unease:

---

[89] "It seems to me that the millions of men who went to war, through their moral authority as much as through their strength, make up an element whose help it is of great interest to obtain," wrote Tixier in a letter to the Secretary-General of the League of Nations on October 7, 1922 (ABIT, MU/7/5/1).

[90] ABIT, MU/3/7/22, Barbusse to Tixier, letter dated August 3, 1920. On May 1, 1920, Barbusse had participated in founding a Veterans' Internationale, whose founding document was quite clearly hostile to the spirit of Geneva: "Veterans agree to not collaborate with anything in favor of the League of Nations, which is incapable of reaching its goals, and they agree to condemn it as well as any similar bourgeois institution willingly established in order to guarantee the safety of imperial conquests, in opposition to all the proletariat."

We reject wholeheartedly the mere idea of making contact with German veterans as long as Germany continues to avoid paying reparations for the damage it inflicted on France and the Allies; as long as it publicly questions the responsibilities it solemnly affirmed at the Versailles Peace Treaty, and as long as the voices coming from beyond the Rhine continue to proffer their lies in a detestable spirit of vengeance. It is possible that some far-sighted Germans may be disposed to understand and to cooperate with inter-allied nations in the interest of a general peace. But they are few in number, and we must wait until they are legion and until they have given indisputable proof of the transformation of the German mentality . . . [91]

What was true for the French was of course also true of other veterans' associations. The German *Reichsbund* and its 750,000 members, the association of disabled Austrian veterans, that of the Italian disabled veterans, the union of Polish disabled veterans and the British Legion—about 4 million disabled veterans altogether in Europe—said they were ready to meet with foreign veterans. But other associations voluntarily kept their distance. In Germany, the International Union, affiliated with the *Fédération Internationale* presided over by Barbusse, changed its mind and decided not to participate. The Union of Romanian Veterans accepted the idea of a meeting but set as a preliminary condition that "the associations of [their] former enemies declare they would respect and commit to honor existing treaties and pay reparations via the governments of their countries."[92] The National Federation of Disabled Belgian Veterans, for its part, judged that "the time of devastation is still too close and that of reparations still too far away to make it possible for the association to consider a cooperation of this kind."[93]

The first international veterans' meeting thus willingly took a practical approach, as if to keep away from controversial topics such as the Germans' responsibility for starting the war and for paying compensations. Along with the disabled veterans who represented their associations, there were officials from the ILO and scientific experts such as Ripert, a physician at the French Army's prosthetics fitting center in Paris, or Meier, head of the prosthetics and orthopedics department at the Ministry of Labor in Berlin. In discussions among veterans, physicians, and officials from various offices serving disabled veterans, the principal topics were the most promising prosthetic devices in post-war Europe, the most suitable materials, the best fitting techniques, and the most effective physical

---

[91] ABIT, MU/7/9/5/4, Malleterre to Tixier, letter dated November 2, 1922.
[92] ABIT, MU/7/5/1, Romanian Veterans' Union to Tixier, letter dated October 10, 1922.
[93] ABIT, MU/7/5/1, Belgian National Disabled War Veterans' Federation to Tixier, letter dated December 6, 1922.

therapy.[94] But the underlying objective was more ambitious: by working to reintegrate disabled veterans into active life, the delegates hoped to "establish a truly humane system of work in the world"[95]—words that effectively called to mind the ILO's mandate and that indicated a global way of thinking about the meaning of human dignity after the war.

The bureaucratic character of the minutes of these meetings, available in the ILO's archives, should not lead us to forget their human aspect or their symbolic importance. Men profoundly affected by the war found themselves face to face: those who had lost an arm, such as Adrien Tixier and the Polish delegate Kikiewicz; men wounded in the abdomen like Cassin; severely disabled men such as Major Cohen from the British Legion. For all of them, confronting former enemies was a new trial: "I know from experience that it is not pleasant to meet people who not long ago were firing bullets and grenades at you while you were firing at them, but it is precisely in the interest of world peace that I judge such meetings necessary,"[96] Tixier wrote.

On June 28, 1919, in the Hall of Mirrors, the German signatories of the Treaty of Versailles were obliged to come face to face with a delegation of French veterans described in French as *gueules cassées* ("men with broken faces")—a living reminder to the enemy of his responsibility for leading such a brutal war.[97] Only 2 years later, the Geneva meeting was to be the occasion to reflect together on the rights common to all veterans of the Great War. "It was not without some anguish that I left the warm environment of the meeting in Annecy in order to fulfill a particularly serious mandate," René Cassin remembered. "Germany and Austria had participated in the ILO since its founding in 1919; the most powerful Disabled Soldiers' Federations of those countries . . . had sent a delegate or two, sharing the stage for the first time with Allied delegates. The initial encounter was polite although marked by an understandable reserve."[98]

What would henceforth be the implications of a shared investigation into the rights of disabled veterans? The first, doubtless the strongest in symbolic terms, was the recognition of equal suffering among French and German disabled veterans. During the entire World War I, the body of the enemy was the locus on which nationalistic hatred focused, as a

---

[94] ABIT, MU/3/2/22, Tixier to Pichot, letter dated August 2, 1920.
[95] ABIT, MU/7/2/2, See also Léon Jouhaux's inaugural speech during the 1921 meeting. He evoked "a great duty to solidarity and a great task for international reconciliation."
[96] ABIT, MU/7/5/1, Tixier to Albert Thomas, letter dated October 31, 1922.
[97] On this episode, see especially Stéphane Audoin-Rouzeau, "Die Delegation der 'gueules cassees' in Versailles am 28. Juni 1919," in Gerd Krumeich (ed.), *Versailles 1919: Ziele, Wirkung, Wahrnehmung* (Essen: Klartext Verlag, 2001), pp. 280–287.
[98] René Cassin, "La réunion de Genève," *La France mutilée*, September 25, 1921.

number of recent studies on the historical anthropology of the Great War have suggested.[99] French physicians published articles explaining that the enemy was a different being, not only in his mind but also in his physiology: his physical appearance, his ways of speaking or eating, and even his smell—all supposedly differed from those of Allied soldiers.[100] Recognizing that disabled veterans from all countries had equal rights made physical suffering a common feature among all veterans, whatever their country of origin. Disfigured bodies were no longer seen solely in light of national combats, disturbing vestiges of the violence of war in Allied countries, incarnations of defeat in Germany and Austria-Hungary.[101] Assessed by doctors and legal scholars, but used above all by the veterans themselves to establish their common claims, these disfigured bodies formed a foundation from which each veteran's rights could be worked out.

Moreover, the first international disabled veterans' conference met with the goal of comparing the prosthetics and physical therapy techniques available in different countries.[102] To read the reports of the experts who met in Geneva makes it possible to see more clearly the state of general improvisation that prevailed at the time. No one could evaluate the results obtained with a particular prosthesis since there was scarcely any follow-up on veterans fitted with prostheses, except in Canada. But the very idea of international cooperation was revolutionary. Several years earlier, applied sciences, especially in the area of prosthetics, was considered to be one of the areas of expression for national genius. The context of the Great War had given rise to one of the great idols of early twentieth-century medicine, the surgeon.[103] The small group of specialists in reconstructive surgery was seen as particularly distinguished, and, among them, the most revered were those who operated on soldiers with severe facial trauma.[104] In all the nations who had gone to war, the ability to reconstruct bodies, send severely wounded men back to the front, and reintegrate disabled veterans into the war economy was praised as a sign

---

[99] For a general synthesis of these works, see Stéphane Audoin-Rouzeau and Annette Becker, *14–18. Retrouver la Guerre* (Paris: Gallimard, 2000), translated by Catherine Temerson as *14–18: Understanding the Great War* (New York: Hill and Wang, 2003).

[100] Juliette Courmont, *L'odeur de l'ennemi, 1914–1918* (Paris: Armand Colin, 2010).

[101] On Germany, see Sabine Kienitz, *Beschädigte Helden. Kriegsinvalidität und Körperbilder 1914–1923* (Paderborn, 2008).

[102] This comparison led to the 1921 publication of a work of international documentation on prosthetics, created by Dr. Florent Martin, director of l'Institut de prothèse et d'appareillage [Institute for Prosthetics] in Brussels (ABIT, MU/5/7/1).

[103] Delaporte, *Les médecins dans la Grande Guerre*.

[104] Sophie Delaporte, *Les gueules cassées. Les blessés de la face de la Grande Guerre* (Paris: Noésis, 1996).

of that country's modern medical techniques and of its surgeons' skill.[105] For example, following a visit to the Roehampton hospital in England, a reporter for the popular magazine *The Illustrated London News* vaunted the "many types of wonderful mechanical arms and legs now on the market" for disabled soldiers, while the catalog of the Inter-Allied Exposition of May 1918 explained: it was "the best artificial substitutes known to science" that would allow the disabled veteran to find "a definite future in civilian life." Through vivid accounts by the journalist Margaret Chute, Roehampton House became "the house of redemption . . . where the maimed and broken are made whole again, the legless are taught to walk, and the armless are taught to work."[106]

The notion among the Allied physicians of one day working with doctors from enemy countries had seemed unthinkable: had German science not been demonized, accused of denying humane values and using scientific knowledge for destructive purposes? The international conferences on disabled soldiers held in 1921 and 1922 thus represented an important turning point in rebuilding relationships among scientists from the former belligerent nations, at a time when Germany and Austria were still excluded from international scientific meetings. Relations among specialists in prosthetics, moreover, evolved more rapidly that the relations among more abstract scientists. During the International Research Council in Brussels in 1925, the French mathematician Émile Picard, who had lost three sons during the Great War, campaigned against admitting Germany to the organization: the 6 years that had passed since the end of the war represented "a very short time in which to draw a veil over so many odious and criminal acts, especially when no regrets were expressed,"[107] he explained.

It was in this moral and intellectual context that a preparatory meeting was held in Geneva in September 1921, and then the first meeting of experts on disabled veterans, in March 1922.[108] The first subject under

---

[105] Bourke, *Dismembering the Male.*

[106] W.B. Robinson, "Replacing lost limbs: marvellous artificial arms and legs," *The Illustrated London News,* November 1915, p. 633; H.D. Roberts (ed.), *The Inter-Allied Exhibition on the After-Care of Disabled Men, Central Hall, Westminster,* May 20–25, 1918, catalogue (London: Avenue Press, 1918); M. Chute, "Roehampton: The House of Redemption—Refitting the Legless Soldier," *The Graphic,* 4, November 1916, pp. 548–549, quoted by Jeffrey S. Reznick, "Prostheses and propaganda: materiality and the human body in the Great War," in Nicholas J. Saunders, *Matters of Conflict: Material Culture, Memory and the First World War* (London and New York: Routledge, 2004), pp. 51–61.

[107] Quoted by Brigitte Schroeder-Gudehus, "Pas de Locarno pour la science. La coopération scientifique internationale et la politique étrangère des États pendant l'entre-deux guerres," *Relations internationales,* 46, 1986, pp. 173–194.

[108] ABIT, MU/7/2/2 and ABIT, MU/7/4/1.

discussion was the international circulation of information on prosthetics. At a time when there were so many disabled veterans living in post-war Europe, it was important that they benefit from competition between the manufacturers of different devices, and that these devices be subject to international standards. The situation of disabled veterans differed significantly from one country to another. In France, since the beginning of the Great War, veterans had had their choice of device and of fitter, but they were often preyed upon by unscrupulous orthopedists who offered discounts on what turned out to be defective devices. In Austria, the government had a monopoly on the manufacture of prosthetic devices, and the lack of competition impeded innovation and progress. As for Russia and newly (again) independent Poland, whose progress in this area was impeded by a gap in technological progress, they simply could not cope with the large number of disabled veterans.[109]

Experts therefore suggested organizing an international documentation center and an exposition on prosthetics and orthopedics, which would be held in Geneva and also travel across Europe: the goal was to respond to the veterans' requests as best they could and eventually to have the disabled men themselves demonstrate how to fit the devices, as had been done in Great Britain. From an ideological standpoint, this was a notable change when compared with the wartime period. During the conflict, exhibits of prosthetic devices were organized in a national framework (in France, as early as 1915) or in an international one (Allied exhibitions in Paris, London, Rome, and Brussels); such exhibits aimed instead to show the public the reassuring image of rebuilt bodies, ready to reintegrate into society and contribute to the war effort. Nationalist discourse always underlay these displays, such as when Justin Godart opened the Val-de-Grâce Museum in 1916, in order to show the public the successes of French military surgery. "By creating painstakingly accurate displays of the surgical repairs that were carried out on soldiers' bodies at hospitals like Val-de-Grâce, the museum framed France's reconstruction in bodily terms," argues the art historian Amy Lyford.[110] In this type of exhibit, disabled soldiers thus found themselves largely instrumentalized. The staging of reconstructive surgery was not aimed at them, but at civilians or at Allies. The meeting in Geneva, on the other hand, had as its goal to put the disabled veteran back in the center of the picture. In particular, one outcome of the meeting was to recommend

---

[109] ABIT, MU/7/4/1, initial meeting of experts to study questions concerning disabled war veterans, March 2–4, 1922.

[110] Amy Lyford, "The aesthetics of dismemberment: surrealism and the Musée du Val-de-Grâce in 1917," *Cultural Critique*, 46, 2000, pp. 45–79.

comparing social policy in different countries in order to promote those polices most favorable to veterans.

Indeed, there were many differences between Germany and Austria, where veterans benefited from a developed system of health insurance, and France, where it was necessary, in the absence of general insurance against illness, to create an entire special bureaucracy for medical assistance to disabled veterans. The question of disabled veterans living abroad also emerged. In a world where political instability and the search for work led many survivors of the conflict to leave their country of origin, and where national identities often fluctuated, due to changing post-war borders, this was naturally a central question. How could reciprocal protection of disabled veterans be guaranteed between countries that had been enemies during the war—for example, in the case of German or Austrian veterans who came to France looking for work? And in a general fashion, how to proceed so that disabled veterans who had gone abroad were not penalized when the laws of their host country were less favorable than those of their country of origin? This subject, as technical as it may seem, raised important theoretical questions for international law, particularly the following one, on which René Cassin spent a great deal of time during the 1930s: is a right linked to one's nationality or to one's domicile—in other words, one's country of residence?[111]

During the meeting in Geneva, on the advice of Cassin, experts recommended giving disabled veterans the benefits of their country of origin, but no country would be obligated to give foreign disabled veterans advantages not provided to its own veterans: in the end, it was the law of the host country that prevailed. Moreover, each state would be responsible for periodically reimbursing the expenses of other states on behalf of its disabled veterans: the recognition of international rights for disabled war veterans thus concluded with bilateral accords, founded on mutual recognition of the pensions granted by the country of origin, and, over the long term, an international agreement prepared by the ILO. Along with this question of the rights of disabled veterans living abroad, the reorganization of post-war international law was outlined, even including countries that had formerly been enemies.

The steps proposed by the Geneva meeting were in essence those of comparative law. Experts were there to instruct each other on the laws in force in each country. The ILO was in charge of collecting this information in the form of syntheses and answering the requests for information

---

[111] René Cassin, "La nouvelle conception du domicile dans le règlement des conflits de lois," *Académie de droit international de La Haye: recueil des cours*, Vol. 4 (Paris: Sirey, 1931).

coming from veterans' associations. On the question of pensions, taken up during the March 1922 meeting, the laws of former belligerents could be divided into three separate kinds of systems. In Germany and Austria, compensation for war injuries followed the model used for workplace accidents. In Great Britain, obtaining a pension depended on the judgment rendered by an administrative commission. France had the most original system, with its classifications of disabilities, unconnected with workplace law, and the establishment of appeal procedures, which did not exist in Great Britain. René Cassin believed that, if the practical interest of these comparisons was not immediately felt in countries already endowed with modern laws, each of these major systems benefited, with time and experience, by borrowing from the others.[112] From the comparison of systems of protective social policies, reciprocal influence was born: such a result was also the hope of the first meeting of experts in March 1922.

It should be noted in passing that the experts no longer thought of disabled war veterans' rights as separate from other types of laws pertaining to social policy. In his opening speech to the 1922 meeting, Albert Thomas, director of the ILO, explained that "the efforts in favor of disabled war veterans...should be used for the benefit of those disabled in a workplace accident, and of all disabled people in general."[113] We should not see this as a sign of downgrading the question of veterans' rights, but instead as a sign of how difficult it was to separate the direct consequences of the war from the other problems that existed in postwar societies. Certainly, veterans formed a distinct social group and for that reason they enjoyed a certain number of rights. But the experience of being handicapped and the stakes it involved (restoring bodily functions, financial coverage while an invalid, lasting reintegration into the workforce) as well as its impact on people (social isolation and loss of self-confidence) applied not only to disabled veterans but also to those injured in workplace accidents, for whom the ILO had been responsible since its founding.

In the summer of 1923, a second meeting of experts convened in Geneva to discuss the question of job placement for disabled veterans. In the economic context of the time, work had become the main concern of veterans. These placement efforts, difficult in and of themselves, were made even more difficult by mass unemployment in the immediate

---

[112] René Cassin, "Le BIT et les invalides de guerre," *Revue française des Affaires sociales*, 23: 2, April–June 1969, p. 125.
[113] ABIT, MU/7/4/1, Speech by Albert Thomas to the first meeting of experts on disabled veterans, March 2, 1922.

post-war period. Veterans' associations awaited information on other countries' policies concerning the employment of disabled veterans. However, the deterioration of the international situation was hardly favorable to such a meeting. Since the beginning of 1923, in response to delays in the payment of German reparations, French and Belgian troops occupied the Ruhr Valley. In March, violent clashes broke out between workers at the Krupp factory in Essen and French soldiers who had come to requisition vehicles. Arrests and expulsions of civilians were carried out in response to various forms of passive resistance used by the inhabitants of the Ruhr, and in response to acts of sabotage by *Freikorps* troops. French veterans' associations were caught between wanting to develop further contact with German veterans' organizations and supporting a policy of firmness. The exchange of letters between the *Reichsbund* and the UF in June 1923 testifies to the intransigence of French veterans:

Our attitude responds faithfully to the peaceful will of the French people. They have been and they are still too exhausted by a war that they in no way wanted, wished for, or provoked—a war started by imperialist powers and conducted for four years on French soil—to wish to start another war. In their efforts to rebuild Europe, French veterans would strongly and sincerely like to find support from the German people and from a true democracy that would have real power in Germany... Alas, much more is needed in order for the efforts that have been made so far to have the expected results, and for the reparations payment policy for which your Federation has always declared its support to be carried out with sincerity in your country.[114]

Tixier was initially pessimistic about the possibility of bringing French and German veterans together again, at least as long as the Ruhr crisis remained unresolved.[115] By the end of August 1923, the representatives of disabled soldiers' associations and the heads of national bureaus in charge of veterans' job placement nevertheless met in Geneva. The circle had grown: Canada, South Africa, Australia, and New Zealand all sent representatives. As in 1922, the meeting essentially consisted of exchanging information on the laws in force in different countries. With the use of films, including one about blind veterans in the Siemens-Schuckert factory in Germany, the participants sought to show that severely wounded war veterans could perfectly well regain an active role in the economy. The real question at the heart of the debates was the validity of the principle of reserving jobs for war victims.

Several months before, in January 1923, French legislators had voted on a law granting preference to disabled veterans, widows, and orphans

---

[114] ABIT, MU/3/2/22, The Union Fédérale to the Reichsbund, June 1923.
[115] ABIT, MU/7/5/1, Tixier to Cassin, letter dated March 16, 1923.

when hiring for government jobs.[116] Unlike the previous law of April 1916 on the placement of disabled war veterans, it was no longer ordinary soldiers who benefited from the law, but all war victims, without regard for age or profession. With the law of 1923, therefore, we see a way of redefining the contract linking the state and individuals, and, in consequence, a redefinition of the social status of victims of the war. At the same time that commemorations of the Great War put the focus on veterans, to the detriment of the civilian victims of occupied regions, as Annette Becker has amply illustrated,[117] the state's aid had a larger scope and reach, in the form of government-sponsored jobs. It was understood as aid to families, whether they had been weakened by the return of a severely wounded soldier or by the death of the head of the family. This extension of the welfare state's benefits to victims as a whole, and not simply to veterans, was moreover one of the recurring themes of the associations' demands: during the first meeting of experts in Geneva in 1922, for example, the delegates recommended that the prosthetics benefit not be limited to those with a disabled veteran's pension, and that the right to prostheses be extended to civilian victims of the war.[118]

It was still necessary for victims of the war to prove that they could benefit from jobs reserved for them. The procedure was long; applicants often perceived it as humiliating, and it was closely monitored by military authorities: all the medical examinations, certificates of professional aptitude, and job interviews were held in barracks. The admissions tests were no different from those for candidates in good health. It was simply that each year a certain number of government jobs were reserved for victims of the war, classified according to the severity of their wounds in the case of disabled veterans, and according to the number of dependent children in the case of war widows.[119] Proof of the difficulty of getting one of the reserved jobs can be seen in the fact that only about half of the applicants, on average, got a job. In fact, the proposed jobs often required professional qualifications of a higher level than those typically held by veterans, since they had gone off to war too young to have gone beyond the most elementary schooling, and higher than those typically held by widows, who also did not have a sufficient educational level. Most beneficiaries of the law thus held low-skills jobs, where the pay was

[116] To the law of January 30, 1923, concerning government jobs, was added that of April 26, 1924 on jobs in the private sector.
[117] Annette Becker, *Oubliés de la Grande Guerre.*
[118] ABIT, MU/7/4/1, meeting of experts on disabled veterans, Geneva, March 2–4, 1922.
[119] Peggy Bette, "Reclasser les victimes de la Première Guerre mondiale: le cas de la loi du 30 janvier 1923 sur les emplois réservés en France (1923–1939)," *Amnis. Revue de civilisation contemporaine*, 6, 2006.

not enough to live on. Reserved jobs generally came as a supplement to pensions, which were themselves rather inadequate. In 1928, a French war widow who had not remarried, and whose husband had been an ordinary soldier, received an annual pension of 1,696 francs, or 4.64 francs per day, which was a little more than the price of 2 kilograms (4.4 pounds) of bread.[120] Reserved jobs thus brought both an essential financial supplement and job security, since they were government jobs.

As it happens, although it was quite important from the perspective of the question of jobs, in view of the number of people affected (1 million disabled soldiers, 600,000 widows, 550,000 orphans), this French law of 1923 also raised significant theoretical questions concerning the rights of war victims. The legislative debates preceding the vote on the law help to illustrate the dual aspect of the concept of the right to work. As with pensions, reserved jobs exemplify the symbolic debt contracted by the nation towards those who sacrificed themselves for it: disabled soldiers had the right to reserved jobs in compensation for the handicaps inflicted on them during the conflict, but disabled soldiers also had the right to participate in rebuilding the country. This was the second meaning of the right to work. "In sum, what do our disabled comrades and those who have suffered from the war want? They simply want to regain their place in society, they want to continue the efforts begun on the front lines, they want to restore our France, which has been sorely tried, to the place she should occupy among the nations, that is to say, first place, which she held before the war," explained Marcel Ferraris, a deputy from the Jura. "They still want to work for the prosperity of the country, which emerged victorious from this terrible war."[121]

In asking that veterans be able to participate in post-war reconstruction, that they all have the right to work for their country, the final declaration of the Geneva meeting in August 1923 held each state responsible for the *bien-être social* or "social welfare" of disabled veterans, a term that at the time was often used as a synonym for *droits sociaux* or "social rights."[122] But each of the participants was persuaded at the time that this improvement in veterans' rights, in various forms (the right to medical care and to prostheses, the right to a pension, the right to work...) depended on consolidating democracy in post-war Europe and peaceful

---

[120] Prost, *Les anciens combattants et la société français*, Vol. II, p. 257.
[121] Marcel Ferraris, *Official Journal, Parliamentary Debates, Chamber of deputies*, June 30, 1921, p. 3015, quoted by Bette, "Reclasser les victimes."
[122] ABIT, MU/7/4/2, Final declaration of the Geneva meeting of August 31, 1923. However, this right to work was progressively extended beyond the area of the public sector, as the French law of April 16, 1924 shows, which required all industrial and agricultural enterprises to employ pensioned war veterans as 10 percent of their workforce.

relations among the nations comprising it. Without this kind of political stability, both national and international, the rights of veterans would be fragile and doomed to disappear.

From victims' rights to peace through justice

In the minds of many of those who participated in the Geneva meetings of 1922 and 1923, these meetings were only a first step in restoring peaceful relations among the veterans of the Great War. "You will certainly understand that the discussions will not be limited to technical considerations," explained Paul Vaillant, secretary-general of the Fédération socialiste des Côtes du Nord, in proposing a first meeting with the Germans. "For my part, I very much hope that it will be possible for us to form a solid foundation for an international veterans' federation, destined to be the strongest element of peace, standing against the hawkishness of the chauvinists, the imperialists, and those hungry for revenge, in every country."[123] Some delegates, however, thought that technical questions were the only kind that could be mutually addressed with former enemies. Until that point, the questions of peace treaties, reparations, and even responsibility for starting the war, had all been carefully avoided. Why risk discord that could threaten the fragile edifice constructed during the first meetings in Geneva?

The answer to this question lies in one of the major transitions brought about by veterans in the 1920s: from an ideology of *la Guerre du droit* [the War for Justice], to a growing faith in peace brought about through justice. During the Great War, the large majority of soldiers, whatever their nationality, had adhered to the idea of a defensive war, conducted by their countries according to the rule of engagement.[124] For the French and their allies, the profound feeling that the Central Powers unilaterally bore responsibility for the beginning of hostilities reinforced this conviction. In their eyes, the war was doubly just, both because it had been provoked by outside aggression and because, on the battlefield, the Germans used methods of war contrary to international law and to which it was therefore legitimate to respond.

Academia played a part in setting up the argument for the "War for Justice." The legal scholar Louis Renault, who had been a member in the French delegation to the Hague Convention in 1907, gave a famous lecture at the Académie des Sciences Morales et Politiques entitled "War and human rights in the twentieth century," in the fall of 1914. During

[123] ABIT, MU/7/2/2, Vaillant to Tixier, June 30, 1921.
[124] This question of a just war is addressed in a special issue of *Mil Neuf Cent*, 1, 2005.

the same period, the accounts of atrocities committed by the German army against Belgian and French civilians formed an entire body of accusations, carefully examined by jurists on a variety of investigative committees, and countered by German intellectuals in the form of the famous Manifesto of the 93 (October 4, 1914), which also belonged to the domain of law.[125] Neutral states were naturally one of the targets of this campaign, led by the *Comité d'études et de documents sur la guerre*, a research committee created under the auspices of the French government. Some of the most respected French intellectuals of the time were part of the committee: Lavisse, Durkheim, Bergson, Seignobos . . . [126] The jurist André Weiss, a well-known specialist of international law, took on the role of legal expert for the committee. In 1915, he published a small treatise on the German violation of Belgian neutrality.[127] In other publications, he dismantled the arguments put forth by German legal scholars. The other target of the Committee was of course French public opinion, whose support of the *Union sacrée* had to be safeguarded. Even the major peace movements, such as the association *La Paix par le droit* (Peace through Justice), run by the philosopher Théodore Ruyssen, a specialist of Kant, did not distance themselves from this patriotic credo.[128]

It is important here to return briefly to the source of this juridical pacifism in order to illustrate the place that international law occupied in pacifist milieus before the war. Founded in 1887 by a group of students preparing for their baccalauréat at Nîmes, the *Association des jeunes amis de la paix* [Association of Young Friends of Peace] had become in 1895 the association *La Paix par le droit*. From the outset, it distanced itself from the radical, anti-militarist pacifism exemplified by Gustave Hervé and it adopted a more juridical and pragmatic approach, sometimes described as "moderate pacifism." The wars of the future would not be avoided by opposing the draft or by refusing the principle of national self-defense, according to the supporters of juridical pacifism, but through the advancement of international law, dialogue among nations, and the development of the practice of arbitration. From this standpoint, two national traditions could almost be opposed: a German pacifism marked

[125] Horne and Kramer, *German Atrocities, 1914.*
[126] Eric Thiers, "Droit et culture de guerre 1914–1918: le Comité d'études et de documents sur la guerre," *Mil Neuf Cent. Revue d'histoire intellectuelle,* 1: 23, 2005, pp. 23–48.
[127] André Weiss, *La violation de la neutralité belge et luxembourgeoise par l'Allemagne* (Paris: Armand Colin, 1915).
[128] Rémi Fabre, "Un exemple de pacifisme juridique. Théodore Ruyssen et le mouvement 'La Paix par le Droit' (1884–1950)," *Vingtieme siècle. Revue d'histoire,* 39, July–September 1993, pp. 38–54.

by an ethical conception of peace that exalted a natural, preexisting harmony among men, and a French tradition that spoke less in terms of morality and more in terms of international law or arbitration.[129] The association *La Paix par le droit* set as its goal to "popularize legal solutions to international conflicts by studying them." In so doing, it was part of a larger trend of thought on the rise at the end of the 1890s, with important figures such as Frédéric Passy, who founded the *Société française pour l'arbitrage entre les nations* [French Society for Arbitration between Nations] in 1867, and Léon Bourgeois, the theorist of *solidarisme* and the head of the French delegation to the Hague Conventions in 1899 and 1906. It was these same men who founded the European office of the Carnegie Endowment for International Peace in 1912; Jules Prudhommeaux, secretary-general of *La Paix par le droit*, also became one of its leaders.

When war broke out, the pacifist forces that had worked in France for a rational agreement with Germany, in the name of law, all supported the *Union sacrée* as one. They first had to mourn the loss of their pre-war pacifist hopes; that is, to accept "the inevitable ruin of all that had been the object of [their] faith, of [their] love, of [their] action," in Ruyssen's words. But by August 10, 1914, the association's journal, also called *La Paix par le droit*, had redefined its goals and recovered its sense of mission. If war had broken out, it was not because the doctrine of juridical pacifism had been false or naïve, but because European powers, beginning with Germany, had not applied this doctrine. "Since they wanted war, let the war—this war of legitimate self-defense—be violent, obstinate, fierce," the famous physiologist Charles Richet wrote. "Let it only end with liberation. In this colossal struggle, we represent the independence of peoples, freedom, the definitive future pacifism of the world. Let us remain soldiers of the law."[130]

In a letter dated August 6, 1914, written with the determination characteristic of those who had decided to go to war, Jules Prudhommeaux confided:

I who made no exceptions in my pacifism and who wanted Franco-German reconciliation with all my strength—I am now surprised by my ardent desire for the destruction of governmental and feudal Prussia, for the fall of the Hohenzollern, for a ferocious Commune [like the Paris Commune of 1871] that would make socialism in Germany leap a century ahead and regenerate that country,

---

[129] Roger Chickering, *Imperial Germany and a World Without War: The Peace Movement and German Society, 1892–1914* (Princeton University Press, 1975).

[130] Charles Richet, "Les représailles," *La Paix par le Droit*, 15–16, August–September 1914, p. 444, quoted by Sophie Lorrain, *Des pacifistes français et allemands, pionniers de l'entente franco-allemande, 1871–1925* (Paris: L'Harmattan, 1999), pp. 126–127.

something, in the end, something in Europe so decisive and so profound that on the remnants of pan-German savagery, the time might come for the United States of Europe."[131] For its part, the *Ligue des Droits de l'Homme* [Human Rights League], whose defense of republican rights dated back to the Dreyfus Affair, vigorously denounced the "atrocious war" led by an imperialist Germany.[132] "The law! Never has an idea seemed more clear, more just, more familiar," Victor Basch wrote in May 1915. "What was formerly denounced as empty ideology has again become, in the hour of danger, the clearest, the most urgent of watchwords [. . .] Germany has done an immense service to our cause.[133]

At the same time, many German pacifists supported the need for a defensive war: "Ever since the question of peace and war has no longer had anything to do with what we want, and since our nation, threatened on the east, the north, and the west, has been engaged in this historic struggle, any German who is a friend of peace must do his duty towards his Fatherland, like any other German," according to a pacifist pamphlet from fall 1914.[134]

In France, the reinvestment in juridical pacifism in a struggle for a just peace would come about in several phases: first in the winter of 1915 and the fall of 1916, when Briand began to sketch out the conditions for a lasting peace "that would protect the freedom of nations from any assault, through international conventions," then with the growth of Wilsonian ideology in early 1918. In the last months of the war, juridical pacifism became an important school of thought, after having been somewhat marginalized. It took up the project of a League of Nations, which had been invented by Léon Bourgeois before the war, and renewed its relevance, in the form of a French Association for the League of Nations, founded in 1918. For all these moderate pacifists, there was no doubt that peace should be based on an Allied victory and on writing the German defeat into legal history. In November 1916, the Conference of the *Ligue des Droits de l'Homme*, held in Paris, had already set out the legal basis for a lasting peace in these terms: "Justice requires that the future peace treaty plan for sanctions against the instigators responsible for the war;

---

[131] Quoted by Jean-Michel Guieu, *Le rameau et le glaive. Les militants français pour la SDN* (Paris: Presses de Sciences Po, 2008), p. 29.

[132] Emmanuel Naquet, "Guerre et Droit. L'inconciliable? L'exemple de la Ligue des droits de l'Homme de l'avant à l'après 14–18," *Mil Neuf Cent. Revue d'histoire intellectuelle*, 1: 23, 2005, pp. 93–110.

[133] Victor Basch, "La Ligue des droits de l'Homme et la guerre," *Bulletin officiel de la Ligue des droits de l'Homme*, May 1, 1915, p. 173.

[134] Pamphlet attributed to Ludwig Quidde, quoted by Sandy Cooper, *Patriotic Pacifism. Waging War on War in Europe, 1815–1914* (Oxford University Press, 1991), p. 190.

penalties against those who carried it out without respect for people's rights; reparations owed by the aggressor states."[135]

But what did veterans think and how did they situate themselves with respect to the debates over peace through justice? During the conflict itself, soldiers as a group were convinced that they were participating in a just war, and were acting within their rights in fighting against the enemy. The letters of French soldiers as seen in the archives of the *Contrôle postal aux armées* or military postal control, despite the subtle cuts of the censors and the soldiers' self-censorship, sometimes reveal feelings of revolt in the face of the difficulties of war or in the face of the absurdities of military life. They never question, or they rarely question, the validity of the national defense argument.[136] The Allied soldiers always held on to the feeling of engaging in a just war, a defensive war to protect their country, their way of life, and their families. As it happens, German soldiers who penetrated enemy territory had the same feeling; they saw their actions as legitimate in view of the surrounding double threat of Russian forces on the eastern front and Franco-British forces on the western front. They gladly saw themselves as their country's advance guard, leading a defense against foreign invasion.[137]

At the moment of the Armistice, the letters of French soldiers express the same sure faith in a just war, confirmed by victory over Germany. In this army grieving so much loss of life, the certainty of having led a war for the triumph of justice subsisted. "The job is done, we are satisfied," a soldier of the Fifth Army wrote. "The crushing of the *Boche* [Hun] is the symbol of the best of victories, that of good over evil, truth over lies," as another soldier summed it up, while many of his comrades awaited Germany's demobilization and punishment with equal impatience.[138] In the eyes of most French soldiers in 1918, Germany now had to be made to pay for what it had done. Germany—that is, its leaders, as President Wilson said—but also its people, including civilians, as numerous soldiers' letters suggest. In a period as unstable as that of the Armistice, it is however impossible to find a coherent and collective idea of justice in soldiers' letters, as this was something necessarily still too abstract for those who had endured the ordeal of war in the flesh.

---

[135] Quoted by Lorrain, *Des pacifistes français et allemands*, p. 127.
[136] Jean Nicot, *Les poilus ont la parole. Lettres du front, 1917–1918* (Paris: Editions Complexe, 1998, 2nd edition, 2003).
[137] Gerd Krumeich, "Le soldat allemand sur la Somme," in Jean-Jacques Becker and Stéphane Audoin-Rouzeau (eds.), *Les sociétés européennes et la guerre de 1914–1918* (Presses de l'Université de Nanterre, 1990), pp. 367–373.
[138] Cabanes, *La victoire endeuillée*, Chapter 1.

The disappointment of French soldiers awaiting demobilization, when they heard about the peace conditions imposed on Germany in the spring of 1919, was quite significant in this regard. If we turn once again to the analyses provided by the archives of the military censors, we learn that most French soldiers thought that the negotiators at the Paris Peace Conference had not gone far enough, that they had not succeeded in translating the need for justice expressed by the victorious troops into the language of international law. "We were too timid, too humble," a French soldier wrote regretfully in a letter to his wife on July 1, 1919. The men in black, the diplomats, "have ruined the work of the men in blue," the soldiers of 1918. And he added, "Our politicians made a shambles of everything. We should have had Foch as a dictator and peacemaker."[139] It is precisely the confusion between law and justice that is problematic here. In the eyes of the French soldiers, peace treaties should do justice to the dead and to the suffering they endured during the war—but how can treaties do this?

Pacifism as an ideology, if one means by this not the refusal of war in and of itself, but veterans' common quest for a lasting peace, thus took several years to take hold. In this sense, the progress of a kind of cultural demobilization, put in place by associations such as *La Paix par le droit*, which returned rather quickly to their pre-war convictions, should not be confused with the veterans' associations' movement towards peace, slower and not as well organized. In France, at the beginning of the 1920s, the veterans' associations formed a complex milieu, where attitudes towards former enemies differed significantly from one association to another. Certainly, a deeply felt need for pacifism, spurred by the trauma of 4 years of war, henceforth transcended political and social boundaries. For the first time in European history, millions of veterans empathized with one another in a common hope that the horrors of war would never return: "Never again," "Nie wieder Kreig," "Plus jamais ça." But pacifist ideology itself was divided, since not everyone could agree on exactly what peace would mean, or on how to bring it about in a lasting manner, or on the role that the League of Nations could or should play in reconciling former enemies.

A minority group, comprised of intransigent pacifists such as Henri Barbusse and Victor Margueritte, held the Allies and the Central Powers equally responsible for the carnage of the Great War. These veterans did not want in any way to connect their fate or that of the international

---

[139] Bruno Cabanes, "Die französischen Soldaten und der Verlust des Sieges," in Gerd Krumeich (ed.), *Versailles 1919: Ziele, Wirkung, Wahrnehmung* (Essen: Klartext Verlag, 2001), pp. 269–279.

veterans' group to which they aspired, to the fate of the League of Nations, a bourgeois institution inherited from the unjust post-war treaties. Most French veterans, for their part, hewed to a tradition that the historian Norman Ingram has called "old-style pacifism."[140] At the beginning of the 1920s, this tradition constituted the main support of the League of Nations, whose values it espoused: arbitration, and disarmament in a military and moral sense. Founded in 1918, the French Association for the League of Nations was more or less run by disabled veterans, which in itself is significant—even if it does not mean, of course, that all veterans were favorably disposed towards the League. In 1923, six large federations of disabled veterans (from the Pas-de-Calais, Meurthe et Moselle, Cantal, Tarn, Puy-de-Dôme and Loiret *départements*) joined the Association, and many members of the UF soon followed.[141] All advocated for *La Paix par le droit* and for international arbitration. René Cassin naturally belonged to this school of thought. The League of Nations for him constituted the "necessary framework for a better humanity, for which [veterans] fought." It would enable "replacing anarchy with an organization suited to making justice reign among nations."[142]

Beginning in 1924, René Cassin became a member of the French delegation to the League, nominated by Édouard Herriot to represent veterans. He thus traveled regularly to Geneva, especially in the fall, when the general assembly was held. It was there that he became friends with several important figures in international relations, such as Paul Mantoux, who had been Clemenceau's translator during the peace conference and who was now a member of the Secretariat of the League, and members of other delegations, such as Wellington Koo from the Chinese delegation and Christian Lous Lange of the Norwegian delegation. The latter was a leading advocate of disarmament, and he was awarded the Nobel Peace Prize in 1921, along with the Prime Minister of Sweden, Hjalmar Branting. Because of the close ties he maintained with veterans' associations in France, especially the UF, which at that time numbered seventy

---

[140] Norman Ingram, *The Politics of Dissent. Pacifism in France, 1919–1939* (Oxford University Press, 1991).

[141] That being said, the work of Jean-Michel Guieu (*Le rameau et le glaive*, pp. 95–106) has shown that organizations supporting the League of Nations brought together distinguished statesmen and intellectuals, but, in the end, they were unable to establish themselves in the provinces and they were few in number. Total individual memberships for all such organizations did not number more than 20,000 in France at the end of the 1920s. This was much fewer than the British League of Nations Union, which went from 4,000 members in 1919 to 650,000 in 1928 (see Christian Birebent, *Les mouvements de soutien à la Société des Nations en France et au Royaume-Uni [1918–1925]*, PhD dissertation in history, Université Paris X-Nanterre, 2002, p. 200).

[142] Published in *La France mutilée*, November 1922, quoted in Agi, *René Cassin*, p. 50.

federations and nearly 320,000 members, Cassin served as an intermediary between French veterans of the Great War and the League of Nations, which took great care not to cut itself off from public opinion. All of the UF's influence and all the weight of Cassin's moral authority were needed in order to arrange a meeting of veterans' associations from nine countries, under the League's auspices, in September 1925. They met not to talk about technical questions such as aid to disabled veterans, but rather the future of peace. This was doubtless one of the most surprising human enterprises of the 1920s, but also one of the least well known.

Nothing was less self-evident from the outset than Franco-German reconciliation: it had to confront persistent enmity between the two countries, internal divisions within pacifist movements, and the fundamental difference between French and German pacifism. The divide was a considerable one. In France, pacifism was progressively diffused in public opinion, to the point of becoming a "shared idea," whereas in Germany, pacifism was held responsible for the defeat. Shaken by the requirements of the treaty of Versailles, which weakened the dogma of "peace through justice," German pacifism was then marginalized by the rise of various strains of nationalism.

The signing of the peace treaty was first followed by a long period of silence, where relations between pacifists in Germany and France were practically broken: the former felt they had been cheated out of the just peace promised by President Wilson, and the latter did not know if they could trust pacifists who had compromised their beliefs by working with the government of the Reich during the war. At international peace conferences, the French systematically refused to participate when German delegates were present. Relations between activists in the two countries were restored very slowly, first at an unofficial level, through organizations such as the Carnegie Endowment for International Peace,[143] then through official visits, such as when the *Ligue des Droits de l'Homme* in Paris welcomed German delegates, and when French peace activists were welcomed to Germany in 1922.[144]

The following year, in 1923, the occupation of the Ruhr was felt to be a real calamity for Franco-German reconciliation, but it had paradoxical results. Many French pacifists did in fact denounce, in the name of international law, France's brutal policy in the Ruhr, and they did come to the aid of German pacifists, who were increasingly regarded as

---

[143] Alain Chatriot, "Une véritable encyclopédie économique et sociale de la guerre. Les séries de la Dotation Carnegie pour la paix internationale," *L'atelier du centre de recherche historique*, 3: 1, 2009.
[144] For a history of this reconciliation, see Lorrain's fine overview in *Des pacifistes français et allemands*, Chapter II.

traitors in their own country. "In the Ruhr, we behaved like Germans—no, not like Germans, but like *Boches*," declared Victor Basch, who would become president of the *Ligue des Droits de l'Homme* in 1926.[145] True, no one questioned the legitimacy of reparations, which German peace activists also supported. But neither did anyone want fresh humiliation for Germany, which might create serious risks to peace in Europe. The victory of the Coalition of the Left in 1924 marked a complete change of policy, with a reduction in compensations and the beginning of the evacuation of the Ruhr. At the same time, the policy of reconciliation undertaken by the German Minister for Foreign Affairs, Gustav Stresemann, and his French counterpart Aristide Briand, led to a kind of cultural demobilization, as evidenced by what has been called the "spirit of Locarno."[146]

Several important international conferences brought French and Germans together, whether it was the Conference of Associations for the League of Nations, held in Lyon in July, or the twenty-third Peace Conference, held in Berlin in October. After the renewal of tension during the occupation of the Ruhr, meetings between French and German activists were seen as the best way to counter the rise of different strains of nationalism. Other initiatives were undertaken, such as public talks held by the *Ligue de Droits de l'Homme* in France and in Germany, where foreign speakers took the floor. But this very clear change in the climate of Franco-German relations should not cause us to overlook either cultural differences between French and German pacifists, or, above all, the skepticism of some sectors of public opinion. In France, the meetings organized by the *Ligue des Droits de l'Homme* in cities in the provinces were often tempestuous; they were held in front of an audience that had not seen or heard a German for 10 years.[147]

The first meeting of the CIAMAC took place in just such a moral context. It is worth stressing from the start the power of such an initiative, though its actual influence should not be exaggerated. The prevailing climate in 1924 was indeed that of reconciliation between former enemies, but this development was neither linear nor irreversible, and it had to overcome a kind of incredulity on the part of many survivors of the first large-scale modern conflict. "The spirit of goodwill, the spirit of a common quest, this is what the spirit of Locarno is at the present moment, much more than a spirit of enthusiasm and lightness of heart,

---

[145] Quoted by Lorrain, *Des pacifistes français et allemands*, pp. 199–200.
[146] John Horne, "Locarno et la politique de la démobilisation culturelle, 1925–1930," *14–18 Aujourd'hui* (Paris: Noésis, 2002), pp. 73–87.
[147] Lorrain, *Des pacifistes français et allemands*, p. 209.

after all the many trials that various peoples suffered for years," as the director of the ILO, Albert Thomas, summed it up.[148] In organizing this historic meeting of the first CIAMAC, the ILO willingly stayed in the background. The questions under discussion did not directly have to do with its mission, and it did not want to become implicated in a discussion whose course and outcome could not be determined ahead of time. Tixier limited himself to renting two rooms at the University of Geneva for hosting the conference. The UF was, in fact, the organizing group.

We can only imagine the feelings of Paul Brousmiche, the president of the UF, when he greeted foreign veterans:

We are here among those who, having known the horrors of war, should have the strength to tell to each other, face to face, truths that are elsewhere not easy to say or express, for reasons of national interest... Peace? Do we not have a common interest in defending it together, not only in the moral interest of a better humanity, but even in the material interests of veterans, disabled or not? For only with economic security, restored through a lasting peace, can measures likely to safeguard and improve our existence be planned and carried out.[149]

Alongside the French of the UF, there were the German delegations from the *Reichsbund* and the Federation of Disabled German Veterans, the Federation of Austrian Disabled Veterans, the National Association of Disabled Italian Veterans, the Polish, Romanian, and Czech delegations, and that of the Kingdom of Serbs, Croats, and Slovenes.

Six hours of heated debate were needed to bring about a final resolution, adopted by all these veterans. The associations committed to collaborate on furthering the spirit of peace, and voted unanimously to ratify the fundamental principles of the League of Nations. Obligatory arbitration and general disarmament were presented as indispensable conditions for a lasting peace. On the part of the Germans, this unequivocal support for an international institution born out of the Treaty of Versailles, called the "Diktat" of Versailles in Germany, represented considerable progress. It was the work in particular of influential members of the delegation such as Erich Rossmann, a socialist deputy to the Reichstag, who was won over by Henri Pichot of the UF. At the end of the conference, Eric Drummond, secretary-general of the League of Nations, welcomed a delegation of veterans, including German veterans, to the League. Other officials of the League participated, such as Joseph Paul-Boncour, which naturally gave much more stature to what had been a relatively informal meeting.

[148] ABIT, CAT/2/26/2, Speech by Thomas on the Locarno accords and the economic future of Europe, University of Belgrade, February 9, 1926.
[149] ABIT, MU/7/9/5, First CIAMAC, Geneva, September 18–19, 1925.

But it was one thing to ratify a common declaration in a meeting room at the University of Geneva, and quite another to defend the League of Nations in the face of public opinion. "Frenchmen and Germans, after returning to their countries, will be very strongly attacked by Communist groups because of their support for the League of Nations, and by right-wing groups with nationalist tendencies," worried Tixier. "On the other hand, we have agreed to put aside for the time the questions that would have made everything break down: a people's right to self-determination; the respect for treaties and the Treaty of Versailles in particular. But we will nonetheless have to talk about them one day."[150] If we set aside the exceptional character of this meeting, its concrete results seem rather feeble. No one took responsibility for setting up a permanent structure, such as an international disabled veterans' organization. A simple administrative bureau was established, under the direction of Tixier and two colleagues from the ILO.

A year later, a new conference of the CIAMAC took place in Geneva. In the wings this time, however, several nationalist French veterans' associations tried to make the initiative fail. Some French delegates to the CIAMAC believed they should impose as a condition of their participation that disabled German veterans had to reaffirm Germany's collective responsibility in starting the war. Tixier had to forestall them on the eve of the conference.[151] During the meetings, a new incident occurred when provocateurs took the floor to publicly discuss article 231 of the Treaty of Versailles, which held Germany responsible for the war. However, after an entire night of discussions, the delegates agreed on a document expressing "their right and their duty to collaborate actively on furthering the spirit of peace" and recalling their commitment "to the respect of peace treaties."

This question of Germany's responsibility for starting the war was, indeed, a central question that divided pacifists. Take the case of one of the most influential French pacifist groups, La Paix par le droit. Its leaders, who were at the head of Franco-German reconciliation efforts, also remained convinced that Germany alone bore responsibility for the conflagration of 1914, due to its deliberate violation of Belgian neutrality. True, Ruyssen thought that Article 231 of the Treaty of Versailles was pointlessly humiliating to former enemies, but, in the end, he found nothing to criticize in this judgment of Germany. In 1919, he refused to participate at an international meeting of peace activists that included

---

[150] ABIT, MU/7/9/5, Memorandum from Tixier to Albert Thomas, September 1925.
[151] ABIT, MU/7/9/5/2, International conference of disabled veterans and veterans, Geneva, September 30–October 2, 1926.

Germans: "My first act in a meeting where I might be likely to encounter German or Austrian pacifists would be to ask them if they completely repudiated all of their actions."[152] For their part, the members of the German League for Human Rights strongly condemned Article 231, all while recognizing the important role of the League of Nations. It was not until 1921 that a more radical pacifist organization, the *Bund Neues Vaterland* (BNV), accepted Article 231. A common manifesto was even signed, in conjunction with the French *Ligue des Droits de l'Homme*, at the initiative of Helmut von Gerlach, one of the leaders of the BNV.

Little by little, international conferences of veterans and disabled veterans, which would have been thought unlikely several years earlier, created their own rituals of peace. Meetings almost always traditionally began with a reminder of the horrors of the Great War. These men who normally hesitated to speak openly about their suffering, who wrote in their organizations' newsletters and newspapers with an ironic distance,[153] now justified reconciliation by acknowledging the wounds the war had inflicted upon them. A solemn silence followed their stories; an emotional silence ensued when their former enemies took the floor. In October 1926, in Geneva, the veterans displayed a kind of symbolic brotherhood by designating a German delegate and a French delegate as joint chairs of the last session. After 3 days of debate, everyone participated together in a minute of silence in memory of the war dead. In September 1927, in Vienna, a memorial wreath decorated with the flags of ten veterans' delegations was placed on the Austrian Tomb of the Unknown Soldier. In August 1928, in Berlin, all of the delegates were welcomed by the German chancellor, Hermann Müller.

The CIAMAC's meetings would thus take place successively, year after year, henceforth welcomed by the former Central Powers, Austria in 1927 and Germany in 1928. The number of participants grew as well, with seventeen national federations representing a total of nearly 4 million veterans. In the mid 1920s, only three major federations remained outside the movement: the American Legion and the British Legion (which moreover was clearly in decline, dropping from 1 million to 250,000 members in the space of 6 years) were both much more conservative than the associations that made up the CIAMAC; the Italian Federation of Veterans was also absent, but this was not surprising since it was one

---

[152] Théodore Ruyssen, "Le mouvement pacifiste: pour et contre la reprise des relations pacifistes internationales," *La Paix du Droit*, 29: 1, January 1919, quoted in Ingram, *The Politics of Dissent*, p. 43.

[153] Sophie Delaporte, "Le corps et la parole des mutilés de la Grande Guerre," *Guerres mondiales et conflits contemporains*, 205, 2002, pp. 5–14, as well as her book, *Les gueules cassées*.

of the pillars of the newly formed fascist regime of Benito Mussolini. The Vienna and Berlin conferences brought nothing new to the question of peace. On both occasions, veterans reaffirmed the importance of arbitration, moral disarmament, and educating the younger generations about peace: all themes that were present in veterans' organizations' newspapers since the end of the war.[154]

On the question of material rights, the same complaints were still there. The resolution passed by the 1927 conference was particularly harsh on the indifference experienced by non-disabled veterans:

> The conference notes that in the majority of states, [they] have not received any true compensation for the damage resulting from the lengthy combat duty, that has made them old before their time; it denounces the immorality of the principle by which those who serve the nation with money or labor are remunerated, whereas those who serve with their blood receive only an insufficient compensation; it proclaims the need for veterans' associations to study ways to institute recognition of the particular debt owed to veterans.[155]

It is difficult to judge whether a speech such as this one, given nearly 10 years after the war, conveys the sluggish passage of legislation in support of veterans, or the fact that no compensation could possibly have met their expectations.

Veterans and their families were the first victims of the economic crisis of the end of the 1920s, particularly in areas severely damaged by inflation and depreciation, such as Germany. It was a time when housewives went grocery shopping with baby carriages weighed down with money, where the price of meals changed hourly in restaurants: as soon as they got their pension, veterans raced to spend it, for fear that it would lose too much value over the next few days. Veterans' meetings were held regularly in the 1930s.[156] Veterans still represented a significant part of the male population: a little more than four adult men out of every ten living in France in 1930. But the severity of the economic crisis dissipated little by little the hope of building, via international collaboration, a society that would be more welcoming to veterans, and a peaceful world. The decline of the League of Nations, weakened after the invasion of Manchuria in 1931, precipitated the fall of the CIAMAC. The competing *Fédération*

---

[154] Antoine Prost, *Les anciens combattants, 1914–1940* (Paris: Gallimard-Julliard, collection "Archives," 1977), translated by Helen McPhail as *In the Wake of War: "Les anciens combattants" and French Society* (Oxford: Berg, 1992).

[155] In France, a retirement pension for veterans was finally instituted in 1930. Veterans' associations had been consistently advocating for such a pension since the early 1920s.

[156] Warsaw in 1929, Paris in 1930, Prague in 1931, Vienna in 1932, Geneva in 1933 and 1934, Bucharest in 1935, Copenhagen in 1936, Paris in 1937. The minutes of these meetings are preserved in the archives of the ILO (ABIT, MU/7/9/6–15).

Internationale des Anciens Combattants [International Veterans' Federa-
tion] or FIDAC, of which the British Legion was a member, became
stronger. In addition, with Mussolini's and Hitler's rise to power, Italian
and German associations could no longer take part in the CIAMAC's
activities; the Nazi regime imprisoned some of the German delegates
who had attended previous international conferences.[157]

Each of the reports written by the ILO delegate to the CIAMAC's
annual meetings shows, if not the loss of an ideal, then at least a
kind of growing disenchantment: "The CIAMAC has only very limited means to act, and it is not in a state to use its own means to influence
opinion."[158] True, the resolutions passed by the veterans during their
meetings were valuable examples; they came from people who enjoyed a
form of experience-based authority,[159] and who played the role of "moral
witnesses" in post-war societies, to use the concept proposed by Avishai
Margalit.[160] However, and this is doubtless the most essential point, the
CIAMAC had no concrete way of imposing its views on governments,
and, most of the time, public opinion was barely kept informed of them.

The overall results of the CIAMAC's meetings are thus mixed. It is
clear that they favored the development of a spirit of peace, by allowing
delegates to get to know each other better and by putting them under the
moral obligation to try and reconcile their views. If we compare the meetings held at the end of the 1920s with the hatred for the enemy that was
still strong in the immediate post-war period, this development is truly
remarkable. On some specific points, such as the reevaluation of pensions
in Bulgaria and Austria, the CIAMAC's meetings even had a concrete
impact. But the initial project of a major pacifist association comprising
all the veterans of the Great War never saw the light of day. "In these
conditions, it seems necessary to limit ourselves to sympathizing with a
movement that, while lacking the size and influence it could have had,
is nonetheless worthy of interest," concluded the ILO's representative to
the CIAMAC in 1929. This report has the ring of powerlessness: "Since
the ILO is no more able than the League of Nations to have any effect on
governments such that they modify their policies toward victims of the
war, the defense of these victims can only be assured effectively through
national associations or institutions, which alone have the means to act

157 ABIT, MU/7/9/5/12, letter from Tixier to the ILO's correspondent in Romania, March
   7, 1935.
158 ABIT, MU/7/9/5/6, 5th meeting of the CIAMAC, August 4–6, 1929.
159 For a critical reading of this idea, see Joan W. Scott's famous article, "The evidence of
   experience," *Critical Inquiry*, 17, summer 1991, pp. 773–797.
160 Avishai Margalit, *The Ethics of Memory* (Harvard University Press, 2002).

at their disposal."[161] In other words, the defense of veterans' rights was sent back to the national or local level. In the 1930s, the whole vision of the CIAMAC as a transnational organization—the forerunner of today's NGOs—was laid to rest, and, perhaps with it, the utopia of an "international public opinion" on which a part of the League of Nations project depended.

Conclusion

With hindsight, the recognition of the rights of war victims can seem like an unfinished battle. At an economic level, first of all, the interwar crisis undermined the social gains of the immediate post-war period. Inflation cut down veterans' pensions little by little; charities suffered from a decline in donations; public subventions diminished to the point of endangering the physical therapy centers supported by the state. For the beneficiaries, these restrictions were all the more painful inasmuch as they often coincided with a new stage of life, such as the entry into adulthood for war orphans, who were in their twenties at the end of the 1930s, and retirement for some veterans. At the moment when aid was needed to face the hazards of life, it was insufficient. The noble ideal that gave rise to the status of *pupilles de la nation* also gave way to a kind of disenchantment. "Our fathers were heroes, this gave us a kind of moral superiority. In talking with other children, one often said, 'My father, he was killed,'" a war orphan recalled. But others only remembered from this period of time the feeling of receiving minimal assistance rather than truly being helped, and the humiliation of feeling different from other children.[162]

Moreover, the dream of international brotherhood among veterans, incarnated by the CIAMAC, was unable to resist the rise of fascism, which swept across Europe. The hopes invested in the League of Nations by an entire generation of veterans, hopes for general disarmament, for the spirit of peace, for stronger international cooperation—all these hopes turned out to be illusory. "The more that direct memories of the [Great War] fade, the more difficult it will be to lay the initial foundation for new international laws on armaments," René Cassin had warned, as early as 1929.[163] Two years later, the international conference on disarmament held in Geneva in February 1932 resulted in a complete

[161] ABIT, MU/7/9/5/6, Report to the ILO at the end of the 5th meeting of the CIAMAC.
[162] Faron, *Les enfants du deuil*, Chapter 9.
[163] Archives Nationales, 382AP14: René Cassin, speech to the 3rd Commission on Disarmament, 1929, quoted by Prost and Winter, *René Cassin*, p. 110.

failure; Mussolini's invasion of Ethiopia in 1935, and the lack of any appropriate response from the League of Nations, would prove Cassin right. The League of Nations turned out to be incapable of preserving a system of collective security, no doubt because it would not challenge the principle of the absolute sovereignty of its member states.[164]

Such are the interpretations traditionally proposed by the history of international relations. I would like to propose a different one, which seeks, on the contrary, to underline the originality of the defense of war victims' rights following the Great War, and its fruitfulness over the long term. Even if the CIAMAC's aims in the 1920s and 1930s ended in failure, the work of the generation of veterans of the Great War nevertheless had the merit of creating a new approach to victims' rights, one which would eventually bear fruit after World War II.

The originality of the defense of war victims following the first large-scale modern conflict lies in its origins. For the first time in the history of Europe, a vast veterans' movement was organized, with a multitude of local organizations as its base. Their goal: to defend the rights of victims of the war—beginning with the most vulnerable among them, such as severely wounded veterans, widows, orphans. With the exception of the UNC, created by the army to support the claims of demobilized soldiers, the other movements, which were more informal, grew out of the deep uncertainty felt by veterans upon their return from the war, and out of the feeling that laws inherited from the nineteenth century were no longer appropriate for a conscript army and a total war. In France, the codification of new rights for war victims in the 1920s resulted from negotiations between a republican state and millions of men returned home from the front. They asserted their rights as citizens in order to have their rights as veterans recognized. The history of war victims' rights is thus first that of political history and national history: it is part and parcel of a long republican tradition, with its rituals, codes, and language. Because of its "total war" aspect, World War I nonetheless created a break in that tradition, since not only officers' rights were defended, but those of all veterans, of all ranks, and, on a larger scale, those of civilians, who also benefited from "war compensations." In fact, in France, the Great War renewed a sense of mysticism regarding equality and brotherhood that had its roots in the Revolutionary ideal.

---

[164] On the failure of delegates to the League of Nations as a "transnational community" and the impact of this failure on disarmament policies, see Andrew Webster, "The transnational dream: politicians, diplomats and soldiers in the League of Nations' pursuit of international disarmament, 1920–1938," *Contemporary European History*, 14: 4, 2005, pp. 493–518.

With the founding of the CIAMAC, the defense of war victims' rights took on an international dimension. Veterans from around the world met in Geneva, with representatives from both Allied and Central Powers countries. The fact that men who had fought each other for 4 years could meet together in this way was in and of itself quite extraordinary. Compared with the enormous ideological clash that was World War I, a discussion between veterans of both camps, severely wounded and disabled veterans, as it happened, was a strong symbol of a kind of universalization of rights. In spite of their different national origins and their diverse roles during the conflict, all these men had one thing in common, which legitimized the message they proclaimed together concerning rights and human dignity: they had all suffered in body, mind, and spirit. They had directly experienced the war and had survived it. They spoke thus not only in their own name, but also in the name of all whom the conflict had injured, physically and mentally, and, on a larger scale, they spoke in the name of those who had died. "Out of all veterans, the disabled are the closest to our dead," the president of a French disabled veterans' association declared in 1924. "Because the physical aspect, their infirmities—in a word, their daily suffering—remind them all the more of those who gave their lives on the battlefield."[165] The war dead were the ultimate creditors of the debt each nation had incurred towards its defenders.

Moreover, in the aftermath of the war, when ideological tensions still ran high, it is not insignificant that the dialogue between veterans addressed technical matters, such as the development of better prosthetics or setting aside jobs for veterans. This technical language, borrowed from the language of reconstructive surgery, from the language of labor law and economic language, went hand in hand with the CIAMAC's moral admonitions to different governments: do not forget the victims of the war; take care of the veterans. In this, the CIAMAC adopted a manner of functioning and a style that would later characterize the organizations known today as NGOs—volunteer citizens' associations, pursuing goals of common interest on an international scale, putting pressure on governments to defend their citizens' interests.[166] This is another

---

[165] Speech by the President of the Vitry-le-François Disabled Veterans (Marne), *Journal de la Marne*, November 5, 1924, quoted by Stéphane Tison, *Comment sortir de la guerre? Deuil, mémoire et traumatisme (1918–1940)*, (Presses universitaires de Rennes, 2011), p. 59.
[166] Such organizations were numerous on the eve of the Great War and during the conflict itself. See Akira Iriye, *Global Community: The Role of International Organizations in the Making of the Contemporary World* (Berkeley: University of California Press, 2002). However, the term "non-governmental organization" does not appear until the aftermath of World War II. Article 71 of Chapter X of the United Nations Charter gives them a consulting role.

original aspect of the movement for the defense of victims' rights in the 1920s.

For all these veterans, the state could no longer be considered the sole guarantor of individual liberties. In the eyes of the most radical among them, the state was responsible for what they called the "butchery" of 1914–18; for the majority of veterans, "politicians," considered devious and unscrupulous, could not be taken at their word. But on top of that, the idea of absolute sovereignty was regarded with great suspicion in pacifist milieus. According to them, it inevitably led to "an arms race, a politics of prestige, then to war."[167] René Cassin worked at length on all these questions, especially in a series of lectures given at the Hague Academy of International Law at the beginning of the 1930s.[168] The best critic of absolute sovereignty nonetheless remains the jurist Nicolas Politis, a naturalized French citizen before the war who became a Greek citizen again, before being named Greece's Minister of Foreign Affairs (1916–20) and one of its representatives to the League of Nations. In a lecture given at the Hague in 1925, Politis announced the end of international law based on the absolute sovereignty of states.[169] The Treaty of Versailles had instituted "mixed, arbitrary tribunals" in order to protect minority populations, he reminded his listeners. They gave ordinary individuals full rights.[170] The solidarity of human relations also seemed to win out over artificially drawn borders. But "that which will assure the final triumph of this new conception of international law is the irremediable ruin sure to come to the other fundamental principle of classic doctrine: sovereignty."

Whatever the strength of this great dream may have been, forged in the wake of the war, the primacy of nation-states would win out in the end, driven by the rise of nationalism. Cassin's criticisms thus became sharper. At the beginning of 1930, he categorically refused the preeminence of nationality over country of residence, for he saw in this an example of the state's supremacy over the individual. "The link of nationality is not

---

[167] Iriye, *Global Community*.

[168] In particular, Cassin, "La nouvelle conception du domicile."

[169] Nicolas Politis, "Le problème des limitations de la souveraineté et la théorie de l'abus des droits dans les rapports internationaux," *Recueil des cours de l'académie de droit international de La Haye* (Paris: Sirey, 1925), pp. 5–121.

[170] The most famous example is the petition presented in May 1933 by Franz Bernheim, a citizen of Upper Silesia, fired because he was Jewish. He asked the League of Nations to enforce a 1922 treaty protecting minority groups in that territory, annexed by Germany. The League ruled in his favor. However, Goebbels traveled to Geneva in order to defend Germany's sovereignty over its citizens. Nazi Germany ended up withdrawing from the League several weeks later. See Lauren, *The Evolution of International Human Rights*, pp. 127–130; Burgers, "The Road to San Francisco," pp. 455–459.

the sole link between members of a Nation," he wrote. "There are other, more fundamental ones: the home, the borough, the city." In April 1940, his position became even more radical, for the danger no longer lay just in the absolute sovereignty of states but also in what Cassin called "the Leviathan State": a state whose absolute power, in totalitarian regimes, was an instrument of political violence and of chaos.[171] This was when Cassin prophesied that the Allies' war against Nazism would have to be led in the name of a new "universal Declaration of the rights of the human being, shored up in every country by specific guarantees." The fight he would lead in London, several weeks later, was an outgrowth of the defense of victims' rights that had begun in the 1920s. The jurist of Free France, the man behind the Universal Declaration of Human Rights in 1948, remained a veteran of the Great War, with a disabled body and an indissolvable bond with the living and the dead: in sum, one with those who had suffered during and because of the Great War.

---

[171] Cassin, "L'État Léviathan," *La pensée et l'action*, pp. 63–71.

2 Justice and peace: Albert Thomas, the International Labor Organization, and the dream of a transnational politics of social rights

"During the French Revolution, the noble principles that constituted the Rights of Man and the Citizen were accepted in a moment of clear awareness; in the same way, at the time of the Armistice [of 1918] and at the urging of the labor movement, principles of justice were written into part XIII of the Peace Treaty, in order to bring about social justice, which is the basis for lasting peace."

Albert Thomas, Conference of the International Federation of Trade Unions, Rome, April 20–26, 1922

"I well remember that in those days the ILO was still a dream. To many it was a wild dream. Who had ever heard of Governments getting together to raise the standards of labor on an international plane? Wilder still was the idea that the people themselves who were directly affected— the workers and the employers of the various countries—should have a hand with Government in determining these labor standards."

Franklin Delano Roosevelt, "Address to the ILO," November 6, 1941

"If it had been within any man's power to halt the march of destiny from 1931 towards the economic crisis, the attacks on human dignity, and the aggression which gave rise to a Second World War, Albert Thomas would have been that man. Never would he have stood inert and silent in the face of the growing dangers to peace. Never would he have gone along with those who anesthetized public opinion at a time when it was necessary to open people's eyes and enlighten them against dictatorships, in order to encourage the attitudes necessary to save peace."[1] When René Cassin paid tribute to Albert Thomas, who had died in 1932, in this speech delivered before the Consultative Assembly of Algiers on May 12, 1944, he saw himself standing at the juncture of two world wars: the Great War, bearer of hopes for peace, hopes betrayed during the 1930s, and the fight of the French Resistance, which kept alive the quest for justice begun by veterans of World War I.

[1] Cassin, *La pensée et l'action*, p. 38.

76

When the fight for the liberation of Europe began in 1944, how indeed could René Cassin forget what he owed to Albert Thomas? In the 1920s and 1930s, veterans' associations had to deal with the ultimate power of national sovereignty, and then the rise of nationalism and fascism. They had, however, benefited from the constant support of the ILO, of which Thomas had been the director since its founding in 1919. Without him, it is unlikely that meetings between veterans from Allied and Central Powers countries would have seen the light of day in the early 1920s. The ILO was one of the rare spaces for dialogue where former enemies could meet and talk.[2] A center of expertise on social and economic questions, the ILO and its general secretariat, the International Labor Office, were at the heart of the rebuilding begun in the 1920s. Before 1914, the world had never seen such a violent conflict or one with such a tremendous number of victims. War pensions, reparations, and reclassifications were all relatively new concepts, which the ILO helped define and translate into political action.

The ILO's work was not, of course, limited to veterans' issues. Part XIII of the Treaty of Versailles, Article 427, acknowledged that "differences of climate, habits, and customs, of economic opportunity and industrial tradition, make strict uniformity in the conditions of labour difficult of immediate attainment." Yet, Part XIII made the ILO responsible for keeping nations up to date on social progress in other countries and for having national legislatures adopt new regulations. The ILO had a civilizing and regulating mission. It established standards founded on a belief in a universal justice.[3] Its sphere of influence was vast. A quick glance at the items on the agenda for the first international labor conference, held in Washington DC in 1919, illustrates the point: an 8-hour workday; unemployment; protection for women before and after giving birth; no nighttime or dangerous work for women and children; a minimum age for industrial workers.[4] The ILO was not concerned merely with "improving the working conditions of industrial wage-earners and

---

[2] The former Central Powers countries joined the ILO in 1919. Two German delegates, one from the government and the other a trade union representative, sat on the executive board, and German civil servants worked at the ILO. Arthur Fontaine, head of the International Labor Office's executive board, was very much in favor of German and Austrian participation in the organization's work. However, his viewpoint was criticized in the name of a kind of maintaining vigilance against the German threat (see Isabelle Moret-Lespinet, "Arthur Fontaine, de l'Office du travail au Bureau International du Travail, un promoteur du droit international du travail," in Jean-Pierre Le Crom [ed.], Les acteurs du droit du travail [Presses universitaires de Rennes, 2004], p. 245).

[3] Jean-Michel Bonvin, L'Organisation Internationale du Travail: essai sur une agence productrice de normes (Paris: Presses universitaires de France, 1998).

[4] Clément Argentier, Les résultats acquis par l'Organisation permanente du Travail de 1919 à 1929 (Paris: Librairie du recueil Sirey, 1930).

sailors," as an early draft of its founding document had it. The Organization was also concerned about the welfare of farmers and intellectual wage-earners, and about the well-being of women, children, the unemployed, and the elderly.

For the ILO, "the starting point of all human activity was man himself."[5] Man, that is to say, his work and the conditions of his intellectual and moral development. "The worker must emancipate himself in order to become fully a man," explained Albert Thomas.[6] This was an ambition that his successor at the head of the ILO, the Englishman Harold Butler, would take up in 1935: "The Organization has as a positive goal to make life freer and better for all those who work in industry and agriculture, to raise their level of material comfort and to make available to them all opportunities for physical, intellectual, and spiritual development."[7] This humanist discourse was not self-evident, however.[8] It would be incorrect to see it as the consequence of a triumph of democratic ideals comparable to the spirit of 1945, since the latter emerged in the wake of the victory over fascism. The ILO of the aftermath of World War II should not be confused with the ILO that emerged from the ruins of the Great War,[9] since the international situation in the 1920s was completely different from that of the 1950s.

At the beginning of the 1920s, the ILO's program was the fruit of lengthy negotiations first carried out under the auspices of the Commission on International Labor Legislation, created at the Paris Peace Conference in order to draft the ILO's constitution, and then under the auspices of the Peace Conference itself. The social climate was tense almost everywhere in industrialized countries, and also in non-industrialized countries such as Poland. Fear was growing that the revolutionary situation in Germany, Central Europe, and Russia would spread to the rest of the world. There were more than 3,600 strikes in the United States in 1919. And at the very moment when the peace negotiations following World War I were ending, Paris and its suburbs experienced some of the

---

[5] Ensio Hiitonen, *La compétence de l'Organisation Internationale du Travail* (Paris: Rousseau & Cie, 1929), p. 193.
[6] Bertus W. Schaper, *Albert Thomas: trente ans de réformisme social* (Assen: Van Gorcum, 1959), p. 308. The primary mission of the ILO was to "establish everywhere a truly humane system of work [. . .], to ensure [. . .] better, and as far as possible, equal conditions for all the workers of the world." Albert Thomas, *L'Organisation Internationale du Travail et la première année de son activité* (Geneva, 1921), p. 5.
[7] Cited by Bonvin, *L'Organisation Internationale du Travail*, p. 49.
[8] Albert Thomas borrowed his conception of working-class humanism from Charles Andler and modified it (Charles Andler, *L'humanisme travailliste: essais de pédagogie sociale* [Paris, 1927]).
[9] Bonvin, *L'Organisation Internationale du Travail*, pp. 14–15.

largest metalworkers' strikes in the country's history.[10] "The bourgeoisie is afraid, the government is trembling . . . If they want to block our way, we'll knock them down!"[11] a union activist declared on the eve of May Day, 1919. The negotiators from the Commission on International Labor Legislation cleverly used this fear of revolution to push for the reforms they wanted from employers and governments: real tripartite representation (governments, workers, employers) within the ILO; ways for the new organization to set specific standards for workers' living conditions; the possibility of acting on member states of the ILO so that they would apply international standards.

In official histories of the ILO, the birth of the Organization is often presented as the inevitable result of social progress.[12] In fact, the ILO was just as much the product of power struggles as it was an illustration of the push for reform based on ideals. In 1919, the countries at war emerged from five years of suffering that had given birth to the hope for a more just world. During this period, in France, the *union sacrée* or sacred union had brought a variety of players together, such as management and unions, all focused on supporting the government. The ILO was a daughter of the war; it embodied the aspirations born out of the war years and their faith in the importance of social dialogue.[13] Take, for example, the words of Albert Thomas when he called to mind the early days of the ILO: "It was the war that made labor legislation a top priority. It was the war that forced governments to commit to eradicating 'the poverty, injustice, and privations' that had been the condition of wage-earners. It was the war, again, that made unionized workers understand that, in order to realize some of their aspirations, they needed legal protection organized on an international scale."[14]

Albert Thomas, the ILO's first director, was certainly one of the most influential figures of the labor reform movement that followed the Great

---

[10] Jean-Louis Robert, *Les ouvriers, la patrie et la Révolution, 1914–1919* (Annales littéraires de l'Université de Besançon; Les Belles Lettres, 1995).

[11] Danielle Tartakowsky, "Manifestations ouvrières et théories de la violence, 1919–1934," *Cultures et conflits*, 9–10, 1993, pp. 251–266.

[12] On the historiography of the ILO, see especially Jasmien Van Daele, "Writing ILO histories: a state of the art," in Jasmien Van Daele, Magaly Rodriguez Garcia and Marcel Van der Linden (eds.), *ILO Histories: Essays on the International Labour Organization and Its Impact on the World in the Twentieth Century* (Bern: Peter Lang, 2010).

[13] ABIT, CAT/2/20/10, Albert Thomas, "Le Bureau International du Travail," Speech given on November 5, 1920. See also his speech in Cambridge, October 27, 1926 (ABIT, CAT/2/26/8).

[14] Albert Thomas, "Organisation Internationale du Travail: origine, développement, avenir," *Revue Internationale du Travail*, 1: 1, 1921, pp. 5–22, cited by Isabelle Moret-Lespinet and Vincent Viet, "Introduction," in *L'Organisation Internationale du Travail: origine-développement-avenir* (Presses universitaires de Rennes, 2011), p. 13.

War.[15] A committed pacifist at the turn of the century, he became equally committed to defending France after the declaration of war. By October 1914, Alexandre Millerand, the Minister of War, put him in charge of overseeing arms production. In May 1915, he was appointed Under-Secretary of State for Artillery and Munitions. From December 1916 to September 1917, he served as Minister of Armament under both Briand and Ribot. Thomas was convinced that the social concerns he defended while organizing munitions factories would continue to be important in peacetime. The *union sacrée* of wartime, he thought, would give way in peacetime to a sense of social solidarity at the national and international scale: that was the ILO's mission.

The Organization focused on expanding the social reforms of wartime from a national to an international scale, all while facing a significant challenge: the considerable influence of the Russian Revolution on a large number of workers and union leaders. In these circumstances, the ILO's discourse on social rights also provided an alternative discourse to the Russian experience. In other words, the Russian Revolution paradoxically served the interests of the International Labor Office's founders, by making it impossible for liberal economies to simply return to pre-war conditions. The Russian Revolution forced Western governments to work to secure workers' goodwill, lest they become susceptible to revolutionary sentiments.

The ILO thus held a unique place in the international public sphere. It was the first organization to adopt a tripartite structure and to break with the traditional diplomatic protocol according to which government plenipotentiaries would negotiate social policy agreements between countries, not the social actors themselves (that is, union and management representatives). The standards established by the ILO were voted on in plenary meetings, then sent to member countries for ratification by national legislatures. In theory, the sovereignty of individual states was respected, but, in the end, what counted just as much was the creation of standards with a universal purpose. Reflections on social rights within the ILO were all the more important because they aimed, in the end, to improve living conditions for workers and their families on a worldwide scale. Exempt from its scope were the two major powers that did not belong to the Organization: the United States, which had

---

[15] Jean-Jacques Becker, "Albert Thomas d'un siècle à l'autre. Bilan de l'expérience de guerre," *Les Cahiers de l'IRICE*, 2: 2, 2008, pp. 9–15. As Jean-Jacques Becker has noted, there are not many biographies of Albert Thomas. Out of the memoirs written by his contemporaries, Edward Phelan's book is noteworthy: *Albert Thomas et la création du BIT* (Paris, Grasset, 1936). The only major academic work on Thomas is still the standard one: Schaper, *Albert Thomas*.

refused to ratify the Treaty of Versailles in November 1919, and Bolshevik Russia.

In order to produce universal standards, it is crucial to share knowledge and information about humankind. This was another new feature of the ILO: its ongoing analysis of politics, economics, and society as a whole. In the words of the legal scholar Georges Scelle: "... deciding on any social program, whether it concerns public health and safety, or the struggle against unemployment, means taking into account, from the onset, the necessity for economic planning."[16] Groups of experts of different nationalities and professional backgrounds were quickly formed within the ILO. They had one thing in common—their status as international civil servants, releasing them in theory from allegiance to their country of origin and requiring them to work together for the same goals— a situation that inevitably created tensions with some member states, jealous of their sovereignty. Moreover, these experts constituted a kind of worldwide elite, which the political scientists Adler and Haas have called an "epistemic community": a group of men and women sharing a common goal of creating knowledge in the service of an ideal–social justice.[17] True, international networks of scholars and experts had a tendency to form as early as the end of the nineteenth century, but the ILO gave them an official status and new political responsibilities.

An even greater ambition was behind this quest for social justice; the Organization's work was not limited to its legal or normative dimension. In the minds of its founders, the development of social rights and the promotion of peace were inseparable. "Disarmament and social justice are closely united," insisted Albert Thomas in a November 1921 speech. "There will be no social progress in a world constantly threatened by war, and if the world continues to suffer from injustice, poverty, and privation, world peace will constantly be compromised."[18] *Si vis pacem, cole justitiam*: if you want peace, work for justice; this official motto was written on a piece of parchment and sealed in 1924 beneath the first stone laid for the headquarters of the International Labor Office in Geneva.

---

[16] Georges Scelle, *L'Organisation Internationale du Travail et le BIT* (Paris: Rivière, 1930), p. 87.

[17] Emanuel Adler and Peter M. Haas, "Epistemic communities, world order and the creation of a reflective research program," *International Organization*, 46: 1, 1992, pp. 367–390. The idea of an "epistemic community" refers to men and women with shared knowledge, who can serve as policy experts—in this case, policies on social protection. See also Sandrine Kott's article, "Une 'communauté épistémique' du social? Experts de l'ILO et internationalisation des politiques sociales dans l'entre-deux-guerres," *Genèses*, 2008, 2: 71, 2008, pp. 26–46.

[18] ABIT, CAT/2/21/5, Albert Thomas, Speech on disarmament, Geneva, November 21, 1921.

To create a truly humane system of work, respectful of the rights of all individuals, and especially the weakest, was the surest guarantee of world peace.[19]

Lastly, this combat for social justice and peace reveals the progressive emergence of a base of shared values. For the first time in history, the universality of certain social values was recognized by a large number of countries and made official in the "general principles" of the Labor Charter of 1919. Even if the member states had the right to ratify or not ratify the conventions voted on by the General Assembly of the ILO, they risked incurring the international community's moral disapproval if they rejected the ILO's standards: this was another post-war innovation. The creation of the ILO sanctioned the universalization of social knowledge, the establishment of common values, and the growth of a kind of international public opinion.[20] Its role in the invention of a new system of rights in the wake of the Great War was central. However, the universal application of these values to include the colonies and non-European countries would prove problematic, as did questions regarding women workers. I will address these limits of the ILO's work in the 1920s at the end of this chapter.

But first I would like to recall the two origins of this new perspective on workers' rights: on the one hand, the international trade union movement, and, on the other, the social reform circles of the early twentieth century. By encouraging the circulation of ideas, these international networks assisted in the creation of a "common culture" that lay at the very foundation of the ILO. In the minds of its supporters, the exchange of information on working conditions would lead to a significant improvement in the living conditions of workers, through a kind of mutual imitation among industrialized countries and under pressure from public opinion. One of the principal agents of this change was the ILO's first director, Albert Thomas. By resituating Thomas' life in the larger context of a sociological analysis of social reform circles, I will thus emphasize the continuity between socialism's experience of the war (1914–17) and the beginnings of the ILO, through several significant elements: the role of the social sciences in the definition of labor law, the importance of

[19] Albert Thomas, "Justice sociale et paix universelle. Réflexions sur un texte," *La Revue de Paris*, 6, 15 March, 1924, pp. 241–261.

[20] Thomas gave an example in his speech to the *Comité National d' Etudes sociales et politiques* on February 15, 1923 (ABIT, CAT/2/23/3). He reminded his audience of the case of Persia, which had signed no conventions concerning children and industrial labor, but, in response to pressure from the ILO and international opinion, forbade children under the age of 6 to work in the carpet industry (see also Thomas' speech in Belgrade, December 7, 1924: ABIT, CAT 2/24/5).

concerted effort among various social partners, and the implementation of a way of thinking that brought together the political, the economic, and the social.

I will then address the creation of international standards within the ILO: in other words, the political and intellectual foundation of the international social law that was undergoing rapid development in the 1920s. My analysis will then turn to the rise of a new social group, the international experts whose status as international civil servants statutorily freed them from the national allegiances—in theory. I will illustrate how, on the contrary, labor law as developed by the ILO revealed tensions between member states and the influence of their respective social traditions. Far from constituting a neutral body of knowledge, this expertise resulted from power struggles that need to be acknowledged in their full complexity. The ILO was run by men who were still deeply scarred by their experience of the war. Even in this milieu, which was international by definition, national feeling still prevailed.

Labor as a legal category: the origins of a transnational organization

When the Paris Peace Conference began in early 1919, the project of a "new diplomacy," as expressed by President Wilson in his famous Fourteen Points speech of January 8, 1918, dominated the discussions.[21] As Margaret MacMillan puts it, "Between January and June, Paris was at once the world's government, its court of appeal and its parliament, the focus of its fears and hopes."[22] At a political level, discussions concerning the peace treaties and the League of Nations were quickly taken over by the Council of Four (Wilson, Clemenceau, Lloyd George, and Orlando). Social concerns were delegated to a special commission charged with establishing the basis for international policies.

This Commission on International Labor Legislation, which would give rise to the ILO, brought together experts from all over Europe; for the most part, they knew each other well and had already worked together. In order to understand the origins of the ILO, as well as its striving towards a new kind of diplomacy that would include social questions, we have to

---

[21] Thomas J. Knock, *To End All Wars. Woodrow Wilson and the Quest for a New World Order* (Princeton University Press, 1995). For a recent study of the debates between Wilson and Lansing on the "new diplomacy" and the question of national sovereignty, see Smith, "The Wilsonian Challenge," pp. 179–208.

[22] Margaret MacMillan, *Paris 1919. Six Months that Changed the World* (New York: Random House, 2003).

go back half a century,[23] when the ambition of improving workers' living conditions could be seen in the establishment of international networks of labor experts. The roots of an international labor organization can be traced back to this internationalization of social questions at the end of the nineteenth century.[24]

Beginning in the 1870s, international conferences popularized the idea of international social legislation, providing a setting where people could speak out, where those in power could meet, and where social knowledge could be legitimized. The conferences played an increasingly important role in fin-de-siècle intellectual life: they encouraged the circulation of ideas, the exchange of feedback, and the creation of networks of experts who specialized in social issues.[25] Workers' conferences were of course the most political, and they met at regular intervals. The real turning point in the rising influence of workers' conferences came in 1889 with the Second International.[26] However, each of the socialist parties remained relatively independent at the national level. The fruitful work of the conferences of the Socialist International and the International Socialist Bureau, run by the Belgian Socialist leader Émile Vandervelde beginning in 1900,[27] should not obscure the internal tensions and the personal conflicts that prevented the establishment of a genuinely shared policy on an international level. The members of the Second International did not manage to agree on the choice between reform and revolution, nor did they agree about whether allegiance to one's nation or international solidarity was more important. This debate would be settled *de facto* when workers on the whole chose to participate in defending their country rather than going on strike in an attempt to stop the war before it could start in the summer of 1914. International socialism thus represented a crucible for debates concerning labor law at the end of the nineteenth century, but it was certainly not an organized, hierarchical community that could formulate shared demands.[28]

---

[23] On "labor diplomacy," see Quentin Delpech's chapter in Moret-Lespinet and Viet (eds.) *L'Organisation Internationale du Travail.*

[24] Jasmien Van Daele, "Engineering social peace: networks, ideas and the founding of the International Labour Organization," *International Review of Social History*, 50, 2005, pp. 435–466.

[25] "Les Congrès: lieux de l'échange intellectuel," *Cahiers Georges Sorel*, 7: 7, 1989.

[26] Eric Hobsbawm, "Working-class internationalism," in Frits Van Hothoon and Marcel Van der Linden (eds.), *Internationalism in the Labour Movement, 1830–1940* (Leiden and New York: Brill, 1988).

[27] Janet L. Polasky, *The Democratic Socialism of Emile Vandervelde: Between Reform and Revolution* (Oxford: Berg, 1995).

[28] Gerhart Niemeyer, "The Second International: 1889–1914," in Milorad M. Drachkovitch (ed.), *The Revolutionary Internationals, 1864–1943* (Stanford University Press, 1966), 95–127.

Individual countries organized still other conferences on social questions. The idea of an "epistemic community" comes to mind here—that
is to say, groups of professionals, identified as such in the public sphere,
who share a common form of knowledge, comparable ideological pre-
suppositions, and a similar expertise.[29] Yet their impact was not limited
to formulating a shared set of scientific knowledge, and their role in setting social policies was quickly deemed decisive. The objective at the
time was for the organizing country to solidify its influence by combining traditional diplomacy with a form of juridical cooperation, as had
formerly been the case for technical issues. For example, the first international postal conference had been held in Paris in 1863, and it sought
to set uniform postal rates at the international level. Twenty years later, a
similar international cooperation was extended to the issues of industrial
property and labor law. Insofar as the latter was concerned, the international labor conference held in Berlin in 1890, presided by the young
German Emperor Wilhem II in his second year on the throne, was a
landmark. Consisting of representatives from fourteen European states,
this conference sought to establish the basis for regulations concerning
women and children in the workforce.

Yet the failures of the Berlin conference underline the difficulties of
the transition from the traditional diplomacy of the nineteenth century
to a diplomacy carried out by experts and legal scholars—the kind of
diplomacy that would prevail within the ILO. In 1890, Germany and
Switzerland favored developing regulations by which the countries represented at the conference would have to abide. Conversely, France and
Great Britain wanted to limit things to a major survey of working conditions in different countries. The conference's very status was ambiguous:
it was not a meeting of plenipotentiaries who had the power to sign a
diplomatic agreement, nor was it an academic conference devoid of any
political power. Diplomats and experts came together in their collective
work on labor law, but without really speaking the same language. The
shock of the Great War would prove decisive in allowing for an alternative
form of diplomacy, as embodied by the ILO, to establish itself. Even if
the Paris Peace Conference of 1919, with its somewhat outdated rituals
and its Old Regime surroundings, could be seen as an attempt to continue pre-war diplomatic culture,[30] World War I signaled the increasing
power of experts, as seen in the public sphere some years before.

Lastly, a third type of international conference, described by Anne Rasmussen, brought social economists together to discuss questions such as

[29] Adler and Haas, "Epistemic communities."   [30] MacMillan, *Paris 1919*.

industrial hygiene, weekly time off, and workplace accidents.[31] These meetings were sometimes held in conjunction with Worlds' Fairs, so that the idea of social regulations could combine with the global project of an era of peace and prosperity.[32] Worlds' Fairs, which served primarily as places to display the products of industry, began to take a greater interest in labor itself—in labor as an activity, and in the living conditions of workers. Social reformers also created their own permanent structures, such as the International Association for Labor Legislation (IALL), which had been founded at the time of the Paris World's Fair in 1900. At the head of the organization was the Belgian jurist and sociologist Ernest Mahaim, a perfect embodiment of the new international elite who had mastered several disciplines: he had studied international law, political science, and political economy successively in Brussels, Berlin, Vienna, Paris, London, and Cambridge. The IALL was initially housed at the Musée Social. This was a true research institute, which prefigured what the ILO would become after the war.[33] Later, the association's headquarters moved to Basel and organized periodic meetings on topics such as the prohibition of nighttime work for women or the use of white phosphorus, a toxic substance, in manufacturing matches. The goal, from one meeting to another, was to encourage the signing of international agreements on labor law (such as the Franco-Italian treaty of 1904), with the long-range goal of creating a "United States of Europe."[34]

In those early years, the IALL hosted mainly professors and high-ranking civil servants, and almost no representatives from the upper ranks of trade unions. Socialist circles viewed experts on social law with suspicion, and the two networks were still quite distinct, socially and ideologically. Nonetheless, the IALL played a very important role in

---

[31] Anne Rasmussen, "Le travail en congrès: élaboration d'un milieu international," in Jean Luciani (ed.), *Histoire de l'Office du Travail, 1890–1914* (Paris: Syros, 1992), pp. 119–134.

[32] Anne Rasmussen, "Les congrès liés aux expositions universelles de Paris, 1867–1900," *Mil Neuf Cent. Revue d'histoire intellectuelle*, 7, 1989, pp. 23–45; Laure Godineau, "L'économie sociale à l'exposition universelle de 1889," *Le Mouvement social*, 149, octobre-décembre 1989, pp. 71–88; and, for a more general approach, Jay Winter, *Dreams of Peace and Freedom: Utopian Moments in the Twentieth Century* (Yale University Press, 2006).

[33] Run by Emile Cheysson, the *Musée social* was both a documentation center, with an extensive library on social issues, and a place where debates and public lectures were regularly held. It also served as the headquarters of several workers' collectives and associations such as the IALL. See Janet R. Horne, *A Social Laboratory for Modern France: The Musée social and the Rise of the Welfare State* (Durham, N.C.: Duke University Press, 2002).

[34] Thomas discussed the direct link between the IALL and the ILO during a speech given when Alexandre Millerand visited the ILO headquarters on September 15, 1920 (ABIT, CAT/2/20/9).

the "scientization of the social," i.e., the scientific approach to social questions typical of the late nineteenth century.[35] One man in particular symbolized this burgeoning of labor law based on a scientific approach to society: Arthur Fontaine, who would head the executive board of the ILO from 1919 to 1931, making him the direct superior of Albert Thomas, who at that time was the Director-General of the International Labor Office. A graduate of the Ecole Polytechnique and the Ecole des Mines in Paris, this engineer by training joined the *Office du Travail* (a precursor of the Ministry of Labor) created in 1891, becoming the head of the *Direction du Travail*, where he remained from 1899 to 1920. A trusted advisor to twenty-two successive Ministers of Labor, Fontaine played a central role in preparing all the social legislation passed in France at the beginning of the twentieth century. Under his leadership at the *Direction du Travail*, important empirical studies were undertaken in France and abroad on subjects as diverse as workers' salaries, the length of the workday, or workers' health and safety.[36]

As France's representative to the IALL, Fontaine explained the strategic importance of deciding on the initial stakes of international labor law: "It was not without apprehension that the topics of the first two conventions were chosen. For one thing, to avoid the failure so often predicted by our adversaries, we had to choose topics that would not require too much discussion, reforms that had already been accepted by many countries and that would not present major difficulties. We had to make modest proposals. But we needed to propose reforms of genuine importance, if we wanted to have an impact on public opinion and make serious use of the tool that we were going to create."[37] During the Great War, he worked with Albert Thomas in creating a wartime workforce, and he was a member of the 1919 Commission on International Labor Legislation.[38]

In the wake of Fontaine's contributions, international labor law became its own legal category, bringing concrete knowledge to bear on the evolution of society. Interestingly, it was also at this time that the field of statistics became a recognized discipline, and a tool that could define social

[35] Lutz Raphael, "Die Verwissenschaftlichung des Sozialen als methodische und konzeptionelle Herausforderung für eine Sozialgeschichte des 20. Jahrhunderts," *Geschichte und Gesellschaft*, 22, 1996, pp. 165–193.

[36] Moret-Lespinet, "Arthur Fontaine"; *L'Office du Travail, la république et la réforme sociale, 1891–1914* (Presses universitaires de Rennes, 2007).

[37] Arthur Fontaine, "La législation internationale du travail," *Revue Politique et Parlementaire*, February 1914.

[38] Malcolm Delevingne, "The pre-war history of the international labor legislation," in James T. Shotwell (ed.), *The Origins of the International Labor Organization* (New York: Columbia University Press, 1934).

realities. The growth of the social sciences at the end of the nineteenth century was particularly evident in the gathering of data on society and in the construction of interpretative categories, such as the notion of "unemployment" in the 1890s, as opposed to the condition of "poverty."[39] Social scientists aimed to create realistic models that would enable social policies to be effective. On an international level, different societies could be compared if they were analyzed with the same statistical tools. Moreover, statisticians structured themselves as an international community early on. The first European statistics conferences date back to the mid 1850s; they led to the creation of the International Statistical Institute in 1885.[40]

Statisticians then took part in international social conferences: their professional networks intersected with those of social economists. According to social reformers, statistics introduced numerical rigor, as opposed to the older method of social surveys, now seen as too subjective. Statistics would also make it possible to anticipate future developments, and, finally, would facilitate the establishment of international social legislation. Thirty years later, the great dream of statistics as a lingua franca of international labor law was still the dream of the ILO.[41] What Albert Thomas wrote in 1921 might have been written by the social reformers of the late nineteenth century: "All the efforts towards peace, all the new relationships, all the questions raised in discussions between countries, sharpened the need for universal knowledge. Never have we so strongly called for uniformity in methods of observation, for identical statistical frameworks. Never has it seemed more necessary to have identical processes of investigation [. . .] Science is henceforth necessary for all governments."[42]

On the eve of the Great War, international thinking on labor law was thus supported by well-organized political, trade union, and academic networks. An "epistemic community" had formed to consider important

---

[39] Christian Topalov, *Naissance du chômeur (1880–1910)* (Paris: Albin Michel, 1994); Malcolm Mansfield, Robert Salais and Noel Whiteside (eds.), *Aux sources du chômage, 1880–1914* (Paris: Belin, 1994); Bénédicte Zimmermann, "Du travail au chômage: éléments pour la genèse d'une catégorie sociale," 19ème Congrès international des sciences historiques, Oslo, 2000.

[40] Éric Brian, "Y-a-t-il un objet Congrès? Le cas du Congrès international de statistique (1853–1876)," *Mil Neuf Cent. Revue d'histoire intellectuelle*, 7, 1989, 9–22.

[41] The great statistician Royal Meeker (1873–1953), who was put in charge of labor statistics in the United States by President Wilson in 1913, was a member of the science department of the ILO from 1920 to 1923. He founded the *Revue internationale du Travail*.

[42] Thomas, "L'Organisation Internationale du Travail," p. 17, cited by Kévonian, "La légitimation par l'expertise," p. 83.

questions; paramount concerns were the protection of the weakest sectors of the workforce (women and children), limits on the workday and workweek, and the struggle against occupational disease and workplace accidents. The outbreak of World War I did not call into question this evolution towards an internationalization of social issues. It was simply that in France the conflict temporarily interrupted Franco-German dialogue and strengthened Anglo-Saxon influence.[43] As early as the end of September 1914, the American Federation of Labor called for an international conference on labor law, to be held in tandem with any future peace conferences. Two years later, in July 1916, trade union representatives from several Allied countries, including France and Great Britain, met in Leeds to ask that social rights be integrated into peace treaties and that the IALL be turned into a permanent body—a demand that Justin Godart and Alexandre Millerand would take up during the Paris Peace Conference. One man would play a central role in putting all these social projects from the turn of the century into motion: Albert Thomas, who functioned as a kind of go-between from what Christian Topalov has called the *nébuleuse réformatrice*,[44] or reformist nebula, of the 1900s, and the international milieu that would blossom in Geneva during the 1920s.

Albert Thomas: from socialist reformism to the Geneva project

There are a certain number of similarities between Albert Thomas' life and René Cassin's. In the case of Cassin, his stature as the father of the Universal Declaration of Rights of 1948 has for a long time eclipsed his role in defending war victims' rights during the 1920s.[45] As for Albert Thomas, while numerous scholarly studies have been devoted to his years as a socialist activist in the early twentieth century,[46] or to his government responsibilities during the Great War,[47] very few have made

---

[43] ABIT, CAT/2/20/1, Albert Thomas, Speech given at the Bedford College for Women, London, March 1, 1920.

[44] For more on this idea, see Christian Topalov (ed.), *Laboratoires du nouveau siècle: la nébuleuse réformatrice et ses réseaux en France* (Paris: Éditions de l'École des Hautes Études en Sciences Sociales, 1999).

[45] One exception is the biography of René Cassin by Prost and Winter.

[46] Madeleine Rebérioux and Patrick Fridenson, "Albert Thomas, pivot du réformisme français," *Le Mouvement social*, 87, April–June 1974, pp. 85–97; Christophe Prochasson, *Les intellectuels, le socialisme et la guerre, 1900–1938* (Paris: Seuil, 1991).

[47] Alain Hennebicque, "Albert Thomas and the war industries," in Patrick Fridenson (ed.), *The French Home Front, 1914–1918* (Oxford: Berg, 1993). More recently, see Florent Lazarovici's article, "L'organisation du ministère de l'armement sous Albert

the connection between these two parts of his career and his work for the ILO.[48] In order to understand the birth of the ILO, it is necessary to take a closer look at the experience that Thomas gained during the period 1898–1917, from the beginning of his studies at the Ecole normale supérieure to his departure from the Ministry of Munitions. It may seem incongruous to take a detour through biography before addressing the history of one of the great post-war transnational organizations. But one cannot really understand the origins and structure of the ILO without considering the life of Albert Thomas, socialist reformer.

When Albert Thomas passed the entrance examination of the Ecole normale supérieure and began his studies there in 1898, it marked his crowning achievement as a brilliant student in what was typically referred to as the republican meritocracy. The Ecole was at that time the high temple of French academia, where the Third Republic shaped its future scholars (Jean Perrin, Charles Seignobos, Paul Langevin), men of letters (Romain Rolland, Charles Péguy), and some of its political elite (Jean Jaurès, Paul Painlevé, Léon Blum, Edouard Herriot). It was also at that time a crucible for socialist reformism.[49] Born in 1878 in a modest suburb of Paris (his father was a baker in Champigny-sur-Marne), Albert Thomas completed high school at the Lycée Michelet in Vanves. There, he became friends with Fernand Maurette, who would become a geographer and the head of the Research Division of the International Labor Office in 1924. He also became friends with his teacher Paul Desjardins, the founder of a somewhat influential reformist circle at the time, the *Union pour la vérité* [Union for Truth].[50] Thanks to Desjardins, Thomas was a regular visitor at the intellectual gatherings hosted by middle-class reformers, especially Aline Ménard-Dorian's circle. He met the great

Thomas: une expérience socialiste ou technocratique?" in Romain Ducoulombier (ed.), *Les socialistes dans l'Europe en guerre: réseaux, parcours, expériences, 1914–1918* (Paris: L'Harmattan, 2010), pp. 55–71; he currently has a dissertation in progress: "Albert Thomas et le ministère de l'armement" (Université Paris XII).

48 From this standpoint, the conference "Albert Thomas, société mondiale et internationalisme, réseaux et institutions des années 1890 aux années 1930," organized in 2007 by Alya Aglan, Olivier Feiertag and Dzovinar Kevonian, was a breakthrough. The conference proceedings were published in *Les cahiers de l'IRICE*, 2, 2008.

49 Christophe Charle, "Les normaliens et le socialisme," in Madeleine Rebérioux and Gilles Candar (eds.), *Jaurès et les intellectuels* (Paris: Éditions de l'Atelier, 1994). On the later period, the standard work is Jean-François Sirinelli, *Génération intellectuelle: Khâgneux et normaliens dans l'entre-deux guerres* (Paris: Fayard, 1988).

50 The *Union pour la vérité* met regularly at Pontigny Abbey in Burgundy, which Desjardins purchased after the separation of Church and State in 1905. Before the war, and then from 1922–1939, the *Décades de Pontigny* (10-day conferences) hosted noted French intellectuals such as André Gide, Roger Martin du Gard, and Jacques Rivière (see François Chaubet, *Paul Desjardins et les Décades de Pontigny* [Villeneuve d'Ascq: Presses universitaires du Septentrion, 2000]).

socialist leader and unifier Jean Jaurès, who would have a decisive influence on his political development. He also met Arthur Fontaine, who would become president of the ILO's executive board in the 1920s.[51]

As a young man, Thomas was still hesitant about his political orientation, and he confided his doubts in a moving letter written to Desjardins in October 1899: "Today, socialist democracy seems to me the young, vibrant, and hard-working party in our country, and in spite of its shortcomings, in spite of its faults and violence, I love our party. Oh! I have wanted to tell you this for a long time; but I was not yet decided and open, as I am today; I hesitated, I still had little knowledge of the doctrines of the men to whom I was instinctively drawn, and in spite of your friendship, I lacked confidence; you will forgive me."[52] Thomas' commitment to socialism grew stronger at the Ecole normale supérieure. The friends he made there went on to distinguish themselves in their chosen fields, and some became Thomas' colleagues at the ILO. For example: Lucien Febvre, soon to become one of the founding fathers of the *Annales* school of historiography;[53] François Simiand, Thomas' future colleague at the Ministry of Munitions, who became an eminent economic historian; Mario Roques, Thomas' future *chef de cabinet* or chief of staff during the war, head of the Paris office of the ILO until 1937, and an eminent scholar of medieval literature; the sociologist Maurice Halbwachs; the economist Edgar Milhaud, whom Thomas put in charge of a major survey of economic production in 1925.[54] Clearly, there was a strong overlap between early twentieth-century graduates of the Ecole normale supérieure and the leaders of the ILO in Geneva. Lucien Herr, librarian of the Ecole normale supérieure as of 1888, served as a kind of spiritual

---

[51] During the war, at the Ministry of Armament, Arthur Fontaine was in charge of the recruitment, placement, and protection of factory workers. He was responsible for negotiating with industrialists concerning the government's needs in arms, aviation, and war equipment.

[52] Schaper, *Albert Thomas*, pp. 19–20.

[53] The correspondence between Lucien Febvre and Albert Thomas has been the subject of several studies, including Bertrand Muller, "Problèmes contemporains et hommes d'action à l'origine des *Annales*: Une correspondance entre Lucien Febvre et Albert Thomas (1928–1930)," *Vingtième siècle. Revue d'histoire*, 35, July–September 1992, pp. 78–91. The letters Febvre and Thomas exchanged during the 1920s are preserved in the ILO's archives (ABIT, CAT/7/326). Having successfully passed the *agrégation* in history, Albert Thomas turned to the history of socialism and contributed to *L'Histoire socialiste de la France contemporaine*, edited by Jean Jaurès and aimed at the general public. See Alya Aglan, "Albert Thomas, historien du temps présent," *Les cahiers de l'IRICE*, 2: 2, 2008, pp. 23–38.

[54] Edgar Milhaud (1873–1964) was a professor of political economy at the University of Geneva beginning in 1902. Founder of the journal *Annales de l'Economie collective* in 1908, he joined Albert Thomas at the ILO, where he ran the Economics Section until 1933.

father and confessor to this little group: religious vocabulary seems the only way to fully describe the nature of the relationship between the young *normaliens* and the man who sparked their interest in socialism.[55] Here is Paul Nizan's famous description of Herr: "When we saw this giant leaning over a hill of books, those clear eyes at the base of a dented forehead, of a steep cliff of thoughts, when we heard his voice, which never lied, uttering judgments with a single goal: to render to everyone what was his due—we knew that it could not be dangerous to live in this shabby dwelling."[56]

The Dreyfus Affair (1894–1906) was without a doubt the great cause of this generation of young intellectuals who met under the tutelage of Lucien Herr, the German literature scholar Charles Andler, and Léon Blum.[57] The Affair sharply divided French society, pitting family members against one another, and stirring up violence in both Paris and in the provinces. It also affected the family of René Cassin, who was 19 years old when Dreyfus was exonerated in July 1906. Dreyfus' trial, the explosion of anti-Semitism that it unleashed, and the successive refusals of the legal system to recognize Dreyfus' innocence—all this left deep marks on the Jewish republican circles of Cassin's youth; it wounded their identity as French citizens and the republican values they believed in. "The Dreyfus Affair took place before I began high school. I did not experience it as deeply as my cousins did, since they were in high school. My uncle was deeply engrossed by it, and he even bought the memoirs of Mornard, who had been a lawyer in the *Cour de Cassation*. I read them all," Cassin recalled.[58] This eminent legal scholar's fight for the recognition of universal human rights had its roots in the Dreyfus Affair.[59] And so it is equally significant that the generation that built the ILO earned its political stripes during the Affair. The intolerable nature of injustice, and faith in the universality of moral values: here we see a kind of ideological relationship between the turn of the century and the aftermath of the Great War.

However, the socialist reformism of Thomas and his friends had other aspects that would also leave their mark on his international work.

---

[55] Charles Andler, *Vie de Lucien Herr, 1864–1926* (Paris: Rieder, 1932); Daniel Lindenberg, *Lucien Herr, le socialisme et son destin* (Paris: Calmann-Lévy, 1977). The correspondence between Charles Andler and Lucien Herr was published by Antoinette Blum, with a preface by Christophe Charle: *Correspondance entre Charles Andler et Lucien Herr, 1891–1926* (Paris: Presses de l'École normale supérieure, 1992).

[56] Paul Nizan, *Aden Arabie* (Paris: Rieder, 1931; repub. Gallimard, Folio, 1996), p. 66.

[57] Vincent Duclert (ed.), *Savoir et engagement: ecrits normaliens sur l'Affaire Dreyfus* (Paris: Éditions de la rue d'Ulm, 2006).

[58] René Cassin, *La pensée et l'action*, p. 180.

[59] Prost and Winter, *René Cassin*, pp. 31–32.

What Christophe Prochasson has called "the Albert Thomas network"[60] brought together socialist activists and left-wing intellectuals interested in social issues. These young men, who for the most part had been students at the Ecole normale supérieure, founded the *Revue syndicaliste* in 1905. This journal was meant to serve as a link between the SFIO (the French socialist party) and trade unions. The goal was to provide a solid, scholarly, go-to journal, more accessible than the *Revue socialiste*, with which it merged in 1910. Following the merger, Lucien Herr set a course for the future of the journal, in a letter to Thomas: "We agree, I think, on what must absolutely be eliminated: baseless systems of the world and theories of value; philosophical nonsense; puerile polemics. The essential, for me, is socialist documentation, economic studies, historical and critical studies, factual surveys, and practical realizations."[61] The reforming socialists were also part of an intellectual group, the *Groupe d'études socialistes*, which included some of the most brilliant minds of their generation such as Marc Bloch and Robert Hertz. They turned their back on the Romantic socialism that had defined the previous generation, and instead developed a scientific socialism, committed to scholarly rigor and to concrete ideas based on social research conducted in the field. This faith in the value of the social sciences, especially in sociology as practiced by Durkheim, left a lasting impression on them; it provided inspiration for Thomas' colleagues at the Ministry of Munitions during the Great War, and then afterwards at the ILO in the early 1920s.

Founded on a scientific analysis of society, socialist reformism was a political vision, ready to exercise power. This is an important point that separates Jaurès and Thomas from other socialist leaders of the same time period. Both men believed in the possibility for social change, and not simply improvement. For them, the rise to power would not take place through violence, unlike the ideas put forth by the Bolsheviks. Access to political power would occur at all levels, through the normal channels of republican institutions and through elections. At the local level in particular, what was called "municipal socialism" made it possible to integrate socialists into the republican system by giving them the chance to carry out electoral mandates, often for the first time. In the case of Thomas, it is interesting to see the effects of his experience as mayor of Champigny-sur-Marne on his later career path. In retrospect, the Champigny town

---

[60] Christophe Prochasson, "Entre science et action sociale: le 'réseau Albert Thomas' et le socialisme normalien, 1900–1914," in Topalov (ed.), *Laboratoires du nouveau siècle*, pp. 141–158.
[61] Archives Nationales, Archives Albert Thomas, 94 AP 473, Lucien Herr to Albert Thomas, January 25, 1910.

hall seems like a kind of "laboratory of social solidarity"[62] where Thomas sought to demonstrate that cooperation between social classes was possible: this would also be the ILO's ideal when it hosted delegates from governments, employers, and workers—the famous tripartite schema—in order to establish labor law on an international scale.

When he was elected to the Chamber of Deputies as a representative from the Seine *département* in 1910, Albert Thomas was also the first socialist to join Champigny's city council, before being elected its mayor in 1912. Champigny was still a partly urban, partly rural district, where market farms and gardens mixed with residential neighborhoods. The population included primarily factory workers and day laborers. The arrival of the railroad at the end of the nineteenth century made it easier for working-class families, drawn by the low cost of housing, to settle there. The small town grew from 2,800 residents in 1878 to more than 10,400 in 1911.[63] Although the family bakery (which faced the town hall) was a prosperous one, Thomas still saw workers' poverty firsthand. His childhood experiences inspired his social convictions, as he frequently recalled during speeches he made on official trips as director of the International Labor Office: "As a young boy, in the office of my father, an old republican of the French variety, I often happened to work in the shadow of a small statue, a "Marianne" from 1848,[64] a small republican woman in bronze. And on the marble base two words were written, two inseparable words, two words whose harmony I must affirm today. On one side was the word "Peace"; on the other, the word "Work."[65]

Thomas transformed the town by establishing numerous social services (school health services, a dispensary, public baths) and by creating district staff and a job center run by the municipality. Clearly situated on the right wing of the SFIO, Thomas believed in the importance of public services, in contractual policies, in social democracy; he sought to put these ideals into practice during the war and after it. He saw anarchism as a childhood disease of socialism, and he compared it unfavorably with the more stable SFIO, the Confédération Générale du Travail (CGT), and cooperatives. For him, the path to a socialist society would be built on universal suffrage, the exercise of political power, even in bourgeois

---

[62] Henri Sellier, Speech given at the inauguration of the Albert Thomas Recreation Center in Champigny, February 7, 1937.

[63] Chloé Letoulat-Chotard, "Albert Thomas: Le député-maire socialiste de Champigny-sur-Marne (1912–1919)," Colloque *Albert Thomas (1878–1932). Homme d'État. D'une politique ouvrière en temps de guerre à la naissance du BIT* (Groupe Régional du Comité d'histoire d'Île de France, 2008).

[64] Beginning in 1848, Marianne was an iconic figure symbolizing the French Republic. See Agulhon, *Marianne au combat.*

[65] ABIT, CAT/2/24/2, Speech on the ILO delivered in Warsaw, February 2, 1924.

governments, following the example of Millerand joining the Waldeck-Rousseau government in 1890, and through reform, not revolution. Thomas' political practice was rooted in a place and in a sociology, familiar to him, due to his upbringing in a small town in the Paris suburbs. But his ideological models came from abroad—that is, from Fabianism in England,[66] and from German socialist reformism. His intellectual contacts with Great Britain were developed through the *Groupe d'études socialistes*. In 1905, the sociologist Robert Hertz, whom Thomas had met at the Ecole normale supérieure, returned from a trip to England full of enthusiasm. "Almost every day, in trade unions, cooperatives, municipalities, a new conception of social democracy takes a step forward. The English—I see this more and more clearly—will create social revolution, as they have done throughout their history: no doubt [...]"[67]

Thomas developed connections with Germany firsthand. In 1902–03, after taking the competitive national examination known as the *agrégation*, in history, he went to Germany for an extended stay, at the urging of Charles Andler. This political initiation through travel was relatively common for intellectuals at the time; it allowed Thomas to meet in person some of the leaders of the German Social-Democratic movement, especially Eduard Bernstein.[68] Thomas thus became a kind of conduit for German reformist ideas, adapting them to French intellectual debates in a process of "cultural transfer" that Emmanuel Jousse has amply shown to contain translations, transformations, and, no doubt, misunderstandings of Bernstein's ideas.[69]

In 1896 and 1897, Bernstein published a series of revisionist articles in *Die Neue Zeit*, a theoretically inclined journal of the German socialist party, calling into question the theory of an exacerbated class struggle leading inexorably to the fall of capitalism, and the insurrectional

---

[66] On the rise of Fabianism, see Alan Marne Macbriar, *Fabian Socialism and English Politics, 1884–1918* (Cambridge University Press, 1962); Jay Winter, *Socialism and the Challenge of War: Ideas and Politics in Britain, 1912–1918* (London: Routledge & Kegan Paul, 1974); Keith Laybourn, *The Rise of Socialism in Britain, 1881–1951* (Stroud: Sutton Studies in Modern British History, 1997). On the influence of Fabianism in France, see Emmanuel Jousse, "Un réformisme travailliste: La société fabienne pendant la Grande Guerre," in Romain Ducoulombier (ed.), *Les socialistes dans l'Europe en guerre: réseaux, parcours, expériences, 1914–1918* (Paris: L'Harmattan, 2010), pp. 141–160.

[67] Archives Nationales, Archives Albert Thomas, 94 AP 471, Robert Hertz to Albert Thomas, 18 March, 1905.

[68] Albert Thomas kept up a steady correspondence with Eduard Bernstein, which is preserved in the French National Archives (AN 94 AP 471).

[69] Emmanuel Jousse, *Réviser le marxisme: d'Eduard Bernstein à Albert Thomas, 1894–1914* (Paris: L'Harmattan, 2007). The idea of "cultural tranfer" is defined by Michel Espagne in his book *Les transferts culturels franco-allemands* (Paris: Presses universitaires de France, 1999).

interpretation of socialism.[70] He advocated reformist tactics instead of the revolutionary ones commonly accepted by German socialists; instead of a class-based socialist party [*parti de classe*], he envisoned a party uniting people from all levels of society [*parti de masse*]. The German social-democratic model was the ultimate result of this violent theoretical quarrel, which split the German socialist party and left a lasting mark on the twentieth-century European political landscape. This revisionist debate was noticeably transformed when it came to France. Translated into French terms, revisionism meant renouncing revolution as a means of gaining political power and accepting political collaboration with other left-wing parties, within the framework of bourgeois governments.

Turn-of-the century social reformism reached its peak with World War I, when Thomas joined the *gouvernement d'union sacrée* (national unity government) along with the Socialist ministers Jules Guesde and Marcel Sembat.[71] Called up in August 1914,[72] Thomas was quickly summoned back to the home front to coordinate the railway system for the military's General Staff and the Ministry of Public Works.[73] This was a strategic area of considerable importance. After the major effort of organizing the draft, men and materials constantly had to be supplied to the front lines. The departure of numerous civilians from Paris had to be managed, without descending into chaos. On the night of September 2–3, 1914, the President of the Republic, the entire French government and all its bureaus, left for Bordeaux in a dozen special trains. The departures of these trains had to be spaced out over 20-minute periods for security reasons, and it was necessary to ensure that government bureaucracy could still continue to function in wartime. In October 1914, the Minister of War, the former socialist Alexandre Millerand, put Thomas in charge of the munitions division, not so much for his socialist credentials as for his organizational skills.

---

[70] *Die Neue Zeit*, October 28, 1896; November 25, 1896; March 8, 1897; April 14, 1897.
[71] Jean-Jacques Becker, "La gauche et la Grande Guerre," in Jean-Jacques Becker and Gilles Candar (eds.), *Histoire des gauches en France* (Paris: La Découverte, 2005), pp. 311–329.
[72] According to the law of August 1913, men aged 20–22 years old were required to do 3 years of active military service; the change from 2–3 years had come about following a particularly heated battle of public opinion. After those 3 years came 11 years during which Frenchmen were to serve in the reserves (aged 23–33), then seven years in the Territorial Army (40–47 years of age). Men judged unfit for military service could join the auxiliary service corresponding to their age group. Beginning in 1917, men as young as 19 and as old as 50 were integrated into the French Army, which now numbered nearly 8 million soldiers.
[73] Thomas knew this area well since before the war he had been in charge of the issue of nationalizing the railways as well as *rapporteur à la Chambre des Députés* for the railways' budget.

In retrospect, it is difficult to imagine how unprepared the French Army was to face the industrial warfare that was the hallmark of World War I. It was firmly believed that the war would be of short duration and that reserves were sufficient to cover every need. For example, no one had thought to increase the production of shells. In 1914, war manufacturing was largely dependent on private industry, which Millerand sought to coordinate, even if the state's influence was limited, at least until the spring of 1915.[74] Great Britain and Germany were in similar situations. In France, some workshops had been closed since the beginning of August 1914, and engineers and specialized metalworkers had been sent to the front. Several weeks later, at the end of the Battle of the Marne, stocks were depleted. No longer were 13,500 shells per day being fired, as the military's General Staff had initially planned for, but nine times that.[75]

Albert Thomas was thus appointed the first strategic planner responsible for the industrial reorganization of France, a country reeling from the heavy casualties of the war's first months, when nearly 70 percent of iron and steel production had fallen into the hands of German troops who occupied large portions of Northern and Northeastern France. Factory production in the Paris region, particularly metal, munitions, and aeronautics factories, had to be moved near Lyon, Saint-Etienne, and Toulouse. It was also of the utmost urgency to bring back a workforce to make these factories run. Recruitment teams went to the front lines in search of specialized workers, and some lucky men without the necessary training managed to get themselves hired.[76] Thomas was appointed an under-secretary of state on May 18, 1915, at the very time when the need for heavy artillery had doubled in a few weeks, following the failure of the Ardennes offensive. In December 1916, he was named Minister of Munitions and War Manufacturing. He rejected the idea of nationalizing production, instead of letting industrialists continue to run their factories, although he partially suspended some of the mechanisms of the free market: the state became the sole buyer, maintaining firm control of prices and of how the workforce was used. Thomas' friend, the historian François Simiand, who was his chief of staff in the Ministry of Munitions and who would later work with him in Geneva, summed up the situation in this way: "to have control over the industry without having to resort to requisitioning."[77]

---

[74] Hennebicque, "Albert Thomas and the war industries," pp. 90–91.
[75] Schaper, *Albert Thomas*, pp. 105–106.
[76] Arthur Fontaine, *L'industrie française pendant la guerre* (Paris: Presses universitaires de France; New Haven: Yale University Press, 1924), Chapter 3.
[77] Archives Nationales, Archives Albert Thomas, AN 94 AP 62, Memorandum from François Simiand, no date, but probably from February 1916.

Thomas emphasized increasing productivity. He drew inspiration from methods used in Great Britain and the United States, such as a scientific organization of labor, workforce training, the rearrangement of space inside the factories, and the use of more modern machines. His main sources of information were the car manufacturer Louis Renault; the economist Max Lazard, a member of the *Service d'Études économiques* who, in that capacity, went regularly to the United States as of 1916; and Robert Pinot, director of the powerful management association, the *Comité des Forges*, who knew Great Britain well.[78] High-level trade union leaders such as Léon Jouhaux, secretary-general of the CGT, joined with this group of major industrialists; Jouhaux would later be a member of the organizing committee of the ILO.

Thomas' office brought together many intellectuals and academics whom he had met in the early 1900s and who were somewhat close to the SFIO: his chief of staff, Simiand; his executive secretary, Roques; Maurette; Mantoux.[79] This was ironic, considering that the Socialist party had been deeply pacifist and internationalist before the war. These *experts du social*, or experts on social questions, to use Christophe Prochasson's term, who later formed the heart of the ILO, were responsible for organizing industrial production to supply the war, from the search for raw materials to the manufacture of munitions. They experimented to find the most efficient labor methods and negotiated with unions on the social costs of the war effort. Thomas adapted labor law to the new conditions imposed by the conflict, with a dual goal: increasing production and forestalling social ills that would have severe consequences for the war effort.[80]

As Minister of Munitions, Thomas did not have an easy task, all the more so because his socialist comrades did not always understand it. As a patriot, Thomas was convinced that the defense of France was

[78] Martin Fine, "Albert Thomas: a reformer's vision of modernization, 1914–1932," *Journal of Contemporary History*, 12: 3, July 1977, p. 562, n. 9. See also Martin Fine, "*Toward Corporatism: the Movement for Capital-Labor Collaboration in France, 1914–1936*" (PhD dissertation, University of Wisconsin, Madison, 1971).

[79] Andler, *Vie de Lucien Herr, 1864–1926*, p. 167.

[80] The historian Richard Kuisel is rather severe on Albert Thomas, whom he compares unfavorably with his successor, Louis Loucheur, Minister of Munitions under Painlevé and Clemenceau. According to him, the team organized by Thomas lacked administrative experience and gave priority to workers' rights, while Loucheur was more concerned with improving production (Richard Kuisel, *Capitalism and the State in Modern France*. New York: Cambridge University Press, 1981. French translation, *Le capitalisme et l'État en France*, Paris, Gallimard, 1984). This interpretation is not very convincing, because it underestimates the continuity between the two ministers' staffs (by December 1916, Louis Loucheur was serving as under-secretary of state for artillery and munitions, under Thomas as Minister for Munitions and War Materials) and it misunderstands the importance of production for Thomas (Hennebicque, "Albert Thomas and the war industries").

a just cause. But he was criticized for his participation in a bourgeois government as part of the war effort, as the letter he sent in February 1916 to the leader of the Italian Socialist Party, Giacinto Serrati, attests: "I would have thought that a shared life in the same organization would have allowed the Italian comrades to understand somewhat the duty that French socialists are currently fulfilling... We have simply agreed to collaborate for the defense of our country, and we think that by acting in this way, we serve the proletariat's cause better than others do."[81] Throughout the war and during the 1920s, Thomas would not change his mind on the legitimacy of his decision. "The war came. Of war policy, for my part, I regret nothing," he said in a speech given in 1921. "Our party, all of us, we did our duty. And whatever interpretations may later be brought to bear on war policy or war socialism, I am conscious of having defended justice, the freedom of our country, and the law of the world."[82]

Initially, the Viviani government had considered suspending social laws, as long as the war lasted, since it was not supposed to last long. Following the call-up, the Minister for Labor and Social Security Provisions, Maurice Couyba, gave directives for labor inspectors not to be too harsh when penalizing infractions against the Labor Code.[83] The law of the 10-hour workday, established by the Law of March 30, 1900, was no longer adhered to, and the same held true for the weekly day off, passed into law in 1906. Women workers could work at night on dangerous jobs, such as manufacturing cartridges and shells. "There are no more workers' rights, no more social laws, there is only the war," the Minister of War, Alexandre Millerand, declared to trade union representatives from the Metals Federation in January 1915. This situation could not last. Social legislation soon had to be adapted to a long-term war. It was thus decided to restore the *mobilisés industriels*, the term for those specialized workers sent home from the front, to their full salary and full rights, including rights won by their unions, with the exception of the right to strike. This task did not fall to the Minister of Labor, who lost influence during the conflict, but rather to those like Albert Thomas, who were in charge of wartime production, in the larger context of extending the state's sphere of intervention.[84]

---

[81] Archives Nationales, Archives Albert Thomas, 94 AP 42, Albert Thomas to Giacinto Serrati, February 22, 1916.
[82] "Politique sociale internationale," International Labor Office, 1947, p. 154, cited in Guérin, *Albert Thomas au BIT*, p. 9, n. 18.
[83] *Bulletin du Ministère du Travail*, 1914: circulars dated August 2, 3, and 14, 1914.
[84] Fontaine, *L'industrie française pendant la guerre*; Fridenson (ed.), *The French Home Front*; Fabienne Bock, "L'exubérance de l'Etat"; John F. Godfrey, *Capitalism at War: Industrial Policy and Bureaucracy in France, 1914–1918* (Oxford: Berg, 1987).

Organizing labor law in wartime was all the more complex inasmuch as different kinds of workers had to co-exist: civilian workers, men and women; the specialized workers who had been sent home from the front; the 500,000 workers from overseas colonies and from foreign countries, disabled veterans, prisoners of war. Each factory contained a diverse group of workers, who each had different legal protections. Here is one example among many. Civilian workers who worked in munitions production benefited from the Law of April 9, 1898, concerning workplace accidents. This law granted the right to payment in case of death, permanent disability resulting from an injury incurred on the job, or a simple temporary leave. Conversely, those referred to as the *mobilisés industriels* were the soldiers sent home to work in the factories, following the Dalbiez Law in 1915 and the Mourier Law in 1917, so that their professional expertise could be put to use. They numbered nearly 345,000 in France in the summer of 1916, and were still officially considered to be soldiers. As such, they were protected by the Law of April 11, 1831 concerning military pensions; this law gave them the right to a payment, but only in cases where an on-the-job injury led to permanent disability. Moreover, insurance companies tended to refer difficult cases back to the army, which in turn often refused to accept any responsibility, referring the case back to those in charge at the factory.[85]

This legal confusion was typical of the war. The rights granted to each category of worker outlined social identities that were sometimes ambiguous: the *mobilisés industriels*, i.e., the specialized workers sent home from the front played an essential role in arms production, but the soldiers in the trenches often saw them as shirkers, as they saw anyone not directly exposed to danger on the front lines.[86] Civilians also viewed the *mobilisés industriels* with hostility, and frequently suspected them of benefiting from favoritism in order to gain protection.[87] In wartime, labor law was inseparable from moral questions that did not have the same weight as in peacetime. The rhetoric of equality among citizens, anchored in a

---

[85] Vincent Viet, "Le droit du travail s'en va t-en guerre (1914–1918)," La Documentation française, *Revue française des Affaires sociales*, 1, 2002, pp. 155–167.

[86] The shirker was a central figure in the war culture of 1914–18. Charles Ridel has amply illustrated the flexibility of this idea in his book *Les Embusqués*. Derived from pre-war slang, the term *embusqué* or "shirker" saw a rapid rise in 1915 and 1916, before slowly disappearing at the end of the conflict. It referred to both those who worked on the home front and those who were not on the front lines: artillerymen, medics, and drivers were called *embusqués du front* or "front-line shirkers."

[87] The preamble of the Dalbiez law recalls "the presence, far from the front, of young and strong men, drafted or not, troubles families who know their own sons are exposed to suffering and danger" (*Journal Officiel*, Débats de la Chambre des Députés, annexes, April 1, 1915).

Jacobin tradition dating back to the French Revolution, ran counter to the war's socioeconomic reality—it was necessary to recall qualified workers from the front lines back to the factory. In any event, the sacrifices of workers always seemed to pale in comparison with the price in blood that soldiers paid every day.[88]

In order not to accentuate the growing divide between soldiers and their families on the one hand, and, on the other hand, the *mobilisés industriels* or specialized workers sent home from the front, government leaders, beginning with Thomas, constantly had to remind people that their goal was productivity, not workers' welfare. A famous speech that Thomas gave in April 1916 testifies to this; it was given in the enormous hall of the Creusot factory, during the height of the battle of Verdun. After recalling the "tragic hours of 1793 and 1794," the Minister of Munitions urged the workers on: "Victory hangs over our heads, in the smoke filling this valley. We count on you, comrades, to seize it. It is your task to work to the bitter end, until death." It was no longer the time for workers' demands and for corporatist struggles. "After a victorious war, which will not abolish all social oppositions, when you will have to assert your legitimate rights once again, comrades in the struggle, comrades in hope, you will find me with you, ready to bring about the ideal of justice and liberty that was and remains ours."[89]

In reality, the Great War was also a laboratory for workers' rights, as much scholarly work on social history has shown.[90] It is something of a paradox that, in a situation where factories ran at full capacity and where workers worked nonstop for thirteen days without a day off, they also thought hard and at length about their working conditions. This no doubt resulted from the extreme fatigue suffered by many workers in munitions factories, creating alarm among public authorities. "I saw my companion, so young, so kind, in her large black apron, pursue her task. For a year, she has practically lived at the factory; 900,000 shells have passed through her hands . . . Fresh and strong when she arrived at the factory, she has lost her youthful bloom and is now just a skinny, worn-out girl," in the words of the journalist Marcelle Capy, who got herself hired in a munitions factory in order to share the working conditions of women munitions workers, known as *munitionettes*.[91] But the movement

[88]   Horne, "L'impôt du sang."   [89]   Schaper, *Albert Thomas*, pp. 118–120.
[90]   There is a large bibliography on this topic; see especially the major work of Laura Lee Downs, *Manufacturing Inequality: Gender Division in the French and British Metalworking Industries, 1914–1939* (Ithaca: Cornell University Press, 1995).
[91]   Marcelle Capy, "La femme à l'usine," *La Voix des femmes*, Novembre 28, 1917. On the working conditions of women in the war industry, see the pioneering work of Mathilde

to reform working conditions did not emerge in response to a simple passing emotion after reading newspaper accounts. In the eyes of Albert Thomas, the great reformer, industrial modernization was inseparable from the modernization of social policies. This is particularly evident in the progress made in workplace health and safety, which sought to improve air circulation and air quality in war factories; in the growth of a movement encouraging a higher birth rate, which sought to make women workers' jobs compatible with motherhood by setting up maternity leaves, nursing rooms, and day care for children within the factory.[92]

To Albert Thomas' way of thinking, the protection of workers' health could not be separated from the increase in productivity: the goal was not only to produce more, but also to reduce the impact of industrial labor on the body, to reduce fatigue and weariness. At least, such was the discourse of socialist reformers on the scientific organization of the workplace, while in reality the need to increase production widened the rift between skilled jobs and an unqualified workforce condemned to repetitive tasks. Moreover, the specific protections accorded to women workers were part of a larger view of women's place in society and on gender relations in a wartime society. The Minister of Munitions thus considered political, social, and economic problems *as a whole*—this is also what he would do as head of the ILO. Nonetheless, the social aspect of Thomas' policies remained incomplete. In his mind, his policies as Minister of Munitions had to be implemented in two steps, first by boosting war production, then by strengthening workers' rights. He would not have the time to fully implement the second part of his program.[93]

The other point of continuity between Thomas' policies as Minister of Munitions and his policies in Geneva in the 1920s was the dialogue he inaugurated between unions and employers, both of which were closely associated with industrial policy. What was called tripartism within the ILO was already at work with the systematic use of arbitration and recon- ciliation during the Great War. However, the arbitration of 1916–18 did not, of course, have the same force or the same goal as it did during the 1920s. During the Great War, Thomas appealed to employers' and unions' patriotism, using to his advantage the progressive marginalization of class solidarity in favor of the *union sacrée*, beginning in the summer of

Dubesset, Françoise Thébaud and Catherine Vincent, "The female munition work- ers of the Seine," in Fridenson (ed.), *The French Home Front*, and of course Downs, *Manufacturing Inequality*.

[92] Françoise Thébaud, "The Great War and the triumph of sexual division," in Georges Duby and Michelle Perrot (eds.), *History of Women in the West* (Cambridge Mass.: Belknap Press of Harvard University Press, 1992–94), Vol. 5, ed. Françoise Thébaud.

[93] Lazarovici, "L'organisation du ministère de l'armement."

1914.[94] In this context, the activist union movement behind the strikes of 1917–18 was quickly contained by evoking the sacrifices soldiers were making on the battlefield, and workers' duty to not betray them. With the ILO, on the other hand, the goal was to bring together workers and management in a *transnational project*, with the aim of recognizing universal social rights. But it is true that, without the dialogues established and the contacts made during the war, the ILO in Geneva would doubtless have been run very differently; and without the different types of workers' identities shaped by the war, the reformist trend that Thomas embodied would not have been as important.

In September 1917, the SFIO decided not to join the Painlevé government. Thomas, faithful to his party's rules, turned his post as Minister of Munitions over to one of his colleagues in that office, Louis Loucheur. The SFIO's new line of thinking rejected any collaboration with a bourgeois government and broke with the ideology of the *union sacrée*. For many socialists, Thomas at that time stood for "wartime revisionism." Moreover, his hostility towards Bolshevism,[95] which he called a "regime of massacres and violence,"[96] set him apart from a large section of the French left. "Either Wilson or Lenin. Either democracy born of the French Revolution, strengthened by an entire century's struggles, or the brutal, incoherent, primitive forms of Russian fanaticism. We must choose," Thomas explained, in a famous article published in the socialist newspaper *L'Humanité*.[97] Politically, the initial results of "wartime socialism" can seem slim. But over a longer term, Thomas' experience in the government of the *union sacrée* indeed transformed socialists into full-fledged actors responsible for government policies. The state became the privileged instrument of social progress.[98]

As the embodiment of the reformist trend in the SFIO, Thomas became invested in international issues when he participated in the Paris Peace Conference. For him, wartime socialism, something he had carried out in the French government for 3 years, had to develop into peacetime socialism, based on Wilsonian peace and on the defense of social rights. To take social issues into consideration during the peace negotiations in

---

[94] John Horne, *Labour at War: France and Britain, 1914–1918* (Oxford: Clarendon Press, 1991).

[95] Albert Thomas, *Bolchevisme ou socialisme?* (Nancy and Paris: Berger-Levrault, 1919).

[96] *L'Humanité*, November 19, 1918.

[97] Albert Thomas, "Démocratie ou bolchevisme," *L'Humanité*, November 9, 1918, pp. 1–2.

[98] Nicolas Rousselier, "Le 'gouvernement de guerre' et les socialistes," in Romain Ducoulombier (ed.), *Les socialistes dans l'Europe en guerre: réseaux, parcours, expériences, 1914–1918* (Paris: L'Harmattan, 2010), pp. 33–44.

fact had a double goal, to establish a kind of defense against the Communist temptation that some Western workers might be susceptible to, and, at the same time, to recompense workers for their sacrifices towards the war effort.

A commission consisting of fifteen experts from nine countries thus met, as part of the peace conference, in order to consider what international labor law in the wake of the war might look like. Most of these men knew each other and had already worked together, before or during the war.[99] They were putting into practice the new diplomacy of experts that was in the process of emerging from the chaos of World War I. It was also a precursor of the sea change later embodied in the ILO's tripartism: together around the same table were government representatives (such as the Frenchmen Louis Loucheur, Minister of Industrial Reconstruction, and Justin Godart,[100] the Belgian Minister of Justice, Émile Vandervelde, and the Czech Minister of Foreign Affairs, Eduard Beneš), trade union representatives (such as the American, Samuel Gompers, president of the American Federation of Labor (AFL), and the Frenchman, Léon Jouhaux, secretary-general of the CGT), and academics (the American James Shotwell and the Belgian Ernest Mahaim). Members of upper management, trade union leaders, and government officials were all equally represented, something that did not exist in any national organization at the time.

Finally, after several months of marathon negotiations at the Ministry of Labor in Paris, the delegations reached an agreement that was in fact a compromise obtained only after a difficult struggle. In his study of the origins of the ILO, Jasmien Van Daele has amply illustrated the tension that members of the commission experienced between their national loyalties and their transnational ideals.[101] The best example of this difficulty is the United States' final decision not to join the ILO: only in 1934 did it finally join. The debates focused on two main questions. The first concerned the respective places of trade union and government representatives in the structure of the new ILO. The American delegates, led

---

[99] Arthur Fontaine, Sir Malcolm Delevingne and Ernest Mahaim served together on the board of the IALL; Léon Jouhaux and Louis Loucheur participated in organizing the war economy when Thomas was a member of the government; at the end of the war, Samuel Gompers and Emile Vandervelde founded the International Labour and Socialist Conference, which met in Bern in tandem with the Paris Peace Conference.

[100] Isabelle Moret-Lespinet, "Justin Godart et le Bureau International du Travail," in Annette Wieviorka (ed.), *Justin Godart, un homme dans son siècle, 1871–1956* (Paris: CNRS éditions, 2004), pp. 81–86.

[101] Van Daele, "Engineering social peace," p. 462; see also Edward Phelan, "The Commission on International Labour Legislation," in Shotwell (ed.), *Origins of the International Labour Organization*.

by Gompers, wanted a structure that would give a larger place to work-ers' representatives, since, for them, social progress would come about through agreements negotiated between employers and unions; but the commission concluded that it would be best to maintain a place for gov-ernment representatives, who could serve as a link to national legislatures, which had to vote on social legislation.

Moreover, the French and Italian delegations would have liked for the ILO to become a kind of Labor Parliament, capable of passing interna-tional laws for its member states; in the end, though, giving up this kind of sovereignty was much less important than other issues, and each coun-try maintained control over carrying out any conventions—as we will see later. The members of the commission gave preference to an agreement on some general principles (shortening the length of the workday, pro-hibiting child labor, setting a minimum wage, the right to join a union, weekly time off) rather than setting up a detailed program for the future ILO. This was doubtless the reason why the Peace Conference so readily accepted the ILO's constitution and integrated it into Part XIII of the Treaty of Versailles. When he became director of the ILO on January 27, 1920, Thomas saw his horizons expand; the ILO would make it possible for him to take the ideas and principles he had defended during the war and give them a lasting institutional form.

The International Labor Organization, the culture of expertise, and the creation of international standards

For Thomas and for socialist reformers as a whole, the Great War rep-resented a significant break. The left wing of the French socialist party, invigorated by the Russian Revolution, saw the reformists as traitors to the working class and its pacifist ideal, since they had collaborated on the war effort. After supporting the policies of the *union sacrée*, the reformists lost their leading role within the SFIO: two-thirds of the delegates to the Tours Congress (December 25–30, 1920) voted to join the Third International, thus giving birth to the French Communist Party.[102] In addition to this internal tension, there existed a certain disillusionment vis-à-vis the hopes for peace nourished at the turn of the century, as several of Thomas' speeches from the 1920s illustrate: "For our work, it would have been ideal to have still retained something of the pre-war world. In the world that existed before the war, we enjoyed noticing how, already, in business transactions and in labor agreements, in financial and

---

[102] On the birth of the French Communist Party, see Romain Ducoulombier, *Camarades! La naissance du Parti communiste en France* (Paris: Perrin, 2010).

industrial agreements, a new kind of humanity was coming into being. Pacifists took pleasure in the fact that there were perhaps thirty or forty international pacifist associations. Everything was swept away by the war, and the mirror in which this new kind of humanity could see its image growing clearer was broken."[103]

Our sense of this nostalgia for the pre-war era should not however mask the formidable energy that drove reformist circles in the 1920s, and, beyond that, the work of rebuilding international relations begun during this period. Experts from ministries of war, from trade unions, from upper management, and an entire new school of specialists in international law joined Thomas in Geneva in order to lay the intellectual groundwork for the ILO. They responded to two major concerns of the post-war period: to establish lasting social stability that would forestall the risk of any new conflicts (this goal was written into the preamble to Part XIII of the Treaty of Versailles), and to address the social vulnerabilities inherited from the Great War.

In the space of several years, many things had changed. To begin with, World War I confirmed that the Westphalian model of international relations had eroded, and that a growing number of states and societies were interdependent: this was the crisis of sovereignty of nation-states, theorized by a number of legal scholars in the 1920s, such as Nicolas Politis, André Mandelstam, and Alejandro Álvarez, themselves the heirs of the preceding generation of philosophers of law such as Antoine Pillet and Léon Duguit.[104]

As a result, traditional diplomacy was called into question; hanging over it was the responsibility for the failure of international conferences such as that held at The Hague in 1899. Traditional diplomacy no longer seemed appropriate for the way the post-war world worked.[105] On a cultural level, the crisis was a profound one. The world of diplomats, with

---

[103] ABIT, CAT/2/20/3, Albert Thomas, Speech given at the Villa Borghese, Rome, May 16, 1920. See also his Warsaw speech, February 2, 1924 (ABIT, CAT/2/24/2): "When we think of all our prewar relationships, when we can call to mind all the international conquests and all the speeches given in order to bar the road to war, it must be said that at this hour of mobilization, at the hour when some have been thrown into the fire, thinking they are acting in the name of justice and others in the name of liberty—it must be said that personal relationships had little weight."

[104] Antoine Pillet, *Recherches sur les droits fondamentaux des États dans l'ordre des rapports internationaux et sur la solution des conflits qu'ils font naître* (Paris: Pedone, 1899); Léon Duguit, *Le droit social, le droit individuel et la transformation de l'État* (Paris: Alcan, 1908). See Martti Koskenniemi, *The Gentle Civilizer of Nations: The Rise and Fall of International Law, 1870–1960* (Cambridge University Press, 2004), especially Chapter 4: "International law as sociology: French solidarism, 1871–1950."

[105] A member of the Legal Department of the League of Nations, the American jurist Manley Hudson, thought that the ILO had put an end to "the monopolistic control of

its own order of precedence, rhetoric, and rituals, gradually gave way to a world of experts: economists, legal scholars, sociologists, and demographers. The social and professional background, the cultural references, and the ideals of these new elites were not the same as those of the former. Lastly, as if to occupy the empty space created by the weakening of nation-states and their traditional representatives, a new kind of social group formed and acquired importance: international legal scholars, who worked to lay the foundations for the ILO's legitimacy and to put standards in place that would apply on a worldwide scale.[106]

In order to understand the ILO's workings, it needs to be seen as a *social and cultural space*, where men from around the world met, and, with time, women as well.[107] Also important was Geneva's status as the heir of a long international tradition.[108] Since 1864, it had been the headquarters of the International Red Cross. It formed a unique social mosaic, where the Protestant middle class of Geneva and a cosmopolitan milieu coexisted without really mixing. Subsequently, when the League of Nations and the ILO established their headquarters there after the war, this brought about a change of scale.[109] In 1920, over a hundred international civil servants had been quickly recruited in order to run the new institutions born out of the Treaty of Versailles. In 1925, the ILO already numbered a thousand staff members, of whom 250 worked for the International Labor Office, run by Thomas. Given the size of its task, the Office tended to keep increasing its specialized technical offices, which ended up working independently of one another, if not in outright competition. Eight years after the ILO was founded, Thomas was still

---

the conduct of international relations by Foreign Offices through diplomatic channels." *Progress in International Organization* (Stanford University Press, 1932), p. 52.

[106] Dzovinar Kévonian, "Les juristes et l'Organisation internationale du Travail, 1919–1939. Processus de légitimation et institutionnalisation des relations internationales," *Journal of the History of International Law*, 12, 2010, pp. 227–266.

[107] At the first international labor conference, held in Washington DC in 1919, twenty-two women were present and two of the six conventions adopted had to do with women, one prohibiting them from night work and the other protecting women workers during pregnancy. In the 1920s, the number of women participants in international conferences remained the same. During this period, one of the most active figures in the ILO was the Englishwoman Margaret Bondfield, named Minister of Labor under Ramsay MacDonald in 1929. Women's influence in the ILO grew larger in the 1930s, and it was thanks to Frances Perkins, the first woman to serve as Secretary of Labor in the United States, that her country joined the ILO in August 1934.

[108] During the Paris Peace Conference, the Belgian delegate Ernest Mahaim had argued in favor of Brussels as the headquarters of the League of Nations and the ILO in order to compensate for Belgium's losses during the Great War (see Van Daele, "Engineering social peace," p. 458). However, the choice of Geneva as an international capital quickly gained favor.

[109] For a sociological approach, see Christine Manigand, *Les Français au service de la Société des Nations* (Bern: Peter Lang, 2003).

lamenting this state of affairs in a letter to his assistant director, Harold Butler: "What bothers me the most is to see that in a large number of offices and departments, the work is all done with no enjoyment, no passion. The poverty of ideas is deplorable. I cannot understand how young men who have had the chance to think about their work and its results seem to drive themselves to work hard, only to end up blandly repeating the same things that were said in a previous report. There are some interesting things here and there, but they are rare."[110]

The leadership of the Organization was well aware of the many practical problems resulting from the *ex nihilo* creation of an institution that had no prior historical equivalent. To begin with, there was inevitable administrative awkwardness and difficulties of translation: in 1921, the staff members of the International Labor Office represented nineteen different nationalities.[111] When it came to publishing the Organization's documents, which were always in French and English, Geneva's printers were not used to composing type in English and they lacked sufficient personnel, which explains the many printers' errors in documents from this period. In 1921, when examinations became part of the application process, candidates had to know at least French and English, or at least have some competency in the two languages. But this was far from being the case, particularly when it came to written French and English. Stenographers struggled to take notes during debates in a language that they did not understand well. In addition, there were even more fundamental cultural differences, as Thomas remarked during a lecture in 1923: "When one goes farther and runs into differences in mindset rather than in language or procedure, try to imagine the obstacles that come up when adapting different ways of thinking: the Anglo-Saxon one, factual and pragmatic; the Latin one, logical and theoretical. I have never been able to make any one of my English colleagues understand the purpose of a *vote de principe* [non-binding vote], or the subtlety of the 'modalities' that are, however, the only way that we can save some ideas and reach some solutions in international life."[112]

---

[110] Archives Nationales, AN 94 AP 377, Letter from Thomas to Butler, April 19, 1927. The strongest critic of the ILO remains the novelist Albert Cohen (himself an international civil servant) in his novel *Belle du Seigneur* (Paris: Gallimard, 1968).

[111] Articles 393 and 394 of Part XIII of the Versailles Treaty gave the Director of the ILO the task of recruiting personnel. However, he was bound by the statutes of the ILO to take national representation into consideration. He in fact worked under dual supervision, that of the ILO's executive board, led by Arthur Fontaine, and that of the budgetary committee, which voted on his annual budget of 8 million Swiss francs and which was dependent on the League of Nations. See Guérin, *Albert Thomas au BIT*, pp. 26–27.

[112] ABIT, CAT/2/23/3, Speech on the ILO given to the *Comité National d'Études sociales et politiques* at the École normale supérieure, Paris, February 15, 1923.

Nonetheless, in spite of these inevitable difficulties, a kind of common culture was established.[113] It was a result of several underlying processes, to which I will now briefly turn. The first and doubtless most important was the emergence of *international organizations as legitimate bodies.* Instead of the absolute sovereignty of states, the prevailing theme of several decades earlier, European legal scholars now increasingly referred to "the common law of humanity." International law thus no longer appeared as a product of the will of states. It became the expression of human solidarity, extended to a global scale. This idea was not new, since several nineteenth-century jurists had already discussed it in their work.[114] But it was all the stronger in the 1920s for having broken with the "nationalization of law" that had operated during the Great War.[115] From 1914 to 1918, the overriding interests of each state provided the basis for international law; from the perspective of the founding fathers of the ILO, it was the overriding interest of humanity that provided such a basis.

It would be wrong, however, to overestimate the influence of international legal scholars, who remained in the minority in academe.[116] It is true that they had the advantage of conducting their scholarly work in institutions founded after the war, such as the Hague Academy of International Law and the Graduate Institute of International Studies (IUHEI) in Geneva, as well as the Institute of International Law founded in Ghent in 1873.[117] But in other universities they regularly encountered the resistance of sovereignist colleagues. "The Law School and the *École libre des Sciences Politiques* are the two bulwarks of reactionary thought in

[113] This idea connects to that of an "epistemic community," as discussed by Adler and Haas in their article "Epistemic communities."

[114] The term "common law of humanity" was used in particular by the French legal scholar Antoine Pillet in *Recherches sur les droits fondamentaux des États.* The British legal scholar Wilfred Jenks took it up again in the 1920s; Jenks joined the legal division of the ILO in 1931 and became Director-General from 1970–73 (see Dzovinar Kévonian, "Les juristes et l'Organisation Internationale du Travail," p. 230).

[115] Stora-Lamarre, "La guerre au nom du droit," pp. 150–160; Thiers, "Droit et culture de guerre."

[116] Not only that, in a country like the United States, legal scholars had to work against public opinion and the official policy of non-participation in institutions created by the Treaty of Versailles. On this trend, see Warren F. Kuehl and Lynne K. Dunn, *Keeping the Covenant: American Internationalists and the League of Nations, 1920–1939* (Ohio: Kent State University Press, 1997). The historian James T. Shotwell was a particularly noteworthy figure among the American legal scholars who worked on the creation of the ILO. He was a member of the American delegation to the Paris Peace Conference and the editor of one of the key works on the ILO's history: *The Origins of the International Labor Organization.*

[117] Guillaume Sacriste and Antoine Vauchez, "Les 'bons offices' du droit international: la constitution d'une autorité non-politique dans le concert diplomatique des années 1920," *Critique Internationale,* 26, January 2005, pp. 101–117.

France,[118] and they are solid bulwarks," remarked Thomas. By his own admission, it would take time to fully establish the idea of law based on shared human rights. "In discussions after the war, the principles and the actions of the French Revolution were frequently brought up. Let me suggest a comparison. The same way that during the French Revolution, in a clear moment of conscience, noble principles were adopted and used to formulate the Declaration of the Rights of Man and of the Citizen, in the same way, at the moment of the Armistice, and under pressure from the working-class world, principles of justice were written into Part XIII of the Peace Treaty in order to bring about social justice, the basis for a lasting peace. But years and years of struggle were needed in order for the principles of 1789 to become reality. In the same way, the agreements in Part XIII of the Peace Treaty oblige us to keep up a constant effort."[119]

At the heart of the ILO's project lay the idea that *international peace and social justice go together*: this was the second element of the "common culture" developing during the 1920s. When Part XIII of the Treaty of Versailles was developed in 1919, it sought to "create a truly humane labor system everywhere . . . as the surest guarantee of universal peace."[120] World peace was dependent on social peace. The founding fathers of the Organization were deeply convinced of this, as the debates over the labor commission during the Paris Peace Conference in 1919 show.[121] Hence the ILO's global nature, which in theory should also have avoided a situation where the more socially advanced nations were economically penalized while other countries reaped economic benefits due to less or no concern for their workers' rights.

But how could such harmony be achieved without clashing with the sovereignty of its member states? It was not acceptable, given the post-war situation, for the ILO to become a kind of super-state and for its annual conferences to become an international labor parliament; national governments would not accept this. There was also a strong risk that the ILO would be reduced to powerlessness. Its founding fathers thus had to come up with "sufficiently flexible and completely new legislative or para-legislative procedures that would inspire the most states possible to join."[122] The staff of theInternational Labor Office, which formed

---

[118] Later referred to as École des Sciences Politiques, or Sciences-po.

[119] ABIT, CAT/2/22/1, Albert Thomas, Speech at the Conference of the International Trade Union Federation, Rome, April 20–26, 1922.

[120] ABIT, CAT/2/20/9, Albert Thomas, Speech welcoming Alexandre Millerand on the occasion of his visit to the International Labor Office, September 15, 1920.

[121] Paul Périgord, *The International Labor Organization* (New York: D. Appleton and Company, 1926), Chapter 5.

[122] Michel Virally, "La valeur juridique des recommandations des organisations internationales," *Annuaire français de droit international*, 2, 1956, p. 79.

the general secretariat of the ILO, prepared conventions and recommendations. The relationship between Thomas, as director of the International Labor Office, and the executive board of the ILO, to whom he reported, was not always an easy one. As much as Thomas could count on his friendship with Arthur Fontaine, president of the executive board, and some of the board members such as the French trade union leader Léon Jouhaux and the Belgian jurist Ernest Mahaim, his relationship with Robert Pinot, who represented French employers, was frequently strained.

In order to draft conventions and recommendations, the staff of the International Labor Office drew inspiration from a variety of national legislations, which suggests a significant effort to obtain the necessary documentation and have recourse to experts. After some back-and-forth with national governments on a particular project, proposals were submitted to each government's delegates and its management and labor representatives, during the International Labor Conferences.[123] The recommendations simply set goals. On the other hand, when a majority approved a convention, it had to be submitted by each country to the appropriate authority, usually its legislature, to be ratified within a year. Thus, any dispossession of the rights of member states was quite relative.[124]

One of Thomas' responsibilities was to convince countries to ratify the conventions voted on during the annual conferences, which explains the considerable number of trips he made abroad, even as far as Asia, at a time when transportation was ill-suited to long-haul travel.[125] "You see, in social policy more than any other area, there is only one method to use: being there in person, personal diplomacy . . . ," Thomas declared.

---

[123] The tripartism at the heart of the ILO's structure was originally an English idea, borrowed from Leonard Woolf and the Fabian Society. Each delegation was thus made up of two government representatives, an employers' representative, and a workers' representative. In a way, adopting this principle made it possible to establish the new organization's legitimacy in the mind of public opinion. In addition, the length of time given to member states to submit conventions for ratification by their national legislatures—unlike initial plans, which proposed automatic ratification except in the case of a negative vote by these legislatures—eased concerns over member states' sovereignty. See Eliane Vogel-Polsky, *Du tripartisme à l'Organisation Internationale du Travail* (Brussels: Éditions de l'Institut de Sociologie de l'Université de Bruxelles, 1966) and Bernard Béguin, *The ILO and the Tripartite System* (New York: Carnegie Endowment for International Peace, 1959).

[124] When he made an initial assessment of his work in 1923, Thomas admitted that the conventions agreed on during international labor conferences were not equally welcomed by all countries. Only sixty-five conventions had been ratified, whereas "in multiplying the number of conventions agreed on, by the number of states who should have ratified them, we should have 700 ratifications." (ABIT, CAT/2/23/3)

[125] Sylvie Massart, *Les voyages d'Albert Thomas directeur du BIT (1919–1932)*, Université Paris-I, 1993.

"When relationships are established and when the administrator shows up, clean-shaven or with a beard according to the custom, then international reality makes some results possible."[126] The director of the ILO often presented himself as "the Wandering Jew of social policy,"[127] "the prisoner transferred about, on international trains,"[128] or "a traveling salesman of social policy."[129] His mission was part of a kind of crusade for social justice throughout the world, where, in his speeches, he cleverly played on both competition among member states and the threat of worldwide chaos if the ILO's mandate were to end in failure.[130]

Thomas frequently invoked public opinion as another way of legitimizing his work. Thus, as director of the ILO, he presented himself as continuing the struggles for social rights that had been undertaken in each country, particularly France, thereby adopting a stance that might seem paradoxical for someone whom the left wing of the SFIO reproached for compromising himself by working with bourgeois governments. In Thomas' eyes, the Labor Charter adopted in 1919 recompensed the sacrifices the working class had agreed to make during the war. It hallowed the hopes expressed by workers at a time when the war effort limited their rights. The ILO's strength thus lay not only in the work of specialists in international law and labor law experts, but also in public opinion—although of course this could not always be easily defined. Alluding to the United States' refusal to join the Organization and to the criticisms from Soviet Russia, Thomas admitted: "Here I am trying to get out in public and conduct diplomacy on the streets, to appeal to public opinion... Some suspect me of stirring up agitation where the public would otherwise be calm, and others see me only as a traitor, only as a man who renounced the entire Socialist past and all that was accomplished to protect workers."[131]

It was then that another idea gradually took hold in the common culture of ILO civil servants, that of *international public opinion*. Its slow emergence marks a turning point in the history of international relations.

[126] ABIT, CAT/2/25/1/4, Albert Thomas, Speech at the University of Montevideo, July 29, 1925.
[127] ABIT, CAT/2/22/6, Albert Thomas, Speech given to the Canadian Club of Ottawa, December 14, 1922.
[128] ABIT, CAT/2/26/2, Albert Thomas, Speech on the Locarno accords and Europe's economic future; University of Belgrade, February 9, 1926.
[129] ABIT, CAT/2/30/2, Albert Thomas, Speech to the Alliance Française in Sofia, February 26, 1930.
[130] ABIT, CAT/2/21/5, Albert Thomas, Speech on disarmament: "There will be no social progress in a society constantly under threat of war, and if the world continues to suffer from injustice, poverty, and privation, world peace will constantly be compromised."
[131] ABIT, CAT/2/25/1/4, Albert Thomas, Speech at the University of Montevideo, July 29, 1925.

We can still see its consequences in various forms today, where it has become a commonplace but without being any more clearly defined. For Albert Thomas, the development of labor law necessarily had to take place through raising awareness throughout the world and by the pressure that people would bring to bear on their governments. "Where our problems are concerned, the problem of protections for labor, are there Europeans and Americans?" Thomas wondered during a trip to Latin America in the summer of 1925.

When the matter at hand involves defending a child against being put to work too young, when it involves defending women against the hell of night work, preventing a situation where they work all day as housewives taking care of home and family before heading to a factory job at night, when it involves defending workers against excessively long workdays in order to allow them some hours of leisure that are their due in modern civilization and industrial progress—can there be a European mentality and an American one? For our part, we are conscious of helping create a common mentality, feelings common to all men, and we are conscious of thus bringing about a little moral unity in humanity.[132]

This universalizing discourse, however, should not create any illusions. The issue of gender, for example, represents one of the limits of the rights promoted by the ILO. On the occasion of the 1919 peace conference, English, Belgian, and American women activists came to Paris to argue for women's rights. Some of their demands included the right to vote, the prohibition of nighttime work, and equal pay for equal work. The International Council of Women (ICW), founded in Washington in 1888, was a leading defender of these demands. Madame Brunschwig of the Allied Women Suffragists and Lady Aberdeen, President of the ICW, asked that women be represented in such new entities as the League of Nations and that women's right to vote be officially recognized in the League of Nations Covenant.[133] While President Wilson acknowledged them as the representatives of "mothers of the world," they received only a polite, vague welcome: the question of women's rights was deemed secondary in respect to other issues at hand in the post-war world.[134]

---

[132] *Ibid.*
[133] The first country to grant women the right to vote was New Zealand in 1893, followed by Australia in 1902. In 1919–20, women won the right to vote in Germany, Austria, Czechoslovakia, Poland, Belgium, Luxembourg, Canada, and the United States. Ireland followed in 1921, Mongolia in 1924, the United Kingdom in 1928, Ecuador in 1929, and Spain in 1931.
[134] International Council of Women, *Women in a Changing World: The Dynamic Story of the International Council of Women Since 1888* (London: Routledge, 1966), p. 45, cited in Carol Riegelman Lubin and Anne Winslow, *Social Justice for Women: The International Labor Organization and Women* (Durham and London: Duke University Press, 1990), p. 24.

The ILO's first annual conference in Washington showed some signs of progress in this regard. Women were better represented there than during the Paris Peace Conference; about one out of every ten delegates was a woman. The proposals put forth by these delegates were very much ahead of existing national standards—for example, insofar as night work was concerned (the Commission on Women's Work wanted to prohibit women working from 10 p.m. to 5 a.m.) and the length of maternity leave (6 weeks before and 6 weeks after birth). However, from the outset, the ILO tended to exclude women from positions of power and to restrict women's roles in the organization to issues involving women's work specifically, not other kinds of work. Moreover, the ILO's discourse perpetuated a gendered vision of society in which women were protected only in their capacity as mothers or potential mothers, not as human beings. At the Washington conference, the Norwegian delegate Betzy Kjelsberg criticized this approach:

I am against special protective laws for women, except pregnant women and women nursing children under one year of age because I believe that we are furthering the cause of good labor laws most by working toward the prohibition of all absolutely unnecessary night work. It is hard to see old worn out men or young boys in the most critical period of development working during the night. Many accidents take place in the middle of the night when the workers are most tired.[135]

In addition to the issue of women's rights, the Labor Charter that served as the ILO's founding document did not apply equally to all parts of the world. In practice, it was relativist. It recognized "differences of climate, customs, usages, economic opportunities, and industrial traditions" across the world and pushed back to some vague future time the goal of "absolute uniformity in working conditions." Thus, the first standards defined by the ILO concerning women workers, child labor, the legal length of the workday, occupational diseases, and workplace safety, were designed for industrialized countries and not their colonies. Since 1919, a "colonial clause" allowed member states to exclude all or part of their colonies from enjoying the rights defined by the ILO. At the same time, however, the ILO was the vanguard of a worldwide campaign against forced labor, and it was joined by the League of Nations, which signed an agreement against slavery in 1926. These two international organizations were part of the heritage of the old abolitionist tradition of humanitarianism. The International Convention for the Suppression of

---

[135] International Labor Conference, *1919: Record of the Proceedings* (Geneva: ILO, 1919), p. 103, cited in Lubin and Winslow, *Social Justice for Women*, p. 30.

the Traffic in Women and Children in 1921, and the Universal Declaration of Children's Rights in 1924, presented to the League of Nations by the English philanthropist Eglantyne Jebb (Chapter 5), are good examples of this global approach. "The legal protection of workers is the very essence of our whole movement. It can only have value if it is universal," was how Albert Thomas summarized it. "The legal protection of workers will always be threatened if there are races who can throw child after child into the industrial furnace while others can hardly keep up with the competition."[136]

In the interwar period, the ILO attacked the most visible assaults to human dignity, such as forced labor. But, at the same time, it refrained from applying to the colonies the more specific standards it had defined (limits on using women and children as labor, and the length of the workday).[137] Significantly, labor in the colonies was designated under the term "native labor." The "Native Labor Code" created in 1930 was a specific area of the labor code, separate from the rest of international labor legislation.[138] Thus, international labor law had universal goals only insofar as industrialized countries were concerned.

The issue of defining what constituted occupational diseases illustrates the difficulties that the ILO encountered when it tried to get workers' rights recognized on a worldwide scale. Since the beginning of the 1920s, the industrial health and safety division of the ILO was in charge of illnesses contracted at work. These differed from infectious diseases, which were the responsibility of the health and safety division of the League of Nations, directed by Ludwik Rajchman.[139] But how could one be sure that an illness was indeed caused by working conditions, when its symptoms could sometimes be confused with those of infectious diseases and could reveal themselves years after a worker had left the job? Could poor health have aggravated an occupational disease, and, in this case, should the employer be held responsible? And above all, could ideas coming from European social reformers easily be transposed

[136] ABIT, CAT 2/20/1, Albert Thomas, Speech given at the Bedford College for Women, London, March 1, 1920, p. 20. At the ILO, Thomas was one of the fiercest opponents of forced labor. Debates on this issue continued throughout the 1920s. They focused in particular on the possibility of continuing to use forced labor in the public sector and the timeline for abolishing it in the private sector.

[137] Daniel R. Maul, "The International Labour Organization and the struggle against forced labour from 1919 to the present," *Labor History*, 48: 4, 2007, pp. 477–500.

[138] Susan Zimmermann, "Special circumstances in Geneva: the ILO and the world of non-metropolitan labour in the interwar years," in Van Daele *et al.* (eds.), *ILO Histories*.

[139] Marta Aleksandra Balinska, *Une vie pour l'humanitaire: Ludwik Rajchman, 1881–1965* (Paris: La Découverte, 1995, translated by Rebecca Howell as *For the Good of Humanity: Ludwik Rajchman, Medical Statesman* (Budapest: Central European University Press, 1998).

to countries where medical knowledge, tolerance levels for occupational risks, the status of physicians, and so many other social realities were radically different?[140]

The debates occurring within the ILO did not date from the 1920s. As early as the second half of the nineteenth century, a social approach to medicine was developed in industrialized countries, with the aim of taking an inventory of occupational illnesses and identifying those jobs that posed risks to health. Using cognitive categories derived from medicine as well as legal categories, health specialists and legal scholars worked together at a time when the first examples of social insurance were being developed throughout Europe. The financial stakes were thus very important, particularly for employers, since identifying occupational illnesses also meant, inevitably, establishing rates of compensation. The official recognition of an illness resulted from negotiations, often long and difficult ones, between management and unions. A whole network of specialists working on social issues was thus set up across Europe: they identified the most pressing problems, popularized them as great "causes" to be defended before public opinion, and gradually formulated a common body of knowledge, founded on the social sciences.[141] An International Commission on Occupational Health was thus founded in Milan in 1906, when a World's Fair was held there. The same year, during the Bern conference, the use of the toxic substance white phosphorus was forbidden for use in manufacturing matches.

Expertise was thus at the very heart of power relationships and spheres of influence. When experts were able to reach a consensus, this made the official recognition of an occupational illness possible, and, with it, the right to compensation. Conversely, without legal recognition, there was no illness, or, at the very least, there were nameless illnesses whose very reality was sometimes called into question by employers and the experts they paid. The parallel here between the legal battles surrounding occupational health and those affecting the medical profession during the Great War is striking. Particularly at issue were "invisible wounds" such as those incurred by mustard gas or the psychological damage of shell shock, categorized by German medical authorities as *Rentenneurose*,

---

[140] For an introductory approach to the social mechanisms at work in recognizing disease and illness, see the pioneering work of Ludwik Fleck, *The Genesis and Development of a Scientific Fact*, translated by Frederick Bradley and Thaddeus J. Trenn (University of Chicago Press, 1979); originally published as *Entstehung und Entwicklung einer wissenschaftlichen Tatsache: Einführung in die Lehre vom Denkstil und Denkkollektiv* (Basel: B. Schwabe, 1935). Fleck's work was a precursor to the work of Thomas Kuhn and Michel Foucault in the 1960s.

[141] On this topic, see especially Madeleine Herren, *Internationale Sozialpolitik vor dem Ersten Weltkrieg* (Berlin: Duncker und Humblot, 1993).

neuroses that result in receiving *Rente*, i.e., a pension or annuity (in this case, for disability). Experts disagreed with each other, especially after the war, about compensation issues. Without legal recognition, wounded men were condemned to silence and suspicion (as I have discussed in Chapter 1). Following World War I, the creation of the ILO put a new dynamic in place. Social policies became internationalized; until then they had been limited to nation-states, to the extent that historiography has long considered them solely within a national framework.[142]

The ILO played the role of a moral authority, with its experts and its technical commissions. It improved existing transnational networks and structured the *nébuleuse réformatrice* around the same goals as those networks.[143] It conducted investigations in the field, centralized information, and exerted pressure on its member states, whether directly, in the form of recommendations, or indirectly, by providing leaflets to local unions. The growth of the ILO did not represent a complete erasure of the national component.[144] On the contrary, the ILO depended on its national bureaus to collect information on the social policies in effect in different countries in order to create international social policy (the Paris, Rome, and London bureaus were set up in 1919–20; the Berlin bureau in 1921, and the Tokyo bureau in 1924). We thus see here a kind of "denationalizing of social policies" but, at the same time, national models—such as that of the German state in the case of social insurance—served as an inspiration for the ILO, as Sandrine Kott's work has well demonstrated.[145]

The ILO also organized major international conferences, such as the 1925 conference on occupational illnesses, which resulted in a simple list of recognized illnesses and not, as one might have hoped, in a definition of the idea of "occupational illness." By centralizing the medical and legal knowledge spread across the world, and with an extensive collection of documents in its library,[146] the ILO became a consulting organization,

[142] Kott, "Une 'communauté épistémique' du social?"
[143] Topalov (ed.), *Laboratoires du nouveau siècle.*
[144] Patricia Clavin, "Defining Transnationalism," *Contemporary European History*, 14: 4, November 2005, pp. 421–439.
[145] Sandrine Kott, "Constructing a European social model: the fight for social insurance in the interwar period," in Van Daele *et al.* (eds.), *ILO Histories*, pp. 173–195. See also her previous work on German social history (*L'État social allemand: représentations et pratiques* [Paris: Belin, 1995]) and Gerhard Albert Ritter, *Der Sozialstaat: Entstehung und Entwicklung im internationalen Vergleich* (Munich: Oldenburg, 1989).
[146] Article 396 of the peace treaty established collecting documentation and information as one of the ILO's official missions, continuing the work of the Labor Office in Basel, which since 1901 had served as a European library on social issues. Article 10 of the ILO's constitution specified, "The functions of the International Labor Office shall include the collection and distribution of information on all subjects relating to the

but its real power stopped there.[147] The scientific discourse it generated was usually consensual and situated on a middle ground acceptable to most experts, since the ILO did not have the personnel or financial resources—nor perhaps the political will—to conduct its own research.[148]

In addition, each country remained in control of its health policies, as illustrated by the battle over the recognition of silicosis, a serious lung condition, as an occupational illness.[149] Even if it was doubtless one of the most lethal occupational illnesses of the twentieth century, several decades went by before it was officially recognized as an illness, since the resistance of management in the mines was so strong. In some countries, like France, Belgium, and the Netherlands, the very existence of the disease was denied until the end of World War II. Conversely, England and the United States accorded it official recognition from the 1920s. In this fight, the ILO played the role of a sounding board for experts' debates and discreetly put pressure on recalcitrant countries.

For a long time, social progress has above all been presented as a consequence of social conflicts,[150] but recent historiography now tends to ascribe equal value to the influence of experts in the birth and rise of social policies. In the 1920s, the expert became a familiar figure in large international organizations, whether he was an economist, a legal scholar, a demographer, or a physician. In the legal domain, for example, some experts participated in the inner workings of the ILO, such as those who were members of the executive board (Ernest Mahaim); those who worked within the legal affairs division (Wilfred Jenks); or those who had a personal relationship with Thomas (Georges Scelle). Others became involved at regular intervals in a consulting capacity, such as Louis le Fur

international adjustment of conditions of industrial life and labor." Such information was made available to the public thanks to a series of publications, such as the *Revue internationale du Travail*, *Informations sociales*, and *Etudes et documents*. In a speech to the International Trade Union Federation in Rome, in April 1922, Thomas explained that "the goal of the International Labor Office is to create documentation and collect information in such a way that it is above party lines, available to everyone, and based solely on a concern for truth" (ABIT, CAT/2/22/1).

[147] Thomas Cayet, Marie Thébaud-Sorger and Paul-André Rosental, "How international organisations compete: occupational safety and health at the ILO, a diplomacy of expertise," *Journal of Modern European History*, 7: 2, 2009, pp. 174–196.

[148] Paul Weindling, "Social medicine at the League of Nations Health Organisation and the International Labour Office compared," in Weindling (ed.), *International Health Organisations and Movements*, pp. 134–153.

[149] Paul-André Rosental, "De la silicose et des ambiguïtés de la notion de 'maladie professionnelle,'" *Revue d'Histoire moderne et contemporaine*, 56: 1, 2009, pp. 83–98; Jean-Claude Devinck et Paul-André Rosental, "'Une maladie sociale avec des aspects médicaux': la difficile reconnaissance de la silicose comme maladie professionnelle dans la France du premier XXème siècle," *Revue d'Histoire moderne et contemporaine*, 56: 1, 2009, pp. 99–126.

[150] Peter Baldwin, *The Politics of Social Solidarity: Class Bases of the European Welfare State, 1875–1975* (Cambridge University Press, 1990).

and Albert Geouffre de Lapradelle.[151] Without a doubt, international experts enjoyed a growing respect, which was connected in particular to the growing success of the social sciences since the turn of the century. Nonetheless, the ILO was not, strictly speaking, a "government of experts." It gave institutional shape to the implementation of expertise, it organized the flow of knowledge, and it put in place ways to validate knowledge on an international scale—but its experts had no political authority to exercise on member states. Moreover, it would be wrong to imagine the ILO as forming a community of experts in perfect agreement, relying on knowledge and information recognized by all. Conversely, the ILO can also be seen as a kind of theater,[152] or arena, where experts with different loyalties clashed, some representing management circles, others trade union circles, not to mention conflicts of interest between the international organization and national loyalties.[153]

Here we come to an important point: the experts' sense of identity. Expertise was never pure scientific knowledge existing on a higher plane, above things like national rivalry, contrary to what the ILO's official history sometimes seems to suggest. Rather, it was a contested area where power struggles played out among the member states of the ILO and their differing national traditions. As a consequence, the organization's entire history in the 1920s can be seen as a mirror of the power struggles developing between states, in straitened economic circumstances marked by the difficult transition from war to peace and then by the crisis of the late 1920s.

The crisis of the 1920s and the limits of a "global governance"

As a transnational organization, the ILO suffered at the outset from the ambiguous relationship it had with its member states. By ambiguity, I

---

[151] Kévonian, "Les juristes et l'Organisation internationale du Travail," pp. 227–266.

[152] The study of international organizations as a kind of theater is a relatively underdeveloped area of research. However, in his article "De la silicose et des ambiguïtés," Rosental analyzes the narrative strategies used by experts in their debates over the recognition of occupational illnesses. On the idea of diplomacy as performance, see Erik Ringmar and Naoko Shimazu; for a sociological approach, see Jeffrey C. Alexander, Bernhard Giesen and Jason L. Mast (eds.), *Social Performance, Symbolic Action, Cultural Pragmatics and Ritual* (Cambridge University Press, 2006).

[153] From this standpoint, determining the ILO's areas of expertise was a major problem. The question was especially pertinent in 1921–22, when the Organization brought up the idea of extending rules concerning the length of the workday to the agricultural sector, in conformity with the Washington conference of 1919. The French Chamber of Deputies completely opposed this and relied on the work of numerous experts in order to assert that agricultural issues did not belong to the ILO's mandate. See Jean Chateau, *De la compétence de l'OIT en matière de travail agricole* (Paris: M. Giard, 1924).

mean here its position as an authority providing informed advice on social questions but dependent on the vote of national legislatures in order to put that advice into practice. By joining the ILO, member states agreed to function within the tripartite structure—which was revolutionary in and of itself—and to give up part of their sovereignty, something that the United States and Soviet Russia refused, for other reasons; they did not join the ILO until the mid 1930s. Albert Thomas found this amusing: "It is truly a comic spectacle to see that on one hand the extremist and revolutionary workers of Eastern Europe accuse us of betraying class principles, while on the other side of the ocean, the same organization is described as an international, Bolshevik, socialist one."[154] That said, giving up some sovereignty was somewhat relative, since member states controlled their legislative calendar and ratification procedures. Thus, documents sent to them for ratification could be endlessly delayed or simply rejected outright, which in consequence required the ILO's leaders to undertake significant lobbying work and spend time following up on whether conventions were being carried out by member states.[155]

In its early years, at least, the history of the ILO was thus marked by a series of ratifications that do not simply show, as it would be tempting to believe, the degree to which different countries held to the transnational ideal. "There are new countries, born after the war, that have joined the ILO; they had to create and unify their legislation based on that of three or four different countries. Poland had to create its laws out of the debris of Russian, Austrian, and German legislation. The conventions put out by the ILO gave them the opportunity to unify their legislation," Thomas explained. During the 1920s, democracy was under threat in countries such as Italy, Greece, and Spain. "Today, it isn't good, even for dictators, to seem unfriendly. They thus thought it worth demonstrating to other countries that they were good internationally minded and socially minded men, and they joined the ILO."[156] Conversely, the spread of international social legislation sometimes met the resistance of traditional diplomacy,

---

[154] ABIT, CAT/2/20/1, Albert Thomas, Speech given at the Bedford College for Women, London, March 1, 1920.

[155] Thomas was aware of the difficulties that the Organization encountered. For example, as illustrated by a speech to the *Comité National d'Études Sociales et Politiques*, delivered at the École normale supérieure on February 15, 1923: "Let us take as a given that the conventions agreed on reach various national legislatures. They will sleep quietly for a long time in the files of parliamentary committees. Let's admit it; at the present moment, legislatures are dealing with delicate questions: financial questions, questions concerning reparations, questions about rebuilding. Who then would dream of consistently taking up the fifteen or sixteen conventions agreed on by the ILO and sent to the legislatures?" (ABIT, CAT/2/23/3).

[156] ABIT, CAT/2/26/3, Albert Thomas, Speech given to the Grand Orient of France, February 20, 1926.

whether in the form of some Ministers of Foreign Affairs or in the form of parliamentary committee members. The best example of this resistance is no doubt France—a situation made all the more difficult in that the ILO's leaders and many in their circle were French.[157] A kind of competition between national loyalty and international status was the result, and it lies at the heart of any history of the ILO, even if historians have begun to address it only relatively recently.[158] "A bad Frenchman"—that was how Thomas ironically referred to himself on several occasions after being accused of disloyalty by his fellow citizens for not sufficiently supporting France's national interests.[159] The situation was especially tense when France fought in 1921 to keep its farm industry out of the sectors under consideration in negotiations over the limits of the workweek. Deputies from rural districts, high-ranking civil servants from the Ministry of Foreign Affairs, and even the Union of Metallurgical and Mining Industries, the successor to the *Comité des Forges*, became involved. In July 1922, France was the first country to file suit against the ILO in the Permanent Court of International Justice, on the matter of the ILO's authority. "If this continues under these conditions, I am resolved to make a public scandal out of it," Thomas announced in a letter to Arthur Fontaine. "I love my country very much, but it is precisely because I love it so much that I cannot accept it being the first to break its agreements, even the most indisputable ones, and the first to break up an organization where it should serve as the inspiration and the leader."[160]

In the summer of 1922, Thomas went to the Hague to plead the ILO's cause in person, although normally a lawyer would have represented him. This proved to be a memorable encounter, in which one of the leading figures on the international scene clashed with one of the greatest legal minds of the time, Albert Geouffre de Lapradelle, who was defending the French government.[161] Their disagreement makes it possible to see two opposite perspectives on international law at work. Geouffre de

---

[157] During the first international labor conference, held in Washington in 1919, seventeen conventions were signed by the participants. Five years later, France had ratified none of them, except the one concerning the 8-hour workday, which was applied on a partial basis until 1925–26. See Dzovinar Kévonian, "Albert Thomas et le Bureau International du Travail (1920–1932): enjeux de légitimation d'une organisation internationale," in Jacques Bariéty (ed.), *Aristide Briand, la Société des Nations et l'Europe, 1919–1932* (Presses universitaires de Strasbourg, 2007), pp. 324–338.

[158] On this topic, see especially the work of Sandrine Kott and Dzovinar Kévonian.

[159] ABIT, CAT/2/26/3, Albert Thomas, Speech given to the Grand Orient of France, February 20, 1926.

[160] ABIT, CAT/4/31, Letter from Albert Thomas to Arthur Fontaine, January 3, 1922.

[161] Phelan, *Albert Thomas*.

Lapradelle asserted that agriculture by its very definition belonged to the national arena. The unpredictability of the climate, along with soil diversity, made it impossible to subject agricultural laborers to the rule of the 8-hour workday. In other words, only activities that could easily be compared from one country to another, such as industrial production, would be submitted to consideration for international social legislation. While he agreed that adjustments were necessary, Thomas thought that, on the contrary, agriculture belonged to the ILO's area of authority. This was the cost of international social justice. Thomas took advantage of the opportunity here to stress the limits of his power: "We are not, oh certainly not, a super-state. We are only humble administrators, obligated to take into account every social movement, every incident in the political and governmental life of fifty states."[162] In the end, the Court decided in favor of the ILO and recognized its authority in agricultural matters. This decision marked the end of tensions between the ILO and France, which in the next eight years ratified eighteen conventions submitted to it by the ILO.[163]

Defining the ILO's areas of authority in fact raises several crucial questions: How can international social legislation be defined, when the voices of national and international experts, those of the political authorities in member states, and those of the ILO's leaders contradict each other more often than they agree? Was the renewal of international law as carried out by the ILO handicapped by its very way of functioning, by a structure that constantly had to negotiate for the support of its member states? And, in addition, how could the transnational aspect of the ILO be articulated in conjunction with the respect for the sovereignty of member states in the domain of social law?

There was another difficulty, of a more conjectural order. After several months of rapid expansion in 1919, all worldwide economic indicators were pointing downward in the spring of 1920. One of the strongest deflations since the beginning of the nineteenth century followed the inflation that had affected industrialized countries during the Great War. Although the law setting an 8-hour workday in several countries in 1919 had created fears of a labor shortage, most national economies were experiencing mass unemployment. The crisis hit the United States first in March of 1920, then Great Britain and its dominions in May, Japan

---

[162] "CPIJ. La compétence de l'OIT dans les questions agricoles. Compte rendu des débats devant la Cour," *Bulletin officiel du BIT*, July 27, 1922, p. 199, cited in Kévonian, "Albert Thomas et le Bureau International du Travail," p. 337. On this same theme, see also ABIT, CAT/2/23/1, Albert Thomas, Speech given at the École normale supérieure, Paris, February 15, 1923.
[163] Kévonian, *Ibid.*

in June, and finally all of Europe at the end of 1920 and the beginning of 1921. In Germany and Central Europe, the crisis hit in 1922 and continued until 1923. The financial weight of North America in the world economy explains the rapidity with which the depression spread, causing stock markets to fall in New York, London, and Paris in the space of several months.

"After the treaty was signed, it quickly became a bad time for a nascent international labor organization," Thomas recalled. "By the end of 1920, the most terrible economic crisis the industrialized world had known since the early nineteenth century halted the rise of economic renewal. Financial markets were out of balance and shaken up. Credit was cut off. Prices fell. Unemployment spread its misery."[164] In the end, did the crisis of the 1920s leave as strong a mark on the ILO's early days as the legacy of the Great War did? Historians continue to debate the economy's impact on the establishment of international social standards. For some, the crisis proved a considerable impediment to the ILO, whose top social reform projects were weakened. Thomas thought so, as he explained:

At the very moment when everyone recognized the necessity for production, in 1920, when everyone was getting organized, the crisis came; instead of production, we witnessed a crisis of universal under-consumption due to falling prices, a formidable crisis in the slowdown of production and in unemployment... This was the time when we were being asked to establish rules of social justice, the time when we were asked to shorten the workday, the time when we were asked to make the huge effort of reorganization that would in a more prosperous time have allowed for maintaining and intensifying production, by establishing more extensive social responsibilities.[165]

Conversely, according to recent scholarship such as that of Olivier Feiertag, this turn of events, from inflation to depression, marked the beginning of a kind of "world government." The crisis was seen as an opportunity that led the ILO to "lay the theoretical and practical groundwork for a transnational regulation of globalization."[166] This was a challenge for an institution that otherwise benefited from a confluence of

---

[164] Thomas, "Justice sociale et paix universelle," pp. 241–261.

[165] ABIT, CAT2/26/4, Speech on economic recovery problems, given to employers' representatives in Lyon, February 23, 1926. See also Thomas' article, "L'Organisation Internationale du Travail": "There was a reaction, a reaction against the spirit of Versailles and Washington, against the burst of social conciliation, against reforms seen as 'too generous'... there is no doubt that for a year now, the universal movement in favor of the 8-hour workday has slowed down. Public campaigns have been conducted. The fear of under-production and lack of consumer spending due to high prices have both been used against this reform..." (ABIT, CAT/3/21/3).

[166] At this time, the terms "governance" and "regulation" were of course not used, but "regularization" was. See Olivier Feiertag, "Réguler la mondialisation: Albert Thomas,

factors: a long tradition of expertise inherited from the social reformers of the turn of the century, effective analytical tools such as statistics, and a transnational position that gave it a panoramic view of the crisis. Therefore, because it was able to see the crisis from a global perspective, the ILO was the first international body to address the complex movement of the globalization and flow of the financial markets in scientific terms. The real turning point in recognizing the ILO as a locus of international expertise came in April–May 1922, when the Organization was an official participant in the Genoa Economic Conference.[167] The ILO was now at the heart of worldwide diplomacy. Only a body such as the Organization could provide statistical expertise on the social impact of the crisis in different countries and thus illustrate the inexorable progress of worldwide unemployment: one out of four workers in Great Britain, the United States, and in France, and one out of six in Canada and the Netherlands in the spring of 1922.[168] Three years after the Washington conference, Thomas wondered: "How did such a change in ideas come about? There is no doubt that the breadth of the 1920–21 crisis and its novel character were the impetus for new research . . . It was no longer solely the feeling of human solidarity or the concern for social peace that necessitated the struggle against unemployment. The problem of unemployment broke through the tight boundaries of each state's borders. It became an element of international politics."[169] In accordance with what had been its duties since its founding, the ILO first answered requests for information from its member states and drew upon the rich collections of its library. If a government, a union, or management association wanted facts about the economic and social situation in a particular country, it contacted the Documentation Services at the Geneva headquarters. For example, in 1922, the South African government decided to create an unemployment insurance program. It asked the ILO for information on the programs in place in Great Britain and in Italy, which were the only two of their kind in Europe at the time.[170]

The ILO also regularly published reports on the development of the world economy. In June 1920, it created a Technical Commission on Unemployment—which was in fact the result of a decision made during

les débuts du BIT et la crise économique mondiale de 1920–1923," *Les Cahiers de l'IRICE*, 2, 2008, pp. 127–155.
[167] International Labor Office, "L'organisation internationale du travail et la Conférence de Gênes," *Supplément aux informations sociales*, Vol. II, 9, 2 June 1922.
[168] International Labor Office, *La crise de chômage, 1920–1923*.
[169] ABIT, CAT/2/23/7, Albert Thomas, "The struggle against unemployment," Speech given in Luxembourg, October 9, 1923.
[170] ABIT, CAT/2/23/3, Albert Thomas, Speech to the *Comité national d'Etudes sociales et politiques*, delivered at the École normale supérieure, Paris, February 15, 1923.

the Washington conference, held in November 1919.[171] A year later, it began a major international investigation into unemployment, the results of which were published in 1924.[172] Olivier Feiertag has also stressed the connection between the beginning of the economic crisis and the beginning of the investigation into worldwide industrial production and its relationship to working conditions and the cost of living (1920–25). In other words, according to Feiertag, the crisis of the 1920s strengthened the ILO's status as a locus of expertise and as an authority on social regulation: "There is no doubt that the development of the worldwide economy helped the young ILO in the sense that beginning in the mid 1920s, it made it incontrovertibly useful."[173]

At stake was the circulation of scientific knowledge concerning the crisis, its economic aspect in particular, and the comparison of national policies against unemployment. But at an even more fundamental level, the experts aimed to shed light on the way the crisis had spread on a worldwide scale, in order to be able to anticipate any future crises. "To draw general conclusions on the workings of industrial and economic storms," in the words of a report from October 1920.[174] Doubtless it was still a long way from the overarching analysis of crises dreamed of by economic experts like Varlez and Lazard, who worked with Thomas. The ILO's reports took the form of compilations of nation investigations rather than true syntheses. The phenomena of interdependence and interconnection, which the recent historiography of transnationalism now emphasizes, were largely ignored. The ILO's experts compared the situations of different nations and organized them in hierarchical fashion, according to social advances or declines. However, anyone who reads these reports closely will see that the various countries affected by the crisis did in fact undergo somewhat comparable economic development, and that they were also subject to a certain number of transnational mechanisms, such as the flow of capital, price and salary levels, and workforce migrations—all of which influenced the global spread of the crisis.[175]

---

[171] This Technical Commission on Unemployment counted several men who were close to Thomas, especially the economist Louis Varlez, director of the unemployment and migrations division at the ILO, and Max Lazard, secretary-general of the International Association Against Unemployment, founded on the eve of World War I.

[172] International Labor Office, *La crise de chômage*, collection "Etudes et documents," Geneva, 1924.

[173] Feiertag, "Réguler la mondialisation," p. 136.

[174] ABIT, U1/1/1, *Rapport provisoire de la commission sur le chômage*, October 1921, cited in Feiertag, "Réguler la mondialisation," p. 137.

[175] Paul-André Rosental, "Géopolitique et État-providence. Le BIT et la politique mondiale des migrations dans l'entre-deux-guerres," *Annales HSS*, 1, 2006, pp. 99–134.

To conduct its research, the ILO relied on an extended network of permanent offices around the world, even in non-member countries such as the United States and Russia; the New York office was in place as early as the founding of the ILO, and the Russian office was established in the late 1920s. On the occasion of the International Labor Conferences, the ILO adopted conventions and recommendations that sought to take into account the unemployment policies and the protections for the unemployed that already existed in member states. The issue of unemployment was a good way to analyze the differences between countries, if only because the term "unemployment," which was relatively new in Western countries, could not automatically be applied to the economic and social structures of other continents. The ILO recommended an entire series of common measures to adopt in response to the crisis, so that the unemployed could be better taken into consideration and better protected: this was done via the extension of unemployment insurance, which existed only in Great Britain and Italy in 1919, and by the creation of free, public job placement offices for the unemployed. Another area of concern for the ILO was the treatment of foreign workers, who were particularly vulnerable in times of crisis; they had to be guaranteed social rights analogous to those of native-born workers. Paradoxically, the clear spike in unemployment rates in the 1920s contributed not only to tensions in national policy, which sought to protect native-born citizens, but also to a burst of creativity in the ILO, which had to defend its social model. The fight that the ILO undertook at this time was carried out by extending its area of intervention in the economic arena, although some members of the League of Nations would have liked to limit the ILO strictly to social concerns.[176]

The crisis had in fact another consequence for the ILO's work— namely, rethinking different ways of organizing industrial labor.[177] Thanks to its New York office and also to the connections that Thomas had developed within American industry during the Great War, the ILO followed the development of Taylorism as a social and economic model very closely. Influenced by the American progressive movement, the ILO took an active interest in scientific labor organization in the United States and its social consequences. For example, in 1927, the ILO created the Institut International d'Organisation Scientifique du Travail (IOST, or

---

[176] Isabelle Moret-Lespinet and Ingrid Liebeskind-Sauthier, "Albert Thomas, le BIT et le chômage: expertise, catégorisation et action politique internationale," Les Cahiers de l'IRICE, 2, 2008, p. 175.

[177] Charles Maier, "Between Taylorism and technocracy: European ideologies and the vision of industrial productivity in the 1920s," Journal of Contemporary History, 5: 2, 1970, pp. 27–61.

International Institute for Scientific Labor Organization) in Geneva, led by a French politician, Paul Devinat.[178] Many employers' organizations joined the Institute, which spread this new doctrine that had been developed across the Atlantic to approximately forty countries. The ILO did not simply serve as a sounding board for projects originating in the United States. In the tripartite spirit that was its distinctive characteristic, the Organization underlined the joint role that states, private enterprises, and trade unions should play in social and economic policy. In the face of the competing models of fascism and communism, the ILO defended a social model negotiated between social partners. The crisis of the 1920s reinforced the Organization's innovative character, with its space for discussions between trade unions, upper management, and political leaders, and its role as a locus for constructing new social knowledge. Nonetheless, the idea of a transnational social regulation also had its limits. During crisis periods, each member state tended to focus on itself and on national solutions. In 1931, for example, Thomas published a memorandum in which he proposed fighting unemployment by launching a pan-European public works project.[179] Inspired by Keynes' ideas, he envisaged the creation of a vast railway and automobile network, which would have a threefold benefit: nearly 500,000 new jobs, the unification of European space, and increased mobility for travelers in Europe—all under the patronage of the ILO. This ambitious project foreshadowed some of the principal aspects of the European Community following World War II. But in the midst of the economic crisis of the 1930s, employers preferred to carry out major projects at the national level, and, in any event, the League of Nations contested the ILO's right to intervene in economic and financial issues. The unexpected death of Albert Thomas on May 8, 1932 put an end to this program of improvements that perfectly summed up the ILO's transnational ambitions.

Conclusion

In the fall of 1941, delegates from the ILO, which had now taken refuge in Montreal, met in the United States to discuss the Organization's future. The League of Nations, with which the ILO had been affiliated since

[178] Thomas Cayet, *Rationaliser le travail, organiser la production: Le Bureau International du Travail et la modernisation économique durant l'entre-deux-guerres* (Presses universitaires de Rennes, 2010).
[179] Albert Thomas, "Mémorandum sur la possibilité de saisir la Commission d'étude pour l'Union européenne des propositions concernant une action pratique dans le domaine du chômage" (1931), cited in Moret-Lespinet and Liebeskind-Sauthier, "Albert Thomas, le BIT et le chômage," p. 177.

it was founded, did not exist any more. No one knew when or how the war would end. President Roosevelt welcomed the delegates to the White House on November 6, 1941—one month before the Japanese attack on Pearl Harbor. When he spoke to them, the President shared a memory of the first International Labor Conference, held in Washington in 1919.[180]

I well remember that in those days the ILO was still a dream. To many it was a wild dream. Who had ever heard of Governments getting together to raise the standards of labor on an international plane? Wilder still was the idea that the people themselves who were directly affected—the workers and the employers of the various countries—should have a hand with Government in determining these labor standards. Now 22 years have passed. The ILO has been tried and tested . . . [181]

The ILO is one of the few institutions created by the Treaty of Versailles that still exists today. It has considerably increased the number of its member states and its range of programs and projects. Yet in order to understand the ILO's role compared with that of other international institutions, it is necessary to go back to the immediate post-World War I period. What place did labor law have in the larger task of redefining international law, which had begun after the Great War? Why did the emergence of a transnational politics of social rights constitute a priority at this time?

Western political leaders wanted to acknowledge the sacrifices agreed to by workers in 1914–18, and to forestall the danger of communist influence: the creation of international social law served as a kind of pledge to trade unions, which were now associated with the Organiza-tion's policies via tripartism—a completely new state of affairs. However, the intellectual origins of the ILO were much older.[182] Prosopographical studies of the ILO have stressed the presence in Geneva of numerous representatives of the *nébuleuse réformatrice*. The life of Albert Thomas, a young socialist reformer before the war, a promoter of "war socialism" in 1914–18, still a reformer when he led the ILO from 1920–32, also suggests that the Organization's history needs to be resituated within the broader framework of the history of ideas. These two approaches, the prosopographical and the biographical, highlight a certain continuity

[180] The Washington conference was held in the offices of the Department of the Navy, at the time when Franklin D. Roosevelt was Assistant Secretary of the Navy (a post to which he was nominated in 1913).
[181] Franklin D. Roosevelt, "Address to the International Labour Organization," November 6, 1941, cited in Gerry Rodgers, Eddy Lee, Lee Swepston and Jasmien Van Daele (eds.), *The International Labour Organization and the Quest for Social Justice, 1919–2009* (Ithaca: Cornell University Press, and Geneva: International Labour Office, 2009), pp. 1–2.
[182] For example, Van Daele, "Engineering social peace," pp. 435–466.

between the reformist circles of the turn of the century and the leadership of the ILO.

The risk then, consists of overestimating the unity of transnational networks, those of reformists and those of experts in labor law. The Great War certainly strengthened the desire for international collaboration in the service of peace, but it also gave rise to national tensions that the slow transition from war to peace did nothing to dissipate.[183] Moreover, the most socially advanced countries sought to avoid being economically penalized while other countries protected their workers less and gained economic benefits by doing so. In other words, the legal protection of workers was influenced as much by humanitarian motives (which were in essence transnational) as by economic competition (which was by definition international). In theory, the ILO was a transnational entity, whose task was to manage global problems; in reality, it was more of an international authority, which functioned in a manner similar to traditional diplomacy in its use of influence and the art of negotiation.

The gradual affirmation of international social law did not result from a natural impulse of the international spirit, as some official histories of the ILO would have it. In a more complex manner, the conventions and recommendations issued by the ILO were the result of lengthy procedures and discussions that sought to reach the largest possible consensus, at the risk of ending up with a weaker agreement. Ratification by national legislatures, which was at the heart of the ILO's internal workings, was one of the principal limits on its normative policies: the leaders of the ILO had to anticipate the difficulties of having the conventions ratified by their member states, or, at the very least, they had to anticipate the time frame necessary for ratification.[184] It was not enough for the ILO to define a particular standard; such standards also had to be shared on an international level and taken up by each member state. Thus, within the ILO, international labor law resulted from power struggles between official representatives of member states to the ILO, workers, employers, and the experts whose studies were often used as arguments in debates. Beyond the confines of the ILO, establishing international labor law depended on the possibility of getting new regulations written into law in each country—thus, on lobbying legislators to ratify these regulations.

[183] Horne, "Démobilisations culturelles," pp. 49–53.
[184] Isabelle Moret-Lespinet, "Hygiène industrielle, santé au travail. L'OIT productrice de normes, 1919–1939," in Moret-Lespinet and Viet (eds.), L'Organisation Internationale du Travail, pp. 63–75. That said, even an unratified convention could have a positive effect in contributing to political debate or providing arguments for reformers and unions.

It was therefore the product of influence, negotiations, and, sometimes, of letting go. In addition, establishing social legislation on an international scale was a response to the push of economic "globalization," during and immediately after the war. This was another unique aspect of the ILO, and it was a key one: Thomas always sought to think about social and economic questions *together*. This was naturally true of his work during the Great War, when he ran the French Ministry of Munitions: the war, by its very nature, required a global perspective on human activity, especially in the context of a total war like World War I. This indissoluble connection between social and economic questions was also a hallmark of Thomas' work as the head of the ILO. The extent of the ILO's areas of expertise from its beginnings attests to this:[185] the social protection of workers and the setup of insurance;[186] the fight against unemployment;[187] health issues;[188] refugee work;[189] organizing the length of the workday and workweek, the defense of the right to unionize, gender parity,[190] housing.[191] Nonetheless, this global perspective on man, as found in international social law, has two limits that are important to keep in mind here. The first has to do with gender. From the beginning of the nineteenth century, legislators made it a priority to protect those deemed the most vulnerable—namely, women and children. The rights of women

[185] The ILO's range of activities was so vast that for a long time historians did not attempt to compile a global understanding of the Organization, until recently, when a large research program was organized in honor of the ILO's centenary. The "ILO century project" has already led to the publication of some important work. Among recent syntheses, see Van Daele *et al.* (eds.), *ILO Histories*; Rodgers *et al.* (eds.), *The International Labour Organization and the Quest for Social Justice*; Moret-Lespinet and Viet (eds.), *L'Organisation Internationale du Travail*.

[186] Kott, "Constructing a European social model," pp. 173–195.

[187] Ingrid Liebeskind-Sauthier, *L'Organisation internationale du travail face au chômage: entre compétences normatives et recherche de solutions économiques, 1919–1939*, PhD thesis. University of Geneva, 2005.

[188] Weindling, "Social medicine," in Weindling (ed.), *International Health Organisations and Movements*.

[189] Dzovinar Kévonian, "Enjeux de catégorisations et migrations internationales. Le Bureau International du Travail et les réfugiés (1925–1929)," *Revue européenne des migrations internationales*, 21: 3, 2005, 95–124; Rosental, "Géopolitique et État-Providence," pp. 99–134.

[190] Lubin and Winslow, *Social Justice for Women*; Ulla Wikander, Alice Kessler-Harris and Jane Lewis (eds.), *Protecting Women: Labor Legislation in Europe, the United States and Australia, 1880–1920* (Urbana and Chicago: University of Illinois Press, 1995); Ulla Wikander, "ILO and Women's Economic Citizenship 1919," presentation given at the conference "The International Labour Organization: Past and Present," held in Brussels, October 12–14, 2007.

[191] Pierre-Yves Saunier, "The ILO as Organizer: Shaping the Transnational Housing Scene in the 1920s," presentation given at the conference "The International Labour Organization: Past and Present," held in Brussels, October 12–14, 2007.

workers thus formed its own area of labor law, whose goal was to make labor conditions for women workers compatible with motherhood, seen as women's "natural" function. In the 1920s, the only women who had a role to play within the ILO were experts on women's work. Men controlled the rest of the Organization. This gendered representation of work makes it impossible to see international social law, as it was defined in the 1920s, as being universally applicable.[192]

The other limit stems from the different standards applied to Western countries versus their colonies, and to less-industrialized countries, such as China or Japan. When it was founded, the ILO was led by industrialized European countries that had directly experienced the Great War. The experts working for the Organization were also Westerners. In 1919, the founding charter of the ILO was thus somewhat relative. In Article 35, it underlined the diversity of climates and ways of life, which prohibited putting analogous standards in place for all countries. The application of international agreements to colonies and protectorates was first of all subject to "local conditions"—which was hardly surprising at a time when the negotiators at the Paris Peace Conference of 1919 refused to ratify the principle of racial equality proposed by the Japanese delegates.[193] The Treaty of Versailles was written by Westerners convinced of the superiority of their way of life. In 1930, the Forced Labor Convention, one of the elements of the "Native Labor Code," sought to restrain abuses in the colonies, which, moreover, had been carefully documented in the ILO's investigations into violence in the colonies.[194] But once again, while trying to improve working conditions in the colonies, the 1930 convention took it as a given that the rules of industrialized countries could not be applied to the rest of the world. It was not until the Declaration of Philadelphia in 1944 that workers' rights would no longer be considered as a means to social justice—as had been the case in 1919 when the ILO was founded—but as the expression of universal human rights.[195]

"There are no superior people . . . there can be no justification for discrimination," declared Walter Nash, Prime Minister of New Zealand, who presided over the Philadelphia meeting. Following the Atlantic Charter of August 14, 1941, the Declaration of Philadelphia expressed the

---

[192] Lubin and Winslow, *Social Justice for Women.*

[193] Naoko Shimazu, *Japan, Race, and Equality: The Racial Equality Proposal of 1919* (London and New York: Routledge, 1998).

[194] James P. Daughton, "Documenting colonial violence: the international campaign against forced labor during the interwar years," *Revue d'Histoire de la Shoah*, 189, 2008; *Humanity So Far Away* (Oxford University Press, forthcoming).

[195] Daniel R. Maul, "The International Labour Organization and the globalization of human rights, 1944–1970," in Hoffmann (ed.), *Human Rights*, pp. 301–320.

principles on which the post-war world should be founded: "the right of all human beings, irrespective of race, creed or sex" to pursue "both their material well-being and their spiritual development in conditions of freedom and dignity, of economic security and equal opportunity."[196] Thus, a new ILO was born; it took its place in the global context of the rise of the idea of human rights after World War II.[197]

There still remains to be discussed the central problem of the ILO's normative work when Thomas was Director-General (1919–32). The wide range of the Organization's areas of expertise can be seen as a sign of its vitality, but it also suggests that the ILO was exploring all possible avenues without prioritizing any of them, constantly trying to expand its sphere of influence with each year's International Labor Conference. Did the ILO respond to the various problems of the post-war period in a disorganized way, or did it truly have a long-term reformist plan at work? To those who criticized the chaotic character of the ILO's work, Albert Thomas generally replied by recalling the ideal that was its driving force:

A great idea has been launched: an economy of labor instead of an economy of profit, the idea that an 'organization uniting all the nations of the world might exist for the common good,' as the eighteenth-century philosophers would have put it, an economy where labor law is the essential principle behind all collective action. Thus, respect for human labor is no longer an insurmountable obstacle to any economic competition between states. It is becoming an area of collaboration between all peoples, the very goal of the peace effort.[198]

---

[196] ILO, *The Declaration of Philadelphia* (1944). One of the key figures in this redefinition of the ILO's mandate to include human rights was the English legal scholar Wilfred Jenks, who joined the legal department of the ILO in 1931 and who would later serve as the organization's director-general from 1970–73. See Wilfred Jenks, *Human Rights and International Labour Standards* (London: Stevens, and New York: Praeger, 1960).

[197] Lauren, *The Evolution of International Human Rights*; Cmiel, "The Recent History of Human Rights," pp. 117–135.

[198] Thomas, "Justice sociale et paix universelle."

3   The tragedy of being stateless: Fridtjof Nansen and the rights of refugees

"I thought I saw a whole city before me with its thousands of lights—it was their camps spread out over the plain, camp-fire by camp-fire, and there they were sleeping on the ground without shelter of any kind... They do not know where they are going and will find no shelter where they come."

> Fridtjof Nansen in Constantinople, September 1922, on the sight of refugees of Greek origin fleeing the massacres of the Turkish army.

"The possibility of obtaining an international passport would be a practical solution, but more than that, it would be an important political and moral act that would free Russian citizens abroad from the Soviet yoke."

> Boris Mirkine-Guetzévitch, "Le passeport international," *La Tribune Juive*, March 13, 1922.

For four long years, from 1914 to 1918, the war had created vast movements of displaced populations, civilians who had to flee ahead of invading troops, or who were driven out by force during military occupations on both the Western and Eastern fronts.[1] From 1918 to 1922, large numbers of refugees continued to be on the move in Europe. The collapse of the vast multi-ethnic Austro-Hungarian, Russian, and Ottoman Empires had given birth to smaller nation-states that often forced ethnic minorities to leave.[2] The refugee groups included many people driven

---

[1] The bibliography on these issues is vast. See especially Annette Becker, *Oubliés de la Grande Guerre*; Peter Gatrell, *A Whole Empire Walking: Refugees in Russia during World War I* (Bloomington: Indiana University Press, 1999); Vejas Gabriel Liulevicius, *War Land on the Eastern Front: Culture, National Identity, and German Occupation in World War I* (Cambridge University Press, 2000); Philippe Nivet, *Les réfugiés français de la Grande Guerre, 1914–1920* (Paris: Economica, 2004); Nick Baron and Peter Gatrell (eds.), *Homelands: War, Population, and Statehood in Eastern Europe and Russia, 1918–1924* (London: Anthem Press, 2004); Annette Becker, *Les cicatrices rouges*; Philippe Nivet, *La France occupée, 1914–1918* (Paris: Armand Colin, 2011).

[2] Aristide Zolberg, "The formation of new states as a refugee-generating process," *Annals of the American Academy of Political and Social Science*, 467, May 1983, pp. 24–38. For a general overview, see Michael Marrus, *The Unwanted: European Refugees in the Twentieth Century* (Oxford University Press, 1985), pp. 51–121, and Claudena M. Skran, *Refugees*

133

from their homes by war, religious persecution, or poverty. Several hundred thousand Magyars were expelled from Romania, Czechoslovakia, and Yugoslavia, and migrated to Hungary. After the war, when Alsace-Lorraine returned to French control, the government classified its population into four categories and deported thousands of ethnic Germans during the winter of 1918–19, even if they no longer had any contact with or ties to Germany.[3] Russian refugees fled from oppression, poverty, and hunger. After the genocide of 1915, in which over a million Armenians died, survivors fled to Soviet Armenia, Syria, and other countries.

In addition to these direct consequences of World War I, two political innovations from the 1920s should be taken into consideration. The first consisted of writing the movement of displaced peoples into peace treaties and bilateral accords: for the first time in European history, the forced movement of refugees—not voluntary, even if the distinction is not always easy to make—was legislated by international law.[4] From 1919 to 1920, signatories to peace treaties sought to limit the risk of future conflict by favoring greater ethnic homogeneity in Europe. This "ethnicizing" of national feeling, already apparent in the war culture of 1914–18,[5] nonetheless had the dangerous consequence of radicalizing the tensions among ethnic communities and multiplying possibilities for violence. Peace treaties thus included protective clauses for ethnic minorities, guaranteed by the League of Nations.[6] The treaties also required individuals to settle in the country whose nationality they had adopted.[7]

in Inter-War Europe: The Emergence of a Regime (Oxford: Clarendon Press, 1995), pp. 13–61.

[3] David Allen Harvey, "Lost children or enemy aliens? Classifying the population of Alsace after the First World War," Journal of Contemporary History, 34, 1999, pp. 537–554; Laird Boswell, "From Liberation to Purge Trials in the 'Mythic Provinces': recasting French identities in Alsace and Lorraine, 1918–1920," French Historical Studies, 23: 1, 2000, pp. 129–162. In her article "The minority problem: national classification in the French and Czechoslovak borderlands," Contemporary European History, 17, May 2008, pp. 137–165, Tara Zahra convincingly demonstrates that from this standpoint, when it came to Alsace-Lorraine, France's policy towards ethnic Germans was much more repressive than the policies towards ethnic Germans in most Central European countries, especially Czechoslovakia.

[4] Stephen P. Ladas, The Exchange of Minorities: Bulgaria, Greece and Turkey (New York: Macmillan, 1932); Dimitri Pentzopoulos, The Balkan Exchange of Minorities and its Impact upon Greece (Paris: Mouton, 1962). For a comparative analysis of forced deportation in the modern era, see Richard Bessel and Claudia B. Haake (eds.), Removing Peoples: Forced Removal in the Modern World (Oxford University Press, 2009), pp. 3–11, 13–32.

[5] Michael Jeismann, Das Vaterland der Feinde. Studien zum nationalen Feindbegriff und Selbstverständnis in Deutschland und Frankreich 1792–1918 (Stuttgart: Klett-Cotta, 1992); Audoin-Rouzeau and Becker, 14–18. Retrouver la Guerre.

[6] Fink, Defending the Rights of Others.

[7] E. Maxson Engeström, Les changements de nationalité d'après les traités de paix de 1919–1920 (Paris: Pédone, 1923).

Ten million people in all had to leave territories that had come under the control of another country. But the mix of languages, ethnicities, and cultures was so complex, particularly in Central Europe and the Balkans, that the situation remained extremely complicated.

In January 1923, the Treaty of Lausanne made official the forced deportation of Greek Christians from Turkey to Greece, and of Muslim Turks from Greece to Turkey, nearly 1.5 million people in total.[8] Some members of the Greek and Turkish delegations, as well as legal scholars present during the peace conference, protested this decision because it contradicted the principle of *droit des gens*, or Law of Nations, which had been defended during the Paris Peace Conference of 1919. Many delegates judged forced deportation as immoral, yet it was carried out nonetheless, and was even considered to be the lesser of two evils. After all, it facilitated the work of nation-states by limiting, theoretically at least, the risk of tensions among ethnic communities and by lessening the weight of the obligation to protect ethnic minorities, now a standard feature of peace treaties.[9]

Another new political aspect of the 1920s was the practice of collectively stripping people of their citizenship, on the basis of their political allegiances, social class, ethnicity, or religion.[10] In 1921, hundreds of thousands of Russians suspected of opposing the Bolshevik regime lost their Soviet citizenship,[11] as did many survivors of the Armenian genocide in 1923. In January 1926, opponents of the Fascist regime in Italy lost their Italian citizenship. In July 1933, German Jews living abroad lost their German citizenship. An ideological definition of territory now

---

[8] Renée Hirschon (ed.), *Crossing the Aegean: An Appraisal of the 1923 Compulsory Population Exchange Between Greece and Turkey* (New York and Oxford: Berghahn Books, 2003).

[9] Kévonian, *Réfugiés et diplomatie humanitaire*, pp. 121–129.

[10] The practice of stripping an individual of his citizenship was, however, an older one. In April 1915, for example, France decided to revoke the French citizenship of naturalized citizens originally from enemy countries (such as Frenchmen of German or Austro-Hungarian origin) suspected of collaborating with their former country. See Eugène Audinet, "Le retrait des naturalisations accordées aux anciens sujets de puissances en guerre avec la France," *Journal de droit international*, 42, 1915, pp. 129–140. These wartime measures were replaced by the Law of August 10, 1927, which made it possible to revoke an individual's citizenship for three reasons: committing acts against the country's internal and external security; acts contrary to the interests of France and incompatible with the status of French citizen; and failure to report for military service. See Patrick Weil, *Qu'est-ce qu'un Français? Histoire de la nationalité française depuis la Révolution* (Paris: Grasset, 2002), p. 118, translated by Catherine Porter as *How to be French: Nationality in the Making Since 1789* (Durham, N.C.: Duke University Press, 2008), p. 108.

[11] Jacques Schefgel, "L'Apatridie des réfugiés russes," *Journal de Droit international*, 61, 1934, pp. 36–69; Timothy Andrew Taracouzio, *The Soviet Union and International Law* (New York: Macmillan, 1935), Chapter 5, "Nationality and citizenship."

seemed to be at work: the right to live in a particular territory was granted to anyone who held to its values, broadly defined as cultural and moral values; anyone suspected of not conforming to its values could be forbidden to reside there.

From this standpoint, the collective loss of nationality instituted in the wake of the Great War represents a major breaking point in moral terms; in the minds of those who carried it out, it seemed like a way to purify their territory. Driven from their homes, stripped of their property, stateless persons were also deprived of the material support of their country of origin and condemned to wander from one country to another, without any means of having their identity and their rights recognized. At first they were the victims of the political authorities, the regular army, or the paramilitary units of their own country; later, they were pursued by the police in other countries, who saw them as illegal and wanted to deport them.

In the aftermath of World War I, the condition of statelessness became more and more widespread. Before the war, it had been a legal anomaly.[12] In the early 1920s, nearly 3 million people could be defined as stateless.[13] Indeed, in several novels from this period, the stateless figure was an emblem of the modern human condition, with man in the grip of the all-powerful state.[14] Statelessness increasingly became a focus of academic research, from the perspective of international law (particularly the right to circulate freely) and civil law (individual rights, family law, inheritance law.)[15] Indeed, legal scholars took a strong interest in the legal

---

[12] The German term *heimatlos*, "homeless," "outcast," "uprooted"; the noun form, *der Heimatlose*, was not used in official documents until the nineteenth century. According to I.G. Lipovano, the first use of the term in a legal document was in the Swiss Federal Constitution of 1848. See the published version of Lipovano's law dissertation, *L'Apatridie* (Paris: Éditions internationales, 1935). In the wake of World War I, the concept of *heimatlos* was increasingly combined with that of *staatenlos*, "stateless," *der Staatenlose*, "stateless person," although the terminology was not yet fully established.

[13] Kévonian, *Réfugiés et diplomatie humanitaire*, p. 230.

[14] For example, *Das Totenschiff* [*The Death Ship*], a gripping novel published in 1926 under the pseudonym B. Traven.

[15] Many legal scholars studied the issue of refugees' rights in the 1920s and 1930s. They included Noël Vindry, *L'Apatridie (absence de nationalité)*, law dissertation (Aix-en-Provence: Makaire, 1925); Jean Delehelle, *La situation juridique des Russes en France*, (Lille: L. Danel, 1926); Viktor Sukiennicki, *Essai sur la souveraineté des États en droit international moderne*, law dissertation (Paris: Pédone, 1926); Alexandre Devedji, *L'échange obligatoire des minorités grecques et turques en vertu de la convention de Lausanne du 30 janvier 1923*, law dissertation (Paris: Impr. du Montparnasse, 1929); André Mandelstam, *La protection internationale des minorités* (Paris: Sirey, 1931a); André Colanéri, *La condition des "Sans-patrie": Étude critique de l'Heimatlosen* (Paris: Librairie générale de droit et de jurisprudence, 1932); Ladas, *The Exchange of Minorities*; Georges Scelle, *Précis de droit des gens* (Paris: Sirey, 1932, 1934); Marc Vichniac, "Le statut international des apatrides," *Académie de droit international de La Haye, Recueil des cours*, 43, 1933, pp. 119–245;

nonexistence of stateless persons, in their "invisibility," to use the metaphor common at the time.[16] They analyzed the implications of losing one's nationality: it meant losing the protections accorded by a state to its citizens, of course; it also meant exclusion from the human community and, over the long term, the loss of human dignity.[17] In the eyes of legal scholars, the increasing number of people without rights in the early 1920s underscored the breadth of the crisis of the nation-state in Central and Eastern Europe, given the breakup of the great empires—the Russian, Austro-Hungarian, German, and Ottoman Empires—and, conversely, Western countries' intense concern with national identity, all of which made for growing complications when crossing national borders.

The post-war world was in a paradoxical situation. On the one hand, the pressure to emigrate had never been so strong, since war, political violence, poverty, and famine drove hundreds of thousands of refugees from their homes; but on the other hand, the system of passports and visas that had been introduced during the war, on top of immigration restrictions in the United States, limited refugees' opportunities. At the end of the 1920s, trans-Atlantic immigration was only a third of what it had been in 1913.[18] The post-war world had "suddenly contracted"[19] and was close to suffocating; the movement of displaced peoples was putting national sovereignty to the test. The right to asylum, which the seventeenth-century Dutch legal theorist Grotius viewed as "one of the rights common to all men,"[20] had become a prerogative of the state: citizens and foreigners were subject to increasingly strict identity criteria, inasmuch as the right to social protections and access to work differed for the two groups. In sum, Western countries rapidly turned inward and focused on themselves in response to the crises besetting

Jacques Schefgel, *L'Apatridie des réfugiés russes* (Paris: Éditions Godde, 1934); Lipovano, *L'Apatridie*; Pierre Nafilyan, *Le Heimatlosat*, law dissertation (Lausanne, 1935); Bernard Lejuif, *Les Apatrides*, law dissertation (Caen: Impr. Ozanne, 1939). For more information on the world of legal scholarship at this time, see Kévonian, *Réfugiés et diplomatie humanitaire*, pp. 252 ff., as well as Kévonian, "Les juristes juifs russes en France et l'action internationale dans les années vingt," pp. 72–94; and "Exilés politiques et avènement du 'droit humain': la pensée juridique d'André Mandelstam (1869–1949)," *Revue d'histoire de la Shoah*, 177–178, January–August 2003, pp. 245–273.

[16] Hannah Arendt, in particular, analyzed the "invisibility" of stateless persons in *The Origins of Totalitarianism* [1951] (London, 1976). See Marieke Borren, "Arendt's politics of in/visibility: on stateless refugees and undocumented aliens," *Ethical Perspectives*, 15: 2, 2008, pp. 213–237.

[17] In his 1929 book *Sur la situation juridique des émigrés italiens en France* (Paris: Pedone, 1929), the jurist G. Nitti refers to a "*mort civile*," or "death in civil law," p. 7.

[18] Rosental, "Géopolitique et État-providence."

[19] I have borrowed this phrase from Rosental, "Géopolitique et État-providence," p. 101.

[20] Hugo Grotius, *De jure belli ac pacis* [*On the Law of War and Peace*] Books I–III. (Indianapolis: Bobbs-Merrill, 1625).

the post-war world, a process that Gérard Noiriel has traced back to the nineteenth century, describing it as "a tyranny of the national."[21] Such a state of affairs, extremely difficult both for refugees and the countries where they sought asylum, required the creation of a new legal category for all those wandering in the limbo of the international legal system.

However, the refugee question was a humanitarian issue as well as a legal one. As such, it was handled at the local level by philanthropical organizations and at the international level by new institutions such as the League of Nations and the International Labor Organization (ILO). The High Commission for Refugees, created in 1921, functioned as an intermediary between these two levels of action.[22] The material needs of refugees, especially of women and children, were a deeply pressing concern for Western society at a moment when the Great War had barely ended. Newspapers published photographs of thousands of people crammed into refugee camps. In the imagery of this "long-distance suffering,"[23] many people thought they recognized the face of the war they had just experienced. Often, the conflicts that put refugees on the march across the roads of Europe were in fact the outgrowths of World War I: the Russian civil war (1917–22); the Russo-Polish war (1919–21); the war between Greece and Turkey (1919–22). Refugees normally elicited empathy and concern on the part of many people. As stateless people, they inspired feelings of compassion as well as fear, and, in the end, they showed that the Great War was not really over—that chaos was still threatening to take the upper hand.

For Western European countries undergoing the process of rebuilding after the Great War, refugees represented the possibility of additional social unrest. Lacking any formal national ties, they were viewed by definition as an unstable, uncontrollable group, untrustworthy and potentially dangerous—and, on top of everything else, an impossibly heavy economic burden. The legal scholar Noël Vindry, in his 1925 dissertation on statelessness, expressed his concerns in these terms: "There is something immoral in the position of an individual who takes advantage of the benefits of a civilized state without fulfilling any corresponding military duty, of someone who lives, so to speak, as a parasite." He added, "It is not pleasant for a state to receive people in such an ambiguous

[21] Gérard Noiriel, *La tyrannie du national: le droit d'asile en Europe (1793–1993)* (Paris: Calmann-Lévy, 1991).
[22] Kévonian, "Enjeux de catégorisations et migrations internationales."
[23] I have borrowed this phrase from Luc Boltanski, *La souffrance à distance: morale humanitaire, médias et politique* (Paris, Métailié, 1993), translated by Graham D. Burchell as *Distant Suffering: Morality, Media, and Politics* (Cambridge University Press, 1999).

situation, people who live on the margins of society and whose loyalties, whether enemy or neutral, are impossible to determine in wartime."[24] The refugee crisis became the symbol par excellence of the post-war world's instability.

In order to confront such an unprecedented crisis, the League of Nations appealed for help to a man who was both a diplomat and one of the leading figures of the humanitarian movement: Fridtjof Nansen, of Norway.[25] In June 1921, when he was named the League of Nations' High Commissioner for Russian Refugees, Nansen's popularity extended far beyond narrow diplomatic circles. For many Europeans, he remained above all one of the greatest polar explorers of his time, the man who had heroically tried to reach the North Pole (1893–96). After the Great War, he organized the exchange and repatriation of nearly 430,000 prisoners of war, from May 1920 to July 1922, between Russia, Germany, and Austria-Hungary.[26] Nansen was not a legal scholar, though he surrounded himself with specialists of international law. He was an adventurer and a scientist who became a diplomat later in life. The solutions he proposed for dealing with the refugee crisis were more often than not borne out of necessity and pragmatism, not necessarily out of a personal perspective on the status of refugees after the war.

The document that bears his name, the Nansen Certificate, also commonly called the Nansen Passport, marks a turning point in the history of international law. The certificate was created in July 1922 during an intergovernmental conference held in Geneva, and was initially designed to assist Russian refugees; later it was issued to assist Armenian refugees (1924), and Assyrian and Assyro-Chaldean refugees (1928). The Nansen Passport made it possible for stateless people to circulate and settle abroad. For the first time, refugees deprived of all assistance and protection from their country of origin were placed under the patronage of the international community—in this case, the League of Nations and the High Commission for Refugees. The passport did, however,

---

[24] Vindry, *L'Apatridie*, p. 89.
[25] There are several biographies of Nansen; in particular, Roland Huntford's *Nansen: The Explorer as Hero* (London, Duckworth: 1977) is an important one. Characteristically, however, Nansen the adventurer tends now to be overshadowed by Nansen the diplomat and humanitarian. Thus, World War I and the post-war transition period are seen as major turning points in Nansen's life. For a more recent approach to Nansen's role on the international stage and to his personality, see the work of the Norwegian historian Carl Emil Vogt, *Fridtjof Nansen: Mannen og verden* [*Fridtjof Nansen: The Man and the World*] (Oslo: Cappelen Damm, 2011).
[26] Martyn Housden, "When the Baltic Sea was a bridge for humanitarian action: the League of Nations, the Red Cross and the repatriation of prisoners of war between Russia and Central Europe, 1920–22," *Journal of Baltic Studies*, 38: 1, March 2007, pp. 61–83.

place certain restrictions on its holders, particularly since it did not allow them to be readmitted to the country issuing the Nansen Passport.[27] Moreover, the passport embodied various lines of reasoning that could conflict with each other: humanitarian assistance; workforce controls; surveillance and management of foreigners. Because of their great number, the various feelings they inspired in the West, and their preeminent role in the creation of the Nansen Certificate, Russian refugees have a central place in this story.

Empire in ruins: Russian refugees in the aftermath of war

To write the history of Russian refugees from the beginning of the Revolution to the end of the Civil War is a challenge for the historian. The refugees' departure was not caused solely by political persecution; refugees came from a variety of social and political backgrounds; they took many different paths. For some years now, specialists of Russian emigration have brought considerable nuance to the image the Russian diaspora created of itself—namely, a community united by its shared tragic fate and by its hostility to the Bolshevik regime.[28] In reality, soldiers of the conquered White Army and the political elite from the conservative and liberal camps represented only a fraction of the hundreds of thousands of people leaving Russia between 1918 and 1922.

The complexity of the violence in post-war Russia also defies any attempt at synthesis. Instead of a simple dichotomy between the Bolshevik regime and its opponents, the situation inside Russia should be seen as one of interlocking episodes of violence: border conflicts such as the Russo-Polish war (1919–21); a civil war in which foreign armies intervened; class conflict at the local level; antagonism between the central Russian government and outlying areas; between urban and rural areas; ethnic tension. All these different forms of violence were aggravated by the "brutalization" of political life that followed the Great War, and by the disintegration of the Russian state, which lost control and was unable to keep in check the violence perpetrated by armed bands and

---

[27] It was not until the Refugee Convention of 1933, Article 2, that the right of return would be recognized as an integral part of the Nansen Passport.

[28] For example, Catherine Gousseff, *L'Exil russe: la fabrique du réfugié apatride* (Paris: CNRS éditions, 2008). Gousseff is especially interested in the refugees' own accounts of their situation, children in particular. See *Les enfants de l'exil: récits d'écoliers russes après la Révolution de 1917*, edited by Catherine Gousseff and Anna Sossinskaïa (Paris: Bayard, 2005).

warlords.[29] "The world war formally ended with the conclusion of the Armistice . . . In fact, however, everything from that point onward that we have experienced, and continue to experience, is a continuation and transformation of the world war,"[30] in the words of the philosopher Piotr Struve, who went from the Bolshevik to the White movement. During this period, known as "War Communism" (1918–21), civilians were the first victims of social and political chaos. It was they who accompanied the White Army troops into exile.

The southern parts of the former Russian Empire (Ukraine, the Don, Kuban) suffered the most from the civil war, since opposition to the Bolshevik regime was strongest in these areas (as I will discuss further in Chapter 4). When the Red Army entered Ukraine in the spring of 1919, more than 10,000 people, including 6,000 soldiers and officers, fled Odessa for Constantinople. They were followed by 135,000–150,000 refugees, including 70,000 civilians, after General Wrangel's defeat in November 1920. In these mass evacuations by sea, there were often more civilians than White Army soldiers: there were owners of landed estates along with officers' families, but a flood of people of more modest means also fled the political chaos. Some were originally from the region surrounding the shores of the Black Sea; others came from as far as Petrograd, and traveled across the country at their own risk. The majority of the refugees, concentrated in the region surrounding Constantinople, were deprived of all means of subsistence. In August 1921, the League of Nations sent Major Marcel de Roover, a Belgian delegate, to the Ottoman capital. "In a big, overcrowded city where the economic crisis has raged, it is not easy to earn one's living," he wrote. "Many are those who would have died of starvation if charitable societies, such as the American Red Cross, the Union of Zemstvos and Cities, and the Russian Red Cross, had not brought the most indispensable assistance." Seven months later, Jean-Charles de Watteville of the International Red Cross made the same trip to Turkey. It was the refugees' distress that made the strongest impression on him. "The refugees could be compared to prisoners of war," he declared at a meeting of private organizations for the relief of Russian refugees. "Constantinople is a prison from which it is impossible to escape. [The refugees] are living in surroundings entirely foreign to them and this results in increased demoralization and growing

---

[29] Joshua Sanborn, "The genesis of Russian warlordism: violence and governance during the First World War and the Civil War," *Contemporary European History*, 19: 3, 2010, pp. 195–213.

[30] Cited by Peter Holquist in *Making War, Forging Revolution: Russia's Continuum of Crisis, 1914–1921* (Harvard University Press, 2002), 2.

inability to work."[31] As late as 1927, the British diplomat Philip Noel-Baker called Constantinople "one of the black spots in the post-war history of Europe."[32]

Near the end of the year 1920, the French government, which had supported Wrangel and the White Army, began to provide food and material support to refugee camps, mostly near Gallipoli. This task was made all the more difficult because the Russian veterans, still loyal to their own commanders and living according to the traditional values of honor, duty, and sacrifice, were reluctant to accept their disarmament. Deprived of their guns, former artillerymen built replicas out of wood. In photographs taken at the time, the soldiers can be seen practicing drills and shooting at targets. In one image, a Russian had nostalgically drawn a picture of the snow-covered Kremlin on a wall.[33] When the French government finally decided that the Russian Army should be disbanded, many Russian veterans protested: "In the eyes of thinking Russians, Europe in general and France in particular have lost their authority as ideologically advanced countries."[34] Because conditions were so difficult on shore, the majority of Russians (more than 120,000 in November 1920) were kept on ships, sailing to and fro in the Sea of Marmara. "The ship *Wladimir* that was meant to carry 600 passengers currently has more than 7,000 people aboard!" a member of the Russian Red Cross complained to his cousin in December 1920. "Most of them live on the open deck, others in the hold, where they are suffocating. Merchants go on board to sell bread and bottles of water. For a little piece of bread, the Russians would give their rings, brooches, guns, shoes . . ."[35]

The Russian refugees were gradually evacuated by the League's delegates to the Balkan states and the Greek islands. In the summer of 1921, 50,000 of these refugees were placed throughout Serbia. There were also 100,000 in Romania, primarily Jews, but also soldiers and former officers from General Wrangel's army, and White Guards who had crossed the border to escape the pursuit of the Red Army. There were 50,000 in Greece, 30,000 in Bulgaria. In March 1920, veterans of General Denikin's army were evacuated with British assistance and placed in camps in Lemnos, Cyprus, and Egypt, then sent to Serbia on condition that the British government pay 600 dinars per head per month

---

[31] International Red Cross Archives, Geneva, CR87/SDN, 1921.

[32] Philip Noel-Baker, *The League of Nations at Work* (London, Nisbet, 1926), pp. 118–119.

[33] League of Nations Archives, R1722, 45/13913.

[34] Paul Robinson, *The White Russian Army in Exile, 1920–1941* (Oxford: Clarendon Press, 2002), p. 41.

[35] International Red Cross Archives, Geneva, CR87–5, Report on Russian refugees in Constantinople.

to support the refugees. A small group of refugees left Constantinople for Brazil. The ship was wrecked, and the men disembarked in Corsica, where many of them found work and decided to settle; the others left for Brazil on another ship. Several months later, an alarming report reached the International Committee of the Red Cross concerning the Russian workers' living conditions on the coffee plantations:

The climate in this region is hard to bear: the heat, mosquitoes, fever, snakes, the coffee dust that rubs fingertips raw, the worms that lodge under one's fingernails and cause abscesses—all of this makes their work a real torture. You are allowed to be ill for only 3 days; beyond that, you are fired.[. . .] The situation is aggravated by the fact that there is no official Russian representative in Brazil, not even a consul, and consequently, the Russians are deprived of all legal recourse.[36]

Other refugees, primarily natives of Ukraine, had succeeded in crossing the Polish-Russian border. Poland took in the greatest number of refugees in this period: approximately 550,000 in July 1921, although Polish authorities tended to underestimate the size of the Russian minority in the eastern provinces of the country.[37] As a result of the anti-Semitic disturbances that had marked the Russian Civil War, Jews comprised about 30 percent of the total population influx. In Ukraine, where the majority of the Russian Empire's Jews lived, mass murder occurred on a scale that was surpassed only during World War II, reaching its peak in August 1919.[38] Most of the killings took place in villages, the work of local peasants engaged in looting and ill-disciplined soldiers from all armies who held the Jews responsible for the miseries of war. According to the Ukranians, Jews were pro-Russians; the Bolsheviks accused them of being capitalists. About 10 percent of Ukrainian Jewry may have been killed during these events.

Two years later, the famine that began in the Volga provinces, Transcaucasia, and Ukraine in 1921 accelerated the return of Polish citizens. They had been previously evacuated eastward from zones of military operation by the German authorities in 1914 or had been forced to leave their homes by the war between Poland and Russia in 1920. In March 1921, the Treaty of Riga established the new frontiers between Russia and Poland. Tens of thousands of Poles tried to escape starvation and fled to Poland; large numbers of Russians followed them. One Polish

---

[36] International Red Cross Archives, Geneva, CR87/SDN, 1921.
[37] Gousseff, *L'Exil russe*, pp. 60–63.
[38] Peter Kenez, "Pogroms and white ideology in the Russian Civil War," in John D. Klier and Shlomo Lambroza (eds.), *Pogroms: Anti-Jewish Violence in Modern Russian History* (Cambridge University Press, 1991), pp. 293–313.

quarantine station, Baranowicze, processed 301,287 people returning to Poland from Russia between March and December 1921.[39]

In the summer of 1921, a memorandum was sent to Geneva describing the situation of Russian refugees in Poland as "extremely worrisome": "The number of Russians who have for several weeks been entering Polish territory is estimated at more than 4,000 a day. Information from a reliable source stated that in the Russian governments of Smolensk and Minsk, hundred of thousands of fugitives are making their way towards the Polish frontier and have blocked the roads to such an extent that their progress has been temporarily interrupted." Most refugees settled in Eastern Poland, closest to the frontier, where the countryside had been devastated by the recent war. In her autobiography, Joyce NanKivell Loch, an Australian relief worker, compared this region to a "vast soldiers' grave." "[The refugees] who had fled from the Eastern provinces of Poland began to stream back again to the forests, trenches, and barbed-wire where their homes had been. Again they died as they travelled, of hunger, typhus and cholera. Those who arrived crawled into underground trenches, dug themselves holes in the ground and made bough shelters."[40] Gloor and Tarassoff, who traveled to Poland in August 1921, reported to the International Committee of the Red Cross that refugees who settled in the region of Baranowicze had found their villages destroyed by the war and had no choice but to live "in trenches that had been partly demolished by the Germans."[41] By 1925, the number of Polish citizens who had been repatriated from Russia stood at 1.3 million.

Finland and the former Baltic provinces, Latvia and Estonia, which effectively won independence at the end of World War I, had also given shelter to refugees. Thousands of Carelians, from a region located between the Gulf of Finland and the White Sea, who had rebelled against the Soviets, as well as the Ingrians of the province of Petrograd, were forced to retreat to Finland.[42] Nineteen thousand Russian refugees arrived during the years 1918–21 either in small groups or en masse, after the evacuation of Arkhangelsk, the fall of General Miller's army in September 1919, and the failure of the Kronstadt rebellion in

[39]   *Ibid.*, p. 76.
[40]   Joyce NanKivell Loch, *A Fringe of Blue: An Autobiography* (London: John Murray, 1968), pp. 70–74.
[41]   International Red Cross Archives, Geneva, Commixt II.5/253 a 324, p. 655.
[42]   Marja Leinonen, "Helsinki: Die russische Emigration in Finland," in Karl Schlögel (ed.), *Der Grosse Exodus: Die russische Emigration und ihre Zentren, 1917 bis 1941* (Munich: C.H. Beck, 1994), pp. 165–193.

1921. Remnants of Yudenich's army, accompanied by several thousand civilians, infected with typhus, sought refuge in Estonia. Veterans of Bermondt-Avalov Pavel's army retreated to Latvia. In total, the Baltic countries provided shelter for approximately 55,000 Russians in 1922. But because it was essential for these newly independent countries to come to a modus vivendi with Bolshevik Russia, their powerful neighbor, anti-Bolshevik activists were forced to leave. Others were exposed to growing anti-Semitism and suffered from discrimination. The family of Isaiah Berlin left Petrograd for Riga in October 1920 and was forced to move to Britain in early 1921. He was later to become one of the great political thinkers of the twentieth century.[43]

Many refugees, among them the political leaders of emigrant communities, made their way to Germany, the closest Central European country where they might be able to find work and assistance. They numbered 560,000 in the autumn of 1920. Berlin was the main population center of this emigration, dominated by the upper classes and the intelligentsia, who soon built a cultural life based on nostalgia and a bourgeois lifestyle.[44] The prosperous residential suburbs of Schoeneberg, Friedenau, Wilhelmsdorf, and Charlottenburg, recently incorporated into Greater Berlin, offered an acceptable home for this group, since they had frequented the area before the war. In one German observer's words, "the Russian emigration in Berlin was a pyramid whose point was the only point which remained."[45] In an attempt to perpetuate Russian culture abroad, refugees published newspapers and books. There were seventy-two Russian publishers in the German capital in 1922.[46] Literary cafés provided gathering places for émigré writers: the second floor of the Leon on the Nollendorfplatz was known by Russian Berliners as "almost our club."[47] Yet because of unemployment and the increased cost of living after 1923, Berlin increasingly became a stopover rather than a permanent home for these intellectuals. Monarchist refugees in particular found the country inhospitable to their political activity. After rising to a population of 500,000 people in 1922, estimates of the total number of Russians in Germany dropped to 250,000 in 1925. According to

---

[43] Michael Ignatieff, *Isaiah Berlin: A Life* (London: Chatto and Windus, 1998).

[44] For a similar situation in France and a study of the myth of the "White Russian," see Gousseff, *L'Exil russe.*

[45] Wipert von Bluecher, *Deutschlands Weg nach Rapallo* (Wiesbaden, 1951), p. 53, quoted by Williams, *Culture in Exile*, p. 112.

[46] Karl Schloegel (ed.), *Chronik russischen Lebens in Deutschland, 1918 bis 1941* (Berlin: Akademie Verlag, 1999).

[47] Robert Williams, *Culture in Exile, Russian Emigrés in Germany, 1881–1941* (Ithaca: Cornell University Press, 1972), p. 131.

Nansen's report to the League of Nations in March 1924, "only the well-to-do and solvent elements have left Germany; the needy have remained. The poverty of these latter has greatly increased. The unemployed form a floating population of beggars and vagabonds, whose increasing strength is regarded by the authorities with apprehension as constituting a danger to public security."[48] Many refugees emigrated to other countries. France absorbed the majority but remained very selective in its choices, never abandoning its desire to control the incoming floods of Russian immigrants. Catherine Gousseff has reached an estimate of 80,000 in her recent study of Russian emigration to France.[49]

The Russian Jews who emigrated to Germany in the early 1920s constituted a special case within the broader post-war Russian emigration. As Steven E. Aschheim has convincingly argued, German Jews had since the early nineteenth century developed notions about the "otherness" of Eastern European Jews in order to exhibit a sense of social distance and reinforce their own qualities of culture and refinement.[50] Ironically, Jewish liberals and German anti-Semites alike shared stereotypes of Eastern Jews as a wild and primitive people. At the end of the nineteenth century, German Zionists were the only ones to idealize Eastern European Jews as a community rooted in authentic Jewish traditions. When masses of Eastern Jews or *Ostjuden* settled in Germany or traveled across the country on their way to the United States after the Great War, many German Jews feared that these new immigrants would threaten their assimilation into German society. The German Jewish communities accepted responsibility for the Eastern Jews but believed that post-war Germany was in no position to absorb more workers. To the German Jews, the *Ostjuden* were a potential "provocation," and, therefore, they should be repatriated as soon as possible. In March 1921, Max Naumann founded the *Deutschnationale Juden*. A few months later, an article published with his support read: "Everywhere we look into their strange eyes . . . Everywhere we hear the coarse noises of their excited conversations . . . In all the cafés they go in gesticulating groups, they proceed shouting, wallet in hand, from table to door to the next notary to buy a house . . . Entire areas of Berlin are falling into their hands . . . "[51] The

---

[48] Official Journal of the League of Nations, March 10, 1924.
[49] Gousseff reexamines the social history of Russian refugees in France in her book *L'Exil russe*.
[50] Steven E. Aschheim, *Brothers and Strangers: The East European Jew in German and German-Jewish Consciousness, 1800–1923* (Madison: University of Wisconsin Press, 1982).
[51] *Koelnische Zeitung*, December 18, 1922, quoted in *Ibid.*, p. 221.

obvious solution, according to Naumann, was that they were to be "ruth-lessly expelled."[52]

Thousands of Russian refugees also ended up as far away as China. The first wave had left Russia after the fall of Kazan in 1918. Other groups included men from the Czechoslovak detachments and the soldiers of General Kappel's army in 1920. After the fall of Vladivostok in 1922, Siberian troops under Smolin retreated over the frontier into Manchuria. Harbin, a Chinese town in Manchuria, was taken over by the Russians when the Trans-Siberian railway was built. After the collapse of the White Movement in Siberia, it became host to troops and refugees of all nations. "It is a paradox that the ejection of tens of thousands of refugees to the east was of great benefit to Harbin," Viktor Petrov recalled in his book *The Town of the Sungari*. He remarked:

The town suddenly came to life and grew; its Russian population increased by two hundred thousand. This new population, in the majority of cases drawn from the Government and the intelligentsia raised the cultural level of this Russian town on Chinese soil to an unusual height . . . Dramatic theater made its appearance, along with opera and musical comedy. The most memorable (performances) were those given by artists famous all over Russia, Mozzhukhin and Lipovsky . . . The opera season usually opened with a performance of Aida. After that came other, no less popular operas: Tosca, Madame Butterfly ('Cho-Cho-San') and of course Carmen . . . This in turn led to the foundation of Harbin's first Higher Musical school. If my memory is correct, this school trained the young Yul Brynner, subsequently the famous Hollywood star.[53]

White troops from the Volga under Molchanov went down the coast to the Korean port of Gensan. About 2,000 sailors from Admiral Stark's Siberian flotilla, who were not allowed to land in Gensan, sailed to Shang-hai, where they received assistance from the Chinese Red Cross. Hundreds of refugees were allowed to disembark; others were forced to leave. En route to Manila, they came up against a tropical storm and lost a ship. They were finally transferred to San Francisco, where the American Red Cross put $30,000 towards the cost of their settling.[54] As late as 1925, the position of those who remained in China was described as "more difficult than in any other part of the world." In 1924, a representative

---

[52] Max Naumann, "Auslaendergefahr und Ostjudengefahr," *Mitteilungsblatt des Verban-des nationaldeutscher Juden*, January–February 1923, quoted in Aschheim, *Brothers and Strangers*, p. 221.
[53] Viktor Petrov, *The Town of the Sungari* (Washington, DC: Russo-American Historical Society, 1984), quoted in Norman Stone and Michael Glenny (eds.) *The Other Russia* (London: Faber and Faber, 1990), pp. 205–221.
[54] The American National Red Cross, *Annual Report* [for the year ending June 30, 1923], pp. 68–70.

of the High Commissioner for Refugees reported: "Medical assistance is only available in large towns and medical supplies are most inadequate. The inability to speak the Chinese language and the rigorous winters of Manchuria, where most refugees are living, make their lot an exceedingly hard one."[55] Being faced with a new language and new cultures tended to further isolate the refugees, who mythified and idealized their country of origin, a phenomenon observed by many psychiatrists and social scientists in more recent times.[56]

A problem beyond the power of humanitarian organizations

Although the European refugee problem did not begin in the early 1920s, its extent had become worrisome. The few available statistics concerning refugees were far from exact: this was due both to the continual movement of people and the lack of administrative organization to obtain precise figures. Meanwhile, many refugees found it impossible to establish their citizenship, or there was some doubt as to their place of origin as a consequence of the disintegration of the old Russian Empire. Moreover, the term "Russian refugee" was in itself deeply ambiguous. It was a term used both to describe those who had fled during the Revolution, as well as those Russian citizens who had fled their country before the war and the Bolshevik Revolution and who now found it impossible to return. Rachmaninoff, who had fled with his family to the United States in 1917, was among the former, and Stravinsky, who had spent most of the year in France and Switzerland since 1910, among the latter. The term "Russian refugee" also applied to other diverse communities within this large, heterogeneous, and extremely complex group. According to the most reliable sources, the total number of Russian refugees varied from 750,000 and 2 million people in the early 1920s.[57]

---

[55] C.A. Macartney, *Refugees: The Work of the League* (London: League of Nations Union, 1930), pp. 15–16.

[56] Jean-Luc Roche, "A multidimensional approach to the exile's persecution experience," in Diana Miserez (ed.), *Refugees: The Trauma of Exile* (Dordrecht, Boston and London: Martinus Nijhoff Publishers, 1988), pp. 223–233.

[57] Two million, according to Madeleine de Bryas, *Les peuples en marche. Les migrations politiques et économiques depuis la guerre* (Paris: Pedone, 1926). In his survey of 1939, Sir John Hope Simpson gave a different evaluation of around 750,000 in 1922, but this figure did not include the refugees in the Far East. Speaking on behalf of the Red Cross, Ador referred to 800,000 Russian refugees scattered throughout Europe in 1922. For Michael Marrus, "the refugees from Bolshevik Russia probably numbered close to a million at the highest point," *The Unwanted: European Refugees from the First World War Through the Cold War* (Philadelphia: Temple University Press, 2002), p. 61.

Given the magnitude of the problem, no single government could solve it alone. The recently constituted Yugoslav and Czechoslovak governments, for instance, spent 20 million gold francs annually on their refugees in 1921.[58] They could hardly spend more. As Sylvain Lévy, President of the *Alliance Israélite de France*, emphasized in a letter on December 8, 1920, "only the League of Nations can undertake this formidable task and all the problems involved. Only the League, which rises above religious and racial interests, and is inspired by generous humanitarian motives, can undertake the task of studying and preparing common remedies applicable to all the various cases."[59]

In 1921, Gustave Ador, President of the International Red Cross, was asked by several volunteer organizations to request the President of the League's Council to appoint a High Commissioner for Russian refugees. In a letter of February 29, he noted that the issue went "beyond the power of exclusively humanitarian organizations" and that the League was the "only supernatural political authority capable of solving it." A few days later, the Council of the League of Nations met in Paris and considered the possibility of establishing a coordinated international plan to assist Russian refugees scattered across Europe, either through repatriation or settlement in host countries. The League sent its questionnaire to all countries hosting refugees, in order to obtain information about the situation in each country and to ask for suggestions. In June 1921, the Council invited Fridtjof Nansen to become the first High Commissioner for Russian refugees. His initial tasks were to define the legal position of refugees, to organize their repatriation to or resettlement outside of Russia, and to coordinate the efforts already undertaken for the assistance of refugees in the countries they had fled to.[60] The High Commission for Russian refugees can thus be situated at the juncture of three distinct areas of concern, although these concerns are of course linked to one another: legal action (giving refugees an international status, especially those who were stateless), which was part of the context of the major changes international law underwent in the 1920s; an effort to bring stability to the new map of Europe drawn after World War I; and, third, humanitarian action.[61] In reality, humanitarian action reflected the long-term evolution of several things: the rise of philanthropy, which

---

[58] Macartney, *Refugees*, p. 19.
[59] Sylvain Lévy to the President of the Council of the League of Nations, December 8, 1920, in Lucien Wolf, *Russo-Jewish Refugees in Eastern Europe* (London: Joint Foreign Committee, 1921), p. 15.
[60] League of Nations Archives, R1717, Secretary-General's memorandum concerning Russian refugees, March 16, 1921.
[61] I will develop this particular aspect at greater length in the next chapter.

progressively replaced charity as a way of organizing relief action; the rise to power of large private organizations such as the Near East Relief, already active in the Middle East from 1915;[62] the structuring of a "humanitarian diplomacy" around several axes, including the International Committee of the Red Cross, founded in 1863, and the League of Nations, to which the High Commission for Russian Refugees was attached.

The League's motivation for creating the High Commission was complex. Some representatives emphasized the necessity for countries that had endured the hardships of total war to collaborate on these matters of great importance. If European countries did not coordinate their efforts, they would soon be overwhelmed by the flow of refugees.[63] Moreover, the fear of the presumed violence of Russians, deeply rooted in enduring cultural stereotypes about Russia and Eastern Europe, was reinforced by a discourse that connected the Russian Revolution and Communism with the breakdown of civilization. Western states and many ordinary Europeans viewed Soviet Russia with suspicion and hostility.[64] The waves of refugees that threatened to sweep through Western Europe seemed not just to be a temporary danger but also to present a real challenge to European "civility."[65] When negotiating with Russian officials, the High Commissioner for Refugees was therefore sometimes suspected of being naïve about the risks of the spread of the Bolshevik Revolution or, even worse, of sympathy with the Soviets. On the other hand, Soviet authorities often considered Nansen and his High Commission to be creatures of the League of Nations. After all, in the eyes of the Soviets, most refugees were potential counter-revolutionaries, no better than the émigrés from the Bolshevik regime who had fled to Paris, London, Berlin, and the United States.

Other members of the League adopted a more idealistic tone. Born to a family of Canadian Quakers in 1889, Philip Baker, also known as Philip Noel-Baker, was among them. He had served as the British delegate at the Paris Peace Conference in 1919 and later in the League of Nations Secretariat. An Olympic athlete, he had competed in the 800 meter and 1,500 meter races at the Stockholm Olympic Games in 1912. Like Nansen, he believed in the moral value of sports and in the

---

[62] Kévonian, *Réfugiés et diplomatie humanitaire*, Chapter 7.

[63] James C. Hathaway, *The Law of Refugee Status* (Toronto and Vancouver: Butterworths, 1991), 2.

[64] Ute Frevert, "Europeanizing Germany's twentieth century," *History and Memory*, 17, 2005, pp. 87–116.

[65] Holger Nehring and Helge Pharo, "A peaceful Europe? Negotiating peace in the twentieth century," *Contemporary European History*, 17: 3, 2008, pp. 277–299, 284.

new internationalism that would soon emerge from the war. For him, refugee assistance could "remove the fear of war" and create the "good understanding among peoples upon which peace depends."[66] He saw international aid as a means of contributing to Europe's stability and alleviating global suffering. Noel-Baker's point of view was captured well by historian Claudena Skran, who points out that the new refugee regime derived from a "combination of humanitarian and security reasons."[67]

The creation of the High Commission for Russian Refugees represented a turning point since it was the first formal acknowledgment of international responsibility for the plight of refugees.[68] Poland, Germany, and the Balkan states provided material aid to those who entered their national territories. They placed barracks at the disposal of the refugees and contributed to their food supplies and medical assistance. For example, from 1919 to 1921, the relief given to Russian immigrants at the various frontier posts in Poland cost more than 250 million marks.[69] However, for countries that hosted fewer refugees, like Belgium, or even France and Britain, the support for refugee assistance revealed the strength of humanitarianism in political culture. The movement could be contextualized within the long-term history of humanitarianism going back to the 1850s–60s and to figures such as Florence Nightingale or Henri Dunant.[70] One could also argue that the belief in the fundamental dignity of all human life was a direct and paradoxical consequence of a total war that had brought unprecedented mass death.[71] For instance, in a letter from Lloyd George to Lord Curzon in May 1921, the British Minister in Belgrade refused to cut services to refugees. This would expose them "to privations and hunger," he wrote, and would damage "the standard of humanity with which the world credits us."[72]

Moreover, the creation of a High Commission for Russian Refugees also made it possible to coordinate the work of various agents of humanitarian aid: Western states, which had come to refugees' assistance since they first arrived in Constantinople in 1919 and thus had perpetuated a tradition of humanitarian intervention dating to the early nineteenth

---

[66] Noel-Baker, *League of Nations at Work.*
[67] Skran, *Refugees in Inter-War Europe*, p. 270.
[68] Gil Loescher, *Beyond Charity: International Cooperation and the Global Refugee Crisis* (Oxford University Press, 1993), Chapter 2, "The Origins of International Refugee Regime."
[69] League of Nations Archives, R1725, 45/14 144.
[70] For a recent (but too Anglocentric) history of humanitarianism, see Bass, *Freedom's Battle.*
[71] Metzger, "The League of Nations."
[72] Letter from Sir C. Alban Young to Earl Curzon, dated 21 May, 1921, British Foreign Office Archives, 371/6867/N6310, cited in Skran, *Refugees in Inter-War Europe*, p. 85.

century;[73] the League of Nations and affiliated international organizations such as the International Labor Office; and private organizations, which, as we saw in Chapter 1 with veterans of the Great War and the CIAMAC, played an increasingly important role in the 1920s. Here we see at work the forerunners of what today are called non-governmental organizations (NGOs). Nansen was at the heart of this tripartite collaboration, similar to the functioning of the ILO, with its representatives from member states, unions, and management groups (see Chapter 2).

Thus, in October 1921, the Advisory Committee of Private Refugee Relief Organizations was established near the High Commission for Refugees. This was a unique space for dialogue between organizations active in the field and international organizations in Geneva.[74] Private groups, such as the Zemgor,[75] passed on information concerning the refugees and kept the High Commission informed about the humanitarian needs in each region; conversely, only diplomats from the League of Nations and officials working for the High Commission had the power to influence immigration policy in different countries and develop an internationally valid legal status for the refugees. Everyone gained from this collaboration: the High Commission, which financed a large part of its work thanks to funds raised by private organizations, and which also gained legitimate status in the refugees' eyes; and private organizations, which could rely on the League of Nations for support when they encountered bureaucratic difficulties at the national level. Nansen's

[73] Brendan Simms and D.J.B. Trim (eds.), *Humanitarian Intervention: A History* (Cambridge University Press, 2011), Part II, "The Great Powers and the Ottoman Empire"; Rodogno, *Against Massacre: Humanitarian Interventions in the Ottoman Empire, 1815–1914.*

[74] Dzovinar Kévonian, "L'organisation non gouvernementale, nouvel acteur du champ humanitaire. Le Zemgor et la Société des Nations dans les années 1920," *Cahiers du monde russe*, 46: 4, October–December 2005, pp. 739–756.

[75] The Union of Zemstvos and the Union of Cities were founded in 1914 with the aim of stepping in where the Russian state had failed in aiding victims of the civil war. They played an important role in establishing a network of hospitals during the war and helping people evacuated from combat zones and areas occupied by Central Powers armies. During the war, they forged links with Western charitable organizations and sent representatives to foreign capitals. During the civil war, they continued their work alongside soldiers of the White Army and civilians living in areas controlled by anti-Bolshevik forces. Forced to disband by the new regime in 1919, they re-formed in exile, under the name "Zemsko-gorodskoj Komitet," or "Zemgor." The Zemgor collaborated with the League of Nations in 1920 during the exchange of Russian, German, and Austrian prisoners of war, which was overseen by Nansen. Politically, the Zemgor's leaders, for the most part liberal, were close to the provisional government's official representatives abroad. Along with the Russian Red Cross, they provided medical assistance for refugees, which facilitated their ability to train for and obtain jobs. See Catherine Gousseff and Olga Pichon-Bobrinskoy, "Les archives du comité directeur du Zemgor," *Cahiers du monde russe*, 43: 2–3, April–September 2002, pp. 529–544.

role at the heart of this unique arrangement was a key one: without his personal contacts in the Russian émigré community, both humanitarians and legal scholars, without his firsthand knowledge of conditions in the field, acquired during the repatriation of prisoners of war in 1919–20, and without his charisma, it is unlikely that the work of the High Commission for Refugees would have had the breadth and impact it did.

Fridtjof Nansen's mission

When Nansen accepted the position of High Commissioner for Russian Refugees in September 1921, he already had established a formidable reputation in Europe. His polar expeditions from 1893–96 had made him an international celebrity. His boat, the "Fram" (meaning "Forward" in Norwegian), was strong enough to be frozen into the ice of Siberia and drift over to the North Pole. When Nansen realized after his first year at sea that his course would not take him as far north as he had hoped, he left his crew and, accompanied by one companion, Hjalmar Johansen, tried to reach the North Pole on skis. They survived two winters by hunting seals and were miraculously rescued by a British expedition led by F.G. Jackson. "I raised my hat, we shook hands heartily. 'How do you do?' 'How do you do?'" Nansen recorded in his diary. His book *Farthest North* became an instant bestseller. One of the most popular wax statues at the Grévin museum in Paris in the 1890s was one of Nansen, surrounded by penguins and bears.

In many ways, the Norwegian adventurer embodied the dreams of his era: the aspiration to explore, study, and organize new territories and to construct a global space in which all nations could find common prosperity.[76] In a ten-page article published in the *Review of Reviews*, W.T. Stead recounted what he called "the Nansen boom."[77] According to him, two things about Nansen stood out: "the indomitable faith of the man in himself" and "the unanimity with which most of the best authorities believed he was going to a living grave." Even the anarchist Peter Kropotkin, who had settled in England after 3 years in a French prison, admitted: "Nansen and Johansen [are the] true heroes of our century."[78]

At the turn of the century, the European public became fascinated by science, and Nansen's fame stemmed in part from his status as a scientist.

---

[76] Sylvain Venayre, *La gloire de l'aventure: genèse d'une mystique moderne, 1850–1940* (Paris: Aubier, 2002).
[77] Vol. 15, February 1897, p. 276.   [78] Huntford, *Nansen*, pp. 442–443.

Both an intellectual and a man of action, the Norwegian explorer began his career as an invertebrate zoologist at the Bergen Museum in Norway. As a direct consequence of new developments in microscopy in the mid 1880s, Nansen was one of the first scientists to express doubts about the reticular theory of the nervous system that prevailed in neurology, and to defend what later became known as the Neuron Doctrine. His interests extended to such diverse subjects as geography, geology, oceanography, meteorology, zoology, botany, nutrition, and physics. During his first crossing of Greenland in 1888 and his Fram expedition in 1893–96, he addressed a number of fundamental scientific questions, such as the nature of ice ages, the formation of valleys and fjords, and climatic changes, a topic that has recently reemerged in public debate today.[79] His Norwegian heritage influenced his outlook on the natural world, making him a pioneer in the promotion of an ecologically sustainable life. This would be later disseminated by what we now term environmentalism. Moreover, he saw scientific discoveries as a means of turning humanity away from its warlike tendencies. "True civilization will not have been reached until all nations see that it is nobler to conquer nature than to conquer each other," he wrote.

Living a frugal lifestyle and refusing any salary for his work at the High Commission, Nansen seemed to be "above politics." British feminist Vera Brittain, who saw him for the first time at a General Assembly of the League of Nations in 1923, called him the "hero of every schoolchild . . . " The indefinable quality that set him above his fellows seemed to belong less to his tall, conspicious figure, with its lean, melancholy face beneath the broad-brimmed hat of grey felt, than to his long swift step and the air of untrammeled freedom that an English woman journalist described to me as "the sleigh-dog manner."[80] In an article published by the *New York Times* in October 1923, journalist Hannah Astrup Larsen described her first impression of a stern personality: "The tall, commanding figure, the strong jaw, the dome-like forehead which seemed to bear down with its own weight, the fine wrinkles coming to a focus in the bright, scintillating eyes—the eyes of a sailor looking out over a sunny sea—all contributed to a look of austerity, which, however, soon resolved itself into intensity and concentration."[81]

---

[79] In September 2006, a group of European scientists, funded by the French company Agnès B., repeated the Fram expedition of 1893–96. The schooner Tara was frozen into the ice north of the Laptev Sea and followed a more northerly route than the Fram. The expedition contributed to our understanding of the Arctic Ocean and of the spectacular retreat of ice cap observed in recent years.

[80] Vera Brittain, *Testament of Youth: An Autobiographical Study of the Years 1900–1925* (London: Penguin, 1994), p. 559.

[81] *New York Times*, October 28, 1923.

Following Norway's independence from Sweden in 1905, Nansen, at first a protector of the nationalist Fatherland League (*Fedrelandslaget*),[82] was appointed the first Norwegian ambassador to Great Britain, where he served from 1906 to 1908. In a small country that had recently become independent, political authorities were quick to understand the benefits of being represented by a national hero known around the world.[83] In 1917, the Norwegian government sent him to the United States in the hopes of obtaining supplies for his country, which remained neutral during the conflict and depended on imports of cereals and other goods. He met with US Food Administrator Herbert Hoover, who would deeply influence his later work, and with President Woodrow Wilson. Nansen, who described the world as divided between living and dying nations—thus in emphatic biological terms—also believed that the United States represented the future of the West. The Americans are "great in everything, also in their idealism," he assessed. Like most Scandinavian internationalists, Nansen thought that small states gained the most from the protection of international law and that they shared a special mission in promoting peace among nations.[84] Moreover, he believed that innovative ideas frequently came from small states, as the historical example of the Greek *poleis* clearly demonstrated.[85] Paradoxically, Nansen was at this time a central figure in Norwegian nationalism, and, at the same time, an ardent supporter of internationalism. He soon became president of the Norwegian League of Nations Society and participated in the Paris Peace Conference in 1919. The tragedy of the Great War inspired his humanitarian approach to international relations. To Nansen, World War I remained "the greatest confession of defeat of humanity, a degradation, devoid of meaning, an orgy of self-destruction in which nothing flourished but the lust for power, hatred and stupidity—the bitter fruits of which mankind must eat for a generation."[86]

In 1920, the League appointed Nansen to be High Commissioner for Prisoners of War. His task, one of the most difficult challenges of the post-war era,[87] was to repatriate the many internees who remained in

---

[82] On the apparent contradiction between Nansen's anti-parliamentarianism and nationalism and his passionnate internationalism, see Carl Emil Vogt, "Fridtjof Nansen, peace 1922," in Olav Njølstad (ed.), *Norwegian Nobel Prize Laureates* (Oslo: Universtitetsforlaget, 2006), pp. 119–153.

[83] In his biography, *Fridtjof Nansen*, Vogt stresses that after the death of the Norwegian poet Bjørnstjerne Bjørnson in 1910, Nansen was the only national hero left in Norway except for the Prime Minister, Christian Michelsen, father of Norwegian independence.

[84] Olav Riste, *Norway's Foreign Relations. A History* (Oslo: Universitetsforlaget, 2001).

[85] Fridtjof Nansen, "The mission of small states," authorized interview in the *American-Scandinavian Review*, VI: 1, January–February 1918.

[86] Jon Sorensen, *The Saga of Fridtjof Nansen* (London: Allen & Unwin, 1932), p. 270.

[87] Marrus, *The Unwanted*, p. 87.

prisoners' camps in Russia, Germany, and the successor states of Austria-Hungary. For the League, whose standing had been diminished by the refusal of the United States Senate to ratify the Treaty of Versailles, the repatriation of prisoners was a chance to prove its own usefulness. As High Commissioner, Nansen was the only mediator between the Western countries that refused to recognize the Bolshevik regime and the Soviets who saw the League of Nations as a "capitalist conspiracy." On several occasions during his talks with Georgy Chicherin, the Soviet People's Commissar for Foreign Affairs, the High Commissioner threatened to abandon negotiations. Nearly 430,000 prisoners of war were finally repatriated in less than 2 years, despite the limited sums of money that the League of Nations could provide and the enormous difficulties in transporting people anywhere in Europe: most land routes were closed by the war between Poland and Russia.[88]

In August 1921, even before the repatriation of the prisoners of war had ended, Gustave Ador, the President of the International Red Cross, asked Nansen to join Herbert Hoover in a far-reaching relief movement for famine-stricken Russia (see Chapter 4). Hoover, now Secretary of Commerce in President Harding's Republican administration and head of the American Relief Administration (ARA), declined. Nansen had already signed an agreement with Soviet authorities on August 27, 1921, which established an executive center in Moscow and helped to send nearly 80,000 tons of grain into Russia. Given his success in negotiations with Russian officials and arranging for the exchange of prisoners, there seemed no better candidate for the League's newly created High Commission for Refugees,[89] although some Secretariat officials would have preferred a prominent American or a representative of another Great Power for the job. Moreover, some of the White Russian relief organizations considered the appointment of a man who supposedly entertained friendly relations with the Bolshevik regime as "an arbitrary and hostile act on behalf of the League towards the unfortunate victims of the (Russian) revolution."[90]

A High Commissioner for Russian refugees

The High Commission for Refugees was not one of the big bureaucratic institutions born of the war. Its financial resources were extremely

[88] Sebastian Balzter, *Repatriierung, 1920–1922. Zur Rückführung der Kriegsgefangenen nach dem Ersten Weltkrieg*, Magisterarbeit, Albert-Ludwigs-Universität, Freiburg im Breisgau, 2004.
[89] Philip Noel-Baker, "Advantages of having Nansen," Secretariat note, undated, Philip Noel-Baker Papers, 4/450a, Churchill College, Cambridge University.
[90] League of Nations Archives, R1713, Letter from Pierre Botkine to the Secretary-General, October 3, 1921.

limited: no more than 250,000 Swiss francs per year in the early 1920s.[91] Nansen received no salary and paid for his own train tickets when traveling in Central Europe for the High Commission. It even proved a challenge to raise the 100 Swiss francs needed to print the 1924 proposal that would supply Armenian refugees with identity certificates. The League only paid for administrative costs. It spent no money on direct relief, which depended fully on assistance from individual governments, voluntary agencies, and private individuals. States never considered direct relief a top priority in the 1920s. Broadly speaking, a politics of solidarity that considered humanitarian rights an essential element in the process of peace building in the wake of the Great War now lost ground with the resurgence of nationalism: humanitarian policies remained tied, more often than not, to domestic policy objectives. For example, at the end of his life, Nansen proved unable to resettle Armenian refugees in Erivan (now Yerevan) and to provide them with a national home. Most countries opposed the plan, and the League of Nations failed to give the necessary funds.[92]

The High Commission's main asset was a small staff of hand-picked representatives, such as Burnier in Constantinople, Schlesinger in Germany, or Major Berdez in Warsaw,[93] who ensured close contact with the refugees and facilitated an understanding of their problems. High Commissioner Nansen was in constant contact with them. The correspondence of the staff, now housed in the archives of the League of Nations in Geneva, helps us better understand the day-to-day difficulties faced by the overburdened staff and the inevitable diplomatic tensions with local authorities.[94] Many refugees or former refugees worked for the High Commission, mostly on the local level, as interpreters or staff members: this is still a key feature of the United Nations High Commission for Refugees (UNHCR) today. Without their participation, the local offices of the High Commission would have been unable to deal with problems such as providing legal assistance to refugees, relief operations, or the prevention of epidemics. In Geneva, Nansen's team was made up of

---

[91] Sir John Hope Simpson, *The Refugee Problem: Report of a Survey* (New York, 1939), pp.195–196; Atle Grahl-Madsen, "The League of Nations and the Refugees," in *The League of Nations in Retrospect* (Berlin and New York: Walter de Gruyter, 1983), 362.

[92] Skran, *Refugees in Inter-War Europe*, p. 274.

[93] "Representatives of the High Commissioner in Various Countries," *Official Journal of the League of Nations*, May 1922, p. 395.

[94] In a letter to the High Commissioner in November 1921, Maurice Gehri, Nansen's representative in Sofia, complained: "After some truly heavy efforts, it seems to me that today we may be nearing a solution. It really is not too soon. I am almost out of patience and strength. I undertook countless tasks, went to see a vast number of people, before fully realizing that I would get nothing out of the government unless I ordered them to carry out their obligations. The inertia of government ministers and their way of handling things, or rather not handling things, is staggering."

people who had already worked with him on the repatriation of prisoners of war and the newly started famine relief to Russia. Frick, who spoke Russian with a near-native fluency, was his assistant. Johnson, a former British officer, served as his personal secretary. In his memoirs, the latter gave a vivid and acute description of Nansen's personality: "No one who travelled with him could reconcile the intrepid North Pole explorer, whose Arctic exploits fired the imagination of middle-aged men ... with the 'windy traveller' who was never happy unless he was at the station long before the due departure of the train and who, at the last minute, sent out SOS in all directions for forgotten articles varying from passport to pajamas."[95]

Nansen supervised refugee aid from Switzerland and traveled all over Europe to secure from governments and voluntary organizations the financial support necessary for his project. He created an advisory committee composed of representatives of sixteen private organizations, including the Near East Relief, the International Committee of the Red Cross (ICRC) and the Russian Zemstvos and Towns Relief Committee.[96] In order to seek international consensus and secure support for his work, he regularly participated in the sessions of the Council, of which Britain, France, Italy, Japan (and Germany after 1926) were permanent members, and in the annual session of the General Assembly held in September.[97] Within the League's Secretariat, the Economic and Financial Section took charge of the loans raised for the settlement of refugees, the Health Section helped to fight epidemics,[98] the Legal Section assisted the High Commission in drafting legal conventions, and the Political Section was in charge of the political implications of refugee movements.[99]

The High Commissioner faced juridical problems of an unprecedented complexity. According to international law, foreigners were usually subject to the laws of their own country with regard to their legal status, their family relationships, and their inheritance of property.[100] Those

---

[95] T.F. Johnson, *International Tramps: From Chaos to Permanent World Peace* (London: Hutchinson, 1938), quoted in Huntford, *Nansen*, p. 634.

[96] *Official Journal of the League of Nations*, May 1922, Annex 321, p. 387.

[97] For a clear presentation of the institutional framework and the decision-making procedures, see Skran, *Refugees in Inter-War Europe*, Chapter 3.

[98] Barbara Metzger, "The League of Nations' Health Organization: A Study into the Origins of International Humanitarian Co-operation and its Political Implication during the Early Interwar Years," unpublished M.Phil. thesis submitted to the University of Cambridge, September 1993.

[99] Metzger, "The League of Nations," p. 227.

[100] Except in Great Britain and in the United States, where the personal status of foreigners was determined by the *lex domicilii* or the *lex loci*, the law of the country of origin continued to prevail in most states of Continental Europe and in Japan.

who had become stateless experienced difficulties in most legal issues of everyday life: marriages and divorces, the rights and obligations of married persons in their personal relations, and the inheritance of personal property. In a letter to Lord Robert Cecil, Russian refugee organizations in London complained: "The humiliation of this absence of legal rights is added to the bitterness of exile."[101]

In these matters, Fridtjof Nansen benefited from the expertise of a circle of Russian legal scholars, who served on the Advisory Committee of Private Organizations, a non-governmental group attached to the High Commission for Refugees. All of them, except Baron Boris Nolde, were Jewish liberals, who had taught or been educated at a law school in St. Petersburg. The oldest generation had suffered from the discrimination against Jewish students between 1890 and 1905. In 1920, they left Soviet Russia for France.[102] Most of them were freemasons and met in the most prestigious lodges in the French capital, where they shared their views on international law and the rights of minorities.[103]

André Mandelstam (1869–1949) was undoubtedly one of the most influential figures of the group.[104] In 1907, he was assistant to Fyodor Martens, the legal expert of the Russian Government, in the Second International Peace Conference held at the Hague. He later drafted the 1914 Armenian Reform Agreement and became one of the most knowledgeable specialists on the Ottoman Empire. The head of the legal office at the Russian Ministry of Foreign Affairs, he documented the massacre of the Armenians during the war in a famous book, *Le sort de l'Empire ottoman*, published in 1917. Furthermore, his work included an extensive study of "the theoretical construction of the right to [humanitarian] intervention," which described World War I as "a struggle for human rights" (*une lutte pour le droit humain*).[105]

---

101 Letter from Russian refugees' organizations to Lord Robert Cecil, August 13, 1923, Philip Noel-Baker Papers, 4/625, Churchill College, Cambridge University.
102 Kévonian, "Les juristes juifs," pp. 72–94.
103 Nina Berberova, *Les Francs-maçons russes au XXème siècle* (Arles: Actes Sud, 1990).
104 On André Mandelstam, see Kévonian, "Exilés politiques"; Lubor Jilek, "Violences de masse et droits de l'Homme: André Mandelstam entre Constantinople et Bruxelles," *Cahiers de la Faculté des Lettres de Genève*, 2000, pp. 64–71.
105 In his historical account, based on Rougier's work (*La théorie de l'intervention d'humanité* [Paris: Pedone, 1910]), Mandelstam portrays the Powers' demands to the Ottoman Empire in the nineteenth century as demands to "respect the rights of man." (André Mandelstam, *Le sort de l'Empire ottoman* (Lausanne and Paris: Payot, 1917), part IV, pp. 413–586). I thank Peter Holquist for bringing this important book to my attention. See his unpublished paper, "The origins of 'crimes against humanity': the Russian Empire, international law and the 1915 Note on the Armenian genocide," presented at the annual meeting of the American Historical Association, New York, January 2009.

After the Bolshevik Revolution, Mandelstam emigrated to Paris and became a prominent member of the International Law Institute (ILI), a famous Belgian academic institution that would play a crucial role in developing the study of human rights. Since its founding at the Ghent town hall in September 1873, the Institute had considered international law as more than simply relationships between states.[106] Its eleven founders, who included the Russian Vladimir Besobrasov, met in the aftermath of the Franco-Prussian War to establish collective action for the promotion of international law, "so that those principles of justice and humanity which should govern the mutual relations of peoples shall prevail" (article 1 of the ILI's statutes). The Institute was to become "the organ of the legal conscience of the civilized world" and to "labor, within its proper sphere, whether for the maintenance of peace or for the observance of the laws of war."

Fifty years later, in the wake of a conflict that had violated the rules of war in every possible way, Mandelstam, Nolde, and other prominent Russian jurists still considered the ILI, which had been awarded the Nobel Prize for Peace in 1904, to be a forum for the promotion of internationally recognized human rights.[107] The Institute's members met every 2 years. Between sessions, academic commissions examined topics that had been previously approved by the General Assembly. The commissions' work generally led to the adoption of resolutions of normative character, which they brought to the attention of governments and international organizations. For the Russian legal scholars as well as for the French influential jurist Georges Scelle, the rights of man had become the main topic in discussions over international law. In an article on refugees published in *La Tribune Juive* in February 1922, Boris Mirkine-Guetzevitch, a young Russian jurist, argued that the Great War had given birth to "a new public consciousness that recognizes aid to refugees and to victims of famine and of epidemics as a task of an international public nature (*une tâche de caractère public international*)."[108]

In August 1921, 5 months before a Soviet decree (December 15, 1921) denationalized thousands of former nationals, thus exacerbating

---

[106] Irwin Abrams, "The emergence of the international law societies," *The Review of Politics*, 19: 3, July 1957, pp. 361–380.

[107] In 1917, the Chilean jurist Alejandro Alvarez submitted to the American Institute of International Law a draft declaration on the future International Law and included a section on "international rights of the individual." Yet, Mandelstam and his Russian colleagues were much more influential. In 1929, Mandelstam drafted the "Declaration for the International Rights of Man" for the Institute of International Law. This declaration is often considered to be a first draft of the 1945 Charter of the United Nations. See Burgers, "The Road to San Francisco," pp. 447–477, 451.

[108] "L'émigration," *La Tribune Juive*, 113, February 24, 1922.

the refugee crisis, Nansen asked Mandelstam to write a memorandum on the legal positions of his fellow countrymen who had fled to Constantinople and Poland and were being progressively evacuated to the Balkans and Western Europe. It sometimes proved difficult, if not impossible, to apply their new national legislation to refugees. After the Soviets abolished the rights of private property and inheritance, what could a French or Italian judge do when he had to decide on the inheritance of property left by a Russian in accordance with the national law of the deceased?[109] Applying the law of their new country of residence would be contrary to the spirit of common law. Choosing to accept former Russian civil law, in accordance with the non-recognition of the Bolshevik regime by most European countries, seemed another possibility. "As things are, the Russian refugees cannot travel, marry, be born, or die without creating legal problems, to which there is no solution," a Secretariat official summarized in May 1921.[110] As a consequence, "refugees were defined in largely juridical terms, which meant that they were treated as refugees because of their membership in a group of persons effectively deprived of the formal protection of the government of its state of origin."[111]

In the early 1920s, most governments viewed repatriation as the best solution to the refugee problem. There were several reasons for this, the first of which had to do with the intellectual framework that diplomats of the 1920s developed. The immediate post-war period was indeed characterized by a notable rise in the international ideal, as evidenced by the creation of the League of Nations. At the same time, a group of international legal scholars, centered around the work of Georges Scelle, called the role of nation-states into question and sought to put the individual and his rights back in the center of international relations. For them, the state was not necessarily the best protector of its citizens; this was an idea that Cassin also theorized in his critique of the Leviathan state's demands of its citizens (see Chapter 1). However, diplomats and politicians, for their part, continued to think in national terms. As we have already seen in the example of the ILO in Chapter 2, even the international officials based in Geneva remained largely faithful to their national allegiances. The post-war spirit was certainly more and more internationalist, since the problems that arose at that time were often global or transnational in nature. It is nonetheless still true that the general framework of diplomatic thought was by nature national. It was not surprising, then, that

---

[109] Simpson, *Refugee Problem*, p. 264.
[110] Memorandum of May 6, 1921 on the "Possible action of the League in connection with Russian refugees," Philip Noel-Baker Papers, 4/450, Churchill College, Cambridge University.
[111] Hathaway, *Law of Refugee Status*, pp. 2–3.

many people saw repatriation as the best solution for the refugees. The idea was that a man was most comfortable among his own people, on his own territory, and that his return should be facilitated by all available means.

In addition, repatriation was an appealing option for economic reasons. Having spent large sums of money to assist the defeated soldiers of the White Armies that had fought in the Civil War,[112] France and Britain saw the appointment of a High Commissioner for Russian Refugees as a means of accelerating the return of refugees to their homelands. Many Secretariat officials favored this solution, which would also facilitate the reconstruction of Russia in the wake of the Civil War. "It is vital to build up a new body of technical experts, a new educated class, who would be able to help in the rebuilding of Russia in the next decade. The Soviets have taken every measure which they could to improve education, but they have not got the personnel. It must therefore be done among the emigres who are in Europe,"[113] Philip Baker wrote in March 1922. The High Commissioner personally hoped that repatriation could be achieved as successfully as the homecoming of prisoners of war in 1920–21. In the long term, the League would "help to remove centers of disaffection and discontent" and help to "raise, by the distribution and settlement of industrious and highly educated refugees, the standards of civilization in various parts of the globe."[114]

At first, the general amnesty granted by Soviet authorities to all returnees seemed to be a good omen for the Nansen-Soviet repatriation plan. But the famine conditions that prevailed in Russia and the Ukraine, and the opposition of two major Russian refugee organizations, the United Committee of the Russian Zemstvos and Town Councils, and the Russian Red Cross Society, dissuaded the League from getting involved in the plan.[115] "It would be quite useless to imagine that there is any possibility of obtaining guarantees from the Soviet Government with regard to the safety of the repatriated refugees," the United Committee of the Russian Zemstvos wrote in a memorandum sent to the International Red Cross. "Russia continues to be the stage of fierce civil war and the

---

[112] By November 1921, the French government had spent already 150 million francs on Russian refugees, essentially the Wrangel army fugitives (*Official Journal of the League of Nations*, November 1921, p. 1011). A British Treasury statement reported that large sums had been spent for the maintenance of Russian refugees (more than 1.5 million pounds), the relief of Assyrian and Armenian refugees in Mesopotamia (5.3 million pounds), and the relief of refugees in Poland (200,000 pounds). See Simpson, *Refugee Problem*, pp. 199 ff.
[113] League of Nations Archives, R1719, 45/12930.   [114] Marrus, *The Unwanted*, p. 91.
[115] "Russian Refugees," August 1, 921, Reports by the High Commissioner for Refugees, C.126 (a). M.72(a).1921.VII, 6–8, in Skran, *Refugees in Inter-War Europe*, p. 151.

repatriation of persons who have taken an active part in this war would amount to abandoning them to the mercy and despotism of a vindictive power."

It was only in October 1922 that repatriation began in Bulgaria with small groups of Cossacks, natives of the Don and Kuban provinces. Each returnee had to sign a paper certifying that he or she would return out of their own free will. Some representatives appointed by the High Commissioner supervised their settlement and assured their personal safety after they returned. Delegations of repatriated refugees were also sent abroad to inform their compatriots about their lives back home. In late 1922, however, after 2 months of fairly successful repatriations, rumors about mass killings in Soviet Russia started to leak out to the Russian émigré newspapers. The High Commission proved unable to confirm them, because Soviet authorities now controlled access to the returning refugees. The Bulgarian government's expulsion of two Soviet Red Cross officials on charges of espionage added to the confusion. In June 1923, the fall of the Stamboliiski regime and the "White terror" in Bulgaria put a brutal end to the repatriation plan, which was limited to 6,000 refugees.[116]

In January 1923, the Polish Minister of the Interior issued a decree ordering the expulsion of all Russian refugees who had entered Poland after October 12, 1920 without qualifying as "political refugees"—even if this idea did not yet have a precise definition at the time.[117] Most of them had lost their Russian citizenship and could not return to their country of origin. According to the High Commissioner's delegate in Warsaw, groups of refugees had been pushed back and forth six times between the two countries.[118] The majority were Jewish. The situation grew worse when Polish authorities, under pressure from the Polish Nationalist Party, decided to start the expulsions on April 15, 1923, leaving little more than a month to organize protective measures for the refugees. In a memorandum written in March 1923, Lucien Wolf, the representative of the Jewish Colonization Association, the Joint Foreign Committee of the Jewish Board of Deputies, and the Anglo-Jewish Association estimated that the expulsions would have a negative influence on the Polish image

---

[116] Joseph Rothschild, *East Central Europe between the Two World Wars* (Seattle: University of Washington Press, 1974), pp. 339–342; John D. Bell, *Peasants in Power: Alexander Stamboliiski and the Bulgarian Agrarian National Union, 1899–1923* (Princeton University Press, 1977).

[117] For a detailed account of this diplomatic and humanitarian crisis, see Metzger, "The League of Nations," Chapter 4.

[118] League of Nations Archives, R1725, Letter from Major Berdez to the High Commission in Geneva, January 23, 1921.

abroad: "The world would be presented with the spectacle of thousands of helpless refugees [. . .] driven forcibly at the bayonet's point into the neutral zone between the lines of Russian and Polish frontier guards and left there to perish from hunger and cold. Add to this the fact that we have reason to believe that [. . .] the Expulsion Decree, although ostensibly aimed at Russian refugees, is only enforced against Jewish refugees, and it will be seen that the Polish Government will have to bear the reproach of an action at once inhuman and intolerant."[119] At the last minute, the decree was postponed on April 20, 1923. This was undoubtedly a success for the High Commission, understood by historian Barbara Metzger as a precursor of the concept of the "physical protection of refugees."[120] Yet the Polish crisis also revealed the limits of the repatriation policy that Nansen had implemented in the previous months. Because the majority of Russian refugees were unlikely to return to their country of origin in the near future, the Commission needed to find other solutions, including their long-term settlement in foreign countries.

The Nansen Passport

Nansen achieved far greater success in his attempt to create a legal status for refugees without documentation who wanted to settle abroad. The majority had fled their homes without any identity papers or possessed papers issued by governments that no longer existed. Moreover, in the former Russian Empire, the Soviet government denationalized thousands of former nationals because of their opposition to the new Bolshevik regime or because they were members of a particular ethnic group. The Soviet decree of December 15, 1921 denationalized Russians who had lived abroad for a period of 5 years and had not obtained a Soviet passport or had failed to register with Soviet representatives by June 1, 1922. All those who had left their country without the permission of Soviet authorities after November 7, 1917, or who had taken part in military activities against the new regime and the Red Army, also lost their nationality.[121] Russian refugees were "in judicial limbo."[122]

The Soviet government invalidated the travel and identity documents of hundreds of thousands of Russian refugees. These people lost freedom

---

[119] League of Nations Archives, R1725, Confidential memorandum written by Lucien Wolf for the Joint Foreign Committee of the Jewish Board of Deputies and the Anglo-Jewish Association, March 29, 1923.

[120] Metzger, "The League of Nations," pp. 229–235.

[121] Jacques Scheftel, "L'apatridie des réfugiés russes," *Journal de droit international*, January–February 1934.

[122] Huntford, *Nansen*, p. 634.

of movement, as well as diplomatic protection when they were abroad. Nansen had become a kind of ultimate defender for the vulnerable, comparable to the protective figure of Woodrow Wilson in post-war Europe.[123] The two men received moving letters from helpless people. Those addressed to the High Commissioner for Russian Refugees asked for protection and, above all, for money, which he could not provide.

Dear Sir, I am an invalid Russian officer who has lost his left arm in the war with communists. I have two babies, an aged mother and invalid brother. It is impossible for me to maintain this family on the salary that I earn. I have the honour of asking the committee of the League of Nations to help me and my family to better their situation. The one way out which I could manage here in Serbia is to open a shop which would require a capital of 750 dollars. [. . .] That I will return this monthly I give you my word as an Officer of the Old Imperial Russian army. Help me to stand on my feet and live like a man—Sergei Lachnitsky.[124]

Claudena Skran convincingly argues that the 1920s were "a time of great creativity and innovation, a time when much was accomplished with minimal resources and a time when millions of refugees were helped to begin new lives."[125] This is probably most true of the "Nansen Certificate" (commonly known as the "Nansen Passport"), the result of lengthy negotiations (August 1921–July 1922) with various countries, Russian associations and the League of Nations, which placed refugees under the protection of an international organization for the first time in history.[126] Some newly independent states such as Poland and Czechoslovakia issued their own documents to refugees on their soil, but these papers were not internationally recognized, making it difficult for refugees to travel. In creating a new document, Nansen hoped to facilitate the movement of refugees from regions where they seemed too numerous to those where they could more easily find asylum and work.

Before 1914, international attitudes towards freedom of movement had been relatively liberal, although by the end of the nineteenth century there

[123] Manela, *The Wilsonian Moment*.
[124] League of Nations Archives, R1717, 45/12542.
[125] Skran, *Refugees in Inter-War Europe*, p. 9.
[126] Refugees were placed under the protection of the League of Nations because of the withdrawal of protection by their state of origin. Only persons applying from outside their country of origin were eligible for refugee recognition. Put otherwise, the unprotected individual who remained within the boundaries of his country could not be included within the scope of the League's protection. See Hathaway, *Law of Refugee Status*, p. 4. See also Louise Holborn, "The legal status of political refugees (1920–1938)," *American Journal of International Law*, 32, 1938, pp. 680–703; and James Hathaway, "The evolution of refugee status in international law (1920–1950)," *International and Comparative Law Quarterly* 33, 1984, pp. 348–380.

was an increase in all forms of identity documents and a stronger distinction between the rights of nationals and foreigners—not to mention the stigmatization of specific groups considered "undesirable" outsiders.[127] The Great War dramatically changed this open atmosphere, and virtually every country introduced restrictive legislation, requiring passports and visas. Passports that were intended to facilitate the movement of people would soon become a means for governments to assert control over their own citizens and to protect their borders in a hostile world.[128] In a famous passage from *Die Welt von Gestern* [*The World of Yesterday*], which he began writing in 1934, the Austrian writer Stefan Zweig links these restrictions on the ability to circulate freely with the diminution of individual civil rights:

Before 1914 the earth had belonged to all. People went where they wished and stayed as long as they pleased. There were no permits, no visas, and it always gives me pleasure to astonish the young by telling them that before 1914 I traveled from Europe to India and to America without passport and without ever having seen one. One embarked and alighted without questioning or being questioned, one did not have to fill out a single one of the many papers which are required today. The frontiers which, with their customs officers, police and militia, have become wire barriers thanks to the pathological suspicion of everybody against everybody else, were nothing but symbolic lines which one crossed with as little thought as one crosses the Meridian of Greenwich.

With the outbreak of World War I, the entire way in which people perceived the world and foreigners changed:

The humiliations which once had been devised with criminals alone in mind now were imposed upon the traveler, before and during every journey. There had to be photographs from right to left, in profile and full face, one's hair had to be cropped sufficiently to make the ears visible; fingerprints were taken, at first only the thumb but later all ten fingers [. . .] If I reckon up the many forms I have filled out during these years, declarations on every trip, tax declarations, foreign exchange certificates, border passes, entrance permits, departure permits, registrations on coming and on going; the many hours I have spent in ante-rooms of consulates and officials, the many inspectors, friendly and unfriendly, bored and overworked, before whom I sat, the many examinations and interrogations at frontiers I have been through, then I feel keenly how much human dignity has

---

[127] John Torpey, *The Invention of the Passport. Surveillance, Citizenship and the State* (Cambridge University Press, 2000), Chapter 4.
[128] John Torpey, "The Great War and the birth of the modern passport system," in Jane Caplan and John Torpey (eds.), *Documenting Individual Identity: The Development of State Practices in the Modern World* (Princeton University Press, 2001), pp. 256–270.

been lost in this century which, in our youth, we had credulously dreamed of as one of freedom, as of the federation of the world.[129]

As early as 1914, the Aliens Restriction Act authorized the British government to impose restrictions on the arrival of aliens, prohibiting them from living in certain areas and limiting their movements within the United Kingdom.[130] Breaking with the liberal 1867 Prussian passport law, Germany enacted a new legislation for aliens entering the country from abroad on July 31, 1914. In mid 1916, everyone entering or leaving the territory of the German Empire required a visa. In France, identification cards became mandatory in April 1917 for all foreigners over the age of 15. The cards were to include "the bearer's nationality, his marital status, photograph, occupation and signature."[131] At stake were not simply the modern states' efforts to monopolize the movements of people, but also their control over individuals. The imposition of passport controls, first undertaken as a temporary measure, stemmed from a war-inspired xenophobia, including the fear of spies and of "the enemy within."[132]

In almost every European country, peace did not bring about a return to the policies of the pre-war period. Decrees in Italy (May 1919), Germany (June 1919), and Britain (1920) made permanent the "temporary restrictions" on movement. For instance, anyone entering or leaving Britain was required to have "either a valid passport furnished with a photograph of himself or some other document satisfactorily establishing his national status and identity."[133] Anyone crossing German borders likewise needed to have a passport with a visa, and any foreigner in German territory needed a passport. Governments now subjected aliens and citizens alike to what Gérard Noiriel has called the "identification revolution."[134] Several intergovernmental conferences were held under the patronage of the League of Nations, on the question of passports (Paris, 1920; Geneva, 1926), and on larger questions such as emigration and immigration (Geneva, 1921; Rome, 1924; Havana, 1928), but they only aimed to coordinate national policy, not to revisit on a fundamental

---

[129] Stefan Zweig, *The World of Yesterday* (New York: Viking Press, 1943), pp. 409–411.
[130] The 1905 law, that was largely directed at East European Jews, had already anticipated the end of the laissez-faire era in Great Britain.
[131] Gérard Noiriel, *Le creuset français. Histoire de l'immigration en France, XIXe–XXe siècles* (Paris: Seuil, 1988), p. 90.
[132] Noiriel, *La tyrannie du national*; Panikos Panayi, *The Enemy in Our Midst: Germans in Britain During the First World War* (Providence and Oxford: Berg, 1991), Chapter 2; Leo Lucassen, "The Great War and the origins of migration control in Western Europe and the United States (1880–1920)," in Anita Boecker (ed.), *Regulation of Migration: International Experiences* (Amsterdam: Het Spinhuis, 1998), pp. 45–72; Torpey, *Invention of the Passport*, pp. 111–117.
[133] Aliens Order 1920, March 25, 1920.   [134] Noiriel, *Le creuset français*, Chapter 2.

level the increasing control over foreigners that had begun during the Great War.[135]

In July 1922, Fridtjof Nansen convened the last in a long series of international conferences that resulted in the creation of a special certificate of identity for Russian refugees, the document that later became known simply as the "Nansen Passport." At first, most Russian emigrants' organizations were reluctant to accept the idea. Some even suggested that passports, issued before the Russian Revolution of 1917 or by non-Bolshevik Russian authorities, should be universally recognized, in order to facilitate the circulation of refugees.[136] But, in the long term, this proposition was clearly infeasible. In the end, sixteen countries (and forty in 1926) recognized the Nansen Passport, a document that enabled its holder to travel to the country where he or she would be more likely to find work and assistance. Securing a travel document was relatively easy since no real question of national sovereignty was involved. The guarantee of residence proved much more difficult to obtain. After all, the right to grant or deny admission, to determine "who is in" and "who is out" remained the prerogative of sovereign states.[137] Naturalization en masse of Russian refugees could have provided a solution. However, such

---

[135] Kévonian, *Réfugiés et diplomatie humanitaire*, pp. 233–234, 238–239.

[136] "Legal position of the Russian refugees." Memorandum by M. André Mandelstam, a member of the Institute of International Law, August 1921. League of Nations Archives, R1725, 45/14387.

[137] Initially, the forefathers of international law, inspired by the Church Fathers, supported the idea of a right to asylum that would be universally applicable to every state. Such a right, however, would be reserved for innocent victims, " . . . beaten down by the hard and oppressive strokes of ill fortune," in the words of Grotius, *De jure belli ac pacis*, Book II, Chapter XXI. "Nor ought a permanent residence to be refused to foreigners, who, driven from their own country, seek a place of refuge," he explains in Book II, Chapter II. The shift from a right to asylum to a definition of asylum as the state's prerogative occurred in the 1670s, it seems, with Samuel von Pufendorf, in *De jure naturae et gentium* [*On the Law of Nature and Nations*] (1672). In 1749, the philosopher Christian Wolff wrote: "Since by nature the right belongs to an exile to live anywhere in the world, moreover since it depends altogether on the will of the people, or on the will of the one who has the right of the people, whether or not he desires to receive an outsider into his state, an exile is allowed to ask admittance, but he cannot assuredly according to his liking determine domicile for himself, wherever he shall please, and if admittance is refused, that must be endured." *Jus gentium methodo scientifica pertractatum [The Law of Nations According to the Scientific Method]*, "Of Asking Admittance." In *Le Droit des Gens, ou, Principes de la loi naturelle [The Law of Nations or the Principles of Natural Law]* (1758), Emmerich de Vattel, for his part, judged that "A man, by being exiled or banished, does not forfeit the human character, nor consequently his right to dwell somewhere on earth. He derives this right from nature, or rather from its Author, who has destined the earth for the habitation of mankind" (Book I, Chapter XIX). Vattel also acknowledged a sovereign's right to maintain control over foreigners' entry into his territory: "The sovereign may forbid the entrance of his territory either to foreigners in general or in particular cases, or to certain persons or for certain particular purposes, according as he may think it advantageous to the state" (Book II, Chapter VII).

naturalization remained strictly limited.[138] Nationality was considered a privilege conferred on an individual basis. Moreover, most refugees had expressed strong feelings of national loyalty to their country of origin, and did not necessarily want to acquire another nationality.[139]

Almost at the same time, in the United States, a large segment of the public supported changes to immigration policies. Immigration to the country had risen from 24,627 in 1919 to 652,364 in 1921. In a context of increasing economic crisis and social instability, the support for a change in the open-door policy on immigration grew, alongside anti-immigrant sentiment. The American Legion called for barriers against immigration. At its 1919 convention, the American Federation of Labor proposed its total prohibition for 2 years. As a result, they strongly opposed any proposal to send Russian labor to the United States. In the words of one congressman, "the present bad condition of agriculture and the lack of demand for agricultural labor of any kind, even seasonal labor" were two of the main reasons. He added: "When to this was added ignorance of the language and the fact that the Russian refugees could not be expected to know anything of American methods of farming, there would be great difficulty in placing refugees on farms or in securing special legislation to admit any considerable number."[140]

The fear that immigrants might spread Bolshevism added to the fear that they might take the jobs of American workers. The culmination of the American anti-immigrant movement was the adoption of the first "national origins" quota system in the 1920s, which was primarily a means for regulating European immigration. Suggested as early as 1911 by Senator William P. Dillingham of Vermont, this system encouraged "the limitation of the number of each race arriving each year to a certain percentage of the average of that race arriving during a given period of years." The Quota Law of 1921 (based on the 1910 census) was signed by President Harding after President Wilson vetoed it during his final days in office. Initially designed as a temporary measure (but extended in 1922 and continuing in force until 1924), the law favored immigrants from Northern and Western Europe over those from Southern and Eastern Europe (limited to 155,000). This signaled a reversal in the previous

---

[138] For instance, the Greek refugees from Turkey, Russia, Bulgaria, and other countries who arrived in Greece between 1913 and 1922 under the Greek law of October 19, 1922 and the Convention of Lausanne of 1923, and Bulgarian refugees arriving in Bulgaria from Greece under the 1919 Convention. See Simpson, *Refugee Problem*, pp. 235–236.

[139] Paul Tabori, *The Anatomy of Exile* (London: Harrap, 1972).

[140] Congressman Sidney Anderson of Minnesota, quoted in ILO liaison report, July 4, 1922, International Red Cross Archives, CR87/SDN.

immigration trends: before World War I, immigration from Southern and Eastern Europe was more than four times as great as that from Northern and Western Europe. It also represented an end to what Albert Thomas, the French Director of the ILO, had once called "the era of the great displacements." European countries could not easily export their Russian refugees overseas.[141] In fact, during the early 1920s, France was the only European country encouraging immigration, owing to its heavy losses in World War I, low birthrates, and the resulting labor shortage.

The arrangement under which the Nansen Passport for Russian refugees was approved on July 5, 1922 restricted its validity to a period of 1 year (2 years in the case of Poland). Only the state issuing the certificate could renew it. The granting of the certificate did not confer the right of return to the country of issue, unless that right was expressly granted.[142] In other words, the Nansen Passport was inferior, in many ways, to a national passport. Moreover, despite the growing number of refugees in Europe and elsewhere, only Russian nationals could be issued a Nansen Passport. Italian political refugees who fled the Mussolini regime and were guilty of "abusive emigration" under fascist law, remained outside Nansen's protection scheme: for giving them a Nansen Passport would have meant criticizing a prominent member of the League of Nations.[143] It would also have required a new definition for the term "refugee"— based on the violation of political rights (as would be the case for the refugees fleeing Nazi Germany in the 1930s) rather than on national affiliation. The High Commissioner's mandate was progressively extended to include Armenians in 1924 and Assyrians and Assyro-Chaldeans in 1928.

The issues surrounding Armenian refugees dated to World War I.[144] In order to flee the massacres, pillaging, and deportations perpetrated by the Young Turks beginning in 1915, an exodus of tens of thousands of Armenians managed to escape abroad, following in the footsteps of their predecessors in the nineteenth century. Some settled in Syria; a minority

---

[141] William S. Bernard (ed.), *American Immigration Policy: A Reappraisal* (New York: Harper and Brothers, 1950), Chapter 2.

[142] The arrangement of May 12, 1926 provided a definition of Russian and Armenian refugees (the latter becoming beneficiaries of the Nansen Passport under the arrangement of May 31, 1924) and recommended the right to return to the country of issue.

[143] Marrus, *The Unwanted*, pp. 124–128. The turning point came only in August 1928 with the intergovernmental conference held in Geneva to improve the Nansen Passport, and the first refugee convention in 1933.

[144] The standard work on Armenian refugees is Kévonian, *Réfugiés et diplomatie humanitaire*. It provides an in-depth perspective on this important issue, which I examine here more from the perspective of the history of international law than from the history of humanitarianism.

settled in Egypt; most of them ended up in territory between the Black
Sea and the Caspian Sea, which was controlled by the Russians. During
the war, the Armenian population of the Russian Empire mobilized and
established a network to provide material assistance and moral support
to these refugees. The weakening and the subsequent fall of the Ottoman
Empire made it possible for an independent Armenian state to establish
itself, temporarily (May 1918–November 1920), until its territory was
shared among modern-day Turkey and the Soviet Union, as a result of
the Treaty of Moscow (March 1921). The failure of the dream of an
independent Armenia was compounded by an enormous humanitarian
catastrophe: the refugees ended up in an overpopulated country, ruined
by war, and they could not flee to the other trans-Caucasian republics
nor return to Turkey, for fear of massacres. Lacking any official support
from Western countries, with the exception of humanitarian aid provided
by private organizations from the United States,[145] such as Near East
Relief,[146] the refugees once again were on the road into exile. Some
went to the Soviet Union at the end of the 1920s, while others, around
110,000, went to Western Europe. France in particular welcomed the
largest number of Armenian refugees. The Nansen Passport granted to
them from 1924 made it easier for all Armenian refugees to travel and
settle in new countries.[147]

The Assyrians and Assyro-Chaldeans were another Christian minority
persecuted by the Ottoman Empire. Some fled to the Caucasus or to Iraq,
which was under a British mandate,[148] while others fled to Greece or
settled in Marseille—but without the hope of permanently settling there.
Compared with the Armenian refugees, they were smaller in number;
in 1928, the Nansen Passport was granted to this minority of about
19,000.

In sum, even if it clearly represents a turning point in the history of
international law, the Nansen Passport had its limits. Its creators deliberately adopted a collective definition of refugee status, not an individual

---

[145] Robert G. Koolakian, *Struggle for Justice: A Story of the American Committee for the Independence of Armenia, 1915–1920* (Wayne State University Press, 2008).

[146] James L. Barton, *Story of Near East Relief (1915–1930): An interpretation* (New York: Macmillan, 1930).

[147] Dzovinar Kévonian, "Les tribulations de la diplomatie humanitaire: la Société des Nations et les réfugiés arméniens," in Hans-Lukas Kieser (ed.), *Die armenische Frage und die Schweiz (1896–1923)* (Zürich: Chronos, 1999), pp. 279–310.

[148] The end of the British mandate and the beginning of Iraqi independence in 1930 gave rise to tensions between Assyrian Christians and Muslim Iraqis, and to a new movement of Assyrian refugees to Syria. The British authorities tried in vain to find a country in South America that would welcome the Assyrian minority. See League of Nations, *The Settlement of the Assyrians: A Work of Humanity and Appeasement* (Geneva, 1935).

one: a refugee was defined as any stateless person of Russian origin, and then Armenian origin as well, beginning in 1924, and Assyrian and Assyro-Chaldean in 1928. It was the fact of belonging to a group that allowed a person to obtain a Nansen Certificate, and not an inalienable right belonging to every human being. Second, the creators of the Nansen Certificate made no reference to the political or religious persecution of which certificate holders had been victims. They limited themselves to making a general allusion to the chaos that followed World War I, which avoided assigning blame to any one country but which also had the effect of denying or undervaluing the political dimension of these mass exoduses. Lastly, the document created in 1922 was a certificate of identity and a travel certificate, not a passport in the strict sense of the word, inasmuch as those who held a certificate were not allowed to return to the country issuing the certificate.

The creation of the Nansen Passport, though helpful, did not eliminate all of the administrative problems that the refugees were experiencing. As Sir John Hope Simpson admitted in the earliest modern study on refugees, "a mere formality in the case of a national is, in the case of a refugee, a matter of administrative discretion, which will not necessarily be exercised in his favour."[149] National governments tended to interpret the 1922 agreement in various ways.[150] For example, until the arrangement of June 30, 1928, Russian and Armenian refugees could be sent to an adjoining country, even if they could not be admitted legally. For refugees, the constant fear of being expelled was exacerbated by the memory of their previous journey and time spent in transmigrant centers all over Europe: "After disembarking from the packed trains, disinfection involved the separation of male and female passengers and consequent breaking up of families, the confiscation of all clothing and possessions, rubbing down with strange, slippery substances, and a shower... For those unfamiliar with modern medical routines, medical inspections could be terrifying, arousing fears of robbery and murder."[151] In the mid 1920s, an emigrant leaving Lvóv, Poland, had to undergo at least twelve successive medical visits: those required by the American consulate, by each of the maritime travel companies, by the

---

[149] Simpson, *Refugee Problem*, p. 265.
[150] For instance, in Germany, Nansen Passports were only granted to Russian refugees arriving before May 6, 1921.
[151] Paul Weindling, "A virulent strain: typhus, bacteriology and scientific racism" (unpublished paper, Social History of Medicine Conference, University of Southampton, September 18, 1996), pp. 6–7, in Tony Kushner and Katharine Knox, *Refugees in an Age of Genocide. Global, National and Local Perspectives during the Twentieth Century* (London and Portland, Oreg.: Frank Cass, 1999), p. 78.

British and Polish authorities, and by the United States public health service.[152]

Greek and Turkish refugees

By the end of 1922, a new refugee crisis, known simply as "the big catastrophe" (*Megali Katastrofi*) in Greece, broke out in the Balkans. The region had been continously at war since 1912. As a consequence, Bulgarians moved from Macedonia, Eastern Thrace, and Turkey to Bulgaria, Greeks from Macedonia, from Western and Eastern Thrace and from Turkey into Greece and, again, as the fortunes of war favored their army, back into Macedonia, Western and Eastern, and Anatolia.[153] At the end of the Great War, the Peace Treaty of Neuilly (November 27, 1919) resulted in the annexation of the province of Western Thrace, ceded to Greece by Bulgaria. The Treaty of Sèvres, signed between Turkey and the Allies in August 1920, gave Greece most of Eastern Thrace and a zone round Smyrna, populated by Greeks, Turks, and Armenians.

When Turkish nationalists led by Mustapha Kemal set up a provisional government in Ankara and demanded the revision of the Treaty of Sèvres, the Greek Army entered into the heart of Anatolia, with the blessing of the Allies. Greek Prime Minister Venizelos believed in the expansion of his country to embrace all the provinces of the old Byzantine Empire into a single Greek state. He would not give up until the Cross stood once more atop the dome of Hagia Sophia. Yet in October 1920, the Greek government was defeated in the general elections, an event soon followed by the return to Greece of ex-king Constantine, one of the most energetic opponents of Venizelos. In August 1921, the Turks triumphed over the Greek Army on the Sakarya River. One year later, they staged an offensive, forcing the invaders back to the sea and invading Smyrna.

Atrocities against civilians were committed on both sides, by the Greeks in their retreat and by the Turks in their conquest of the Anatolian coast. When the Turks finally entered the city of Smyrna on September 9, 1922, they burned it to the ground, starting with the city's Armenian quarter. Approximately 12,000 people perished in the flames. Mrs. Mills, the dean of an American college in the city, later reported: "I could plainly see the Turks carrying tins of petroleum into the houses, from which, in each instance, fire burst forth immediately afterward. There was not an Armenian in sight, the only persons visible being the Turkish

---

[152] Rosental, "Géopolitique et État-providence," p. 115, n. 42.
[153] Simpson, *Refugee Problem*, p. 13.

soldiers of the regular army, in smart uniforms."[154] In a letter sent to the Dominion Prime Ministers, Winston Churchill condemned what he called an "infernal orgy": "For a deliberately planned and methodically executed atrocity, Smyrna must . . . find few parallels in the history of human crime."[155]

These events swelled the number of refugees in Europe. "Filled with hereditary panic which had naturally been aggravated by the recent massacres at Smyrna and elsewhere, the refugees, contrary to the projected arrangements made for them, were arriving simultaneously with the retreating Greek army which they absolutely declined to lose from sight," a *Times* correspondent commented. "The result was what might have been expected . . . With very few exceptions, such as those persons who were either too poor or too old to travel, the entire Greek population had left by sea or had emigrated on foot across the Maritza. Whole villages had been left without a single remaining inhabitant, and it was possible to travel for miles on end without seeing a single human being."[156] Ernest Hemingway, reporting for the *Toronto Daily Star*, also described this exodus: "Twenty miles of carts drawn by cows, bullocks and muddy-flanked water buffalo, with exhausted, staggering men, women and children, blankets over their heads, walking blindingly along in the rain beside their wordly goods . . . It is a silent procession. Nobody even grunts. It is all they can do to keep moving."[157]

Only two or three days after the fall of Smyrna, the League of Nations placed a small emergency credit at Nansen's disposal. When he arrived in Constantinople, the High Commissioner for Refugees drove to the outskirts of the city and observed, from a hilltop, the continuous flow of civilians fleeing to Greece. "I thought I saw a whole city before me with its thousands of lights—it was their camps spread out over the plain, camp-fire by camp-fire, and there they were sleeping on the ground without shelter of any kind . . . They do not know where they are going and will find no shelter where they come."[158] Some of the refugees were fleeing to Salonica, others, "herded upon every kind of craft that could float," to the Greek islands. Many died during the journey. One 10-year-old boy who had fled to Salonica later remembered: "We starved. The boat stopped

---

[154] Quoted in George Horton, *The Blight of Asia* (New York, 1926), p. 145. See also the *New York Times*, September 27, 1922.
[155] Martin Gilbert, *Winston Churchill*, Vol. IV, Part 3, April 1921–November 1922 (London: Heinemann, 1977), p. 2070.
[156] Maxwell H.H. Macartney, *Five Years of European Chaos* (New York: E.P. Dutton, 1923), pp. 230–234.
[157] Ernest Hemingway, *Toronto Daily Star*, October 22, 1922.
[158] Quoted in Bruce Clark, *Twice a Stranger. How Mass Expulsion Forged Greece and Turkey* (London: Granta Books, 2006), p. 48.

in Cavala for water only. Older people and younger ones, about four or five of them, died. Their bodies were thrown into the sea."[159] Most refugees converged on Athens, transforming the capital city overnight. "The city had been almost somnolent before this irruption. It had been living the staid life of an orderly small capital where business had grown into established channels and where life had settled into an easy and familiar routine," wrote Henry Morgenthau, former American Ambassador in Constantinople and the head of the Greek Refugee Resettlement Commission. "Now the streets were thronged with new faces. Strange dialects of Greek assailed the ear. The eye was caught by outlandish peasant costumes from interior Asia Minor [...] At the base [of the Acropolis] sprung up a new Angora [*sic*], a new marketplace, packed with tiny shops displaying all the varieties of small merchandise that refugees could scrape together for sale."[160]

In his November 1922 report, the High Commissioner described the situation as potentially explosive:

The problem of the refugees in Greece is a most formidable one for the Greek Government. There are probably 800,000 or more, who have now arrived on Greek territory from Asia Minor and Eastern Thrace [...] 3,000 Armenians from the North Coast of Asia Minor arrived recently at Constantinople, panic-stricken, stating that all their males had been either killed or detained, and that they themselves had the choice either of leaving within a few days or of being deported to the interior. They furthermore expressed the fear that it was the intention of the Turks to expel or exterminate all the Christians in Asia Minor. Such an eventuality must be considered, and the consequent prospect of a further 300,000 Greeks and at least 100,000 Armenians being turned out of their country.[161]

Facing unprecedented chaos in the Balkans, Fridtjof Nansen, who had been awarded the Nobel Peace Prize in 1922, advocated a formal population exchange that would restore some kind of order (what Lord Curzon once called the "unmixing of populations") and permanently eliminate the source of ethnic tensions. On January 30, 1923, the resulting Lausanne Convention organized "a compulsory exchange of Turkish nationals of the Greek Orthodox religion settled in Turkish territory and of Greek nationals of the Muslim religion established in Greek territory." The purpose of the exchange was "to bring a final close to the state of war

---

[159] Quoted in Mark Mazower, *Salonica, City of Ghosts: Christians, Muslims and Jews, 1430–1950* (New York: Alfred A. Knopf, 2005), p. 335.

[160] Henry Morgenthau, Sr., *I Was Sent to Athens* (Garden City, NY: Doubleday, 1929), p. 50.

[161] League of Nations Archives, R1761, Report on the refugee situation in the Near East, November 17, 1922.

which has existed in the East since 1914." Religious affiliation provided the official test for nationality. Within a few months, after the Muslims left Greek territory for Turkey, most areas in Northern Greece were suddenly dominated by Greeks. Ironically, this process resembled what the Young Turks had planned in 1910 for the Muslim colonization of Macedonia. The "homogenization" of populations in both Greece and the emerging Turkish state was essentially legalized.

The decision to proceed with a forcible population exchange nonetheless encountered widespread resistance from jurists and delegates to the Lausanne Conference, who thought it was an inhumane, immoral, and baseless solution from a legal standpoint. The French legal scholar Georges Scelle was one of the strongest critics of this decision. In his famous *Précis de droit des gens* [*Précis of the Law of Nations*] published in 1932, he supported an alternative vision of international law, not based on relations among sovereign states but instead putting the individual at the center of things. Inspired by this humanist ideal, it is not surprising that he would condemn a decision that to him seemed like an extraordinary moral step backwards: "[The population exchange] constitutes a kind of extremism in the theory of nationality [. . .] a practice of transplantation and uprooting [that] seems to go so violently against human liberty, at least, when it is forced and obligatory. It is astonishing that this principle, even in weakened form, could meet with approval after the torment of 1914–18, except when we recall that every war brings with it unbelievable steps backward."[162]

This powerful passage, from one of Scelle's fundamental works—along with the entire school of thought it represents—makes it possible for us to see the full impact the shock of the Great War had on legal scholars in the 1920s. Paradoxically, even if historians have recently taken a strong interest in these theorists of international law, the way these men experienced World War I has been almost completely ignored. In my opinion, this is a sign of a disconnect between the history of international relations, which pioneered the study of international law, and the cultural history of the Great War. Born in Avranches in 1878, Scelle was a little older than René Cassin, who was born in 1887. Before the war, he was a professor of law at the University of Dijon. He was called up as a lieutenant in August 1914 and underwent his baptism by fire during the deadliest months of the war, at the end of summer 1914. He then served as a legal expert for the General Staff of the Eighth Army beginning in 1917.[163]

---

[162] Scelle, *Précis de droit des gens*, Vol. II, p. 174.
[163] Koskenniemi, *The Gentle Civilizer of Nations*, p. 327, n. 279.

There is no doubt that the Great War was one of the key elements in Scelle's thinking on international law. The experience of war fed his hopes for a better international protection of individual rights, which the nation-state was not capable of guaranteeing (and here Scelle is in agreement with Cassin when he condemns the "Leviathan State"; see Chapter 1). But moreover, Scelle claimed that the Great War modified the threshold for tolerating violence—hence his point that, over the long term, the forcible transfer of populations in 1923 was rendered banal by virtue of previous similar experiences, such as the deportation of various groups from Belgium, Northern France, the Balkans, and Eastern Europe, during the period 1914–18. As early as the 1930s, Scelle's scholarship had formalized the idea of civilization's regression in the aftermath of the Great War. Norbert Elias, although he fought on the eastern front in 1915 and during the First Battle of the Somme in September 1916, did not integrate this idea into his own analysis of the "civilizing process" until after World War II, some 20 years later.[164]

Though problematic in many regards and contrary to the minority rights supported by the League, the exchange of populations was considered by most diplomats to be the only realistic solution to the crisis. It would help Greece, destabilized by the arrival of hundreds of thousands of new inhabitants, to find room for the influx of refugees. It would also make it easier to offer compensation to people for the property they were leaving behind. Furthermore, the process seemed acceptable given the forcible relocation of other populations in the recent past, notably residents of Alsace-Lorraine who were found to have German blood in late 1918.[165] What position ought the League to take when it received daily protests against atrocities, which had been committed on both sides during the war? In a letter sent to Nansen in October 1922, a few weeks after the fall of Smyrna, Eric Drummond, the League's Secretary-General, rejected any official intervention: "Any connection of the League with massacres or atrocities which have occurred in the past may endanger or render more difficult firstly the protection of minorities in the Near East which may at any moment devolve on the League, and secondly, the humanitarian work of dealing with refugees and their possible repatriation with adequate guarantees at a future date [. . .] It seems to me that it would be a mistaken policy for the League to deal with atrocities and massacres at present at any rate [. . .] The refugee problem should

[164] Stéphane Audoin-Rouzeau, "Norbert Élias et l'expérience oubliée de la Première Guerre mondiale," *Vingtième Siècle. Revue d'histoire*, 106, April–June 2010, pp. 105–115. See also Stéphane Audoin-Rouzeau, *Combattre. Une anthropologie historique de la guerre moderne (XIXème–XXIème siècle)*, (Paris: Seuil, 2008), pp. 40–68.
[165] Zahra, "The minority problem," pp. 137–165.

not become involved with that of responsibilities for events which have already taken place."[166] This is a clear expression of the League's refusal to promote a defense of human rights based on the individual, inasmuch as an individual may have been the victim of atrocities, and inasmuch as that individual was a member of the human race. Conversely, the League defended human rights insofar as they were based on collective rights, acknowledged as such, and insofar as the individuals in question belonged to a minority group.

The change in the balance of military power and ongoing negotiations between Greece, Turkey, and the League led to a Peace Treaty signed in Lausanne on July 24, 1923, which revised the Treaty of Sèvres and redrew territorial boundaries. The mandatory character of the transfer differentiated it from the previous exchange of 100,000 refugees between Greece and Bulgaria that had followed the Treaty of Neuilly. The exact origin of this determination, based on the increasingly unpopular notion of "compulsory exchanges," however, remains contested.[167] The result was the largest population exchange of the post-World War I period, involving over 1.5 million people.[168] Displaced Greeks and Turks, however, were not considered "refugees" according to the new body of international law. Rather, they were called "emigrants," who had "lost the nationality of the country which they were leaving and acquired the nationality of the country of their destination, upon their arrival," according to Article 7 of the Lausanne Convention. Consequently, "it was not necessary to introduce international protection under refugee law as a replacement for state protection," except for those who found shelter in third countries such as the Greeks who had fled to Egypt.[169]

For the emigrants, housing was the first priority, particularly since they were not always welcome in already overcrowded cities. With a population of 5 million persons, Greece was expected to absorb more than a

---

[166] League of Nations Archives, Etienne Mantoux Papers, Box 154, File 7.

[167] C.G. Tenekidès, "Le statut des minorités et l'échange obligatoire des populations gréco-turques," *Revue générale de droit international public*, Vol. XXXI, 1924, pp. 72–88; S. Seferiadès, "L'échange des populations," *Recueil des cours*, Vol. XXIV, Paris, Académie de droit international, 1928, p. 373; C. Meindersma, "Population exchanges: international law and state practice," *International Journal of Refugee Law*, 9: 1, 1997, pp. 335–653.

[168] The exchange of populations between Greece and Turkey in 1923 foreshadowed other massive compulsory transfers of population in the twentieth century, notably the transfer of German populations after the Potsdam conference in the summer of 1945 and the exchange of Hindus, Muslims, and Sikhs after the New Delhi accords signed by India and Pakistan on April 8, 1950 (see A. de Zayas, "A historical survey of twentieth century expulsions," in A. Bramwell [ed.], *Refugees in the Age of Total War* [London: Unwin Hyman, 1988]).

[169] Michael Barutciski, "Lausanne revisited. Population exchanges in international law and policy," in Hirschon (ed.), *Crossing the Aegean*, pp. 23–38, 26.

million immigrants. The existing population of Old Greece considered the Mikrasiates (Asian Minor refugees) to be "Anatolian Christians" at best, and "Turkish-seeds" or "yogurt-baptized" at worst.[170] In Athens, Henry Morgenthau discovered a "refugee horde [. . .] huddled in tents pieced out of burlap bags, or in huts extemporized out of the ubiquitous 5-gallon Standard Oil cans.[171] "The movement of displaced persons led to the widespread use of refugee camps, where refugees were identified, segregated from the rest of the population, housed, and fed. White Army soldiers near Constantinople, Armenian refugees from Turkey in the Caucasus, Syria, and Lebanon, and later refugees from Greece, Turkey, and Bulgaria all faced similar situations.

The birth of refugee relief programs

The post-war period was characterized by the growing professionalization of refugee aid, including the first official census of the refugee population in 1922 (conducted by the High Commissioner for Refugees in conjunction with the ILO), the organization of major intergovernmental conferences on refugees, the introduction of doctors, nurses and social workers to refugee camps, and the emergence of the field of refugee studies from the 1920s onwards.[172] But the professionalization of refugee management had its limits. While many specialists in refugee studies have used the concept of "governmentality" coined by Michel Foucault to describe the workings of displaced persons camps after 1945,[173] this concept is not easily applied to the early 1920s. Refugee camps were seen largely by the League as temporary shelters for migrant populations and not as highly regulated spaces that could provide refugees with a degree of normalization. Moreover, the general climate that prevailed in the early 1920s was one of improvisation when facing a situation of crisis. The reports sent to Nansen by his representatives in Central Europe and the Balkans, preserved in the archives of the League of Nations in Geneva, illustrate the limits of the humanitarian policy and the day-to-day approach for most refugee issues. In Michael Marrus' words, the League's efforts at refugee protection were "like using bedroom sheets to block a hurricane."[174]

[170] Mazower, *Salonica*, p. 337.   [171] Morgenthau, *I Was Sent to Athens*, p. 50.
[172] Claudena Skran and Carla N. Daughtry, "The study of refugees before 'Refugee Studies,'" *Refugee Survey Quarterly*, 26: 3, 2007, pp. 15–35.
[173] Guglielmo Verdirame and Barbara Harrell-Bond (eds.), *Rights in Exile. Janus-Faced Humanitarianism* (New York: Berghahn Books, 2005); Randy Lippert, "Governing refugees: the relevance of governmentality to understanding the international refugee regime," in *Alternatives*, 24: 3, 1999, pp. 295–329.
[174] Marrus, *The Unwanted*, p. 52.

Private humanitarian organizations also played a pivotal role in the early 1920s. Recent studies on post-war refugees tend to emphasize the importance of Russian organizations in the field, as well as the role that Russian elites played in the definition of new rights for refugees.[175] But the refugee crisis of the early 1920s and the birth of a new international refugee regime reflected the fluidity in the relationships between the leading actors in humanitarian aid: the nation-states, the League of Nations (and its High Commission for Refugees), and the private voluntary organizations. As the humanitarian field reorganized itself after World War I, no single actor came to dominate another. It was only after World War II that the international community would play a dominant role in refugee aid, and this came at a high price: the development of heavily bureaucratized refugee relief programs.[176]

Because the High Commission for Russian Refugees lacked financial resources, its action in the field largely depended on the support of private welfare institutions, based primarily in France, Britain, and, interestingly enough, in the United States, a country that did not recognize the Nansen Passport.[177] In 1922, the League had only $38,000 available to provide food to refugees on the Greek islands, while the American Red Cross spent 2.6 million dollars on food and clothing alone.[178] The evacuation of tens of thousands of Russian refugees from Constantinople to other countries would have been impossible without the support of American organizations. The Save the Children Fund and the Near East Relief took an active part in relief work on behalf of Greek refugees in 1923. They organized so-called "Golden Rule dinners" in which American philanthropists dined, for one night, on simple food, consisting of rice pilaff and potatoes that the unfortunate children of the Near East were supposed to eat in their orphanages.[179] When the American Red Cross withdrew from Greece in the summer of 1923, its decision led to a humanitarian crisis, which put Nansen in a difficult position.

As early as 1921, Fridtjof Nansen knew that refugee relief should lead to development aid. In November 1922, he suggested that an international loan be raised for refugee settlement in Greece, a "pioneering venture in economic development... that was only rediscovered by United Nations agencies in the 1980s," in Claudena Skran's words.[180] In

---

[175] This is the case with Dzovinar Kévonian's works and Gousseff, *L'Exil russe*.
[176] Tony Waters, *Bureaucratizing the Good Samaritan. The Limitations of Humanitarian Relief Operations* (Boulder, Colo. : Westview Press, 2001).
[177] Kévonian, *Réfugiés et diplomatie humanitaire*.
[178] Skran, *Refugees in Inter-War Europe*, p. 159.
[179] League of Nations Archives, R1758, 45/23788.
[180] Skran, *Refugees in Inter-War Europe*, p. 286.

October, Colonel Procter, Nansen's representative in the Balkans, had established a pilot project in Western Thrace for 11,000 Greek refugees, making them self-supporting after the 1923 harvest.[181] The refugees in question, who arrived from Eastern Thrace, were in relatively good condition. They were able to carry with them at least some of their movable possessions including for the most part their cattle, wagons, clothing, and in some cases their agricultural implements. Refugees from Asia Minor, on the other hand, had left their homes in such haste that they had no possessions of any kind other than the light summer clothes that they wore. Moreover, they consisted principally of women and children and old men who, even if they were farmers for the most part, proved more difficult to settle. Most men between 15 and 55 years of age remained captives of the Turks.

Separated from homeland and deprived of any legal status, women and children suffered from homesickness. Schools, churches, monasteries, and private houses were requisitioned to shelter the refugees. Several observers described them as passive and discouraged, although it is impossible to know whether such observations derived from ignorance and prejudice. A process of resocialization started when the men were reunited with their families. Most refugees were able to find a sense of home in the kinship environment that came from belonging to a community of exiles. Houses belonging to Turks and Bulgarians who had left Greece were seized to house the refugees. In the southwestern part of Athens, refugees from Smyrna founded the town of Nea Smyrni, in memory of their city of origin. They would later undertake the construction of commemorative monuments in a Pontian-Greek style, dedicated to the "unforgettable" memory of the 1923 events.[182]

Besides allocating land (the Greek Government donated 500,000 hectares, largely in swampy, malaria-ridden parts of Macedonia and Thrace), their first priority was the creation of new village communities, headed by a *proedros* or village chief. It was seldom possible to re-establish the old communities, which had been decimated by the war or were scattered all over Greece. Each family received one allotment, but the financial question remained of fundamental importance. In August 1923, the Bank of England agreed to loan £100,000 to the Greek government on the condition that the Refugee Settlement Commission, headed by

---

[181] For a detailed account of the Greek settlement, see Macartney, *Refugees*, Chapter 4.
[182] These monuments were built from 1961 onwards, along with replicas of Anatolian monasteries in Macedonia. See Michel Bruneau and Kyriakos Papoulidis, "La mémoire des 'patries inoubliables.' La construction de monuments par les réfugiés d'Asie mineure en Grèce," *Vingtième siècle, revue d'histoire*, April–June 2003, pp. 35–57.

Henry Morgenthau, supervised the loans and the settlement operation. Seven years later, over 27,000 homes had been built, primarily in Athens, Piraeus, and Salonica, and almost 600,000 refugees had been placed on agricultural settlements. When combined with their traditional forms of handicraft, such as carpet weaving, they made a significant contribution to Greek agriculture and industry.

In 1924, Nansen recommended to the League that the ILO be entrusted with the task of combating the issue of jobless refugees, while the High Commission would take care of their legal status (see Chapter 2). For Nansen, the general question of unemployment in post-war Europe would play a key role in the successful circulation and redistribution of refugees. Between 1925 and 1929, the ILO refugee section offered loans to refugees to start small businesses or matched refugees looking for jobs with employers in foreign countries. Yet there was no widespread agreement that refugee aid should be institutionalized. In accepting to take over the Refugee Service, the governing body of the ILO insisted that the service undertaken be considered temporary. Moreover, no definition of what determined the status of Russian refugees existed until 1926; before that, no one had bothered to adopt any universal definition, "because it was assumed that only one group was being addressed and that in any case the problem would be solved before too long."[183]

Conclusion

The question of refugee rights represents one of the most important geopolitical issues of the post-war period. Because of their sheer number, refugees were seen as a threat to the stability of Western societies just barely beginning the process of recovering from the war. The ambiguous status of refugees, especially those who were stateless, illustrated the fragility of the international legal system, based as it was on the premise that an individual's rights and obligations were conferred by the country to which he belonged, and by his own attachment to a particular area or region. As a population on the move, refugees were in essence people without rights, but also without obligations, and therefore public authorities in Western European countries viewed them with a mix of compassion and worry. In 1922, the Nansen Passport, a travel and identity certificate, sought to reintegrate refugees back into the framework of international law.

Nonetheless, this document had its limitations. To begin with, it simply perpetuated a nation-state approach to the refugee question, since it

---

[183] Marrus, *The Unwanted*, p. 89.

was meant not for individuals (as would later be the case in the Universal Declaration of Human Rights in 1948) but for national groups. Such a classification can seem paradoxical: refugees were by definition women and men who had likely left their country under dramatic circumstances; yet when they obtained a Nansen Passport, they were identified with the state to which they had first belonged. The case of Armenian refugees, who received Nansen Passports in 1924, provides a good example; an Armenian, originally from territories that had belonged to the Russian Empire before 1914, was considered a "Russian refugee"; conversely, an Armenian from territories that had been part of the Ottoman Empire was considered an "Armenian refugee." "Refugees" were also defined collectively, not individually, at the intergovernmental conference of 1926.[184]

The individual did not factor into discussions of the refugee question until the 1930s. Since the Nansen Passport issued to German refugees from the Sarre (1935), political activists and German Jews (1936), and Austrian Jews (1938) retained the collective definition of the idea of "refugee," the refugee as an individual was not yet written into international law.[185] However, if we consider the way refugee aid was administered, the rise of the concept of political refugees certainly suggests that there was an approach to the question through individual cases. Such a concept was unknown in the 1920s but it became increasingly present in the 1930s. A good example of this is the "Political Refugee Certificate" provided by the legal services division of the *Ligue des Droits de l'Homme* in France, which made it possible for the holder to obtain a residency visa. This type of certificate was obtained on the basis of an individual dossier, created in both the host country and country of origin. In the same way, in the 1930s, when a refugee living in France was threatened with expulsion, the *Ligue des Droits de l'Homme* sought to persuade the French Interior Ministry, on a case-by-case basis, that such refugees would be in danger if they returned to their country of origin.[186] In addition to the individualization of refugees' status during this time, increasing numbers of refugees provided testimony about their situation, necessitated by the emerging category of "political refugee." For the 1920s, literary sources are often the only ones that provide us a sense of the experience of exile, and a partial one. With the Nansen Passport, refugees

---

184 Dzovinar Kévonian, "Représentations, enjeux politiques et codification juridique: les réfugiés des années vingt," *Relations internationales*, 101, Spring 2000, pp. 21–39, 26.
185 Skran, *Refugees in Inter-War Europe*, pp. 113–116, 194–223.
186 Dzovinar Kévonian, "Question des réfugiés, droits de l'homme: éléments d'une convergence pendant l'entre-deux-guerres," *Matériaux pour l'histoire de notre temps*, 72, 2003, pp. 40–49.

collectively gained rights, but their voices still remained for the most part unheard.[187]

Along with classification based on national origin, the 1920s also witnessed a pragmatic approach to the refugee question. The countries that acknowledged the Nansen Passport increased in number from sixteen in 1922 to forty in 1926; they were no doubt motivated by humanitarian ideals. They wanted to come to the aid of hundreds of thousands of people who had been forced into exile and deprived of any legal status in international law and, consequently, deprived of any rights. Nonetheless, host countries sought above all to prevent refugees from becoming too concentrated in border areas or on the outskirts of large cities like Constantinople and Athens, which would quickly lead to an increase in poverty levels. Conversely, the international agreement of July 1922 was supposed to make it easier for refugees to circulate freely and settle in areas in need of laborers. Characteristically, the Nansen Passport did not initially allow its holders to be readmitted to the country that had issued them the passport. The document was meant to facilitate a refugee's ability to settle in another country, which of course was contingent on that country's goodwill.

Such a technical approach made it difficult to see the refugee question as a political one: the League of Nations never called countries to account for the actions that had created refugees in the first place. No one thought to denounce the real causes of exile: political repression, religious persecution, and ethnic conflict. The League made every effort to assist refugees, all the while respecting the sovereignty of individual states; maintaining the fragile balance put in place by the peace treaties of 1919–20 depended on the League's respecting this sovereignty. In addition, in the 1920s, the refugee problem was thought to be a temporary one. No one at that time could foresee that it would become a permanent, global problem, as would be the case during the Cold War and the wars of de-colonization.[188]

In fact, for most people in the Nansen era, the refugee represented a jarring, anachronistic figure, since the peace treaties of 1919 had been

---

[187] In her now classic book, *Réfugiés et diplomatie humanitaire*, Kévonian notes; "These sources [documents from the French Mandate in Syria and Lebanon, 1918–1920] now make it possible to undertake a micro-history of population movements. Usually condemned to the margins of history, the refugee is often only understood in light of his exemplary fate or when he or she belongs to a cultural elite" (p. 23).

[188] When the High Commission for Refugees was founded in 1950, it was also given only a 3-year mandate. It was thought that the question of 40 million refugees in post-war Europe would be settled in the near future. In 2012, it was estimated that there were 15,200,000 refugees throughout the world, and 27,100,000 displaced persons—that is, those forced to flee from their homes but without crossing any borders.

negotiated with the view to carefully redrawing borders in the hope of homogenizing and stabilizing various territories. Faced with the refugee crisis of the 1920s, then, three options were possible: a repatriation policy, as in the case of Russian and Armenian refugees; a policy of forcible transfer, as in the case of Greece and Turkey in 1923; a policy of settling refugees in a territory designated for them—hence the ILO's particular interest in Latin America and in the exploratory committees it sent there. In all these cases, diplomats aspired to settle each refugee among their own people, on land designated for them. The traditional link between identity and territory was not questioned, even in the face of the chaos that drove hundreds of thousands of people on the road into exile. On the contrary, this line was reaffirmed as the only possible solution.

However, in the second half of the 1920s, the leaders of the League of Nations had to acknowledge that the policy of repatriating Russian refugees was a failure. For its part, the population exchange between Greece and Turkey created massive economic and humanitarian problems. Beginning in September 1924, the mandate to assist refugees with reintegration into the workforce was assigned to the ILO. From now on, the goal was less to find a territorial solution to the refugee question than to regulate an economic problem, which would become especially pressing during the 1929 crisis: the ILO advanced the necessary funds for transferring refugees to countries in need of laborers, and oversaw their settlement in these countries.[189]

The Nansen Passport should not be seen as more modern than it was, given its limited goals, and the refugee problem of the 1920s should not be seen as a global one, since this did not happen until the 1950s. In the same way that labor law did not gain a truly universal dimension until the Philadelphia Declaration—the "second birth," so to speak, of the ILO in 1944—the Nansen Passport did not have the same breadth or the same global aims as the 1951 Geneva Convention on the Status of Refugees. Yet, the interwar period was also marked by innovations that would have long-term implications for humanitarian policy—and this is a point that the historiography of human rights often tends to overlook.

The dramatic plight of Russian and Armenian refugees, as well as the measures adopted to protect minority groups after the Great War, inspired a certain number of legal scholars, including Georges Scelle, André Mandelstam, Boris Mirkine-Guetzévitch and Égidio Réale, to

---

[189] In 1922, Great Britain had also signed an Empire Settlement Act, which was supposed to facilitate refugee resettlement in the Dominions—for example, in Canada. See Stephen Constantine (ed.), *Emigrants and Empire: British Settlement in the Dominions between the Wars* (Manchester University Press, 1990).

reflect on reformulating international law. In their minds, the international law born out of the war should free itself of the particular interests of each state and make the international protection of the individual a "postulate of modern legal thinking."[190] For Égidio Réale and Bernard Lejuif, in their writings on statelessness, this evolution of refugees' legal status took place via an affirmation of the League of Nations' "moral protection," which would take the place of protection by a sovereign state, now called into question. For Georges Scelle and André Mandelstam, the rights of minorities would progressively be extended to include the rest of the world, not simply the signatories to the 1919–20 peace treaties. All of these legal minds, most of whom belonged to the Russian immigrant community in France, thought they were living in an intermediary period: to them, international law as it existed in the 1920s seemed to be a "law in transition."[191]

In October 1929, the members of the International Law Institute (ILI) met at Briarcliff Lodge in New York State's Hudson Valley, in order to draft a "declaration of international human rights," an important document that would sanction the "relative independence [of sovereign states], limited by the common goals of humanity." Insofar as refugee rights were concerned, Article 6 of this solemn declaration set forth that "no state will have the right to strip an individual of his nationality for reasons of sex, race, language, or religion."[192] Several months later, in March–April 1930, an international conference was organized in The Hague, under the auspices of the League and in order to further develop international law in three areas: nationality, maritime law, and the state's responsibilities towards foreigners. In accordance with the Hague agreements, each

---

[190] Égidio Réale, *Le régime des passeports et la Société des Nations* (Paris: A. Rousseau, 1930), p. xiii.

[191] For example, in his *Précis de droit des gens* (1932), p. 252, Scelle writes: "The system for protecting minority groups seems, due to its very inadequacies, to be a kind of transition law. A transition between the old practice of intervention and the inter-State procedure of guaranteeing freedoms; a transition between jurisdictional guarantees and diplomatic guarantees; between the system based on an individual judge's decision and that based on government protection; between the specialized functions of a supra-national community and the concurrent use of an inter-State system; finally, a transition between forced allegiance to the State and the right of people to exercise self-determination."

[192] In parallel to the work begun at the Institute of International Law in 1921 by the French jurist Albert Geouffre de Lapradelle and solidified by the declaration drafted at Briarcliff Lodge in October 1929, another international organization, the Academy for International Diplomacy, founded in 1926, supported the idea of an international convention on human rights. The jurist André Mandelstam played a key role in defending the global aspect of such human rights. See André Mandelstam, "La déclaration des droits internationaux de l'homme," *Revue de droit international*, 13, January–March 1930, pp. 59–78. See also Kévonian, "Exilés politiques."

state kept the prerogative of determining, in accordance with its own laws, who were its nationals, but other states were under no obligation to recognize these criteria for defining nationality, except insofar as they were "in agreement with international conventions, international custom, and generally recognized principles of law concerning nationality."[193] In other words, the state's sovereign authority on questions of nationality was increasingly circumscribed by international law and the interests of the individual, at least in theory, since the 1930s were also marked by increasingly serious violations of human rights and by situations where entire groups of people were stripped of their nationality.

The growing role of private refugee aid organizations was the other major change of the 1920s. In the same way that the International Labor Office established a unique collaboration between governments, workers, and employers, thus renewing what had been called "labor diplomacy," (see Chapter 2), the High Commission for Refugees, founded in 1921, established conditions for dialogue between diplomats, international civil servants from the League of Nations, and private humanitarian organizations (the forerunners of today's non-governmental organizations [NGOs]). Fridtjof Nansen played a personal role in forging connections between Geneva's diplomatic circles, experts in international law, and those working for aid organizations. The Norwegian diplomat had an acute political sense, which he put to good use when negotiating with the Soviets; he was also able to rely on legal thinkers of a White Russian background in order to define refugees' rights. He was quite familiar with the complicated workings of the League of Nations, and he was also a man with experience who did not hesitate to travel all over Europe.

---

[193] In an article published in 1930, the Salvadorean diplomat José Gustavo Guerrero, later the first president of the International Court of Justice from 1946–49, sheds an interesting light on the debates that occurred at the Hague conference (*Revue de droit international*, 14, April–June 1930, pp. 478–491). He first reminds his readers that this project of codifying international law dates back to a decision of the Assembly of the League of Nations in September 1924 to form a committee of experts assigned to make recommendations concerning revisions to international law, especially in three areas: nationality, territorial waters, and the State's responsibility for damage incurred against the person or property of foreigners residing in its territory. The main questions taken up by the first committee, chaired by the Greek legal thinker Nicolas Politis, were the struggle against statelessness and the limitation of dual nationality. The committee suggested that choosing to become the naturalized citizen of another country automatically meant the loss of prior citizenship (pp. 481–485). In addition, the committee on the responsibility of the State, chaired by the French legal scholar Jules Basdevant, developed an interesting argument based on the necessity of preserving both the sovereignty of the State and international standards based on international treaties, customary law, and what members of the commission called "general principles of law" (pp. 489–490). In his article, Guerrero nonetheless regretted that what he called "general principles of law" remained somewhat vaguely defined, and that it was not more clearly defined in relationship to "respect for man as an individual" (p. 490).

Indeed, Nansen's empirical approach to crisis management, along with his preference for getting things done via personal relationships instead of through the League of Nations' heavy bureaucracy, both call to mind Albert Thomas' leadership style at the International Labor Office. In both cases, the success of international organizations such as the ILO and the High Commission for Refugees was largely due to their founders' personalities: a dynamic reformist anchored in the experience of World War I, in Thomas' case; in Nansen's case, an iconoclast—both a diplomat and an adventurer. Nansen died in 1930, and Thomas passed away 2 years later. With their deaths, the management style of their respective organizations naturally changed. Post-war Europe had to come to grips with significant problems, such as the tension between the increasing numbers of refugees and the tendency of many countries to turn inward, and so, if it were to have any influence, the international ideal had to be lived out in the work and personality of these two men. Such was the strength as well as the limitation of these new international institutions, founded in the wake of the League of Nations.

4   The hungry and the sick: Herbert Hoover, the Russian famine, and the professionalization of humanitarian aid

"It was our privilege to forfend infinite suffering from these millions of people, to save millions of lives, and it was our opportunity to demonstrate America's ability to do it in a large, generous and efficient way, befitting our country."

Herbert Hoover, "America's obligations in Belgian relief."[1]

In the summer of 1921, news of one of the worst famines in Russian history began to reach Europe and the United States. For months the Volga valley—Russia's breadbasket—had not received a drop of rain.[2] The agricultural crisis spread progressively, extending into southern Ukraine, the Transcaucasus, and the Urals. Starvation threatened

---

[1] Address of Herbert C. Hoover, Chairman of the Commission for Relief in Belgium before the Chamber of Commerce of the State of New York, February 1, 1917.

[2] The Russian famine of 1921–23 and its dramatic consequences have long been neglected, especially when compared with the more extensive body of scholarship on the famine of 1932–33. The classic study on the latter is still Robert Conquest, *The Harvest of Sorrows: Soviet Collectivization and the Terror-Famine* (Oxford University Press, 1986). The first scholars to address the 1921–23 famine are Charles M. Edmondson, "The politics of hunger: the Soviet response to famine, 1921," *Soviet Studies*, 29: 4, 1977, pp. 506–18, and Roman Serbyn, "The famine of 1921–1923: a model for 1932–1933?" in Roman Serbyn and Bowdan Krawchenko, *Famine in Ukraine, 1932–1933* (Edmonton: Canadian Institute of Ukrainian Studies, University of Alberta, 1986). The traumatic event that was the 1921–23 famine has been discussed in only several paragraphs, at best, in general histories of the Russian Revolution and the Civil War. Beginning in the 1990s, several scholars began to study the famine's impact at the local level. However, Richard Pipes observed, "At the time of writing, there exists not one scholarly monograph on the 1921 famine." See also Richard Pipes, *Russia Under the Bolshevik Regime* (New York: Alfred A. Knopf, 1993), p. 410. The first demographic analyses of the famine were published several years later—for example, by Markus Wehner, in *Cahiers du monde russe*, 38: 1–2, 1997, pp. 223–241, and by Stephen G. Wheatcroft, in *Cahiers du monde russe*, 38: 4, 1997, pp. 525–557. For a synthesis of the demographic impact of the 1921–23 famine, see Serguei Adamets, *Guerre civile et famine en Russie: le pouvoir bolchevique et la population face à la catastrophe démographique, 1917–1923* (Paris: Institut d'études slaves, 2003), which has an extensive bibliography of works published in Russian. Harold H. Fisher's *The Famine in Soviet Russia, 1919–1923* (New York: Macmillan, 1927) was an official history of the ARA's work in Russia, and it offers a good account of American humanitarian aid. The standard work is Bertrand M. Patenaude, *The Big Show in Bololand: The American Relief Expedition to Soviet Russia in the Famine of 1921* (Stanford University Press, 2002).

more than 25 million people. In the villages, the oldest inhabitants remembered the famine of 1891–92, which had caused some 375,000 to 400,000 deaths. Many thought that this time the situation was worse. "An unprecedented calamity, such perhaps as we have not seen since the days of Czar Alexis," lamented the writer Vladimir Korolenko, aged 68, referring to the great agrarian crises of the mid seventeenth century.

Weakened by the years of civil war from which it had only just emerged, Russia was also isolated from the world by a wall of hostility and suspicion. The political risks of a severe humanitarian crisis were clear to Russian authorities. The greatest threat was that trouble in the countryside would be compounded by urban famine riots, triggered by the influx of refugees. The Soviet regime's survival was at stake.[3] Along with this initial risk of escalating urban and rural rioting, there was also the fear that internal enemies would use the situation to their advantage, or that foreign armies would use it as a new opportunity to destabilize the regime. In his message "To all honest people," published with Lenin's approval on July 13, 1921, the writer Maxim Gorky did not hesitate to attribute partial responsibility for the situation to Western powers: "If humanitarian ideas and feelings—faith in whose social import was so shaken by the damnable war and its victors' unmercifulness toward the vanquished—if faith in the creative force of these ideas and feelings, I say, must and can be restored, Russia's misfortune offers humanitarians a splendid opportunity to demonstrate the vitality of humanitarianism."[4]

---

[3] At the Tenth Congress of the Russian Communist Party in March 1921, Lenin was aware of how risky an agricultural and humanitarian crisis might prove for the regime: "If there is a crop failure, it will be impossible to appropriate any surplus because there will be no surplus. Food will have to be taken out of the mouths of the peasants. If there is a harvest, then everybody will hunger a little, and the government will be saved; otherwise, since we cannot take anything from people who do not have the means of satisfying their own hunger, the government will perish." Vladimir Ilyich Lenin, "Doklad o zamene razvyorstki naturalnym nalogom," March 15, 1921, *Polnoe sobranie sochineny*, 43, p. 71, quoted in Weissman, *Herbert Hoover*, p. 2.

[4] *American Relief Administration Bulletin*, Series 2, No. 16, September 1, 1921, p. 2. During a trip to Los Angeles in September 1959, Nikita Khrushchev used more or less the same theme in a speech: "We remember [the help given by the ARA] and we thank you. I consider it necessary to add, however, one "but." And this "but" consists of the fact that our people remember not only that America helped us through the ARA, and that, thanks to them, thousands of people were rescued from famine on the Volga; they also remember that, in the difficult time after the October Revolution, American soldiers under the leadership of their generals landed on Soviet soil in order to help the White Guards in their struggle against the Soviet system . . . If you and your Allies had not landed their armies, we would have finished off the White Guards immediately, and we would not have had a civil war, we would not have had destruction, we would not have been starving. And it would not have been necessary, therefore, for you to help the Soviet people through the ARA." Speech at Twentieth-Century Fox Studios, Los Angeles, Calif., September 19, 1959. Quoted in Weissman, *Herbert Hoover*, p. 190.

But who could bear the burden of the humanitarian sentiment to which Gorky appealed? In early August 1921, responding to pleas from the Committee of Zemstvos and Cities, the International Committee of the Red Cross and the League of Red Cross Societies proposed the creation of an international committee—under its authority—to oversee the aid that would be provided by governments and charitable associations: this was how the International Committee for Assistance to Russia was formed.[5] The entire history of the Red Cross had destined it for this role. After caring for the wounded on the battlefield and establishing a policy of aiding victims of war, the Red Cross' scope of operations gradually extended to include victims of natural disasters—at a time when countries rarely became involved in such circumstances outside their own borders.[6] In 1873–74, in 1891–92, and again in 1906 and 1911, the Russian Red Cross had intervened to assist famine victims. In 1905–06, it participated in the fight against a cholera epidemic that had begun in India and quickly spread to Southeast Asia and Russia. World War I and the immediate post-war period had increased the international importance of the Red Cross, which had provided aid to civilians living in occupied areas, distributed packages to prisoners of war and then repatriated those prisoners, and collected information on those killed in combat.[7]

Besides gaining international legitimacy from these experiences, the Red Cross had acquired the expertise necessary for the organization and deployment of aid on a massive scale. In the case of Russia in 1921–23, the gravity of the situation was further complicated by the problem of transporting foodstuffs. "The state of the Russian rail system is deplorable," a Red Cross report observed. "The tracks went practically

---

[5] Charline Dekens, "Refaire de ces abandonnés des hommes: le comité international de secours à la Russie et la famine de 1921–1922," MA thesis, University of Geneva, Faculty of Letters, 2002.

[6] The Red Cross, as a movement, comprised three distinct organizations in the 1920s: the national Red Cross Societies, known as the Red Crescent in Muslim countries; the International Federation of the Red Cross and Red Crescent Societies, also called the "League of Red Cross Societies" or LRCS; the International Committee of the Red Cross, seen as the leadership element of the Red Cross movement, even if its hierarchical relationship to the LRCS was not clearly defined until the end of the 1920s. For a good synthesis of the history of the Red Cross, see John F. Hutchinson, *Champions of Charity: War and the Rise of the Red Cross* (Boulder, Colo: Westview Press, 1996).

[7] On the redefinition of humanitarianism during World War I, see Annette Becker, *Oubliés de la Grande Guerre*. As recognition for its humanitarian work during the war, the ICRC was awarded the Nobel Peace Prize in 1917. In 1919, Article 25 of the Covenant of the League of Nations recognized the Red Cross' preeminent role: "The Members of the League agree to encourage and promote the establishment and co-operation of duly authorized voluntary national Red Cross organisations having as purposes the improvement of health, the prevention of disease and the mitigation of suffering throughout the world." League of Nations: The Covenant of the League of Nations, 1920.

without repairs during the years of the Civil War, which, on the contrary, largely contributed to their degradation."[8] Putting the Red Cross in charge of responding to the 1921 famine had another advantage. It allowed countries that did not recognize the Bolshevik government—in other words, almost all Western governments at the time—to provide aid while bypassing traditional diplomatic channels. The humanitarian effort needed to be led by a man of demonstrated competence, who was at once respected by Western embassies, well known to donors, and acceptable to the Russian government. The International Committee of the Red Cross (ICRC) therefore decided to call on the services of Fridtjof Nansen (see Chapter 3). During the last 2 years, the Norwegian diplomat had successfully overseen the repatriation of Russian, German, and Austrian prisoners of war. He had already proved himself capable of organizing large-scale operations, since he had mobilized thousands of trains in order to carry prisoners from one end of Europe to the other. He was familiar with the inner workings of Russian diplomacy, and he had an extensive network of local contacts. Moreover, he was on good terms with private humanitarian organizations, and he hoped to convince European countries to provide Russia with the necessary credit to buy grain.

In reality, no country other than Norway would agree to lend money. The Bolshevik threat was deemed too strong. Anti-Communism was a powerful feeling dominating post-war public opinion.[9] In an appeal published in September 1921, the representatives of the Second International expressed their indignation on this score:

The obligation rests with the national trade union centres to exercise the strongest pressure on their governments for unhesitating action to assist the Russian people. But that alone is not sufficient. The Russian people reckon upon the spirit of brotherhood and generosity of the workers of all lands. Give freely, give the last penny you can spare to the authorised trade union collecting centres. Comrades, fight for a real international brotherhood! Down with reaction and militarism! Help the Russian people![10]

[8] Archives of the ICRC, Geneva, Commixt II.5, 1921, "Secours à la Russie" [Aid to Russia].
[9] The European press, especially in France and Great Britain, vigorously opposed aid to Russia, fearing that the money and food collected would be used by the Bolshevik regime to its advantage. In Norway, the conservative daily paper *Aftenposten* launched a fundraising campaign to help needy Norwegian fishermen, to illustrate that priority should be given to Norwegians rather than to Russian peasants. See Carl Emil Vogt, "'Først vore egne!' Da Aftenposten saboterte Nansens nødhjelp til Russland" ["'Our own people first!' How the *Aftenposten* newspaper sabotaged Nansen's charity to Russia]," *Historisk Tidsskrift*, 87: 1, 2008.
[10] ABIT, Geneva, R301/13, Starvation in Russia, Second International, Amsterdam, September 26, 1921. The Second International demanded that European socialist

The International Committee for Russian Relief (ICRR), Nansen's organization, thus had to make do with private financing and with negotiating on a day-to-day basis with Soviet authorities, who shared oversight for logistical operations. The lack of funds, the absence of political support from the West, the suspicions of Russian authorities, and the tensions between various private humanitarian organizations (Save the Children, the American Friends Service Committee [i.e., the Quakers], etc.) made Nansen's job especially difficult. The supplies of medicine and food available to him were in the end rather limited. In spite of efficient joint coordination between the Geneva bureau, run by Edouard August Frick, and the Moscow bureau, run by the Englishman John Gorvin, the ICRR's work tended to get bogged down in bureaucracy. The ICRR was responsible for only 10 percent of the provisions delivered to Russia from abroad.

The other 90 percent of humanitarian aid was provided by a much more powerful organization, established in the United States in 1919: the American Relief Administration (ARA). Herbert Hoover had distinguished himself at the head of the ARA for his handling of food aid to occupied Belgium in 1914–18, and later in the immense rebuilding and stabilization effort that Americans set in place in Western Europe following the Great War. He knew Russia reasonably well, having traveled there in 1908–10 in connection with his business interests in the mining sector.[11] Unlike Nansen's ICRR, which depended solely on private groups for its funds, the ARA had funding allocated by the United States Congress, and it coordinated both public and private relief efforts. It had enormous reserves of provisions stockpiled in North America and Europe. Its logistical infrastructure on the ground was considerable. Nansen, however, had to structure the bases of his humanitarian work from the ground up, even though he benefited from the know-how of the Red Cross along with private groups. He was a diplomat and an adventurer; Hoover was a businessman.

In Riga, on August 20, 1921, the head of the ARA's European division, Walter Lyman Brown, was the first to sign an agreement with the Soviet authorities.[12] The food, clothing, and medicine brought by the

---

papers regularly use slogans such as "Every helper of the Russian people is a supporter of the world-wide working class unity," or "Every sacrifice made to assist the starving Russian workers is a move for Labour's emancipation," or "The workers are pioneers of humanitarianism throughout the world."

[11] On Hoover's work in Russia before the war, see David Burner, *Herbert Hoover: A Public Life* (New York: Alfred A. Knopf, 1979), pp. 55–57.

[12] The agreement signed by Maxim Litvinoff and Walter Lyman Brown is reprinted in Surface and Bland (eds.), *American Food*, pp. 926–927.

Americans would remain the ARA's property (article 8). They would be distributed exclusively to children and to the sick, "without regard to race, religion, or social or political status" (article 24). The costs of storing and distributing aid within the country would be borne by the Russians (article 13). On the other hand, the ARA's representatives agreed not to carry out any political or trade activity on Russian territory (article 25). An agreement between Nansen and Georgy Chicherin, the People's Commissar for Foreign Affairs, was signed a week later, on August 27; it allowed the Russian authorities much stricter control over the transport and distribution of aid.

In any event, the ICRC and the ARA had different goals. As far as aid distributed under the sponsorship of the Red Cross was concerned, Nansen seemed to be motivated by the humanitarian idealism characteristic of his work in the wake of the Great War.[13] "The peoples of the world are learning hard things: they are learning through the League of Nations to curb the dogs of war. They are learning through your great liberal organization to co-operate in fighting social injustice and wrongs," he explained in a speech to the ILO. "Let them show that they can act together, before it is too late, to prevent the most terrible of the tragedies that have followed in the train of war."[14] For Nansen, the humanitarian operation in Russia was meant to help the Russians as human beings, not as Bolsheviks.[15] Although his detractors saw him as providing significant assistance to the Communist regime, he refused to consider such an argument: "I do not think it will strengthen the Soviet Government if we show the Russians that charity still exists in Europe. But even if it did, is there any man who dares to say that it is better to let 20 million people starve to death than to strengthen the Soviet regime?"[16]

Hoover's motivations were much more ambiguous. On the one hand, humanitarian discourse made it possible to legitimize intervention in Russia. In a letter to George Haskell, the ARA's director of Russian operations, Hoover stressed that "the service that we are able to perform must be given in a true spirit of charity. There must be no discrimination

---

[13] Vogt, *Fridtjof Nansen.*
[14] ABIT, CAT/7–523, ILO conference, third session, Geneva, November 12, 1921.
[15] In September 1921, the International Union of the Save the Children Fund presented the debates over the moral issues surrounding aid to Russia as follows: "It is clear that aiding the cause of the starving amounts to indirectly helping the current regime in Russia. Given the Soviet government's admirable capabilities where propaganda is concerned, we cannot deny that it will use for its benefit the immense prestige that comes with foreign aid. Yet we believe that the question of helping the innocent victims of hunger should be separated completely from the actions of those who govern them." (ABIT, R 301/5, Starvation in Russia).
[16] National Library, Oslo, Ms. Fol. 1988 N6.

as to politics, race or creed. Charity can take no interest in international politics, and any individual who does not so conceive his work should immediately be withdrawn upon your initiative."[17] On the other hand, Hoover, a conservative man, did not conceal his desire to destabilize the Soviet regime by using food as a weapon against Communism. For him as for most Western leaders at the time, Bolshevism was a disease bred by poverty. Fighting Communism and hunger stemmed from the same humanitarian impulse. By bringing food and supplies to areas hard hit by famine, Hoover hoped to demonstrate both the negligence of Communist authorities and the generosity of American capitalists—all while creating markets for American products in the years to come.

It is thus not surprising that Soviet authorities tried to play the two humanitarian organizations against each other, in order to maintain some control over the situation. After World War I, the Soviets were favorably disposed towards Nansen. In a letter to Lenin in June of 1920, after the repatriation of prisoners of war, Chicherin wrote:

You no doubt recall that Nansen was always one of the most outstanding representatives of the leftist intelligentsia which insisted on reconciliation with Soviet Russia. The role of such radical intellectuals is, of course, somewhat complicated, and the Entente governments at one time tried to entangle and exploit Nansen for their own purposes. Litvinov rightly notes that if we manage to take Nansen into our hands, he could prove highly useful to us. His renown in the leftist bourgeois world and his major role would make close contact with him highly valuable for us politically. Litvinov correctly notes that the main thing that has to be watched is that no pernicious escorts accompany Nansen. Nansen alone can be very useful, but the escorts attached to him could be extremely harmful.[18]

Hoover's visceral anti-Communism, however, was well known. After all, American socialists had called him "the most obstinate anti-Bolshevik [in the Harding administration],"[19] because he had opposed re-establishing diplomatic and trade relations between the United States and Soviet Russia in 1921.[20] But it was he, much more than Nansen, who had

---

[17] Hoover Institution Archives, Stanford University, ARA, Russian Operations, 1919–25, Box 19, Folder 6.

[18] Chicherin to Lenin, June 23, 1920, quoted in Richard Pipes (ed.), *The Unknown Lenin: From the Secret Archives* (New Haven: Yale University Press, 1996), p. 84.

[19] *The New Statesman*, May 20, 1921, p. 3, quoted in Robert W. McElroy, *Morality and American Foreign Policy* (Princeton University Press, 1992), p. 67.

[20] Following the October Revolution, the United States, along with many other Western countries, refused to recognize the Bolshevik regime or to maintain trade relations with it. See Frederick Schuman, *American Policy Toward Russia Since 1917* (New York, 1928). There are several explanations for this attitude: the threat of a worldwide revolution fomented by Russian communists, the refusal of the new regime to recognize the debts incurred under the czarist regime, and the confiscation of all foreign property and goods in the former Russian Empire. In a 1919 letter to President Wilson, Hoover supported

the financial and material means to come to Russia's assistance. Lenin had no other choice than to accept the ARA's work in Russian territory, albeit under the surveillance of the Bolshevik authorities, as defined by the terms of the Riga Accords.

"Death was now more in evidence than life"

The dramatic reports from travelers, the extent of the black-shaded zones on maps of Russia, the photographs of children with their bellies swollen by hunger—all these made the Russian famine a striking event. Furthermore, those familiar with Russia's history knew that for the past three centuries, cycles of famine had succeeded one another almost nonstop. Despite its reputation as a major grain exporter, Russia conceivably had the lowest agricultural productivity in all of Europe on the eve of the Great War. The beginning of the war further increased the threat of famine. Eighteen million Russian men, most of them peasants, were mobilized during the conflict; 2 million horses were requisitioned. The peasants who had not been mobilized could no longer obtain manufactured goods, and their deliveries of agricultural products to the cities slowed. Beginning in 1916, Moscow and Petrograd endured periods of famine.

The question of hunger therefore lay at the heart of the Russian Revolution. The Petrograd authorities' decision to institute ration cards brought on a series of bread riots that sparked the Revolution of February 1917.

a policy of complete firmness with regard to Russia: "We cannot even remotely recognize this murderous tyranny without stimulating activist radicalism in every country in Europe and without transgressing . . . every national ideal of our own." But he quickly added, alluding to Nansen, "Some Neutral of international reputation for probity and ability should be allowed to create a second Belgian Relief Commission for Russia. He should ask the Northern Neutrals, who are especially interested both politically and financially in the restoration of better conditions in Russia, to give to him diplomatic, financial and transportation support." Quoted in Benson Greyson, *The American Image of Russia: 1917–1977* (New York: Frederick Praeger, 1978), p. 47. On August 10, 1920, Bainbridge Colby, the US Secretary of State, confirmed this foreign policy stance in a letter to the Italian ambassador: "The existing regime is based upon the negation of every principle of honor and good faith and every usage and convention underlying the whole structure of international law—the negation, in short, of every principle upon which it is possible to base harmonious and trustful relations, whether of nations or individuals [. . .] In the view of this government, there cannot be any common ground upon which it can stand with a power whose conceptions of international relations are so entirely alien to its own, so utterly repugnant to its moral sense. There can be no mutual confidence or trust, no respect even, if pledges are to be given and agreements made with a cynical repudiation of their obligations already in the mind of one of the parties." Quoted in Xenia Joukoff Eudin and Harold H. Fisher, *Soviet Russia and the West, 1920–1927: A Documentary Survey* (Stanford University Press, 1957), pp. 66–69.

The provisional government was forced to set up a state monopoly on grain commerce, but with the decree of May 13, 1918 the Bolshevik government took the decisive step of establishing a far-reaching government monopoly on food distribution, often considered the cornerstone of "War Communism." Committees of poor peasants were put in charge of requisitioning agricultural surpluses from well-off peasants. Military food brigades or *voenprodotriady*, composed of militant Bolsheviks, workers, and demobilized soldiers—nearly 300,000 men in 1920—enforced the new order. In speeches, Lenin initiated a "crusade" for bread, calling for a "merciless and terroristic struggle and war against peasants and other bourgeois concealing grain surpluses."[21]

At the local level, this class warfare against *kulaks* or rich peasants and merchants led to an outbreak of violence that left lasting traces in Russian society.[22] Villagers who dared to resist the requisitions (*prodrazverstka*) were beaten and threatened with death. The military food brigades took families hostage, imposed heavy fines, searched houses, and did not hesitate to burn the villages of those who might try to hide part of the harvest. The Red Army sometimes participated in these operations, using their weapons.[23] Initially, the requisitions only affected grains and animal feed. But following the introduction of new directives in January 1919, fruits, vegetables, meat, eggs, and milk were requisitioned. Occasionally, peasants' horses were taken for the army, which proved catastrophic for them. A decree punished by death all who opposed such measures.

The Bolsheviks' stated objectives throughout these operations were the provisioning of workers and the war against *kulaks*, who were portrayed as hoarders. But in a completely disorganized internal market, the redistribution of foodstuffs was chaotic. Without the trains necessary to transport it, the wheat extorted from peasants was left piled on station platforms, rotting in its bags. Their food supply was so precarious that city dwellers took to the roads by the thousands with a few goods, hoping to barter with villagers for food. "All kinds of people, belonging to different classes of society, took part in these expeditions, all professions and all ages, men, women, children: cabman and composer of music, journeyman and university professor, old [seamstresses] and schoolboys—all

---

[21] Vladimir Ilyich Lenin, *Polnoe sobranie sochineny*, 36, pp. 395–418, quoted in Patenaude, *Big Show in Bololand*, p. 20.

[22] Richard Pipes, *The Russian Revolution* (New York: Knopf, 1990), Chapter 16: "War on the village."

[23] On the work of the food brigades in the southern Volga region, see Orlando Figes, *Peasant Russia, Civil War: The Volga Countryside in Revolution* (Oxford: Clarendon Press, 1989), pp. 262–267.

formerly decent people now mix in one crowd of hungry, ragged beggars," reported Western observers.[24]

At the same time, the countryside rose up in resistance to the requisitions. Passive resistance often consisted of hiding part of the harvest or making under-the-table payments to local Communist Party officials. But also, inevitably, active and violent resistance broke out, a measure of the villagers' despair as they faced the threat of hunger.[25] On March 4, 1919, a food brigade was greeted by the sound of church bells in the little village of Novodevichy, on the banks of the Volga. The villagers came out of their houses and attacked the head of the local Bolshevik military and security apparatus or *Cheka*, who was leading the troops. There was a terrible fight. The *Cheka* man was tortured and his body thrown into the icy waters of the nearby river.[26]

These "peasant wars" unleashed demons on both sides: the Communists against the "hoarders" and "enemies of the people"; the villagers against all symbols of collectivization. These violent acts spoke to the deterioration of social relations between peasants and the representatives of state power. "In Tambov province," Gorky reported, "Communists were nailed with railway spikes by their left hand and left foot to trees a meter above the soil, and [the peasants] watched the torments of these deliberately oddly-crucified people."[27] The tortured bodies signaled the peasantry's willingness to attack the enemy's humanity (genitals, eyes, and ears ripped off), or to symbolically designate him as a pillager of foodstuffs (belly torn open and filled with wheat), or to impose a Christian identity upon him (the symbol of the cross branded onto palms and chests with a hot iron).[28]

For the duration of the Civil War, the fight against the state requisitions of food surpluses compounded the opposition to forced conscription, to the arbitrariness of local Communist Party potentates, and to the introduction of collective farms. Beginning in 1920, the revolts, fueled by the specter of famine, focused above all on the question of grain. Many

---

[24] Hoover Institution Archives, Stanford University, ARA, Russian Operations, 1919–25, Box 19, Folder 6.

[25] For a theoretical introduction to forms of resistance in peasant societies, see James C. Scott, *Weapons of the Weak: Everyday Forms of Peasant Resistance* (New Haven: Yale University Press, 1985).

[26] Taisia Osipova, "Peasant rebellions: origins, scope, dynamics, and consequences," in Vladimir N. Brovkin (ed.), *The Bolsheviks in Russian Society* (New Haven: Yale University Press, 1997), p. 164.

[27] Maxim Gorky, "On the Russian peasantry," in Robert E.F. Smith (ed.), *The Russian Peasant, 1920 and 1984* (London, 1977), pp. 16–18.

[28] Orlando Figes, *A People's Tragedy: The Russian Revolution, 1891–1924* (London: Jonathan Cape, 1996), p. 757.

Russian peasants had received their land from the Bolsheviks through the decree of October 26, 1917. Now, the Communists were stealing the products of peasant labor. "We demand the return of the Bolsheviks," the peasants declared, not realizing that the thieves and benefactors were one and the same.

In the village of Kamenka, in the Tambov province, southeast of Moscow, a troop of local Communists arrived in August 1920 to proceed with requisitions.[29] The local peasants were rumored to be rich, and the Communists demanded that they immediately deliver almost all of their harvest, which was in fact mediocre because of weather conditions that spring. Villagers and members of the food brigade exchanged insults. Then the peasants seized their pitchforks and killed several tax collectors. While the rest of the brigade fled, the villagers armed themselves and waited for the brigade's reinforcements to come from Tambov. In a few weeks, the entire region rose up against the Bolsheviks and conducted a kind of guerrilla warfare for which it was ill prepared. The rebels were "scarcely vulnerable, extraordinarily invisible, and so to speak ubiquitous," worried Antonov-Ovseenko, the Bolshevik leader in charge of the repression. The special forces of the *Cheka* crushed these "peasant wars" with brutality; its ranks swelled from 1,000 men in April 1918 to more than 250,000 by the spring of 1921. Cases of extreme violence multiplied: massacres of civilians, bombings of villages, use of gas warfare against insurgent peasants. These examples illustrate the use on the domestic front of practices learned in the Great War and the radicalization of the perception of an enemy within.[30]

Lacking the means to forcibly resist the requisition of their crops by the state, some rural communities made the decision to reduce their cultivated acreage, to limit agricultural surpluses as much as possible and produce only what was strictly necessary for their own survival. In the European portion of the Soviet Union, land cultivated in 1920 was only 70 percent of the pre-war acreage. In Ukraine, 80 percent of the pre-war acreage was put to plow. But this was a hazardous strategy. The Bolshevik authorities did not hesitate to draw from the villages' subsistence stores, an act that immediately condemned the residents to famine.

In the fall of 1920, local authorities in several regions began to send alarming reports to Moscow, indicating the impact of the requisitions.

[29] Delano Dugarm, "Peasant wars in Tambov Province," in Vladimir N. Brovkin (ed.), *The Bolsheviks in Russian Society: The Revolution and the Civil Wars* (New Haven: Yale University Press, 1997), pp. 177–197.
[30] Nicolas Werth, "L'ex-Empire russe, 1918–1921: les mutations d'une guerre prolongée," in Audoin-Rouzeau and Prochasson (eds.), *Sortir de la Grande Guerre*, pp. 285–306.

"It is already clear that any measures to collect the levy will be doomed to failure from the start and that the results, if there are any at all, will be extremely insignificant: there is simply no grain left to take," warned the central procurement service of a German community in the Volga. "The comrades who read my report will no doubt suspect me of localism; but that is not the point—I have lived through more than one year of hunger in Moscow, and I am just as eager as they are to take as much surplus grain as possible for the starving proletariat in the north; but I repeat, whatever measures are taken, it will be impossible to achieve any positive result."[31]

Still, nothing changed in central government policy; indeed, it seems that requisitions increased, affecting half the grain harvested in the Volga basin. The Bolsheviks operated on the assumption that the peasants hid one third of their surplus, so the resulting pillage of the countryside was absolutely catastrophic. "[The city of Saratov] was filled with destitute Germans who had abandoned their homes, put their families and belongings on to wagons and fled . . . without any other plan than to get away from the scenes of blood, torture and ruin," recalled a witness. "They camped on the banks of the Volga, sold their animals (a good horse was sold in one case for five loaves of bread) . . . This was a sight that had never before been seen in Russia."[32]

The New Economic Policy (NEP) that Lenin instituted in 1921 was supposed to allow the Bolshevik regime a chance to catch its breath. It relied upon the idea of a "worker and peasant alliance" and on the parallel development of the industrial and agricultural sectors, without one being sacrificed to the other. In the agricultural sector, the NEP was to be supplemented by the improvement of agricultural tools and machines that would, it was hoped, lead to a rapid increase in productivity. But the reforms came too late. In many regions, the impact of the Civil War, closely followed by that of the "peasant wars," was already so dire that the entire rural economy was unstable. The 1921 famine was not due to a deliberate decision to starve a portion of the peasant population, as would be the case in 1931–33.[33] But certainly the massive requisitions levied against the villages by the state weakened the rural world to the point that it stood defenseless in the face of natural disaster.

In the spring of 1921, a wave of drought hit Ukraine and the regions of the Don and the Volga. This followed the bad harvest of 1920 and

---

[31] Quoted in Figes, *Peasant Russia*, p. 272.
[32] A. Rabine, "The Bolsheviks in Russia," Library of Congress Manuscript Division, 26, quoted in Figes, *Peasant Russia*, p. 273.
[33] Conquest, *Harvest of Sorrow*.

the especially harsh winter of 1920–21. The rainfall in April, May, and June 1921 was barely a fifth of the past decade's average, while the temperatures were as high as those of July. A scorching wind swept across the thousands of acres already planted with grain, transforming the rich agricultural lands into a vast and arid wasteland, parched by the sun. The regions of the lower and middle Volga were the first affected. The river fell to its lowest level in several decades. But soon, all of Ukraine and a portion of European Russia sank into chaos. In July 1921, Soviet reports listed the provinces affected by the catastrophe: Astrakhan, Samara, Simbirsk, Saratov, Tsaritsin, the German regions of the Volga, the Tatar Republic, the Chuvash region, parts of Ufa and Vyatka, as well as the republic of Maris. In a report dated August 1921, the American Department of Commerce confirmed that the situation was dire: "In the province of Kazan, 95,000 acres usually cultivated were not sown at all. To the west of the Volga Valley less than 50 per cent of the arable territory of the Province of Orel was sown, and in the Province of Tula, only 20 to 35 per cent of the necessary seed for sowing was available."[34] A quarter of the Russian peasantry prepared itself for a slow death by starvation.

In the cities, obtaining food became more complicated, especially in the new Russian capital of Moscow, which Harold Fisher described thus in the first months of the famine: "The people were listless, anemic, heavily depressed; they were laboriously active only in the struggle for food . . . Few shops were open and these scantily stocked. Starvation, such as was later encountered along the Volga and in Ukraine, did not appear on the surface in Moscow. There was food to be had at prices not much above the American level, but far beyond the means of most of those to whom it was offered. The majority of persons met, therefore, were obviously undernourished, hungry, weary and disheartened."[35] Women, children, and the elderly were the most vulnerable, but so too were those whose professions ill prepared them to cope with food shortages, such as academics. In the view of one Russian correspondent of the ARA, the entire Russian intelligentsia was threatened with extinction: "Death was now more in evidence than life. Before my eyes died Feodor Batiushkov, the famous professor of philology, poisoned from eating uneatably filthy cabbage. Another one to die from hunger was S. Bengerov, professor of history and literature, he who gave to the Russian people entire editions of Shakespeare, of Schiller and of Pushkin . . . I saw the talented critic A. A. Ismailov die of hunger. At the same period the philosopher V.V.

---

[34] *American Relief Administration Bulletin*, Series 2: 16, September 1921, p. 7.
[35] Fisher, *Famine in Soviet Russia*.

Rosanov succumbed to starvation in Moscow. Before this death the latter roamed the streets in search of cigarette ends with which to appease his hunger . . . ."[36]

In ordinary times, peasants would have been at least somewhat able to cope with a capricious climate. Before the great crisis of 1921, the Volga basin had known periods of drought, usually every four or five years.[37] But this time the granaries were empty after being methodically pillaged by the food brigades over the two previous years, especially during the fall and winter of 1920. "All houses, barns, stables, cellars, lofts, were searched, and literally swept of everything they contained, down to the last dried apple, and the last egg," a resident of the region recalled.[38] Nothing was left to feed the peasants or their livestock, or to sow in the fields. In the case of the German populations in the Volga, recent scholarship has underlined the central government's hostility towards the community and the weight of anti-German prejudices in the general Russian population. The Bolsheviks withheld news of the catastrophe and even banned the word "famine" (*golod*) from the press.[39] The first official reports of the disaster date back to the winter of 1920, but only in the following summer did *Pravda*, the Communist Party's official newspaper, reluctantly acknowledge the extent of the crisis in the Volga basin and the disastrous impact of the preceding months' requisitions.

By this time, news of the calamity had already crossed the Russian border. In early July, Dr. Georges Lodygensky, director of the Russian Red Cross in Geneva, drew the first map of the famine in Russia and Ukraine. A month later, a similar map was published in the pages of *The Times* of London. In 1922, the area outlined in black had greatly increased, and now covered more than 1 million square miles—the equivalent of twenty Russian provinces with their 25 million inhabitants. In the most affected regions, such as Samara, which had had practically no spring rain, grain production was a third of normal levels and the wheat spikes were minuscule. By September 1921, 2 million people, three-fourths of the population of Samara, were dying of starvation and disease. "The population is feeding mainly on substitutes: all the grass is eaten, corn is considered a luxury, and bread is being baked from horse-radishes. Field rats are also being eaten," stated an official report published in *Izvestia*.[40]

---

[36] *American Relief Administration Bulletin*, Series 2: 43, December 1923, p. 107.
[37] James W. Long, *From Privileged to Dispossessed: The Volga Germans, 1860–1917* (Lincoln: University of Nebraska Press, 1988), pp. 2–4.
[38] James W. Long, "The Volga Germans and the famine of 1921," *The Russian Review* 51: 4, 1992, pp. 510–525, 514.
[39] *Ibid.*   [40] Archives of the ICRC, Geneva, Commixt II.5, 1921, Aid to Russia.

The French scholar Etienne Gilson, a renowned specialist in medieval philosophy, traveled to Russia for several months on behalf of the *Comité Français de Secours aux Enfants* [French Committee for Aid to Children]. He described the rapid decline in living conditions: "If we go into the villages, we see a large number of destroyed houses: these ravages are not made by war, but by the famine. After having sold their animals, their furniture, and their clothes to buy grain or flour, the peasants sold the roofs, doors and windows from all the houses whose inhabitants had died. They then began to take the beams from their own roofs to burn or to sell. The last winter was such that everything was sold or eaten; next winter, the peasants will have nothing to eat, and won't even have the means to sell anything or destroy their houses to insure their survival . . . "[41]

The Bolsheviks were determined to use any means to prevent this environmental catastrophe from turning into a large-scale political crisis. Certainly, by the beginning of the summer of 1921, most of the peasant revolts had been crushed by military means. But some rebel leaders had managed to flee and continued to harass the Red Army into 1922–23. This was the case for Alexander Antonov, who with a small group of men continued his guerrilla war until June 1922, when he finally fell into an ambush laid by the *Cheka*.[42] The Bolsheviks feared that the food crisis might reawaken old enemies and spur on new ones. The government maintained its pressure on regions thought to be prone to rebellion and on those where, in the recent past, peasant rebellions had been strongest. Ukraine, for example, was under martial law for all of 1921.

The famine of 1921–22 was also an opportunity to launch a vast campaign against the Orthodox Church. A February 1922 decree ordered local Soviets to seize objects of worship, including sacred relics, so that they could be sold to finance the purchase of food from the Americans—or so the Bolsheviks claimed. This was a way to discredit the work of the ARA in the eyes of the most religious peasants. "Turn gold into bread!" proclaimed the Communist regime. Russian peasants often reacted violently to these anti-religious campaigns by defending their churches, their clergy, and their icons.[43] In a small village near Votkinsk, in the east of the Viatka province, the inhabitants interrogated the local Communist

[41] Etienne Gilson, "Enquête sur la situation actuelle des enfants en Ukraine et dans les régions de la Volga, 15 août–15 septembre 1922," *Revue internationale de la Croix Rouge*, October 1922, IV.46, pp. 883–896.

[42] Oliver H. Radkey, *The Unknown Civil War in Soviet Russia : A Study of the Green Movement in the Tambov Region, 1920–1921* (Stanford: Hoover Institution Press, Stanford University, 1976), pp. 372–374.

[43] Glennys Young, *Power and the Sacred in Revolutionary Russia: Religious Activists in the Village* (The Pennsylvania State University Press, 1997).

Party representative and asked him if it was true that Lenin was the Antichrist.[44] Throughout the country, churches were systematically visited by gangs of looters who left with their arms full of crucifixes, chalices, and icons. Sometimes residents banded together to defend their places of worship, as on March 12, 1922 in the city of Shuya, northeast of Moscow. Violence broke out and the looters, armed with rifles and machine guns, fired into the crowd. Official reports, kept secret until the 1990s, enumerate more than a thousand bloody incidents causing the deaths of 7,000 clergymen and the arrests of 10,000 priests. "The more members of the reactionary bourgeoisie and clergy we manage to shoot, the better," Lenin declared.

At the same time, the Bolshevik state was well aware that it had to use any means at its disposal to ease the death grip of the famine; to do so meant appealing to international solidarity. For Lenin, the famine "was a disaster that threatened to nullify the whole of [the Bolsheviks'] organizational and revolutionary work." The danger did not come solely from the peasants, often presented as counter-revolutionary agents, but also from starving workers. Lenin, unlike the left wing of the Russian Communist Party, did not oppose asking the United States for help if necessary, even if this meant inviting a Trojan horse into the land of Communism. After all, foreign investments were necessary for the success of his NEP.[45]

On July 11, 1921, the patriarch Tikhon, the leader of the Russian Orthodox Church, wrote an appeal to the West that was reprinted in the *New York Times* at the end of the month. On July 13, Gorky's appeal "To all honest people" was published in the *New York Times*. Citing Russia's contribution to the world's cultural heritage, he urged the West to come to the aid of the "country of Tolstoy, of Dostoyevsky, of Mendeleyev, of Pavlov, of Mussorgsky . . . " In the span of a few months, the Russian famine had become an international issue.

Hoover and the power to feed

At the onset of the food crisis, the White Russian organizations reacted quickly. In a call to the International Committee of the Red Cross (ICRC), the Committee of *Zemstvos* and Cities accused the Bolshevik government "of having plunged the country into misery and ruin" and of "having shown itself incapable of containing the horror." "The

---

[44] Aaron B. Retish, *Russia's Peasants in Revolution and Civil War: Citizenship, Identity and the Creation of the Soviet State, 1914–1922* (Cambridge University Press, 2008), p. 259.
[45] Weissman, *Herbert Hoover*, pp. 11–15.

autonomous organizations of the *zemstvos* that have always supported the fight against misery no longer exist in Russia, where all private enterprise has been stifled,"[46] the group lamented. Other voices were raised to warn Western powers of the advantages the Communist regime could reap from international aid if the distribution of foodstuffs were not closely monitored. "Humanitarian action is necessary, but it needs to be restricted to relieving the victims of famine, without permitting the Soviets to use the occasion to help themselves consolidate their situation," cautioned Gustave Ador, president of the ICRC.[47]

On the other hand, the Russian crisis sparked a series of mobilizations in the heart of the European workers' movement. The International Federation of Trade Unions met in Berlin in mid August under the direction of Léon Jouhaux, one of the founders of the ILO. "The workers of the world should be the first to respond to the appeal of the workers and peasants of Russia," stated the trade unionists. "If in this public calamity the international working classes should fail to do their duty and even more than their duty, they would be unworthy of the glorious mission which history assigns them: the liberation of labor."[48] For sympathetic organizations, the famine was a grave threat to the stability of the Communist regime. The future of Bolshevik Russia—as well as that of the worldwide communist revolution—was at stake.

Western countries saw the Russian famine as much more than a simple economic crisis. The environmental disaster in Ukraine and the Volga basin presented an opportunity to increase their ability to influence events in Bolshevik Russia. At the end of July, Herbert Hoover received his government's authorization to respond to the Russian appeals. As Secretary of Commerce, he was a key figure in American political life and one of the most knowledgeable on questions of food supply. During World War I, he had put in place an enormous humanitarian aid program for occupied Belgium, even before the United States officially entered the conflict. In the spring of 1917, Hoover took over the leadership of the US Food Administration. It was unfortunate timing that he became President of the United States in March of 1929, 6 months before his country underwent the most serious economic crisis in its history. Hoover has been criticized for not having foreseen the crisis and for not having understood its depth. In America's collective memory, Hoover's

---

[46] Archives of the ICRC, Geneva, Commixt II.5, year 1921, Aid to Russia, Appeal of the Committee of Zemstvos and Cities to the ICRC, August 1, 1921.
[47] Archives of the ICRC, Geneva, Commixt II.5, year 1921, Aid to Russia.
[48] Archives of the ICRC, Geneva, Commixt II.5, year 1921, Aid to Russia, Resolution at the Conference of the International Federation of Trade Unions, Berlin, August 15–16, 1921.

name remains linked to unemployment, poverty, and substandard housing (the famous "Hoovervilles"). His opponents in the Democratic party seized the opportunity to create new words in order to discredit him: in 1929, "Hoover leather" referred to cardboard soles used to repair holey shoes, and the term "Hoover blanket" was used for old newspapers used to protect oneself from the cold. But in 1921, when the Russian famine broke out, Hoover was still a hero of humanitarian work in everyone's eyes. He had saved millions of French and Belgians from famine while they were living under German occupation, and beginning in 1917 he had succeeded in inspiring Americans to reduce their food consumption in order to adapt to the war effort.

The food supply in Belgium had become precarious by the end of 1914; in peacetime, the country had depended largely on the importation of agricultural materials to satisfy its needs. Following invasion and methodic pillaging by the German army, Belgium was further isolated from the rest of the world by the British blockade.[49] "Anything and everything that men could consume or that the German factories could utilize were seized and transported to the Fatherland . . . Belgium was gutted," reported an American resident of Antwerp.[50] A group of Belgian businessmen created the *Comité Central de Secours et d'Alimentation* [Central Committee for Aid and Food], with the goal of assisting the 800,000 inhabitants of Brussels, many of whom were beginning to suffer from hunger.

But by the end of September, the Committee had to admit its powerlessness in the face of a vastly overwhelming problem. Belgium needed the intervention of the United States, with its financial power, its agricultural resources, and its diplomatic influence. On the advice of the American ambassador to Great Britain, the Committee contacted Herbert Hoover, now an engineer based in London.[51] He had already distinguished himself by organizing the repatriation of 200,000 Americans stranded in Europe at the beginning of the hostilities.

Hoover undertook what would become a profound redefinition of humanitarian work. The Commission for Relief in Belgium (CRB), which he had created in October 1914, was a private entity, completely

---

[49] Sophie De Schaepdrijver, *De Groote Oorlog: het Koninkrijk België in de Eerste Wereldoorlog [The Great War: The Kingdom of Belgium in the First World War]* (Amsterdam: Atlas, 1997). Revised French translation: *La Belgique et la Première Guerre Mondiale* (Berlin and New York: PIE-Peter Lang, 2004); Annette Becker, *Les cicatrices rouges*.

[50] Edward Eyre Hunt, *War Bread: A Personal Narrative on the War and Relief in Belgium* (New York: Henry Holt and Company, 1916), p. 111.

[51] George Nash, *The Life of Herbert Hoover*, Vol. 1: *The Engineer, 1874–1914* (New York: W.W. Norton, 1983).

independent of the American government and therefore removed from traditional channels of influence.[52] Hoover had to invent a way to bring his organization's weight to bear on the belligerents, especially Great Britain, which insisted on maintaining its blockade of the Central Powers, and Germany, which hoped that a starving Belgian population would eventually turn against the British. "Our only court of appeal is public opinion," Hoover proclaimed in the press. He sought the support of VIPs from the neutral countries and strengthened his informal relations with authorities on both sides of the conflict in order to force them to ease the blockade.

With its offices in New York, Buenos Aires, London, Paris, and Rotterdam, the CRB had the capacity to procure provisions in India and Latin America, to transport nearly 5 million tons of food to occupied countries, to negotiate agreements at the highest levels, to ensure diplomatic immunity for its personnel in the countries at war, and to distribute aid to civilians—all thanks essentially to a network of 50,000 volunteers. The efficiency of the CRB lay in a rational organization of humanitarian aid: the purchase of raw materials, mainly in North America and South America; the transport of these materials across the Atlantic via a convoy of fifty to sixty cargo ships, which bore the Committee's flag in order to demonstrate their neutral status and to avoid submarine attacks; the unloading of the merchandise at the port of Rotterdam; stocking it in the warehouses of 4,000 Belgian and French cities and villages; distributing the aid through the use of ration cards. This new method of organization, which revolutionized the way humanitarian aid was distributed, was used again by Hoover during the time of the Russian famine in 1921–23.

Hoover was sincerely moved by the distress of French and Belgian civilians, but he did not lose sight of the political and economic advantages of the entire operation. Food aid was financed by loans from England and France to the Belgian government, and then by the US Treasury beginning in 1917.[53] Hoover also hoped that the work of the CRB would eventually create new markets for American exports. In his mind, moral and economic motivations could not be separated from one another.

---

[52] For firsthand accounts of the CRB's work, see Herbert Hoover, *Memoirs*, Vol. I: *Years of Adventure, 1874–1920* (New York: Macmillan, 1951); Vernon L. Kellogg, *Fighting Starvation in Belgium* (Garden City, NY: Doubleday, Page & Company, 1918); the Kellogg-Dickie Papers, Manuscripts and Archives, Sterling Memorial Library, Yale University; Edward E. Hunt, *War Bread*. See also Gay and Fisher (eds.), *Public Relations* and Surface and Bland (eds.), *American Food*.

[53] Surface and Bland (eds.), *American Food*, p. 14.

"It was our privilege to forfend infinite suffering from these millions of people, to save millions of lives, and it was our opportunity to demonstrate America's ability to do it in a large, generous and efficient way, befitting our country; but far beyond this, it was our opportunity to demonstrate that great strain of humanity and idealism which built up and in every essential crisis saved our Republic," he explained in February 1917 in a speech to the Chamber of Commerce of New York City.

We felt that it was the national duty of America, who stood out unharmed in this vast swelter to keep alight the lamp of humanity. The result of this war will be that America will be rich, prosperous, wealthy, and will have made untold millions of this wealth out of the woe and swelter of Europe. It is true enough that we were not responsible for this war. On the other hand, we have made large profits out of this misfortune. The justification of any rich man in the community is his trusteeship to the community for his wealth. The justification of America to the world-community to-day is her trusteeship to the world-community for the property which she holds [. . .] We have tried to keep the lamp of humanity alight and to implant true Americanism in Europe. If we fail, it will be the failure of the American people.[54]

The cult of personality surrounding Hoover during the Great War illustrates a personalization of humanitarian aid that differs somewhat from the anonymity of today's NGOs. As director of the CRB, Hoover received thousands of letters, and grain sacks were regularly sent back by aid recipients—decorated with messages of thanks and with drawings by children.[55] And yet, the man was hardly charismatic. "He is abnormally shy, abnormally sensitive, filled with an impassioned pride in his personal integrity and ever apprehensive that he may be made to appear ridiculous," noted one of his biographers. "He rises awkwardly as a visitor is shown to his desk, and extends his hand only halfway, in a hesitant fashion . . . He stares at his shoes, and because he looks down so much of the time, the casual guest obtains only a hazy impression of his appearance."[56] Even as the leader of one of the most powerful humanitarian organizations in the world, the American businessman from the little town of West Branch, Iowa, who had been orphaned at the age of nine, remained true to his Quaker upbringing.[57] The landscape of his

[54] "America's obligations in Belgian relief: address of Herbert Hoover, February 1, 1917," (New York Chamber of Commerce, 1917), pp. 4–5, 8–10.
[55] Belgium Gratitude File 1914–1918, Commission for Relief in Belgium Records 1914–1930, Box Nos. 516–529, Hoover Institution Archives, Stanford University.
[56] Henry F. Pringle, "Hoover: an enigma easily misunderstood," *World's Work*, 56 (June 1928), pp. 131–143.
[57] David Hinshaw, *Herbert Hoover: American Quaker* (New York: Farrar Straus, 1950). For a good description of the milieu in which Hoover was raised, see Louis Thomas Jones, *The Quakers of Iowa* (State Historical Society of Iowa, 1914).

youth amounted to a few plain wooden houses nestled in the hollow of a small valley, lost among the vast fields of the American Midwest. "Those who are acquainted with the Quaker faith, and who know the primitive furnishing of the Quaker meeting-house, the solemnity of the long hours of meeting awaiting the spirit to move someone, will know the intense repression upon a ten-year-old boy who might not even count his toes," Hoover recalled.[58]

During the Great War, the 260-year-old non-conformist Christian "Religious Society of Friends," as the Quakers called themselves, was caught between patriotic duty and a long-standing commitment to peace that forbade members to bear arms.[59] How could you defend your country and remain a pacifist? This was the inner conflict that most Quakers had to face. In England, Philip Noel-Baker, who at that time led the Cambridge Union Society and later would play an influential role at the League of Nations, created a way for his co-religionists to serve without fighting. He founded the Friends Ambulance Unit, which brought medical and moral support to wounded soldiers.

In the United States, humanitarian aid to Belgium was also a way to intervene in the conflict, without violating the government's officially neutral stance. Hoover's initiative gave the American people a just cause, compatible with the United States' perception of itself as "an exceptionally altruistic nation," as historian David Kennedy wrote.[60] During the war years, Hoover intended the work of the CRB to be part of a wider movement of solidarity, especially after President Wilson put him in charge of the US Food Administration in the spring of 1917. The goal of this organization was not only to export to the European allies the agricultural products they lacked (meat, flour, butter, and sugar), but also to encourage Americans to limit their food consumption and thus increase the exportable surplus.[61] Voluntary sacrifice and solidarity went hand in hand: "Meatless Mondays, wheatless Wednesdays, and when in doubt, eat potatoes." Food rationing was never seriously considered in the United States. "The last thing that any American could contemplate with equanimity would be the introduction of anything resembling Prussian autocracy into the food control of his country," Wilson solemnly

[58] Hoover: *Memoirs: Years of Adventure*, p. 7.
[59] Peter Brock, *The Quaker Peace Testimony, 1660 to 1914* (New York: Syracuse University Press, 1990).
[60] David M. Kennedy, *Over Here: The First World War and American Society* (Oxford University Press, 1980), p. 153.
[61] Helen Elizabeth Veit, "'We were a soft people.' Asceticism, self-discipline, and American food conservation in the First World War," *Food, Culture and Society*, 10: 2, summer 2007, pp. 167–190; and *Victory Over Ourselves: American Food and Progressivism in the Era of the Great War*, PhD dissertation, Yale University, 2008.

declared while reaffirming his belief in "[our] ability to defend ourselves without being Prussianized."

World War I marked a major turning point in the globalization of agricultural markets. That same globalization inspired Hoover to open Commission offices in 40 American states and around the world—from the Scandinavian countries to the great agricultural regions of South America, Australia, New Zealand, and South Africa. And the shift of humanitarian aid to Russia in the early 1920s was conceived in the same spirit.

The British economist J.A. Hobson had lamented in a 1909 treatise: "When each village was a virtually self-sufficing economic unit, some sense that he was helping to feed his neighbor must have accompanied the work of the husbandman who tilled the soil; but the Dakota farmer, whose wheat will pass into an elevator in Chicago and after long travel will go to feed some unknown family in Glasgow or in Hamburg, can hardly be expected to have the same feeling for the social end which his tilling serves."[62] America's entry into total war reversed this trend. Henceforth, intensive agricultural production, wartime dietary changes, and the fight against food waste all contributed to a sense of individual responsibility. The way people produced and consumed food defined them as citizens. Never in the history of the Western world had so many food packages been prepared and shipped to prisoners of war, occupied populations, and urban victims of hunger. This practice changed the symbolic significance of food, increasingly understood as nourishment meant to be shared, as a vital part of living together or *vivre ensemble*, in Barthes' phrase.[63] The boundary between the public and the private—including the most intimate spaces—was also redrawn. Nothing would escape the war effort: neither work in the fields nor agricultural commerce, nor even the meals served at the family dinner table.

This globalization also stimulated debate about whether there might actually be a right to food, and raised questions about the legitimacy of using hunger as a weapon against civilian populations in wartime. Since the second half of the nineteenth century, the blockade of an enemy country was seen as legitimate only if it were limited to merchandise with military applications, a theory elaborated by the famous English jurist William Hall.[64] Agricultural production was therefore theoretically

---

[62] J.A. Hobson, *The Industrial System: An Inquiry into Earned and Unearned Income* (London, Longmans, Green & Co., 1909), p. 320.

[63] Roland Barthes, *Comment vivre ensemble: cours et séminaire au Collège de France (1976–1977)* (Paris: Seuil/IMEC, 2002), p. 152.

[64] William Edward Hall, *A Treatise of International Law* (Oxford: Clarendon Press, 1904).

excluded, except in certain cases, such as the war France waged in China in 1881–85, or the Russo-Japanese war of 1904–05. With the promulgation of the Hague Conventions in 1899 and 1907, what previously had been forbidden solely on moral grounds (attacking unarmed populations) was gradually transformed into a judgment based on international rights (distinguishing between combatants and non-combatants).[65] Nevertheless, when the Committee of Imperial Defense met in London on December 4, 1908, the participants considered the total blockade of Germany, foodstuffs included. "All is fair in war," said the plainspoken Sir John Fisher, commander of the Royal Navy since 1904. "Hitting in the belly or anywhere else . . . Moderation in war is imbecility!" The admiral had never masked his hostility towards international conferences on the laws of war: "The inevitable result of conferences and arbitrations is that we always give up something. It's like a rich man entering into a conference with a gang of burglars."[66]

Furthermore, the line separating combatants from non-combatants was blurred during the first weeks of World War I, which saw the crimes perpetrated by the German troops in the summer of 1914, the pillage of Belgium and Northern France, and the Allies' imposition of the economic blockade in 1915.[67] The British could very well claim that their target was Germany's military might, but of course the German civilian population was the first victim. The blockade's effect on daily life in Germany was dramatic, especially during the famous "turnip winter" of 1916–17.[68] The debate about whether food could be used as a weapon was postponed until the end of the war, when Germany and the United States exchanged diplomatic notes in the fall of 1918. On the morning of November 8, 1918, in a train parked in the Rethondes Forest, the German plenipotentiaries attended a reading of the conditions of the Armistice. They were stunned to discover Article XXVI, which stated: "The existing blockade conditions set up by the Allied and Associated Powers are to remain unchanged, German merchant ships found at sea

---

[65] Geoffrey Best, *Humanity in Warfare* (New York: Columbia University Press, 1980).

[66] Avner Offer, "'Jacky' Fisher: economic warfare and the laws of war," *Journal of Contemporary History*, 23: 1, January 1988, pp: 99–118, 100.

[67] John Horne (ed.), *Vers la guerre totale*. See especially Sophie de Schaepdrijver, Annie Deperchin, and Laurence Van Ypersele's essays on the occupations, and Gerd Krumeich on the blockade.

[68] On this issue see the following, which focus on specific regions: Anne Roerkohl, *Hungerblockade und Heimatfront: Die kommunale Lebensmittelversorgung in Westfalen während des Ersten Weltkriegs* (Stuttgart: Franz Steiner, 1991); Belinda J. Davis, *Home Fires Burning: Food, Politics and Everyday Life in Berlin* (Chapel Hill: University of North Carolina Press, 2000).

remaining liable to capture." Germany had lost the war largely on the economic front. Far from ending the war against civilians that the blockade had represented, the Armistice prolonged it.

Then Herbert Hoover arrived in France, as advisor to the American delegation at the peace conference. While the European nations bitterly debated the question of post-war food aid in Europe, he suggested that the mission be assigned to a single organization—and that this organization be directed by a sort of Allied commander-in-chief, comparable to what Marshal Foch had been at the end of the war. "This man should be an American—the disinterested nation; the nation having to furnish the bulk of the supplies; the nation that could increase its supplies by call from its own citizens," he explained.[69] In January, Wilson placed him at the head of the ARA, a gigantic government-sponsored, humanitarian agency supported by thousands of donors. In the 9 months following the Armistice, 4 million tons of food were delivered to European ports. The ARA's personnel was made up of volunteers who had participated in the distribution of humanitarian aid to Belgium during the Great War, as well as recently demobilized American soldiers.

One goal of the ARA was to reduce the enormous agricultural surpluses that the United States had accumulated during its intensified wartime production. Another goal was to increase European demand for American products. In any case, the ARA's objectives were political. Providing food to the former German and Austrian enemies would ensure that neither country fell into anarchy or Bolshevism. "Bolshevism is steadily advancing westward. It cannot be stopped by force but it can be stopped by food," Hoover wrote in January 1919. Slowly the blockade loosened.[70] The first boatloads of supplies arrived in the port of Hamburg on March 22, 1919. In a pamphlet entitled "Why We are Feeding Germany?" Hoover justified ending the blockade with his usual pragmatism: "From the point of view of an economist, I would say that it is because there are seventy millions of people who must either produce or die... their production is essential to the world's future and they... cannot produce unless they are fed. From the point of view of a governor... it is because famine breeds anarchy, anarchy is infectious, the infection of such a cesspool will jeopardize France and Britain, will yet spread to the United States. From the point of view of a peace

---

[69] Herbert Hoover, Interoffice memorandum to American officials, November 14, 1918, in Suda L. Bane and Ralph H. Lutz (eds.), *Organization of American Relief in Europe, 1918–1919* (Stanford University Press, 1943), p. 50.

[70] The history of the lengthy diplomatic negotiations that led to the end of the blockade is chronicled in C. Paul Vincent, *The Politics of Hunger: The Allied Blockade of Germany 1915–1919* (Athens, Ohio: Ohio University Press, 1985), Chapter IV.

negotiator, it is because we must maintain order and stable government in Germany if we would have someone with whom to sign peace."[71]

During the conflict, the slogan of the US Food Administration had been "Food will win the war." For Hoover, food was also the way to win the post-war. It was also Hoover who recommended that President Wilson refuse diplomatic recognition to Bolshevik Russia and that he take a hard line with the new masters of the Kremlin, in contrast to the more conciliatory plan proposed by the American diplomat William C. Bullitt.[72] In April 1919, Hoover met with his friend Nansen to put in place a neutral aid mission to Russia. The relief effort was to "be devoted solely to the humanitarian purpose of saving life" and "would raise no question of political recognition or negotiations between the Allies with the existing authorities in Russia,"[73] he promised—in vain, as the Russians rejected Hoover's plan as too political, while the Allies pressured Nansen to end his contacts with the Bolsheviks.

Hoover, like Nansen, had tried to replace traditional diplomacy with humanitarian action: the former by wielding the weapon of food to limit the influence of the Bolshevik regime, the latter by hoping to reconcile Russia with the rest of the world thanks to Western aid.[74] Meanwhile the Russian Civil War raged on, with the West engaged on the side of the White armies. The Bolsheviks suspected that behind the invocation of humanitarianism lurked the much more political goal of destabilizing the Communist regime.

In the summer of 1919, there emerged a new, wholly private ARA. It replaced the government agency while keeping its name and the mission to aid the starving people of Central Europe. In 1920, the ARA distributed relief supplies in twenty-one European nations. "The sole object of relief should be humanity. It should have no political objective or other aim than the maintenance of life and order," Hoover promised.[75] The reality was different. Efficiency and performance were the ideas at the heart of the ARA's work, which the "food regulator of the world" (as General Pershing called Hoover) understood above all as an enterprise, a

---

[71] Herbert Hoover, "Why we are feeding Germany?" March 21, 1919, quoted in Herbert Hoover, *The Ordeal of Woodrow Wilson* (Baltimore: Johns Hopkins University Press, 1992), pp. 172–173.
[72] William C. Bullitt, *The Bullitt Mission to Russia: Testimony before the Committee on Foreign Relations, United States Senate, of William C. Bullitt* (New York: B.W. Huebsch, 1919).
[73] Weissman, *Herbert Hoover*, p. 32.
[74] *Ibid.*, Chapter 2: "The roles of Herbert Hoover."
[75] Herbert Hoover, "Analysis and comparison of the plans of President Wilson and the plans of the allied representatives," December 16, 1918, in Bane and Lutz (eds.), *Organization of American Relief*, p. 93.

business. Hoover sought to reduce the organization's operating costs by limiting the number of American personnel (in Central Europe, and later in Russia, humanitarian aid was administered by several hundred young Americans) and by calling on a significant part of the local workforce, who were generally paid in food.

At the same time, the ARA furnished the White armies with fuel, food, and clothing. For example, in a letter addressed to "Mr. Hoover, Food Dictator of Europe," the commander of the Army of the Northwest rejoiced over the aid that the American organization had provided "in our struggle with the bitterest enemy of mankind, law and order— Bolshevism."[76] In 1921, Hoover became the Secretary of Commerce in President Harding's Republican administration. This was a surprising political appointment for someone who had been such a close collaborator of the Democratic President Woodrow Wilson, but the new president appreciated Hoover's talents as a negotiator as well as his international connections.

In the United States, the Red Scare reached a high point under the influence of Attorney General Mitchell Palmer.[77] "Bolshevism in most minds did not represent a political or economic theory, but the destruction of public order, the end of all security of person and property, the reign of bloody violence," observed the historian Harold H. Fisher.[78] In a rather ironic twist, Herbert Hoover—the man who only weeks before had looked forward to the overthrow of the Bolshevik regime—had to answer the call Maxim Gorky issued in July 1921. No doubt he continued to hope that food would prove an effective weapon against the regime, as he had suggested in 1919. The peasant revolts, Lenin's introduction of the NEP, the outbreak of famine in Ukraine and Volga: in Hoover's eyes, all seemed to indicate that Bolshevism's days were numbered. An American humanitarian intervention would allow the promotion of a political and economic alternative to Bolshevism, and could ultimately subvert the current regime.

---

[76] Commander, Northwest Russian Army, to Herbert Hoover, July 26, 1919, Herbert Hoover Archives Special Testimonials File, quoted in Weissman, *Herbert Hoover*, p. 37.

[77] Robert K. Murray, *Red Scare: A Study in National Hysteria, 1919–1920* (Minneapolis: University of Minnesota Press, 1955) is still the classic study of the "Red Scare"; Murray Levin draws on his conclusions in *Political Hysteria in America* (New York: Basic Books, 1971). For Regin Schmidt, in *Red Scare: FBI and the Origins of Anticommunism in the United States, 1919–1943* (Copenhagen: Museum Tusculanum Press, 2000), the "Red Scare" was largely the creation of the FBI, which set it before the American public as a paranoid reading of political life. Beverly Gage has recently analyzed a key episode of the "Red Scare"—namely, the Wall Street attack of September 16, 1920; see Gage, *The Day Wall Street Exploded: A Story of America in its First Age of Terror* (Oxford University Press, 2009).

[78] Fisher, *Famine in Soviet Russia*, p. 25.

One of the difficulties Hoover encountered was how to find financing sufficient to support a sizable operation in Russia. Aid would be provided mainly by the federal government, which transferred $20 million to the budget of the United States Grain Corporation in a law passed on December 22, 1921. Hoover made President Harding realize that the massive purchase of grain destined for Russia would make it possible to stabilize the market for foodstuffs, which had seen a precipitous drop in the United States due to the abundant harvest of 1921.[79] In addition to the advantages for American farmers, Hoover also hoped that the Soviet government would bring its share to the table by drawing on the gold reserves of the Czarist regime; an agreement was thus signed in December 1921, first with Moscow, then with the Soviet Republic of the Ukraine, for payment in ingots, worth $12 million.[80] In addition to food supplies, clothing and medicines worth $4 million were to be distributed; these came from the American army surplus following the Great War.[81]

However, a good part of aid to Russia was dependent on numerous private charitable organizations that collaborated with the ARA, by late 1921: the American Red Cross ($3,800,000), the Near East Relief, the YMCA and the YWCA, the American Friends Service Committee (Quakers), the Federal Council of Churches, the American Jewish Joint Distribution Committee, the Knights of Columbus, the Volga Relief Society ... For all these organizations, experienced in fundraising and in organizing aid distribution on the ground, the Russian crisis presented a specific set of problems. The economic difficulties that many Americans were facing in the early 1920s tended to limit their charitable giving. Moreover, the members of these philanthropic organizations had to deal with their compatriots' hostility to the Communist regime. "Russian atrocities were now as dear to the sensationalists of press and platform as German atrocities had been a few years before," Fisher wrote. To win over his compatriots, Hoover had to invoke the civilian's—and particularly the child's—humanitarian rights. "We must make some distinction between the Russian people and the group who have seized the Government," he asserted.[82] A keen sympathy on the part of the American public towards

---

[79] According to the American Secretary of Agriculture, the average price of a bushel of corn produced in Nebraska thus went from 25 cents in November 1921 to 50 cents in February 1922. See Surface and Bland (eds.), *American Food*, p. 246.

[80] ARA, Russian Operations, 1919–1925, Box No. 9, Folder No. 3, Hoover Institution Archives, Stanford University. Fisher addresses the issue of Russian gold in *Famine in Soviet Russia*, pp. 154–159.

[81] *American Relief Administration Bulletin*, Series 2, No. 19, December 1921, p. 1.

[82] Fisher, *Famine in Soviet Russia*, p. 141.

the Russian people was achieved through a massive propaganda campaign in the media, especially through the use of photography and film.

Fighting against indifference to Russian suffering

When the Russian famine began, feeling of pity for victims of hunger was a relatively new phenomenon. Up to the beginning of the nineteenth century, Malthusian theory held starving populations solely responsible for their fate.[83] Famine was seen as a necessary evil that checked overpopulation and encouraged the poorest people to abandon their apathy and get to work. In the words of the economist Joseph Townsend, famine taught "decency and civility, obedience and subjection, to the most brutish, the most obstinate and the most perverse."[84] Only in the second half of the 1840s when confronted with the great Irish famine, and especially during the 1880s, did Malthusian discourse begin to give way to what the historian Thomas Laqueur has called the "humanitarian narrative."[85]

A new generation of investigative journalists went to war against famine, considered a "hideous wound," a "major calamity," a "human tragedy." The ravages wrought by hunger were described in detail and their demographic impact represented in lines and curves. Regions affected by famine were carefully mapped: a "geography of hunger" was born. At the turn of the century, journalists Vaughan Nash and Henry Nevinson were sent to India to cover the great famines of 1899–1901 and 1907–08 for the *Manchester Guardian*. A.S. Krausse immersed himself for three weeks in London's poorest neighborhoods and then wrote a riveting report on hunger that was published as a series in the *Globe*.[86] These articles were not based on economic arguments about the distribution of wealth, but took a more subjective approach that allowed readers to imagine the suffering of individuals and the emaciated bodies of the famished.

Particular attention was paid to children, whose skeletal silhouettes, distended bellies, and blank gazes were featured by journalists. In 1896–98, Julian Hawthorne, *Cosmopolitan*'s correspondent and the son of the

---

[83] James Vernon, *Hunger: A Modern History* (Cambridge, Mass.: Belknap Press of Harvard University Press, 2007), Chapter 2.

[84] Joseph Townsend, *A Dissertation on the Poor Laws. By a Well Wisher to Mankind* (London, 1786). Republished version (Berkeley: University of California Press, 1971).

[85] Thomas Laqueur, "Bodies, Details and the Humanitarian Narrative," in Lynn Hunt (ed.), *The New Cultural History* (Berkeley: University of California Press, 1989), pp. 176–204.

[86] A.S. Krausse, *Starving London: The Story of a Three Weeks' Sojourn Among the Destitute* (London: Remington, 1886).

author of *The Scarlet Letter*, crossed paths with a 5-year-old child on an Indian road: "Its arms were not so large round as my thumb; its legs were scarcely larger; the pelvic bones were plainly shown; the ribs, back and front, started through the skin, like a wire cage. The eyes were fixed and unobservant; the expression of the little skull-face solemn, dreary and old...."[87] Fifteen years later, these same words were used by travelers to Russia, no doubt with the same goal of arousing the sympathy of Western readers for the agony endured by a faraway people.[88] Dispatched at the first signs of the worsening famine in Volga, Western newspaper correspondents described at length the damage the famine inflicted on the bodies of Russian children. Their articles dwelled on individual stories, which allowed them to personalize the suffering. The American philanthropist Lilian Brandt analyzed this technique in her 1921 monograph, *How Much Shall I Give?* "The fundamental, primitive, probably instinctive desire to relieve physical suffering is still no doubt the most general and the strongest of all motives," Brandt wrote. "When an earthquake or a fire or a flood destroys property and lives, money pours in—sometimes much more than is needed—to provide shelter for the homeless, food for the hungry, clothing for the naked, and burial for the Dead [...] Successful appeals—in annual reports, circular letters—are directed primarily toward exciting sympathy for the suffering of individuals and desire to relieve or prevent that suffering [...] The more vividly the individuals are pictured, the greater the returns."[89]

Brandt nevertheless saw a limit to this natural sympathy, which she explained by the great numbers of catastrophes, which attenuated donors' feelings of responsibility, as well as their frequency, which desensitized them to the suffering of others. "The emotions become fatigued, like the frog's muscle in an experiment; increasing doses of stimulation must be applied to produce equal reactions; and finally the point is reached at which it is impossible to excite any response."[90] As long ago as 1759, in his essay on the theory of moral sentiments, Adam Smith had warned his readers that excessive exposure to the suffering of others would only lead to indifference.[91] But, at the close of the nineteenth century, debates over the limits of natural sympathy were conducted in a different context, part of a collective questioning of the excesses of the modern world. For

---

[87] Julian Hawthorne, "India starving," *Cosmopolitan*, 23: 4, August 1897, pp. 379–382.
[88] Boltanski, *La souffrance à distance.*
[89] Lilian Brandt, *How Much Shall I Give?* (New York: The Frontier Press, 1921), p. 12.
[90] *Ibid.*, p. 27.
[91] Adam Smith, *The Theory of Moral Sentiments*, edited by D.D. Raphael and A.L. Macfie (Oxford: Clarendon Press, 1976), p. 30.

the American neurologist George Beard, who in the 1870s invented the notion of neurasthenia, "the sorrows of any part of the world, many parts greater geographically than the old world as known to the ancients, through the medium of the press and the telegraph are made the sorrows of individuals everywhere. One morning newspaper, as we read with our breakfast, has the history of the sorrows of the whole world for a day; and a nature but moderately sympathetic is robbed thereby, consciously or unconsciously, of more or less nervous strength."[92]

In a letter to Nansen about the famine in Russia, the author George Bernard Shaw perfectly described this state of mind: "The worst of it is that I can no longer feel anything about these calamities that are overwhelming the world. I think I should still be a little distressed if I drove my car over a British baby, or even a British dog; but when you tell me that another five million infants are starving in Russia, or another five thousand Greeks perishing in Asia Minor, I just say 'Dear me!' I forget about it as soon as I can. On a very fine day I am perhaps cheerful enough to greet the news with a hollow laugh, especially when people ask me to stop it, as if I were God Almighty."[93] How to combat this general tendency of indifference to the suffering of others, which Susan Moeller has described as "compassion fatigue"?[94] How to make the Western—and particularly American—public understand that access to food was a right that, in the context of the end of the Great War, Western powers had a duty to enforce? Conscious of their limited impact on public opinion, the Red Cross and Hoover's ARA sought to improve their fundraising techniques in order to reach a larger number of donors.

The end of the nineteenth century and the beginning of the twentieth had been marked by an advancement in philanthropy, with the Babies Milk Funds, the Salvation Army (1865), the New York Society for the Prevention of the Cruelty to Children (1874), the American Society for the Prevention of Cruelty to Animals (1886), and the Volunteers of America (1896). America collected for foreign missions, old-age homes, hospitals, and orphanages, victims of natural disasters at home and abroad.[95] In a great, disorganized outpouring of energy, armies of well-intentioned volunteers sold stamps to fight tuberculosis and organized

---

[92] George M. Beard, *American Nervousness, Its Causes and Consequences* (New York: G.B. Putnam's Sons, 1881), p. 134.
[93] National Library, Oslo, Ms. Fol. 1988 RUP3, Letter from George Bernard Shaw to Nansen, March 2, 1923.
[94] Susan Moeller, *Compassion Fatigue: How the Media Sell Disease, Famine, War and Death* (New York and London: Routledge, 1999).
[95] Austin Sarat and Javier Lezaun (eds.), *Catastrophe: Law, Politics and the Humanitarian Impulse* (Amherst and Boston: University of Massachusetts Press, 2009).

auctions for the Red Cross, while during its enormous campaigns ("Y" drives) of the 1910s, the YMCA went door-to-door to meet the collection quotas that had been set at the beginning of each month.

The advent of World War I caused a thorough restructuring and professionalization of charitable organizations.[96] For example, Hoover's CRB had been manned by thousands of volunteers, who worked under a team composed of engineers, like Hoover himself, and Rhodes scholars. In April 1917, when the United States entered the war, more than 130 American organizations were already raising money for Belgian children, refugees, and prisoners of war. Their subscription drives were planned like military campaigns. One man in particular represented this shift in the way the humanitarian sector functioned: Henry P. Davison, a former director of the J.P. Morgan Bank, who took over the War Council of the American Red Cross in the spring of 1917.[97] To collect the hundreds of millions of dollars for the 1917 campaign—that is to say, fifty times the amount collected by the American Red Cross in the previous 3 years—Davison surrounded himself with the top YMCA fundraisers. He increased press campaigns, issued a considerable number of posters, and assigned to each American city and state donation quotas to be met before the end of the year.

A new amendment to tax law offered deductions to donors, and the results were spectacular. The American Red Cross campaign raised $175 million in 1918, while the United War Work Fund, an umbrella organization of seven American charities, raised $200 million. In his survey of charitable practices in New Haven, Connecticut, the economist Willford Isbell King confirmed the funds collected locally by philanthropic societies had doubled between 1914 and 1921.[98] Before World War I, gifts inspired by what was then termed "charity" were still the prerogatives of the very rich. On the eve of the conflict, far more numerous contributions, made now in the name of "philanthropy," came from all levels of society.[99]

Yet when famine swept over Russia, it was not easy to redirect wartime charitable habits towards peacetime objectives. From an American point of view, raising money for the starving people of Volga or Ukraine

[96] Robert H. Bremner, *American Philanthropy* (Chicago and London: The University of Chicago Press, 1960), Chapter VIII.

[97] Henry Pomeroy Davison, *The American Red Cross in the Great War* (New York: Macmillan, 1919).

[98] Willford Isbell King, *Trends in Philanthropy: A Study in a Typical American City* (National Bureau of Economic Research, 1928).

[99] Scott M. Cutlip, *Fund Raising in the United States: Its Role in America's Philanthropy* (New Brunswick: Rutgers University Press, 1965), chapter 6, "The 1920's: Exit Charity, Enter Popular Philanthropy."

did not come as naturally as supporting Belgian or French allies. Once again, advertising techniques succeeded in stimulating American generosity. All the members of the American Red Cross (their numbers increased from 20 thousand in 1914 to 20 million in 1918)[100] received the *American Red Cross Magazine* in which the spectacle of suffering on every page clamored for readers' compassion and charity. The Geneva-based *Union Internationale de Secours aux Enfants* [International Union of Aid to Children] edited a collection of nine postcards, distributed around the world, that represented all stages of hunger, up to and including death. In one, an emaciated child spoon-feeds a younger boy—his brother?—while the caption states, "The skeletal limbs, the distended belly (by grass, straw, tree bark, worms, dirt). These children cannot be saved; it is too late. To have saved them, one would have needed to feed them before they reached this degree of exhaustion."[101]

Hoover's ARA also made massive use of photography and film. Forceful images, touching individual stories, moralistic narration: everything about the humanitarian films of the 1920s recalled the visual propaganda produced during World War I, especially by the Committee on Public Information created by President Wilson in April 1917. Bruce Barton, one of the great publicists of the day, who was in charge of propaganda for the United War Work Fund during the war, also worked for several humanitarian organizations, including the Salvation Army and the Knights of Columbus.

In 1921, the ICRC had already produced almost sixty films to publicize its work on behalf of prisoners of war, refugees, victims of typhus, or the starving populations of central Europe.[102] Red Cross organizations from Italy, Great Britain, and the United States made their own films. A public lecture delivered by a Red Cross representative in a theater, a meeting hall, or a school had once been the primary method of spreading humanitarian propaganda. Now, in the 1920s, the slideshow or film became the preferred means of spreading information. More riveting than even the most eloquent speech, images of the starving circled the globe. No matter that the people in the photographs seemed to be posing, or that the weight of movie cameras limited the shots the filmmakers could take. No matter that the films were systematically cut and

[100] *The Work of the American Red Cross During the War,* Washington DC, American Red Cross, 1919, quoted in Kevin Rozario, "'Delicious horrors.'"

[101] Union Internationale de Secours aux Enfants (UISE), "Famine in Russia-III," Geneva, 1921–23.

[102] Enrico Natale, "Quand l'humanitaire commençait à faire son cinéma: les films du CICR. des années 20," *International Review of the Red Cross,* 86: 854, June 2004, pp. 415–438.

then spliced together using scenes from various sources to create new, more spectacular, films. What mattered was the shock of the image—like the crazed eyes of children suspected of having eaten their parents to avoid starvation—transformed into iconic figures of human misery. The dissolution of family ties and the reduction of the human body to mere food fascinated and horrified public opinion in the West. The pictures confirmed the belief that Russia was peopled by savages.

In the winter of 1921–22, when the first cases of cannibalism began to be known,[103] G.H. Mewes, who had been a *Daily Mirror* reporter on the eastern front during the Great War, visited the affected regions for the Save the Children Fund (SCF). "Often I saw children who had gone far beyond the stage where English food and medicine would help, children in such a condition that, had they been animals, one would have destroyed them where they lay," he reported. The film he shot in Saratov province, in southern Russia, showed scenes of desolation, some children dying of hunger, others hastily buried, crowds of refugees fleeing the region in hopes of escaping the famine.[104] On a snowy road, a dog threw itself on the frozen carcass of a horse. A camel pulled a wagon, loaded with coffins. Four bodies, abandoned on the side of a road, awaited collection. The second half of the film showed the rescue effort. There on screen was Nansen directing the distribution of food, as well as Laurence Webster, a young British administrator of the SCF, checking that the train cars loaded with food were securely sealed. Dr. Farrar, the representative of the League of Nations' Epidemiological Commission, was captured on film giving bread to a group of children, 3 weeks before he himself died from typhus in December 1921. Other children were shown seated at a table in front of bowls of soup. Behind them, large Save the Children posters were displayed.

Commissioned to bestow legitimacy on the aid mission to Russia— aimed at a Western public that was fundamentally wary of the Bolshevik authorities—Mewes' film had remarkable success, far greater than that of other humanitarian films of the 1920s. It was translated into several languages and shown all over Europe and in Japan in order to raise money. In

---

[103] ARA, Russian Operations, 1919–25, Box No. 94, Folder No. 10, Hoover Institution Archives, Stanford University.

[104] G.H. Mewes, *Famine: A Glimpse of the Misery in the Province of Saratov*, 32 mins (9 mins and 23 mins), black and white, silent; 35 mm, 1922, The National Archives, Kew, Richmond, Surrey. This film is also available at the archives of the ICRC under the title "Famine en Russie (film Nansen)." On this humanitarian film, see Roland Cosandey, "Eloquence du visible: la famine en Russie, 1921–1923. Une bibliographie documentée," *Archives*, 75/76, June 1998, Institut Jean Vigo, Perpignan, and Lukas Straumann, *L'humanitaire mis en scène: la cinématographie du CICR des années 1920*, ICRC, 2000.

January 1922, Nansen organized a screening in London. "No advertisements, articles, verbal or printed appeals could have produced such an overwhelming impression upon the audience as did the staggering realism of these pictures," observed the *Daily News*. In Liverpool, "hundreds of people could not get into the theater and the films and projections had to be shown twice. The success was such that the audience donated their jewelry at the exit, and Dr. Nansen's car was lengthily cheered."[105]

A scientific approach to hunger

While humanitarian propaganda films used sensationalism to arouse the pity of the West, the experts of the charitable organizations sought a scientific method to evaluate the effects of hunger on bodies. At what point can you say that a person is suffering from hunger? How to rate victims' nutritional deficiencies on an internationally accepted scale? In the search for a standardized language, groups such as the ILO (see Chapter 2) and the League of Nations' Health Organization played a key role.[106] They pressured national governments to raise civilian populations' standards of living. They also spread worldwide the new knowledge of nutrition, especially concerning vitamins and proteins.

To understand the debates of the early 1920s, one must return once again to the intellectual laboratory that was World War I. In 1914, the "science of nutrition" was 20 years old. It had been developed in the 1890s with the goal of quantifying the amount of food an individual—in particular a member of the working class—required to maintain good health and to continue to produce efficiently for the benefit of industrial society.[107] In his pioneering study on the population of York, the British sociologist Seebohm Rowntree asked several families of workers to give him a detailed account of their food budget, and of the types and quantities of food they ate.[108] He based his conclusions on a thermodynamic model: the human body functions as a kind of motor that must be furnished with sufficient quantities of fuel.[109] From this perspective, what mattered was the quantity of food, although Rowntree

[105] Archives of the ICRC, Geneva, Commixt II.5/1107 and 1109, February 3–10, 1922.
[106] Weindling, "Social medicine," in Weindling (ed.), *International Health Organisations and Movements*, pp. 134–153.
[107] Dietrich Milles, "Working capacity and calorie consumption: the history of rational physical economy," in Harmke Kamminga and Andrew Cunningham (eds.), *The Science and Culture of Nutrition* (Amsterdam and Atlanta, Georgia: Rodopi, 1995), pp. 75–96.
[108] B. Seebohm Rowntree, *Poverty: A Study of Town Life* (London: Macmillan, 1901).
[109] Anson Rabinbach, *The Human Motor: Energy, Fatigue and the Origins of Modernity* (Berkeley: University of California Press, 1992).

recognized that needs differed greatly based on age, sex, and professional activity.

Not until the eve of World War I did the American E.V. McCollum and the Pole Casimir Funk finally argue for the crucial importance of qualitative nutritional deficiencies.[110] Several diseases, such as beriberi, scurvy, rickets, and pellagra (an illness caused by niacin [vitamin B_3] deficiencies) were then attributed to the lack of certain substances called "vitamins" (vital amines or amino acids)—the first of these to be identified was vitamin A in 1912. The discovery of vitamins marked a turning point in the history of nutritional science. The body-as-motor gradually was replaced by another model, based on the importance of a balanced diet. In an article published in the *British Medical Journal*, a researcher from the Lister Institute in England summarized the state of knowledge on the eve of the war: "The nutrition of an animal is seen to depend not only upon the supply of proteins, carbohydrates, fats and inorganic material, but also upon the presence in the diet of certain accessory substances, small amounts of which are sufficient to supply the needs of the organism."[111]

At that stage, only American and British scientists were acknowledging the role played by vitamins. Their German colleagues still remained faithful to the tradition of foods with high caloric value, as was especially shown in the work of Max Rubner (1854–1932), one of the most influential experts of the pre-war period. Elected in 1891 to the prestigious chair of hygiene at the University of Berlin, Rubner was one of the German imperial state's primary advisors on health policy. He envisioned a vast project of "rational nutrition," which would combine new knowledge from the "science of nutrition" with an economic approach. In a passage in his book, *Changes in the People's Nutrition* (1913), he attacked the meat sandwich that Berlin workers bought on the street as too poor in protein, too rich in fats, and much too expensive for its actual supply of calories.[112]

In October 1914, with chemist Fritz Haber and physicist Max Planck, Rubner was part of a group of ninety-three German intellectuals who defended the German Army when it was accused of having committed

[110] Leslie Harris, "The Discovery of Vitamins," in J. Needham, ed., *The Chemistry of Life: Eight Lectures on the History of Biochemistry* (Cambridge University Press, 1970).

[111] E.A. Cooper, *The British Medical Journal* (April 5, 1913), quoted in Mikulas Teich, "Science and food during the Great War: Britain and Germany," in Kamminga and Cunningham (eds.), *Science and Culture of Nutrition*, p. 223.

[112] Max Rubner, *Wandlungen in der Volksernaehrung* [*Changes in the People's Nutrition*], (Leipzig, 1913), quoted in Corinna Treitel, "Max Rubner and the biopolitics of rational nutrition," *Central European History*, 41, 2008, pp. 1–25.

atrocities against Belgian and French civilians. In December 1914, he gave a speech to the Reichstag in which he presented his plan to ensure German nutritional self-sufficiency in the event of an Allied blockade. On the eve of the conflict, didn't Germany import a fourth of her caloric needs? Household consumption therefore had to be strictly rationed and housewives taught to cook with less butter and meat, while communal kitchens had to be developed.

The serious food crisis that befell Germany in 1917 and the political troubles that followed revealed the limits of "rational nutrition" as Rubner had imagined it.[113] His definition of hunger was also problematic. Whereas Rubner and his German colleagues emphasized the caloric value of foods, British researchers stressed the nutritional importance of vitamins and the harm that could be caused by an unbalanced diet, especially in the young.[114] At the beginning of the 1910s, British scholars had used the Empire as a laboratory for the study of the diseases of hunger.[115] With the end of the war, the tragic state of the urban populations of central Europe, particularly in Vienna, presented a new field of study. The reports received by the English scientists detailed severe cases of rickets among Viennese children, which led to irreversible deformities. As for the elderly, they suffered from acute varieties of calcium deficiency.

A small team left for the Austrian capital and arrived in the fall of 1919. Its conclusions were particularly alarming. There were numerous instances of rickets and scurvy among children, which could be explained by the diminished consumption of milk, replaced in the diet by cereal-heavy meals. The British doctors also noted retarded growth in infants and cases of blindness (keratomalacia) caused by vitamin A deficiencies. Their German and Austrian counterparts remained skeptical. In their opinion, rickets was caused by an infectious agent present in food, which attacked the most vulnerable subjects. Some doctors, who had spent part of the war working in camps for Russian prisoners of war, noticed similarities between the symptoms of their current patients and those of prisoners. But for a while no one connected these symptoms with nutritional deficits. The British doctors then introduced experimental treatments that brought good results.

At the end of the war, the English physiologist Edward Mellanby had done an experiment on a group of dogs to prove the non-infectious origin

---

[113] Avner Offer, *The First World War: An Agrarian Interpretation* (Oxford: Clarendon Press, 1989); Belinda Davies, *Home Fires Burning: Food, Politics and Everyday Life in World War I Berlin* (Chapel Hill: University of North Carolina Press, 2000).

[114] Sally M. Horrocks, "The business of vitamins: nutrition science and the food industry in inter-war Britain," in Kamminga and Cunningham (eds.), *Science and Culture of Nutrition*, pp. 235–258.

[115] Vernon, *Hunger*, pp. 104–117.

of rickets. He had locked them in a dark, sunless room and had fed them nothing but porridge for several weeks. Then he had added cod liver oil to their diet. The dogs, which had developed all the symptoms of rickets, were cured in a few days. Rickets, therefore, was clearly caused by a nutritional deficiency—a lack of vitamin D, which was discovered only in 1922. We now know that it is produced naturally by the body through sun exposure and that it is present in large quantities in certain foods, such as cod liver oil. In Vienna, children ill with scurvy were treated with lemon juice, and those with rickets were fed vegetable stew and cod liver oil. Those suffering from bone loss were put on a diet based on dairy products. Progress was monitored using a relatively new discovery, X-rays, the use of which had spread thanks to military application in the Great War.

For the first time, the definition of hunger—previously explained as a lack of nourishment, or under-nutrition—gave way to the more complex notion of malnutrition, which involved a qualitative nutritional deficiency. However, when the Russian famine broke out in 1921, the discoveries made by British scientists were still too recent to be effectively applied to humanitarian aid. In addition, the scientific definition of hunger rarely corresponded to its legal definition, as given by Russian experts from the Pomgol Central Commission—which had the power to assign a status of "Starving" to a district, as a function of its net harvest per person divided by the number of inhabitants, at least in theory.[116]

Many charitable organizations, once in the field, failed to provide balanced meals. For example, the Quakers, who were very active in Russia at the onset of the famine, served cacao-based meals, whose high caloric value they extolled. Massively exported from the United States, corn was eaten in the form of bread or mush.[117] "[Its] value as a source of energy to the body is the highest of all the cereals, being approximately 1,800 calories per pound, or about 100 calories above the average,"[118] according to the American Secretary of Agriculture. Certain experts nevertheless called attention to the fact that a diet exclusively based on the

[116] Adamets, *Guerre civile et famine en Russie*, pp. 122–125.
[117] The choice of corn instead of another cereal grain was the result of lengthy negotiations between Hoover and American farmers. Certain producers told him that the Russians did not have enough mills to grind the corn and that they did not know how to cook it. One wrote that it would be necessary to teach them how to make tortillas. The Russian government itself would have preferred rice, wheat, or millet. In the end, the importance of the United States' corn surplus, its low cost, and the lobbying of corn growers made the difference. See John R. Ellingston, "The use of corn and its success in Russia," *American Relief Administration Bulletin*, Series 2, No. 41, October 1923, pp. 13–16.
[118] "Corn meal as a food and ways of using it," United States Department of Agriculture, *Farmers' Bulletin*, 565, 1914, p. 5.

consumption of corn presented health risks: pellagra had caused the deaths of several thousand people in South Carolina and Georgia during the Great War.

Only slowly did the SCF and the ARA apply a more scientific approach to food aid. In this regard, Herbert Hoover was especially reliant on biologist Vernon L. Kellogg and bacteriologist Hans Zinsser to evaluate the deficiencies afflicting the Russian people and develop ways to cure them. In September 1921, the two men made a trip to the Volga valley. On their return to New York 1 month later, Kellogg described children's institutions where the children were so worn out by hunger that they no longer had the strength to cry. Their heads shaved to avoid lice, the children slept huddled together on the ground, without mattresses. Most had the swollen bellies of famine victims.[119] At Hoover's initiative, humanitarian aid was thus rapidly broadened to include medical care, which had not been the case for the ARA in its programs in Central Europe following the war.

In comparison to the situation in Vienna in 1919, the state of sanitation in Russia 3 years later was much more worrisome. Russian medical personnel had experienced heavy losses during the Bolshevik Revolution and the Russian Civil War. Hospitals were few and poorly equipped. There was neither chloroform nor anesthetics. Lacking bandages, doctors covered wounds and incisions with newspapers.[120] The ARA's medical mission was connected to the Red Cross; upon arrival in Russia in September 1921, it had to confront a recurrence of epidemics such as malaria, which was difficult to cure without quinine. There were cases of tuberculosis and typhus as well.

Colonel Henry Beeuwkes was the head of the ARA's medical commission. During World War I, he had served as the personal physician of General John J. Pershing. In August 1921, the president of the American Red Cross introduced Hoover and Beeuwkes to each other. Several weeks later, Hoover assigned Beeuwkes the task of creating the ARA's medical team, essentially composed of doctors who had served with the American army in World War I. "[Beeuwkes] established central warehouses in Moscow into which our immense medical imports were received and thence dispatched to the areas in need," Hoover recalled. "He established stations in each of the famine districts and also at points where the refugees could be treated. [. . .] His major methods of attacking the

---

[119] ARA, Russian Operations, 1919–1925, Box No. 96, Folder No. 5, Hoover Institution Archives, Stanford University.
[120] Goodrich to Hoover, November 1, 1921, ARA, Russian Operations, 1919–1925, Box No. 95, Folder No. 3, Hoover Institution Archives, Stanford University.

scourge was to equip existing institutions with food, medicine and medical instruments in order to bring life and tools to Russia's own doctors and technicians."[121]

After several months of famine, the inhabitants of the affected regions had to resort to a wide variety of food substitutes, with the sole goal of staving off the hunger pangs that gripped them. Beeuwkes described these strategies at length in a report published in 1926: "A white clay resembling stone, containing a small proportion of organic matter, was extensively used as an adulterant for making bread throughout the Volga area. In numerous villages which I visited during the Spring of 1922 many families made bread exclusively of bones, rushes and clay."[122] "Their bread, which they pathetically held out in their hands for exhibition, disclosed in every specimen examined an admixture of clay or [and?] straw," according to the district supervisor for Kazan, James Rives Childs. "It was the most repulsive-looking substitute for food which I have ever seen."[123] Cats, dogs, and rats were also trapped and eaten. Cases of cannibalism were attested in the districts of Odessa, Donetz, Zaporosh, Nicolaev, and Ekaterinoslav. Beeuwkes reported that in Orenburg a law required that meat be sold with minimal butchering, so that it could clearly be identified as being of animal origin.[124]

The effects of malnutrition began to appear en masse in the fall of 1921. In a report sent in September, Laurence Webster of the SCF described the visual shock he felt upon his arrival in southern Russia: "I was walking through the streets of Saratov when I spotted three peasants walking in front of me. Their appearance was so extraordinary that I stopped near them. The men were of a nice height, but extraordinarily fleshless and emaciated. Only with difficulty did they put one foot in front of the other. Their eyes, covered by a strange film, stared fixedly with the rigidity of absolute exhaustion. One instinctively sensed that these were men in an advanced state of inanition. This encounter was my first contact with the famine."[125] Beeuwkes confirmed: "The faces with puffed eyelids, the white waxy pallor of the skin, sometimes tinged with

---

[121] Herbert Hoover, *An American Epic*, Vol. 3 (Chicago: H. Regnery Co., 1961), pp. 473–477.

[122] Henry Beeuwkes, *American Medical and Sanitary Relief in the Russian Famine, 1921–1923* (New York: ARA, 1926), p. 20.

[123] Jamie H. Cockfield (ed.), *Black Lebeda: The Russian Famine Diary of ARA Kazan District Supervisor J. Rives Childs, 1921–1923* (Macon, Ga.: Mercer University Press, 2006), p. 24. Childs here describes *lebeda*, a kind of bread made from a mix of clay, grass, and straw.

[124] Beeuwkes, *American Medical and Sanitary Relief*, p. 21.

[125] ABIT, R301/5, Starvation in Russia. International Union of the Save the Children Fund.

jaundiced yellow, the swollen feet, legs and abdomen, and the labored movements of the extremities together with the peculiar mental apathy and lethargy characterizing these individuals, once seen are not soon forgotten."[126]

Faced with so many children to feed, the American doctors had to establish a way to rate the degree of malnutrition and thus prioritize the distribution of foods. They referred to Dr. Clément Pirquet's "Pelidisi system"[127] developed in 1919 during his work in Vienna. By calculating "the cubic root of the tenfold weight of the body divided by that body's sitting weight," Pirquet had managed to establish the level of malnutrition in the Viennese population. A healthy adult level was 100, children were 94.5. During the Russian crisis, children's level generally fell to 92, or even lower.[128] Based on this information and a complementary medical examination (muscular development, elasticity of the skin . . .), the young patient would in theory receive a nutrition card and a more or less sizeable ration.

The scholarly effort to understand the physiological mechanism of hunger, to evaluate an individual's degree of malnutrition, and to apply the correct remedies nevertheless clashed with the reality of the situation in the field. Lacking manpower and time, the American doctors could not perform the Pelidisi tests. Almost everywhere, the urgency of the situation required them to abandon the scientific study of the food crisis. In the villages where everyone knew each other, it was impossible to set priorities for food distribution that were acceptable to all, or to enforce the system of nutrition cards. Most often, the villagers in charge of the distribution of rations gave preference to their family or friends. Or else the rule of "might makes right" prevailed. Furthermore the League of Nations' Health Organization was too new to wield any authority on an international scale. Its director, Ludwik Rajchman, who had previously worked with Casimir Funk, one of the discoverers of vitamins, had wanted first to establish universally recognized nutritional standards. This project would have to wait for progress in the field of biochemistry,[129] and for a new global food crisis (the Great Depression of the 1930s), before it was finally achieved.

---

[126] Beeuwkes, *American Medical and Sanitary Relief*, p. 54.
[127] H. Violle and Theodore C. Merrill, "Recent applications of the principles of nutrition," *American Journal of Public Health*, 1922, pp. 568–574.
[128] *American Relief Administration Bulletin*, Series 2, No. 18, November 1921.
[129] Between 1931 and 1934, a series of conferences led to the recognition of vitamins by the scientific community. See Paul Weindling, "The role of international organizations in setting nutritional standards in the 1920s and 1930s," in Kamminga and Cunningham (eds.), *Science and Culture of Nutrition*, pp. 319–332.

The men of the American Relief Administration— between idealism and pragmatism

In the fall of 1921, aid began to flow in from throughout the world. The key to success in distributing this aid in the far-flung regions hit by famine (nearly 770,000 square miles, 1,000,000 in 1922), lay in mastering logistics. Herbert Hoover had extensive experience in this area, acquired notably during World War I and the immediate post-war period. The methods he employed in Russia were the same ones he had successfully established in Belgium beginning in 1914 and in Central Europe in 1919–20.

According to a veritable battle plan, the entire territory hit by famine was divided into 18 districts, each placed under the authority of an American official, assisted by a district physician. Their role was to set up committees of local volunteers, assigned to distribute aid and regularly send reports to the Moscow headquarters concerning the status of what was in stock and what was needed. The breadth of the crisis made it necessary for the ARA's agents to have a basic knowledge of statistics—hence a rise in applying scientific knowledge and techniques to humanitarian work—as well as a mastery of concrete problems such as the transport and storage of considerable quantities of food, which risked spoiling if not distributed in timely fashion. The shipment of packages from the sizeable Russo-American community to individual recipients was also negotiated with Soviet authorities. For $10, a package containing flour, rice, oil, milk, sugar, and tea was held for the Russian recipient at the ARA center closest to his home.[130] In areas where it had less of a presence, such as the Caucasus, the ARA appealed for help to private groups such as the Near East Relief, which already had a good knowledge of the region. Soon, all the regions affected by the famine were divided among the charities: the Society of Friends (Quakers) in the Samara region, as well as around Moscow and Minsk; the SCF around Saratov, and so on.

However, the situation in Russia presented a certain number of specific problems. The Baltic ports of Petrograd, Reval, and Danzig were not equipped to handle cargo ships carrying significant tonnage, and so goods from the United States were often sent to Hamburg, where they were divided among smaller ships that then went to Russia. During the winter—that is, from the end of October to the beginning of April—ice blocked access to the Baltic ports. Four Black Sea ports—Odessa,

---

[130] Archives of the ICRC, Geneva, Commixt II.5/G12bis: ARA—Food remittances to Russia, November 1921.

Theodosia, Novorossiysk, and Batum—were thus used to distribute aid to southern Russia and Ukraine. The packages then had to be unloaded and shipped in a regular rotation via trains headed to the regions awaiting Western aid.

The first deliveries of food were marked by difficulties. Upon the arrival of the American cargo ship *Phoenix*, the Russians unloaded the food sacks so carelessly that a portion of the shipment was lost, and the rest was stolen by dockworkers. "Openly and deliberately, in the face of the guards who were standing about to prevent pilferage, the workmen proceeded systematically to fill all available parts of their clothing—their hats, their pockets, the tied legs of their trousers—with flour, sugar and tins of preserved milk."[131] In November 1923, a report by Sidney Brooke, a former engineer of the Baltimore and Ohio railroad who was now in charge of transport for the ARA, gave a particularly severe account of the first months of humanitarian aid in action:

Each day brought new surprises, such as the sudden arrival of a relief ship unheralded by the advance telegram which should precede it, with no cars ready for its cargo, most of the warehouses full, no stevedoring gangs ready, and none of the other numerous preparations made [. . .] Or perhaps the long protesting rails would eventually give way in some vital part of the yard, derailing a string of cars and holding up the unloading of a ship for five or six hours. Then if all else went well for a change, perhaps the customs authorities would suddenly find reason to suspect that the ARA was importing machine guns and other dangerous arms and insist on opening various innocent cases of condensed milk to search for these weapons for a suspected counter-revolutionary plot.[132]

River transport on the Volga, the Don, and the Dnieper would have been the most obvious choice for getting aid from the north to the south, but a good part of the commercial fleet had been destroyed during the Civil War. It was thus necessary to use the railways. It was at this stage that the logistics set up by the Americans tended to fray. Indeed, the general condition of the Russian railways was absolutely calamitous. The railway network was already underdeveloped in 1914, which had created serious mobilization problems; it had since been partially destroyed, due to the movements of troops during the Great War and the Civil War. Barely 40 percent of locomotives were still functioning. On top of that, they ran on wood fire, since carbon production had decreased by 80 percent during the war years. The areas in southern Russia that had been hit by famine also suffered from a lack of fuel, since wood came for the most part from the forests of northern Russia. The Russian railways ran

[131] Fisher, *Famine in Soviet Russia*, p. 80.
[132] *American Relief Administration Bulletin*, Series 2, No. 42, November 1923, p. 34.

too slowly; it normally took 3 weeks to transport cargo from the Baltic ports to Moscow. The poor state of cargo wagons, the overloading of the railway network, the rise in administrative checkpoints and controls, the lack of willingness on the part of railway personnel, who sought to be paid in food for their participation, all explain the slow movement of food and supplies in the first months of 1922.

The main preoccupation of the ARA's leaders was to ensure a strict control over the supply transport lines. At headquarters in Moscow, giant wall maps of European Russia were dotted with little colored flags, in order to follow the daily progress of convoys of food, aid to children, and medicine.[133] In reality, since many telegraph lines had been destroyed during the war, it was impossible to know exactly where a particular cargo train was at a given time. In addition to the risk of losing convoys in transit, there was the risk of pillage. The Riga accords held the Russians responsible for the convoys' security. The cargo cars were weighed before departure and at arrival, and their doors were locked. According to the rules of revolutionary justice, theft was punishable by death. In all, the number of thefts was much less than anticipated by the Americans. When theft occurred, it was often the work of the armed guards accompanying the convoys. The army only provided rations for the planned length of the trip; the guards reached their final destination starving, or after drawing on the cargo they were supposed to keep watch over.[134]

Upon arrival, the aid still had to be distributed to cities and villages. The men of the ARA, isolated from the Moscow hierarchy, were obliged to negotiate with local authorities, who sought payment for the use of secondary rail networks. Roads were difficult in winter because of snow, and in spring because of mud. "Official statistics tell us there are over 300,000 miles of road in European Russia but in truth less than 3 per cent of these are paved and 80 per cent do not deserve the name of roads at all,"[135] one American observer noted. Aid was thus transported by sleigh or horse-drawn carriages. Yet in the areas hit by famine, the number of horses was clearly declining. Of the 33 million horses in Russia in 1913, it seems that there were only 17.5 million in 1921.[136] The rest had been killed during World War I and the Civil War, or they had starved to death. Finding feed for horses was at least as important as finding food for people during this major humanitarian crisis; horses were

---

[133] *Ibid.*, p. 29.   [134] *Ibid.*, p. 88.   [135] *Ibid.*, p. 82.
[136] Major General Sir John Moore estimated that there were 220,096,000 horses in Russia before the war: John Moore, "Wastage of animals in war," *The Journal of the United Service Institution of India*, 49: 221, October 1920. Although such statistics should be viewed with caution, it is still likely that there were catastrophic losses on the Eastern front.

indispensable for bringing aid to villages and for working in the fields, to find what food could be harvested. The Russian government thus set up a vast network for delivering feed, bought or requisitioned from areas spared by the drought. In reality, animal feed was sometimes used as a food substitute for people, or horses were killed for food by starving peasants.

The ARA established its base of operations at the end of August 1921 under the command of Colonel William N. Haskell, who had had wide experience in aid relief as Director of the ARA in Romania and Armenia in 1919–20. Carlton Bowden was one of the first to arrive in Russia. A former Rhodes Scholar, he had worked with the CRB during the war, and later with the ARA in Hungary. His early objectives were to find places for the kitchens, hire Russian staff, and make contact with local governments. "We have certainly come to the right place," he noted after a quick evaluation of the situation in Petrograd.[137] "The situation here is far worse than I had imagined. It is incredible that people can live on as little food as they receive here [. . .] The average ration even of grown-ups is not more than 1,200 calories daily. The food consists principally of very black bread and of a soup made from dry vegetables, with no fat content whatever."

Amazed by the influx of refugees fleeing the famine, the men of the ARA were convinced that the big cities, where need was most concentrated, should have priority in receiving aid. The spectacle offered by the train stations of Moscow and Petrograd was terrifying: "Imagine a compact mass of sordid rags, among which are visible here and there, lean, naked arms, faces already stamped with the seal of death. [. . .] The waiting room, the corridor, every foot thickly covered with people, sprawling, seated, crouched in every imaginable position . . . No registration is attempted . . . It is impossible to close the railway station. There is no way to stop this great wave of starving peasants who come to the city to die . . . "[138] When he arrived in Moscow in early September 1921, Philip Carroll was stupefied to see the chaos reigning in the city: "Everybody appears to have but one object in life and that is to get sufficient food and clothing. The market places are crowded, everyone trying to sell or exchange some small knickknack or trinket. Practically all shops are closed, though a few are opening up at the present time. Food is obtainable if one has money, but the prices are very high."[139] An

---

[137] *American Relief Administration Bulletin*, Series 2, No. 18, November 1921, Carlton G. Bowden, "Arrival of the first American Unit in Petrograd," pp. 7–11.

[138] *Ibid.*, p. 90.

[139] *American Relief Administration Bulletin*, Series 2, No. 18, November 1921, Philip H. Carroll, "ARA headquarters established in Moscow," p. 14.

enormous food kitchen was opened in Moscow in the space vacated by the Hermitage Restaurant, which had been famous before the revolution for the cuisine prepared by its French chef, Lucien Olivier.

At September's end, alarming reports began to arrive from the villages of the Volga basin. There, the situation was clearly even more dire. Hundreds of thousands of peasants were dying of hunger. In an article published in November 1921 in the *Bulletin* of the ARA, Will Shafroth made a particularly somber observation concerning the government of Kazan: "Two things stand out as of an importance which it is almost impossible to realize, without actual visual contact with these or similar conditions, as of an importance which cannot be over-estimated: first, that the present allocation is wholly inadequate to cover the need, and second, that speed in sending out the food and organizing its distribution means the saving of many lives."[140]

Most of the 380 Americans working for the ARA—a small number when in the context of the vastness of the affected regions—were young men between the ages of 20 and 30. By August 1921, hundreds of job application letters arrived at the ARA's headquarters at 42 Broadway, New York City. These letters, kept in the Hoover Archives in Palo Alto, give a portrait of a generation of educated young men, imbued with Wilsonian ideals, but also incredibly naïve about a country that they did not know well and that they frequently referred to as "Bololand," or "Bolshevik country." Their motives, tinged with feelings of Western superiority and of anti-Communism, were all loosely equivalent: "come to the aid of the Russian people," "fight famine in the name of Humanity." Many had just graduated from college. For those who had not seen combat during the Great War, a tour with the ARA looked like a chance to do something with their lives. Others had fought on the western front, like Dudley H. Hale, born in 1893, who took part in the Argonne offensive; or George N. McClintock, born in 1897, decorated with the *Croix de guerre*. For them, the humanitarian aid operation in Russia was a way to escape the boredom that had followed demobilization. Others had already participated in relief work, like Philip Carroll, formerly of West Point, who directed the operations of the ARA in Serbia and then in Hamburg in 1919–20. But most of the men of the ARA were inexperienced and arrived in Russia armed only with their idealism.[141]

---

[140] *American Relief Administration Bulletin*, Series 2, No. 18, November 1921, Will Shafroth, "An inspection trip to the Volga," p. 25.
[141] "Personnel of the ARA," ARA, Russian Operations, 1919–1925, Box No. 266, Folder Nos. 2, 3 and 4, Hoover Institution Archives, Stanford University.

Imagine, for example, the lack of preparedness of someone like Frank Golder, a former history major who went to Russia to buy books for the Hoover War Collection (predecessor of the Hoover Archives) in Stanford, and who was recruited to the ARA simply because he spoke fluent Russian: born near Odessa in 1877, when he was at the age of eight his family had fled the pogroms following the assassination of Czar Alexander II. They then settled in the United States. Golder wrote a thesis on Russian history at Harvard, but nothing had prepared him for participating in a humanitarian operation of such breadth.[142] Even Mayer Raskin, who had fought on the western front during the war, was obliged to admit, "The only instructions I received were from Colonel Grove (the district supervisor of Ukraine) who stated in a crisp military tone that the only instruction that he could give me was to sink or swim."[143] In the month of May 1922, at age 24, he found himself in charge of humanitarian aid in Nikolayev, a province with a population of 1.4 million, of which 580,000 were classified as suffering from hunger.

In every village, a kitchen was hastily set up in a school or a house that had been abandoned after the death of its occupants; here, bread was to be baked and meals prepared. The ARA regulations were strict: all food had to be prepared and eaten on site, in the collective kitchens and dining rooms. Otherwise, how could one ensure that the weakest—particularly the children—would not be robbed of their food? The meals essentially consisted of a piece of white bread, a little rice, corncakes, a little milk, sugar, and sometimes cocoa. Russian inspectors were entrusted by the ARA to make rounds in the villages in all weather conditions, checking the quality of the food and the efficiency of distributions. At the height of its activity, in the summer of 1922, the ARA served meals to more than 10 million people.[144]

The young Americans sent to Russia were well fed and comfortably housed. Because they were volunteers, they were free to end their work at any time. "It is like seeing a great tragedy on the stage while sitting on soft upholstered seats with a box of chocolates in your lap and a limousine waiting outside to take you home," confessed an American Quaker, working in the Samara region.[145] Even so, medical personnel frequently

---

[142] Frank Alfred Golder and Lincoln Hutchinson, *On the Trail of the Russian Famine* (Stanford University Press, 1927).

[143] Mayer Raskin, "Bringing relief to Nikolaiev," in H.H. Fisher and Suda L. Bane (eds.), *Documents of the American Relief Administration, Russian Operations, 1921–1923* (Stanford, 1931), p. 9.

[144] The most reliable statistics, also organized by region, can be found in Surface and Bland (eds.), *American Food*, pp. 862–927.

[145] Edwin H. Vail Papers, 1922–1924, Hoover Institution Archives, Stanford University.

observed signs of depression, called "famine shock" (an adaptation of the Great War's "shell shock"), among the staff. "The boys of the ARA were in a really hyper nervous condition from hard work and memories of the horrors that they worked night and day to alleviate last winter," noted one doctor sent to the town of Orenburg. "I took the liberty of asking a big strong American why he showed such signs of suffering when there was no doubt in [my] mind that he had had good food, a warm place to sleep and a good bed . . . Among other things he said . . . How in hell can a real man eat or sleep in comfort when he knows that in the morning the first thing that will greet his eyes when he looks out of the window will be corpses along the street?"[146]

In the province of Samara in the fall of 1921, an American and several Russian inspectors had to stop work following nervous breakdowns, as did the district supervisor of Zaporizhia in Ukraine. "Many clever young Americans had to be sent out of Russia with nerves completely wrecked or on the verge of insanity due not only to the horrible suffering which they were forced to witness but to the interference and annoyance to which they were unnecessarily subjected by the very Soviet officials who should have been their helpers," remembered William Haskell.[147] Besides the difficulty inherent in an enormous task, and the danger of epidemics, the men of the ARA soon found themselves burdened with all the complexities of the Russian bureaucracy. When they arrived in Russia, the Americans were greeted with suspicion by the Bolshevik authorities. The memory of the Civil War and the Western support of the White armies was on everyone's mind. The Russian press depicted the Westerners as capitalists hoping to help themselves to Russia's natural resources. "Taught as an A-B-C principle that all human conduct is guided purely by motives of self interest, how can the good Communistic Soviet government official be expected to think that such a thing as a relief organization animated by philanthropic motives is possible—the more so when that organization is from the most capitalistic of all states, and headed by a man who has been the kind of capitalist they most dislike and fear . . . ?" wondered James Somerville.[148]

At the same time, the letters the Americans wrote home to their families contradicted the idealized picture put forward by Hoover's propaganda, that of a great collective epic. The letters speak of feelings of isolation, and of always being watched. "My great trouble was that I was all alone,"

---

[146] Bakhmetev Archives, Columbia University, New York., [Henry O. Eversole] to Selskar Gunn, October 8, 1922, Allen Wardwell Papers, p. 7.

[147] William Haskell Papers, 1932, vol. I, 157, ARA, Russian Operations, 1919–1925, Hoover Institution Archives, Stanford University.

[148] Quoted in Patenaude, *Big Show in Bololand*, p. 640.

confessed Mayer Raskin. "I had no one to tell my troubles to, and I hardly need to assure anyone that I had enough worries to keep me from oversleeping mornings." In Moscow and other large urban centers, the relationships between Americans and their Russian counterparts were based on a kind of mutual mistrust, but also on the certainty that both sides had to collaborate. In the countryside, the situation was generally more complex. Local Communist officials were completely ignorant of the Riga Accords and had never seen an American in their entire lives. They were struck by the humiliation of watching foreigners, speaking a language they did not understand, interfering in Russia's internal affairs. The Russians were indignant that their government had been forced to pay for the equipment costs of the aid operation, as well as for the transportation of food and the salaries of the local employees of the ARA "Something like that was to be expected from the practical, business-like Yankees," they claimed.

"It is the common experience of ARA men that the farther you get from the center, either of the Soviet government itself or of the *Gubernia* or ARA District Headquarters, the greater generally are the difficulties with the local authorities. What might seem reasonable to [the Soviet government plenipotentiary representative] Karl Lander in Moscow will be disputed by the second-rate representatives sent out by Moscow to the District," confessed the ARA inspector Arthur Ruhl.[149] The best way to avoid tensions with the local authorities was to organize frequent informal meetings—which Cyril Quinn called "diplomacy of the samovar" in a memo to the representatives of the ARA in January 1923. The Americans not only needed to learn to drink the traditional tea, they had to be able to endure, for better or worse, the ingestion of copious amounts of vodka while remaining lucid enough to avoid the pitfalls of conversation. Theoretically, it was forbidden to talk politics. How did one answer a local official when he toasted "the day when the United States will recognize Russia"? By lifting his glass in honor of "the day when Russia will balance her budget," quipped Thomas Barringer, who had arrived in Russia in February 1922.[150] Some ARA men, like Frank Golder, were bilingual and others, like James Rives Childs, took intensive Russian language courses, but many had to use the services of an interpreter, who was often later revealed to be a Communist Party spy.

149 "Memorandum on inspection trip to Tsaritsyn, 17 July–12 August 1922," by Arthur Ruhl, ARA, Russian Operations, 1919–1925, Box 83, Folder 2, Hoover Institution Archives, Stanford University.
150 Thomas C. Barringer Papers, 1922–1925, "An American's impression of Soviet Russia," 1923, ARA, Russian Operations, 1919–1925, Hoover Institution Archives, Stanford University.

Six months after the arrival of the first Americans on Russian territory, relations between ARA men and the Bolsheviks were considerably
strained. In Samara, Plenipotentiary Representative Karklin demanded
access to all telegrams sent by the Americans. In Orenburg, the local
Communist Party chief asked the ARA to feed the Red Army, a violation of the Riga accords. In April 1922, several Russian employees of
the ARA were detained in Tsaritsyn, Samara, and Moscow. At the same
time, the railroad workers went on strike to protest their living conditions
and refused to move the cars loaded with humanitarian aid. Therefore,
with the ARA's agreement, Soviet authorities took nearly 5,000 tons of
wheat and corn from the food supply, valued at a total $230,000, so that
the workers might end the strike.[151]

In fact, the ARA men learned that a different definition of rights ruled
their day-to-day existence, one far from the idealism that had compelled
them to come to Russia. The Americans spoke of free access to food.
They hoped that the daily labor of the ARA and its tens of thousands of
Russian co-workers, most of them drawn from educated, bourgeois circles, would soon give birth to a new democratic Russia. On the contrary,
their Russian counterparts accused them of choosing beneficiaries on an
ideological basis. "Out of a total of 393,273 packages received by July
(1922), 60 percent of ARA packages were received by intellectuals, professors and city residents, leaving 40 percent for workers and peasants of
the countryside and rural areas," one official Soviet report complained.
"By nationality, the packages were distributed thus: 50 percent of the
total went to Jews, and moreover, not to the poorest ones but to members of the petty bourgeoisie and tradesmen, the remaining 50 percent to
the other nationalities of the RSFSR [Russian Soviet Federative Socialist
Republic]."[152] The accusation that the ARA gave priority to Jews was
frequent. In Ekaterinoslav (Ukraine), Thomas Barringer was accused
by a local representative of helping "exclusively the speculators."[153]
In Kiev, a rumor held that the acronym "ARA" had been selected
so that it could be read from right to left by its Jewish beneficiaries.
Humanitarian aid was called *Zhidopomoshch*, which translates as "Yid-
Relief."[154]

In the midst of the tragedy of the Russian famine, therefore, remained
the more fundamental question of who had the power to feed. Nourishment is a parental function, explained anthropologist Margaret Mead in

---

[151] Surface and Bland (eds.), *American Food*, p. 250.
[152] Weissman, *Herbert Hoover*, p. 121.
[153] Thomas C. Barringer, May 25, 1923, ARA, Russian Operations, 1919–1925, Box No.
138, Folder No.12, Hoover Institution Archives, Stanford University.
[154] Patenaude, *Big Show in Bololand*, p. 633.

another context. She thought that "no other operation, even the provision of hospitalization and emergency care, is so effective in proving to an anxious and disturbed people that the powers... have their welfare at heart."[155] Nourishment also appeared as a providential power at a time when all the suffering of the world seemed to have fallen on Russia. The peasants who thought the ARA men were "messengers from God" were not altogether wrong. After a period of suspicion during the fall of 1921, followed by the first disputes in that winter, there came a time when the people of Ukraine and Volga fervently welcomed the Americans.

American corn, expected since the beginning of the year, finally arrived in April 1922. "People fall on their knees and kiss the earth upon which the relief workers walk," reported young Will Shafroth, clearly very impressed by the welcome he received. "The United States can have a solemn feeling of pride in saving the Russian race from extinction [...] To the [simple peasants] American inspectors were almost gods. I have seen them crowd around and fall on their knees trying to kiss my feet, because I symbolized to them the nation which was saving them from death. And I believe that they will always feel unceasing gratitude to the American people."[156] "To the mind of the Russian common people, the American Relief Administration was a miracle of God which came to them in their darkest hour under the stars and stripes," Colonel Haskell intoned in a letter to Hoover, in August 1923.[157] No doubt one must read these sorts of testimony—and they frequently appeared in the pages of the American press and the ARA bulletins—with care, since they say as much about the idealism of the men of the ARA as about the emotions actually experienced by the Russians, which are of course difficult to evaluate without reliable sources.[158]

The cries of joy from women and children, the tears of the aged, the falling to knees and making the sign of the cross: all these rituals of collective gratitude, told and retold by the Americans, also served to give meaning to the mission in which the ARA was invested. Contradictory

---

[155] Margaret Mead, "Food and feeding in occupied territory," *The Public Opinion Quarterly* 7: 4, Winter 1943, pp. 618–628.
[156] ARA, Russian Operations, 1919–1925, Box No. 81, Folder No. 8, Hoover Institution Archives, Stanford University.
[157] ARA, Russian Operations, 1919–1925, Box No. 340, Folder No. 3, Hoover Institution Archives, Stanford University.
[158] In his diary, James Rives Childs, district supervisor for Kazan, noted: "Even when the people of Karakulinsky *volost* were told that the food which we were distributing came from America, there were many to whom this meant nothing as they had no conception of America or of anything outside the narrow little circle in which they moved." Cockfield (ed.), *Black Lebeda*, p. 167.

accounts, however, come from American doctors, who discerned a certain apathy in the Russian population, characteristic of the shock of famine. "These people have borne so much that their emotions have long since been exhausted," noted the district physician William Dear, visiting a small village of the *volost* of Norkeyevskaya.[159]

Russia was a place where power had long expressed itself through the function of nourishing;[160] he who fed the people, especially he who fed them in times of famine, also wielded true power. Russian peasants accepted paying tax in exchange for state protection in case of famine. The 1921–23 crisis changed the relationship between the peasants and state power. Neither central government nor local authority was capable by itself of responding to the humanitarian disaster. In response to the urgency of the food crisis, the Bolsheviks invoked the "patriotic duty" of all citizens to come to the aid of regions touched by famine. The moral economy that was the very foundation of rural Russian society was shaken.[161] Local Communist Party officials tried also to minimize the ARA's contributions by emphasizing the vastness of the United States' resources. Some suggested that the Americans had only acted under pressure from their own working class. In several speeches, Lenin praised the work of the International Workers' Committee for Aid to the Starving in Russia, a charity that he had inspired and that brought together many sympathetic individuals including Käthe Kollwitz, George Bernard Shaw, Henri Barbusse, and Paul Vaillant-Couturier.[162] It was his way of demonstrating that the overarching triumph of the relief effort was not the establishment of humanitarian values, that were considered "bourgeois," but the strength of proletarian solidarity and the endurance of the Russian Revolution.

The relief operations in Russia ended in mid June 1923 with reassuring predictions for the future. "Samara, the blackest spot of last year's Volga famine, is emerging from the catastrophe with an excellent chance of having a surplus of grain when the summer crop is harvested," according to district supervisor Ronald Allen.[163] Between 10 and 11 million Russians had been saved thanks to international humanitarian aid, but the loss of life had been very heavy: between 1.5 and 2 million people in 1921–22, tens of thousands the following year, and several thousand

---

[159] Medical Reports, ARA, Russian Operations, 1919–1925, Box No. 29, Folder No. 6, Hoover Institution Archives, Stanford University.

[160] Tamara Kondratieva, *Gouverner et nourrir: du pouvoir en Russie (XVIème–XXème siècles)* (Paris: Les Belles Lettres, 2002).

[161] Retish, *Russia's Peasants*, p. 257.   [162] Weissman, *Herbert Hoover*, p. 168.

[163] Hoover Institution Archives, Stanford University, ARA, Russian Operations, 1919–1925, Box 89, Folder 1, ARA News Release, April 19, 1923.

in 1923, according to the best estimates.[164] Many villages in Volga and Ukraine vanished from the map, their inhabitants driven to the cities or decimated by hunger. In the deserted streets, the silence was deafening.

Since 1921, the dramatic circumstances of the Russian famine had given birth to the greatest humanitarian aid program in the history of the world, involving dozens of nations and as many charitable organizations. Paradoxically, the most advanced thinking on humanitarianism came from a man known worldwide for his anti-Communist views. "The sole object of relief should be Humanity," Herbert Hoover had explained. Secretary of Commerce and a businessman, Hoover was also the head of a private humanitarian aid agency, and at risk of confusing public and personal interests. Yet for him, there was no contradiction between invoking humanitarian themes and hoping for the rapid downfall of the Communist regime. Hoover considered Communism "a symptom of people in distress" and the food crisis as the paroxysmal expression of the Russian tragedy. To assert humanitarian rights for the starving people of Russia—as he had done for the former German and Austrian enemies 2 years earlier—was to affirm their right to political stability and give them the chance to rejoin the ranks of civilized nations. Or, as one ARA volunteer, James Goodrich, wrote: "We are again proving to all the world that in America human sympathy outweighs material achievement, and in the heart of a giant nation, which is about to awaken from a long sleep, we are planting seeds of affection, of common understanding, that some day will flourish and stand us in good stead, materially as well as sentimentally and morally."[165]

In July 1922, Maxim Gorky, living in exile in Italy because of his differences with Lenin, wrote to Hoover to congratulate him on the early results achieved by the ARA. "In all the history of human suffering I know of nothing more trying to the souls of men than the events through which the Russian people are passing, and in the history of practical humanitarianism, I know of no accomplishment which in terms of magnitude and generosity can be compared to the relief that you have actually accomplished . . . The generosity of the American people resuscitates the dream of fraternity among people at a time when humanity greatly needs charity and compassion."[166]

---

[164] A. Berelowitch and V. Danilov (eds.), *Sovetskaâ derevnâ glazami VCK-OGPU-NKVD. Dokumenty i materialy* (Moscow, 1998), Vol. I (1918–1922), p. 14, quoted in Kondratieva, *Gouverner et nourrir*, pp. 233–234.

[165] James P. Goodrich, "The True Communists of Russia," *Current History* (September 1922), p. 931.

[166] *American Relief Administration Bulletin*, Series 2, No. 28, p. 6.

A year later, the victory over the famine left Hoover with a bitter after-taste. Certainly, Lenin had opened his country to capitalism with his NEP. The Russian government held up the name of Henry Ford as a model of modernity and efficiency. "We need Marxism plus American-ism," Bukharin had said.[167] But the Bolshevik dictatorship remained solidly in place. The hope of its impending downfall, so strong at the moment when the relief effort was launched in the summer of 1921, gradually evaporated. "Mr. Hoover said that he had never been so glad to finish a job as this Russian job," noted one of his correspondents, "that he was completely disgusted with the Bolsheviks and did not believe that a practical government could ever be worked out under their leader-ship."[168]

Conclusion

The ARA's humanitarian work in Russia ended in diplomatic failure. At the end of the summer of 1923, President Harding reaffirmed his refusal to recognize the Communist government of Russia.[169] Hoover himself shared the President's resolve. In the absence of any indemnity for for-eign property seized by the Bolsheviks during the October Revolution, it was useless to hope for a normalization of diplomatic and trade rela-tions between the two countries; this would not occur until November 1933.[170] Nevertheless the extent and the duration of aid to Russia in the 1920s was impossible to ignore. By bringing nearly 768,000 tons of food, medicine, and clothing, the Americans succeeded in establish-ing the most important humanitarian operation of the early twentieth century within the space of several months.[171] The men of the ARA saved several million human lives. Thanks to his experience as an engi-neer and as a businessman, Hoover created a new kind of humanitarian

---

[67] Hans Rogger, "*Amerikanizm* and the economic development of Russia," *Comparative Studies in Society and History*, 23, July 1981, pp. 382–420.

[68] DeWitt Clinton Poole to Charles Evans Hughes, May 4, 1923, General Records of the Department of State, Record Group 59, National Archives, Washington DC, File 861.48/2215, quoted in Patenaude, *Big Show in Bololand*, p. 706.

[69] *New York Times*, August 1, 1923, p. 1.

[70] The steps towards normalization of diplomatic and trade relations between the USSR and Western countries were a March 16, 1921 trade agreement between Great Britain and the USSR; the Rapallo treaty between the USSR and Germany signed on April 16, 1922; and the Herriot government's formal recognition of the USSR on October 28, 1924. For an analysis of these events, see Jan F. Triska and Robert M. Slusser (eds.), *The Theory, Law and Policy of Soviet Treaties* (Stanford University Press, 1962), pp. 181–210.

[71] Surface and Bland, *American Food*, p. 239.

aid, one capable of responding quickly and efficiently to humanitarian disasters.

Even if the general structure of humanitarian aid in Russia was based on models that were created in wartime, Hoover's motivations were more complex in 1921 than they had been during his previous experiences. In the case of the countries assisted by the ARA in 1919–20,—Germany, Austria, Hungary, Poland, Bulgaria, and Czechoslovakia—the goals of the Americans were both economic (to participate in rebuilding Central Europe) and political (to limit the spread of Communism). These goals were clearly in line with American national interests. Insofar as aid to Russia was concerned, the ARA's work was in contradiction with the diplomatic and trade isolation that the United States had consistently practiced with regard to Russia since the October Revolution. Paradoxically, the ARA ran the risk of strengthening the Bolshevik regime at the moment when it was most threatened. For a staunch anti-Communist like Hoover, the decision to intervene in Russia could be summed up in a central question: how to help Russia without helping the Bolsheviks?

Humanitarian intervention in Russia in 1921–23—a massive, lengthy, and costly operation—can be explained in various ways. Hoover has often been portrayed as a pragmatic entrepreneur who wanted to find commercial outlets for American agricultural surpluses and open new markets for the United States. In December 1921, addressing the Committee on Foreign Affairs of the House of Representatives, he declared, "The food supplies that we wish to take to Russia are all in surplus in the United States, and are without a market in any quarter of the globe . . . We are today feeding milk to our hogs; burning corn under our boilers."[172] Several weeks earlier, when the Secretary of State, Charles Evans Hughes, suggested that Germany serve as an intermediary for future trade exchanges between the United States and Russia, Hoover unveiled a long-term strategy: "The relief measures already initiated [. . .] will build a situation which, combined with other factors, will enable the Americans to undertake the leadership in the reconstruction of Russia when the proper moment arrives."[173] Here, Hoover is speaking in his role as Secretary of Commerce, a position he held from March 1921 to August 1928. He was counting on the short-term collapse of the Communist regime. He hoped to contribute to the fall of Communism by bringing concrete proof of Bolshevik incompetence and American

---

[172] US Congress, House of Representatives. *Russian Relief: Hearings Before the Committee on Foreign Affairs*, 67th Congress, 2nd Session, 1921, p. 39.

[173] Hoover to Hughes, December 10, 1921, quoted in Patenaude, *Big Show in Bololand*, p. 637.

efficiency to Russian peasants—which explains his disillusionment in the summer of 1923, when the Americans left and the regime was still in place.

Other scholars have stressed Hoover's idealism and his humanitarian convictions, which would put him closer to Nansen.[174] The natural solidarity among human beings, the distinction Hoover made between the Russian population and its leaders, and the innocence of the famine victims are themes that recur regularly in his public speeches. In fact, these two interpretations of Hoover's work, the pragmatic and the idealistic, do not necessarily contradict each other. In his relationship with President Harding and with Congress, Hoover skillfully drew on both approaches, sometimes stressing the benefit to the United States in helping Russia, sometimes emphasizing the moral greatness of the mission; yet it is not easy to discern whether one aspect held a greater importance for him than the other.[175] Indeed, in an interview with a Russian newspaper in September 1921, Trotsky had already underlined the ambiguity of the ARA's project, and sketched the outlines of humanitarianism as we know it today: "Of course, help to the starving is spontaneous philanthropy, but there are few real philanthropists—even among American Quakers. Philanthropy is tied to business, to enterprises, to interests—if not today, then tomorrow."[176]

It is important to move beyond speculating on Hoover's own motives, since aid to Russia clearly represents also a major turning point in the emergence of a feeling of international solidarity in response to natural disasters. In the nineteenth century, the idea of intervening abroad to come to the aid of others was commonly accepted, especially where minority populations were concerned, as in the question of the Near East.[177] The words "humanitarianism" and "humanitarian" appeared in

[174] See, for example, McElroy, *Morality and American Foreign Policy*. Somewhat surprisingly, in the 1950s, the diplomat George F. Kennan (the father of the containment doctrine) praised the ARA's work as a "forgotten chapter" in the history of American benevolence, whereas the Soviets of that same era tended to relativize the importance of the ARA. See George Kennan, "Our aid to Russia, a forgotten chapter," *New York Times Magazine*, July 19, 1959. See also John Gaddis, *George F. Kennan: An American Life* (New York: Penguin Press, 2011).

[175] According to David Burner, Hoover's biographer, the latter was someone who "in a philosophical way liked to perceive concurrences of morality and self-interest and in practice knew something about managing people, did indeed use the fact of the surplus to obtain Congressional approval of funds for the ARA. But it is not easy to say whether his own thoughts were on unloading the surplus, or on manipulating Congress for the sake of the hungry or both." Burner, *Herbert Hoover*, pp. 132–133.

[176] Leon Trotsky, *Sputnik Kommunista* (Moscow), 3 (September 4, 1921), p. 15, quoted in Weissman, *Herbert Hoover*, p. 18.

[177] In his book *Freedom's Battle,* Bass traces the first example of humanitarian intervention back to the Greek revolt of 1821–32, to the 1860–61 expedition in Syria, and to the

English in the years 1840–50. At the same time, the French popularized the idea of "*intervention d'humanité*" [humanitarian intervention].[178]
These new concepts signaled an important development in the ethics of
action, which was no longer motivated solely by the case of an individual
in distress, as with traditional charity, or by a vaguely defined social group
(the "poor," the "indigent"), but by *a crisis situation*, such as an armed
conflict, that affected a specific population group (for example, prisoners
of war or disabled veterans). At work in nineteenth-century humanitarianism, especially after Henri Dunant created the Red Cross in 1863,
was the desire to confront and respond to human suffering for a short
period of time, during a war, and to reestablish conditions favorable to
the dignity of the individual.[179]

Yet, until 1914, environmental catastrophes such as earthquakes and
famines were rarely part of humanitarian intervention beyond national
borders.[180] There were of course some exceptions, such as when col-
onized territories were affected by a humanitarian crisis,[181] or when a
country's sensibilities were especially touched by a catastrophe, such as
the emergency relief funds that the US Congress approved following
earthquakes in Venezuela in 1812 and in Sicily in 1908.[182] Most often,
diasporic populations organized among themselves to provide aid to their
country of origin, as when Russians who had settled in Europe and the
United States sent aid to Russia during the famine of 1891.[183]

In the wake of the Great War, article 25 of the League of Nations
Covenant stressed the preeminent role the International Red Cross
played in "the improvement of health, the prevention of disease and

early days of the Armenian question. See also Rodogno, *Against Massacre*. For its part
Simms and Trim (eds.), *Humanitarian Intervention* offers a remarkable synthesis of the
emerging notion of "humanitarian intervention." See also Michael Barnett, *Empire o*
Humanity: A History of Humanitarianism (Ithaca: Cornell University Press, 2011).

178 Antoine Rougier, *La théorie de l'intervention d'humanité* (Paris: Pedone, 1910).
179 On the eve of the Great War, the role of the national Red Cross organizations in futur
conflicts was anticipated by each of the belligerents, who took it into account in thei
war plans. For more on this militarization of humanitarianism in Europe prior to 1914
see Hutchinson, *Champions of Charity*, p. 198.
180 The Lisbon earthquake of November 1755, which played an important role in th
philosophical debates between Voltaire and Rousseau concerning the nature of evi
resulted in the first use of humanitarian aid in European history: the British parliamer
offered £100,000; the city of Hamburg sent four ships carrying clothes, and woo
for rebuilding; Spain sent money. See Grégory Quenet, *Les tremblements de terre au*
XVIIème et XVIIIème siècles: la naissance d'un risque (Paris: Champ Vallon, 2005).
181 Alessa Johns (ed.), *Dreadful Visitations: Confronting Natural Catastrophe in the Age*
Enlightenment (New York: Routledge, 1999), Part II, pp. 81–181.
182 McElroy, *Morality and American Foreign Policy*, p. 59.
183 Emily Rosenberg, "Missions to the world: philanthropy abroad," in *Charity, Phila*
thropy and Civility in American History (ed.), Lawrence Friedman and Mark McGarv
(New York: Cambridge University Press, 2004), p. 248.

the mitigation of suffering throughout the world." In March 1921, the League established a Bureau of Relief in charge of organizing international cooperation during humanitarian crises. At the same time, the League recognized "a *human right* of nations stricken by calamities which could not be foreseen, to be assisted by [international governmental] solidarity, if the mobilization of their own powers is found insufficient to succor the suffering within their territory."[184]

However, this "right to assistance" remained vague, since it was recognized *collectively* with respect to nations, and not *universally* with respect to individuals affected by catastrophe. It was not accompanied by the codification of a "right to humanitarian intervention," or, *a fortiori*, by a "duty to intervene for humanitarian reasons"—concepts which are still widely debated today.[185] Countries intervened individually, in accordance with their own diplomatic imperatives.[186] The case of the 1921–23 Russian famine illustrates the limits of the international solidarity defined by the League in the spring of 1921; several months later, Fridtjof Nansen encountered an almost complete European resistance to financing aid to Russia, which he had set up under the auspices of the ICRC. The virulent anti-Communism of the early 1920s, the fear that the Bolsheviks would turn the aid to their own gain, and the desire to maintain Russia's diplomatic isolation all prevailed over any feeling of humanitarian obligation in Western countries.

It was not until the fall of 1923, several months after the end of the ARA's mission in Russia, that the League of Nations created a commission in charge of organizing "an international federation of states, for the mutual assistance of peoples stricken by calamity." The senator Giovanni Ciraolo, president of the Italian Red Cross, led the commission. A native of Calabria, he had lost several family members during the 1908 earthquake in Messina. For several months, the practical aspects of this new

---

[184] League of Nations, *Official Journal of the League of Nations*, Geneva, 1922, p. 1216.

[185] For a general introduction to these debates, see Didier Fassin, *La raison humanitaire: une histoire morale du temps présent* (Paris: Gallimard/Seuil/Hautes Etudes, 2010), translated by Rachel Gomme as *Humanitarian Reason: A Moral History of the Present Times* (Berkeley: University of California Press, 2012).

[186] In September 1923, President Calvin Coolidge decided to send aid to Japan, where 145,000 people had been victims of an earthquake. Tons of food were transported to the port of Yokohama by a dozen American warships. The American Red Cross launched a fundraising campaign, which brought in nearly $12 million. This significant humanitarian catastrophe was one of a series of earthquakes that caused Western attitudes towards natural disasters to change: Lisbon in 1755, San Francisco in 1906, and Messina in 1908. See François Walter, *Catastrophes: une histoire culturelle, XVIème–XXIème siècles* (Paris: Seuil, 2008). On the San Francisco earthquake of 1906, see Ted Steinberg, "Smoke and mirrors: the San Francisco earthquake and seismic denial," in Steven Biel (ed.), *American Disasters* (New York University Press, 2001), pp. 103–126.

organization were the subject of lively debate:[187] what role should the International Committee of the Red Cross and the League of Red Cross Societies play? How should states finance aid to countries affected by humanitarian crises, and, in addition, what exactly were the "calamities" that Ciraolo wanted to address?[188] Despite widespread opposition, especially from the British, the Council of the League of Nations approved the statutes of the International Relief Union (IRU) in 1926, and they became effective in December 1932.

At the end of the 1930s, the IRU had been strangled by the economic crisis, which dried up its funds. It "was like an army magnificently equipped, with an iron discipline and the most modern armaments, but with the serious defect, in the firing line, of being almost entirely without ammunition,"[189] in the words of a member of its executive committee. Following World War II, the IRU ceased to exist. Its mission was taken up by UNESCO, in charge of world heritage and education, and by the International Red Cross. But the essential issue here is not the difficulties encountered by the IRU in the 1930s. It is in the effect of the message that the organization wished to convey following the Great War: charity no longer dictated aid to countries affected by humanitarian crises; justice and solidarity did. The "right to assistance," to use Ciraolo's term, was no longer applied solely to victims of war, in the tradition of humanitarian law.[190] It now also concerned victims of natural disasters in peacetime.

One French jurist in particular, who was part of the working committee organized by Ciraolo, advocated for defining aid to victims as an "obligation of humanity." For René Cassin, all peoples ought to be able to

---

[187] John F. Hutchinson, "Disasters and the international order: earthquakes, humanitarians and the Ciraolo Project," *The International History Review*, 22: 1, March 2000, pp. 1–36.

[188] The term "calamity" covered a large range of possible meanings. Article 3 of the organization's provisional statutes stated that it would intervene each time an urban community was overcome "by upheavals due to natural forces . . . the spread of dangerous epidemics; a disturbance of the social conditions . . . which unexpectedly cuts off the minimum supplies indispensable for normal existence; the consequences of war, in so far as they may have deprived a people of the resources or the power to meet, without assistance, the immediate needs of its collective life; [or] the threatened exhaustion of the race through the lack, in the hour of need, of the barest provision for the safety of its children." Giovanni Ciraolo, *An International Organization of Mutual Aid among the Nations for Succour and Assistance to Peoples Stricken by Calamities: Project and Explanatory Notes* (Rome, 1923).

[189] Camille Gorgé, *The International Relief Union: Its Origin, Aims, Means and Future* (Geneva, 1938), p. 35.

[190] Sassoli, "Le droit international humanitaire."

benefit from international solidarity in calamitous situations.[191] In June 1924, he wrote that it was necessary to "put into practice the equal application of the right to mutual aid for all peoples in cases of calamity."[192] For Germans and Austrians, as well as for the rest of post-war Europe; for Russians as well as for other victims of famine. This was, after all, exactly what Cassin had demanded several years earlier, for veterans of the Great War.

[191] Peter Macalister-Smith, *International Humanitarian Assistance. Disaster Relief Actions in International Law and Organization* (Dordrecht/Boston/Lancaster: Martinus Nijhoff, 1985), pp. 18–21.
[192] Commission d'étude du projet Ciraolo, June 27–29 1925, p. 19, quoted in Prost and Winter, *René Cassin*, p. 100.

5 Humanitarianism old and new: Eglantyne Jebb and children's rights

"The soldiers are the 'Heroes of Europe,' but it is the thousands of sick and starving and helpless and deserted folk, whose misery is unrelieved by the sense of adventure and victory, who pay the price for war's arbitrament."

Eglantyne Jebb, "Where war has been lady's work in Macedonia," May 30, 1913.

At the end of September 1924, the League of Nations met for its fifth General Assembly in the Salle de la Réformation, located in the very heart of Geneva. The Ministers of Foreign Affairs from twenty-one European countries had made the journey there, in addition to the British and French Prime Ministers, Ramsay MacDonald and Edouard Herriot. They had come to discuss the recently finished London Reparations Conference as well as the Dawes Plan, which had just taken effect several days earlier.[1]

On the morning of September 26, the delegates examined a short document entitled the "World Child Welfare Charter." It was the work of an international association founded in 1920, the Save the Children International Union (SCIU), and, more specifically, the work of a British activist, Eglantyne Jebb, then 48 years old. The preamble's first words rang out with the promise of a new era: "Mankind owes to the Child the best that it has to give . . . beyond and above all considerations of race, nationality, or creed."

Most of the League's delegates were quite familiar with the SCIU's work. Some were even members of its executive board, such as Giuseppe Motta of Switzerland, the president of the League's 1924 General Assembly. Save the Children, the British organization that was the precursor of the SCIU, had earned a solid reputation through its work in Germany and Austria in 1919 and in Russia during the famine of 1921–23. Its renown was part of the larger story of humanitarian work undertaken in

---

[1] Francis P. Walters, *A History of the League of Nations*, 2 vols. (Oxford University Press, 1952; reprinted 1960), pp. 268 ff.

248

the whole of Central Europe after the Great War. At the beginning of the League's session on September 26, 1924, the Hungarian delegate took the floor. With the support of several members of the British delegation, he asked the Assembly to solemnly ratify the World Child Welfare Charter; they voted unanimously in favor of ratification. As a journalist from the *New York Times* put it: "The children of the world will be under the protection of the League of Nations."

The welfare of children was a central preoccupation in the early 1920s. For anyone involved in charitable and humanitarian work, children represented the future in a world still mourning World War I. Defending children's rights, although still a vague concept at the time, was seen as a major transnational cause that could bring former enemies together. In the wake of the Great War, many humanitarian figures thus fought for the protection and welfare of children. In Central Europe, the goal was to confront the ravages wrought by the war and the Allied blockade. The Polish doctor Ludwik Rajchman set up large-scale vaccination programs, first in Poland and then in Russia, both of which had been devastated by epidemics.[2] The activist Emily Hobhouse organized fund drives in aid of German women and children, 20 years after she had denounced the living conditions of Boer children in British concentration camps during the Second Boer War (1899–1902).[3]

The Near East was another area of intense humanitarian activity. After witnessing the atrocities against Armenians in 1915–16 and trying to raise awareness in Western public opinion, several Protestant missions and their successors, such as the powerful Near East Relief, founded in 1919,[4] established aid programs for refugees and organized search and rescue missions for the missing. During the deportations of World War I, thousands of Armenian children died of starvation or fatigue. Others were taken away by Ottoman families and forced to convert to Islam and to work as slaves. The American nurse Emma Cushman and the British physician W.A. Kennedy were part of the Commission on the Deportation of Armenian Women and Children, established by the

---

[2] Ludwik Rajchman became Director of the Health Section of the League of Nations in 1921. In 1924, he helped found the International School of Geneva, which sought to promote humanist values among children and to educate them on the importance of peace. See Balinska, *Une vie pour l'humanitaire*.

[3] Jennifer Hobhouse Balme, *To Love One's Enemies: The Work and Life of Emily Hobhouse, Compiled from Letters and Writings, Newspaper Cuttings and Official Documents* (Cobble Hill, British Columbia: Hobhouse Trust, 1994).

[4] Barton, *Story of Near East Relief*; Robert L. Daniel, *American Philanthropy in the Near East (1820–1960)* (Athens: Ohio University Press, 1970); Joseph L. Grabill, *Protestant Diplomacy in the Near East: Missionary Influence on American Policy, 1810–1927* (Minneapolis: University of Minnesota Press, 1971); Watenpaugh, "The League of Nations' rescue."

League of Nations in February 1921.[5] Several years later, in 1924, the Danish missionary Karen Jeppe, who was part of the same Commission, founded an agricultural colony in the Aleppo region for the women and children who had survived the Armenian genocide.[6]

In Germany, Austria, Central and Eastern Europe, and the Near East, the International Red Cross, the Near East Relief, the Protestant missions, the Quakers, and many other charitable organizations of various importance all increasingly tended to create aid programs specifically intended for children, or for children and their mothers. These large-scale programs were part of a larger reorganization taking place in humanitarian work following the Great War: the League of Nations, founded in 1919, played an increasingly important role in conjunction and sometimes in competition with the International Red Cross and other organizations.[7] But was the protection of children, as a significant transnational cause, also part of a concomitant rise in the promotion of children's rights on an international scale? In other words, how were the strategies used by humanitarian groups, along with their work on the ground, translated into international law?

The protection of child welfare on an international scale was not new. It could be discerned as early as the first international pediatrics conferences in the 1890s, a consequence of the convergence of two movements: the rise of humanitarianism, which saw in children the very symbol of innocence and vulnerability; and progress in medicine and the social sciences, part of a construction of childhood as a key moment in human development. At the end of the nineteenth century, a shared community of knowledge was progressively established in order to bring expert analysis to bear on the needs of children—a global category still in the process of being defined—and to better guarantee their rights. Humanitarianism motivated by religious or moral principles gave way to a new kind of

---

[5] The work of this commission was based on two legal documents—Article 23 of the Covenant of the League of Nations, which entrusted the organization with putting into practice international agreements on the trafficking of women and children; and Article 142 of the Treaty of Sèvres, signed by the Allies and the Ottoman Empire on August 10, 1920 but never ratified, which obligated the Turkish government to cooperate with efforts to locate those who were missing and ensure their freedom. See Vahram L. Shemmassian, "The League of Nations and the reclamation of Armenian genocide survivors," in Richard G. Hovannisian (ed.), *Looking Backward, Moving Forward: Confronting the Armenian Genocide* (New Brunswick: Transaction Publishers, 2003), pp. 81–110.

[6] Hebe Spaull, *Women Peace-Makers* (London: George G. Harrap, 1924).

[7] See Kévonian, *Réfugiés et diplomatie humanitaire*, Chapter 7. Kévonian distinguishes between several networks in the humanitarian world, which was undergoing reorganization. These networks, such as Protestant missionary groups, the International Red Cross, the League of Nations, and French humanitarian diplomacy, were at times partners, and at other times in competition with each other.

secular humanitarianism, based on modern scientific knowledge (pediatrics, child psychology, nutrition science). After the Franco-Prussian War of 1870–71, the founder of the British National Society for Aid to the Sick and Wounded in War, Colonel Robert Lloyd-Lindsay, had already pointed out that "It is possible to be as precise in the administration of relief [. . .] as it is to be in ordinary mercantile transactions."[8]

This shift from religious to secular humanitarianism (1880–1920) was slow and complex. A significant religious component continued to be part of the defense of children's rights, during and after the Great War. Even when scientific methods were used to further the cause of child welfare, fundamental anthropological issues were still at work, such as the survival of family structures and faith in the future. Because of the emotion they inspired, children were considered almost sacred. Innocent victims par excellence of war, they represented a fundamental focus of concern in the post-war period.[9] Even at the beginning of World War I, Allied publications denouncing the war linked the young victims of the German invasion and occupation to the "holy innocents" massacred by Herod after the birth of Christ.[10] In addition, missionary ideals often motivated the philanthropists behind many of the humanitarian movements in the 1920s. Following the Great War, religious and moral discourse combined with scientific and legal discourse in defense of children's rights. Religious solidarity continued to be one of the principal motivations for humanitarian work abroad, as in the case of Protestant missions to Christian Armenian refugees. The Near East Relief viewed aid to the survivors of the Armenian genocide, especially children and orphans, as a civilizing crusade against the Turkish "barbarians" as well as a humanitarian task.[11] In the agricultural colony she set up near Aleppo, Karen Jeppe sought to re-socialize Armenian women and children through manual labor, but also to restore their original identity to them and to re-Christianize them. "It is hard to believe your eyes when you compare the people in rags, dirty and of a savage bearing who arrive here, with the more or less civilized

8 *Report of the Operations of the British National Society for Aid to the Sick and Wounded in War During the Franco-Prussian War, 1870–71* (London: Harrison and Sons, 1871), p. 151, cited in Rebecca Gil, "'The rational administration of compassion': the origins of British relief in war," *Le Mouvement social*, 227, April–June 2009, p. 10.

9 David Archard and Colin M. Macleod (eds.), *The Moral and Political Status of Children* (Oxford University Press, 2002).

10 Horne and Kramer, *German Atrocities, 1914.*

11 Flora A. Keshgegian, "'Starving Armenians': the politics and ideology of humanitarian aid in the first decades of the twentieth century," in Richard Ashby Wilson and Richard D. Brown (eds.), *Humanitarianism and Suffering: The Mobilization of Empathy* (Cambridge University Press, 2009), pp. 140–155. See especially the important work of Watenpaugh, "The League of Nations' rescue," as well as his *Bread from Stones.*

people who leave us a few months later," she explained. "At first, our protégés often tend to try to run away if life here doesn't completely suit them; but soon 'the Armenian' within begins to reappear. Before they leave us, they are completely returned to their nationality."[12]

In Europe, the SCIU also combined a scientific approach to children's needs and rights with religious and moral discourse. Central Europe and Russia were seen as places to carry out missionary work, where compassion for children would win out over the hatred and chaos of the post-war period. It is therefore important to add some nuance to the idea that the protection of children's rights was secularized, and that this secularization was the dominant characteristic of humanitarian work in the 1920s.[13] Because of her social background and her ideology, Eglantyne Jebb perfectly embodied the ambiguous nature of the transition from nineteenth-century charitable activity to a new kind of humanitarianism, scarred by the tragedies of the early twentieth century.

A Victorian education

The elation that followed the League's vote in September 1924 nearly obscured the fact that the concept of children's rights was not self-evident. This concept arose in the nineteenth century and slowly took shape as a particular category of human rights after World War II. There are several reasons for this. One was the influence of an emerging scientific discourse, spread by philanthropists, social workers, teachers, and doctors, stressing the specificity of childhood relative to adulthood. Another was the experience of the Great War, during which children suffered in many ways: through the violence of invasion and occupation, the death of their fathers, the destruction of their way of life, and the food shortages caused by the blockade. Eglantyne Jebb was marked by both of these influences. A pacifist, during the war she had campaigned against the blockade affecting German civilians, and then for humanitarian work in Central Europe. But above all, she was a product of the late nineteenth century, and, like many young women of her background at that time, she found a way to escape the constraints of domestic life through philanthropy—a

---

[12] Karen Jeppe, "Rapport du Président de la Commission de la Société des Nations pour la protection des femmes et des enfants dans le Proche-Orient," [Report of the President of the League of Nations Commission for the protection of women and children in the Near East], July 1923–July 1924, quoted in Tara Zahra, *The Lost Children: Reconstructing Europe's Families after World War II* (Harvard University Press, 2011), p. 34.

[13] For example, Gil, "'The rational administration of compassion,'" pp. 9–26.

scientific philanthropy, to whose modernization and professionalization she significantly contributed.

Born in 1876 to a family of the rural gentry, Eglantyne Jebb spent the first 20 years of her life on a Shropshire manor. Her parents were conservative Anglicans, with an ingrained social conscience that motivated them to act on behalf of the poorest of the poor. Her mother, also named Eglantyne but known as "Tye," founded the Home Arts and Industries Association. She crisscrossed the Shropshire countryside, organizing workshops where women and children made traditional crafts, and she went to London to sell, on their behalf, the objects they made. Working with one's hands, and the teaching of new techniques, was supposed to combat idleness and make a disciplined life triumph: "Happier lives and lighter hearts, tidier children, cleaner cottages, and a better moral tone all around," assured Tye. Eglantyne Jebb's father Arthur was a wealthy landowner, more liberal with his tenants than with his children, especially his daughters. He opposed higher education for them, seeing it as a waste of time and money when they should instead concentrate their energies on making a good marriage. "If a woman were marked with smallpox and had good abilities, if she were short-sighted as to make spectacles a perpetual necessity and had great common sense, if she were obliged hereafter to gain her livelihood as a teacher at some sad seminary, there might be something to be said for Cambridge," he explained. "Otherwise a ladies' college seems to me only a ladies' school with all its evils intensified."[14]

Arthur Jebb's sister, Louisa "Bun" Jebb, was one of the first students at Newnham, a women's college founded at Cambridge University in 1871. Never married, she came to live with her brother's family in order to supervise the education of their six children, as was usual for maiden aunts in Victorian England. Aunt Bun was an impressive figure: an enthusiastic reader of Charles Darwin, an activist for women's rights, and good with her hands. One of the children remembers her this way: "A disused back bedroom was her workshop where she introduced those who had a wish to carpentry, wood turning, glass-cutting and glazing; and she taught us besides how to make and use boomerangs, kites, popguns, bows and arrows, toboggans, stilts and fishing nets, and—supreme joy—over her bedroom fire—to melt lead and cast bullets."[15] Bun protected the young

---

[14] Letter from Arthur Jebb to his wife, October 4, 1891, quoted in Clare Mulley, *The Woman Who Saved the Children: A Biography of Eglantyne Jebb, Founder of Save the Children* (Oxford: Oneworld, 2009), p. 29.

[15] Francesca M. Wilson, *Rebel Daughter of a Country House: The Life of Eglantyne Jebb, Founder of the Save the Children Fund* (London: George Allen and Unwin Ltd., 1967), pp. 33–34.

Eglantyne from her father's wrath when she grew rebellious. She was her confidante and governess. In return, the little girl, who spent her days playing at soldiers in the park on the grounds of the estate, affectionately bestowed on her the title of Field Marshal.

When Arthur Jebb died in December 1894, it was Bun who convinced her sister-in-law to let Eglantyne pursue a university education. Tye, however, was not especially in favor of it. "A woman's right . . . to live a life worth living, demands that she shall live as a help 'meet' to man, using her special faculties and endowments to perform that part of the world's work as is fitted to woman rather than man," she wrote. Louisa "Lill" Jebb, one of her elder daughters, left home to study agronomy at Cambridge. In the fall of 1895, Eglantyne Jebb matriculated at Lady Margaret Hall, Oxford University, one of the few women's colleges in England. It had been founded several years earlier by Elizabeth Wordsworth, the great-niece of the Romantic poet.[16]

At that time, the city of Oxford was a narrow-minded and conservative place. Oxford professors did not have the right to marry until 1872, a change that discreetly brought the presence of women into the margins of academic life. Women students, for their part, were few in number: only 48 at Lady Margaret Hall in 1897.[17] They were governed by additional regulations that forbade them to go outside college grounds without a chaperone or to go out after ten o'clock in the evening. They had to be satisfied with special certificates, since they were not awarded university degrees like men (Oxford began awarding degrees to women in 1920; Cambridge, in 1948). Jebb studied history, participated in the Oxford Women's Intercollegiate Debating Society, and escaped university life on long bicycle rides across the countryside. In 1898, she left Oxford to teach in a primary school in Marlborough, Wiltshire. She was very bored there. "I have none of the natural qualities of a teacher," she admitted. "I don't care for children, I don't care for teaching." Three years later, in 1901, she returned to the family home, and then moved with her mother to Cambridge. The goal was to find her a husband.

When they arrived in Cambridge, mother and daughter met up again with Sir Richard Jebb, Tye's brother and one of the most prominent young Greek scholars at Trinity College. His wife Caroline was an American. Their circle of friends included such outstanding minds as the Darwins (the son of the naturalist, and his wife), the Keyneses, and the Trevelyans,

16 Martha Vicinus, *Independent Women: Work and Community for Single Women, 1850–1920* (The University of Chicago Press, 1985), Chapter 4: "Women's colleges: an independent intellectual life."
17 Mrs. Henry Sidgwick, *The Place of University Education in the Life of Women* (London: Transactions of the Women's Institute, 1897).

among many others. "The first man I spoke with, vaguely cast off epigrams in the air," Jebb remembered. "The second had been studying savages in New Guinea and he lectured me on the Papuans; the third had just arrived from Uganda, and he drew aside a bit of the veil from the Great Lakes." She attended various public lectures, and, thanks to her Aunt Caroline's connections, she became close to Cambridge wives and their philanthropic organizations. Among them was Florence Keynes, one of the most influential figures in pre-war Cambridge. Married to the philosopher John Neville Keynes and the mother of three children, including the famous economist, she was also an enthusiastic advocate for social rights. She needed an assistant, and she was introduced to Jebb, who quickly joined the local branch of the Charity Organization Society (better known as the COS).

The goal of this society, founded in 1869 by the philanthropists Bosanquet and Loch, consisted of coordinating the work of charitable organizations at a local level.[18] Its work was thus based on interviews with poor families, in order to determine their needs and the kind of public or private aid that could be given to them. Moreover, the COS tried to promote a sense of responsibility among the poor. Through work and individual initiative, it sought to lift the needy out of poverty and to turn them away from a mentality of depending on outside assistance. For the first time in a long while, Jebb felt useful: "You know the feeling when you have been cold and somebody rubs you warm. I felt once more the steady strong pulsation of life—I had never thought it would come back."[19]

The Cambridge years marked a turning point in her life. At Oxford, though she had rebelled against any form of authority, she remained true to her father's conservative ideas and knew nothing about the causes of women's suffrage or of socialism. From now on, she moved in Liberal spheres, openly supporting the party's local candidate in the 1906 election. "I came to believe that no social reform could be of use which did not promote the independence of the people," she declared.[20] Her sensitivity to social issues grew stronger; her approach to the question of poverty became more methodical and rigorous. The COS' work was based on a whole series of local monographs and investigations in the

[18] Geoffrey Finlayson, *Citizen, State and Social Welfare in Britain, 1830–1990* (Oxford: Clarendon Press, 1994), p. 71; Frank Prochaska, *Christianity and Social Service in Modern Britain: The Disinherited Spirit* (Oxford University Press, 2006), p. 76.
[19] Save the Children Fund Archives, Gardiner Papers, Eglantyne Jebb to Dorothy Kempe, Letter 192, p. 10.
[20] Cambridge Independent Press, *c.* July 8, 1910, quoted in Linda Mahood, *Feminism and Voluntary Action. Eglantyne Jebb and Save the Children, 1876–1928* (London: Palgrave Macmillan, 2009), p. 147.

field. In 1904, Jebb tackled the first sociological study of the population of Cambridge, which she published several months later.[21] Writing this book of more than 270 pages would later influence the rest of her work. She learned to coordinate teams of investigators, gather statistical information on the working-class population, and outline the major aspects of a policy on aid for the destitute.

There was more to Cambridge than its university. It had also become a working-class city—or, rather, an ancient rural town that grew in a sudden and chaotic fashion as a result of the development of the building industry. Its population quadrupled between 1830 and 1905. The city certainly escaped the problems of overcrowding that characterized the industrial cities in the north of England or in London. But in spite of their efforts to improve the sanitation, lighting, and security of the more plebeian neighborhoods, the municipal authorities failed to create an organized and coherent urban plan. Living conditions remained inadequate. Drawing on theories of air purity popular at the end of the nineteenth century,[22] Jebb stressed the heightened risk of epidemic due to the stagnant and fetid air of the slums' backyards. "Here is the blackened stump of an old fruit-tree forlorn amongst the litter and the rubbish heaps, here a bit of bare ground with more paper than grass," she lamented. "The names alone recall the past—Orchard Street, Flower Street, Blossom Street."[23] With the naïveté one might expect from a young woman of the gentry discovering the reality of working-class England for the first time, she acknowledged, "We make our occasional descent into the slums as from another world, and are like men from Mars for the inhabitants."

Town and gown: the two communities coexisted but remained unaware of each other. Jebb went around the working-class neighborhoods in order to map them, as Henry Mayhew and Charles Booth had done earlier in London,[24, 25] or Seebohm Rowntree in York.[26] She questioned

---

[21] Eglantyne Jebb, *Cambridge: A Brief Study in Social Questions* (Cambridge: Macmillan and Bowes, 1906).

[22] The miasma theory of disease, which had become dogma by the nineteenth century, considered polluted air to be an essential factor in disease; hence, the necessity of opening up enclosed, confined spaces. See Alain Corbin, *Le miasme et la jonquille: l'odorat et l'imaginaire social, XVIIIème–XIXème siècles* (Paris: Aubier, 1982), translated as *The Foul and the Fragrant: Odor and the French Social Imagination* (Harvard University Press, 1988).

[23] Jebb, *Cambridge*, p. 9.

[24] Henry Mayhew, *London Labour and the London Poor: A Cyclopaedia on the Condition and Earnings of Those that will Work, Those that cannot Work and Those that will not Work* (London: Griffin Bohn, 1861–62).

[25] Charles Booth, *Life and Labour of the People in London* (London: Williams and Norgate, 1889–91).

[26] Rowntree, *Poverty*.

the inhabitants and suggested solutions—in particular, the education of young children through teaching them to work with their hands and through sports. Using the concept of citizenship dear to British Liberals, Jebb redrew the outlines as to what collective responsibility towards the poor entailed. "We are all citizens bound to make the best of our town, our duties of citizenship . . . the task of dealing with social problems, involves us all," she emphasized. This form of inter-class solidarity prefigures the transnational solidarity that she would proclaim several years later, when she would be consumed by the plight of children in Europe, during and after the Great War.

It is important to note the role gender played in social action. Edwardian-era philanthropy made it possible for many women of the middle classes to move out of the private sphere to which they were traditionally constrained and play a public role, at a time when they still did not have the right to vote.[27] It gave them the opportunity to get together, meet other like-minded women, and exchange ideas on the future of society. They could exercise the abilities they had acquired thanks to higher education, just as traditional charitable work was giving way to a more modern, professional form of philanthropy.[28] At the time, women were said to have a natural aptitude for compassion.[29] They were also thought to have a stronger religious sensibility, which led them to take an interest in the poor. In her sociological study of Cambridge, for example, Jebb notes: "We forget our brothers and sisters in distress, those who are perishing under the conditions which we have created, or succumbing to temptations to which our actions have exposed them. Year by year much suffering continues which might be alleviated, year by year lives are wrecked which might have been saved, and the responsibility for the sufferings and the failure rests with us."[30]

---

[27] Lynn Hollen Lees, *The Solidarities of Strangers: The English Poor Laws and the People, 1700–1948* (Cambridge University Press, 1998).

[28] In Eglantyne Jebb's case, the courses on political economy that she took at Cambridge had an important effect on her future career path. Her professor Mary Marshall recommended that she become engaged in social action and encouraged her to pursue her project of a monograph on Cambridge. On the role of women in the making of the European welfare states, see Gisela Bock and Pat Thane (eds.), *Maternity and Gender Policies* (London and New York: Routledge, 1991); see also Linda Gordon (ed.), *Women, the State and Welfare* (Madison: University of Wisconsin Press, 1990); Finlayson, *Citizen, State and Social Welfare in Britain*; and Susan Pedersen, *Eleanor Rathbone and the Politics of Conscience* (New Haven: Yale University Press, 2004).

[29] Lynda Nead, *Myths of Sexuality, Representations of Women in Victorian Britain* (Oxford: Blackwell, 1988), p. 28. On the emerging "culture of sensibility" and the construction of gendered identities in the eighteenth century, see G.J. Barker Benfield, *The Culture of Sensibility: Sex and Society in Eighteenth-Century Britain* (University of Chicago Press, 1992).

[30] Jebb, *Cambridge*, p. 263.

Although scientific in nature, her analysis of poverty did not lack for moralizing discourse. "The girls who can find no better happiness than that of parading the streets in their best clothes grow up into women who spend their day gossiping on their doorsteps or in reading penny novelettes. The boys who loaf at the street corners grow up into men who spend their evenings in the public-houses," Jebb wrote. "The charity organizationist knows how hopeless it is to expect thrift and industry from those who have squandered away their youth . . . For better or worse, what men and women are at twenty, that they generally are for life."[31] At this stage of her thinking, Jebb defended society's right to protect itself against young delinquents, rather than defending children's rights.

Through her contact with her sister Dorothy and her brother-in-law Charles Buxton, she put the finishing touches on her political education. The Buxtons were another influential couple in pre-war Cambridge, like the Keyneses; he was a brilliant lawyer, great-grandson of the abolitionist Sir Thomas Fowell Buxton, who had helped bring an end to slavery in the British Empire in 1833;[32] she was an energetic young woman who had studied economics and political science at Newnham College. Charles and Dorothy decidedly did not fit the image of a traditional Victorian couple. Dorothy Buxton did not conform to the model of the "angel in the house," which still held sway in her social milieu.[33] Husband and wife were on equal footing in private and public life, each contributing in turn to the other's career. Charles called his wife his "dear comrade." He respected her opinions and admired her determination to change society. "She has made her brain a keen sword and kept it sharp," he wrote of her. "She is a bringer of discomfort—so people think, and rightly think."[34] After their marriage in 1904, they set up house in a working-class neighborhood of London and decided not to have servants. Giving up poetry, his real passion, Charles Buxton began a political career, along with his brother Noel, who would later become part of Ramsay MacDonald's Labour government in 1924. Dorothy and Charles were especially active in the People's Suffrage Federation, which had just been

[31] *Ibid.*, pp. 129, 156.

[32] The Buxton family history illustrates the abolitionist origins of the humanitarian movement of the late nineteenth century. See Reginald Coupland, *The British Anti-Slavery Movement* (London: T. Butterworth, 1933; 2nd edition, London: F. Cass, 1964).

[33] That being said, the model of the "angel in the house" was more of an idealized representation than a reality in bourgeois Victorian families, as M. Jeanne Peterson has so well demonstrated. See M. Jeanne Peterson, "No angel in the house: the Victorian myth and the Paget women," *American Historical Review*, 89: 3, June 1984, pp. 677–708. See also M. Jeanne Peterson, *Family, Love and Work in the Lives of Victorian Gentlewomen* (Bloomington: Indiana University Press, 1989).

[34] V. De Bunsen, *Charles Roden Buxton* (London: George Allen & Unwin, 1948), p. 49.

created in support of women's suffrage. After two unsuccessful attempts, Charles Buxton became a Member of Parliament in 1910. "Charlie's mission, as everyone knows, is to hasten the day of juster social relations, greater equality of opportunity, a wider diffusion of happiness and well-being," Jebb wrote.

Charles Buxton and his brother Noel first concentrated their attention on the Balkans, where war had just broken out between four Allied countries—Bulgaria (independent in 1908), Serbia (1878), Greece (1830), Montenegro (1878)—and the Ottoman Empire. An initial conflict ended in December 1912 with the defeat of the Ottoman troops. Another conflict began 6 months later between the conquerors, and ended with the Peace of Bucharest on August 10, 1913. These two successive wars represented not only a turning point in Balkan history, bringing new territorial divisions, but also a new threshold in the evolution of the violence of war.[35] After the Boer War and the Russo-Japanese War, the Balkan Wars put modern, destructive weapons into action, which meant the beginning of the end of traditional battles and the heavy casualties associated with them. The frequency and brutality of the damage sustained by civilians struck many observers. "Nowhere in international law is there a clause relative to war on the ground and the treatment of the injured which has not been violated by all the belligerents, even by the Romanian Army, which, strictly speaking, was not a belligerent," reported the Carnegie Foundation after the war.[36] Massacres of prisoners, rape, destruction of villages and cemeteries: civilian populations served as an outlet for the defeated armies. This violence also aimed at triggering the flight of ethnic minorities, in the interest of enforcing the homogenization of conquered territories.

Sensitive to the fate of these minorities, the Buxton brothers created a humanitarian structure in Macedonia to help refugees. In March 1913, Charles Buxton succeeded in persuading Jebb to go to Monastir and supervise the work in a hospital. For a young woman who had never left England, this experience was a shock. Upon her return, she described in a lengthy report the waves of refugees fleeing the fighting, the devastating

[35] Richard Hall, *The Balkan Wars: Prelude to the First World War* (London and New York: Routledge, 2000). Olivier Cosson, "Expériences de guerre du début du XXème siècle (guerre des Boers, guerre de Mandchourie, guerre des Balkans)," in Stéphane Audoin-Rouzeau and Jean-Jacques Becker (eds.), *Encyclopédie de la Grande Guerre, 1914–1918: Histoire et culture* (Paris: Bayard, 2004), pp. 97–108. Olivier Cosson, "Violence et guerre moderne dans les Balkans à l'aube du vingtième siècle," in Annette Becker (ed.), "Violences coloniales, violences de guerre, violences extrêmes," *Revue d'histoire de la Shoah*, special issue, July–December 2008.
[36] Report of the International Commission to inquire into the causes and conduct of the Balkan Wars (Washington DC: Carnegie Endowment for International Peace, 1914).

effects of hunger and epidemic, and the courage of the nurses.[37] Not many women were active in the combat zones; Mabel Annie Stobart tended to the wounded from the Bulgarian Army,[38] Katherine Hodges worked for the Macedonian Relief Fund, and there were a few others. But they played a key role in the organization of humanitarian aid, as they would later in the 1920s.[39] For Jebb, this brief sojourn in the Balkans was also an opportunity to see firsthand the extreme vulnerability of women and children in wartime. "The soldiers are the 'Heroes of Europe,' but it is the thousands of sick and starving and helpless and deserted folk, whose misery is unrelieved by the sense of adventure and victory, who pay the price for war's arbitrament," she wrote. On the one hand, there was the heroic masculinity of the soldiers, whose suffering was given meaning through patriotic rhetoric and the inscriptions on war memorials. On the other hand, there were women and children, whose rights urgently needed to be recognized.[40] The key to understanding Jebb's work lies in this shift in perspective.

The child as a legal category

The idea of children's rights has a history. In his groundbreaking work, the historian Philippe Ariès demonstrated in depth that this idea took hold in tandem with what he calls "le sentiment de l'enfance": the recognition or understanding that there exists a particular age group, with fluid contours, to be sure, but distinct from adulthood; and, moreover, that adults have a specific interest in or attachment to the very young.[41] For Ariès, a major turning point in the history of childhood can be situated in the sixteenth and seventeenth centuries, when children are no longer lumped together with adults, but endowed with their own social existence through a more openly expressed maternal love. Ariès' book has been widely discussed and challenged since its publication in the 1960s.[42]

---

[37] Eglantyne Jebb, "The barbarous Balkans," *Brown Book. Lady Margaret Hall Chronicle* (1913).

[38] Mabel Annie Stobart, *War and Women, from Experience in the Balkans and Elsewhere* (London: G. Bell and Sons, Ltd., 1913).

[39] Eglantyne Jebb, "Where war has been lady's work in Macedonia," unknown publication, May 30, 1913.

[40] This disproportionate emphasis on military victims as opposed to civilian victims of the war persisted throughout the Great War, as Annette Becker has shown in *Oubliés de la Grande Guerre*.

[41] Philippe Ariès, *L'enfant et la vie familiale sous l'Ancien Régime* (Paris: Seuil, 1960), translated by Robert Baldick as *Centuries of Childhood* (New York: Vintage, 1962).

[42] Jean-Louis Flandrin, "Enfance et société," *Annales ESC*, 1964, 19: 2, pp. 322–329; Irene Q. Brown, "Philippe Ariès on education and society in seventeenth- and eighteenth-century France," *History of Education Quarterly*, 7: 3, autumn 1967, pp. 357–368

Some scholars criticize him for not taking into account evidence of affectionate attitudes towards children in early modern Europe; others for seeing the "child" as a single entity, without considering the differences between girls and boys. Here, however, I want to focus on one essential point: the history of children's rights cannot be separated from a larger history, that of the family, of mentalities, of feeling. It was this new focus on children that lay behind the need to codify their rights. The child was seen at one and the same time as an individual being formed within the family unit, as an innocent being threatened by the world around it, and as a future citizen upon whose stability and prosperity society would depend in the long run.

From 1830–40, debates over children's rights focused above all on the issue of juvenile delinquency, one of the great concerns of the time. By acknowledging the specific rights of children who were delinquent, neglected, or criminal, society sought to remedy the dysfunctional aspects of their social background and prevent future delinquency. The French Inspector-General of Prisons, Charles Lucas (1803–89) and social reformers such as Edouard Ducpétiaux of Belgium (1804–68) were concerned about the corrupting influence of older inmates when children were incarcerated in the same places as adults. Children's prisons were thus created, such as the Petite-Roquette, established in Paris in 1835.[43] At the same time, the alternative project of agricultural camps was developed, along the Mettray model of 1839, created by Frédéric-Auguste Demetz (1796–1873) near Tours, which emphasized reeducation rather than repression. At the end of the nineteenth century and the beginning of the twentieth, this increasing tendency to issue a separate kind of justice for children led to the creation of the first juvenile courts, first in the United States, in the Chicago area, in 1899,[44] then in Europe (England, 1905; Germany and Belgium, 1908; France, 1912). In practice, the principle of a special jurisdiction reserved for minors went along with recognizing their lack of responsibility, from a legal standpoint; in France,

Urban T. Holmes, "Medieval children," *Journal of Social History*, 2: 2, winter 1968, pp. 164–172; Lawrence Stone, "The massacre of the innocents," *New York Review of Books*, 21: 18, November 1974, pp. 25–31; Adrian Wilson, "The infancy of the history of childhood: an appraisal of Philippe Ariès," *History and Theory*, 19: 2, February 1980, pp. 132–153; Ludmilla Jordanova, "Children in history: concepts of nature and society," in Geoffrey Scarre (ed.), *Children, Parents, and Politics* (Cambridge University Press, 1989), pp. 3–24.

[43] Michelle Perrot, "Les enfants de la Petite-Roquette," in *Les Ombres de l'histoire: crime et châtiment au XIXème siècle* (Paris: Flammarion, 2001), pp. 337–349. See also Kathleen Mary Nilan, *Incarcerating Children: Prison Reformers, Children's Prisons and Child Prisoners in July Monarchy France*, PhD dissertation, Yale University, 1992.

[44] Judith Sealander, *The Failed Century of the Child: Governing America's Young in the Twentieth Century* (Cambridge University Press, 2003), p. 21.

beginning with the Law of 1912, children younger than 13 were spared punishment such as fines or prison and could now only be required to submit to "measures designating them wards of the state, and measures involving supervision, reform, and assistance" (Article I).[45]

Hygiene and health were other areas of research connected to children's rights in the period 1870–80. Delinquent children were no longer at the heart of the debate; rather, at issue was the right of children to living conditions favorable to their psychological and moral development— whatever their social background.[46] In defending this right, social reformers invoked children's natural weakness and their dependence on adults, which made it necessary for legislators to make child welfare a part of the law. The family unit, particularly a child's relationship with its mother, was seen as the natural framework for child development.[47] But when parental neglect or mistreatment endangered a child's health, morality, or life, the state could assume parental authority and place the child in a foster family (the French model) or in a children's institution (the American model).

In addition, interest in child welfare was linked to the severe anxiety surrounding the demographic decline in Western societies at the turn of the century.[48] France's defeat in the Franco-Prussian War of 1870–71

---

[45] Dominique Dessertine, "Aux origines de l'assistance éducative: Les tribunaux pour enfants et la liberté surveillée, 1912–1941," in Michel Chauvière, Pierre Lenoël and Éric Pierre (eds.), *Protéger l'enfant: raison juridique et pratiques socio-judiciaires, XIXème–XXème siècle* (Presses universitaires de Rennes, 1996), pp. 138–139. In the United States, most states since the mid nineteenth century had recognized lack of legal responsibility for children under age 10. See Andrew Walkover, "The 'infancy defense' in the new juvenile court," *UCLA Law Review*, 31, 1984, pp. 503–562.

[46] Patricia T. Rooke and Rudy L. Schnell, "Uncramping child life: international children's organisations, 1914–1939," in Weindling (ed.), *International Health Organisations and Movements*, pp. 177–178.

[47] This valorization of the family as the best place for a child to develop explains why in the early nineteenth century humanitarian circles were especially interested in missing or stolen children. Thus, abolitionists decried the separation of children from their parents on plantations and in slave markets. Parental rights were seen as natural rights that must be protected. In her book *The Lost Children*, pp. 14–15, Tara Zahra reminds us that separating parents and children could also be seen as a way to protect the latter. She cites the case of the mid nineteenth-century activists who supported the Home Children program in England: dozens of thousands of poor or orphaned children were sent to Canada, Australia, New Zealand, and South Africa, with the goal of increasing population in the Dominions and rescuing the younger generation from the dangerous influence of life in the working-class suburbs.

[48] Michael S. Teitelbaum and Jay Winter, *The Fear of Population Decline* (Orlando: Academic Press, 1985); see also Deborah Dwork, *War is Good for Babies and Other Young Children: A History of the Infant and Child Welfare Movement in England, 1898–1918* (London and New York: Tavistock Publications, 1987).

led to a resurgence of fears about a low birth rate and national decline.[49] What better way to confront these possibilities than to concentrate on the education of young mothers and on the health of their children? In Great Britain, the large percentage of working-class recruits declared unfit for service in the Boer War (1899–1902) raised serious concern over the physical state of the younger generations.[50] In this context, alcoholism, syphilis, tuberculosis, and domestic violence were seen as hereditary illnesses, transmitted from adults to children, from one generation to another. Protecting child welfare also meant fighting against population decline, social disorder, and national decline. Most Western countries adopted an entire series of so-called "protection" laws, which also applied to infants and mothers. The term *enfant en danger* or "endangered child," frequently used at the end of the nineteenth century, covered a wide variety of situations: mistreatment by one's family, abandonment, the exploitation of children in the workforce, and child prostitution.

Medicine, education, and social policy had all made children an object of study. In the second half of the nineteenth century, the development of pediatrics led to a more precise definition of the stages of child development, children's specific diseases, and the care necessary for the first years of life.[51] Following the creation of the *Hôpital des Enfants Malades* [Children's Hospital] in Paris in 1802, and of pediatric clinics in Berlin and St. Petersburg in the 1830s, other hospitals for children were founded in the United States and Britain in the 1850s: London (1852), New York (1854), Philadelphia (1855), and Chicago (1865). Along with the creation of hospitals for children, medical schools began to offer pediatrics courses (starting in France in 1878), and to develop new therapeutic techniques. Pediatrics became professionalized and was soon recognized as a specialty of its own. In 1880, the American Medical Association created a section specializing in children's diseases, prior to the creation of

---

[49] Robert A. Nye, *Crime, Madness and Politics in Modern France: The Medical Concept of National Decline* (Princeton University Press, 1984).

[50] Anna Davin, "Imperialism and motherhood," *History Workshop Journal*, 5, spring 1978, pp. 14–18. In an article published in 1903, General Frederick Maurice wrote, "Whatever the primary cause . . . we are always brought back to the fact that . . . the young man of 16 to 18 years of age is what he is because of the training through which he has passed during his infancy and childhood. 'Just as the twig is bent, the tree's inclined'. Therefore it is to the condition, mental, moral and physical, of the women and children that we must look if we have regard to the future of our land . . . " Frederick Maurice, "National health: a soldier's study," *Contemporary Review*, January 1903.

[51] In her book *The Science of Woman: Gynaecology and Gender in England, 1800–1929* (Cambridge University Press, 1990), Ornella Moscucci convincingly shows how gynaecology developed in parallel with pediatrics at the end of the nineteenth century.

an autonomous organization in 1888, the American Pediatric Society.[52] At the end of the nineteenth century, the state of medical knowledge concerning childhood disease nonetheless remained relatively weak. For example, in 1891, the first holder of the Chair in Pediatrics at Harvard Medical School described his discipline as "a poor subterfuge of unreal facts forming structures of misleading results which in the scientific medicine of adults would not for a second be tolerated."[53]

In the United States, but also in Great Britain, France, and Germany, the study of the child's body, its particular nutritional needs, growth patterns, and pathologies reinforced the idea that children are specific beings. In the words of the great pediatrician Abraham Jacobi, when he took over the American Pediatric Society in 1889, "Pediatrics does not deal with miniature men and women, with reduced doses and the same class of diseases in smaller bodies, but . . . it has its own independent range and horizon . . . There is scarcely a tissue or an organ which behaves exactly alike in the different periods of life . . . There are anomalies and diseases which are encountered in the infant and child only. There are those which are mostly found in children, or with a symptomatology and course peculiar to them."[54] He concluded by calling for social policies that would protect children, with his country leading the way: "Unless the education and training of the young is carried on according to the principles of sound and scientific physical and mental hygiene, neither the aim of our political institutions will ever be reached nor the United States fulfill its true manifest destiny."

Many throughout the world sought to make the ideas expressed by Jacobi a reality. In France, the Roussel Law of 1874 established

---

[52] Sydney A. Halpern, *American Pediatrics: The Social Dynamics of Professionalism, 1880–1980* (Berkeley: University of California Press, 1988).

[53] Thomas Morgan Rotch, "Iconoclasm and original thought in the study of pediatrics," *Transactions of the American Pediatric Society*, 3, 1891, pp. 6–9.

[54] Abraham Jacobi, "The relations of pediatrics to general medicine," *Transactions of the American Pediatrics Society* 1, 1889, p. 8. See also Peter C. English, "'Not miniature men and women': Abraham Jacobi's vision of a new medical specialty a century ago," in Loretta M. Kopelman and John C. Moskop (eds.), *Children and Health Care: Moral and Social Issues* (Dordrecht: Kluwer Academic, 1989), pp. 247–273. Jacobi's life was an interesting one. Born to a Jewish family in Westphalia in 1830, he studied medicine at the University of Göttingen and the University of Bonn. He was sentenced to 2 years in prison for participating in the 1848 Revolution. His radical politics led him to emigrate to England and then to the United States, where he taught pediatrics at several universities in the New York area beginning in 1861. His medical practice went hand in hand with social activism in favor of a more just society, one that would recognize children's rights. See Julie Miller, *Abandoned: Foundlings in Nineteenth-Century New York City* (New York University Press, 2008), Chapter 5.

protections for children who were entrusted to wet nurses.[55] In Great Britain, the Children's Charter of 1889 defended minors against the violence they could be subject to within their own families—physical violence, and then psychological violence—and these social issues were combined with an 1894 legislation guarding against the absence of medical care for a sick child.[56] The demographic context of the late nineteenth century played an important role in developing this protective legislation. Following a rapid decline in infant mortality around 1800, an inverse rise could be seen beginning in 1850, due in particular to an upsurge in the spread of contagious diseases. Around 1880, when most of the protective legislation was passed, infant mortality rates rose 95 percent in Ireland, 142 percent in England, 168 percent in France, and 226 percent in Germany.[57] In the United States, 2 out of 10 children died before the age of 5.[58] The persistence of high infant mortality levels was a major concern in countries where the birth rate itself was already low, as in France.

Economic development at the end of the nineteenth century also contributed to improvements in living conditions for children. In most industrialized countries, the use of better machines led to a reorganization of the workforce. In 1851, children under age 15 still comprised 6.9 percent of the industrial workforce in Great Britain; they represented only 4.5 percent of workers in 1881.[59] Children's rights, especially the minimum work age and the length of the workday, were therefore not solely dictated by a rise in humanitarianism; they also stemmed from changes in the means of production. "Compulsory education was a necessity by the 1870s not because children were at work, but because increasingly they were not," in the words of the sociologist Frank Musgrove.[60]

The protection of child welfare received high priority in philanthropic circles. It rallied nearly 500,000 volunteers in the England of the 1890s,

---

[55] Rachel Ginnis Fuchs, *Abandoned Children: Foundlings and Child Welfare in Nineteenth-Century France* (Albany: State University of New York Press, 1984).

[56] George K. Behlmer, *Child Abuse and Moral Reform in England, 1870–1908* (Stanford University Press, 1982), pp. 78–110.

[57] Michel Poulain and Dominique Tabutin, "La mortalité aux jeunes âges en Europe et en Amérique du Nord du XIXème siècle à nos jours," in Paul-Marie Boulanger and Dominique Tabutin (eds.), *La mortalité des enfants dans le monde et dans l'histoire* (Université catholique de Louvain: Ordina Éditions, 1980), p. 120.

[58] Samuel H. Preston and Michael R. Haines, *Fatal Years: Child Mortality in Late Nineteenth-Century America* (Princeton University Press, 1991), p. 3.

[59] Behlmer, *Child Abuse and Moral Reform in England*, p. 46.

[60] Frank Musgrove, "Population changes and the status of the young in England since the eighteenth century," *The Sociological Review*, 11, 1, March 1963, pp. 69–93.

Eglantyne Jebb and her mother among them.[61] In 1910, more than 250 private American organizations, such as the New York Society for the Prevention of Cruelty to Children, founded in 1874, led a crusade against violence against children. The vast majority of these volunteers were women, troubled by the disparity between their vision of childhood and the reality they experienced on their visits to working-class neighborhoods.[62] The British philanthropist Florence Davenport-Hill confessed, "It is painful to set aside our ideal of a childhood of innocence and bright playfulness, and to realize that there are among us thousands of children familiar with shocking vice."[63] In Eglantyne Jebb's England, defending children's rights meant defending the right of each child to have a childhood that was a carefree time of innocence and purity. "A happy childhood is an unspeakably precious memory. We look back upon it and refresh our tired hearts with the vision when experience has cast a shadow over the full joy of living," according to Kate Wiggin, author of children's stories, in a small book she published in 1892 called *Children's Rights*.[64] She added, "A child has an inalienable . . . right to his childhood."

This idealized representation of childhood was born in the second half of the eighteenth century, with the publication of Jean-Jacques Rousseau's *Émile* in 1760, and it spread throughout the nineteenth century. Such a representation doubtless had varying levels of success in various countries. In the United States, for example, it ran counter to Puritan ideology, which stated that children just as much as adults were tainted by original sin. However, there were many, like the Romantic poets Blake and Wordsworth, who saw the child as a sort of noble savage, naturally more sensitive and moral, and as an asexual being (at least during early childhood). The smallest influence was thought to make an impression on these individuals both so pure and so fragile. The Boston Children's Friend Society judged that "[their] plastic natures may be molded into images of perfect beauty, or as perfect repulsiveness."[65] It was therefore appropriate to weave a "network of good influence" around children in schools, orphanages, parishes, and youth clubs, which would make it

---

[61] Frank Prochaska, *Women and Philanthropy in Nineteenth-Century England* (Oxford University Press, 1980), pp. 30–32.

[62] Ellen Ross (ed.), *Slum Travelers: Ladies and London Poverty, 1860–1920* (Berkeley: University of California Press, 2007).

[63] Florence Davenport-Hill, *Children of the State* (2nd edition, London, 1889), p. 22, quoted in Hugh Cunningham, *Children and Childhood in Western Society Since 1500* (2nd edition, Harlow, UK, and New York: Pearson Longman, 2005), p. 139.

[64] Kate Wiggin, *Children's Rights* (Boston and New York: Houghton, Mifflin, 1892).

[65] Quoted in David J. Rothman, *The Discovery of the Asylum: Social Order and Disorder in the New Republic* (Boston and Toronto: Little, Brown, 1971), p. 213.

possible to isolate children from the outside world, keep an eye on their development, and protect them.

Philanthropic societies were not the only ones to take action. The promotion of children's rights was closely linked to growing state intervention in the structure of society, the management of industrial labor, and even family life.[66] The 1878 Factory and Workshop Act passed by the British parliament forbade children under the age of 10 from working; school was compulsory up to that age. The Act also limited children between ages 10 and 14 to part-time work. Thirty years later, in 1908, the British government voted on a series of laws that aimed to safeguard the interests of children and to defend society against juvenile delinquency. Jebb followed this legislative action with special attention because it was the work of the Liberal Party, which had won the 1906 election, and to which her brother-in-law Charles Buxton and her sister Dorothy were close. Charles would later be elected a Liberal MP in 1910. "A great cause is entrusted to this generation: as great as to the generation of Cromwell and Wesley—the emancipation of the working classes," Jebb enthused.[67] The Children and Young Persons Act of 1908 established juvenile courts, forbade the sale of tobacco and alcohol to children, punished those who abused them or forced them to beg, and gave free meals to needy children in schools.

Henceworth the rights of children became an international cause.[68] Almost everywhere, the defense of the very young was seen as a priority. For example, in an essay titled "The century of the child," the Swedish feminist Ellen Key wrote, "The next century will be the century of the child, just as much as this century has been the woman's century. When the child gets his rights, morality will be perfected."[69] Between 1890 and 1910, numerous international conferences made possible the sharing of scientific knowledge concerning children, whether legal or medical.[70] One initial reformist network, made up of legal scholars and judges in juvenile cases, such as the Frenchman Henri Rollet (1860–1934),

[66] In the United States, President Taft created the Children's Bureau in 1912, with a mandate to consider "all matters pertaining to the welfare of children and child life among all classes of our people."

[67] Quoted in Mulley, *The Woman who Saved the Children*, p. 111.

[68] Catherine Rollet, "La construction d'une culture internationale autour de l'enfant," in *Comment peut-on être socio-anthropologue? Autour d'Alain Girard* (Paris: L'Harmattan, 1995), pp. 143–168.

[69] Ellen Key, *The Century of the Child* (New York and London: G.P. Putnam's Sons, 1900, 1909), p. 45.

[70] On the role of conferences in international scientific exchange in the nineteenth century, see Christophe Prochasson, "Les Congrès, lieux de l'échange intellectuel. Introduction," *Cahiers Georges Sorel*, 7: 7, 1989, pp. 5–8, and Rasmussen, "Le travail en congrès," pp. 119–134.

grappled with the question of how to set international standards for juvenile justice. The experts envisaged the creation of an International Bureau for Children, in the same way that the International Labor Organization (ILO) had been established for workers (see Chapter 2). However, the outbreak of the Great War put this project on hold. At the same time, international conferences on hygiene and demography were adopting a more empirical approach to children's rights, by exchanging data and information on nutrition and medical care for children.[71] The medical and the legal approaches coalesced around the questions of how to protect children sent out to wet nurses and how to protect children who were mistreated at home; international experts discussed how to address both of these issues.

In fact, a variety of goals were at stake in this internationalization of the cause of children on the eve of the Great War. For physicians and social workers specializing in children, the establishment of international networks protecting child welfare would make it possible to collect data on infant mortality, to compare the statistics for different countries, and to establish benchmark standards for the protection of minors. Since the problems arising from poverty were in essence transnational, experts thought to improve things by making it possible to compare different national experiences and inspire a kind of competition for the improvement of the condition of children. For philanthropists and charitable organizations, however, progress in living conditions for children would come about differently: by educating mothers through films, brochures, and regular visits from social workers.[72] This campaign aimed at mothers was based on a belief in the universal feminine and maternal love, which was thought to be the same in every country, whatever the circumstances.[73]

International expositions were held in London in 1913 and 1914 "to illustrate the progress that has been made all over the world in providing for the mental, physical and social welfare of children." The Belgian Union for the Protection of Infant Life was formed in 1900 in order to compile statistics on infant mortality. The Swiss hoped to create an International Office for the Protection of Children, but the plan was

[71] Catherine Rollet, "La santé et la protection de l'enfant vues à travers les Congrès internationaux (1880–1920)," *Annales de démographie historique*, 1: 101, 2001, pp. 97–116.

[72] The international "Drop of Milk" conferences (Paris, 1905; Brussels, 1907; Berlin, 1911) testify to the growing interest of public authorities in aiding very young children.

[73] Many authors have long since called into question this vision of maternity. See Elisabeth Badinter, *L'amour en plus: histoire de l'amour maternel (XVIIème–XXème siècle)* (Paris Flammarion, 1980), translated by Roger DeGaris as *Mother Love: Myth and Reality. Motherhood in Modern History* (New York: Macmillan, 1981).

abandoned after the declaration of war.[74] Finally, an international conference on eradicating the white slave trade was held in Paris in 1902. It
led to two more conferences, in May 1904 and May 1910, which sought
to impose sanctions on international trafficking in women, young girls,
and children "for prostitution or other immoral activities."[75]

Nonetheless, if there was an area of international cooperation from
which children were largely absent, it was the laws of war.[76] In July
1899 and October 1907, the Hague Conventions had addressed the
protection of individual rights in wartime. Until this point, the laws of

---

[74] Dominique Marshall, "The construction of children as an object of international relations: the Declaration of Children's Rights and the Child Welfare Committee of the
League of Nations, 1900–1924," *The International Journal of Children's Rights*, 7, 1999,
pp. 103–147, 110–120.

[75] After the creation of the International Bureau for the Traffic in Women and Children in
1899, two international agreements for the suppression of white slavery were adopted
on May 18, 1904 and May 4, 1910. They proposed sanctions against the trafficking of
women younger than 20. After the war, these two agreements were taken up in Article
XXII of the Covenant of the League of Nations, then by the International Convention
for the Suppression of the Traffic in Women and Children (adopted on September
30, 1921). See Nitza Berkovitch, *From Motherhood to Citizenship: Women's Rights and
International Organizations* (Baltimore: Johns Hopkins University Press, 1999). However, several American philanthropists were concerned by the fact that the fight against
prostitution was connected to the cause of children, as this 1925 letter to the League
of Nations from Raymond Fosdick, president of the Rockefeller Foundation, shows:
"The point is that in combining child welfare with the committee for the suppression
of the traffic in women and girls, the whole movement is getting off on the wrong foot.
Such a combination represents an idea that was prevalent perhaps 25 or more years ago
when child welfare was conceived to be exclusively a business of protecting children
from external assault. Newer ideas, however, have been introduced, and now when we
here in America speak of child welfare, we think of it in more positive and affirmative
terms—not only health, but in the general release of those forces in childhood which
make for happiness and balanced life. The emphasis has come to be not so much to
protect the child from external situations as to develop the child and remove the inhibi-
tions, which might cramp and narrow its life. [. . .] It really is deplorable that the new
committee should be handicapped in its first attempts by so unfortunate a name as the
Committee on Traffic in Women and Protection of Children." Archives of the League
of Nations, R681/34652 /42399.

[76] Granting specific protections to children in wartime is a relatively recent development,
dating back to the June 1977 adoption of an additional protocol to the Geneva Conventions. In Part IV, concerning civilians, Article 77 on the protection of children states that
"children shall be the object of special respect and shall be protected against any sort of
indecent assault [. . .] The parties to the conflict shall take all feasible measures in order
that children who have not attained the age of fifteen years do not take a direct part in
hostilities and, in particular, they shall refrain from recruiting them into their armed
forces . . . " The 1977 document is the first one to address the issue of child soldiers. In
the 1949 Geneva Conventions, children were included under the rubric of civilians and
protected as were "all persons taking no active part in hostilities." See Denise Plattner,
"Protection of children in international humanitarian law," *International Review of the
Red Cross*, 24: 240, 1984, pp. 140–152. See also Best, *Humanity in Warfare* and Michael
Howard, George J. Andreopoulos and Mark R. Shulman, *The Laws of War: Constraints
on Warfare in the Western World* (New Haven: Yale University Press, 1994).

war had essentially been based on common law—that is, a certain number of practices fixed by custom and liable to be contested by the warring parties. With the two Hague Conventions (the 1907 Convention was more detailed and restrictive), the goal was to humanize the practice of war at a time when weapons were becoming more and more destructive.

Indeed, the status of the laws of war remained largely uncertain following these two international conferences. Major powers such as Germany had not succeeded in reaching agreements with smaller nations on the way civilians should be treated during an invasion. In other words, the Hague Conventions, part of the long humanitarian tradition of the nineteenth century, were not binding on belligerent countries. They only sketched out the direction to take, which was in favor of respect for the "droit des gens" or Law of Nations—the as yet poorly defined principle invoked by the Russian jurist Fyodor Martens, president of the commission in charge of laws and customs of war.[77]

However fluid the Hague Conventions were, it is not surprising that they never mentioned the rights of children. There is a reason for this: the status of children during wartime still remained vague. As unarmed victims of conflict, nothing distinguished them from women or the elderly. The case of child soldiers was also foreign to the Hague Conventions, although it was not unusual for children to participate in military conflicts in the nineteenth century.[78] When World War I broke out, the welfare of children during wartime largely remained an untouched question.

Feeding the enemy's children?

During the summer of 1914, Eglantyne Jebb suffered from a serious depression that did not lift for several years. Afflicted by a thyroid condition, she lived like a recluse in her mother's house, paradoxically absent from the events that were tearing Europe apart—she who had been so troubled by the plight of the Balkan refugees. She wrote in her journal: "Seclusion is to me a heaven on earth... Never all day the voice of a human. Who would not be a hermit?" While World War I was turning the daily lives of most women upside down, it seemed to have had little impact on Jebb. "I have absolutely no cause for personal grief," she confessed, "... I who have no near relation at the front."[79]

---

[77] Rupert Ticehurst, "La clause de Martens et le droit des conflits armés," *Revue internationale de la Croix Rouge*, 79, 1997, pp. 133–142.

[78] James Marten, *The Children's Civil War* (Chapel Hill: University of North Carolina Press, 1998).

[79] For example, Eglantyne Jebb is quite different from the famous activist Vera Brittain, a product of the same social background, whose wartime letters and journals express her

The Great War passed her by, at least at first. The other members of her family were much more active. With her training in agronomy, Jebb's sister Lill founded the Women's National Service Corps, later known as the Women's Land Army, which enlisted women to work on farms in the absence of men away at war.[80] Emily "Em" Jebb, the eldest sister, had married an Irishman, Beverly Ussher. She lived in Waterford County in the south of Ireland and became a passionate supporter of Irish independence. Dorothy and Charles Buxton actively supported the cause of peace. They helped create a new political movement, the Union of Democratic Control. At a time when the fear of spies had led British authorities to incarcerate nearly 10,000 German residents of England in camps, Dorothy Buxton, in a contrarian spirit, invited a German family to live in her house.[81] Her husband published numerous anti-war pieces and gave a series of talks in favor of a negotiated peace. An activist from the Anti-German Union protested, "I have heard him speak before and he ought to be hanged by the neck until he is dead." It is no surprise that the Buxtons left the Liberal party for the Independent Labour Party, which favored peace, and the Church of England, which they considered too pro-war, for the pacifist Quakers.

However, pacifist groups remained marginalized. In April 1915, a handful of British feminists managed to obtain passports to go to Holland for the Women's Peace Congress.[82] For these activists, only transnational solidarity between women could triumph over the war. The English press fulminated against what it called "a shipload of hysterical women" or "women peace fanatics." Dorothy Buxton joined the group several months later. She began to devote herself to a project that would give the British a more accurate picture of the German enemy, especially the life of civilians under the Allied blockade. According to Dorothy, who believed in the virtues of compulsory education, the English press was directly responsible for prolonging hostilities. With some naïveté, she believed that an honest account of the situation of civilians in Germany would disarm the bellicose spirit of her fellow citizens. Therefore, she translated and summarized articles from German newspapers, which she published in the *Cambridge Magazine*. Directed by Charles Kay Ogden,

---

shock at being separated from her fiancé and her regret at not being a man who could go fight. See *Letters from a Lost Generation: First World War Letters of Vera Brittain and Four Friends* (eds.) Alan Bishop and Mark Bostridge (Abacus, 1999); Brittain, *Testament of Youth*.
[80] Pamela Horn, *Rural Life in England in the First World War* (New York: St. Martin's Press, 1984), pp. 124–136.
[81] Panayi, *The Enemy in Our Midst*, p. 72.
[82] Leila J. Rupp, *Worlds of Women: The Making of an International Women's Movement* (Princeton University Press, 1997).

this weekly had the widest circulation of any intellectual publication in the country.[83] Dorothy soon had some twenty or thirty collaborators, her sister Eglantyne Jebb among them, who labored day and night to translate the two hundred newspapers from all over Europe that arrived every week.

The first difficulty the translators faced was getting a supply of foreign newspapers, which were subject to censorship in light of the Defence of the Realm Act (DORA) of August 8, 1914. It was impossible to get them without authorization. Charles Buxton thus intervened on his wife's behalf with the Prime Minister, David Lloyd George, to get a special accreditation for her from the Board of Trade. Newspapers piled up in the mailbox of the Buxtons' London home. One of their children remembers: "From 1915 onwards our house in the garden suburb... became a political and editorial office—a hive of industry, where, however, any normal domestic or social life was virtually unknown."[84] Dorothy Buxton and Eglantyne Jebb took care to avoid publishing any information of a military nature, which would have been censored. They concentrated on measures in favor of peace and the plight of civilians.

Within the small circle of pacifist activists, the international section of the *Cambridge Magazine* quickly gained recognition. Its effect beyond the academic world was, however, limited. How was it possible to get the word out about the terrible situation of people suffering under the blockade when the leading papers proclaimed stories of "German atrocities" and reinforced the anti-German prejudices of the British? The *Daily Mail*, with a million copies sold every day, made a specialty of this. Without any circumspection, it reprinted the more or less exaggerated stories of the destruction committed by the German Army during the invasion. In an editorial on "German brutality" dated August 12, 1914, for example, the *Mail* explains, "They are also reported in many places to have mistreated civilians on whom they have waged unprovoked war with appalling brutality. Our Special Correspondent in Belgium, Mr. Jeffries says he cannot bring himself to believe these stories and hopes they will not be confirmed, but the grim account, which we reproduce today from *Le Temps* proves that the Germans have shot unarmed Frenchmen for the sole crime of crying 'Vive la France!'"[85]

In these tales of atrocities, children played a major role: "children with their hands cut off" in one story that likens the German invader to an

[83] W. Terrence Gordon, *C.K. Ogden. A Bio-Bibliographic Study* (Metuchen, N.J. and London: The Scarecrow Press, 1990), pp. 12–20.
[84] Mulley, *The Woman Who Saved the Children*, p. 217.
[85] Quoted in Adrian Gregory, *The Last Great War: British Society and the First World War* (Cambridge University Press, 2008), p. 48.

ogre;[86] a child with a wooden toy gun shot by an enemy patrol; Belgian children on the road to exile in the summer of 1914; forced child labor in the occupied regions. The sinking of the "Lusitania," brought down by a German submarine on May 7, 1915 also led to the death of nearly a hundred children: a "massacre of innocents," energetically denounced by the Allied press. Children became the symbol of persecuted innocence, proof that Germany could no longer be considered a civilized nation, and the ultimate justification for a war against barbarism. An American poster from 1917 shows a woman and her child, clinging to each other, falling down to the bottom of the ocean. A single word, blood-red in color, "Enlist," is written across the drawing, which alludes to the sinking of the Lusitania. In the end, the culture of war made World War I a war about children—to avenge those persecuted by the enemy, and to ensure a future without war for others.

The theme of victimized children was also the means that Buxton and Jebb used to stir public opinion. It was no easy task. They had to manage to make people forget that the children living under the blockade were the "enemy's" children and promote instead an image of the universal child, which was difficult to reconcile with the nationalist climate of the Great War. In France, hatred of the German race, expressed on a large scale in war-related publications, included both adults and children. Since the Germans were characterized by physical defects and moral depravity, the defects they were said to have would inevitably be transmitted from one generation to the next. Moreover, war-related rapes, especially during the invasion, gave rise to the fear of contamination of the French race by the German via the intermediary of children.[87] In Great Britain, the figure of the enemy's child provoked less of a sense of aversion, since the country was not directly threatened by invasion, but also because the relationship between Great Britain and Germany was not marked by the same racism as France's was with its German neighbor.[88]

Nevertheless, British public opinion needed convincing on the subject of the iniquities of the economic blockade of Germany and the humanitarian disaster it entailed for the civilian population, especially its youngest members. In fact, when the Allies set up the blockade in 1915, no one thought to criticize a strategy that never had been judged immoral or inhumane. Indeed, as the war continued, viewpoints on Germany hardened, due to what the historian John Horne has called a

---

[86] Horne and Kramer, *German Atrocities, 1914*, pp. 196–211.
[87] Ruth Harris, "The child of the barbarian: rape, race and nationalism in France during the First World War," *Past and Present*, October 1993, pp. 170–206; Stéphane Audoin-Rouzeau, *L'enfant de l'ennemi* (Paris: Aubier, 1995; repub. 2009).
[88] Jeismann, *Das Vaterland der Feinde*.

movement of "cultural remobilization" in 1918.[89] The war seemed endless. For many, food was seen as a decisive weapon to bring about victory. In September 1918, the English journalist F.W. Wile gave voice to fantasies of a massive destruction of the German population, in an article for the *Weekly Dispatch*: not only some tens of thousands of "unborn Germans are destined for a life of physical inferiority," but thousands of others who had not even been conceived yet would suffer the same fate. "The disease that will have to be treated most often in Germans after the war will indeed be the English disease."[90] Several weeks later, Robert Baden-Powell, the founder of the Scout Movement, confirmed it: "We will have to wait until 1940 to see who has really won the war . . . The true consequences of the blockade aimed at Germany, that criminal nation shall not feel till the future." He added: "The German race is being ruined: though the birth rate, from the German point of view, may look satisfactory, the irreparable harm done is quite different and much more serious."[91]

Such was the climate in which the Jebb sisters tried to make a different voice heard. The first descriptions of famine in German and Austrian cities appeared in Swiss newspapers, under the byline of Frédéric Ferrière, a Swiss doctor and delegate of the International Committee of the Red Cross. But soon, all of Central Europe was assailed by hunger, from Romania to Poland. The *Cambridge Magazine* tirelessly reported it. Jebb and Buxton were active on all fronts—the regular procurement of foreign newspapers, the heavy workload for translators, the refusal of numerous bookstores to sell copies of the *Magazine*, the need to increase their readership—in order to arrive at an unhoped-for run of 20,000 weekly copies sold in 1918. "There are only two methods that occur to me, of teaching the actual position of affairs," the writer Jerome K. Jerome noted. "One is to compel every adult civilian in Europe to spend three or four months in the fighting line, the other is to compel them to read The *Cambridge Magazine*."[92]

In the intellectual and artistic circles that made up most of its readership, the journal benefited from the enthusiastic support of George Bernard Shaw, John Galsworthy, and John Maynard Keynes, but it was

[89] John Horne, "Remobilizing for total war: France and Britain, 1917–1918," in Horne (ed.), *State, Society and Mobilization*, pp. 195–211.

[90] F.W. Wile, "The Huns of 1940," *Weekly Dispatch*, September 8, 1918, quoted in Werner Schaeffer, *Guerre contre les femmes et les enfants: blocus décrété par l'Angleterre pour affamer l'Allemagne, 1914–1920* (Bruxelles: Maison internationale d'édition, 1940), p. 5. The year of publication is worth noting.

[91] Quoted in Max Rubner, *The Starving of Germany* (Berlin: Berliner medizinische Gesellschaft, 1919), p. 6.

[92] Mulley, *The Woman Who Saved the Children*, p. 221.

also the object of open hostility. Charles Kay Ogden, its editor, was portrayed as a shirker, since his recurring attacks of rheumatic fever excused him from military service. "Cambridge is no place for people such as you, nor indeed is England. You might feel more at home in Germany," a master at the Perse School, a famous private school in the city, wrote to him.[93] A grieving mother sent him a letter of protest in a black-bordered envelope. News of the Armistice did not lessen the hatred directed at the newspaper. On the evening of November 11, 1918, the offices of the *Cambridge Magazine* were vandalized and Ogden's office destroyed, an illustration of the hostility that had been growing for several years.

For the Jebb sisters, the Armistice did not mean the end of the fight either. The terms of the Armistice presented to the Germans in the clearing of Rethondes prolonged the blockade until the peace was signed. Germany's economic situation was severely deteriorating. At the time when the German Army's soldiers were discharged, the food supply of a city like Berlin had fallen into chaos, all the more so since the November Revolution was raging. The daily arrival of food in the capital's warehouses was a good indicator of the situation. By January 1919, some foods such as wheat, rye, flour, and turnips had been restored to their pre-war levels. On the other hand, this was far from true for fresh foods like milk, meat, vegetables, and fruit. A witness remembers: "In spite of all warnings and punishments, the milk delivered was almost always considerably watered. Partly too the lack of fats in the milk was the result of cows getting no nourishing food; in fact, hardly enough of any sort of food [. . .] Owing to difficulties in transport and distribution arising out of centralizing and rationing, the milk regularly arrived sour, or curdled when it was boiled."[94] In June of 1919, the situation had worsened further and food supplies had reached levels noticeably below those of the summer of 1914.[95]

Up until now, conditions brought on by war had taught German civilians that what seemed intolerable could nevertheless be borne. Hunger, that daily companion beginning in the winter of 1916–17, had been endured in view of a victory to come. Were not the soldiers at the front the most to be pitied, since they had to face death and injury on top of everything else? In the fall of 1918, this social contract fell apart. The authorities' inability to organize the distribution of meager food resources

[3] *Ibid.*, p. 222.
[4] Lina Richter, *Family Life in Germany Under the Blockade* (London: National Labour Press, 1919), p. 22.
[5] Thierry Bonzon and Belinda Davis, "Feeding the cities," in Jay Winter and Jean-Louis Robert (eds.), *Capital Cities at War: Paris, London, Berlin, 1914–1919* (Cambridge University Press, 1997), p. 339.

added to the civilians' poverty. The hunger that had united the German nation, soldiers, and civilians, in the name of common sacrifice, began to divide it: city dwellers against country dwellers, consumers against supposed "profiteers."[96]

Above all, the short-term future of children was now threatened. "In the second year of the war the effects of the blockade showed themselves very clearly, but school doctors and nurses all agreed that there were no serious results to be seen in the children," a witness observed. "This was, as a municipal doctor in Chemnitz writes, 'mainly due to the self-sacrifice of the parents, and especially of the mothers, in their anxiety for their children'... In the following year the picture changed. The school doctor already quoted sums up in 1918 as follows: 'Thin and pale as corpses, the children shoot up, mere skin and bone... the child's body must grow, and if it has no material to build with, it builds with bad.'"[97]

A major shift was taking place in the relationship between the generations: the sacrifices made by parents no longer sufficed to protect the youngest children. At the heart of a hardening social climate, it was women—mothers—who bore the weight of the strife. The news of the Armistice indicated that their sacrifices had come to nothing. The total number of civilian deaths on the European continent due to famine from the blockade has been hotly disputed since the end of the war. But the best estimates that we have gauge that about 500,000 people died—some authors say 630,000—and how many children were among them?[98]

The plight of civilians in Germany and in other defeated countries received little coverage in the English press. The British were preoccupied with celebrating victory and mourning their dead. At the end of 1918, a general election organized by Lloyd George confirmed the ruling Liberal party's hold on power. The entire electoral campaign was organized around the theme "Germany will pay to the last penny." Hatred of the enemy was at its height. In his working-class constituency of West Ham, in London, the Liberal coalition's candidate, Clem Edwards, promised to work "for the death of the Kaiser and other guilty parties, to make Germany pay, to boycott Germans and German products."[99] Among other slogans were: "Hang the Kaiser" and "We'll squeeze Germany til'

---

[96] Belinda Davis, "Homefront: food, politics and women's everyday life during the First World War," in Karen Hagemann and Stefanie Schuler-Springorum (eds.), *Home/Front: The Military, War, and Gender in Twentieth-Century Germany* (Oxford and New York: Berg, 2002), pp. 115–138.

[97] Richter, *Family Life in Germany*, pp. 15–16.

[98] Offer, *First World War*. In his book *The Starving of Germany*, published in 1919, Rubner proposed the number of 800,000 dead in Germany alone.

[99] Quoted in Adrian Gregory, "Adieu à tout cela: comment les Anglais sortirent de l guerre," in Audoin-Rouzeau and Prochasson (eds.), *Sortir de la Grande Guerre*, p. 54.

the pips squeak." In this context, the *Cambridge Magazine*'s efforts to inspire sympathy for the fate of German children were in vain. "Why feed children who will only rise up and kill us 25 years hence?" asked a reader of the newspaper. In addition, with the political chaos rocking the defeated countries, it was increasingly difficult to get a good sense of the situation.

In the spring of 1919, Jebb was determined to send a medical team to Germany to gather information. "We must have figures," she wrote to her sister. "It is the only way to combat political influences. It is the only way to prove our honesty . . . and therefore the only way to rally public opinion behind us." A London physician, Dr. Hector Munro, was sent to Vienna. He was a pacifist of long standing, a supporter of women's rights, and had worked with the Belgian Red Cross to organize a private ambulance unit on the western front. His report on the humanitarian catastrophe in the Austrian capital was devastating. "Children were actually dying in the street," he wrote after his return. "The children's bones were like rubber . . . Clothing was utterly lacking. Children were wrapped in paper and in the hospitals there was nothing but paper bandages."[100]

Other accounts, like that of Lina Richter, based on the testimony of Viennese doctors and teachers, confirmed the severity of the situation. In his preface to Richter's book, the writer George Bernard Shaw castigated his contemporaries' attitude with his usual irony: "In the early years of voluntary recruiting, we were exhorted from every hoarding to remember that some day our children would ask us what we did in the great war. That question was dropped when compulsory military service was instituted. It might very well be revived in the form: 'Daddy, what did you do when the war was over?' The man who can say: 'I shared my ration with the poor starving children in Germany' will have a considerable moral advantage over the ardent patriot who has nothing better to say than 'I voted for hanging the Kaiser; and he was not hanged after all.'"[101]

Save the Children: the birth of a non-governmental organization

The end of the war freed Eglantyne Jebb from the effects of the Victorian education that had shaped her. From 1909 to 1912, she had followed her mother from one spa town to another in Switzerland and Italy. Her stay in the Balkans in 1913 and then her work for the *Cambridge Magazine*

---

[100] Hector Munro, "Memories of the time after the war," quoted in Mulley, *The Woman Who Saved the Children*, p. 237.
[101] George Bernard Shaw, Preface to Richter, *Family Life in Germany*, pp. 6–7.

opened her eyes to the world around her. Under the influence of her sister Dorothy Buxton, she was now ready to take on government censorship and her fellow citizens' hostility in order to raise awareness of the plight of German children. On May 15, 1919, she and a suffragette named Barbara Ayrton Gould were arrested in Trafalgar Square for distributing material calling for an end to the blockade. The pamphlet, entitled "A starving baby," contained the photograph of a child who seemed more like a skeleton, only able to stand up with a nurse's help. "The child is 2½ years old, and his weight is only 12 lbs 2 oz. The normal weight of a child of this age is 28 lbs 2 oz," read the caption. "There are millions of such children starving today. The only way to bring real help to starving Europe is to restore free intercourse between the nations and allow the starving countries to feed themselves." Because of the censorship laws then still in effect in England, Jebb was sentenced to pay a fine of £5, and the National Labour Press, which printed the pamphlet, a fine of £80.

This relatively light punishment amounted to a victory, and, above all, it brought Jebb out of her anonymity. "Recently, I was prosecuted for not having submitted to the Censor a leaflet with a photo of a starving child ... What I regret is this—that if such a simple humanitarian document is to be regarded as a 'leaflet likely to be used for propagandist purposes in relation to the present war,' then the implication is that the starvation of children is a war weapon still in use, and that the relief of their suffering is a political and not, as I contend, a purely humanitarian object," she wrote in a piece published in the *Daily News*.[102] Jebb also pointed out that her trial had taken place on the very same day as the state funeral for the famous British heroine Edith Cavell, executed in Belgium by the Germans in the fall of 1915. "I feel that patriotism is not enough. We must have no hatred or bitterness in our hearts towards anyone," she wrote, quoting Cavell's last words as a call to reconciliation. She concluded, "Let us take this message, and live it out in practical action ... with the saving of the children of Europe, irrespective of their nationality."

On May 19, the Royal Albert Hall overflowed with people who had come for the first public meeting of a new organization created by Jebb and her sister Dorothy Buxton, the Save the Children Fund (SCF). In a symbolic gesture, Buxton held up a container of milk in front of the enthusiastic crowd and said, "There is more practical morality in this tin than in all the creeds." Outside, a crowd of demonstrators had gathered in front of the doors to throw rotten apples at those whom it deemed "traitors." In a country still grieving, passions ran high. The SCF's

---

[102] Mahood, *Feminism and Voluntary Action*, p. 164.

mission had been the subject of lively discussion among its founders. Should they simply put the emphasis on children? Jebb had been convinced of this since her trip to the Balkans in 1913, and since Dr. Munro's reports had shown her the extreme state of weakness afflicting the children of Vienna. For her, children were the measure of a better social order: "Every generation of children . . . offers mankind anew the possibility of rebuilding his ruin of a world." But at a time when there were so many problems in post-war Britain, how could she persuade people that the problems of Central Europe, especially the problems of former enemies, should also matter? And was not taking care of the enemy's children in some way ensuring that those countries had a future, while everything in post-war Allied diplomacy aimed squarely at preventing the former Central Powers from regaining their influence? As an opponent of the SCF wrote at the time, they should not count on her to help "the enemies of England to recover from the effects of their own lack of honour and humanity . . . Only half-hearted patriots would wish to relieve enemies."[103]

While the peace negotiations were being conducted in Paris, the success of the Jebb sisters' project depended on relentlessly lobbying political authorities and on providing material relief on the ground, thanks to donations. The Fight the Famine Council, created by Charles and Noel Buxton, took on the task of campaigning for lifting the blockade. During that time, the SCF collected funds. Jebb wanted to achieve for children what the Red Cross had done for wounded soldiers and prisoners of war: "War which stops in front of wounded soldiers must even more respect the innocent child."[104] In February 1920, the SCF opened its first office in London in a shabby building in Golden Square, a stone's throw from Piccadilly Circus. A year later, it moved to the Paddington neighborhood.

The organization's headquarters at 42 Langham Street resembled a beehive, buzzing with dozens of employees and volunteers, mostly women from the London bourgeoisie, recognizable as such because of the elegant hats they wore to work. A certain austerity prevailed inside: no carpets, no decorations. Most of the furniture was obtained from army surplus stores. Every day, requests for help came by the thousands from all over Europe, and were piled in clothes boxes stacked in the hallways. It was only in 1924 that the SCF would move to more spacious quarters in

[103] Quoted in Linda Mahood, "Feminists, politics and children's charity: the formation of the Save the Children Fund," *Voluntary Action: The Journal of the Institute of Volunteering Research*, 4: 1, 2002, p. 77.
[104] Dominique Marshall, "Humanitarian sympathy for children in times of war and the history of children's rights, 1919–1959," in James Marten (ed.), *Children and War* (New York University Press, 2002), p. 187.

Bloomsbury.[105] In fact, the SCF was run like any charitable organization of the Edwardian era, with its executive board and its patrons drawn from members of the government, high-ranking officials and the aristocracy. Some choices might seem surprising, such as that of Lord Robert Cecil, the minister in charge of the blockade from 1916 to 1918 and, in that role, directly responsible for the humanitarian situation in Central Europe. "It is as if a murderer were to head the public subscription list for a coffin for his victims," protested a friend of the organization.[106] But the SCF was also a force to be reckoned with when it launched calls for donations, a precursor of what humanitarian work would become fifty years later. Due to her obsession with frugality, Jebb initially seemed little inclined to spend time and money to raise awareness of her cause.

As it happened, the SCF soon made an impact with its advertising campaigns. It was one of the first charitable organizations to understand the importance of images in capturing donors' attention: it featured photographs of malnourished children on posters all over London, except on the Underground, which refused to give permission for a poster campaign in 1924, calling the images "too gruesome." Jebb and Buxton hired a former press attaché from the *Daily Mail* to handle public relations for the SCF, something previously unheard of in philanthropic groups. Confronted with the objections of some volunteers disconcerted by the use of advertising, Jebb offered this justification: "The new charity . . . must be scientific and possess the same thoroughness, the same intelligence as are to be found in the best commercial and industrial enterprises."[107]

The SCF's advertising campaigns put the focus on the gaunt faces of young famine victims, using heartrending captions ("Won't You Help Us?") and individual stories. Figuring that the dramatic story of a single child would be more effective than the description of a starving crowd, the SCF's directors sent investigators to take photographs and collect witness accounts. At the same time, supporters of the Armenian cause were using similar measures. The Near East Relief financed films inspired by real life, but produced in Hollywood studios. *Alice in Hungerland*, *One of These Little Ones*, and *Stand By Them a Little Longer* came out in American movie theaters in the early 1920s. Charitable organizations sold stamp books, with all profits going to support Armenian refugees. Sunday schools organized fund drives all across the United States. "Clean your plate. Remember the starving Armenians," was a refrain at

---

[105] *Save the Children Fund* (SCF) archives, London, E. Lawrence, "Random memories of the Save the Children Fund."

[106] Jebb Family Papers (private collection), F. Houghton to Dorothy Buxton, October 25, 1919, quoted in Mahood, *Feminism and Voluntary Action*, p. 171.

[107] *The World's Children*, January 1, 1921.

American dinner tables. The child actor Jackie Coogan, who became a huge celebrity after starring with Charlie Chaplin in *The Kid* (1921), launched a "children's crusade" that raised $1 million in 1924. The theaters showing his film also sponsored collection drives for condensed milk. Coogan toured the country in his own private railroad car. In Boston, he was given the key to the city. In Albuquerque, N.M., the Navajo Indians made him a Medicine Man. In 1924, he himself left New York for Greece on board a "milk ship," headed towards the refugee camps.[108]

This new humanitarian narrative, which Thomas Laqueur traces back to the end of the eighteenth century and the early nineteenth century, was based on a detailed description of the sufferings of others. Such a description made it possible to feel connected to other people, in this case, to sense a bond between children suffering from hunger and one's own children.[109] It was the *detail* of the sentimental novel, then of photography and film (the look in a child's eyes, its belly swollen with hunger, its skeleton-like frame) that facilitated empathy, even if linking donor and beneficiaries together this way could sometimes have the opposite effect and inspire feelings of disgust or else make the donor grow weary of images that had become almost ordinary from overuse.[110] On a model

---

[108] Suzanne E. Moranian, "The Armenian genocide and American missionary relief efforts," in Jay Winter (ed.), *America and the Armenian Genocide of 1915* (Cambridge University Press, 2003), p. 207; Barton, *Story of Near East Relief*, p. 391.

[109] Laqueur, "Bodies, details and the humanitarian narrative." There is a rich bibliography on the role of the sentimental novel in the emergence of humanitarian feeling in the eighteenth century. See, for example, David Marshall, *The Surprising Effects of Sympathy: Marivaux, Diderot, Rousseau and Mary Shelley* (University of Chicago Press, 1988); Ann Jessie Van Sant, *Eighteenth-Century Sensibility and the Novel: The Senses in Social Context* (Cambridge University Press, 1993); Markman Ellis, *The Politics of Sensibility: Race, Gender and Commerce in the Sentimental Novel* (Cambridge University Press, 1996). On the role of abolitionist discourse in the rise of humanitarianism, see Thomas Haskell, "Capitalism and the origins of the humanitarian sensibility," *American Historical Review*, 1985, 90: 2, pp. 339–361; 90: 3, pp. 547–566.

[110] On the effect that distance in space and time can have on the capacity to feel pity for another's suffering, see Carlo Ginzburg's classic article "Killing a Chinese mandarin: the moral implications of distance," *Critical Inquiry*, 21, autumn 1994, pp. 47–60, now reprinted in Carlo Ginzburg, *Wooden Eyes: Nine Reflections on Distance*, translated by Martin Ryle and Kate Soper (New York: Columbia University Press, 2001). On the moral ambiguity of the spectacle of suffering, see Karen Halttunen, "Humanitarianism and the pornography of pain in Anglo-American culture," *American Historical Review*, 100, April 1995, pp. 303–334 and Susan Sontag's classic *Regarding the Pain of Others* (New York: Farrar, Straus and Giroux, 2003). On the limits of empathy, see especially the work of Carolyn Dean—in particular, *The Fragility of Empathy after the Holocaust* (Ithaca: Cornell University Press, 2004). Samuel Moyn also provides a useful discussion in "Empathy in history, empathizing in humanity," *History and Theory*, 45, October 2006, pp. 397–415, in which he links the history of emotional regimes (pity, compassion, sympathy, empathy) to the history of humanitarianism.

similar to that of the "war godmothers" or *marraines de guerre* in France, who "adopted" a soldier at the front and corresponded with him, the SCF offered its donors the opportunity to "adopt" a German, Polish, or Russian child for two shillings a week, thus establishing a symbolic familial relationship that gave emotional weight to the donor's financial gift.[111] The SCF published a newsletter, *The Record of the Save the Children Fund*, renamed *The World's Children* in July 1922. It also organized fund drives, especially charity dinners, where a symbolically empty high chair occupied the place of honor at the dinner table. Remarkably, the SCF was one of the first humanitarian organizations to appeal not only to bourgeois philanthropy, but also to seek out working-class support by collecting donations from factory workers as they left their shifts—indeed, with some success.[112]

Jebb considered the international aspect of her work to be fundamentally important. On one hand, the SCF was a philanthropic organization in the Victorian tradition, but open to new techniques of fundraising, especially the use of advertising in newspapers and the creation of humanitarian films. On the other hand, there was the SCIU, founded in 1920, whose job was to create new branches of the SCF in other countries, to coordinate the distribution of information and aid operations at an international level, and to represent the SCF's interests to non-governmental organizations (NGOs) such as the International Committee of the Red Cross (ICRC) and to international organizations in Geneva, such as the League of Nations. In fact, Dorothy Buxton thought that the SCIU represented a much more developed form of internationalism than the League of Nations did: "the power of the many concentrated in the hands of the few," was her severe judgment of the League. In 1921, the SCIU had already formed national SCF committees in twelve different countries. Less hierarchical than the League, the SCIU managed to free itself from the constraints of traditional diplomacy and admit members from former enemy nations.[113]

Initially, the SCF did not operate directly in the field. It provided financial and material support to other humanitarian organizations.[114]

---

[111]   On the moral implications of child sponsorship, see Laura Suski, "Children, suffering and the humanitarian appeal," in Richard Ashby Wilson and Richard D. Brown (eds.), *Humanitarianism and Suffering: The Mobilization of Empathy* (Cambridge University Press, 2009), pp. 212–216.

[112]   Marshall, "Humanitarian sympathy," p. 190.

[113]   Emily Baughan, "Save the Children: constructing an international humanitarian movement in interwar Britain," dissertation in progress, University of Bristol. See also Emily Baughan, "'Every citizen of empire implored to save the children!' Empire, Internationalism and the Save the Children Fund in interwar Britain," *Historical Research*, 86: 231, February 2013, pp. 116–137.

[114]   The day after its founding meeting at the Royal Albert Hall, the SCF had collected £35,000. In 1922, donations totaled £700,000, and in 1924, £1,895,000.

From the outset, it benefited from influential supporters—most notably, Pope Benedict XV, with whom Jebb had a private audience on December 27, 1919. This marked the first time that the Sovereign Pontiff had agreed to sponsor a non-Catholic organization. In addition, Benedict XV's support for the SCF reinforced the Catholic Church's position in the area of humanitarian diplomacy, which in the 1920s was dominated by English-speaking countries and by Protestant missions.[115] The Pope then devoted two successive encyclicals to the subject of children in Central Europe: *Paterno Iam Diu*, published on November 24, 1919, and *Annus Iam Plenus*, on December 1, 1920. Lastly, he decided to organize a fund drive to benefit the SCF in conjunction with the Feast of the Holy Innocents, on December 28.

This symbolic connection of the famine victims to the massacre of newborns ordered by Herod after Jesus' birth legitimized Jebb's message: the children living under the Allied blockade were innocent victims; to help them was not a political act but a moral obligation.[116] For a Christian, Christ's countenance is on every child's face. The symbol of the SCIU, a newborn wrapped in swaddling clothes, was itself inspired by the fifteenth century *tondi* or circular panel sculptures of infants created by the artist Andrea della Robbia to adorn the arches of the Foundling Hospital in Florence. The theme of innocence, everywhere present in the SCF's discourse, combined with the more political discourse of neutrality. But what could be the real value of neutrality in a world still torn apart by the memory of the Great War? The SCF was based on the premise that children, more so than adults, had been spared from national antagonisms and that they could be a model of neutrality and innocence for the post-war world.

Recently, historical scholarship has tended to argue the reverse. That is, that the "culture of war" impregnated the educational system along with children's games and reading, spreading wide the xenophobic discourse

---

[115] Kévonian, *Réfugiés et diplomatie humanitaire*, pp. 374–385.

[116] A religious discourse on the "martyrdom" of children was common during the Great War. It was also a widespread theme in patriotic literature. In the spring of 1918, the progressive Catholic activist Marc Sangnier devoted several speeches to the topic of German atrocities in Belgium and the civilian victims of bombing in Paris. The Church of Saint-Gervais was bombed on March 29, 1918—Good Friday—and many children lost their lives; Sangnier called it a "sacrilege." When he discussed the bombing of the Baudelocque maternity hospital on April 11, 1918, Sangnier referred with horror to the "innocent white cradles" stained with blood. Religious metaphors often connected the massacre of children to Christ's sacrifice. In wartime France, the Catholic Church gave its wholehearted support to the fight against "German barbarism." See Gearóid Barry, "Marc Sangnier's war, 1914–1919: portrait of a soldier, Catholic and social activist," in Pierre Purseigle (ed.), *Warfare and Belligerence: Perspectives in First World War Studies* (Leiden and Boston: Brill, 2005), p.183.

and nationalistic exhilaration forged during the conflict.[117] Sometimes, war was merely rendered banal and presented as a sort of big game: childrens' uniforms that were realistic reproductions of adults' became extremely popular; tanks, used for the first time in the Somme in 1916, were available as toys in France the very next year.[118] But often, ideological mobilization took place via hate-filled discourse towards the enemy, even in children's newspapers and magazines. France illustrates this phenomenon particularly well, on account of its invasion by German troops and the memory of the war of 1870–71. Here, the militarization of education was doubtless stronger than elsewhere, and the saturation of children's culture by nationalism was more violent. Children certainly were victims, since they suffered from the material hardships of war and the absence of their fathers. The image of neutrality that the SCF conferred on them is, therefore, much more debatable, even if it took center stage in the organization's rhetoric in the aftermath of the conflict.

In early 1919, the SCF concentrated its efforts on Austria, especially Vienna. The city that had been at the head of a giant empire of some 50 million inhabitants in 1914 had now become the over-sized capital of a small country. A third of the Austrian population lived in Vienna. The rich farming regions of Bohemia no longer felt inclined to send their crops to German Austria, as they had been obliged to do under the Habsburg monarchy. At the end of 1918, therefore, the population of Vienna lived under the daily threat of hunger.[119] Long lines outside stores, along with the black market, were still part of daily life until the early 1920s. Material instability, political violence, and the humiliating dissolution of the empire—all the familiar reference points had been shaken. "In that winter it seemed a city of the dead, a huge and silent mausoleum," said one witness.

It was not that one saw children dead in the street or death-carts piled with corpses as one saw in the Russian famine. Nothing so dramatic. Its wounds were hidden. The silence struck me. The streets were deserted, except for queues of people waiting for rations of wood and sour bread, all of them, women and children as well as men, huddled in old patched army coats: all of them pale, hungry, cold, silent and waiting. This was defeat: this was how a great empire

---

[117] Stéphane Audoin-Rouzeau, *La guerre des enfants (1914–1918)* (Paris: Armand Colin, 1993); Maureen Healy, *Vienna and the Fall of the Habsburg Empire: Total War and Everyday Life in World War I* (Cambridge University Press, 2004), Chapter 5; Manon Pignot, *Allons enfants de la patrie! Génération Grande Guerre* (Paris: Seuil, 2012).

[118] George Mosse, *Fallen Soldiers. Reshaping the Memory of the World Wars* (Oxford University Press, 1990), pp. 139–140.

[119] Healy, *Vienna and the Fall of the Habsburg Empire*, p. 309; Rauchensteiner, "L'Autriche entre confiance et résignation," pp. 165–185. According to the ARA, 96.2 percent of Viennese children were undernourished in 1919.

ends, not with a bang, not even it seemed with a whimper. Nothing here but hunger, cold and hopelessness.[120]

Classified as a "liberated nation," Austria received American food aid in exchange for payments in gold. The goal of the American Relief Administration (ARA), directed by Herbert Hoover, was to prevent the spread of Bolshevism in Central Europe. Food was considered a weapon against poverty, and thus against political instability and Communism as well. In the case of children, a program was put into effect in January 1919 under the name of the European Children's Fund, based on the model of the Commission for Relief in Belgium (CRB) that Hoover had created during World War I. Humanitarian organizations gave top priority to children, who could not be held responsible for the war, unlike their parents. In their Vienna canteens, the staff of the ARA forced children to clean their plates, and went so far as to examine their pockets to make sure they weren't taking bread home to share with their families.[121] The program covered all of Central Europe, from the Baltic states (Estonia, Lithuania, Latvia), Poland, the former territories of the Austro-Hungarian Empire (Austria, Czechoslovakia, and Hungary), to Balkan states such as Romania and Serbia. In the spring of 1919, nearly 4 million children benefited from the distribution of food supplies, vaccination programs, and education: 1,500,000 in Poland alone, 600,000 in Czechoslovakia, 500,000 in Romania, 400,000 in Serbia, 400,000 in Austria, 200,000 in Russian Armenia.[122]

In the Hoover archives, hundreds of letters testify to the impact food aid had on the children of Central Europe. They were addressed to the director of the ARA or care of him to "The Children of America." Sometimes, Polish, Austrian, and Russian children decorated empty flour sacks with American flags and eagles as a sign of gratitude. Schools also sent class photographs, surrounded with drawings and signatures. This is all that remains to us today of children caught up in the maelstrom of the post-war period; this is the only way we can still hear their voices, although it is not clear what role their teachers played in sending these gifts all

---

[120] Wilson, *Rebel Daughter of a Country House*, p. 198. Francesca Wilson became involved in humanitarian work among refugees during World War I, the Spanish Civil War, and World War II. She is also the author of a magnificent eyewitness account of the situation in Czechoslovakia, Yugoslavia, and Austria from 1945–46, published under the title *Aftermath* (London: Penguin Books, 1947).

[121] ARA, European Operations Records, 1919–23, Box No. 632, Folder No. 2, Dr. Clemens Pirquet, Hoover Institution Archives, Stanford University.

[122] Hoover Presidential Library, West Branch, Iowa, ARA-European Relief, "The American Relief Administration. America's Care of Millions of European Children since the Armistice."

around the world.[123] The somewhat grave tone of the messages, however, implies the vigilant presence of adults. "To the children of America! On the occasion of the Fourth of July, a solemn day for you and also for us, we send you all our gratitude. Even with the passage of time, the memory of your kindness will never fade. We will carry it from generation to generation," declared a group of schoolchildren from the region of Podlachia, in northeast Poland. "We will never forget your help," other children wrote. "If you are ever one day in the same situation—God forbid—we will send you sugar, milk, and medicine. Come visit us in Kobryn. Long live American children!"[124]

In the spring of 1919, the US Congress decided to stop its humanitarian programs in Europe, before refusing to ratify the Treaty of Versailles at the beginning of 1920.[125] In addition, the population of the United States followed this isolationist tendency and fears were expressed that help for European children would come at the expense of American children. "The sending of food for the relief of the children of Central Europe was highly commendable; in fact it was one of the most generous things that history records. Yet we should not overlook the fact that many of our children, judged by the same standards employed by the ARA are in need of supplemental food," an American observer opined in retrospect.[126] A massive privatization of humanitarian aid to Central Europe then occurred. Without changing its name, the ARA became a private organization, run by volunteers. This was also the moment when numerous humanitarian groups, such as the American Friends Service Committee (the Quakers), intensified their efforts in the field. In Austria, a program called "Cows for Vienna" made it possible for Austrian farmers to obtain cows, bought in Holland or Switzerland by the SCF on the farmers' behalf, so that the farmers could send the milk at no charge to Infant Welfare Centers set up in Vienna by the Quakers. The Americans of the ARA provided meals to all school-age children in Germany and Austria. The Quakers, with the financial help of the SCF, saw to the needs of children under the age of six. In 1920, to save them

[123] On the use of children's drawings as a source of information on wartime experiences, see Pignot, *Allons enfants de la patrie!*

[124] ARA, European Operations Records, 1919–23, Box No. 702, Folder No.1, Hoover Institution Archives, Stanford University. I thank my friend Professor Piotr Wandycz of Yale University for kindly translating the letters of Polish children.

[125] On the defeat of Wilsonianism, see John Milton Cooper, Jr., *Breaking the Heart of the World: Woodrow Wilson and the Fight for the League of Nations* (New York: Cambridge University Press, 2001).

[126] William E. Carter in the *Journal of the American Medical Association*, 77, 1921, p. 1541, quoted in Richard Wagner, *Clemens von Pirquet: His Life and Work* (Baltimore: Johns Hopkins University Press, 1968), p. 159.

from the famine, more than 100,000 Austrian children were evacuated to Denmark, Holland, and Switzerland, where they were settled with host families.[127]

The real turning point for the SCF's efforts came later, however, during the terrible Russian famine of the 1920s. For the first time, Jebb's organization created its own relief programs, feeding centers, medical clinics, and schools.[128] It was a daring initiative. "Feeling runs very high over here in regard to the relief of Bolshevik children—almost higher than in the case of German children," Jebb admitted. "On our committee I think the majority are anti-Bolshevik."[129] Nonetheless, there was an outpouring of donations in support of Russian children, which can be explained partly by an increase in the SCF's advertising budget and the undertaking of an energetic advertising campaign that stressed the exceptional severity of the Russian famine and the need to act quickly. In an article published in the SCF's newsletter, the Archbishop of Canterbury described the Russian famine as "perhaps the vastest problem of human suffering which Christendom has ever had to face."[130] Another SCF pamphlet quoted the League of Nations' High Commissioner for Russian Relief: "Nansen's Clarion Call: Every Minute is Precious."

In September 1921, the *SS Torcello*, laden with 600 tons of food supplies, left London for Riga, which it reached at the end of the month, just before the water in the port froze over for the winter. Less than a year later, the SCF was running 1,450 feeding centers and providing daily meals for 300,000 children in the province of Saratov, where the famine was the most catastrophic. This region, on the right bank of the Volga, extends farther than all of Great Britain. Following the wishes of its founders, Eglantyne Jebb and Dorothy Buxton, the SCF professionalized its work. Laurence Webster, a young British businessman who knew Russia well and who would later pursue a long humanitarian career in Bulgaria, directed operations. In Great Britain, the SCF had recourse to a large variety of ways to raise money, such as press campaigns, gala dinners, and concerts. The magazine *The World's Children* printed the names of those who donated more than £100, and feeding centers set up in Russia were named after them.[131]

[127] Zahra, *The Lost Children*, p. 37.
[128] The SCF was active within the framework of the international program put in place by Fridtjof Nansen, the High Commissioner for Russian Refugees, at the end of August 1921. Nansen gave the SCF responsibility for the Saratov region, "in the heart of the Russian famine zone."
[129] SCF Archives, London, Letter to Suzanne Ferrière, May 11, 1921.
[130] *The Record of the Save the Children Fund*, March 1, 1922, p. 190, SCF Archives, London.
[131] Rodney Breen, "Saving enemy children: Save the Children's Russian relief operation, 1921–23," *Disasters*, 18: 3, pp. 221–237.

The SCF also sent filmmakers such as George Mewes, a former *Daily Mail* photographer, to film the Russian children in distress. Humanitarian propaganda generally contrasted images of dead children with images of those who had been saved, the victims of hunger versus the beneficiaries of Western generosity: "The little waif on the left crept into a deserted house to die. He might have been saved had food arrived on time, like the child in the second picture." Always the same note of urgency, the same appeal to a donor's sense of responsibility: "If these children are to be rescued from death they must be fed till September next."[132] In the fall of 1922, in spite of the resolute opposition of some media outlets like the *Daily Express*, which protested against the aid sent to Bolshevik Russia, the SCF had already collected more than £484,000 in donations.

The SCF's campaign in Russia was completed in summer 1923, at the time when other humanitarian groups, particularly Hoover's ARA, were leaving the country. The famine had been stifled; aid work would cease. Another humanitarian crisis was already claiming the SCF's attention: the population exchange following the Greco-Turkish War and the arrival of nearly a million refugees in Greece. The SCF made a film in order to increase public awareness, as it had done with the Russian famine: *The Tragedy of the Near East* described the sacking of the city of Smyrna by the Turks in September 1922 and the refugees' flight to Greece. True to its strategy of encouraging individual responsibility, the SCF established model villages in Bulgaria (Atolovo) and in Albania (Xhebana—the Albanian transcription of Jebb's last name). It distributed weaving materials to the refugees, whose carpets were then sold to finance the aid they were receiving.[133] In 1923, it also responded to crises in Egypt, Chile, and even Japan, when a large earthquake caused 145,000 deaths in the Kanto region. This expansion of its zone of operation and types of activities (help to refugees and victims of natural disasters) was part of a broader reflection on the SCF's mission. "We cannot possibly go on maintaining children by charity for ever and ever," Jebb had already written to the economist John Maynard Keynes in July 1920. "Our funds are certain to become exhausted, and it will be heartbreaking indeed if it comes about that we have only saved them from starvation one year in order to leave them to starve the next."[134] The founder of Save the Children thought it crucial to be free of the tyranny of emergencies in order to reflect upon having children's rights acknowledged on an international scale.

---

[132] *The Record of the Save the Children Fund*, March 15, 1922, p. 140, SCF Archives, London.

[133] Edward Fuller, *The Right of the Child: A Chapter in Social History* (Boston: Beacon Press, 1951), pp. 95–96.

[134] Quoted in Mulley, *The Woman Who Saved the Children*, pp. 294–295.

The invention of international rights for children

Jebb was not a lawyer like Cassin, nor was she a diplomat like Nansen. She did not have the war experience Thomas did when he created the ILO to defend workers' rights in the aftermath of the war. Her ideological convictions were less fixed than those of Hoover when, hoping to contribute to the overthrow of the Bolshevik regime, he sought to promote the Russians' humanitarian rights. Yet it is to her that we owe the first internationally recognized declaration of children's rights, adopted by the SCIU on May 17, 1923, then ratified by the General Assembly of the League of Nations in September 1924: a codified text, unlike the "humanitarian rights" defended by Hoover; not restricted to one social group, unlike Cassin's veterans' rights; and not restricted to certain national groups, unlike the Nansen Passport. The Declaration of the Rights of the Child was universal, without any distinction on the basis of religion, race, or nationality.

What a change, compared with the time when Jebb and Buxton were translating articles from the German press to raise awareness of the suffering of children living under the Allied blockade. Since 1918, Jebb had become aware of the interdependence of the post-war world. In January 1922, she wrote: "It has passed almost into a commonplace of post-war relief work that if the relief of suffering, disease ridden humanity on the continent were neglected, even Britain's geographical insularity would not preserve her from the possibility of a scourge analogous to the Black Death of the fourteenth Century."[135] To save Russian children (and the German or Austrian children before them) was to reinforce the stability of the world's future at the very time when the intensifying nature of international exchange was dissipating the illusion that what was happening in a country at one end of Europe could not affect a country at the other end. "We have only to recall the establishment within the past few days, of a regular air service between Berlin and Moscow to realize how geographical distance is being annihilated by the hand of modern science and commercial enterprise," said the SCF's newsletter. "Now all this means that we cannot, even if we would, ignore the children of Russia for they are destined to play an important part, for good or ill, in the future of Europe and of the world."[136]

The protection of children had already been a major international cause since the end of the nineteenth century, with numerous conferences on the issue organized by social reformers and pediatricians. However, the international organizations founded in the wake of the Great War,

---

[135] *The Record of the Save the Children Fund*, January 15, 1922, p. 135, SCF Archives, London.
[136] *Ibid.*

such as the League of Nations and the International Labor Office, contributed to strengthening existing networks of experts. They gave them fresh energy by prioritizing support for children. The Health Organization of the League of Nations, under the leadership of Ludwik Rajchman in the 1920s, took up the fight against contagious disease and infant mortality; Rajchman would later become one of the founders of UNICEF after World War II.[137] The Consultative Committee on the Trafficking of Women and Children took up the fight against child prostitution.[138] The paramount question at the heart of international policy protecting children, however, had to do with labor.

During the Paris conference, a commission was set up to prepare the foundation of what would become the ILO (see Chapter 2). Among its recommendations was the prohibition of employment of children under 14, with child labor now considered an international problem, and restrictions on the employment of women who had just given birth.[139] Between 1919 and 1939, the ILO put forth no less than sixteen conventions on child labor. But paradoxically, although no other issue was subject to so many international regulations, the regulation setting the minimum working age at 14 was also the one that was the least well applied. Between 1919 and 1924, only eight countries ratified this convention. It is true that the situation of child workers differed considerably from country to country. In Great Britain, for example, the mechanization of industry and the division of labor progressively eliminated young children from the workforce. It was different in Mediterranean countries, which were not as industrialized, and in France, where small and mid-sized industries, a major share of the industrial sector, still largely had recourse to child labor. France thus initially refused to ratify a minimum working age of 14, even though most experts saw it as fundamental to the protection of child welfare.[140]

[137] Maggie Black, *Children First: The Story of UNICEF, Past and Present* (Oxford University Press, 1996). UNICEF's first director, Maurice Pate (1894–1965) worked for the CRB during World War I, then in Poland for Herbert Hoover's ARA.

[138] According to the historian Mark Connelly, after an active fight against "white slavery" at the end of the nineteenth century, concern for the scourge of prostitution "dissipated [in the 1920s] almost as rapidly as it had emerged two decades earlier." *The Response to Prostitution in the Progressive Era* (Chapel Hill: University of North Carolina Press, 1980), p. 153. Several recent studies emphasize, on the other hand, the internationalization of the fight against prostitution in the interwar era, especially Metzger, "The League of Nations"; "Towards an international human rights regime," pp. 54–79; Katarina Leppänen, "Movement of women: trafficking in the interwar era," *Women's Studies International Forum*, 30: 6, 2007, pp. 523–533; and Dan Gorman, "Empire, internationalism and the campaign against the traffic in women and children in the 1920s," *20th Century British History*, 19: 2, 2008, pp. 186–216.

[139] Shotwell (ed.), *Origins of the International Labour Organization*.

[140] Clark Nardinelli, *Child Labor and the Industrial Revolution* (Bloomington: Indiana University Press, 1990).

In fact, the entire international community took up the question of rights for young people, children, and adolescents. In 1922, the International Union of Socialist Youth Organizations and the Young Workers International convened together in Salzburg, with the goal of drafting "a minimum programme for the protection of youth." [Capitalism] is "directing its systematic offensive in the first place against the apprentices and young workers: their wages are the first to be reduced; their working hours the first to be increased; their rights the first to be disregarded,"[141] proclaimed the final version of the declaration. A year later, the International Council of Women (ICW) drew up a charter of children's rights, containing fifty-one clauses, "based on the principle that every child is born with the inalienable right to have the opportunity of full physical and spiritual development."[142]

Two approaches to the protection of children can thus be clearly differentiated. For the British government, organizations such as the SCIU mainly had an advisory role. Conversely, smaller countries like Belgium and Switzerland wanted to break with the European diplomatic model in which the major powers dominated. They proposed locating the headquarters of humanitarian child welfare organizations in Brussels or Geneva, and giving them a much more ambitious role: defining international standards and ratifying international conventions. In the summer of 1921, an international conference was held in Brussels to coordinate distribution of aid to children, as the Frenchman Henri Rollet had proposed before the war.[143] The International Association for the Promotion of Child Welfare was born. In 1923, this association, comprised of various private groups, was finally attached to the League of Nations, in spite of initial hesitance on the part of the British, who feared for their national sovereignty.

---

[141] Philip E. Veerman, *The Rights of the Child and the Changing Image of Childhood* (Dordrecht: Kluwer, 1992) p. 318.

[142] The idea of considering a children's charter was expressed first in motions submitted to the 5th Yearly Assembly of the International Council of Women (1920), by the International Women's Councils of Poland and the United States. This charter was intended to give the minimum of rights accorded to the children of all nations. A special committee, which met at the Hague in 1922, was set up and instructed to prepare a draft to the Executive Committee of the International Council of Women. The Executive Committee adopted this draft and decided that it should be communicated to the National Councils. (Archives of the League of Nations, Geneva, R681/34652/40484.)

[143] In a report sent to Albert Thomas, the ILO delegate William Martin was skeptical about the association's chances for success: "I would be quite surprised if anything positive for the near future resulted from this conference. The statutes have been voted on by the delegates, most of whom have no power. No diplomatic formalities were observed and all the states seem to have some reserves concerning the payment of contributions—which however are so low that they would in no way make any real work possible." (ABIT, D600/571, Congrès international pour la protection de l'enfance, Bruxelles, July 1921.)

For its part, the SCIU prepared a solemn declaration, with the goal of assuring a leading role for the organization in the field of humanitarian assistance.[144] Jebb insisted that it be a short text—several fundamental principles rather than a long list of rights to be respected. One story portrays her as climbing Mont Salève, in the suburbs of Geneva, "one cloudless summer Sunday in 1922." She was said to have come down several hours later, after drafting the World Child Welfare Charter in silence, on the mountain.[145] The canonization of this foundational text in philanthropic circles could not be more clearly expressed. The preamble solemnly expresses the concept of "the right of the child" in a famous phrase: "Mankind owes to the Child the best that it has to give . . . beyond and above all considerations of race, nationality or creed." The Declaration itself consists of five points. Article I reminds us that "each child must be provided with the requisite means for his or her normal development, both materially and spiritually," which Article II specifies as: "The child that is hungry must be fed; the child that is sick must be nursed; the child that is backward must be helped; the delinquent child must be reclaimed; and the orphan and waif must be sheltered and succoured."

Article III is doubtless the most important, insofar as it, like the preamble, legitimizes the existence of specific rights for children by virtue of their position in society: "The child must be the first to receive relief in times of distress." The experience of the Great War and the symbol of the child as a martyr that grew out of it left their mark on the Declaration of the Rights of the Child. "The misery of the child surpasses that of the adult. The latter has in him the strength to resist and to endure; he can subsist without falling, while the child is often overcome by the first wave of horror and suffering that crashes over it; or, if it escapes from that wave, it is with wounds that will leave scars on all its future development," observed a commentator on the Geneva Declaration, at the beginning of the 1920s.[146] We should not exaggerate this point, however, by overestimating the extent to which children's psychological wounds were actually taken into consideration in the wake of the Great War. Still in its early stages, the psychiatry of war was completely uninterested in the plight of civilians, children in particular.[147] War novels and films

[144] On these issues surrounding humanitarian politics, see Joëlle Droux, "L'internationalisation de la protection de l'enfance: acteurs, concurrences et projets transnationaux (1900–1925), *Critique internationale*, 3: 52, 2011, pp. 17–33.
[145] Mulley, *The Woman Who Saved the Children*, p. 301.
[146] Quoted in Marshall, "The construction of children," p. 133.
[147] The first studies of the traumatic effects of war on children date back to the Spanish Civil War. Alfred and Françoise Brauner used children's drawings to criticize the war.

produced during the conflict or immediately afterwards, for their part, offer an ambivalent picture of childhood. Infants and young children are seen as victims of the breakup of the family circle (the father killed in combat, the mother brutalized by the invading forces, the family dispersed at the beginning of the war),[148] but older children, and naturally adolescents, are presented less often as victims than as entirely separate actors in the conflict: young heroes of the struggle against the invader or occupier, given as an example for the children left behind, young boys especially.[149]

Article IV acknowledges the child as an independent being whose vocation does not consist of being exploited by adults; taking into consideration a child's physical and psychological weakness, it evokes a right to protection: "The child must be in a position to earn a livelihood and must be protected against every form of exploitation." Lastly, Article V does not express a right, in the strict sense of the word, so much as an ideal, characteristic of the early days of the League of Nations: "The child must be brought up in the consciousness that its talents must be devoted to the service of its fellow-men."

All that remained—and it was a great deal—was to give legal weight to this declaration of principles. Jebb was perfectly aware of the difficulty of this task, if only because the universality of rights to which she aspired ran counter to the diversity of cultures in the world as well as individual conceptions regarding the education of one's own children. "Everything should be done to avoid imposing a uniform type of culture," she explained. "The methods of child nurture must necessarily vary greatly according to differences of climate, race, traditions, beliefs, etc. But nevertheless there are certain fundamental principles which should be respected, however much the means of their practical application may differ in different localities."[150] In fact, the future of the SCIU's 1923 declaration lay with the League of Nations, the only body capable of giving it international recognition.

It should be noted, however, that even if Françoise Brauner were a pediatrician, the collection of drawings that she and her husband assembled had no theoretical or therapeutic context. This is not an example, properly speaking, of the beginning of child psychiatry in war, which came later, with World War II and the work of Melanie Klein, Anna Freud, and Donald Winnicott. See Yannick Ripa, "Naissance du dessin de guerre. Les époux Brauner et les enfants de la guerre civile espagnole," *Vingtième siècle*, 1: 89, 2006, "Enfances en guerre," edited by Stéphane Audoin-Rouzeau, pp. 29–46. See also the international conference "Enfances en guerre. Témoignages d'enfants sur la guerre," UNESCO, Paris, December 2011.

[148] For example, Abel Gance's famous film, *J'accuse*, (1919) on wartime rape.
[149] Audoin-Rouzeau, *La guerre des enfants*.
[150] Quoted in Mulley, *The Woman Who Saved the Children*, p. 307.

Initially, the leaders of the SCIU had hoped that the League of Nations would guarantee them logistic support in their operations in the field. During the first General Assembly in 1920, Gustave Ador, a member of the Swiss Delegation and former President of the Swiss Confederation, had asked the League to make the defense of children's rights its priority. He added, "These millions of children rescued from death and deprivation will remember, when they become men, the debt they have contracted towards the League of Nations when it [was] just beginning, and they will work to cement this construction... of universal brotherhood."[151] While admitting the importance of helping children, the League refused to take on this responsibility, limiting itself to expressions of moral support for the relevant humanitarian groups, which certainly fell short of what the SCIU had wanted.

Only in September 1924 did the League officially adopt the Declaration of the Rights of the Child, on the recommendation of the Labour Prime Minister Ramsay MacDonald, a personal friend of Jebb's brother-in-law Charles Buxton. The League also created an internal Child Welfare Committee for the purpose of documenting the problems specific to children and suggesting international regulations. Naturally, the SCIU was represented on the committee, in the person of Jebb herself. This universalizing of children's rights set in motion in the 1920s was at first limited to Europe. The SCIU essentially concentrated its efforts on Eastern and Central Europe, first within the context of initial post-war reconstruction, then during the Russian famine and the typhus epidemic in those regions. And only at the end of the 1920s and the early 1930s did the SCIU's leaders turn their attention to the rest of the world, particularly Africa, which now represented its principal sphere of action. In 1931, the first conference on African children was held in Geneva, with nearly two hundred participants. Five years later, during the invasion of Ethiopia by Mussolini's troops, the SCIU launched a press campaign and a series of initiatives in the field in order to raise public awareness of the situation of refugee children in Addis Ababa.[152]

For an organization like the SCIU, which depended on donor support, recognition by the League of Nations signified a probable increase in its financial resources and the number of its volunteers—just at the moment when public interest seemed to be fading. "Collections are less successful, individual donations are becoming more rare in spite of new and

---

[151] Document 160 of the General Assembly of the League, A.20/48/160. [IV], 2 December 1920, quoted in Marshall, "Humanitarian sympathy," p. 191.

[152] Frédérique Small, "Union internationale de secours aux enfants. Mission en Ethiopie," *Revue internationale de la Croix Rouge*, 18, April 1936, quoted in Marshall, "Humanitarian sympathy," p. 192.

pressing calls for help," noted a French SCIU volunteer at the end of 1922. In the summer of 1924, Jebb began a triumphant tour of Europe, visiting each new country that had adopted her charter of children's rights. In Hungary, she climbed the great staircase of Parliament, surrounded by dozens of children in the national costume, and, more surprisingly, by young prisoners in their prison uniforms. In France, the Minister of Public Education had the Geneva Declaration posted in schools. In Paris, Gustave Ador read the text over the radio, from the top of the Eiffel Tower. Exhausted by her travels and by the great effort of her struggle, Jebb soon chose to stay in Geneva, where she studied Chinese and Esperanto.[153]

Conclusion

The official recognition of children's rights by the League of Nations in the mid 1920s marked an important step. Until this point, the fate of children had depended on the legislative bodies of individual countries and on the work of charitable organizations. The vote of the League's Assembly General singled out the protection and welfare of children as priorities for the international community, and could serve as a reference point for the improvement of their living conditions. According to the Japanese delegate, Yotaro Sugimura, the 1924 Declaration forcefully illustrated how "so many nations in the different continents—nations of most varied customs, traditions, systems of morality, and civilizations—have joined forces, with that sense of responsibility of the human conscience which is the spiritual treasure of all mankind." "[The League of Nations] had a twofold task—that of keeping peace, the peace of to-day, and that of preparing the peace of to-morrow," he added. "A nation which does not protect its future generations is bound to fall. The League, too, must watch like a mother over the fate of future generations which to-morrow will decide the fate of the world. To care for neglected children, to bring up young people in the love of peace and justice, that is one of the League's chief tasks . . . "[154]

[153] In the 1880s, several projects aimed at creating a universal language were being carried out, particularly Volapük and Esperanto, which was the invention of a young Polish doctor, Lazar Ludwik Zamenhof. The first Esperanto dictionary, with translations into five European languages, was published in 1894. In the 1920s, supporters of Esperanto argued that it should be recognized as an official language at international conferences. See Young S. Kim, "Constructing a global identity: the role of Esperanto," in John Boli and George M. Thomas (eds.), *Constructing World Culture. International Nongovernmental Organizations since 1875* (Stanford University Press, 1999), pp. 127–148.
[154] League of Nations, *Official Journal*, Special Supplement No. 33, Records of the Sixth Assembly (Geneva, 1925), p. 131.

Children were distinguished from adults not just as an age group but also because of their presumed "natural innocence" as well as their physical and moral vulnerability. Society made children the object of special protections; by protecting their welfare, society sought to protect its own future stability and prosperity. From this point of view, the League of Nations caught up with the work that had been ongoing for several decades in medicine with the invention of pediatrics and in the social sciences with advances in physiology and psychology of children. In retrospect, it would be tempting to call the Geneva Declaration the beginning of what has been called the "century of the child," which saw its apogee after World War II with the creation of UNICEF in 1946, then with the adoption of the Declaration of the Rights of Children by the United Nations on November 20, 1959. To do so, however, would be to mistake the particular import of Jebb's text.

The 1924 Declaration is more significant for its moral import than for its legal weight. Its goal was not to bind the signatories in the way an international treaty would have done, but to establish relatively general principles for the protection of child welfare. The articles comprising the Declaration amount to a list of the basic obligations adults have towards children: to nourish, care for, protect, and educate them, especially when they are starving, sick, or in danger. At issue here are welfare rights, meant to answer the specific needs of children.[155] By explicitly placing children under adult protection, the text of the Declaration outlines the shape of an ideal society where the weakest may live in safety, free from want. Children were perceived as fragile and innocent beings to be protected, particularly "in cases of distress" (Article III). Children here were not seen as legal subjects or as future citizens. In other words, the Geneva Declaration was part of a long paternalist tradition inherited from the eighteenth century, rather than from the tradition of international law: the international community stepped in and offered the protection traditionally offered by parents.

Moreover, even if the Declaration was adopted by fifty countries, under the auspices of the League of Nations, the signatories did not sign as representatives of clearly designated member states but as part of a larger group, "men and women of all nations"—a somewhat vague way of putting it. This particularity of the 1924 Declaration has several implications. The members of the League of Nations were not obligated to integrate the provisions of the Geneva Declaration into their own national legislation. No supervisory body was set up to ensure the protection of children's rights. No recourse to the League was provided for in cases of

---

[155] Bob Franklin (ed.), *The Rights of Children* (New York: Basil Blackwell, 1986), p. 14.

clear violations of these rights. Even if we limit ourselves to the Declaration's moral dimension alone, the relationship of men and women to the children who must be protected remains vague: does the text of the Declaration simply recall the duty of parents towards their children, as many charitable organizations of the nineteenth century did? Or rather, was the Declaration addressed in broader terms to adults as a whole, calling on them to protect children because they were vulnerable and they were the future of society?

Finally, the absence of children themselves from this declaration of their rights is noteworthy. No children witnessed the signing, no children were represented within the SCIU; it would be difficult to hear their voices here. It was not until the 1970s that the paternalist tone dominating the discourse on children's rights gave way to a more emancipatory viewpoint that recognized children as autonomous subjects.[156] The 1924 Declaration makes no allusions in its preamble to the dramatic inheritance of the Great War and of the post-war period, and no allusion to the efforts of charitable organizations such as Save the Children. Its very brevity helped give the text adopted by the League of Nations an indisputable symbolic weight. However, it remained too imprecise and too general to effect any real change. It employed familiar stereotypes of children as vulnerable and innocent beings, reaffirmed the duty of adults to protect them, and established easily acceptable standards for protecting them. Unlike the scientific, medical language that many humanitarian organizations had been using since the end of the nineteenth century, the 1924 Declaration relied above all on the language of sentiment and emotion.

The Geneva Declaration is also of interest for its tone and for the atmosphere in which it was ratified. The work of documentation and rule making accomplished by the Child Welfare Committee of the League of Nations met with a collective elation, which was in the end rather characteristic of the utopias that developed in the 1920s. The cult of the universal child, a fiction drawn up by international law, was spread, and with it that of neutrality and innocence—values that World War I had violated with extraordinary brutality, but which the SCF's founders still wanted to honor. Without exaggerating the point, it can be said that the Geneva Declaration was adopted at the price of voluntary blindness to what World War I had been: not only a conflict of which children were the victims, as they assuredly were, but also a total war, in which children were active participants in adults' ideological combat, in their own way

---

[156] Geraldine Van Bueren, *The International Law on the Rights of the Child* (Amsterdam: Kluwer, 1998).

and in as much as they were able.[157] The reality of children mobilized for war, via education and patriotic rhetoric, does not fit with the simplistic image of the "innocent victim" promoted by the SCF.

Of course, the theme of the child as an innocent martyr or victim had an obvious function in the post-war world; it made it possible to rebuild international relations on peaceful foundations.[158] By making the defense of children a top priority, new organizations such as the League of Nations and the International Labor Office thought they could establish a common ground among all societies—namely, children as the embodiment of the future.[159] The 1924 Declaration clearly belongs to the post-war context, in which children were at the heart of all the various efforts for peace and rebuilding, precisely because their fate went beyond national borders. The issue of children's rights was in essence transnational. The child as a universal figure, a fiction to which all of the signatories to the 1924 Declaration subscribed, was conceived of as an apolitical being who could unify peace efforts. Children were portrayed as the ultimate beneficiary of post-war reconciliation.

But there is something more at work: the 1924 Declaration came into being at a time when children were seen as entirely separate actors in the promotion of peace.[160] Following World War I, Swiss child psychologists such as Adolphe Ferrière (1879–1960) and Jean Piaget (1896–1980) emphasized the need to educate children on the importance of peace, from a very young age. According to them, the best way society could ensure a better future for children was to assign them the mission of working for peace. In 1925, they created the International Bureau of Education in Geneva, which was part of the Jean-Jacques Rousseau Institute, founded in 1912. The goal of these research centers was to improve knowledge on the origins of the human psychological self and to apply that knowledge to pedagogy.[161] In Prague in the summer of 1927, an international conference was held on "pedagogy of peace," which analyzed and criticized the warlike tone of school textbooks. According to these specialists of child psychology, traditional schools

---

[157] Audoin-Rouzeau, *La guerre des enfants*.

[158] Dominique Marshall, "Dimensions transnationales et locales de l'histoire des droits de l'enfant: la Société des Nations et les cultures politiques canadiennes, 1910–1960," *Genèses*, 2: 71, 2008, pp. 47–63.

[159] Marshall, "The construction of children," p. 122.

[160] I thank Emmanuel Saint-Fuscien for pointing out to me this "pedagogy of peace" in the 1920s.

[161] Regina Helena de Freitas Campos, "Les psychologues et le mouvement d'éducation pour la paix à Genève (1920–1940)," in Élisabeth Chapuis, Jean-Pierre Pétard and Régine Plas (eds.), *Les psychologues et les guerres* (Paris: L'Harmattan, 2010), pp. 95–109.

encouraged prejudice against foreigners instead of combating it. The psychologist Pierre Bovet delivered the opening address in Esperanto. He explained that the fighting instinct typical of young children should be controlled, and class discussion should be encouraged. Mutual respect, intellectual exchange, and shared work were all values cultivated by "active schools," an experiment originally begun by the Italian physician and educator Maria Montessori (1870–1952), who had close connections to the League of Nations.[162] The 1924 Declaration was supported by a broader intellectual and moral climate in which the future of children was connected to the future of peace. Several child welfare organizations carrying out work on the ground also emphasized the stake of education in promoting peace for the future; such was the case, for example, with the International Near East Association and with programs like those established by Karen Jeppe for Armenian refugees.[163]

In August 1924, a month before the League of Nations adopted the Geneva Declaration on the Rights of the Child, Jebb was invited to deliver a sermon in the Protestant Cathedral of St. Pierre—a rare privilege for a woman. In front of a large audience, she asked participants to pray "for the children of God . . . neglected, exploited, starved, persecuted, tortured, their innocent minds have been poisoned and their white souls dragged through the vilest mud." For Jebb, the children suffering from war and poverty were truly the descendants of the Holy Innocents persecuted by Herod, as the symbol of the SCIU illustrates: a swaddled newborn. Even if Save the Children was influenced by contemporary research on children in the areas of pediatrics, psychology, and pedagogy, and on a larger scale by a scientific approach to humanitarian work, the SCIU's vision remained religious and moral in nature. The defense of children's rights had become a crusade—the crusade par excellence, doubtless, through which Eglantyne Jebb hoped she could enable the world to turn the page on the Great War.

---

[162] In 1949, Maria Montessori published *Educazione e Pace* [*Education and Peace*]. At the end of the 1920s, other social reformers connected education with the promotion of peace, such as the Swedes Alva and Karl Gunnar Myrdal, who later went on to defend the cause of nuclear disarmament. Alva Myrdal received the Nobel Peace Prize in 1982.

[163] "The world may have its choice between a voluntary, constructive, peace-time educational program now, or destructive warfare later," as a document of the International Near East Association put it in September 1923. CICR, MISS/69–5/2 ter., quoted by Kévonian, *Réfugiés et diplomatie humanitaire*, p. 385.

Conclusion: Human dignity: from humanitarian rights to human rights

One morning in April 1921, the citizens of a small town in New England awoke to the sight of 2,000 white crosses, planted in rows on their town green. Each cross symbolized the imminent death of a child suffering from famine in Central Europe. A representative of the Hoover Committee waited behind a stand. For a donation of $10, he would remove a cross and replace it with an American flag. Within a week, the symbolic graveyard had become a sea of red, white, and blue flags.[1]

Although it's impossible to say exactly what the individual donors felt as those crosses disappeared, the vision of the flags offered a strong symbol of lives saved by the power of charity. Those who chose to donate must have been moved by the thought of innocent children suffering in the chaos of the post-war period; they empathized with these children, no matter how little they knew about the faraway countries where they lived or the tragedies they had endured.

The growth of humanitarian feeling stood in sharp contrast to the brutality of the Great War and its aftermath. All over Europe, World War I shattered the lives of millions of families and led to horrific political violence. It also forged links among people who did not know each other and imposed a sense of moral duty towards victims of the war. However, the true turning point of World War I can be found neither in this intensification of humanitarian feeling nor in the growing professionalization of humanitarian assistance, but rather in the assertion of humanitarian rights that occurred in the wake of the war. "Rights, not charity" was the guiding principle of this movement.

Inspired by new international organizations such as the League of Nations and the International Labor Office and their experts, by activists from humanitarian organizations, and sometimes by the war victims themselves, this movement led to the international recognition of several fundamental rights: the right to pensions for war victims; to social

---

[1] "The children's graveyard," *The Record of the Save the Children Fund*, Series 1, April 15, 1921, p. 167, cited in Zahra, *The Lost Children*, p. 38.

rights for workers; the right to identity papers—and to safe transit—for stateless refugees; the right to humanitarian aid for victims of famine and epidemic; the right of children to be protected by society. Some of these rights became official following long ratification procedures in various national legislative bodies of, for example, the standards proposed by the ILO; some acquired official status through the more classic route of an agreement among nation-states, such as the Nansen Passport. Other rights were adopted as a result of lobbying by organizations that were pre-cursors of today's non-governmental organizations (NGOs), such as the Conférence Internationale des Mutilés et Anciens Combattants [International Conference of Associations of Disabled War Veterans] (CIAMAC). Still other rights existed only at the stage where they were declared as principles, as in the Declaration of the Rights of the Child in 1924. Such rights did not have concrete content; instead, they announced specific moral engagements. All of these rights, as they were developed in the 1920s, were not yet universal—even if the Declaration of the Rights of the Child (1924) came the closest to a declaration of rights applying to all those in a particular age cohort. They applied to groups, not to individuals. But the fact that they were invented nonetheless represents a decisive turning point.

These rights were developed, asserted, and defended in response to the chaos that Europe experienced in the aftermath of the Great War. There were to be sure earlier developments in this field, but World War I made a major difference, evident especially in the post-war world. The transition period of the 1920s (what I have referred to in a previous book as the *sortie de guerre*)[2] was marked by the disruption of collective identities, new borders resulting from the breakup of empires, and uncertainties in the passage from war to peace. In the early 1920s, the violence of the war still remained present, sometimes flaring up in the form of wars between nation-states, civil wars and revolutions, paramilitary violence, the per-secution of ethnic minorities, and bloody combat against various internal enemies.[3] From these paroxysms of violence came refugee movements of a magnitude that Europe had not seen since the Thirty Years' War, and the spread of deadly epidemics and famines, which had a serious impact on the most vulnerable population groups and on children. The global reach and nature of the post-war era's problems required not only

---

[2] Cabanes, *La victoire endeuillée*.

[3] Mark Mazower, *Dark Continent: Europe's Twentieth Century* (New York: Knopf, 1998); Peter Gatrell, "War after the war: conflict, 1919–1923," in John Horne (ed.), *A Companion to World War I* (Oxford: Blackwell, 2010). For a study of recent historiography, see Robert Gerwarth and John Horne, "The Great War and paramilitarism in Europe, 1917–23," *Contemporary European History*, 19: 3, pp. 267–273.

a transnationalization of humanitarian practices on the ground, but also a reform of international law. The assertion of new rights can be understood as both an attempt to bring a symbolic closure to World War I and as a way to stem the violence of the post-war period.

In the face of the threat posed by the Bolshevik revolution, social democracy had to fight for its future, and what better way to do so than on a transnational level? The crisis situation reinforced the fears of Western public opinion: the Red Scare and the fear of anarchists; the fear of both political and epidemic contamination; the fear of an overwhelming influx of immigrants, which could lead to unemployment and poverty. Driven out of their homes by civil war and famine, Russian refugees alone were the focus of many of these fears. By the tens of thousands, they grouped together on the outskirts of Constantinople, in the towns of Central Europe, and on the German-Russian border. Once citizens of the Russian Empire, a country that no longer existed, then the victims of a loss of citizenship in their new country, the Soviet Union, they were without papers, incapable of legally crossing borders and settling abroad.

Their status as stateless people intrigued legal scholars as much as it caused concern in Western countries. Lacking all rights connected to nationality, Russian refugees were also people without obligations, without clear affiliation in the event of a new conflict. By creating an identity certificate for them in 1922, Fridtjof Nansen introduced a major reform into international law, since he separated the right to move freely from the fact of having a particular nationality. He also sought to identify, classify, and support a population on the move, uncontrollable and potentially dangerous. In a world where identity checks had been reinforced since the beginning of World War I, statelessness was perceived as a worrisome phenomenon.

The revolution in rights in the 1920s was driven by an urgent response to a state of crisis. This sense of urgency was shared by all human rights activists in the wake of the war, but it was felt even more strongly by those who worked directly with the victims of humanitarian disasters: Eglantyne Jebb with German and Austrian children; Fridtjof Nansen with Russian and Armenian refugees; and Herbert Hoover with victims of the Russian famine. The very notion of a "humanitarian crisis," with its own temporality and its division of space into zones of intervention, emerged in this period. Along with the victim, the rescuer was the other important figure born of the new humanitarian activism.

The redefinition of rights did not, indeed, arise solely in the milieu of international legal scholars nor from the League of Nations and its international functionaries. In the past, international law had traditionally resulted from binding agreements among various nation-states; such was the viewpoint that the American Secretary of State, Robert Lansing, continued to defend in the wake of the war. Lansing was, of course, one of the strongest opponents of Wilsonianism.[4] In the 1920s, work carried out in the field by humanitarian organizations working in Central Europe and in the Near East also contributed to the growth of humanitarian rights. International law came about as a result of *doing*. Through regular investigations and reports, the personnel of humanitarian organizations provided operational centers in New York, London, and Geneva with specific information on the breadth of humanitarian crises, the number of victims, and the means to be employed to resolve the situation. These organizations had networks of influence at their disposal within the League of Nations and the ILO, not only for obtaining financial and material aid, but also for influencing the development of international law. This was how Eglantyne Jebb succeeded in having the Declaration of the Rights of the Child adopted by the General Assembly of the League of Nations on September 26, 1924. In the same way, by participating in the French delegation to the League of Nations beginning in 1924, René Cassin was able to spread the ideas developed by the CIAMAC. The work of these NGOs has been little studied, until recently. With the exception of the Near East Relief, the subject of several significant scholarly studies,[5] the history of other organizations, such as the International Red Cross in the 1920s, has remained largely unexplored.[6]

Post-war humanitarianism can only be truly understood as part of the continuity of World War I. The early 1920s and the Great War belong to the same chronological sequence. In 1914–18, for example, a relatively recent literary genre was born: the literature of denunciation, which took on a paramount importance in the wake of the war. In his famous report published in May 1915, Lord Bryce sought to establish the reality of "German atrocities" in Belgium and Northern France in the summer of 1914; the same year, the historian Arnold Toynbee revealed the criminal intent at work during the Armenian genocide.[7] In the early 1920s, the journalists who brought to public attention the drama of famine in Berlin, Vienna, and Budapest, and in the Ukraine, were part of this tradition. All

[4] Smith, "The Wilsonian Challenge."
[5] Kévonian, *Réfugiés et diplomatie humanitaire*; Watenpaugh, "The League of Nations' rescue" and *Bread from Stones*.
[6] See Kimberly Lowe's "The Red Cross and the new world order, 1918–1924," PhD dissertation, Yale University, 2013.
[7] On the origins of the literature of denunciation in the nineteenth century, see Bass, *Freedom's Battle*, and Ann Marie Wilson, "In the name of God, civilization and humanity: the United States and the Armenian massacres of the 1890s," *Le Mouvement social*, 2: 227, 2009, pp. 27–44.

these writers made it possible to transform regional humanitarian crises into international *causes célèbres*.

The organization and functioning of humanitarian aid in the 1920s was also largely inspired by the experience of World War I. The work of the American Relief Administration (ARA) in Central Europe and then in Russia in 1921–23 owed much to the organizational methods put in place by Hoover when he ran the Commission for Relief in Belgium (CRB) beginning in 1915: the same logistics for the transport and distribution of aid; the same use of local volunteers; the same reliance on advertising to motivate donors. In some instances, the same men who had worked under Hoover in Belgium during the war assisted him during the famine in Russia in the 1920s. Although it is important not to make the humanitarian organizations founded by Nansen, Jebb, and Hoover more modern than they really were—they never developed the bureaucracy nor benefited from financial resources that would be put in place after World War II—the 1920s nonetheless represent a significant turning point in the history of humanitarian aid.

Humanitarian policies carried out by various nations, by the League of Nations, and by humanitarian organizations (what we today would call NGOs) all necessitated the collection of precise data and an ordering of priorities. This was when experts stepped in: their task was to develop standards that would be applicable from one humanitarian crisis to another, and from one country to another. Where the rights of victims were concerned, questions of bodily harm had to be evaluated. Faced with various humanitarian emergencies, medical experts gradually supported the development of a common scientific culture. Where social rights were concerned, the growth of the social sciences, which had begun in the nineteenth century, made it possible to construct interpretative models applicable to all humanitarian crises.[8] The growth of statistics as a field nourished the dream of universal science that could benefit all human societies.

International networks of specialists on social questions certainly existed well before World War I.[9] The first conferences on children's rights were held in the 1890s. The first Pan-American Health Organization was founded in 1902, and the first International Sanitary Convention in 1903. By the end of the nineteenth century, scientific exchange had

---

[8] Thomas L. Haskell, *The Emergence of Professional Social Sciences: The American Social Science Association and the Nineteenth-Century Crisis of Authority* (Baltimore: Johns Hopkins University Press, 2000).

[9] Herren, *Internationale Sozialpolitik*; Akira Iriye, *Global Community: The Role of International Organizations in the Making of the Contemporary World* (Berkeley: University of California Press, 2002), Chapter 1.

created "epistemic communities," that is, groups of individuals with shared expertise.[10] Through international treaties and accords, the nations of the world sought to create a global community in order to protect their shared interests. Nevertheless, the chaos of the post-war period intensified these collective efforts and led to more efficient collaboration, since no one country could deal with epidemics or famine on its own; nor clarify the status of refugees; nor reintegrate war victims back into society. The international organizations created in 1919 aimed to develop new legal and health standards that would set the foundation for a new world. They took over from the reformist movements active before 1914—sometimes relying on the same experts, as we can see in the case of Albert Thomas' staff at the International Labor Office. These experts were responsible for proposing rational solutions that would make it possible to move beyond the war. National feeling was to be banished: the goal was to work for the good of humanity.

We should be careful, however, and avoid the simplistic image of a harmonious, international community of thinkers, guided by the higher principle of scientific research. Nearly thirty years ago, historians of science first began to question this received idea.[11] In the 1920s, it was not experts driven by a universal ideal who opened the way to "cultural demobilization," to use John Horne's phrase; it was politicians who put pressure on scientists to reconnect with former enemies. In November 1918, an Inter-Allied Conference of Scientific Academies was held in Paris. Participants were quick to invoke "the nameless crimes that will leave a stain on the histories of the guilty nations, a stain that signatures affixed to [peace] treaties will not wash away."[12] The International Research Council (IRC) was founded in July 1919 to bring scientific standards into accord on a worldwide scale, but the Academies of Science in Germany, Austria, Hungary, and Bulgaria were excluded from the IRC, for an initial period of 12 years.

In July 1925, the eminent Dutch physician Hendrik Antoon Lorentz proposed extending a welcome to scientists from the former Central Powers. "We judge that the time has come to give scientific research the universal character that it should have, as much as it possibly can, given the nature of science," he explained. At the same time, the mathematician

[10] Adler and Haas, "Epistemic communities."
[11] Brigitte Schroeder-Gudehus, *Les scientifiques et la paix: La communauté scientifique internationale au cours des années vingt* (Montréal: Presses de l'université de Montréal, 1978) and her article: "Pas de Locarno pour la science," pp. 173–194.
[12] "La deuxième conférence interalliée des académies scientifiques," *Comptes rendus hebdomadaires de l'Académie des sciences*, p. 167, December 1918. Two successive conferences were held, the first in London in October 1918, the second in Paris in November 1918.

Émile Picard, perpetual secretary of the French Academy of Sciences and a member of the Académie Française, categorically opposed a return to the pre-war norm. In his view, 6 years constituted "a very short time to throw a veil over so many odious and criminal acts, especially when no regret was expressed."[13] Only in the summer of 1926 were German and Austrian scientists allowed to join the IRC.[14]

These divisions in the scientific community also affected legal scholars. Specialists of international law sought to establish a scientific method that would make it possible to understand the problems of the post-war world in a rational way. The redefinition of international law in the 1920s was based on the premise that the work of international jurists from 1870 to 1914 had failed, as Martti Koskenniemi has shown in his socio-historical study of this field.[15] Antoine Pillet, one of the most brilliant French theorists of international law before the war, bitterly noted, "Nothing remains then of what used to seem so firmly established, and we servants of international law have come to this, to wondering if, after this vast destruction, anything can be rebuilt for the future."[16] For legal scholars in the post-war period such as Alvarez, Scelle, and many others, the goal was to respond to the crisis in international law, to provide an alternative to the absolute sovereignty of states, and to create a conceptual apparatus for the new utopia embodied in the League of Nations. Peace and justice, defined not by individual states but by transnational norms, were the new guiding principles of this new generation of jurists.

From their perspective, traditional diplomacy had failed legally, both in the 1899 and 1907 Hague Conventions in the realm of humanitarian law, and in the international conferences held before the war on the realm of labor law. Before 1914, international relations were the sole purview of diplomats, who sought to conciliate and arbitrate. Now it was time to replace their practices with collaborative work carried out by experts in international law, freed from the constraints of oversight by nation-states.

Founded in 1863, the Paris Institute for International Law initially seemed a promising place to establish dialogue among legal scholars. Yet when a meeting was convened in the French capital during the peace negotiations in 1919, it began by excluding scholars from Germany and Austria, which led to the immediate departure of scholars from neutral countries. Other institutions for the promotion of international law were

---

[13] International Research Council, Third Assembly, Brussels, 1925, cited in Schroeder Gudehus, "Pas de Locarno pour la science," p. 183.
[14] I thank Anne Rasmussen for bringing to my attention these debates at the beginning of the 1920s.
[15] Koskenniemi, *The Gentle Civilizer of Nations*.   [16] Pillet, "La guerre actuelle," p. 12.

subsequently established, such as The Hague Academy of International Law (1923) and the Graduate Institute of International Studies in Geneva (1927). A new generation of jurists, including Nicolas Politis, André Mandelstam, Égidio Réale, and René Cassin, took up the work begun by pre-war thinkers such as Léon Duguit and Antoine Pillet. They affirmed the need to go beyond the framework of the nation-state and to establish the individual as the primary focus of law. The fight for human dignity was a key concern.[17]

Yet those who promoted international law represented only a minority of legal thinkers in Europe. Their viewpoints often contrasted sharply with the nationalism and conservatism of many colleagues in their home countries. Thus, it is important to take a nuanced view of the true impact of international spirit after the war. The workings of the new organizations created by the peace treaties suggest that a careful approach is needed. It is certainly true that the ILO, run by Albert Thomas, succeeded in establishing a new kind of dialogue among representatives from government, business, and trade unions. The Organization's initial goal was ambitious: to further world peace by promoting social justice. It recruited its experts from among the best legal minds of the day. However, the ILO also had to deal with the reluctance of numerous countries to actually apply its conventions. Within the very heart of the institution, national interests sometimes had a tendency to prevail over the ideal of social justice. Moreover, this ideal was quite relative, since it was not applied in the same way to men and to women, to Western countries and to their colonies. The revolution of rights in the 1920s was carried out through an emerging culture of experts in the areas of international law, social engineering, and medicine. But this transnational approach to post-war problems also ran up against the resistance of national sovereignty and the tensions inherited from World War I.

This phase in the elaboration of rights that took place in the 1920s is more than simply a pragmatic response to humanitarian crises in the post-war period, and more than just a reaction to the intellectual crisis in international law. The *sortie de guerre* or post-war transition period was also a time for sustained reflection on the damage to human dignity wrought by the war, on the foundation for this dignity, and on how to best protect it. Here was one of the sources of the post-1945 assertion of human rights as the bulwark of human dignity, both for victims of the war and for the history of international law. This is one of the sources of the transition from humanitarian rights that protected specific groups (victims of war, persecution, famine, and natural disasters) to human rights

[17] Kévonian, "Les juristes."

applicable to each person, as an individual.[18] A new ethics of reciprocity and a new definition of international law resulted from recognizing the equal dignity of former enemies, of French and German veterans, of German and Austrian children suffering under the Allied blockade, and of inhabitants of Bolshevik Russia enduring famine. The transition from war to peace in the course of the 1920s was a key moment in the emergence of a new sense of human rights that would lead in time to the Universal Declaration of Human Rights of 1948.

In the early 1920s, Europe was a continent in the throes of reconstruction, still experiencing civil war and conflicts such as the Russo-Polish War (1919–21) and the Greco-Turkish War (1919–22), and further weakened by major humanitarian catastrophes such as the epidemics in Central Europe and the famine in Russia. All over Europe, collective identities were in flux; the end of the Russian, German, Austro-Hungarian, and Ottoman Empires sent millions of people on the road, into exile. They had become strangers in their own country. New countries emerged on the map of Europe, giving rise to new laws and new loyalties. This reorganization of collective identities also affected survivors of the conflict. Over the course of a lengthy transition from war to peace, soldiers became "dischargeable," then they became veterans; disabled war veterans were carefully categorized according to the type of wounds suffered and degree of disability. War widows and orphans received symbolic pensions and benefits. In the wake of a conflict as violent as World War I, granting such rights represented an attempt to guarantee a kind of social order in an otherwise chaotic and threatening world. To assign victims a new place or status, since they could not return to their pre-war status, was a way to reintegrate survivors into the post-war world as fully as possible under the circumstances. The rights of war victims were all the more important in that they affected a significant number of people: nearly 20 million wounded in Europe, for example, of whom 8 million were invalids. Beyond this initial circle of direct victims of the war, the survival of millions of families relying on collective aid was at stake—an unprecedented situation.

The rights of war victims were not limited to material concerns. As early as 1918, the German psychiatrist Karl Abraham described the "inextinguishable thirst" for recognition on the part of disabled soldiers.[19] What pension could ever compensate for their sacrifice? The strength of veterans' groups was to channel this need, which was by definition impossible

---

[18]   On the link between human dignity and human rights, see George Kateb, *Human Digni*... (Cambridge, Mass.: Belknap Press of Harvard University Press, 2011).

[19]   *Zur Psychonalyse der Kriegsneurosen.*

to fulfill, into action. Moreover, by adding an international dimension to war victims' rights, René Cassin, Adrien Tixier, and many other veterans opened up new horizons: the moral responsibility towards victims was no longer limited to the state's duties towards its citizens. It also fell to the international community to take on this responsibility. They did so in the name of universal principles such as human dignity. Following a war where every possible attempt was made to inflict the maximum number of losses on enemy ranks, veterans all across Europe recognized the need to unite for the defense of the rights of disabled veterans. In their eyes, all disabled veterans suffered equally, whether they were conquerors or conquered, whether they were citizens of member countries in the League of Nations or citizens of nations excluded from the League, such as Germany.

In an article published in April 1919, the French writer Jean Guéhenno, an infantry officer during the years 1914–18, wondered to what extent the end of the war represented a turning point: "Just as the concept of the nation had been a nineteenth-century concept, the concept of the world seems to be the concept of the twentieth century [. . .] The identity of men on all continents, in all their diversity . . . Everywhere, it is the same human flesh, suffering and sacred, and everywhere, the same heart [. . .] Will we finally recognize at last this coalition of pain, joy, and goodwill, creating the same rights and the same duties for all men?"[20] The nationalization of bodies, pushed to an extreme in 1914–18, gradually gave way to a transnational conception of the rehabilitation of wounded bodies, and the rights of disabled veterans, war widows, and orphans. Nowhere was the reconciliation of former enemies more moving than when French and German veterans met for the first time in Geneva, in the fall of 1922, to discuss their rights and work for peace. Severely wounded men from both sides met face to face—amputees such as Tixier, who had lost an arm, and men wounded in the abdomen, such as Cassin. The dialogue that took place among these men, who had been at war with each other only 4 years previously, focused on technical questions: the quality of prostheses, their cost, the medical support for disabled veterans in each country. Because of this exchange of information, national comparisons could be made, and common demands formulated. The collective struggle to defend peace soon became the primary goal.

The suffering body, the body of each victim on both an individual and universal level, served as a starting point for thinking about human rights. However, it still remained for this common humanity to be recognized everywhere. To put oneself in the other man or woman's place, to imagine

[20] Jean Guéhenno, "Le sens du monde," *La grande revue*, April 1919, pp. 177–192.

their suffering as if it were one's own—required considerable effort.[21] It required even more effort when that other man or woman was a former enemy, to whom material and symbolic rights needed to be granted—an act that went far beyond simple empathy. The recognition of rights common to all veterans opened the way to forgiveness. In his work, the philosopher Paul Ricœur has often highlighted the risks of what he calls "difficult forgiveness" and the "odyssey of the spirit of forgiveness."[22] The rights common to all war victims were difficult to conceive, difficult to grant; so too was the forgiveness that was the endpoint of the joint struggle for these rights, which brought former enemies together and rekindled a relationship that war had extinguished. Historians have not fully considered either the moral stakes of this transition from war to peace, or the paths taken in order to define new international rights in the 1920s.

In 1914–18, the body of the enemy was a focus of nationalist hatred. He was humiliated, degraded, and ridiculed. His features and appearance, deformed by caricature, identified him as monstrous. As early as the summer of 1914, the crimes committed by German troops seemed to confirm Allied ideas about the enemy's animal nature. In response, Germany denounced attacks by imaginary Belgian "francs-tireurs," depicting them as wild animals. Scientific discourse and medical literature reinforced the prejudices of public opinion. French physicians, for example, published articles explaining that the psychological immaturity of the German made him less sensitive to suffering—a similar argument was used to reject the idea that newborns could feel pain. The enemy was seen through scientific fictions as inferior—less sophisticated, more primitive.

The enemy included civilians as well as soldiers, children as well as adults. Numerous articles defended the legitimacy of a total war, involving all generations; would children not be called upon someday to take the place of adults? Were physical and mental defects not passed on from parents to children?[23] When set against the violent cultures of war in 1914–18, the growth of humanitarian rights in the 1920s emerges in its full measure—as a major break with what came before, although it occurred slowly and chaotically. Just as it is difficult to evaluate the true extent of the spread of racist stereotypes during the war, it is also

---

[21] Elaine Scarry, *The Body in Pain: The Making and Unmaking of the World* (Oxford University Press, 1985).

[22] Paul Ricœur, *La Mémoire, l'Histoire, l'Oubli* (Paris: Seuil, 2000), 591–956; Translated by Kathleen Blamey and David Pellauer as *Memory, History, Forgetting* (University of Chicago Press, 2006).

[23] Harris, "Child of the Barbarian"; Audoin-Rouzeau, *L'enfant de l'ennemi.*

difficult to measure the extent to which former enemies were rehabilitated in each other's minds. One thing is certain, however. The awareness of the suffering endured by the enemy and the emergence of a kind of empathy towards him or her gradually made way for a new mentality—a new psychic landscape. This was one of the conditions that made the affirmation of new international rights possible, and, beyond that, enabled a transition from humanitarian to human rights, individual and universal in nature.

The defense of peace took place, inevitably, in recognizing that former enemies also possessed human dignity. For too long the history of humanitarianism in the interwar years has been written without reference to the works of the historians of World War I. Yet, recent works on the cultural history of the Great War have emphasized how much enemies have been dehumanized by the "cultures of war" in 1914–18.[24] They help us better understand the complexities of the process of "cultural demobilization" after the war, and what was really at stake in the redefinition of humanitarian rights in the early 1920s. The pacifism of veterans played a major role in this process, which also had a moral element that has largely gone unnoticed. The biblical precept "Love thy neighbor as thyself," also called the Golden Rule, is sometimes referred to as one of the foundational elements of thinking on human rights; it is at the very heart of the ethics of reciprocity.[25] For many veterans who had grown up in the Christian or Jewish tradition, recognizing the rights of former enemies after the Great War meant rebuilding a moral universe that the conflict had profoundly degraded.[26] In the early 1920s, the progressive Catholic activist Marc Sangnier, who had served in the French army during the war, exhorted veterans "not to lose the price of victory—peace." Between 1921 and 1932, he organized a dozen conferences advocating "International Democratic Peace." His assistant Georges Hoog declared that "before disarming the combatants, it is necessary to disarm hatred."[27]

---

[24] Audoin-Rouzeau and Becker, *14–18: Understanding the Great War.*

[25] René Cassin, "From the ten commandments to the rights of man," in Shlomo Shoham (ed.), *Of Law and Man. Essays in Honor of Haim H. Cohn* (New York and Tel Aviv: Sabra Books, 1971).

[26] Samuel Moyn, "Personalism, community and the origins of human rights," in Hoffmann (ed.), *Human Rights*, pp. 85–106.

[27] Marc Sangnier, *La Démocratie*, June 22, 1919; Georges Hoog, *Compte rendu complet du Premier congrès démocratique international de la paix*, Paris, December 4–11, 1921 (Paris: La Démocratie, 1922), p. 235, cited in Barry, "Marc Sangnier's war," p. 186. See also Olivier Prat, "Marc Sangnier et la paix à la Chambre bleu horizon, 1919–1924," in Claude Carlier and Georges-Henri Soutou (eds.), *1918–1925. Comment faire la paix?* (Paris: Économica, 2001), pp. 53–79; and Gearóid Barry, *The Disarmament of Hatred. Marc Sangnier, French Catholicism and the Legacy of the First World War* (Basingstoke: Palgrave Macmillan, 2012).

For others like Eglantyne Jebb, who witnessed the violence of war from a civilian perspective, the religious aspect of the struggle for human rights was even clearer.

Indeed, Jebb frequently compared the young victims of the Allied blockade to the Holy Innocents of the New Testament—that is, to the Jewish children massacred by Herod after the birth of Christ. The British and the Americans were called upon to help the children of the enemy as if they were their own children. Donations were collected during "Golden Rule Dinners," where participants ate meals of rice pilaf and potatoes similar to those eaten by orphans in Central Europe and the Near East. With support from both Protestant churches and Pope Benedict XV, the Save the Children Fund (SCF) worked hard to focus donors' attention on children in enemy countries. Humanitarian cinema, which was created during this time, focused its lens on the emaciated bodies and empty gazes of starving children. An appeal addressed to the League of Nations in 1920 put it this way: "All rivalries, all racial or religious antagonisms have vanished in the face of the agony of the children—who are the sacred heritage of the human race."[28] In these words we can clearly discern a new sense not only of humanitarian rights but of *human rights*.

René Cassin, Albert Thomas, Fridtjof Nansen, Herbert Hoover, and Eglantyne Jebb all embody a crucial moment in the development of a collective attitude towards humanitarian rights. This attitude was inspired by the memory of World War I and the chaos of the 1920s. The experience of the Great War left its mark on all five of them: combat, injury, and the brotherhood of veterans, for Cassin; social reform and wartime government for Thomas; humanitarian aid to prisoners of war, refugees, and famine victims for Nansen, Hoover, and Jebb. The struggle for peace, inseparable from the struggle for justice, lay at the heart of their engagement in the post-war world. But it was inspired above all by a powerful call for the respect of human dignity that was issued in Western societies in the aftermath of World War I. In this transition period, pre-war humanitarian practice and humanitarian law, which set standards for the protection of victims of war, gradually gave birth to an assertion of "humanitarian rights," which would change not only the lives of millions of war victims but also the field of international law. From this recognition of the equal dignity of former enemies, there came an even more radical idea, which would only assume universal value and recognition in the aftermath of World War II: what we today refer to as human rights—that

---

[28] "Intervention en faveur des enfants des pays éprouvés par la guerre," [Speech in support of children in countries suffering from the war] December 2, 1920, quoted in Lauren, *The Evolution of International Human Rights*, p. 116.

is, the rights of each individual, in peace and in war. The 1920s mark a decisive step in the transition from one basic understanding of rights to the other.

The great legal scholar André Mandelstam bore witness to this transition and to the violence of the early twentieth century. Exiled to France to escape the pogroms against Jews in the Russian Empire, he devoted his life's work to protecting the rights of the individual against the modern state. As one of the most eminent members of the Institute of International Law, he responded to the persecution of civilians in a powerful October 1921 speech: "In the Near East, the Turks took advantage of the Great War in order to massacre a million and a half Armenians, Greeks, and Assyro-Chaldeans; they continue their work by exterminating the Christians who remain under their yoke. In the Russia of the Soviets, the Bolsheviks continue to methodically suppress the bourgeoisie and especially Russian intellectuals." He added, "I am convinced that, without resorting to the political arena, the Institute's duty is to raise its voice loudly and to proclaim without delay the great new principle [. . .]: human rights exist, and it is the duty of each state to respect them."[29]

[29] André Mandelstam, speech delivered to the ILL, October 8, 1921, cited by Jilek, "Violences de masse et droits de l'homme."

Further reading

Introduction

On the history of humanitarianism and humanitarian sensibility: Geoffrey Best, *Humanity in Warfare* (New York: Columbia University Press, 1980); Thomas Haskell, "Capitalism and the origins of the humanitarian sensibility," *American Historical Review*, 90: 2, 1985, pp. 339–361; 90: 3, pp. 547–566; Thomas Laqueur, "Bodies, details and the humanitarian narrative," in Lynn Hunt (ed.), *The New Cultural History* (Berkeley: University of California Press, 1989), pp. 176–204; Luc Boltanski, *La souffrance à distance: morale humanitaire, médias et politique* (Paris: Métailié, 1993), translated by Graham D. Burchell as *Distant Suffering: Morality, Media and Politics* (Cambridge University Press, 1999); Karen Halttunen, "Humanitarianism and the pornography of pain in Anglo-American culture," *American Historical Review*, 100, April 1995, pp. 303–334; Annette Becker, *Oubliés de la Grande Guerre: humanitaire et culture de guerre, 1914–1918* (Paris: Noésis, 1998; repub. Pluriel, 2003); Kevin Rozario, "'Delicious horrors': mass culture, the Red Cross and the appeal of modern American humanitarianism," *American Quarterly*, 55: 3, September 2003, pp. 417–455; Richard Ashby Wilson and Richard D. Brown (eds.), *Humanitarianism and Suffering: The Mobilization of Empathy* (Cambridge University Press, 2009); Rebecca Gil, "'The rational administration of compassion': the origins of British relief in war," *Le Mouvement social*, 227, April–June 2009, pp. 9–26.

For an introduction to the debates on the history of human rights, see Jan Herman Burgers, "The road to San Francisco: the revival of the human rights idea in the twentieth century," *Human Rights Quarterly*, 14: 4, November 1992, pp. 447–477, and Kenneth Cmiel, "The recent history of human rights," *American Historical Review*, 109: 1, February 2004, pp. 117–135. Paul Gordon Lauren, *The Evolution of International Human Rights: Visions Seen* (Philadelphia: University of Pennsylvania Press, 1998) offers a rich synthesis of this field of research. For a critical reading of the moralizing discourse on human rights, see Mark Mazower,

314

"The strange triumph of human rights," *New Statesman*, February 4, 2002, and *No Enchanted Palace: The End of Empire and the Ideological Origins of the United Nations* (Princeton University Press, 2009). In an important book situated at the intersection of intellectual history and cultural history, *Inventing Human Rights: A History* (New York: W.W. Norton, 2007), Lynn Hunt studies the cultural origins of human rights, the language of rights, and the evolution of humanitarian sensibilities. Samuel Moyn, *The Last Utopia: Human Rights in History* (Belknap Press of Harvard University Press, 2010) has offered an important new perspective on the history of human rights and modified its chronology. Stefan-Ludwig Hoffmann (ed.), *Human Rights in the Twentieth Century* (Cambridge University Press, 2011) is the best critical synthesis on the topic (see especially Hoffmann's introduction, "Genealogies of human rights," pp. 1–26). See also Akira Iriye, Petra Goedde and William I. Hitchcock (eds.), *The Human Rights Revolution: An International History* (Oxford University Press, 2012). On the distinction between humanitarian rights and human rights, see Marco Sassoli, "Le droit international humanitaire, une *lex specialis* par rapport aux droits humains?" in Andreas Auer, Alexandre Flueckiger and Michel Hottelier, *Les droits de l'homme et la constitution: études en l'honneur du Professeur Giorgio Malinverni* (Geneva: Schulthess, 2007), pp. 375–395.

On the history of the 1920s, a standard work is Charles Maier, *Recasting Bourgeois Europe: Stabilization in France, Germany and Italy in the Decade after World War I* (Princeton University Press, 1975). See also Stéphane Audoin-Rouzeau and Christophe Prochasson, *Sortir de la Grande Guerre. Le monde et l'après-1918* (Paris: Tallandier, 2008). Erez Manela's *The Wilsonian Moment: Self-Determination and the International Origins of Anti-colonial Nationalism* (Oxford University Press, 2007) is a good example of renewed scholarly attention to the international landscape after the Great War. For a synthesis of the new history of international relations, see Zara Steiner, *The Lights that Failed: European International History, 1919–1933* (Oxford University Press, 2005). On the new approaches to the history of the League of Nations, see Susan Pedersen, "Back to the League of Nations," *American Historical Review*, 112: 4, October, 2007, pp. 1091–1117. On the key question of the rights of minority groups, see Carole Fink, *Defending the Rights of Others: The Great Powers, the Jews, and International Minority Protection, 1878–1938* (Cambridge University Press, 2004).

For an initial approach to transnational history, see Patricia Clavin, "Defining transnationalism," *Contemporary European History*, 14: 4, November 2005, pp. 421–439 and "On transnational history," *American Historical Review*, 111: 5, December 2006, pp. 1441–1464; Akira Iriye and Pierre-Yves Saunier (eds.), *The Palgrave Dictionary of Transnational History* (Basingstoke: Palgrave Macmillan, 2009).

On the history of international law, see Francis Anthony Boyle, *Foundations of World Order: The Legalist Approach to International Relations (1898–1922)* (Durham NC: Duke University Press, 1999); Martti Koskenniemi, *The Gentle Civilizer of Nations: The Rise and Fall of International Law, 1870–1960* (Cambridge University Press, 2001); Jean-Michel Guieu, "Les juristes français, la Société des Nations et l'Europe," in Jacques Bariéty (ed.), *Aristide Briand, la Société des Nations et l'Europe, 1919–1932* (Presses universitaires de Strasbourg, 2007), pp. 185–199. See also Leonard V. Smith, "The Wilsonian challenge to international law," *Journal of the History of International Law*, 13: 1, 2011, pp. 179–208.

On transnational networks in the nineteenth and twentieth centuries: Madeleine Herren, *Internationale Sozialpolitik vor dem Ersten Weltkrieg* (Berlin: Duncker und Humblot, 1993); Paul Weindling (ed.), *International Health Organisations and Movements, 1918–1939* (Cambridge University Press, 1995); Kevin Grant, Philippa Levine and Frank Trentmann (eds.), *Beyond Sovereignty: Britain, Empire, and Transnationalism, c.1880–1950* (Basingstoke: Palgrave Macmillan, 2007); Sebastian Conrad and Dominic Sachsenmaier (eds.), *Competing Visions of World Order: Global Moments and Movements, 1880s–1930s* (Basingstoke: Palgrave Macmillan, 2007).

On the cultural history of the Great War: Stéphane Audoin-Rouzeau and Annette Becker, "Violence et consentement: la 'culture de guerre' du premier conflit mondial," in Jean-Pierre Rioux and Jean-François Sirinelli (eds.) *Pour une histoire culturelle* (Paris: Seuil, 1997), pp. 251–271; John Horne, "Démobilisations culturelles après la Grande Guerre," *14–18 Aujourd'hui* (Paris: Noésis, 2002), pp. 49–53; Stéphane Audoin-Rouzeau and Annette Becker, *14–18: Understanding the Great War* (New York: Hill and Wang, 2003); Bruno Cabanes, "Grande Guerre," in Christian Delporte, Jean-Yves Mollier and Jean-François Sirinelli (eds.), *Dictionnaire d'histoire culturelle de la France contemporaine* (Paris: Presses universitaires de France, 2010), pp. 368–371.

Chapter 1

On veterans of the Great War: Stephen R. Ward (ed.), *The War Generation: Veterans of the First World War* (Port Washington, NY: Kennikat Press, 1975); Antoine Prost, *Les anciens combattants et la société française, 1914–1939* (Paris: Presses de la Fondation nationale des Sciences Politiques, 1977); Bruno Cabanes, *La victoire endeuillée: la sortie de guerre des soldats français (1918–1920)* (Paris: Seuil, 2004). On veterans' pacifism: Norman

Ingram, *The Politics of Dissent. Pacifism in France, 1919–1939* (Oxford University Press, 1991); Sophie Lorrain, *Des pacifistes français et allemands, pionniers de l'entente franco-allemande, 1871–1925* (Paris: L'Harmattan, 1999); Andrew Webster, "The transnational dream: politicians, diplomats and soldiers in the League of Nations' pursuit of international disarmament, 1920–1938," *Contemporary European History*, 14: 4, 2005, pp. 493–518; Jean-Michel Guieu, *Le rameau et le glaive. Les militants français pour la SDN* (Paris: Presses de Sciences Po, 2008); Gearóid Barry, *The Disarmament of Hatred. Marc Sangnier, French Catholicism and the Legacy of the First World War* (Basingstoke: Palgrave Macmillan, 2012).

The standard biography of René Cassin is now the one by Antoine Prost and Jay Winter (Paris: Fayard, 2011). See also Marc Agi, *René Cassin: Prix Nobel de la paix, 1887–1976* (Paris: Perrin, 1998); Gérard Israel, *René Cassin: 1887–1976, la guerre hors la loi. Avec de Gaulle. Les droits de l'Homme* (Paris: Desclée de Brouwer, 1990); and *René Cassin, 1887–1976: une pensée ouverte sur le monde moderne* (Paris: Honoré Champion, 2001). In addition, René Cassin's book *La pensée et l'action* (Paris: Éditions F. Lalou, 1972) is also useful, particularly the "Autobiographical fragments." For this chapter, I used the Cassin archives held at the International Labor Organization (ILO) (ABIT, MU/3/7; ABIT, CAT/2) and the archives of the League of Nations, in Geneva. The newsletters and newspapers of disabled veterans' organizations are available on the French National Library's "Gallica" database, accessible on the internet. The *Bibliothèque de Documentation Internationale Contemporaine* (BDIC) in Nanterre has a significant collection of pamphlets on human rights published in the interwar period. Of these, see in particular René Cassin's "La nouvelle conception du domicile dans le règlement des conflits de lois," *Académie de droit international de La Haye: Recueil des cours* (Paris: Sirey, 1931) and "L'État Léviathan," in *La Pensée et l'Action* (Paris: Éditions F. Lalou, 1972), pp. 63–71.

On disabled veterans: Robert Weldon Whalen, *Bitter Wounds: German Victims of the Great War, 1914–1939* (Ithaca: Cornell University Press, 1984); Joanna Bourke, *Dismembering the Male: Men's Bodies, Britain and the Great War* (University of Chicago Press, 1996); Sophie Delaporte, *Les gueules cassées. Les blessés de la face de la Grande Guerre* (Paris: Noésis, 1996); David A. Gerber (ed.), *Disabled Veterans in History* (Ann Arbor: University of Michigan Press, 2000); Deborah Cohen, *The War Come Home: Disabled Veterans in Britain and Germany, 1914–1939* (Berkeley: University of California Press, 2001); Jeffrey S. Reznick, "Prostheses and propaganda: materiality and the human body in the Great War," in Nicholas J. Saunders, *Matters of Conflict: Material Culture, Memory and the First World War* (London and New York:

Routledge, 2004), pp. 51–61; Sabine Kienitz, *Beschädigte Helden: Kriegsinvalidität und Körperbilder 1914–1923* (Paderborn, 2008); Marina Larsson, *Shattered Anzacs: Living with the Scars of War* (University of New South Wales Press, 2009); Beth Linker, *War's Waste: Rehabilitation in World War I America* (University of Chicago Press, 2011).

On war widows and orphans: Joy Damousi, *The Labour of Loss: Mourning, Memory and Wartime Bereavement in Australia* (Cambridge University Press, 1999); Olivier Faron, *Les enfants du deuil. Orphelins et pupilles de la nation de la Première Guerre mondiale* (Paris: La Découverte, 2001); Stéphane Audoin-Rouzeau, *Cinq deuils de guerre: 1914–1918* (Paris: Noésis, 2001); Virginia Nicholson, *Singled Out: How Two Million British Women Survived Without Men After the First World War* (Oxford University Press, 2008), and Erica A. Kuhlman, *Of Little Comfort: War Widows, Fallen Soldiers and the Remaking of the Nation after the Great War* (New York University Press, 2012).

Chapter 2

On the origins of international labor law: James T. Shotwell (ed.), *The Origins of the International Labor Organization* (New York: Columbia University Press, 1934) and Isabelle Moret-Lespinet, *L'Office du travail, la République et la réforme sociale, 1891–1914* (Presses universitaires de Rennes, 2007). On reformist circles before the war, the standard work is still Christian Topalov (ed.), *Laboratoires du nouveau siècle: la nébuleuse réformatrice et ses réseaux en France* (Paris: Éditions de l'École des Hautes Études en Sciences Sociales, 1999)—especially Christophe Prochasson's article "Entre science et action sociale: le 'réseau Albert Thomas' et le socialisme normalien, 1900–1914," in Topalov (ed.), *Laboratoires du nouveau siècle*, pp. 141–158.

Little scholarly work on Albert Thomas exists, and it is often out of date. See, however, Edward Phelan, *Albert Thomas et la création du BIT* (Paris, 1936) and the standard biography by Bertus W. Schaper, *Albert Thomas: trente ans de réformisme* (Assen: Van Gorcum, 1959). On Thomas' work as a minister in the *'gouvernement d'union sacrée'* during the Great War, see Martin Fine, "Albert Thomas: a reformer's vision of modernization, 1914–1932," *Journal of Contemporary History*, 12: 3, July 1977; Christophe Prochasson, *Les intellectuels, le socialisme et la guerre, 1900–1938* (Paris: Seuil, 1991); Alain Hennebicque, "Albert Thomas and the war industries," in Fridenson (ed.), *The French Home Front*; Jean-Jacques Becker, "La gauche et la Grande Guerre," in Jean-Jacques Becker and Gilles Candar (eds.), *Histoire des gauches en France* (Paris: La Découverte, 2005), pp. 311–329; and Florent Lazarovici,

"L'organisation du ministère de l'armement sous Albert Thomas: une expérience socialiste ou technocratique?" in Romain Ducoulombier (ed.), *Les socialistes dans l'Europe en guerre: réseaux, parcours, expériences, 1914–1918* (Paris: L'Harmattan, 2010), pp. 55–71.

To write this chapter, I worked in the archives of the ILO in Geneva, which contain exceptional source material that has been little studied. The bibliography on the ILO has been enriched by many recent studies. For an initial approach, see Gerry Rodgers, Eddy Lee, Lee Swepston and Jasmien Van Daele (eds.), *The International Labour Organization and the Quest for Social Justice, 1919–2009* (Ithaca: Cornell University Press, and Geneva: International Labor Office, 2009); Jasmien Van Daele, Magaly Rodriguez Garcia and Marcel Van der Linden (eds.), *ILO Histories: Essays on the International Labour Organization and its Impact on the World in the Twentieth Century* (Bern: Peter Lang, 2010); and Isabelle Lespinet and Vincent Viet (eds.), *L'Organisation Internationale du Travail* (Presses universitaires de Rennes, 2011).

On the workings of the ILO: Bernard Béguin, *The ILO and the Tripartite System* (New York: Carnegie Endowment for International Peace, 1959); Eliane Vogel-Polsky, *Du tripartisme à l'Organisation Internationale du Travail* (Bruxelles: Éditions de l'Institut de Sociologie de l'Université de Bruxelles, 1966); Jean-Michel Bonvin, *L'Organisation Internationale du Travail: essai sur une agence productrice de normes* (Paris: Presses universitaires de France, 1998) and Dzovinar Kévonian, "Albert Thomas et le Bureau International du Travail (1920–1932): enjeux de légitimation d'une organisation internationale," in Jacques Bariéty (ed.), *Aristide Briand, la Société des Nations et l'Europe, 1919–1932* (Presses universitaires de Strasbourg, 2007), pp. 324–338. On the role of women in the ILO, see Carol Riegelmann Lubin and Anne Winslow, *Social Justice for Women: The International Labor Organization and Women* (Duke University Press, 1990).

On the ILO's health policies: Paul Weindling, "Social Medicine at the League of Nations Health Organisation and the International Labour Office compared," in Paul Weindling (ed.), *International Health Organisations and Movements, 1918–1939* (Cambridge University Press, 1995), pp. 134–153; Isabelle Moret-Lespinet, "Hygiène industrielle, santé au travail. L'OIT productrice de normes, 1919–1939," in Moret-Lespinet and Viet (eds.), *L'Organisation Internationale du Travail*. On the ILO and large-scale migration, see Dzovinar Kévonian, "Enjeux de catégorisations et migrations internationales: Le Bureau International du Travail et les réfugiés (1925–1929)," *Revue européenne des migrations internationales*, 21: 3, 2005, and Paul-André Rosental, "Géopolitique et État-providence. Le BIT et la politique mondiale des migrations dans l'entre-deux-guerres,"

Annales HSS, 1, 2006, pp. 99–134. On the ILO's economic models, Ingrid Liebeskind-Sauthier, *L'Organisation internationale du travail face au chômage: entre compétences normatives et recherche de solutions économiques, 1919–1939*, PhD thesis, University of Geneva, 2005; Thomas Cayet, *Rationaliser le travail, organiser la production: Le Bureau International du Travail et la modernisation économique durant l'entre-deux-guerres* (Presses universitaires de Rennes, 2010). On the ILO and forced labor: James P. Daughton, "Documenting colonial violence: the international campaign against forced labor during the interwar years," *Revue d'Histoire de la Shoah*, 189, 2008.

On networks of experts: Jasmien Van Daele, "Engineering social peace: networks, ideas and the founding of the International Labour Organization," *International Review of Social History*, 50, 2005, pp. 435–466; Sandrine Kott, "Une 'communauté épistémique' du social? Experts de l'ILO et internationalisation des politiques sociales dans l'entre-deux guerres," *Genèses*, 2: 71, 2008, pp. 26–46; Dzovinar Kévonian, "La légitimation par l'expertise: Le Bureau International du Travail et la statistique internationale," *Les cahiers de l'IRICE*, 2: 2, 2008; Thomas Cayet, Marie Thébaud-Sorger and Paul-André Rosental "How international organisations compete: occupational safety and health at the ILO, a diplomacy of expertise," *Journal of Modern European History*, 7: 2, 2009, pp. 174–196; Dzovinar Kévonian, "Les juristes et l'Organisation internationale du Travail, 1919–1939. Processus de légitimation et institutionnalisation des relations internationales," *Journal of the History of International Law*, 12, 2010, pp. 227–266; Davide Rodogno, Bernard Struck and Jakob Vogel (eds.), *Shaping the Transnational Sphere: Networks of Experts and Organisations, 1840–1930* (New York: Berghahn Books, forthcoming).

Chapter 3

For a general overview of the history of refugees after the Great War, a good starting point is Michael Marrus, *The Unwanted: European Refugees in the Twentieth Century* (Oxford University Press, 1985) and Claudena M. Skran, *Refugees in Inter-War Europe: The Emergence of a Regime* (Oxford: Clarendon Press, 1995).

See also Annette Becker, *Oubliés de la Grande Guerre: humanitaire et culture de guerre, 1914–1918* (Paris: Noésis, 1998; repub. Pluriel, 2003); Peter Gatrell, *A Whole Empire Walking: Refugees in Russia During World War I* (Bloomington: Indiana University Press, 1999); Philippe Nivet, *Les réfugiés français de la Grande Guerre, 1914–1920* (Paris: Economica, 2004); Nick Baron and Peter Gatrell (eds.), *Homelands: War, Population and Statehood in Eastern Europe and Russia, 1918–1924* (London: Anthem

Press, 2004); Catherine Gousseff, *L'Exil russe: la fabrique du réfugié apatride* (Paris: CNRS éditions, 2008); Annemarie H. Sammartino, *The Impossible Border: Germany and the East, 1914–1922* (Ithaca: Cornell University Press, 2010).

The standard work on refugees in the Near East is Dzovinar Kévonian, *Réfugiés et diplomatie humanitaire: les acteurs européens et la scène proche-orientale pendant l'entre-deux-guerres* (Paris: Publications de la Sorbonne, 2004). See also Dzovinar Kévonian, "Les tribulations de la diplomatie humanitaire: la Société des Nations et les réfugiés arméniens," in Hans-Lukas Kieser (ed.), *Die armenische Frage und die Schweiz (1896–1923)* (Zürich: Chronos, 1999), pp. 279–310; and Keith David Watenpaugh, "The League of Nations' rescue of Armenian genocide survivors and the making of modern humanitarianism, 1920–1927," *American Historical Review*, 115: 5, December 2010, pp. 1315–1339—as well as his book *Bread from Stone: The Middle East and the Making of Modern Humanitarianism* (University of California Press, forthcoming).

On population exchanges: Renée Hirschon (ed.), *Crossing the Aegean: An Appraisal of the 1923 Compulsory Population Exchange between Greece and Turkey* (New York and Oxford: Berghahn Books, 2003); Richard Bessel and Claudia B. Haake (eds.), *Removing Peoples: Forced Removal in the Modern World* (Oxford University Press, 2009). On the issue of minorities, Fink, *Defending the Rights of Others*, and Tara Zahra, "The minority problem: national classification in the French and Czechoslovak borderlands," *Contemporary European History*, 17, May 2008, pp. 137–165. On the loss of Russian citizenship, see Jacques Schefgel, "L'Apatridie des réfugiés russes," *Journal de Droit international*, 61, 1934, pp. 36–69; Timothy Andrew Taracouzio, *The Soviet Union and International Law* (New York: Macmillan, 1935), Chapter 5, "Nationality and citizenship."

On the creation of passports and immigration policy: Gérard Noiriel, *La tyrannie du national: Le droit d'asile en Europe, 1793–1993* (Paris: Calmann-Lévy, 1991); John Torpey, *The Invention of the Passport: Surveillance, Citizenship and the State* (Cambridge University Press, 2000); John Torpey, "The Great War and the birth of the modern passport system," in Jane Caplan and John Torpey (eds.), *Documenting Individual Identity: The Development of State Practices in the Modern World* (Princeton and Oxford: Princeton University Press, 2001), pp. 256–270.

On refugees' rights and human rights in the 1920s, Dzovinar Kévonian, "Les juristes juifs russes en France et l'action internationale dans les années vingt," *Archives Juives*, 34: 2, 2001, pp. 72–94; "Exilés politiques et avènement du droit humain: la pensée juridique d'André Mandelstam (1869–1949), *Revue d'histoire de la Shoah*, 177–178, January–August 2003, pp. 245–273; and "Question des réfugiés, droits de l'homme:

éléments d'une convergence pendant l'entre-deux-guerres," *Matériaux pour l'histoire de notre temps*, 72, 2003, pp. 40–49.

On non-governmental organizations (NGOs): Dzovinar Kévonian, "L'organisation non gouvernementale, nouvel acteur du champ humanitaire. Le Zemgor et la Société des Nations dans les années 1920," *Cahiers du monde russe*, 46: 4, October–December 2005, pp. 739–756. See also James L. Barton, *Story of Near East Relief (1915–1930): An Interpretation* (New York: Macmillan, 1930); Robert L. Daniel, *American Philanthropy in the Near East (1820–1960)* (Ohio University Press, 1970); Joseph L. Grabill, *Protestant Diplomacy in the Near East: Missionary Influence on American Policy, 1810–1927* (Minneapolis: University of Minnesota Press, 1971). On the International Red Cross, John F. Hutchinson, *Champions of Charity: War and the Rise of the Red Cross* (Boulder, Colo: Westview Press, 1996) and David P. Forsythe, *The Humanitarians: The International Committee of the Red Cross* (Cambridge University Press, 2005).

On the League of Nations and refugees: Sir John Hope Simpson, *The Refugee Problem: Report of a Survey* (New York: Oxford University Press, 1939); Gil Loescher, *Beyond Charity: International Cooperation and the Global Refugee Crisis* (Oxford University Press, 1993), Chapter 2, "The origins of international refugee regime"; Barbara Metzger, "The League of Nations and human rights: from practice to theory," unpublished PhD thesis, University of Cambridge, 2001; Dzovinar Kévonian, "Enjeux de catégorisations et migrations internationales," pp. 95–124; and Rosental, "Géopolitique et État-providence," pp. 99–134.

On Nansen, the League of Nations' High Commissioner for Russian Refugees, see Roland Huntford, *Nansen: The Explorer as Hero* (London: Duckworth, 1997), and especially the recent work of the Norwegian historian Carl Emil Vogt. In order to write this chapter, I stayed in Oslo for several months, where I used the archives of the Nobel Foundation and the National Archives (Ms. Fol. 1988). In Geneva, the archives of the League of Nations hold important documents relative to Nansen and Russian refugees. I also worked in the archives of the International Committee of the Red Cross, which contain numerous reports on humanitarian work in the Near East, in Constantinople, the Balkans, Russia, and Central Europe in the 1920s.

Chapter 4

The standard work on the American Relief Administration (ARA) is Bertrand M. Patenaude, *The Big Show in Bololand: The American Relief Expedition to Soviet Russia in the Famine of 1921* (Stanford University Press, 2002). See also Benjamin M. Weissman, *Herbert Hoover and Famine*

Relief to Soviet Russia, 1921–23 (Stanford, Calif.: Hoover Institution Press, 1974).

On Hoover and the Commission for Relief in Belgium (CRB) during the Great War, see Annette Becker, *Les cicatrices rouges, 14–18: France et Belgique occupées*. See also Edward Eyre Hunt, *War Bread: A Personal Narrative on the War and Relief in Belgium* (New York: Henry Holt, 1916); Vernon L. Kellogg, *Fighting Starvation in Belgium* (Garden City, NY: Doubleday Page, 1918), as well as the Kellogg-Dickie Papers, Manuscripts and Archives, Sterling Memorial Library, Yale University; and George I. Gay and Harold H. Fisher (eds.), *Public Relations of the Commission for Relief in Belgium: Documents*, 2 vols. (Stanford University Press, 1929); Frank M. Surface and Raymond L. Bland (eds.), *American Food in the World War and Reconstruction Period* (Stanford University Press, 1931); Herbert Hoover, *Memoirs*, Vol. I: *Years of Adventure, 1874–1920* (New York: Macmillan, 1951).

The Hoover Institution Archives are located in Stanford, California, and the Hoover Presidential Archives are in West Branch, Iowa. They contain the official papers of the ARA's work in Europe and Russia, as well as numerous personal papers of ARA members such as Thomas C. Barringer, James Rives Childs, Harold H. Fisher, Frank A. Golder, James P. Goodrich, and William N. Haskell. For this chapter, I also used the archives of the International Committee of the Red Cross in Geneva (Commixt, II.5), the ILO's archives (ABIT/R.301, Starvation in Russia), and the Nansen Archives at the National Library in Oslo (National Library, Ms. Fol. 1988). The *American Relief Administration Bulletin* provides important information on how operations on the ground were carried out. See also Henry Beeuwkes, *American Medical and Sanitary Relief in the Russian Famine, 1921–1923* (New York, 1926) and Frank Alfred Golder and Lincoln Hutchinson, *On the Trail of the Russian Famine* (Stanford University Press, 1927).

On the demographic impact of the 1921–23 famine: Sergueï Adamets, *Guerre civile et famine en Russie: le pouvoir bolchevique et la population face à la catastrophe démographique, 1917–1923* (Paris: Institut d'études slaves, 2003), with a rich bibliography on the work of Russian historians. For a general overview of the political context: Richard Pipes, *The Russian Revolution* (New York: Knopf, 1990); Orlando Figes, *Peasant Russia, Civil War: The Volga Countryside in Revolution* (Oxford: Clarendon Press, 1989), and *A People's Tragedy: The Russian Revolution, 1891–1924* (London: Jonathan Cape, 1996). On the crisis of the early 1920s as a continuation of World War I, see Peter Holquist, *Making War, Forging Revolution: Russia's Continuum of Crisis, 1914–1921* (Harvard University Press, 2002). On the power to feed in contemporary Russia: Lars T. Lih,

Bread and Authority in Russia, 1914–1921 (University of California Press, 1990); Tamara Kondratieva, *Gouverner et nourrir: du pouvoir en Russie (XVIè–XXème siècles)* (Paris: Les Belles Lettres, 2002).

On Hoover's motivations during the Russian famine, see Robert W. McElroy, *Morality and American Foreign Policy* (Princeton University Press, 1992).

On the idea of humanitarian intervention, see Gary J. Bass, *Freedom's Battle: The Origins of Humanitarian Intervention* (New York: Alfred A. Knopf, 2008); Michael Barnett, *Empire of Humanity: A History of Humanitarianism* (Ithaca: Cornell University Press, 2011); Brendan Simms and D.J.B. Trim (eds.), *Humanitarian Intervention: A History* (Cambridge University Press, 2011), Part II, "The Great Powers and the Ottoman Empire"; Davide Rodogno, *Against Massacre: Humanitarian Interventions in the Ottoman Empire, 1815–1914* (Princeton University Press, 2012). On the role of the United States in humanitarian policy, see Merle Curti, *American Philanthropy Abroad* (New Brunswick, New Jersey: Transaction Books, 1988).

Chapter 5

The history of childhood in the modern era has been the object of major scholarly works. The turning point came with the publication of Philippe Ariès, *L'enfant et la vie familiale sous l'Ancien Régime* (Paris: Seuil, 1960), translated by Robert Baldick as *Centuries of Childhood* (New York: Vintage, 1962). This book was widely read and inspired lively debate— for example: Jean-Louis Flandrin, "Enfance et société," *Annales ESC*, 1964, 19: 2, pp. 322–329; Lawrence Stone, "The massacre of the innocents," *New York Review of Books*, November 1974, 21: 18, pp. 25–31; Adrian Wilson, "The infancy of the history of childhood: an appraisal of Philippe Ariès," *History and Theory*, 19: 2, February 1980, pp. 132–153. On the social history of childhood, see also George K. Behlmer, *Child Abuse and Moral Reform in England, 1870–1908* (Stanford University Press, 1982); Deborah Dwork, *War is Good for Babies and Other Young Children: A History of the Infant and Child Welfare Movement in England, 1898–1918* (London and New York: Tavistock Publications, 1987); Catherine Rollet, *La politique à l'égard de la petite enfance sous la IIIème République* (Paris: Presses universitaires de France, 1990); Samuel H. Preston and Michael R. Haines, *Fatal Years: Child Mortality in Late Nineteenth-Century America* (Princeton University Press, 1991); Michel Chauvière, Pierre Lenoël and Éric Pierre (eds.), *Protéger l'enfant: raison juridique et pratiques socio-judiciaires, XIXème–XXème siècle* (Presses universitaires de Rennes, 1996); Judith Sealander, *The Failed Century of the Child: Governing America's Young in the Twentieth Century* (Cambridge University Press, 2003); Hugh Cunningham, *Children and Childhood in Western Society Since 1500* (2nd edition) (Harlow, UK, and New York: Pearson Longman, 2005).

For this chapter, I used the Save the Children Fund Archives in London, the archives of the Advisory Committee on the Traffic in Women and the Protection of Children in the League of Nations archives, and the State Archives of Geneva. On Eglantyne Jebb, see Clare Mulley, *The Woman Who Saved the Children: A Biography of Eglantyne Jebb, Founder of Save the Children* (Oxford: Oneworld, 2009) and especially Linda Mahood, *Feminism and Voluntary Action. Eglantyne Jebb and Save the Children, 1876–1928* (London: Palgrave Macmillan, 2009).

On the role of women in philanthropy, see Frank Prochaska, *Women and Philanthropy in Nineteenth-Century England* (Oxford University Press, 1980); Linda Gordon (ed.), *Women, the State and Welfare* (Madison: University of Wisconsin Press, 1990); Gisela Bock and Pat Thane (eds.), *Maternity and Gender Policies* (London and New York: Routledge, 1991); Geoffrey Finlayson, *Citizen, State and Social Welfare in Britain, 1830–1990* (Oxford: Clarendon Press, 1994); and Susan Pedersen, *Eleanor Rathbone and the Politics of Conscience* (New Haven: Yale University Press, 2004).

On children during the Great War: Stéphane Audoin-Rouzeau, *La guerre des enfants (1914–1918)* (Paris: Armand Colin, 1993); Stéphane Audoin-Rouzeau (ed.), "Enfances en guerre," *Vingtième siècle*, 1: 89, 2006; Manon Pignot, *Allons enfants de la patrie! Génération Grande Guerre* (Paris: Seuil, 2012).

On the Save the Children Fund (SCF), Patricia T. Rooke and Rudy L. Schnell, "Uncramping child life: international children's organisations, 1914–1939," in Weindling (ed.), *International Health Organisations and Movements*, pp. 176–202; Emily Baughan, "Save the Children: constructing an international humanitarian movement in interwar Britain," dissertation in progress, University of Bristol. See also Emily Baughan, "'Every citizen of empire implored to save the children!' Empire, internationalism and the Save the Children Fund in interwar Britain," *Historical Research*, 86: 231, February 2013, pp. 116–137. On the rise of children's rights, see Dominique Marshall, "The construction of children as an object of international relations: the Declaration of Children's Rights and the Child Welfare Committee of the League of Nations, 1900–1924," *The International Journal of Children's Rights*, 7, 1999, pp. 103–147; "Humanitarian sympathy for children in times of war and the history of children's rights, 1919–1959," in James Marten (ed.), *Children and War* (New York University Press, 2002), and "Dimensions transnationales et locales de l'histoire des droits de l'enfant: la Société des Nations et les cultures politiques canadiennes, 1910–1960," *Genèses*, 2: 71, 2008, pp. 47–63; see also Joëlle Droux, "L'internationalisation de la protection de l'enfance: acteurs, concurrences et projets transnationaux (1900–1925), *Critique internationale*, 3: 52, 2011, pp. 17–33.

Bibliography

PRIMARY SOURCES

ARCHIVES

FRANCE

Bibliothèque de Documentation Internationale Contemporaine, Nanterre
National Archives of France, Paris
René Cassin Papers, 382 AP
Albert Thomas Papers, 94 AP 197–220; 94 AP 232 (creation of the ILO); 94 AP
    377–394 (correspondence)
National Library, Paris

GREAT BRITAIN

Save the Children Fund (SCF) Archives, London

NORWAY

National Library, Oslo
Fridtjof Nansen Papers, Ms. Fol. 1988

SWITZERLAND

Archives of the International Committee of the Red Cross (ICRC)
ACICR/Commixt, II. 5: Aid to Russia
ACICR, CR 87, Russian Refugees
Archives of the International Labor Organization (ILO)
ABIT/Cabinet Albert Thomas (CAT) Series
ABIT/D600: International Conference for the Protection of Childhood
ABIT, MU/7: Disabled Veterans
ABIT, R301: Starvation in Russia
The League of Nations Archives
A/SDN/Refugees Mixte Archival Group/Nansen Fonds
A/SDN/Archives of the International Relief Union
A/SDN/R 681: Child Welfare
A/SDN/Mantoux Papers, 1919–26, Box 154
A/SDN/Politis Papers, Box 213

The State Archive of Geneva:
International Union of Save the Children Papers

UNITED STATES OF AMERICA

Hoover Institution Archives, Stanford University
American Relief Administration, European Operations
American Relief Administration, Russian Operations
Hoover Presidential Archives, West Branch, Iowa
American Relief Administration

PUBLISHED PRIMARY SOURCES

Newspapers and periodicals
Académie de droit international de La Haye, Recueil des cours
American Journal of International Law
Annales de l'Economie collective
Annuaire de l'Institut de Droit International
Après la bataille
Cahiers des Droits de l'Homme
Cahiers de l'Union fédérale
Etudes et documents
La Croix
La France mutilée
Journal de Droit international
Journal des mutilés et réformés
Recueil de Droit international
Revue de Droit international et de législation comparée
Revue générale de droit international public
La Revue de Paris
Revue Politique et Parlementaire
La Revue socialiste
La Tribune Juive
La Voix du combattant

Official publications
American Relief Administration Bulletin
Les Documents du Travail
Informations sociales
Official Journal of the League of Nations
The Record of the Save the Children Fund
Revue internationale de la Croix Rouge
Revue internationale du Travail

Books, pamphlets and articles
Guide de la victime de guerre (pensions, gratifications, allocations) (Paris, 1916).
Guide pratique des droits des militaires et de leurs familles victimes de la guerre aux recours, pensions, gratifications et autres avantages accordés par l'Etat (Paris, 1917).

Pour obtenir une pension militaire. Ce qu'il faut savoir, ce qu'il faut faire. Guide indispensable aux veuves, orphelins et réformés (Paris, 1915).

Alvarez, Alejandro, *La codification du droit international – ses tendances, ses bases* (Paris, 1912).

Alvarez, Alejandro and Albert de la Pradelle, "L'Institut des Hautes Études Internationales et l'enseignement du droit des gens," *Revue générale de droit international public*, 46, 1939, pp. 666–669.

Andler, Charles, *L'humanisme travailliste: essais de pédagogie sociale* (Paris, 1927).

Andler, Charles, *Vie de Lucien Herr, 1864–1926* (Paris, 1932).

Audinet, Eugène, "Le retrait des naturalisations accordées aux anciens sujets de puissances en guerre avec la France," *Journal de droit international*, 42, 1915, pp. 129–140.

Barton, James L., *Story of Near East Relief (1915–1930): An interpretation* (New York, 1930).

Basch, Victor, "La Ligue des droits de l'Homme et la guerre," *Bulletin officiel de la Ligue des droits de l'Homme*, May 1, 1915, p. 173.

Beeuwkes, Henry, *American Medical and Sanitary Relief in the Russian Famine, 1921–1923* (New York, 1926).

Bourgeois Léon, *Pour la Société des Nations* (Paris, 1910).

Bourgeois, Léon, "La morale internationale," *Revue générale de droit international public*, 29, 1922, pp. 5–22.

Bourgeois, Léon, *L'œuvre de la Société des Nations, 1920–1923* (Paris, 1923).

Brandt, Lilian, *How Much Shall I Give?* (New York, 1921).

Brunet, René, *La Société des Nations et la France* (Paris, 1921).

Bullitt, William C., *The Bullitt Mission to Russia: Testimony before the Committee on Foreign Relations, United States Senate, of William C. Bullitt* (New York, 1919).

Capy, Marcelle, "La femme à l'usine," *La Voix des femmes*, Novembre 28, 1917.

Cassin, René "La réunion de Genève," *La France mutilée*, September 25, 1921.

Cassin, René, Commission d'étude du projet Ciraolo, 1925.

Cassin, René, "La nouvelle conception du domicile dans le règlement des conflits de lois," *Académie de droit international de La Haye: recueil des cours*, Vol. 4 (Paris, 1931).

Cassin, René, "Le B.I.T. et les invalides de guerre," *Revue française des Affaires sociales*, 23: 2, April–June 1969.

Cassin, René, "From the ten commandments to the rights of man," in Shlomo Shoham (ed.), *Of Law and Man. Essays in Honor of Haim H. Cohn* (New York and Tel Aviv, 1971).

Cassin, René, *La pensée et l'action* (Paris, 1972).

Chateau, Jean, *De la compétence de l'OIT en matière de travail agricole* (Paris, 1924).

Ciraolo, Giovanni, *An International Organization of Mutual Aid among the Nations for Succour and Assistance to Peoples Stricken by Calamities: Project and Explanatory Notes* (Rome, 1923).

Colanéri, André, *La condition des "Sans-patrie." Étude critique de l'Heimatlosen* (Paris, 1932).

Davison, Henry Pomeroy, *The American Red Cross in the Great War* (New York, 1919).

Delehelle, Jean, *La situation juridique des Russes en France* (Lille, 1926).

Delevingne, Malcolm, "The pre-war history of the international labor legislation," in Shotwell (ed.), *Origins of the International Labor Organization*.

Devedji, Alexandre, *L'échange obligatoire des minorités grecques et turques en vertu de la convention de Lausanne du 30 janvier 1923*, law dissertation (Paris, 1929).

Duguit, Léon, *Le droit social, le droit individuel et la transformation de l'Etat* (Paris, 1908).

Dupuis, Charles, *Le droit des gens et les rapports des grandes puissances avec les autres états avant le pacte de la Société des Nations* (Paris, 1921).

Durkheim, Emile and Ernest Denis, *Qui a voulu la guerre? Les origines de la guerre d'après les documents diplomatiques* (Paris, 1915), pp. 61–63.

Engeström, Maxson E., *Les changements de nationalité d'après les traités de paix de 1919–1920* (Paris, 1923).

Fisher, Harold H. *The Famine in Soviet Russia, 1919–1923* (New York, 1927).

Fontaine, Arthur, "La législation internationale du travail," *Revue Politique et Parlementaire*, February 1914.

Fontaine, Arthur, *L'industrie française pendant la guerre* (Paris and New Haven, 1924).

Garner, James W., "La reconstitution du droit international," *Revue générale de droit international public*, 28, 1921, pp. 413–440.

Gay, George I. and Harold H. Fisher (eds.), *Public Relations of the Commission for Relief in Belgium: Documents*, 2 vols. (Stanford, 1929).

Ghali, Paul, *Les nationalités détachées de l'Empire ottoman à la suite de la guerre* (Paris, 1934).

Gilson, Etienne, "Enquête sur la situation actuelle des enfants en Ukraine et dans les régions de la Volga, 15 août–15 septembre 1922," *Revue internationale de la Croix Rouge*, IV: 46, October 1922, pp. 883–896.

Golder, Frank Alfred and Lincoln Hutchinson, *On the Trail of the Russian Famine* (Stanford, 1927).

Gorgé, Camille, *The International Relief Union: Its Origin, Aims, Means and Future* (Geneva, 1938).

Hall, William Edward, *A Treatise of International Law* (Oxford, 1904).

Hauck, Henry, "En souvenir d'Adrien Tixier," *La Revue socialiste*, February 1956.

Hiitonen, Ensio, *La compétence de l'Organisation Internationale du Travail* (Paris, 1929).

Hoover, Herbert, *An American Epic* (Chicago, 1961).

Hoover, Herbert, *Memoirs*, Vol. I: *Years of Adventure, 1874–1920* (New York, 1951).

Address of Herbert C. Hoover, Chairman of the Commission for Relief in Belgium before the Chamber of Commerce of the State of New York, February 1, 1917.

Hudson, Manley, *Progress in International Organization* (Stanford, 1932).

Hunt, Edward Eyre, *War Bread: A Personal Narrative on the War and Relief in Belgium* (New York, 1916).

Jebb, Eglantyne, *Cambridge: A Brief Study in Social Questions* (Cambridge, 1906).

Jebb, Eglantyne, "The barbarous Balkans," *Brown Book. Lady Margaret Hall Chronicle* (1913).

Jebb, Eglantyne, "Where war has been lady's work in Macedonia," unknown publication, 30 May, 1913.

Johnson, T.F., *International Tramps: From Chaos to Permanent World Peace* (London, 1938).

Kellogg, Vernon L., *Fighting Starvation in Belgium* (Garden City, NY, 1918).

Key, Ellen, *The Century of the Child* (New York, 1900, and London, 1909).

King, Willford Isbell, *Trends in Philanthropy: A Study in a Typical American City* (National Bureau of Economic Research, 1928).

Krauel, A., "L'applicabilité du droit des gens à la Chine," *Revue de droit international et de législation comparée*, 9, 1877, pp. 387–401.

La Pradelle, Albert de, *La paix moderne (1899–1945). De La Haye à San Francisco* (Paris, 1947).

La Pradelle, Albert de, *La place de l'Homme dans la Construction du Droit international* (London, 1948).

Lauterpacht, Hersch, *The Function of Law in the International Community* (Oxford, 1933).

Lauterpacht, Hersch, *International Law and Human Rights* (New York, 1950).

League of Nations, *The Settlement of the Assyrians: A Work of Humanity and Appeasement* (Geneva, 1935).

Le Fur, Louis, *Guerre juste et juste paix* (Paris, 1920).

Lejuif, Bernard, *Les apatrides*, law dissertation (Caen, 1939).

Lehmann, Marcel, *Le droit des mutilés* (Paris, 1918).

Lipovano, I.G., *L'Apatridie* (Paris, 1935).

Macartney, C.A., *Refugees: The Work of the League* (London, 1930).

Macartney Maxwell H.H., *Five Years of European Chaos* (New York, 1923).

Mandelstam, André, "La déclaration des droits internationaux de l'homme," *Revue de droit international*, 13, January–March 1930, pp. 59–78.

Mandelstam, André, *Le sort de l'Empire ottoman* (Lausanne and Paris, 1917).

Mandelstam, André, *La société des Nations et les puissances devant le problème arménien* (Paris, 1926).

Mandelstam, André, *La protection internationale des minorités* (Paris, 1931a).

Mandelstam, André, *Les droits internationaux de l'Homme* (Paris, 1931b).

Mead, Margaret, "Food and feeding in occupied territory," *The Public Opinion Quarterly*, 7: 4, winter 1943, pp. 618–628.

Montessori, Maria, *Educazione e Pace* [*Education and Peace*], 1949.

Morgenthau, Henry, Sr., *I Was Sent to Athens* (Garden City, NY, 1929).

Nafilyan, Pierre, *Le Heimatlosat*, law dissertation (Lausanne, 1935).

Noel-Baker, Philip, *The League of Nations at Work* (London, 1926).

Périgord, Paul, *The International Labor Organization* (New York, 1926).

Phelan, Edward, *Albert Thomas et la création du BIT* (Paris, 1936).

Phelan, Edward, "The Commission on International Labour Legislation," in Shotwell (ed.), *Origins of the International Labour Organization*.

Pillet, Antoine, "La guerre actuelle et le droit des gens," *Revue Generale de Droit International Public*, 1916, p. 12.

Pillet, Antoine, *Recherches sur les droits fondamentaux des États dans l'ordre des rapports internationaux et sur la solution des conflits qu'ils font naître* (Paris, 1899).

Pillet, Antoine, *Les leçons de la guerre présente au point de vue de la science politique et du droit des gens* (Paris, 1915).

Pillet, Antoine, "La guerre actuelle et le droit des gens," *Revue Generale de Droit International Public*, 1916, p. 12.

Pillet, Antoine, *Le traité de paix de Versailles* (Paris, 1920).

Politis, Nicolas, "Le problème des limitations de la souveraineté et la théorie de l'abus des droits dans les rapports internationaux," *Recueil des cours de l'académie de droit international de La Haye* (Paris, 1925), pp. 5–121.

Politis, Nicolas, *Les nouvelles tendances du droit international* (Paris, 1927).

Querenet, René, *Conférence faite au Comité d'entente des œuvres venant en aide aux veuves et aux orphelins de la guerre* (Paris, 1918).

Réale, Égidio, *Le régime des passeports et la Société des Nations* (Paris, 1930).

Renault, Louis, *Les premières violations du droit des gens par l'Allemagne: Luxembourg et Belgique* (Paris, 1917).

Richter, Lina, *Family Life in Germany Under the Blockade* (London, 1919).

Roberts, H.D. (ed.), *The Inter-Allied Exhibition on the After-Care of Disabled Men*, May 1918.

Rolin, Albéric de, *Les origines de l'Institut de Droit international, 1873–1923. Souvenirs d'un témoin* (Brussels, 1923).

Rougier, Antoine, "La théorie de l'intervention d'humanité," *Revue générale de droit international public*, 17 (Paris, 1910).

Rougier, Antoine, *La théorie de l'intervention d'humanité* (Paris, 1910).

Rubner, Max, *The Starving of Germany* (Berlin, 1919).

Ruyssen, Théodore, "Le mouvement pacifiste: pour et contre la reprise des relations pacifistes internationales," *La Paix du Droit*, 29: 1, January 1919.

Scelle, Georges, *Le pacte des nations et sa liaison avec le Traité de paix* (Paris, 1919).

Scelle, Georges, *La Morale des Traités de Paix* (Paris, 1920).

Scelle, Georges, *L'Organisation Internationale du Travail et le BIT* (Paris, 1930).

Scelle, Georges, *Précis de droit des gens*, 2 vols. (Paris, 1932, 1934).

Scheftel, Jacques, "L'apatridie des réfugiés russes," *Journal de droit international,* 61, 1934, pp. 36–69.

Scheftel, Jacques, *L'Apatridie des réfugiés russes* (Paris, 1934).

Scherrer, A., *La condition juridique de l'orphelin de la guerre de 1914–1919* (Nancy, 1933).

Scott, James Brown, *Les Conférences de la Paix de La Haye de 1899 et 1907*, 3 vols (Carnegie Endowment for International Peace, 1932).

Seferiadès S., "L'échange des populations," *Recueil des cours*, Vol. XXIV (Paris, 1928).

Shotwell, James T. (ed.), *The Origins of the International Labor Organization* (New York, 1934).

Sorensen, Jon, *The Saga of Fridtjof Nansen* (London, 1932).

Spaull, Hebe, *Women Peace-Makers* (London, 1924).

Spiropoulos, Jean, "L'individu et le droit international," *Académie de droit international de La Haye, Recueil des Cours*, 30, 1929, pp. 195–269.

Stobart, Mabel Annie, *War and Women, from Experience in the Balkans and Elsewhere* (London, 1913).

Stowell, Ellery C., "Humanitarian intervention," *American Journal of International Law*, 33, 1939.

Sukiennicki, Viktor, *Essai sur la souveraineté des États en droit international moderne*, law dissertation (Paris, 1926).

Surface, Frank M. and Raymond L. Bland (eds.), *American Food in the World War and Reconstruction Period* (Stanford, 1931).

Taracouzio, Timothy Andrew, *The Soviet Union and International Law* (New York, 1935).

Tenekidès C.G., "Le statut des minorités et l'échange obligatoire des populations gréco-turques," *Revue générale de droit international public*, Vol. XXXI, 1924, pp. 72–88.

Thomas, Albert, *Bolchevisme ou socialisme?* (Nancy and Paris, 1919).

Thomas, Albert, *L'Organisation Internationale du Travail et la première année de son activité* (Geneva, 1921).

Thomas, Albert, "Organisation Internationale du Travail: origine, développement, avenir," *Revue Internationale du Travail*, 1: 1, 1921, pp. 5–22.

Thomas, Albert, "Justice sociale et paix universelle. Réflexions sur un texte," *La Revue de Paris*, 6, 15 March, 1924, pp. 241–261.

Valentino, Charles, *Accidents du travail et blessures de guerre* (Bordeaux, 1917).

Vichniac, Marc, *La Protection des Droits des Minorités dans les traités internationaux de 1919–1920* (Paris, 1920).

Vichniac, Marc, "Le statut international des apatrides," *Académie de droit international de La Haye, Recueil des cours*, 43, 1933, pp. 119–245.

Vindry, Noël, *L'Apatridie (absence de nationalité)*, law dissertation (Aix-en-Provence, Makaire, 1925).

Virally, Michel, "La valeur juridique des recommandations des organisations internationales," *Annuaire français de droit international*, 2, 1956, p. 79.

André Weiss, *La violation de la neutralité belge et luxembourgeoise par l'Allemagne* (Paris: Armand Colin, 1915).

Wiggin, Kate, *Children's Rights* (Boston and New York, 1892).

Wolf, Lucien, *Russo-Jewish Refugees in Eastern Europe* (London, 1921).

Zweig, Stefan, *The World of Yesterday* (New York, 1943).

SECONDARY SOURCES

Abrams, Irwin, "The emergence of the international law societies," *The Review of Politics*, 19: 3, July 1957, pp. 361–380.

Adamets, Sergueï, *Guerre civile et famine en Russie: Le pouvoir bolchevique et la population face à la catastrophe démographique, 1917–1923* (Paris, 2003).

Adler, Emmanuel and Peter M. Haas, "Epistemic communities, world order and the creation of a reflective research program," *International Organization*, 46: 1, 1992, pp. 367–390.

Agi, Marc, *René Cassin. Prix Nobel de la paix, 1887–1976* (Paris, 1998).

Aglan, Alya, "Albert Thomas, historien du temps présent," *Les cahiers de l'IRICE*, 2, 2, 2008, 23–38.

Agulhon, Maurice, *Marianne au combat. L'imagerie et la symbolique républicaines de 1789 à 1880* (Paris, 1979). Translated by Janet Lloyd as *Marianne into Battle: Republican Imagery and Symbolism in France, 1789–1880* (Cambridge, 1981).

Alcock, Antony, *History of the ILO* (New York, 1971).

Alexander, Jeffrey C., Bernhard Giesen and Jason L. Mast (eds.), *Social Performance, Symbolic Action, Cultural Pragmatics and Ritual* (Cambridge, 2006).

Andreyev, Catherine and Ivan Savicky, *Russia Abroad. Prague and the Russian Diaspora, 1918–1938* (New Haven, 2004).

Archard, David and Colin M. Macleod (eds.), *The Moral and Political Status of Children* (Oxford, 2002).

Arendt, Hannah, *The Origins of Totalitarianism* [1951] (London, 1976).

Arendt, Hannah, "The Stateless People," *Contemporary Jewish Record*, 8 (April 1945), 137–153.

Argentier, Clément, *Les résultats acquis par l'Organisation permanente du Travail de 1919 à 1929* (Paris, 1930).

Ariès Philippe, *L'enfant et la vie familiale sous l'Ancien Régime* (Paris, 1960), translated by Robert Baldick as *Centuries of Childhood* (New York, 1962).

Aschheim, Steven E., *Brothers and Strangers: The East European Jew in German and German-Jewish Consciousness, 1800–1923* (Madison, 1982).

Audoin-Rouzeau, Stéphane, *Les combattants des tranchées* (Paris, 1986).

Audoin-Rouzeau, Stéphane, *La guerre des enfants (1914–1918)* (Paris, 1993).

Audoin-Rouzeau, Stéphane, *L'enfant de l'ennemi* (Paris, 1995; repub. 2009).

Audoin-Rouzeau Stéphane and Annette Becker, "Violence et consentement: la 'culture de guerre' du premier conflit mondial," in Jean-Pierre Rioux and Jean-François Sirinelli (eds.), *Pour une histoire culturelle* (Paris, 1997), pp. 251–271.

Audoin-Rouzeau, Stéphane and Annette Becker, *14–18. Retrouver la Guerre* (Paris, 2000), translated by Catherine Temerson as *14–18: Understanding the Great War* (New York, 2003).

Audoin-Rouzeau, Stéphane, "Die Delegation der 'gueules cassées' in Versailles am 28. Juni 1919," in Gerd Krumeich (ed.), *Versailles 1919: Ziele, Wirkung, Wahrnehmung* (Essen, 2001), pp. 280–287.

Audoin-Rouzeau, Stéphane, *Combattre. Une anthropologie historique de la guerre moderne (XIXème–XXIème siècle)* (Paris, 2008).

Audoin-Rouzeau, Stéphane, "Les cultures de guerre," in Benoît Pellistrandi and Jean-François Sirinelli (eds.), *L'histoire culturelle en France et en Espagne* (Madrid, 2008), pp. 289–299.

Audoin-Rouzeau, Stéphane, "Norbert Élias et l'expérience oubliée de la Première Guerre mondiale," *Vingtième Siècle. Revue d'histoire*, 106 (April–June 2010), pp. 105–115.

Audoin-Rouzeau, Stéphane and Christophe Prochasson (eds.), *Sortir de la Grande Guerre. Le monde et l'après-1918* (Paris, 2008).

Baldwin, Peter, *The Politics of Social Solidarity: Class Bases of the European Welfare State, 1875–1975* (Cambridge, 1990).

Balinska, Marta Aleksandra, *Une vie pour l'humanitaire: Ludwik Rajchman, 1881–1965* (Paris, 1995), translated by Rebecca Howell as *For the Good of Humanity: Ludwik Rajchman, Medical Statesman* (Budapest, 1998).

Balme, Jennifer Hobhouse, *To Love One's Enemies: The Work and Life of Emily Hobhouse, Compiled from Letters and Writings, Newspaper Cuttings and Official Documents* (Cobble Hill, British Columbia, 1994).

Bane, Suda L. and Ralph H. Lutz (eds.), *Organization of American Relief in Europe, 1918–1919* (Stanford University Press, 1943).

Barnett, Michael, *Empire of Humanity: A History of Humanitarianism* (Ithaca, 2011).

Baron, Nick and Peter Gatrell (eds.), *Homelands: War, Population, and Statehood in Eastern Europe and Russia, 1918–1924* (London, 2004).

Barrois, Claude, *Psychanalyse du guerrier* (Paris, 1999).

Barry, Gearóid, "Marc Sangnier's war, 1914–1919: portrait of a soldier, Catholic and social activist," in Pierre Purseigle (ed.), *Warfare and Belligerence: Perspectives in First World War Studies* (Leiden and Boston, 2005).

Barthes, Roland, *Comment vivre ensemble: cours et séminaire au Collège de France (1976–1977)* (Paris, 2002).

Barutciski, Michael, "Lausanne revisited. Population exchanges in international law and policy," in Hirschon (ed.), *Crossing the Aegean*.

Bass, Gary, *Stay the Hand of Vengeance: The Politics of War Crimes Tribunals* (Princeton, 2001).

Bass, Gary J., *Freedom's Battle: The Origins of Humanitarian Intervention* (New York, 2008).

Bassiouni, M. Cherif, *Crimes against Humanity: Historical Evolution and Contemporary Application* (Cambridge, 2011).

Bassiouni, M. Cherif, "World War I, 'the war to end all wars' and the birth of a handicapped international criminal justice system," *Denver Journal of International Law and Policy*, 30: 3, 2002, pp. 244–291.

Bayly, C.A., Sven Beckert, Matthew Connelly, Isabel Hofmeyr, Wendy Kozol and Patricia Seed, "*AHR* conversation: on transnational history," *American Historical Review*, 111: 5, December 2006, pp. 1441–1464.

Beaud, Olivier and Patrick Wachsmann (eds.), *La science juridique française et la science juridique allemande de 1870 à 1918* (Strasbourg, 1997).

Becker, Annette, "Conclusion," in David El-Kenz and François-Xavier Nérard, (eds.), *Commémorer les victimes en Europe, XVIème–XXIème siècles* (Paris, 2011), pp. 328–329.

Becker, Annette, *Les cicatrices rouges, 14–18, France et Belgique occupées* (Paris, 2010).

Becker, Annette, "Les victimes, entre 'innocence,' oubli et mémoire," *Revue suisse d'histoire*, 57, 1, 2007.

Becker, Annette, *Oubliés de la Grande Guerre: humanitaire et culture de guerre, 1914–1918* (Paris, 1998; repub. 2003).

Becker Jean-Jacques, "Les procès de Leipzig," in Annette Wieviorka (ed.), *Les Procès de Nuremberg et de Tokyo* (Brussels, 1996), pp. 51–60.

Becker, Jean-Jacques (ed.), *Histoire culturelle de la Grande Guerre* (Paris, 2005).

Becker, Jean-Jacques, "La gauche et la Grande Guerre," in Jean-Jacques Becker and Gilles Candar (eds.), *Histoire des gauches en France* (Paris, 2005), pp. 311–329.

Becker, Jean-Jacques, "Albert Thomas d'un siècle à l'autre. Bilan de l'expérience de guerre," *Les Cahiers de l'IRICE*, 2: 2, 2008, pp. 9–15.

Béguin, Bernard, *The ILO and the Tripartite System* (New York, 1959).

Behlmer, George K., *Child Abuse and Moral Reform in England, 1870–1908* (Stanford, 1982).

Bell, John D., *Peasants in Power. Alexander Stamboliiski and the Bulgarian Agrarian National Union, 1899–1923* (Princeton, New Jersey, 1977).

Berberova, Nina, *Les Francs-maçons russes au XXème siècle* (Arles, 1990).

Berkovitch, Nitza, *From Motherhood to Citizenship: Women's Rights and International Organizations* (Baltimore and London, 1999).

Bernard, William S. (ed.), *American Immigration Policy: A Reappraisal* (New York, 1950).

Bessel, Richard, *Germany after the First World War* (Oxford, 1993).

Bessel, Richard, "Die Heimkehr der Soldaten. Das Bild der Frontsoldaten in der Öffentlichkeit der Weimarer Republik," in Gerhard Hirschfeld, Gerd Krumeich and Irina Renz (eds), *"Keiner fühlt sich hier mehr als Mensch . . ."* *Erlebnis und Wirkung des Ersten Weltkriegs* (Essen, 1993), pp. 221–240.

Bessel, Richard and Claudia B. Haake (eds.), *Removing Peoples: Forced Removal in the Modern World* (Oxford, 2009).

Best, Geoffrey, *Humanity in Warfare* (New York, 1980).

Bette, Peggy, "Reclasser les victimes de la Première Guerre mondiale: le cas de la loi du 30 janvier 1923 sur les emplois réservés en France (1923–1939)," *Amnis. Revue de civilisation contemporaine*, 6, 2006.

Bette, Peggy, "Des maîtresses en leur demeure? Le pouvoir de tutelle des veuves de guerre au sein de la sphère familiale au lendemain de l'Armistice (1918–1921)," in Bruno Cabanes and Guillaume Piketty (eds.), *Retour à l'intime au sortir de la guerre* (Paris, 2009), pp. 245–257.

Black, Maggie, *Children First: The Story of UNICEF, Past and Present* (Oxford, 1996).

Blais, Marie-Claude, *La solidarité. Histoire d'une idée* (Paris, 2007).

Blum, Antoinette, *Correspondance entre Charles Andler et Lucien Herr, 1891–1926* (Paris, 1992).

Bobrinskoy-Pichon, Olga, "Action publique, action humanitaire pendant le premier conflit mondial: les zemstvos et les municipalités," *Cahiers du monde russe*, 46: 4, 2005, pp. 673–698.

Bock, Fabienne, "L'exubérance de l'Etat en France de 1914 à 1918," *Vingtième siècle revue d'histoire*, 3, July 1984, pp. 41–51.

Bock, Gisela and Pat Thane, *Maternity and Gender Policies* (London and New York, 1991).

Boltanski, Luc, *La souffrance à distance: morale humanitaire, médias et politique* (Paris, 1993), translated by Graham D. Burchell as *Distant Suffering: Morality, Media, and Politics* (Cambridge, 1999).

Bonvin, Jean-Michel, *L'Organisation Internationale du Travail: essai sur une agence productrice de normes* (Paris, 1998).

Bonzon, Thierry and Belinda Davis, "Feeding the cities," in Jay Winter and Jean-Louis Robert (eds.), *Capital Cities at War: Paris, London, Berlin, 1914–191* (Cambridge, 1997), pp. 305–341.

Borren, Marieke, "Arendt's politics of in/visibility: on stateless refugees and undocumented aliens," *Ethical Perspectives*, 15: 2, 2008, pp. 213–237.

Boswell, Laird, "From liberation to purge trials in the 'Mythic Provinces': recasting French identities in Alsace and Lorraine, 1918–1920," *French Historica Studies*, 23: 1, 2000, pp. 129–162.

Bourke, Joanna, *Dismembering the Male: Men's Bodies, Britain and the Great War* (Chicago, 1996).

Breen, Rodney, "Saving enemy children: Save the Children's Russian Relief Operation, 1921–23," *Disasters*, 18: 3, pp. 221–237.

Bremner, Robert H., *American Philanthropy* (Chicago and London, 1960).

Brian, Éric, "Y-a-t-il un objet Congrès? Le cas du Congrès international de statistique (1853–1876)," *Mil Neuf Cent. Revue d'histoire intellectuelle*, 7, 1989, pp. 9–22.

Bruneau, Michel and Kyriakos Papoulidis, "La mémoire des 'patries inoubliables.' La construction de monuments par les réfugiés d'Asie mineure en Grèce," *Vingtième siècle, revue d'histoire*, April–June 2003, pp. 35–57.

Burgers, Jan-Herman, "The road to San Francisco: the revival of the human rights idea in the twentieth century," *Human Rights Quarterly*, 14: 4, November 1992, pp. 455–459.

Burner, David, *Herbert Hoover: A Public Life* (New York, 1979).

Cabanes, Bruno, "Die französischen Soldaten und der Verlust des Sieges," in Gerd Krumeich (ed.), *Versailles 1919: Ziele, Wirkung, Wahrnehmung* (Essen, 2001), pp. 269–279.

Cabanes, Bruno, *La victoire endeuillée: la sortie de guerre des soldats français (1918–1920)* (Paris, 2004).

Calhoun, Craig, "The imperative to reduce suffering: charity, progress, and emergencies in the field of humanitarian action," in Michael Barnett and Thomas G. Weiss (eds.), *Humanitarianism in Question: Politics, Power, Ethics* (Ithaca, 2008), pp. 73–97.

Cayet, Thomas, *Rationaliser le travail, organiser la production: Le Bureau International du Travail et la modernisation économique durant l'entre-deux-guerres* (Rennes, 2010).

Cayet, Thomas, Marie Thébaud-Sorger and Paul-André Rosental, "How international organisations compete: occupational safety and health at the ILO, a diplomacy of expertise," *Journal of Modern European History*, 7: 2, 2009, pp. 174–196.

Charle, Christophe, "Les normaliens et le socialisme," in Madeleine Rebérioux and Gilles Candar (eds.), *Jaurès et les intellectuels* (Paris, 1994).

Chatriot, Alain, "Une véritable encyclopédie économique et sociale de la guerre. Les séries de la Dotation Carnegie pour la paix internationale," *L'atelier du centre de recherche historique*, 3: 1, 2009.

Chaubet, François, *Paul Desjardins et les Décades de Pontigny* (Villeneuve d'Ascq, 2000).

Chickering, Roger, *Imperial Germany and a World Without War: The Peace Movement and German Society, 1892–1914* (Princeton, 1975).

Clark, Bruce, *Twice a Stranger. How Mass Expulsion Forged Greece and Turkey* (London 2006).

Clavin, Patricia, "Defining transnationalism," *Contemporary European History*, 14: 4, November 2005, pp. 421–439.

Clavin, Patricia and Jens-Wilhelm Wessel, "Transnationalism and the League of Nations: understanding the work of its financial and economic organisation," *Contemporary European History*, 14: 4, 2005, pp. 465–492.

Cmiel, Kenneth, "The recent history of human rights," *American Historical Review*, 109: 1, February 2004, pp. 117–135.

Cohen, Deborah, *The War Come Home: Disabled Veterans in Britain and Germany, 1914–1939* (Berkeley, 2001).

Conklin, Alice L., "Colonialism and human rights: a contradiction in terms? The case of France and West Africa, 1895–1914," *American Historical Review*, 103: 2, April 1998, pp. 419–442.

Connelly, Mark, *The Response to Prostitution in the Progressive Era* (Chapel Hill, 1980).

Conquest, Robert, *The Harvest of Sorrows: Soviet Collectivization and the Terror-Famine* (Oxford, 1986).

Constantine, Stephen, *Emigrants and Empire: British Settlement in the Dominions between the Wars* (Manchester, 1990).

Cooper, John Milton, Jr., *Breaking the Heart of the World: Woodrow Wilson and the Fight for the League of Nations* (Cambridge, 2001).

Cooper, Sandy, *Patriotic Pacifism. Waging War on War in Europe, 1815–1914* (Oxford and New York, 1991).

Cosandey, Roland, "Eloquence du visible: la famine en Russie, 1921–1923. Une bibliographie documentée," *Archives*, 75–76, June 1998, Institut Jean Vigo, Perpignan.

Cosson, Olivier, "Expériences de guerre du début du XXème siècle (guerre des Boers, guerre de Mandchourie, guerre des Balkans)," in Stéphane Audoin-Rouzeau and Jean-Jacques Becker (eds.), *Encyclopédie de la Grande Guerre, 1914–1918: Histoire et culture* (Paris, 2004), pp. 97–108.

Cosson, Olivier, "Violence et guerre moderne dans les Balkans à l'aube du vingtième siècle," in Annette Becker (ed.), "Violences coloniales, violences de guerre, violences extrêmes," *Revue d'histoire de la Shoah*, special issue (July–December 2008), pp. 57–74.

Courmont, Juliette, *L'odeur de l'ennemi, 1914–1918* (Paris, 2010).

Cunningham, Hugh, *Children and Childhood in Western Society Since 1500* (2nd edition) (Harlow, UK, and New York, 2005).

Curle, Clinton Timothy, *Humanité: John Humphrey's Alternative Accounts of Human Rights* (Toronto, 2007).

Curti, Merle, *American Philanthropy Abroad: A History* (New Brunswick, 1963).

Cutlip, Scott M., *Fund Raising in the United States: Its Role in America's Philanthropy* (New Brunswick, 1965).

Daniel, Robert L., *American Philanthropy in the Near East (1820–1960)* (Athens, Ohio, 1970).

Daughton, James P., "Documenting colonial violence: the international campaign against forced labor during the interwar years," *Revue d'Histoire de la Shoah* 189, 2008.

Daughton, J.P. *Humanity So Far Away* (Oxford University Press, forthcoming).

Davin, Anna, "Imperialism and motherhood," *History Workshop Journal*, 5, spring 1978, pp. 9–65.

Davis, Belinda, "Homefront: food, politics and women's everyday life during the First World War," in Karen Hagemann and Stefanie Schuler-Springorum (eds.), *Home/Front: The Military, War, and Gender in Twentieth-Century Germany* (Oxford and New York, 2002), pp. 115–137.

Davis, Belinda J., *Home Fires Burning: Food, Politics and Everyday Life in World War 1 Berlin* (Chapel Hill, 2000).

Dean, Carolyn, *The Fragility of Empathy after the Holocaust* (Ithaca, 2004).

de Bryas, Madeleine, *Les peuples en marche. Les migrations politiques et économiques depuis la guerre* (Paris, 1926).

De Freitas Campos, Regina Helena, "Les psychologues et le mouvement d'éducation pour la paix à Genève (1920–1940)," in Élisabeth Chapuis, Jean-Pierre Pétard and Régine Plas (eds.), *Les psychologues et les guerres* (Paris, 2010), pp. 95–109.

Dekens, Charline, "Refaire de ces abandonnés des hommes: le comité international de secours à la Russie et la famine de 1921–1922," MA thesis, University of Geneva, Faculty of Letters, 2002.

Delaporte, Sophie, *Les gueules cassées. Les blessés de la face de la Grande Guerre* (Paris, 1996).

Delaporte, Sophie, "Le corps et la parole des mutilés de la Grande Guerre," *Guerres mondiales et conflits contemporains*, 205, 2002, pp. 5–14.

Delaporte, Sophie, *Les médecins de la Grande Guerre, 1914–1918* (Paris, 2003).

De Schaepdrijver, Sophie, *De Groote Oorlog: het Koninkrijk België in de Eerste Wereldoorlog* [*The Great War: The Kingdom of Belgium in the First World War*] (Amsterdam, 1997). Revised French translation: *La Belgique et la Première Guerre Mondiale* (Berlin and New York, 2004).

Dessertine, Dominique, "Aux origines de l'assistance éducative: les tribunaux pour enfants et la liberté surveillée, 1912–1941," in Michel Chauvière, Pierre Lenoël and Éric Pierre (eds.), *Protéger l'enfant: raison juridique et pratiques socio-judiciaires, XIXème–XXème siècle* (Rennes, 1996).

Devinck, Jean-Claude and Paul-André Rosental, "'Une maladie sociale avec des aspects médicaux': la difficile reconnaissance de la silicose comme maladie professionnelle dans la France du premier XXème siècle," *Revue d'Histoire moderne et contemporaine*, 56: 1, 2009, pp. 99–126.

Dodenhoeft, Bettina, *"Laßt mich nach dem Rußland heim": Russische Emigranten in Deutschland von 1918 bis 1945* (Frankfurt am Main, 1993).

Downs, Laura Lee, *Manufacturing Inequality: Gender Division in the French and British Metalworking Industries, 1914–1939* (Ithaca and London, 1995).

Droux, Joëlle, "L'internationalisation de la protection de l'enfance: acteurs, concurrences et projets transnationaux (1900–1925), *Critique internationale*, 52: 3, 2011, pp. 17–33.

Dubesset, Mathilde, Françoise Thébaud and Catherine Vincent, "The female munition workers of the Seine," in Fridenson (ed.), *The French Home Front*, pp. 183–218.

Duclert, Vincent (ed.), *Savoir et engagement: ecrits normaliens sur l'Affaire Dreyfus* (Paris, 2006).

Ducoulombier, Romain, *Camarades! La naissance du Parti communiste en France* (Paris, 2010).

Dugarm, Delano, "Peasant wars in Tambov Province," in Vladimir N. Brovkin (ed.), *The Bolsheviks in Russian Society: The Revolution and the Civil Wars* (New Haven, 1997), pp. 177–197.

Dutton, Paul V., *Origins of the French Welfare State: The Struggle for Social Reform in France (1914–1947)* (Cambridge, 2002).

Dwork, Deborah, *War is Good for Babies and Other Young Children: A History of the Infant and Child Welfare Movement in England, 1898–1918* (London and New York, 1987).

Edmondson, Charles M., "The politics of hunger: the Soviet response to famine, 1921," *Soviet Studies*, 29: 4, 1977, pp. 506–18.

Eghigian, Greg, "The politics of victimization: social pensioners and the German social state in the inflation of 1914–1924," *Central European History*, 26: 4, 1993, pp. 375–403.

English, Peter, C. "'Not miniature men and women': Abraham Jacobi's vision of a new medical specialty a century ago," in Loretta M. Kopelman and John C. Moskop (eds.), *Children and Health Care: Moral and Social Issues* (Dordrecht, 1989), pp. 247–273.

Fabre, Rémi, "Un exemple de pacifisme juridique. Théodore Ruyssen et le mouvement 'La Paix par le Droit' (1884–1950)," *Vingtieme siècle. Revue d'histoire*, 39, July–September 1993, pp. 38–54.

Faron, Olivier, *Les enfants du deuil. Orphelins et pupilles de la nation de la première guerre mondiale (1914–1941)* (Paris, 2001).

Faron, Olivier, "Aux côtés, avec, pour les pupilles de la Nation. Les formes de mobilisation en faveur des orphelins de la Première Guerre mondiale," *Guerres mondiales et conflits contemporains*, 205, January–March 2002.

Fassin, Didier, *La raison humanitaire: une histoire morale du temps présent* (Paris, 2010), translated by Rachel Gomme as *Humanitarian Reason: A Moral History of the Present Times* (Berkeley, 2012).

Fassin, Didier and Richard Rechtman, *L'Empire du traumatisme* (Paris, 2007), translated by Rachel Gomme as *The Empire of Trauma: An Enquiry into the Condition of Victimhood* (Princeton, 2009).

Feiertag, Olivier, "Réguler la mondialisation: Albert Thomas, les débuts du BIT et la crise économique mondiale de 1920–1923," *Les Cahiers de l'IRICE*, 2, 2008, pp. 127–155.

Figes, Orlando, *Peasant Russia, Civil War: The Volga Countryside in Revolution* (Oxford, 1989).

Figes, Orlando, *A People's Tragedy: The Russian Revolution, 1891–1924* (London 1996).

Fine, Martin, "Albert Thomas: a reformer's vision of modernization, 1914–1932," *Journal of Contemporary History*, 12: 3, July 1977, pp. 545–564.

Fink, Carole, "Minority rights as an international question," *Contemporary European History*, 9, 2003, pp. 385–400.

Fink, Carole, *Defending the Rights of Others: The Great Powers, the Jews, and International Minority Protection, 1878–1938* (Cambridge, 2004).

Finlayson, Geoffrey, *Citizen, State and Social Welfare in Britain, 1830–199* (Oxford, 1994).

Fitzpatrick, Sheila, *Educational and Social Mobility in the Soviet Union, 1921–193* (Cambridge, 1979).

Forsythe, David, *Humanitarian Politics: The International Committee of the Red Cross* (Baltimore, Maryland: 1977).

Franklin, Bob (ed.), *The Rights of Children* (New York, 1986).

Frevert, Ute, "Europeanizing Germany's twentieth century," *History and Memory*, 17, 2005, pp. 87–116.

Fridenson, Patrick (ed.), *The French Home Front, 1914–1918* (Oxford, 1993).

Fuchs, Rachel Ginnis, *Abandoned Children: Foundlings and Child Welfare in Nineteenth-Century France* (Albany, 1984).

Fuller, Edward, *The Right of the Child: A Chapter in Social History* (Boston, 1951).

Gage, Beverly, *The Day Wall Street Exploded: A Story of America in its First Age of Terror* (Oxford, 2009).

Gatrell, Peter, *A Whole Empire Walking: Refugees in Russia during World War I* (Bloomington, 1999).

Gerwarth, Robert and John Horne, "The Great War and paramilitarism in Europe, 1917–23," *Contemporary European History*, 19: 3, pp. 267–273.

Ghebali, Victor-Yves, *The International Labour Organization* (Dordrecht, 1988).

Gil, Rebecca, "'The rational administration of compassion': the origins of British relief in war," *Le Mouvement social*, 227, April–June 2009, pp. 9–26.

Glendon, Mary Ann, *A World Made New: Eleanor Roosevelt and the Universal Declaration of Human Rights* (New York, 2001).

Godfrey, John F., *Capitalism at War: Industrial Policy and Bureaucracy in France, 1914–1918* (Oxford, 1987).

Godineau, Laure, "L'économie sociale à l'exposition universelle de 1889," *Le Mouvement social*, 149 (octobre–décembre 1989), pp. 71–88.

Gordon, Linda (ed.), *Women, the State and Welfare* (Madison, 1990).

Gorman, Dan, "Empire, internationalism and the campaign against the traffic in women and children in the 1920s," *20th Century British History*, 19: 2, 2008, pp. 186–216.

Gousseff, Catherine, "Ouverture et fermeture des frontières soviétiques dans les années 1920: la NEP à tâtons," *Cahiers de l'Institut d'Histoire du Temps Présent* (January 1997), pp. 119–134.

Gousseff, Catherine, *L'Exil russe: la fabrique du réfugié apatride* (Paris, 2008).

Gousseff, Catherine and Olga Pichon-Bobrinskoy, "Les archives du comité directeur du Zemgor," *Cahiers du monde russe*, 43: 2–3 (April–September 2002), pp. 529–544.

Gousseff, Catherine and Anna Sossinskaïa (eds.), *Les enfants de l'exil: récits d'écoliers russes après la Révolution de 1917* (Paris, 2005).

Grabill, Joseph L., *Protestant Diplomacy in the Near East: Missionary Influence on American Policy, 1810–1927* (Minneapolis, 1971).

Grahl-Madsen, Atle, "The League of Nations and the refugees," in *The League of Nations in Retrospect* (Berlin and New York, 1983).

Grant, Kevin, *A Civilised Savagery: Britain and the New Slaveries in Africa, 1884–1926* (London, 2005).

Grant, Kevin, Philippa Levine and Frank Trentmann (eds.), *Beyond Sovereignty: Britain, Empire, and Transnationalism, c.1880–1950* (Basingstoke, 2007).

Gregory, Adrian, "Adieu à tout cela: comment les Anglais sortirent de la guerre," in Audoin-Rouzeau and Prochasson (eds.), *Sortir de la Grande Guerre*.

Gregory, Adrian, *The Last Great War: British Society and the First World War* (Cambridge, 2008).

Greyson, Benson, *The American Image of Russia: 1917–1977* (New York, 1978).

Groves, Charles Pelham, "Missionary and humanitarian aspects of imperialism," in L.H. Gann and Peter Duignan (eds.), *Colonialism in Africa* (Cambridge University Press, 1969), Vol. I, pp. 462–496.

Guérin, Denis, *Albert Thomas au BIT, 1920–1932* (Geneva: Institut européen de l'Université de Genève, 1996).

Guieu, Jean-Michel, "Les juristes français, la Société des Nations et l'Europe," in Jacques Bariéty (ed.), *Aristide Briand, la Société des Nations et l'Europe, 1919–1932* (Strasbourg, 2007), pp. 185–199.

Guieu, Jean-Michel, *Le rameau et le glaive. Les militants français pour la SDN* (Paris, 2008).

Hall, Richard, *The Balkan Wars: Prelude to the First World War* (London and New York, 2000).

Halpern, Sydney A., *American Pediatrics: The Social Dynamics of Professionalism, 1880–1980* (Berkeley, 1988).

Halttunen, Karen, "Humanitarianism and the pornography of pain in Anglo-American culture," *American Historical Review*, 100, April 1995, pp. 303–334.

Harris, Leslie, "The discovery of vitamins," in J. Needham (ed.), *The Chemistry of Life: Eight Lectures on the History of Biochemistry* (Cambridge, 1970).

Harris, Ruth, "The child of the barbarian: rape, race and nationalism in France during the First World War," *Past and Present*, October 1993, pp. 170–206.

Hartigan, Richard Shelly, *Lieber's Code and the Laws of War* (Chicago, 1983).

Harvey, David Allen, "Lost children or enemy aliens? Classifying the population of Alsace after the First World War," *Journal of Contemporary History*, 34, 1999, pp. 537–554.

Haskell, Thomas, "Capitalism and the origins of the humanitarian sensibility," *American Historical Review*, 1985, 90: 2, pp. 339–361; 90: 3, pp. 547–566.

Hassel, James E., *Russian Refugees in France and in the United States between the World Wars* (Philadelphia, 1991).

Hathaway, James, "The evolution of refugee status in international law (1920–1950)," *International and Comparative Law Quarterly*, 33, 1984, pp. 348–380.

Hathaway, James C., *The Law of Refugee Status* (Toronto and Vancouver, 1991).

Hatzfeld, Henri, *Du paupérisme à la sécurité sociale* (Nancy, 1971, repub. 1989).

Hausen, Karin, "The German nation's obligations to the heroes' widows of World War I," in Margaret Higonnet, Jane Jenson, Sonya Michel and Margaret Collins Weitz (eds.) *Behind the Lines: Gender and the Two World Wars* (New Haven, 1987), pp. 126–140.

Healy, Maureen, *Vienna and the Fall of the Habsburg Empire: Total War and Everyday Life in World War I* (Cambridge, 2004).

Henkin, Louis, *The Age of Rights* (New York, 1990).

Hennebicque, Alain, "Albert Thomas and the war industries," in Fridenson (ed.), *The French Home Front*, pp. 57–132.

Herren, Madeleine, *Internationale Sozialpolitik vor dem Ersten Weltkrieg* (Berlin, 1993).

Hinshaw, David, *Herbert Hoover: American Quaker* (New York, 1950).

Hirschon, Renée (ed.), *Crossing the Aegean: An Appraisal of the 1923 Compulsory Population Exchange Between Greece and Turkey* (New York and Oxford, 2003).

Hobsbawm, Eric, "Working-class internationalism," in Frits Van Hothoon and Marcel Van der Linden (eds.), *Internationalism in the Labour Movement, 1830–1940* (Leiden and New York, 1988).

Hoffmann, Stefan-Ludwig (ed.), *Human Rights in the Twentieth Century* (Cambridge, 2011).

Holborn, Louise, "The legal status of political refugees (1920–1938)," *American Journal of International Law*, 32, 1938, pp. 680–703.

Holquist, Peter, *Making War, Forging Revolution: Russia's Continuum of Crisis, 1914–1921* (Cambridge, Mass., 2002).

Hoover, Herbert, *The Ordeal of Woodrow Wilson* (Baltimore, 1992).

Horne, Janet R., *A Social Laboratory for Modern France: The Musée Social and the Rise of the Welfare State* (Durham, North Carolina, 2002).

Horne, John, "L'impôt du sang: republican rhetoric and industrial warfare in France, 1914–18," *Social History*, 14: 2, May 1989, pp. 201–223.

Horne, John, *Labour at War: France and Britain, 1914–1918* (Oxford, 1991).

Horne, John, "Remobilizing for total war: France and Britain, 1917–1918," in John Horne (ed.), *State, Society and Mobilization* (Cambridge, 1997), pp. 195–211.

Horne, John, "Démobilisations culturelles après la Grande Guerre," *14–18 Aujourd'hui* (Paris, 2002), pp. 49–53.

Horne, John, "Locarno et la politique de la démobilisation culturelle, 1925–1930," *14–18 Aujourd'hui* (Paris, 2002), pp. 73–87.

Horne, John, (ed.), *Vers la guerre totale: le tournant de 1914–1915* (Paris, 2010).

Horne John and Alan Kramer, *German Atrocities, 1914: A History of Denial* (New Haven, 2001).

Horrocks, Sally M., "The business of vitamins: nutrition science and the food industry in inter-war Britain," in Harmke Kamminga and Andrew Cunningham (eds.), *The Science and Culture of Nutrition* (Amsterdam and Atlanta, Georgia: Rodopi, 1995), pp. 235–258.

Housden, Martyn, "When the Baltic Sea was a bridge for humanitarian action: the League of Nations, the Red Cross and the repatriation of prisoners of war between Russia and Central Europe, 1920–22," *Journal of Baltic Studies*, 38: 1, March 2007, pp. 61–83.

Howard, Michael, George J. Andreopoulos and Mark R. Shulman, *The Laws of War: Constraints on Warfare in the Western World* (New Haven, 1994).

Hunt, Lynn, *Inventing Human Rights: A History* (New York, 2007).

Huntford, Roland, *Nansen. The Explorer as Hero* (London, 1997).

Hutchinson, John F., *Champions of Charity: War and the Rise of the Red Cross* (Boulder, Colo, 1996).

Hutchinson, John F., "Disasters and the international order: earthquakes, humanitarians and the Ciraolo Project," *The International History Review*, 22: 1, March 2000, pp. 1–36.

Ignatieff, Michael, *Isaiah Berlin: A Life* (London, 1998).

Ingram, Norman, *The Politics of Dissent. Pacifism in France, 1919–1939* (Oxford, 1991).

Iriye, Akira, *Cultural Internationalism and World Order* (Baltimore, Maryland, 1997).

Iriye, Akira, *Global Community: The Role of International Organizations in the Making of the Contemporary World* (Berkeley, 2002).

Iriye, Akira, Petra Goedde and William I. Hitchcock (eds.), *The Human Rights Revolution: An International History* (Oxford, 2012).

Iriye, Akira and Pierre-Yves Saunier (eds.), *The Palgrave Dictionary of Transnational History* (Basingstoke, 2009).

Irvine, William, *Between Justice and Politics: The Ligue des Droits de l'Homme, 1898–1945* (Stanford, Calif., 2007).

Israel, Gérard, *René Cassin: 1887–1976, la guerre hors la loi. Avec de Gaulle. Les droits de l'Homme* (Paris, 1990).

Israel, Gérard, *René Cassin: 1887–1976: une pensée ouverte sur le monde moderne* (Paris, 2001).

Jablonka, Ivan, *Ni père, ni mère. Histoire des enfants de l'Assistance publique (1874–1939)* (Paris, 2006).

Jeismann, Michael, *Das Vaterland der Feinde. Studien zum nationalen Feindbegriff und Selbstverständnis in Deutschland und Frankreich 1792–1918* (Stuttgart, 1992).

Jenks, Wilfred, *Human Rights and International Labour Standards* (London and New York, 1960).

Jilek, Lubor, "Violences de masse et droits de l'Homme: André Mandelstam entre Constantinople et Bruxelles," *Les cahiers de la faculté des Lettres de Genève*, 2000, pp. 64–71.

Jordanova, Ludmilla, "Children in history: concepts of nature and society," in Geoffrey Scarre (ed.), *Children, Parents, and Politics* (Cambridge, 1989), pp. 3–24.

Jousse, Emmanuel, "Un réformisme travailliste: la société fabienne pendant la Grande Guerre," in Romain Ducoulombier (ed.), *Les socialistes dans l'Europe en guerre: réseaux, parcours, expériences, 1914–1918* (Paris: 2010), pp. 141–160.

Jousse, Emmanuel, *Réviser le marxisme: d'Eduard Bernstein à Albert Thomas, 1894–1914* (Paris, 2007).

Kateb, George, *Human Dignity* (Cambridge, Mass., 2011).

Kenez, Peter, "Pogroms and white ideology in the Russian Civil War," in John D. Klier and Shlomo Lambroza (eds.), *Pogroms: Anti-Jewish Violence in Modern Russian History* (Cambridge, 1991), pp. 293–313.

Kennedy, David M., *Over Here: The First World War and American Society* (Oxford, 1980).

Keshgegian, Flora A., "'Starving Armenians': the politics and ideology of humanitarian aid in the first decades of the twentieth century," in Richard Ashby Wilson and Richard D. Brown (eds.), *Humanitarianism and Suffering: The Mobilization of Empathy* (New York, 2009), pp. 140–155.

Kévonian, Dzovinar, "Les tribulations de la diplomatie humanitaire: la Société des Nations et les réfugiés arméniens," in Hans-Lukas Kieser (ed.), *Die armenische Frage und die Schweiz (1896–1923)* (Zürich, 1999), pp. 279–310.

Kévonian, Dzovinar, "Représentations, enjeux politiques et codification juridique: les réfugiés des années vingt," *Relations internationales*, 101 (spring 2000), pp. 21–39.

Kévonian, Dzovinar, "Les juristes juifs russes en France et l'action internationale dans les années vingt," *Archives Juives*, 34: 2, 2001, pp. 72–94.

Kévonian, Dzovinar, "Exilés politiques et avènement du droit humain: la pensée juridique d'André Mandelstam (1869–1949)," *Revue d'histoire de la Shoah* 177–178, January–August 2003, pp. 245–273.

Kévonian, Dzovinar, "Question des réfugiés, droits de l'homme: éléments d'une convergence pendant l'entre-deux-guerres," *Matériaux pour l'histoire de notre temps*, 72, 2003, pp. 40–49.

Kévonian, Dzovinar, *Réfugiés et diplomatie humanitaire: les acteurs européens et la scène proche-orientale pendant l'entre-deux-guerres* (Paris, 2004).

Kévonian, Dzovinar, "Enjeux de catégorisations et migrations internationales. Le Bureau International du Travail et les réfugiés (1925–1929)," *Revue européenne des migrations internationales*, 21: 3, 2005, pp. 95–124.

Kévonian, Dzovinar, "L'organisation non gouvernementale, nouvel acteur du champ humanitaire. Le Zemgor et la Société des Nations dans les années 1920," *Cahiers du monde russe*, 46: 4, October–December 2005, pp. 739–756.

Kévonian, Dzovinar, "Albert Thomas et le Bureau International du Travail (1920–1932): enjeux de légitimation d'une organisation internationale," in Jacques Bariéty (ed.), *Aristide Briand, la Société des Nations et l'Europe, 1919–1932* (Strasbourg, 2007), pp. 324–338.

Kévonian, Dzovinar, "La légitimation par l'expertise. Le Bureau International du Travail et la statistique internationale," *Les cahiers de l'IRICE*, 2: 2, 2008, pp. 81–106.

Kévonian, Dzovinar, "Les juristes et l'Organisation internationale du Travail, 1919–1939. Processus de légitimation et institutionnalisation des relations internationales," *Journal of the History of International Law*, 12, 2010, pp. 227–266.

Kévonian, Dzovinar, "Les juristes, la protection des minorités et l'internationalisation des droits de l'homme: le cas de la France (1919–1939)," *Relations Internationales*, 149: 1, 2012, pp. 57–72.

Kienitz, Sabine, "Beschädigte Helden. Zur Politisierung des kriegsinvaliden Soldatenkörpers in der Weimarer Republik," in Jost Dülffer and Gerd Krumeich (eds.), *Der verlorene Frieden. Politik und Kriegskultur nach 1918* (Essen, 2002), pp. 199–214.

Kienitz, Sabine, *Beschädigte Helden. Kriegsinvalidität und Körperbilder 1914–1923* (Paderborn, 2008).

Kim, Young S., "Constructing a global identity: the role of Esperanto," in John Boli and George M. Thomas (eds.), *Constructing World Culture. International Nongovernmental Organizations since 1875* (Stanford, 1999), pp. 127–148.

Knock, Thomas J., *To End All Wars. Woodrow Wilson and the Quest for a New World Order* (Princeton, New Jersey, 1995).

Kondratieva, Tamara, *Gouverner et nourrir: du pouvoir en Russie (XVIème–XXème siècles)* (Paris, 2002).

Koolakian, Robert G., *Struggle for Justice: A Story of the American Committee for the Independence of Armenia, 1915–1920* (Wayne State University Press, 2008).

Koskenniemi, Martti, *The Gentle Civilizer of Nations: The Rise and Fall of International Law, 1870–1960* (Cambridge, 2004).

Kott, Sandrine, *L'État social allemand: représentations et pratiques* (Paris, 1995).

Kott, Sandrine, "Une 'communauté épistémique' du social? Experts de l'ILO et internationalisation des politiques sociales dans l'entre-deux guerres," *Genèses*, 2: 71, 2008, pp. 26–46.

Kott, Sandrine, "Constructing a European social model: the fight for social insurance in the interwar period," in Van Daele *et al.* (eds), *ILO Histories*, pp. 173–195.

Krumeich, Gerd, "Le soldat allemand sur la Somme," in Jean-Jacques Becker and Stéphane Audoin-Rouzeau (eds.), *Les sociétés européennes et la guerre de 1914–1918* (Nanterre, 1990), pp. 367–373.

Kuehl, Warren F. and Lynne K. Dunn, *Keeping the Covenant: American Internationalists and the League of Nations, 1920–1939* (Kent, Ohio, 1997).

Kuisel, Richard, *Capitalism and the State in Modern France* (New York, 1981). French translation: *Le capitalisme et l'Etat en France* (Paris, 1984).

Ladas, Stephen P., *The Exchange of Minorities: Bulgaria, Greece and Turkey* (New York, 1932).

Langdom, Mary Ann, *A World Made New. Eleanor Roosevelt and the Universal Declaration of Human Rights* (New York, 2001).

Laqueur, Thomas, "Bodies, details and the humanitarian narrative," in Lynn Hunt (ed.), *The New Cultural History* (Berkeley, 1989), pp. 176–204.

Larsson, Marina, *Shattered Anzacs: Living with the Scars of War* (Sydney, 2009).

Lauren, Paul Gordon, *The Evolution of International Human Rights: Visions Seen* (Philadelphia, 1998).

Laybourn, Keith, *The Rise of Socialism in Britain, 1881–1951* (Stroud, 1997).

Lazarovici, Florent, "L'organisation du ministère de l'armement sous Albert Thomas: une expérience socialiste ou technocratique?" in Romain Ducoulombier (ed.), *Les socialistes dans l'Europe en guerre: réseaux, parcours, expériences, 1914–1918* (Paris, 2010), pp. 55–71.

Lees, Lynn Hollen, *The Solidarities of Strangers: The English Poor Laws and the People, 1700–1948* (Cambridge and New York, 1998).

Leinonen, Marja, "Helsinki: Die russische Emigration in Finland," in Karl Schlögel (ed.), *Der Grosse Exodus: Die russische Emigration und ihre Zentren, 1917 bis 1941* (Munich, 1994), pp. 165–193.

Leppänen, Katarina, "Movement of women: trafficking in the interwar era," *Women's Studies International Forum*, 30: 6, 2007, pp. 523–533.

Letoulat-Chotard, Chloé, "Albert Thomas: Le député-maire socialiste de Champigny-sur-Marne (1912–1919)," Colloque *Albert Thomas (1878–1932). Homme d'Etat. D'une politique ouvrière en temps de guerre à la naissance du BIT* (Groupe Régional du Comité d'histoire d'Île de France, 2008).

Lih, Lars, *Bread and Authority in Russia, 1914–1921* (Berkeley, 1990).

Lindenberg, Daniel, *Lucien Herr, le socialisme et son destin* (Paris, 1977).

Link, Arthur S., *The Papers of Woodrow Wilson* (Princeton University Press, 1966–1994), Vol. 58, pp. 598–600.

Lippert, Randy, "Governing refugees: the relevance of governmentality to understanding the international refugee regime," in *Alternatives*, 24: 3, 1999, pp. 295–329.

Liulevicius, Vejas Gabriel, *War Land on the Eastern Front: Culture, National Identity, and German Occupation in World War I* (Cambridge, 2000).

Loescher, Gil, *Beyond Charity: International Cooperation and the Global Refugee Crisis* (Oxford, 1993).

Long, James W., *From Privileged to Dispossessed: The Volga Germans, 1860–1917* (Lincoln, 1988).

Long, James W., "The Volga Germans and the famine of 1921," *The Russian Review*, 51: 4, 1992, pp. 510–525.

Lorrain, Sophie, *Des pacifistes français et allemands, pionniers de l'entente franco-allemande, 1871–1925* (Paris, 1999).

Lubin, Carol Riegelman and Anne Winslow, *Social Justice for Women: The International Labor Organization and Women* (Durham and London, 1990).

Lucassen, Leo, "The Great War and the origins of migration control in Western Europe and the United States (1880–1920)," in Anita Boecker (ed.), *Regulation of Migration: International Experiences* (Amsterdam, 1998), pp. 45–72.

Lutz, Raphael, "Die Verwissenschaftlichung des Sozialen als methodische und konzeptionelle Herausforderung für eine Sozialgeschichte des 20. Jarhhunderts," *Geschichte und Gesellschaft*, 22 (1996), pp. 165–193.

Lyford, Amy, "The aesthetics of dismemberment: surrealism and the Musée du Val-de-Grâce in 1917," *Cultural Critique*, 46, 2000, pp. 45–79.

Macalister-Smith, Peter, *International Humanitarian Assistance. Disaster Relief Actions in International Law and Organization* (Dordrecht, Boston and Lancaster, 1985).

Macartney, Maxwell H.H., *Five Years of European Chaos* (New York: 1923).

Macbriar, Alan Marne, *Fabian Socialism and English Politics, 1884–1918* (Cambridge, 1962).

Macmillan, Margaret, *Paris 1919. Six Months that Changed the World* (New York, 2003).

Mahood, Linda, "Feminists, politics and children's charity: the formation of the Save the Children Fund," *Voluntary Action: The Journal of the Institute of Volunteering Research*, 5: 1, 2002, pp. 71–82.

Mahood, Linda, *Feminism and Voluntary Action. Eglantyne Jebb and Save the Children, 1876–1928* (London, 2009).

Maier, Charles, "Between Taylorism and technocracy: European ideologies and the vision of industrial productivity in the 1920s," *Journal of Contemporary History*, 5: 2, 1970, pp. 27–61.

Maier, Charles, *Recasting Bourgeois Europe: Stabilization in France, Germany and Italy in the Decade after World War I* (Princeton University Press, 1975).

Maier, Charles, "Consigning the twentieth century to history: alternative narratives for the modern era," *American Historical Review*, 105: 3, 2000, pp. 807–31.

Malik, Habib C., (ed.), *The Challenge of Human Rights: Charles Malik and the Universal Declaration* (Oxford, 2000).

Manela, Erez, *The Wilsonian Moment. Self Determination and the International Origins of Anticolonial Nationalism* (Oxford and New York, 2007).

Manigand, Christine, *Les Français au service de la Société des Nations* (Bern, 2003).

Mansfield, Malcolm, Robert Salais and Noel Whiteside (eds.), *Aux sources du chômage, 1880–1914* (Paris, 1994).

Margalit, Avishai, *The Ethics of Memory* (Cambridge, Mass., 2002).

Marrus, Michael, *The Unwanted: European Refugees in the Twentieth Century* (New York, 1986).

Marshall, Dominique, "The construction of children as an object of international relations: The Declaration of Children's Rights and the Child Welfare Committee of the League of Nations, 1900–1924," *The International Journal of Children's Rights*, 1999, pp. 103–147.

Marshall, Dominique, "Humanitarian sympathy for children in times of war and the history of children's rights, 1919–1959," in James Marten (ed.), *Children and War* (New York, 2002).

Marshall, Dominique, "Dimensions transnationales et locales de l'histoire des droits de l'enfant: la Société des Nations et les cultures politiques canadiennes, 1910–1960," *Genèses*, 2: 71, 2008, pp. 47–63.

Marrus, Michael, *The Unwanted: European Refugees from the First World War Through the Cold War* (Philadelphia: Temple University Press, 2002).

Maul, Daniel R., "The International Labour Organization and the struggle against forced labour from 1919 to the present," *Labor History*, 48: 4, 2007, pp. 477–500.

Maul, Daniel R., "The International Labour Organization and the globalization of human rights, 1944–1970," in Hoffmann (ed.), *Human Rights*, pp. 301–320.

Maurer, Trude, *Ostjuden in Deutschland, 1918–1933* (Hamburg, 1986).

Mayer, Arno J., *Wilson vs. Lenin: Political Origins of the New Diplomacy, 1917–1918* (New Haven, 1959).

Mazower, Mark, "Minorities and the League of Nations in interwar Europe," *Daedalus*, 126, 1997, pp. 47–61.

Mazower, Mark, *Dark Continent: Europe's Twentieth Century* (New York, 1998).

Mazower, Mark, "The strange triumph of human rights," *New Statesman*, February 4, 2002.

Mazower, Mark, "The strange triumph of human rights, 1933–1950," *Historical Journal*, 47: 2, 2004, pp. 379–398.

Mazower, Mark, *Salonica, City of Ghosts: Christians, Muslims and Jews, 1430–1950* (New York, 2005).

Mazower, Mark, *No Enchanted Palace: The End of Empire and the Ideological Origins of the United Nations* (Princeton, 2009).

McAuley, Mary, *Bread and Justice: State and Society in Petrograd, 1917–1922* (Oxford, 1991).

McClintock, Megan J. "Civil War pensions and the reconstruction of union families," *Journal of American History*, 83, September 1996, pp. 456–480.

McElroy, Robert W., *Morality and American Foreign Policy* (Princeton, 1992).

Meindersma, C., "Population exchanges: international law and state practice," *International Journal of Refugee Law*, 9: 1, 1997, pp. 335–653.

Metzger, Barbara, "Towards an international human rights regime during the inter-war years: the League of Nations' combat of traffic in women and children," in Kevin Grant, Philippa Levine and Frank Trentmann (eds.), *Beyond Sovereignty: Britain, Empire and Transnationalism, c.1880–1950* (Basingstoke, 2007), pp. 54–79.

Miller, Carol, "Geneva – the key to equality": Inter-war feminists and the League of Nations," *Women's History Review*, 3, 2, 1994, pp. 219–245.

Miller, Julie, *Abandoned: Foundlings in Nineteenth-Century New York City* (New York, 2008).

Milles, Dietrich, "Working capacity and calorie consumption: the history of rational physical economy," in Harmke Kamminga and Andrew Cunningham (eds.), *The Science and Culture of Nutrition* (Amsterdam and Atlanta, Georgia: Rodopi, 1995), pp. 75–96.

Moeller, Susan, *Compassion Fatigue: How the Media Sell Disease, Famine, War and Death* (New York and London, 1999).

Mommsen, Hans (ed.), *Der Erste Weltkrieg und die europäische Nachkriegsordnung: Sozialer Wandel und Formveränderung der Politik* (Cologne, 2000).

Montès, Jean-François, "L'office national des anciens combattants et victimes de guerre: création et actions durant l'entre-deux-guerres," *Guerres mondiales et conflits contemporains*, 205, January–March 2002, pp. 71–83.

Moranian, Suzanne E., "The Armenian genocide and American missionary relief efforts," in Jay Winter (ed.), *America and the Armenian Genocide of 1915* (Cambridge, 2003), p. 207.

Moret-Lespinet, Isabelle, "Arthur Fontaine, de l'Office du travail au Bureau International du Travail, un promoteur du droit international du travail," in Jean-Pierre Le Crom (ed.), *Les acteurs du droit du travail* (Rennes, 2004).

Moret-Lespinet, Isabelle, "Justin Godart et le Bureau International du Travail," in Annette Wieviorka (ed.), *Justin Godart, un homme dans son siècle, 1871–1956* (Paris: 2004).

Moret-Lespinet, Isabelle, *L'Office du Travail, la république et la réforme sociale, 1891–1914* (Rennes, 2007).

Moret-Lespinet, Isabelle, "Hygiène industrielle, santé au travail. L'OIT productrice de normes, 1919–1939," in Moret-Lespinet and Viet (eds.), *L'Organisation Internationale du Travail*, pp. 63–75.

Moret-Lespinet, Isabelle and Ingrid Liebeskind-Sauthier, "Albert Thomas, le BIT et le chômage: expertise, catégorisation et action politique internationale," *Les Cahiers de l'IRICE*, 1, 2008, pp. 157–179.

Moret-Lespinet, Isabelle and Vincent Viet (eds.), *L'Organisation Internationale du Travail: origine-développement-avenir* (Rennes, 2011).

Mosse, George, *Fallen Soldiers. Reshaping the Memory of the World Wars* (New York, 1990).

Mosse, George L., "Shell-shock as a social disease," *Journal of Contemporary History*, 35: 1 (January 2000), pp. 101–108.

Moyn, Samuel, "Empathy in history, empathizing in humanity," *History and Theory*, 45, October 2006, pp. 397–415.

Moyn, Samuel, "Spectacular wrongs: Gary Bass' '*Freedom's Battle*,'" *The Nation*, October 13, 2008.

Moyn, Samuel, "Personalism, community and the origins of human rights," in Stefan-Ludwig Hoffmann (ed.), *Human Rights in the Twentieth Century* (Cambridge, 2011), pp. 85–106.

Moyn, Samuel, *The Last Utopia: Human Rights in History* (Cambridge, Mass., 2010).

Muller, Bertrand, "Problèmes contemporains et hommes d'action à l'origine des *Annales*: une correspondance entre Lucien Febvre et Albert Thomas (1928–1930)," *Vingtième siècle. Revue d'histoire*, 35, July–September 1992, pp. 78–91.

Mulley, Clare, *The Woman Who Saved the Children: A Biography of Eglantyne Jebb, Founder of Save the Children* (Oxford, 2009).

Naquet, Emmanuel, "Guerre et Droit. L'inconciliable? L'exemple de la Ligue des droits de l'Homme de l'avant à l'après 14–18," *Mil Neuf Cent. Revue d'histoire intellectuelle*, 1: 23, 2005, pp. 93–110.

Nardinelli, Clark, *Child Labor and the Industrial Revolution* (Bloomington, 1990).

Nash, George, *The Life of Herbert Hoover* (New York, 1983).

Natale, Enrico, "Quand l'humanitaire commençait à faire son cinéma: les films du CICR des années 20," *International Review of the Red Cross*, 86: 854, June 2004, pp. 415–438.

Nead, Lynda, *Myths of Sexuality, Representations of Women in Victorian Britain* (Oxford, 1988).

Nehring, Holger and Helge Pharo, "A peaceful Europe? Negotiating peace in the twentieth century," *Contemporary European History*, 17: 3, 2008, pp. 277–299.

Niemeyer, Gerhart, "The Second International: 1889–1914," in Milorad M. Drachkovitch (ed.), *The Revolutionary Internationals, 1864–1943* (Stanford, Calif., 1966), pp. 95–127.

Nilan, Kathleen Mary, *Incarcerating Children: Prison Reformers, Children's Prisons and Child Prisoners in July Monarchy France*, PhD dissertation, Yale University, 1992.

Nivet, Philippe, *La France occupée, 1914–1918* (Paris, 2011).

Nivet, Philippe, *Les réfugiés français de la Grande Guerre, 1914–1920* (Paris, 2004).

Noiriel, Gérard, *Le creuset français. Histoire de l'immigration en France, XIXe–XXe siècles* (Paris, 1988).

Noiriel, Gérard, *Réfugiés et sans papiers. La République face au droit d'asile, XIXe–XXe siècles* (Paris, 1998).

Noiriel, Gérard, *La tyrannie du national: le droit d'asile en Europe (1793–1993)* (Paris, 1991).

Nourrissier, François, *L'homme humilié: sort des réfugiés et des personnes déplacées, 1912–1950* (Paris, 1950).

Offer, Avner, "'Jacky' Fisher: economic warfare and the laws of war," *Journal of Contemporary History*, 23: 1, January 1988, pp. 99–118.

Offer, Avner, *The First World War: An Agrarian Interpretation* (Oxford, 1989).

Osipova, Taisia, "Peasant rebellions: origins, scope, dynamics, and consequences," in Vladimir N. Brovkin (ed.), *The Bolsheviks in Russian Society* (New Haven, 1997).

Panayi, Panikos, *The Enemy in Our Midst. Germans in Britain During the First World War* (Providence and Oxford, 1991).

Panayi, Panikos (ed.), *Minorities in Wartime* (Oxford, 1993).

Patenaude, Bertrand M., *The Big Show in Bololand: The American Relief Expedition to Soviet Russia in the Famine of 1921* (Stanford, 2002).

Paugal, Serge (ed.), *Repenser la solidarité. L'apport des sciences sociales* (Paris, 2007).

Pedersen, Susan, *Family, Dependence, and the Origins of the Welfare State: Britain and France (1914–1945)* (Cambridge, 1993).

Pedersen, Susan, "The maternalist moment in British colonial policy: the controversy over 'child slavery' in Hong Kong, 1917–1941," *Past & Present*, 171, May 2001, pp. 171–202.

Pedersen, Susan, *Eleanor Rathbone and the Politics of Conscience* (New Haven, 2004).

Pedersen, Susan, "Back to the League of Nations," *American Historical Review*, 112: 4, October, 2007, pp. 1091–1117.

Pentzopoulos, Dimitri, *The Balkan Exchange of Minorities and its Impact upon Greece* (Paris, 1962).

Perrot, Michelle, "Les enfants de la Petite-Roquette," in *Les Ombres de l'histoire: crime et châtiment au XIXème siècle* (Paris, 2001), pp. 337–349.

Peterson, M. Jeanne, "No angel in the house: the Victorian myth and the Paget women," *American Historical Review*, 89: 3, June 1984, pp. 677–708.

Peterson, M. Jeanne, *Family, Love and Work in the Lives of Victorian Gentlewomen* (Bloomington, 1989).

Pignot, Manon, *Allons enfants de la patrie! Génération Grande Guerre* (Paris, 2012).

Pipes, Richard, *The Russian Revolution* (New York, 1990).

Pipes, Richard, *Russia Under the Bolshevik Regime* (New York, 1993).

Pipes, Richard (ed.), *The Unknown Lenin: From the Secret Archives* (New Haven, 1996).

Plattner, Denise, "Protection of children in international humanitarian law," *International Review of the Red Cross*, 24: 240, 1984, pp. 140–152.

Polasky, Janet L., *The Democratic Socialism of Emile Vandervelde: Between Reform and Revolution* (Oxford, 1995).

Poulain, Michel and Dominique Tabutin, "La mortalité aux jeunes âges en Europe et en Amérique du Nord du XIXème siècle à nos jours," in Paul-Marie Boulanger and Dominique Tabutin (eds.), *La mortalité des enfants dans le monde et dans l'histoire* (Louvain, 1980).

Prat, Olivier, "Marc Sangnier et la paix à la Chambre bleu horizon, 1919–1924," in Claude Carlier and Georges-Henri Soutou (eds.), *1918–1925. Comment faire la paix?* (Paris: 2001), p. 53.

Preston, Samuel H. and Michael R. Haines, *Fatal Years: Child Mortality in Late Nineteenth-Century America* (Princeton, 1991).

Prochaska, Frank, *Women and Philanthropy in Nineteenth-Century England* (Oxford, 1980).

Prochaska, Frank, *Christianity and Social Service in Modern Britain: The Disinherited Spirit* (Oxford, 2006).

Prochasson, Christophe, "Les Congrès, lieux de l'échange intellectuel. Introduction," *Cahiers Georges Sorel*, 7: 7, 1989, pp. 5–8.

Prochasson, Christophe, *Les intellectuels, le socialisme et la guerre, 1900–1938* (Paris, 1991).

Prochasson, Christophe, "Entre science et action sociale: le 'réseau Albert Thomas' et le socialisme normalien, 1900–1914," in Topalov (ed.), *Laboratoires du nouveau siècle*, pp. 141–158.

Prost, Antoine, "Combattants et politiciens. Le discours mythologique sur la politique entre les deux guerres," *Le Mouvement social*, 85, October–December 1973, pp. 117–154.

Prost, Antoine, *Les anciens combattants et la société française, 1914–1939* (Paris, 1977).

Prost, Antoine, *Les anciens combattants, 1914–1940* (Paris, 1977), translated by Helen McPhail as *In the Wake of War: "Les anciens combattants" and French Society* (Oxford, 1992).

Prost, Antoine, "Le service de santé militaire pendant la Première Guerre mondiale," in Annette Wieviorka (ed.), *Justin Godart, un homme dans son siècle* (Paris, 2004).

Prost, Antoine, "Ils ont des droits sur nous," in Jean-François Muracciole and Frédéric Rousseau (eds.), *Combats. Hommage à Jules Maurin historien* (Paris, 2010), pp. 369–380.

Prost, Antoine and Jay Winter, *René Cassin* (Paris, 2011).

Pryor, Elizabeth, *Clara Barton: Professional Angel* (Philadelphia, 1987).

Rabinbach, Anson, *The Human Motor: Energy, Fatigue and the Origins of Modernity* (Berkeley, 1992).

Radkey, Olivier H., *The Unknown Civil War in Soviet Russia: A Study of the Green Movement in the Tambov Region, 1920–1921* (Stanford, 1976).

Raeff, Marc, *Russia Abroad: A Cultural History of the Russian Emigration, 1919–1939* (New York and Oxford, 1990).

Rasmussen, Anne, "Les congrès liés aux expositions universelles de Paris, 1867–1900," *Mil Neuf Cent. Revue d'histoire intellectuelle*, 7, 1989, pp. 23–45.

Rasmussen, Anne, "Le travail en congrès: élaboration d'un milieu international," in Jean Luciani (ed.), *Histoire de l'Office du Travail, 1890–1914* (Paris, 1992), pp. 119–134.

Rauchensteiner, Manfried, "L'Autriche entre confiance et résignation, 1918–1920" and "La Hongrie, 1918–1920: dix gouvernements en vingt mois," in Audoin-Rouzeau and Prochasson (eds.), *Sortir de la Grande Guerre*, pp. 165–206.

Rebérioux, Madeleine and Patrick Fridenson, "Albert Thomas, pivot du réformisme français," *Le Mouvement social*, 87, April–June 1974, pp. 85–97.

Reniolet, Jean-Jacques, *L'UNESCO oubliée: la Société des Nations et la coopération intellectuelle, (1919–1946)* (Paris, 1999).

Renouvin, Pierre, *Le traité de Versailles* (Paris, 1969).

Retish, Aaron B., *Russia's Peasants in Revolution and Civil War: Citizenship, Identity and the Creation of the Soviet State, 1914–1922* (Cambridge, 2008).

Reznick, Jeffrey S., "Prostheses and propaganda: materiality and the human body in the Great War," in Nicholas J. Saunders, *Matters of Conflict: Material Culture, Memory and the First World War* (London and New York, 2004), pp. 51–61.

Ricœur, Paul, *La Mémoire, l'Histoire, l'Oubli* (Paris, 2000), translated as *Memory, History, Forgetting* (Chicago, 2006).

Ridel, Charles, *Les Embusqués* (Paris, 2007).

Ripa, Yannick, "Naissance du dessin de guerre. Les époux Brauner et les enfants de la guerre civile espagnole," *Vingtième siècle*, 1: 89, 2006, "Enfances en guerre," edited by Stéphane Audoin-Rouzeau, pp. 29–46.

Ritter, Gerhard Albert, *Der Sozialstaat: Entstehung und Entwicklung im internationalen Vergleich* (Munich, 1989).

Robert, Jean-Louis, *Les ouvriers, la patrie et la Révolution, 1914–1919* (Besançon, 1995).

Robinson, Paul, *The White Russian Army in Exile, 1920–1941* (Oxford, 2002).

Roche, Jean-Luc, "A multidimensional approach to the exile's persecution experience," in Diana Miserez (ed.), *Refugees: The Trauma of Exile* (Dordrecht, Boston and London, 1988), pp. 223–233.

Rodgers, Gerry, Eddy Lee, Lee Swepston and Jasmien Van Daele (eds.), *The International Labour Organization and the Quest for Social Justice, 1919–2009* (Ithaca and Geneva, 2009).

Rodogno, Davide, *Against Massacre: Humanitarian Interventions in the Ottoman Empire, 1815–1914* (Princeton, 2012).

Rodogno, Davide, Bernard Struck and Jakob Vogel (eds.), *Shaping the Transnational Sphere: Networks of Experts and Organisations, 1840–1930* (New York: Berghahn Books, forthcoming).

Roerkohl, Anne, *Hungerblockade und Heimatfront: Die kommunale Lebensmittelversorgung in Westfalen während des Ersten Weltkriegs* (Stuttgart, 1991).

Rogger, Hans, "*Amerikanizm* and the economic development of Russia," *Comparative Studies in Society and History*, 23, July 1981, pp. 382–420.

Rollet, Catherine, "La construction d'une culture internationale autour de l'enfant," in *Comment peut-on être socio-anthropologue? Autour d'Alain Girard* (Paris, 1995), pp. 143–168.

Rollet, Catherine, "La santé et la protection de l'enfant vues à travers les Congrès internationaux (1880–1920)," *Annales de démographie historique*, 1, 101, 2001, pp. 97–116.

Rooke, Patricia T. and Rudy L. Schnell, "Uncramping child life: international children's organisations, 1914–1939," in Weindling (ed.), *International Health Organisations and Movements*.

Rosenberg, Clifford, *Policing Paris: The Origins of Modern Immigration Control between the Wars* (Ithaca, 2006).

Rosenberg, Emily, "Missions to the world: philanthropy abroad," in *Charity, Philanthropy and Civility in American History* (ed.), Lawrence Friedman and Mark McGarvie (New York, 2004), p. 248.

Rosental, Paul-André, "Géopolitique et État-providence. Le BIT et la politique mondiale des migrations dans l'entre-deux-guerres," *Annales HSS*, 1, 2006, pp. 99–134.

Rosental, Paul-André, "De la silicose et des ambiguïtés de la notion de 'maladie professionnelle,'" *Revue d'Histoire moderne et contemporaine*, 56: 1, 2009, pp. 83–98.

Roshwald, Aviel, *Ethnic Nationalism and the Fall of Empires: Central Europe, Russia and the Middle East, 1914–1923* (London, 2001).

Ross, Ellen (ed.), *Slum Travelers: Ladies and London Poverty, 1860–1920* (Berkeley, 2007).

Rothman, David J., *The Discovery of the Asylum: Social Order and Disorder in the New Republic* (Boston and Toronto, 1971).

Rothschild, Joseph, *East Central Europe between the Two World Wars* (Seattle, 1974).

Rousselier, Nicolas, "Le 'gouvernement de guerre' et les socialistes," in Romain Ducoulombier (ed.), *Les socialistes dans l'Europe en guerre, réseaux, parcours, expériences, 1914–1918* (Paris, 2010), pp. 33–44.

Rozario, Kevin, "'Delicious horrors': mass culture, the Red Cross and the appeal of modern American humanitarianism," *American Quarterly*, 55: 3, September 2003, pp. 417–455.

Rupp, Leila J., *Worlds of Women: The Making of an International Women's Movement* (Princeton, New Jersey, 1997).

Sacriste, Guillaume and Antoine Vauchez, "Les 'bons offices' du droit international: la constitution d'une autorité non-politique dans le concert diplomatique des années 1920," *Critique Internationale*, 26, January 2005, pp. 101–117.

Sammartino, Annemarie H., *The Impossible Border: Germany and the East, 1914–1922* (Ithaca, 2010).

Sanborn, Joshua, "The genesis of Russian warlordism: violence and governance during the First World War and the Civil War," *Contemporary European History*, 19: 3, 2010, pp. 195–213.

Sarat, Austin and Javier Lezaun (eds.), *Catastrophe: Law, Politics and the Humanitarian Impulse* (Amherst and Boston, 2009).

Sassoli Marco, "Le droit international humanitaire, une *lex specialis* par rapport aux droits humains?" in Andreas Auer, Alexandre Flueckiger and Michel Hottelier, *Les droits de l'homme et la constitution: études en l'honneur du Professeur Giorgio Malinverni* (Geneva, 2007), pp. 375–395.

Scarry, Elaine, *The Body in Pain: The Making and Unmaking of the World* (Oxford, 1985).

Scelle, Georges, "Une ère juridique nouvelle," *La paix par le droit*, July–August 1919, pp. 297–298.

Schaper, Bertus W, *Albert Thomas: trente ans de réformisme social* (Assen, 1959).

Schloegel, Karl, *Chronik russischen Lebens in Deutschland, 1918 bis 1941* (Berlin, 1999).

Schlögel, Karl (ed.), *Der grosse Exodus: Die russische Emigration und ihre Zentren 1917 bis 1941* (Munich, 1994).

Schroeder-Gudehus, Brigitte, *Les scientifiques et la paix: la communauté scientifique internationale au cours des années vingt* (Montréal, 1978).

Schroeder-Gudehus, Brigitte, "Pas de Locarno pour la science. La coopération scientifique internationale et la politique étrangère des États pendant l'entre-deux-guerres," *Relations internationales*, 46, 1986, pp. 173–194.

Scott, Joan W., "The evidence of experience," *Critical Inquiry*, 17, summer 1991, pp. 773–797.

Sealander, Judith, *The Failed Century of the Child: Governing America's Young in the Twentieth Century* (Cambridge, 2003).

Sellars, Kirsten, *The Rise and Rise of Human Rights* (Stroud, 2002).

Serbyn, Roman, "The famine of 1921–1923: a model for 1932–1933?" in Roman Serbyn and Bowdan Krawchenko, *Famine in Ukraine, 1932–1933* (Edmonton, 1986).

Sheehan, James, "The problem of sovereignty in European history," *American Historical Review*, 111: 1, 2006, pp. 1–15.

Sheehan, James, *Where Have all the Soldiers Gone? The Transformation of Modern Europe* (Boston, 2008).

Shelton, Dinah (ed.), *Commitment and Compliance. The Role of Non-Binding Norms in the International Legal System* (Oxford, 2000).

Shemmassian, Vahram L., "The League of Nations and the reclamation of Armenian genocide survivors," in Richard G. Hovannisian (ed.), *Looking Backward, Moving Forward: Confronting the Armenian Genocide* (New Brunswick, 2003), pp. 81–110.

Shimazu, Naoko, *Japan, Race, and Equality: The Racial Equality Proposal of 1919* (London and New York, 1998).

Shoham, Shlomo (ed.), *Of Law and Man. Essays in Honor of Haim H. Cohn* (New York and Tel Aviv, 1971).

Simms, Brendan and D.J.B. Trim (eds.), *Humanitarian Intervention: A History* (Cambridge, 2011).

Simpson, John Hope, *The Refugee Problem: Report of a Survey* (New York, 1939).

Sirinelli, Jean-François, *Génération intellectuelle: Khâgneux et normaliens dans l'entre-deux guerres* (Paris: Fayard, 1988).

Skran, Claudena, *Refugees in Inter-war Europe: The Emergence of a Regime* (Oxford, 1995).

Skran, Claudena and Carla N. Daughtry, "The study of refugees before 'Refugee Studies,'" *Refugee Survey Quarterly*, 26: 3, 2007, pp. 15–35.

Skocpol, Theda, *Protecting Soldiers and Mothers: The Political Origins of Social Policy in the United States* (Cambridge, Mass., 1992).

Smith, Leonard V., *Between Mutiny and Obedience: The Case of the French Fifth Infantry Division during World War I* (Princeton, 1994).

Smith, Leonard V., "Remobilizing the citizen-soldier through the French army mutinies of 1917," in John Horne (ed.), *State, Society and Mobilization during the First World War* (Cambridge, 1997), pp. 144–159.

Smith, Leonard V., "The Wilsonian challenge to international law," *Journal of the History of International Law*, 13: 1, 2011, pp. 179–208.

Snyder, Timothy, *The Reconstruction of Nations: Poland, Ukraine, Lithuania, Belarus, 1569–1999* (New Haven, 2003).

Sontag, Susan, *Regarding the Pain of Others* (New York: Farrar, Straus and Giroux, 2003)

Steiner, Zara, *The Lights that Failed: European International History, 1919–1933* (Oxford, 2005).

Stone, Norman and Michael Glenny (eds.), *The Other Russia* (London and Boston, 1990).

Stora-Lamarre, Annie, "La guerre au nom du droit," *Revue d'histoire du XIXème siècle*, 30, 2005, pp. 150–160.

Straumann, Lukas, *L'humanitaire mis en scène: la cinématographie du CICR des années 1920*, ICRC, 2000.

Suski, Laura, "Children, suffering and the humanitarian appeal," in Richard Ashby Wilson and Richard D. Brown (eds.), *Humanitarianism and Suffering: The Mobilization of Empathy* (New York, 2009), pp. 212–216.

Tabori, Paul, *The Anatomy of Exile* (London, 1972).

Tartakowsky, Danielle, "Manifestations ouvrières et théories de la violence, 1919–1934," *Cultures et conflits*, 9–10, 1993, pp. 251–266.

Teitelbaum, Michael S. and Jay Winter, *The Fear of Population Decline* (Orlando, 1985).

Thébaud, Françoise, "The Great War and the triumph of sexual division," in Georges Duby and Michelle Perrot (eds.), *History of Women in the West* (Cambridge, Mass., 1992–94), Vol. 5, edited by Françoise Thébaud.

Thiers, Eric, "Droit et culture de guerre 1914–1918: le Comité d'études et de documents sur la guerre," *Mil Neuf Cent. Revue d'histoire intellectuelle*, 1: 23, 2005, pp. 23–48.

Ticehurst, Rupert, "La clause de Martens et le droit des conflits armés," *Revue internationale de la Croix Rouge*, 79, 1997, pp. 133–142.

Tison, Stéphane, *Comment sortir de la guerre? Deuil, mémoire et traumatisme (1918–1940)* (Rennes, 2011).

Topalov, Christian (ed.), *Laboratoires du nouveau siècle: la nébuleuse réformatrice et ses réseaux en France* (Paris, 1999).

Topalov, Christian, *Naissance du chômeur (1880–1910)* (Paris, 1994).

Torpey, John, *The Invention of the Passport. Surveillance, Citizenship and the State* (Cambridge, 2000).

Torpey, John, "The Great War and the birth of the modern passport system," in Jane Caplan and John Torpey (eds.), *Documenting Individual Identity. The Development of State Practices in the Modern World*, (Princeton and Oxford, 2001), pp. 256–270.

Traini, Christophe, "Les victimes entre émotions et stratégies," in Sandrine Lefranc et Lilian Mathieu (eds.), *Mobilisations de victimes* (Rennes, 2009).

Treitel, Corinna, "Max Rubner and the biopolitics of rational nutrition," *Central European History*, 41, 2008, pp. 1–25.

Triska, Jan F. and Robert M. Slusser (eds.), *The Theory, Law and Policy of Soviet Treaties* (Stanford, 1962).

Tuck, Richard, *The Rights of War and Peace. Political Thought and the International Order from Grotius to Kant* (Oxford, 1999).

Turner, Brian, *Vulnerability and Human Rights* (University Park, Penn., 2006).

Van Bueren, Geraldine, *The International Law on the Rights of the Child* (Amsterdam, 1998).

Van Daele, Jasmien, "Engineering social peace: networks, ideas and the founding of the International Labour Organization," *International Review of Social History*, 50, 2005, pp. 435–466.

Van Daele, Jasmien, Magaly Rodriguez Garcia and Marcel Van der Linden (eds.), *ILO Histories: Essays on the International Labour Organization and Its Impact on the World in the Twentieth Century* (Bern, 2010).

Veerman, Philip E., *The Rights of the Child and the Changing Image of Childhood* (Dordrecht, 1992).

Veit, Helen Elizabeth, "'We were a soft people.' Asceticism, self-discipline, and American food conservation in the First World War," *Food, Culture and Society*, 10: 2, summer 2007, pp. 167–190.

Veit, Helen Elizabeth, *Modern Food, Moral Food: Self-Control, Science, and the Rise of Modern American Eating in the Early Twentieth Century* (University of North Carolina Press, 2013).

Verdirame, Guglielmo and Barbara Harrell-Bond (eds), *Rights in Exile. Janus-Faced Humanitarianism* (New York, 2005).

Vernon, James, *Hunger: A Modern History* (Cambridge, Mass., 2007).

Vicinus, Martha, *Independent Women: Work and Community for Single Women, 1850–1920* (Chicago and London, 1985).

Viet, Vincent, "Le droit du travail s'en va t-en guerre (1914–1918)," La Documentation française, *Revue française des Affaires sociales*, 1, 2002, pp. 155–167.

Vincent, C. Paul, *The Politics of Hunger: The Allied Blockade of Germany, 1915–1919* (Athens, Ohio, 1985).

Vogel-Polsky, Eliane, *Du tripartisme à l'Organisation Internationale du Travail* (Brussels, 1966).

Vogt, Carl Emil, "Fridtjof Nansen, peace 1922," in Olav Njølstad (ed.), *Norwegian Nobel Prize Laureates* (Oslo, 2006), pp. 119–153.

Vogt, Carl Emil, "'Først vore egne!' Da Aftenposten saboterte Nansens nødhjelp til Russland" ["'Our own people first!' How the *Aftenposten* newspaper sabotaged Nansen's charity to Russia]," *Historisk Tidsskrift*, 87: 1, 2008.

Vogt, Carl Emil, *Fridtjof Nansen: Mannen og verden* [*Fridtjof Nansen: The Man and the World*] (Oslo, 2011).

Wagner, Richard, *Clemens von Pirquet: His Life and Work* (Baltimore, 1968).

Walkover, Andrew, "The 'infancy defense' in the new juvenile court," *UCLA Law Review*, 31, 1984, pp. 503–562.

Walter, François, *Catastrophes: une histoire culturelle, XVIème–XXIème siècles* (Paris, 2008).

Walters, Francis P., *A History of the League of Nations*, 2 vols. (London, 1952; reprinted 1960).

Ward, Stephen (ed.), *The War Generation. Veterans of the First World War* (Port Washington, New York, 1975).

Watenpaugh, Keith David, "The League of Nations' rescue of Armenian genocide survivors and the making of modern humanitarianism, 1920–1927," *American Historical Review*, 115: 5, December 2010, pp. 1315–1339.

Watenpaugh, Keith David, *Bread from Stones: The Middle East and the Making of Modern Humanitarianism* (University of California Press, forthcoming).

Waters, Tony, *Bureaucratizing the Good Samaritan. The Limitations of Humanitarian Relief Operations* (Boulder, Colo., 2001).

Webster, Andrew, "The transnational dream: politicians, diplomats and soldiers in the League of Nations' pursuit of international disarmament, 1920–1938," *Contemporary European History*, 14: 4, 2005, pp. 493–518.

Weil, Patrick, *Qu'est-ce qu'un Français? Histoire de la nationalité française depuis la Révolution* (Paris, 2002), p. 118, translated by Catherine Porter as *How to be French: Nationality in the Making Since 1789* (Durham, North Carolina, 2008).

Weindling, Paul, "A virulent strain: typhus, bacteriology and scientific racism" (unpublished paper, Social History of Medicine Conference, University of Southampton, September 18, 1996), pp. 6–7, in Tony Kushner and Katharine Knox, *Refugees in an Age of Genocide. Global, National and Local Perspectives during the Twentieth Century* (London and Portland, Oreg.: Frank Cass, 1999), p. 78.

Weindling, Paul (ed.), *International Health Organisations and Movements, 1918–1939* (Cambridge, 1995).

Weindling, Paul, "The role of international organizations in setting nutritional standards in the 1920s and 1930s," in Harmke Kamminga and Andrew Cunningham (eds.), *The Science and Culture of Nutrition* (Amsterdam and Atlanta, Georgia: Rodopi, 1995), pp. 319–332.

Weindling, Paul, "Social medicine at the League of Nations Health Organisation and the International Labour Office compared," in Paul Weindling (ed.),

International Health Organisations and Movements, 1918–1939 (Cambridge, 1995), pp. 134–153.

Weissman, Benjamin M., *Herbert Hoover and Famine Relief to Soviet Russia, 1921–23* (Stanford, 1974).

Weitz, Eric D., "From the Vienna to the Paris system: international politics and the entangled histories of human rights, forced deportations, and civilizing missions," *American Historical Review*, 113: 5, December, 2008, pp. 1313–1343.

Werth, Nicolas, "L'ex-Empire russe, 1918–1921: les mutations d'une guerre prolongée," in Audoin-Rouzeau and Prochasson (eds.), *Sortir de la Grande Guerre*, pp. 285–306.

Whalen, Robert Weldon, *Bitter Wounds: German Victims of the Great War, 1914–1939* (Ithaca and London, 1984).

Wikander, Ulla, Alice Kessler-Harris and Jane Lewis (eds.), *Protecting Women: Labor Legislation in Europe, the United States and Australia, 1880–1920* (Urbana and Chicago, 1995).

Williams, Robert, *Culture in Exile: Russian Emigrés in Germany, 1881–1941* (Ithaca, 1972).

Willis, James F., *Prologue to Nuremberg: The Politics and Diplomacy of Punishing War Criminals of the First World War* (Westport, Conn., 1982).

Wilson, Adrian, "The infancy of the history of childhood: an appraisal of Philippe Ariès," *History and Theory*, 19: 2, February 1980, pp. 132–153.

Wilson, Ann Marie, "In the name of God, civilization and humanity: the United States and the Armenian massacres of the 1890s," *Le Mouvement social*, 2: 227, 2009, pp. 27–44.

Wilson, Francesca M., *Rebel Daughter of a Country House: The Life of Eglantyne Jebb, Founder of the Save the Children Fund* (London, 1967).

Winter, Jay, *Socialism and the Challenge of War: Ideas and Politics in Britain, 1912–1918* (London, 1974).

Winter, Jay "Forms of kinship and remembrance in the aftermath of the Great War," in Jay Winter and Emmanuel Sivan (eds.), *War and Remembrance in the 20th Century* (Cambridge, 1998), pp. 25–40.

Winter, Jay, *Dreams of Peace and Freedom: Utopian Moments in the Twentieth Century* (New Haven, 2006).

Winter, Jay and Antoine Prost, *Penser la Grande Guerre. Un essai d'historiographie* (Paris: 2004).

Winter, Jay and Antoine Prost, *The Great War in History, Debates and Controversies, 1914 to the Present* (Cambridge University Press, 2005).

Woloch, Isser, *The French Veterans from the Revolution to the Restoration* (Chapel Hill, 1979).

Woloch, Isser, "A sacred debt: veterans and the state in Revolutionary and Napoleonic France," in David Gerber (ed.), *Disabled Veterans in History* (Ann Arbor, 2000), pp. 145–162.

Yerly, Frédéric, "Grande Guerre et diplomatie humanitaire: la mission catholique suisse en faveur de prisonniers de guerre, 1914–1918," *Vingtième siècle*, 58, 1998, pp. 13–28.

Zahra, Tara,"The minority problem: national classification in the French and Czechoslovak borderlands," *Contemporary European History*, 17, May 2008, pp. 137–165.

Zahra, Tara, *The Lost Children: Reconstructing Europe's Families after World War II* (Cambridge, Mass., 2011).

Zimmermann, Susan, "Special circumstances in Geneva: the ILO and the world of non-metropolitan labour in the interwar years," in Van Daele *et al.* (eds.), *ILO Histories* (Bern: 2010).

Zolberg, Aristide, "The formation of new states as a refugee-generating process," *Annals of the American Academy of Political and Social Science*, 467, May 1983, pp. 24–38.

Zolberg, Aristide, *A Nation by Design: Immigration Policy in the Fashioning of America* (Cambridge, Mass., 2006).

Theses and dissertations

Balzter, Sebastian, *Repatriierung, 1920–1922. Zur Rückführung der Kriegsgefangenen nach dem Ersten Weltkrieg*, Magisterarbeit, Albert-Ludwigs-Universität, Freiburg im Breisgau, 2004.

Birebent, Christian, *Les mouvements de soutien à la Société des Nations en France et au Royaume-Uni (1918–1925)*, PhD dissertation in history, Université Paris X-Nanterre, 2002.

Léonetti, Antoine-Jean, *Georges Scelle. Étude d'une théorie juridique*, PhD thesis, Université Nice-Sophia Antipolis, 1992.

Liebeskind-Sauthier, Ingrid, *L'Organisation internationale du travail face au chômage: entre compétences normatives et recherche de solutions économiques, 1919–1939*, PhD thesis, University of Geneva, 2005.

Lowe, Kimberly, *The Red Cross and the New World Order, 1918–1924*, PhD dissertation, Yale University, 2013.

Massart, Sylvie, *Les voyages d'Albert Thomas directeur du BIT (1919–1932)*, Master's thesis, Université Paris-I, 1993.

Metzger, Barbara, *The League of Nations and Human Rights: From Practice to Theory*, PhD thesis, University of Cambridge, 2001.

Miller, Carol, *Lobbying the League: Women's International Organizations and the League of Nations*, PhD thesis, University of Oxford, 1992.

Veit, Helen Elizabeth, *Victory Over Ourselves: American Food and Progressivism in the Era of the Great War*, PhD dissertation, Yale University, 2008.

Zeyer, Marie-Adelaide, *Léon Bourgeois, père spirituel de la Société des Nations. Solidarité internationale et service de la France (1899–1919)*, thesis, École des Chartes, Paris, 2006.

Index

Aberdeen, Lady, 113
Abraham, Karl, 22, 308
Academies of Science, 305
activism
    French peace welcomed to Germany
        (1922), 64
    Humanitarian, 14
    International, 7
    protection of war victims, 1
    religious, 4
    rights', 7
    women's, 113–115, 253
Addis Ababa, 294
Adler, Emanuel, 81
Ador, Gustave, 149, 156, 205, 294, 295
advertising, to motivate donors, 216, 220,
    221, 280, 304
Advisory Committee of Private Refugee
    Relief Organizations, 152, 159
Africa, 294
agricultural camps, 29, 182, 250
    Mettray model (1839), 261
agriculture, 121, 122
    globalization of markets, 210
    Russian, 196, 198
    and Russian refugees in United States,
        169
Agulhon, Maurice, 19
aid
    birth of a refugee program, 179–182
    defined as an obligation of humanity,
        246
    emergency relief for natural disasters,
        244
    financing of international, 246
    international, 14, 157, 158, 229–241
    international for refugees, 150, 151,
        171, 179–182
    private organizations, 150, 152, 171,
        180, 187
    programs for children and mothers,
        250

    to civilians under occupation, 191
    see also humanitarian aid
aid policies
    for disabled veterans, 37
    for families of soldiers killed in action,
        37
    German, 22
    United States' for Russia, 213, 215,
        241
air service, 289
Aix-en-Provence, veterans' association, 28
Albania, 288
Aleppo, agricultural colony, 250, 251
Alexander II, Czar, assassination, 234
Aliens Restriction Act (British 1914), 167
Allen, Ronald, 239
Alliance Israélite de France, 149
Allied Women Suffragists, 113
Allies
    blockade against Germany, 5, 252, 271,
        273, 283, 312
    and Bolsheviks, 213
    Germany grants right to prosecute war
        criminals to (1919), 1
    ideas of the enemy, 310
    soldiers' belief in just war, 61
    and Turkey, 2
    veterans and German veterans, 44
Alsace-Lorraine, 134, 177
Álvarez, Alejandro, 7, 106, 306
American Civil War, 35
American Federation of Labor, 89
    convention on immigration (1919), 169
American Friends of France, 42
American Friends Service Committee
    (Quaker), 215, 286
American Jewish Joint Distribution
    Committee, 215
American Journal of International Law, 13
American Legion, 68, 169
American Medical Association, 263
American Pediatric Society, 264